SCHAUM'S OUTLINE OF

THEORY AND PROBLEMS

of

BEGINNING PHYSICS I:
Mechanics and Heat

ALVIN HALPERN, Ph.D.

Professor of Physics
Brooklyn College
City University of New York

This book is dedicated to my wife, Mariarosa Halpern

ALVIN HALPERN is a Ph.D. He is a Professor of Physics at Brooklyn College of the City University of New York (CUNY). Dr. Halpern has had extensive teaching experience in college physics at all levels, elementary through doctoral. He was chairman of the physics department at Brooklyn College for ten years and presently has a university-wide role as vice president for research development at the Research Foundation of the university. He is also Executive Director of the Applied Science Coordinating Institute of the university.

 This book is printed on recycled paper containing 10% postconsumer waste.

Schaum's Outline of Theory and Problems of

BEGINNING PHYSICS I: Mechanics and Heat

1 2 3 4 5 6 7 8 9 10 11 12 13 14 15 16 17 18 19 20 BAW BAW 9 8 7 6 5

ISBN 0-07-025653-5

Sponsoring Editor: Arthur Biderman
Production Supervisor: Leroy Young
Editing Supervisor: Maureen Walker

Library of Congress Cataloging-in-Publication Data

Halpern, Alvin M.
    Schaum's outline of theory and problems of beginning physics I :
mechanics and heat / Alvin Halpern.
        p.   cm. — (Schaum's outline series)
    Includes index.
    ISBN 0-07-025653-5
    1. Mechanics.   2. Heat.   I. Title.
QC127.H24   1995
531—dc20   94-44819
                                                                 CIP

Preface

Beginning Physics I: Mechanics and Heat is intended to help students who are taking, or are preparing to take, a first year College Physics course that is quantitative in nature and focuses on problem solving. The book is specifically designed to allow students with relatively weak training in mathematics and science problem solving to quickly gain the needed quantitative reasoning skills as well as confidence in addressing the subject of physics. A background in high school algebra and the rudiments of trigonometry are assumed, but the first chapter of the book is a mathematical review for those not comfortable with their command of the needed mathematics. The book is written in a "user friendly" style so that even those initially terrified of physics can develop mastery of the subject. It develops the subject matter and methodology slowly and gently and maintains a "coaxing" ambiance all the way through. Nonetheless, the material is not "watered down." The intention is to raise the level of ability of the students to the point where they can handle the material of a rigorous noncalculus-based course, including dealing with sophisticated problems.

In particular, *Beginning Physics I* should be useful to preprofessional (e.g., premedical and predental) students, engineering students, and science majors. It also is suitable for liberal arts majors who are required to satisfy a rigorous science requirement, and choose physics. Volume I of the book covers the material in a typical first semester of such a course. Volume II, which is in preparation, will cover the material of the typical second semester of the course.

Beginning Physics I will also serve as an excellent support book for engineering and science students taking a calculus-based physics course, even though the book does not use calculus. The major stumbling block for students in such a course is typically not the calculus itself but rather the same weak background in problem-solving skills that faces many students taking noncalculus-based courses. Indeed, many of the physics problems found in the calculus-based course are of the same type as, and comparable in sophistication to, those in a rigorous noncalculus course. This book will thus help engineering and science students raise their physics problem-solving skill levels, so that they can more easily handle a calculus-based course.

ALVIN HALPERN

To the Student

The Preface gives a brief description of the subject matter level, the philosophy and approach, and the intended audience for this book. Here I wish to give you, the student, some brief advice on how to use the book. *Beginning Physics I: Mechanics and Heat* consists of an interweaving of text with solved problems that is intended to give you the opportunity to learn through exploration and example. The most effective way to gain mastery of the subject is to go through each problem as if it were an integral part of the text (which it is). The section in each chapter called *Problems for Review and Mind Stretching* gives a few additional worked-out problems that both review and extend the material in the chapter. It would be a good idea to try to solve these problems on your own before looking at the worked-out solutions, just to get a sense of where you are in terms of mastery of the material. Finally, there are supplementary problems at the end of the chapter, which give only the numerical answers. You should try to do as many of these as possible, since problem solving is the ultimate test of your knowledge in physics. If you follow this regimen faithfully, you will not only master the subject, but you will sense the stretching of your intellectual capacity and the development of a new dimension in your ability to think. Good luck.

ALVIN HALPERN

Contents

Chapter 1

Introduction and Mathematical Background

1.1 INTRODUCTION TO THE STUDY OF PHYSICS AND ITS RELATIONSHIP TO MATHEMATICS

What Is Physics?

Physics is the study of all physical phenomena—phenomena experienced through the human senses, either directly or with the aid of instruments. Among the topics studied are the following: (*a*) the motion and distortion of objects due to interaction with their environment (mechanics); (*b*) heat and thermodynamics; (*c*) sound and other wave motions; (*d*) light and optical phenomena; (*e*) electrical and magnetic phenomena; and (*f*) atomic and molecular properties of matter. The typical general physics sequence, consisting of two or three courses, usually covers all these subjects at an elementary level, often in the order listed.

Physics Is a Science

It is based on experiment and observation. It is a *quantitative* science; relationships between physical quantities (such as position and time for a moving object) are expressed as precisely as possible. That is why physics uses the language of mathematics. Only mathematical formulas can give the relationships between physical quantities in precise form. Thus, for example, if we wish to describe what happens to an object that is dropped from a certain height, we can do so with different degrees of precision. At the lowest level of precision we can say that the object falls until it hits the ground. At a somewhat more detailed level we can say that the object speeds up as it falls. At the most detailed level we want to know exactly where it is located and how fast it is moving at every instant of time. For this last case we need a mathematical relationship between the height and the time and between the speed of fall and the time.

1.2 MATHEMATICAL REVIEW

Notation

We will often use a center dot (·) to signify the product of two numbers and a slash (/) to signify their division. When no ambiguity can exist, the center dot for multiplication will be omitted [for example, when multiplying terms in parentheses: 3(10) to be read "three times ten" or when multiplying by a variable: $2x$ to be read "two times x"]. The **absolute value** or **magnitude** of a number, or of a variable x, is its value with a positive sign. Using the notation "absolute value of x" = $|x|$, we have, for example: $|-6| = 6$; $|3| = 3$; for x negative, $x = -|x|$, while for x positive, $x = |x|$.

Mathematical Functions

Suppose we have a mathematical relationship between two quantities (for example, the relationship between the distance that an object moves and the time that has elapsed or the relationship

1

between two purely mathematical quantities). Then, if one of the quantities takes on a particular value, the relationship tells us the corresponding value of the other quantity. Suppose the two quantities are represented by the symbols x and t; then for every value of t there is a definite value of x. The quantities x and t are called **variables** because they can take on a range of values. The variable x is said to be a **function** of the variable t, or symbolically, $x = f(t)$, which is read "x equals a function of t," or in shorthand, x equals "eff" of t.

Problem 1.1. The quantity x is related to the quantity t by the relationship $x = f(t) = 3t + 4$. Find the value of x when t takes on each of the following values: $t = 0$, $t = 1$, $t = 2$, $t = 2.5$, $t = 10$.

Solution

For the first value we have

$$x = f(0) = 3 \cdot 0 + 4 = 0 + 4 = 4$$

Similarly, for the other values we have

$$x = f(1) = 3 \cdot 1 + 4 = 3 + 4 = 7 \qquad x = f(2) = 3 \cdot 2 + 4 = 6 + 4 = 10$$

$$x = f(2.5) = 3(2.5) + 4 = 7.5 + 4 = 11.5 \qquad x = f(10) = 3 \cdot 10 + 4 = 30 + 4 = 34$$

Problem 1.2. The quantities z and x are related by the function $z = f(x) = 12x - 7$. Find the values of z corresponding to the following values of x: $x = 3$, -3, $\frac{1}{2}$, $-\frac{1}{2}$, 1.2.

Solution

We carry out the calculation for each value of x:

$$z = f(3) = 12 \cdot 3 - 7 = 29 \qquad z = f(-3) = 12(-3) - 7 = -43$$

$$z = f\left(\tfrac{1}{2}\right) = 12\left(\tfrac{1}{2}\right) - 7 = -1 \qquad z = f\left(-\tfrac{1}{2}\right) = 12\left(-\tfrac{1}{2}\right) - 7 = -13$$

$$z = f(1.2) = 12(1.2) - 7 = 14.4 - 7 = 7.4$$

Problem 1.3. The quantities y and x are related through the equation $y = f(x) = 2x^2$. Find y for $x = -4$, -2, -1, 0, 1, 2, 4, 4.5.

Solution

We calculate y for each value of x, in the order given. To save space we won't write the $f(x)$ expression for each case.

$$y = 2(-4)^2 = 2 \cdot 16 = 32 \qquad y = 2(-2)^2 = 2 \cdot 4 = 8$$

$$y = 2(-1)^2 = 2 \qquad y = 2(0)^2 = 0 \qquad y = 2(1)^2 = 2$$

$$y = 2(2)^2 = 8 \qquad y = 2(4)^2 = 32 \qquad y = 2(4.5)^2 = 2 \cdot 20.25 = 40.5$$

Problem 1.4. y and t are related by the function $y = f(t) = 4t^2 - 2t + 6$. Find y when $t = -3$, -2, -1, 0, 1, 2, 3.

Solution

In the order given,

$$y = 4(-3)^2 - 2(-3) + 6 = 36 + 6 + 6 = 48$$
$$y = 4(-2)^2 - 2(-2) + 6 = 16 + 4 + 6 = 26$$
$$y = 4(-1)^2 - 2(-1) + 6 = 4 + 2 + 6 = 12$$
$$y = 4(0)^2 - 2(0) + 6 = 0 + 0 + 6 = 6$$
$$y = 4(1)^2 - 2(1) + 6 = 4 - 2 + 6 = 8$$
$$y = 4(2)^2 - 2(2) + 6 = 16 - 4 + 6 = 18$$
$$y = 4(3)^2 - 2(3) + 6 = 36 - 6 + 6 = 36$$

Graphs

Whenever one has a mathematical relationship between two variables, say x and t, one can represent the function $x = f(t)$ by a two-dimensional graph. To do this, one typically draws two straight lines, called **axes** at right angles to each other—one horizontal and the other vertical, as shown in Fig. 1-1. The horizontal axis is marked off to some scale, as shown, for the variable t (called the **independent variable**) with negative and positive values as shown. The zero point, where the two axes cross, is called the **origin** and is denoted by the letter O for origin or the numeral 0. Traditionally the right half of the horizontal axis is chosen as positive and the left half as negative. Similarly, the values of x (called the **dependent variable**) are marked off on some scale on the vertical axis, with upward traditionally chosen as positive.

For each value of t on the horizontal axis, one imagines a line drawn vertically upward to a point (point A in Fig. 1-1, for example) whose height corresponds to the value of $x = f(t)$ as measured on

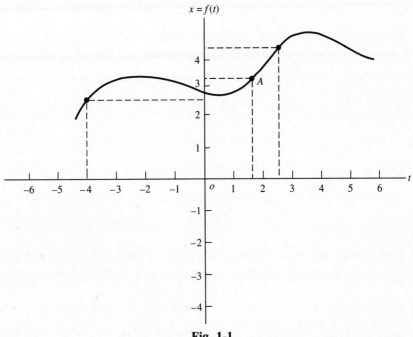

Fig. 1-1

the vertical axis. One can imagine a horizontal line from the vertical axis also drawn to the point A. (The two imaginary lines are represented by dashed lines in Fig. 1-1). If one constructs points this way for each value of t (two more examples are shown in the figure), the points can be fitted by a smooth curve as shown. This curve is the **graph** of the function $x = f(t)$. Each point on the graph is directly above (or directly below, for negative x) a value of t. The same point is then directly to the right (or to the left) of the corresponding value of x. Thus all the information contained in the relationship between x and t [that is, the function $x = f(t)$] is displayed on the graph.

Problem 1.5.   Plot the graph of the function in Problem 1.1 between the values $t = -5$ and $t = +5$.

Solution

We first plot some of the values already calculated in Problem 1.1. These are shown in Fig. 1-2. As can be seen they lie on a straight line. The x intercept, defined as the point at which the line crosses the vertical axis, is at $x = 4$. The **slope** of the line, defined as the number of vertical units between two points on the line divided by the corresponding number of horizontal units, is just $\frac{6}{2} = 3$, as demonstrated in the figure by means of the dashed lines. (Since the scale of our graph was chosen differently for the horizontal and the vertical axes, the vertical distance doesn't *look* three times as big as the horizontal distance.)

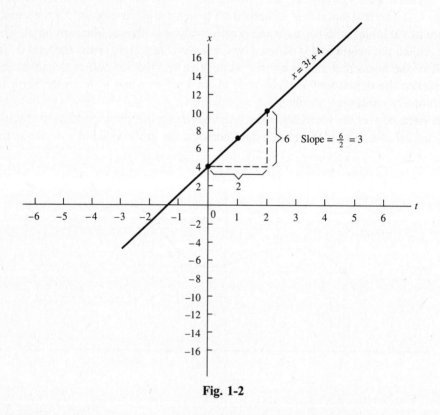

Fig. 1-2

A straight line is always specified uniquely on a graph by giving the slope and the intercept with the vertical axis. In fact the general equation of a straight line with slope m and intercept b is just $x = mt + b$.

Problem 1.6.   Plot the function $z = f(x)$ found in Problem 1.2.

Solution

The function is $z = 12x - 7$. We plot x on the horizontal and z on the vertical and see that this is clearly a straight line whose vertical intercept is at $z = -7$ and whose slope is 12. We have to plot only two points to draw the straight line, and this is illustrated in Fig. 1-3.

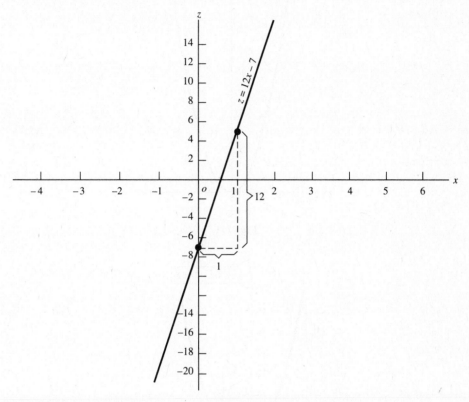

Fig. 1-3

Problem 1.7.   Plot the function $y = f(x)$ found in Problem 1.3.

Solution

Since $y = 2x^2$, this is clearly *not* a straight line. Figure 1-4 shows the graph of this function; note some of the values calculated in Problem 1.3. This is the curve of a parabola that is symmetric about the vertical axis and touches the origin at its lowest point.

Problem 1.8.   Plot the function $x = f(t)$ where $f(t)$ is given in Problem 1.4.

Solution

Here the function is $x = 4t^2 - 2t + 6$ and it is shown plotted in Fig. 1-5. Again we have a parabola, but now it is symmetric about a vertical axis through the point $t = \frac{1}{4}$, which corresponds to its lowest point $x = 5.75$.

Inverse Functions

When we have a function $x = f(t)$, for every t value we can determine the corresponding x value. Is it possible to turn this around so that for every x value we can find a corresponding t value? The

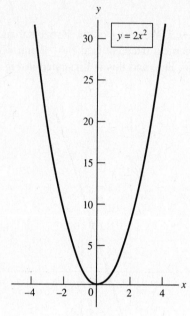

Fig. 1-4

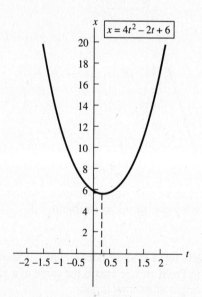

Fig. 1-5

answer is a qualified yes. Sometimes there is no ambiguity, but at other times one must exercise caution. If we succeed in doing so, then t has become a function of x. To acknowledge that this new function was obtained by turning around or "inverting" the function $x = f(t)$, it is usually labeled $t = f^{-1}(x)$ and is called the **inverse function**.

Problem 1.9.   Find the inverse function for the case of Problem 1.1.

   Solution

   The original function $x = f(t)$ is given by the equation $x = 3t + 4$. To get t in terms of x we want to isolate the t in the equation. First we subtract 4 from both sides of the equation, to get $3t = x - 4$. Next

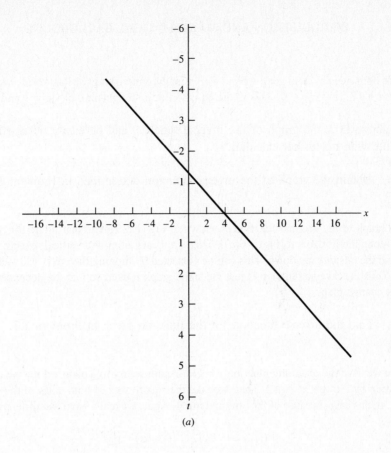

(a)

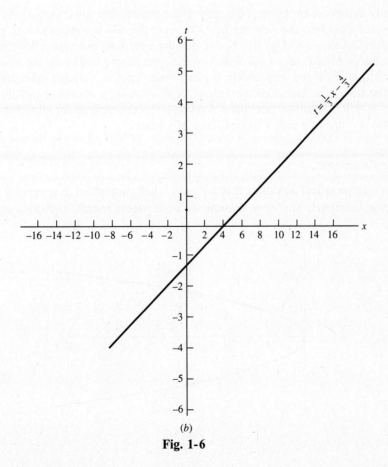

$t = \frac{1}{3}x - \frac{4}{3}$

(b)

Fig. 1-6

7

we divide both sides by 3, to get $t = (x - 4)/3$. Finally, simplifying this last result, we get for our inverse function, $t = f^{-1}(x) = \frac{1}{3}x - \frac{4}{3}$. This is the equation of a straight line of slope $\frac{1}{3}$ and t intercept $(-\frac{4}{3})$.

Problem 1.10 shows how the graph of the inverse function can be easily obtained from that of the original function, with no further calculation.

Problem 1.10.   Obtain the graph of the inverse function determined in Problem 1.9.

Solution

The graph of the original function is shown in Fig. 1.2. Rotate that figure 90° clockwise so that x appears along the horizontal [Fig. 1-6(a)]. Then t appears along the vertical, except the negative values are up and the positive are down. This can be corrected by flipping the t axis 180° about the x axis [Fig. 1-6(b)]. Thus the inverse function is just the same graph rotated so that the dependent and independent variables change place.

Problem 1.11.   Find the inverse function for the function given in Problem 1.3.

Solution

Here we have the quadratic function $y = 2x^2$. Again we try to isolate x. First we divide both sides of the equation by 2 to get $x^2 = y/2$. Then we take the square root of both sides of the equation to get $x = \pm\sqrt{y/2}$. In this case, because of the plus and minus signs, we really have two different inverse functions:

$$\text{(i)}\quad x = +\sqrt{\frac{y}{2}} \qquad \text{(ii)}\quad x = -\sqrt{\frac{y}{2}}$$

This can be understood by inverting the graph of the original function (Fig. 1-4). As in Problem 1.10, we rotate by 90° clockwise and then flip by 180° about the new horizontal axis to get the graph for the inverse function shown in Fig. 1-7. Notice that there are now two values of x, one positive and one negative, for each value of y. Each branch of the curve, above and below the axis, corresponds to the choice of (i) or (ii) above, respectively, as the inverse function. Another interesting feature is that the inverse function (either branch) is not defined for all values of y, but rather only for positive values of y (see Fig. 1-7). It is often the case that a function $y = f(x)$ is defined for all x, but the inverse function $x = f^{-1}(y)$ is defined for only a limited range of y values.

Trigonometric Functions

Among the mathematical functions that are particularly important in a general physics course are the trigonometric functions. The most commonly used trigonometric functions are the sine, cosine,

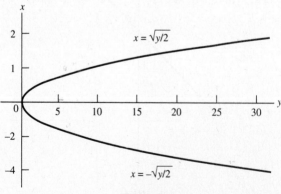

Fig. 1-7

and tangent functions. They are most usually defined in terms of ratios of sides of a right triangle, in which an angle (say, θ) plays the role of the independent variable. Figure 1-8 shows the rules for obtaining the sine, cosine, and tangent of angles between $\theta = 0°$ and $\theta = 360°$. The angle is always measured counterclockwise from the positive horizontal axis to the hypotenuse of the right triangle.

sine of θ $\sin \theta = \dfrac{\text{opposite}}{\text{hypotenuse}} = \dfrac{o}{h}$

cosine of θ $\cos \theta = \dfrac{\text{adjacent}}{\text{hypotenuse}} = \dfrac{a}{h}$ (1.1)

tangent of θ $\tan \theta = \dfrac{\text{opposite}}{\text{adjacent}} = \dfrac{o}{a}$

Also, from (1.1)

$$\tan \theta = \frac{o/h}{a/h} = \frac{\sin \theta}{\cos \theta} \qquad (1.2)$$

The trigonometric functions are positive or negative depending on the quadrant. The correct signs ($\pm$) for the functions in all four quadrants can be determined by using Fig. 1-8. The rule is that the opposite and adjacent sides of the triangles shown are to be considered positive or negative depending on which side of the axis they are on, while the hypotenuses are always considered positive. (Note that only in the first quadrant is the angle of interest θ inside the triangle.) The graphs of the trigonometric functions are shown in Fig. 1-9(a), (b), and (c), where we have plotted $x = \sin \theta$, $x = \cos \theta$, and

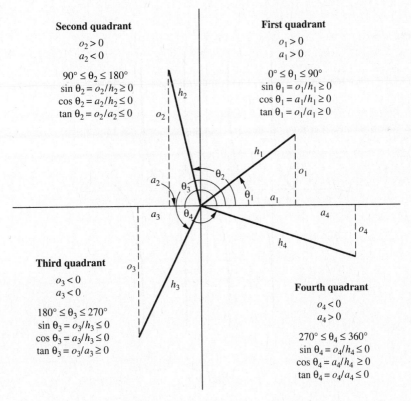

Second quadrant

$o_2 > 0$
$a_2 < 0$

$90° \leq \theta_2 \leq 180°$
$\sin \theta_2 = o_2/h_2 \geq 0$
$\cos \theta_2 = a_2/h_2 \leq 0$
$\tan \theta_2 = o_2/a_2 \leq 0$

First quadrant

$o_1 > 0$
$a_1 > 0$

$0° \leq \theta_1 \leq 90°$
$\sin \theta_1 = o_1/h_1 \geq 0$
$\cos \theta_1 = a_1/h_1 \geq 0$
$\tan \theta_1 = o_1/a_1 \geq 0$

Third quadrant

$o_3 < 0$
$a_3 < 0$

$180° \leq \theta_3 \leq 270°$
$\sin \theta_3 = o_3/h_3 \leq 0$
$\cos \theta_3 = a_3/h_3 \leq 0$
$\tan \theta_3 = o_3/a_3 \geq 0$

Fourth quadrant

$o_4 < 0$
$a_4 > 0$

$270° \leq \theta_4 \leq 360°$
$\sin \theta_4 = o_4/h_4 \leq 0$
$\cos \theta_4 = a_4/h_4 \geq 0$
$\tan \theta_4 = o_4/a_4 \leq 0$

Fig. 1-8

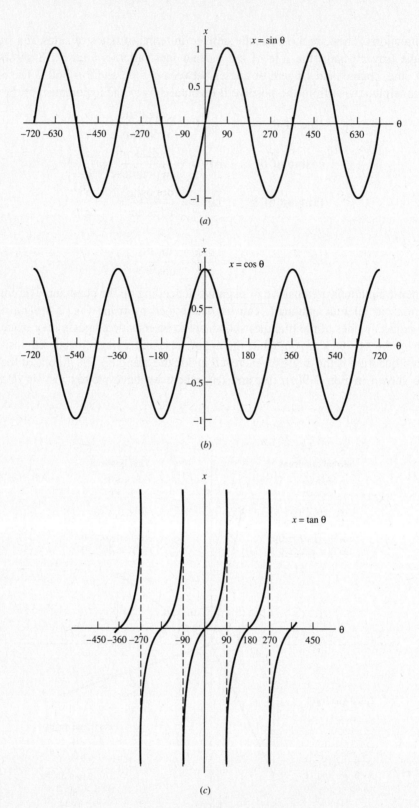

Fig. 1-9

$x = \tan \theta$, respectively. It is seen that the functions repeat themselves every time θ winds through $360°$, clockwise or counterclockwise:

$$\sin \theta = \sin(\theta + 360°) = \sin(\theta + 720°) = \cdots$$
$$\cos \theta = \cos(\theta + 360°) = \cos(\theta + 720°) = \cdots \qquad (1.3)$$
$$\tan \theta = \tan(\theta + 360°) = \tan(\theta + 720°) = \cdots$$

Thus, for example, if $\theta = 300°$, we have

$$\sin(300°) = \sin(-60°) \qquad \cos(300°) = \cos(-60°) \quad \text{and} \quad \tan(300°) = \tan(-60°) \quad (1.4)$$

Figure 1-9 indicates that the maximum and minimum values of the sine and cosine functions are ± 1. This is a consequence of the fact that the length of the sides a and o can never exceed that of the hypotenuse. The tangent, however, can vary from minus infinity to plus infinity, since $\tan \theta = \sin \theta / \cos \theta$ and the expression becomes infinite when the cosine becomes zero.

Problem 1.12. What is the sign of the sine, cosine, and tangent in each quadrant?

Solution

From Fig. 1-8, using the sign convention discussed, we see that in the first quadrant (where θ is an acute angle) o, a, and h are all positive, so all three functions are positive. In the second quadrant (where θ is between $90°$ and $180°$), o and h are positive, but a is negative. Thus, $\sin \theta$ is positive, while $\cos \theta$ and $\tan \theta$ are negative. In the third quadrant (where θ is between $180°$ and $270°$), both o and a are negative, and only h is positive. Thus, $\sin \theta$ and $\cos \theta$ are both negative, while $\tan \theta$ is positive. In the fourth quadrant (where θ is between $270°$ and $360°$), o is negative, while a and h are positive. Thus, $\sin \theta$ and $\tan \theta$ are negative, while $\cos \theta$ is positive.

Problem 1.13. Show that $\sin \theta = \cos(90° - \theta)$; $\cos \theta = \sin(90° - \theta)$; $\tan(90° - \theta) = \cot \theta$ (where $\cot \theta$ is defined as $\cos \theta / \sin \theta$, and thus $\cot \theta = 1/\tan \theta$).

Solution

Consider the right triangle in Fig. 1-10. Since opposite and adjacent sides for angle θ are adjacent and opposite sides, respectively, for angle $(90° - \theta)$, we get all three results.

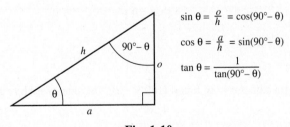

$$\sin \theta = \frac{o}{h} = \cos(90° - \theta)$$
$$\cos \theta = \frac{a}{h} = \sin(90° - \theta)$$
$$\tan \theta = \frac{1}{\tan(90° - \theta)}$$

Fig. 1-10

Problem 1.14. Show that (a) $\cos \theta = -\cos(180° - \theta)$; (b) $\sin \theta = \sin(180° - \theta)$.

Solution

(a) We consider the second-quadrant triangle depicted in Fig. 1-11(a). For angle θ we must consider o and h positive and a negative. Then $a = -|a|$ and $\cos \theta = -|a|/h$. On the other hand, $(180° - \theta)$ is an acute angle in a triangle with positive sides o, $|a|$, and h (dotted triangle in first quadrant). Therefore $\cos(180° - \theta) = |a|/h$. Comparing, we get the result $\cos \theta = -\cos(180° - \theta)$.

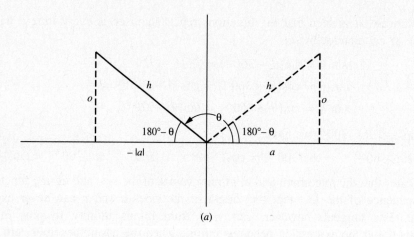

(a)

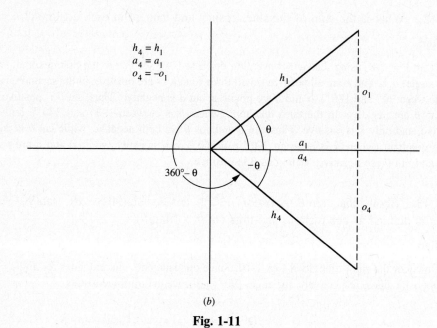

(b)

Fig. 1-11

(b) Since side o is positive for both θ and $(180° - \theta)$, the sine of each angle equals o/h, and they are equal.

Problem 1.15. Show that $\sin^2 \theta + \cos^2 \theta = 1$ for all values of θ.

 Note. $\sin^2 \theta$ stands for $(\sin \theta)^2$, etc., and is the accepted way of writing the square of a trigonometric function.

Solution

 $\sin^2 \theta + \cos^2 \theta = (o/h)^2 + (a/h)^2 = (o^2 + a^2)/h^2$. But, by the pythagorean theorem, $o^2 + a^2 = h^2$, or $(o^2 + a^2)/h^2 = 1$.

Problem 1.16.   Show that $\cos(-\theta) = \cos\theta$; $\sin(-\theta) = -\sin\theta$; $\tan(-\theta) = -\tan\theta$.

Solution

By examining the graphs in Fig. 1-9, we see that the cosine is symmetric about the $\theta = 0$ mark, while the sine and tangent are antisymmetric (i.e., if they assume a value at a given positive angle, they will assume the exact negative of that value at the corresponding negative angle). This is precisely what had to be shown. The same results follow directly from the definitions (Fig. 1-8). Consider an angle θ in the first quadrant and the corresponding angle $-\theta$ below the horizontal in the fourth quadrant, as shown in Fig. 1-11(b). Angle $(360 - \theta)$ is the counterclockwise angle to the hypotenuse in the fourth quadrant, so the trigonometric functions for $(-\theta)$ can be obtained from the triangle shown in the fourth quadrant with the usual sign convention. The two triangles shown are congruent, so the sides a, o, and h have the same magnitudes in both quadrants, but side o has opposite signs in the two quadrants. Thus, since sine and tangent involve side o, we have $\sin\theta = -\sin(-\theta)$, $\tan\theta = -\tan(-\theta)$. For the cosine, which does not involve side o, $\cos\theta = \cos(-\theta)$.

In general, to find the sine, cosine, or tangent of a particular angle, one has to use trigonometric tables or a calculator. However, for certain angles that often come up in general physics problems, one can obtain the values of the trigonometric functions from Fig. 1-12. The triangle in Fig. 1-12(a) is referred to as a "30-60-90" degree triangle; Fig. 1-12(b) shows the isosceles right triangle; and Fig. 1-12(c) is the "3-4-5" sides triangle. (In this last triangle, the angles given are not exact, but they are a good approximation.)

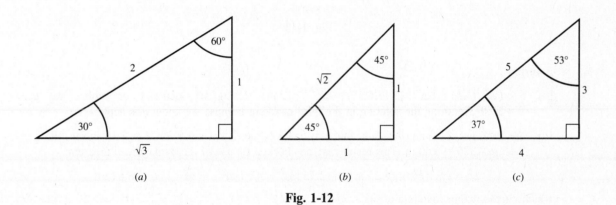

Fig. 1-12

Problem 1.17.

(a)   Find the following from Fig. 1-12: $\sin 30°$, $\cos 30°$, $\tan 60°$, $\cos 45°$, $\sin 37°$, $\cos 53°$.

(b)   Find the following values of the inverse trigonometric functions: $\sin^{-1}(\tfrac{1}{2})$, $\cos^{-1}(\sqrt{3}/2)$, and $\tan^{-1}(1)$.

Solution

(a)   From Fig. 1-12(a) and Eqs. (1.1): $\sin 30° = o/h = \tfrac{1}{2} = 0.500$; $\cos 30° = a/h = \sqrt{3}/2 = 0.866$; $\tan 60° = o/a = \sqrt{3}/1 = 1.73$. From Fig. 1-12(b): $\cos 45° = a/h = 1/\sqrt{2} = 0.707$. From Fig. 1-12(c): $\sin 37° = o/h = \tfrac{3}{5} = 0.600$; $\cos 53° = a/h = \tfrac{3}{5} = 0.600$.

(b)   From the definition of inverse functions: $x = \sin\theta \Leftrightarrow \theta = \sin^{-1} x$. So $\theta = \sin^{-1}(\tfrac{1}{2}) \Rightarrow \sin\theta = \tfrac{1}{2}$. From Fig. 1-12(a) [or part (a)] we have $\theta = 30°$. However, since the sine is also positive in the second quadrant, we get a second solution: $\theta = 180° - 30° = 150°$. Similarly, $\theta = \cos^{-1}(\sqrt{3}/2) \Rightarrow \cos \theta = \sqrt{3}/2 \Rightarrow \theta = 30°$. Since cosine is also positive in the fourth quadrant, we have a second solution: $\theta = 360° - 30° = 330°$. Repeating for the next case: $\theta = \tan^{-1} 1 \Rightarrow \tan \theta = 1$. From Fig. 1-12(b): $\tan 45° = \frac{1}{1} = 1$, so $\theta = 45°$. Tangent is also positive in the third quadrant, so we have another solution: $\theta = 180° + 45° = 225°$.

Actually there are an infinite number of solutions to part (b) if we include angles outside the range from 0° to 360°, as can be seen from Eqs. (1.3), or by turning Figs. 1-9 (a), (b), (c) on their sides as in Problems 1.10 and 1.11. However, since the angles repeat every 360°, it is usually sufficient to consider only angles in the range 0° to 360°.

Problem 1.18. Figure 1-13 shows a ramp of length L and angle θ, whose base is $b = 6.25$ m and whose height is $h = 2.15$ m. Find (a), θ, (b) L.

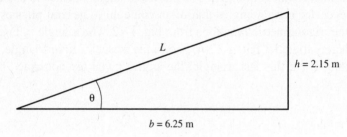

L

$h = 2.15$ m

θ

$b = 6.25$ m

Fig. 1-13

Solution

(a) $\theta = \tan^{-1}(h/b) = \tan^{-1}(2.15/6.25) = \tan^{-1}(0.344)$. Using a calculator or tables, we get $\theta = 19.0°$, ignoring the solution in the third quadrant because we know θ is acute.

(b) We can get L from the fact that $\sin \theta = h/L$, so $L = h/\sin \theta$ or $L = 2.15$ m/$\sin 19.0° = 2.15$ m/0.326 = 6.60 m. This result may be checked by use of the pythagorean theorem:

$$L^2 = b^2 + h^2 = (6.25 \text{ m})^2 + (2.15 \text{ m})^2 = 43.7 \text{ m}^2 \qquad \text{or} \qquad L = 6.61 \text{ m}$$

which checks within rounding errors.

Simultaneous Equations

Often in solving physics problems one encounters two relationships involving the same two variables. Then both relationships can be valid only for specific values of the variables. To see this we look at Figure 1-14, which shows the graphs of two functions between the variables y and x: $y = f_1(x)$ and $y = f_2(x)$. As can be seen, for an arbitrary value of x the corresponding y values will be different for the two functions. There is, however, one particular value of x (call it x_A) for which the two functions give the same value of y (call it y_A). This is the only pair of values of x and y that are valid for (or "satisfy") both relationships. We say that the two "simultaneous" equations between y and x (given by the two functions) are "solved" by the values x_A and y_A. (If the curves cross in more than one place, there exist additional pairs of values that satisfy both relationships, so there are additional solutions to the pair of equations.)

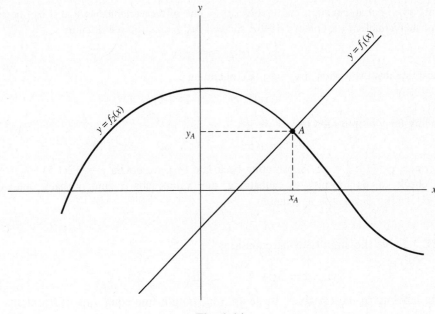

Fig. 1-14

Sometimes the two relationships can be expressed in the particularly simple form

$$a_1x + b_1y = c_1 \qquad \text{and} \qquad a_2x + b_2y = c_2 \qquad\qquad (1.5a,b)$$

where a_1, b_1, c_1 and a_2, b_2, c_2 are constants, and x, y are the variables. (A specific example would be

$$6x + 3y = 8 \qquad \text{and} \qquad 2x - 3y = 4 \qquad\qquad (1.6a,b)$$

Here $a_1 = 6$, $b_1 = 3$, $c_1 = 7$, $a_2 = 2$, $b_2 = -3$, $c_2 = 4$.) Such equations are represented by straight lines on a graph, since one can rewrite them in the standard slope and intercept form

$$y = mx + b \qquad\qquad (1.7)$$

(See Problem 1.19.) Equations of the form (*1.5*) are therefore called **linear equations**. Since two straight lines can cross at most once, there is either a single solution to the pair of equations or no solution when they don't cross at all.

Problem 1.19.   Show that Eq. (*1.6a*), $6x + 3y = 8$, is a straight line on a y vs. x graph.

Solution

Subtracting $6x$ from both sides of the equation we get $3y = -6x + 8$. Then we divide both sides by 3 to get $y = -2x + \frac{8}{3}$, which is the equation of a straight line expressed in standard form. It has slope $m = -2$ and vertical intercept $b = \frac{8}{3}$.

Problem 1.20.   Find the solution of the pair of Eqs. (*1.6a*) and (*1.6b*).

Solution

The two equations are

$$\text{(i)} \quad 6x + 3y = 8 \qquad \text{and} \qquad \text{(ii)} \quad 2x - 3y = 4$$

We must try to get an equation that involves only one of the variables so that it can be solved for the value of the variable. In Problem 1.19 we showed that (i) can be rewritten as

$$\text{(iii)}\quad y = -2x + \tfrac{8}{3}$$

We substitute this expression for y into (ii), obtaining

$$\text{(iv)}\quad 2x - 3\left(-2x + \tfrac{8}{3}\right) = 4$$

Performing the multiplication by -3 we get

$$\text{(v)}\quad 2x + 6x - 8 = 4 \qquad \text{or} \qquad 8x = 12$$

which yields $x = \frac{12}{8} = \frac{3}{2} = 1.5$. Substituting back into (iii), we obtain $y = -2(1.5) + \frac{8}{3} = -3 + \frac{8}{3} = -\frac{1}{3}$. As a check of our results we substitute our values for x and y back into (ii) and get $2(1.5) - 3(-\frac{1}{3}) = 3 + 1 = 4$, as required.

Problem 1.21. Solve the simultaneous equations

$$\text{(i)}\quad z = 3t + 4 \qquad\qquad \text{(ii)}\quad z = 12t - 7$$

Except for the labeling of the variables, these are the straight-line equations of Problems 1.1 and 1.2 above.

Solution

The two expressions for z must be equal, or $3t + 4 = 12t - 7$. Bringing the terms with t to one side of the equation and the constant terms to the other yields $9t = 11$ or $t = \frac{11}{9}$. Then, substituting the value of t into, say (i), we get $z = 3(\frac{11}{9}) + 4 = \frac{11}{3} + 4 = 7\frac{2}{3}$.

Problem 1.22. Solve the simultaneous equations

$$\text{(i)}\quad 3z + 4t = -2 \qquad\qquad \text{(ii)}\quad 2z - 12t = 3$$

Solution

We could solve these equations by the techniques of Problems 1.20 and 1.21, but let us use another method instead. We note that if we multiply both sides of (i) by 3 we get

$$\text{(iii)}\quad 9z + 12t = -6$$

So the coefficient of t has the same magnitude but opposite sign in both equations. We now add the left sides of (ii) and (iii), so the variable t cancels out. The result must equal the addition of the right sides of the two equations, and we get $11z = -3$ or $z = -\frac{3}{11}$. Substituting the value of z back into (i) yields

$$3\left(-\tfrac{3}{11}\right) + 4t = -2 \qquad \text{or} \qquad 4t = -2 + \tfrac{9}{11} = -\tfrac{13}{11} \qquad \text{or} \qquad t = -\tfrac{13}{44}$$

[Check these results for z and t by showing they satisfy (ii).]

Problem 1.23. Solve the simultaneous equations

$$\text{(i)}\quad y = 2x^2 \qquad\qquad \text{(ii)}\quad 2x + y = 12$$

Solution

Here only one of the equations is linear, the other is a quadratic. We can still solve for x and y, as follows: First we isolate y on one side of (ii): $y = -2x + 12$. Then we substitute this for y in (i) to get

$$\text{(iii)}\quad 2x^2 = -2x + 12 \qquad \text{or} \qquad \text{(iv)}\quad 2x^2 + 2x - 12 = 0$$

This is the well-known quadratic equation, of the general form

$$\text{(v)}\quad ax^2 + bx + c = 0$$

where a, b, and c are constants. Its solution is given by

$$\text{(vi)}\quad x = \frac{-b \pm (b^2 - 4ac)^{1/2}}{2a}$$

For our case $a = 2$, $b = 2$, and $c = -12$, so

$$x = \frac{-2 \pm (4 + 96)^{1/2}}{4} = \frac{-2 \pm \sqrt{100}}{4} = \frac{-2 \pm 10}{4}$$

Thus $x_1 = 2$ and $x_2 = -3$ are the two solutions for x. As luck would have it, (iv), which can be reduced to $x^2 + x - 6 = 0$, can be factored into $(x + 3)(x - 2) = 0$, yielding the two values of x directly. We now find the corresponding y values by substituting each x value into either (i) or (ii). Using (i) we get

$$y_1 = 2x_1{}^2 = 2(2)^2 = 8 \qquad y_2 = 2x_2{}^2 = 2(-3)^2 = 18$$

1.3 MEASURING PHYSICAL QUANTITIES

Measurement and Units

To find precise relationships that describe physical phenomena we must be able to measure physical quantities such as length, area, volume, velocity, acceleration, mass, time, and temperature. To do this we need **units of measurement** for all the quantities we are interested in. For example, the most commonly used unit of time is the *second*, that of length is the *meter* or the *foot*, and that of mass is the *kilogram*. Not all measurable quantities require their own units. Often the unit is automatically defined in terms of other units. For instance, if we have a unit of length, say the meter, then we already have units of area and volume: the square meter (a square 1 meter on a side) and the cubic meter (a cube 1 meter on a side), respectively. Another example is the unit of velocity, the meter per second, which is already defined in terms of units of length and time. Such units are called **derived units**. It turns out that in the subject of mechanics (motion and distortion of objects), only three physical quantities must have their units defined independently. These three quantities are usually taken to be length, mass, and time, and their units are called **fundamental units**.

Standards

To define a fundamental unit, everyone must agree to pick some physical example of the quantity to be measured and say that by definition it corresponds to one unit. Thus, for example, the unit of mass, the kilogram, is defined as a mass equal to that of a particular platinum-iridium cylinder housed in Sèvres, near Paris, France. That physical specimen is called the *standard* which defines the unit. The unit of length, the meter, used to be defined as the length of a particular platinum-iridium bar, but it has since been redefined in terms of the length of a certain wavelength of light, and most recently in terms of the distance light travels in a certain time interval. The standard for time has always been defined in terms of some repetitive phenomenon, such as the spin of the earth on its axis, the revolution of the earth about the sun, and most recently in terms of the oscillations of an atomic clock. The idea of the standard is that everyone can check their measuring apparatus against the standard for accuracy. In the case of time our everyday clocks can always be checked against the *standard* to make sure that they tell the right time. Thus, the most reliable and reproducible object or process makes the best standard.

History of Units

Not too long ago, units for the same physical quantities were defined independently in different countries and were all based on different standards. Today we still have different units used in different countries, but they are now all based on the same standards. This was essential to avoiding confusion and discrepancies in comparing measurements made in different parts of the world. The set of units most commonly used throughout the world, and which is almost exclusively used in scientific work, is called the *International System of units*, and abbreviated SI, from the French name, Système International d'Unités. In mechanics the units are the meter (m), the kilogram (kg), and the second (s), and are what is commonly called the *metric or mks (meter-kilogram-second) system.*

The units of the metric system are multiplied and subdivided by powers of 10 into commonly used subunits. Examples are the **gram** (g), which is one-thousandth of a kilogram; the **nanometer** (nm), which is one-billionth of a meter; the **centimeter** (cm), which is one-hundredth of a meter; the **kilometer** (km), which is one thousand meters; and the **millisecond** (ms), which is one-thousandth of a second. Indeed, the prefixes to the basic unit indicate what power of 10 to multiply or divide by.

In addition to the SI units, another common set of units used in the United States and a few other countries is referred to as the *English System*. Here the fundamental units are length, time, and force, which are respectively the **foot** (ft), the **second** (sec or s), and the **pound** (lb). The foot is now defined to be precisely 0.3048 meter, the second is the same in all systems, and the pound is defined in terms of the weight of a certain mass (given in kilograms) at a certain location on the earth's surface. (The relation between *weight* and *mass* will be discussed in Chap. 5.)

Systems of Units

All measurements involve specifying a multiplicative number and the associated unit as in, for example, "the length of the table is 10 ft" or "the car traveled at 30 m/s." One must be especially careful in relating different measured quantities. For example, if the length of a table is 10 ft and an extension of length 3 m is added on, what is the combined length? Clearly we cannot simply add the two numbers: 10 ft + 3 m = 13? Before adding we must either convert 10 ft to the equivalent length in meters or convert 3 m to the corresponding length in feet.

It is usual to use a consistent set of units when dealing with a given problem. Thus if we use the mks system, it means not only that the fundamental units are the meter, kilogram, and second but also that all the derived units are based on these three. Thus, the unit of velocity is the meter per second (m/s) and the unit of force is the newton (N) (this unit will be discussed in Chap. 5). This assures us that all mathematical equations will be consistent.

Units as Algebraic Quantities

Whenever we multiply or divide physical quantities, we have to figure out what happens to the units. For example, we know that for something moving at constant speed, *distance = speed × time*. Suppose the speed is 50 feet per second (50 ft/s). To find the distance traveled in 10 s we multiply the speed by the time to get: distance = (50 ft/s) (10 s) = 500 ft.

Notice that the units were treated as algebraic quantities; the seconds canceled out in the numerator and denominator, giving the result in feet.

Consider a conversion from one unit to another. Suppose we are told that a certain backyard is 30 ft long, and we want to express the length in meters. We multiply the length in feet by the number of meters per foot (m/ft) to get the length in meters: (30 ft) (0.3048 m/ft) = 9.144 m.

Problem 1.24. A certain task takes 12 min to accomplish. Find the time it takes in seconds; in hours.

Solution

To get the time in seconds we multiply the time in minutes by the number of seconds per minute: $t = (12 \text{ min}) (60 \text{ s/min}) = 720$ s. To get the time in hours we multiply by the number of hours per minute: $t = (12 \text{ min}) [(\frac{1}{60}) \text{ h/min}] = 0.20$ h. Equivalently, we could divide the time in minutes by the number of minutes per hour: $t = (12 \text{ min})/(60 \text{ min/h})$. Separating the numerical and unit parts: $t = (\frac{12}{60})$ [min/(min/h)] = 0.20(min) (h/min) = 0.20 h, as before.

Problem 1.25. Convert the speed $v = 60$ miles per hour to ft/s.

Solution

$v = 60$ mi/h. We must change both the length unit and the time unit to convert this to ft/s. Recalling that there are 5280 feet in a mile (5280 ft/mi) and 3600 seconds in an hour (3600 s/h), we calculate as follows:

$$v = \frac{(60 \text{ mi/h}) (5280 \text{ ft/mi})}{3600 \text{ s/h}} = \frac{60 \cdot 5280}{3600} (\text{mi/h}) (\text{ft/mi}) (\text{h/s}) = 88 \text{ ft/s}$$

Problem 1.26. The dimensions of a rectangular block are width $w = 0.10$ m, length $l = 0.20$ m, and height $h = 0.30$ m. Find the volume in cubic centimeters (cm^3).

Solution

Method 1. We convert each dimension to cm: $w = (0.10 \text{ m}) (100 \text{ cm/m}) = 10$ cm, $l = (0.20 \text{ m}) (100 \text{ cm/m}) = 20$ cm, $h = (0.30 \text{ m}) (100 \text{ cm/m}) = 30$ cm. Then the volume $v = w \cdot l \cdot h = (10 \text{ cm}) (20 \text{ cm}) (30 \text{ cm}) = 6000$ cm^3.

Method 2. We first get the volume in cubic meters (m^3): $v = (0.10 \text{ m}) (0.20 \text{ m}) (0.30 \text{ m}) = 0.0060$ m^3. Next we determine how many cubic centimeters (cm^3) there are in a cubic meter (m^3). We note that 1 m = 100 cm, so $(1 \text{ m})^3 = (100 \text{ cm})^3 = (100 \text{ cm}) (100 \text{ cm}) (100 \text{ cm})$, or 1 m^3 = 1,000,000 cm^3. Thus the conversion factor is 1,000,000 cm^3/m^3. Then $v = (0.0060 \text{ m}^3) (1,000,000 \text{ cm}^3/\text{m}^3) = 6000$ cm^3.

It turns out that **units can be treated algebraically** in any physics equation; provided the units are consistent, they will combine to give the correct final unit. As an example of a more complicated situation, let us take the equation describing how far an object travels under constant acceleration (acceleration will be discussed in Chapter 2). The equation is

$$x = v_0 t + \tfrac{1}{2}at^2 \qquad\qquad (1.8)$$

where v_0 is the velocity at the starting time ($t = 0$ s), a is the constant acceleration, t is the time elapsed in seconds, and x represents how far the object has moved in the elapsed time.

Problem 1.27. In Eq. (1.8) we are given that $v_0 = 20$ m/s and that the acceleration corresponds to an increase in velocity of 3 m/s every second. Thus, $a = (3 \text{ m/s})/\text{s} = 3$ m/s^2. Find x when $t = 10$ s.

Solution

To find x we substitute all the known information into Eq. (1.8), getting

$$x = (20 \text{ m/s}) (10 \text{ s}) + \tfrac{1}{2}(3 \text{ m/s}^2) (10 \text{ s})^2$$

According to our general rule, seconds cancel out of the numerator and denominator in the first expression on the right and (seconds)^2 cancel out of the numerator and denominator of the second expression on the right:

$$x = (20 \text{ m/}\cancel{s}) (10 \cancel{s}) + \tfrac{1}{2}(3 \text{ m/}\cancel{s^2}) (100 \cancel{s^2}) = 200 \text{ m} + 150 \text{ m} = 350 \text{ m}$$

Always include units in your manipulations, and carry the algebra through on the units. This helps you to keep track of the units and indicates an error in your work if the units don't come out right.

Problem 1.28. In (*1.8*) find x, in meters, if $v_0 = 50$ ft/s, $a = 200$ cm/s^2, and $t = 1.5$ min.

Solution

We can't just enter the information into the equation, since the units are not consistent. Since we want x in meters, we convert all distances to meters

$$v_0 = (50 \text{ } \cancel{\text{ft}}/\text{s}) (0.3048 \text{ m/}\cancel{\text{ft}}) = 15.24 \text{ m/s} \qquad a = (200 \text{ } \cancel{\text{cm}}/\text{s}^2) (0.01 \text{ m/}\cancel{\text{cm}}) = 2.00 \text{ m/s}^2.$$

Similarly we convert minutes to seconds: $t = (1.5 \text{ } \cancel{\text{min}}) (60 \text{ s/}\cancel{\text{min}}) = 90$ s. Now (*1.8*) gives

$$x = (15.24 \text{ m/s}) (90 \text{ s}) + \tfrac{1}{2}(2.00 \text{ m/s}^2) (90 \text{ s})^2 = 1372 \text{ m} + 8100 \text{ m} = 9472 \text{ m}.$$

Significant Figures

Whenever a measured value is given for a physical quantity, it can only be an approximation because it is not possible to measure anything with "infinite" accuracy. For example, in measuring the length of a table with a meterstick one is limited to the accuracy of the rule lines on the stick [see Fig. 1-15(a)]. Even if the meterstick were absolutely accurate (an impossibility), one would still have to estimate the fraction of the smallest interval etched on the stick [see Fig. 1-15(b)]. Even if the person had the "superhuman" ability to read an "infinitely" accurate ruler, there would still be uncertainty since the apparently smooth edge of the table has some irregularities [Fig. 1-15(c)].

A scientist or engineer who specifies the numerical value of a physical quantity keeps only as many figures in the number as are justified by the accuracy to which the physical quantity is known. Thus, if in measuring the length of a table one uses a good meterstick with centimeter gradations etched on it and estimates the fraction of an interval between centimeter marks, one gives the measured value to a tenth of a centimeter, say $L = 3.427$ m. The 7 represents an estimate that may be off by one- or two-tenths of a centimeter. In other words specifying that $L = 3.427$ m implies that one is sure about the first three digits (3.42) but somewhat uncertain about the last digit. Nonetheless, because one has *some* knowledge about the last digit, the length is said to have been measured to four significant figures. For any measured quantity there is always some uncertainty in the last digit given.

The rules for dealing with uncertainties in measured quantities is typically discussed in detail in the laboratory section of a course. We give an overview of the subject in the following problems.

Problem 1.29. Five lengths have been measured and recorded as follows:

$$L_1 = 3.427 \text{ m} \qquad L_2 = 3.5 \text{ m} \qquad L_3 = 0.333 \text{ m} \qquad L_4 = 12 \text{ m} \qquad L_5 = 32.000 \text{ m}$$

(*a*)   Approximately what uncertainty is there in each measurement?

(*b*)   What is the approximate percentage uncertainty in each measurement?

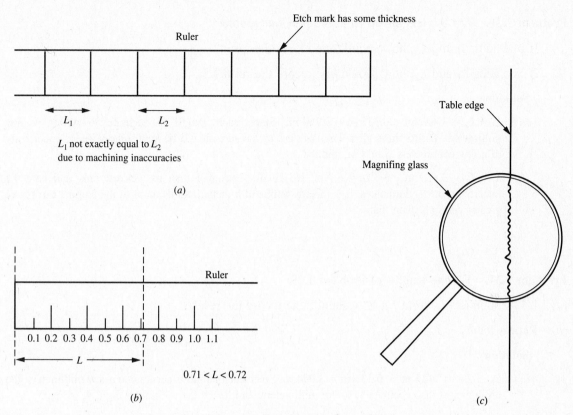

Fig. 1-15

Solution

(a) About one or two millimeters for L_1, L_3, and L_5; about one or two-tenths or a meter for L_2; and about one or two meters for L_4. Note the significance of placing the zeros after the decimal point in L_5. Although mathematically they don't change the value of L_5, they indicate the accuracy to which L_5 has been determined.

(b) For L_1 suppose that the uncertainty is two millimeters. Two out of 3427 corresponds to about six out of ten thousand, or multiplying by 100 to get percent, six hundredths of one percent. Because two millimeters is merely an estimate of the uncertainty, we can say that the percentage uncertainty in 3.427 m is several hundredths of one percent. Similarly for L_2 we have an uncertainty of, say two out of 35, which corresponds to several percent. For L_3 we have an uncertainty of about two out of 333, which corresponds to several tenths of one percent. For L_4 we have about two out of twelve uncertainty, which is about 20 percent. For L_5 we have about two parts in 32,000 uncertainty, which corresponds to several thousandths of one percent.

The number of significant figures thus provides a rough measure of percent uncertainty: two significant figures indicates several percent uncertainty, three significant figures indicates several tenths of a percent uncertainty; etc. The uncertainty itself indicates that the true value can be greater than or less than the recorded value by the amount of the uncertainty. The same holds for percent uncertainties.

Problem 1.30.   For the lengths given in the previous problem:

(*a*)   If one adds L_1 and L_3, how should one record the result?

(*b*)   If one adds L_1 and L_2, how should one record the result?

Solution

(*a*) $L_1 + L_3 = 3.427$ m $+ 0.333$ m $= 3.760$ m.   Since each length is accurate to within a few millimeters, their sum is also. The last zero in the sum should be kept; otherwise an uncertainty of a few centimeters would be implied.

(*b*) $L_1 + L_2 = 3.427$ m $+ 3.5$ m $= 6.9$ m. No chain is stronger than its weakest link, and here the uncertainty in L_2 dominates. It is already tenths of a meter, and the sum of the lengths can't have greater certainty than that.

Problem 1.31.   For the lengths of Problem 1.29:

(*a*)   If one subtracts L_3 from L_1, how should one record the result?

(*b*)   Repeat for $L_2 - L_1$.

Solution

(*a*) $L_1 - L_3 = 3.427$ m $- 0.333$ m $= 3.094$ m. Since each length is accurate to a few millimeters, the difference is also accurate to a few millimeters, and hence the millimeter digit, 4, is kept.

(*b*) $L_2 - L_1 = 3.5$ m $- 3.427$ m $= 0.1$ m. As in Problem 1.30(*b*) we need to keep only one place to the right of the decimal point.

In this case it is interesting to examine the percentage uncertainty in the result. Since there is only one significant figure, the uncertainty is one or two parts out of one! Thus the uncertainty is greater than 100%, even though the percent uncertainty in L_2 is only a few percent. The result of 0.1 m may actually be as high as 0.3 m or as low as -0.1 m (meaning that L_2 might actually have been smaller than L_1). This drastic loss of accuracy occurs when one subtracts two measured quantities that are very close in value, producing a difference that is comparable to the uncertainties in the individual values.

Problem 1.32.   Suppose that L_1 and L_2 of Problem 1.29 refer to the length and width of a rectangular tabletop. What is the area of the tabletop and how should it be recorded?

Solution

Area $= L_1 \cdot L_2 = ?$ The question is how many significant figures should be kept in the product. This can be answered by noting that the percent uncertainty in the product should be roughly the same as the larger of the percent uncertainties in the two factors. To understand why this is reasonable, let as assume that L_1 is known perfectly (not a real possibility). Then if L_2 were increased by 10% the area would be increased by 10% also (see Fig. 1-16). If, on the other hand, L_2 were reduced by, say, 20%, then the area would be reduced by 20% also. If L_1 were not exactly known but had an error of, say, several hundreths of a percent, as in our actual case, this would have a negligible effect on the percent uncertainty in the product. Thus, the percent uncertainty in the product is indeed approximately the same as the larger of the individual percent uncertainties.

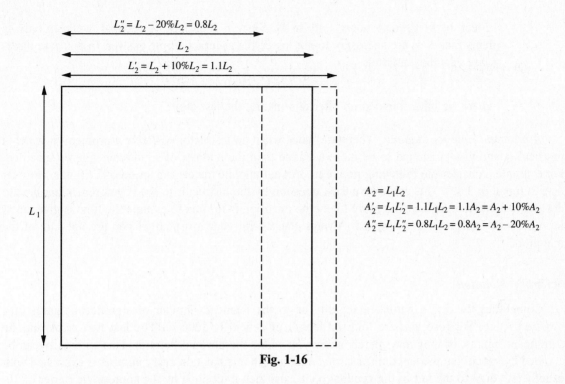

Fig. 1-16

For our case the larger percent uncertainty is in L_2, where it was shown in Problem 1.29 to be several percent. Then, following our analysis (after Problem 1.29) we should keep *at most* three significant figures in the product:

$$A = (3.427 \text{ m}) (3.5 \text{ m}) = 12.0 \text{ m}^2$$

One could argue that we should keep only two significant figures in Problem 1.32 but this would imply a larger percentage uncertainty than is justified. While one can always determine in a given problem whether to do so or not, keeping one more significant figure in the product than found in the cruder factor is often a reasonable thing to do.

The same rule that holds for the number of significant figures in the product of two numbers holds for the quotient of two numbers as well. This is because, as in multiplication, the percent uncertainty in the quotient is roughly the same as the larger of the percent uncertainties in the quantities being divided.

Problem 1.33.   A bicycle travels 634.73 ft in 42 s. What is the speed of the bicycle?

Solution

$$\text{Speed} = \frac{\text{distance}}{\text{time}} = \frac{634.73 \text{ ft}}{42 \text{ s}} = 15.1 \text{ ft/s}$$

Note.   Often in a physics problem certain numbers appear that are to be presumed exact. Consider the circumference of a circle $C = 2\pi R$, where R is the measured radius. The 2 and the π are exact mathematical quantities, not measured quantities. Suppose, for example, R is given as $R = 2.16$ m. What is the circumference C? The number of significant figures in the answer will be the same as or at most one more than that of R (to reflect the *percentage* uncertainty in *R*). Since π is an infinite decimal, we keep only as many places as are necessary to not lessen the accuracy of the answer. In this case three-place accuracy suffices:

$$C = 2(3.14)\,(2.16\text{ m}) = 13.6$$

where we have rounded up after eliminating the last digit.

A practical note for students. There are times when an instructor will give a problem in which a physical quantity is presumed to be more accurate than the number of significant figures specified. For example, consider the following problem: "An automobile travels at a speed of 32.5 m/s. How far does it travel in 3 s?" This could be a trick question by the instructor to see if you remember how to deal with significant figures, but more likely the intention is for you to assume the time is given to at least the same accuracy as the speed. Always check with your instructor if you are not sure of the intention.

Scientific Notation

Sometimes there is a natural ambiguity as to the intended number of significant figures in a reported value. Suppose you are told the length of a field is 3200 m. The last two zeros may be significant figures, or they may merely show you where the decimal point is. This ambiguity can be avoided by specifying the length in *scientific notation*. In this notation every number is expressed with exactly one digit to the left of the decimal point, and then multiplied by the appropriate power of 10. For example, the number 356 is expressed as $3.56 \cdot 10^2$, and the length 0.0003246 cm is expressed as $3.246 \cdot 10^{-4}$ cm. The power of 10, called the **exponent**, can be positive or negative, and tells you how many digits to move the decimal point to the right or left, respectively. To add or subtract two numbers in scientific notation, one first has to convert them to numbers with the same exponent. For example,

$$3.56 \cdot 10^2 + 2.437 \cdot 10^3 = 0.356 \cdot 10^3 + 2.437 \cdot 10^3 = 2.793 \cdot 10^3$$

To multiply or divide two numbers is particularly easy since multiplying or dividing powers of 10 is accomplished by adding or subtracting the exponents, respectively.

Problem 1.34. Express in scientific notation the product of (*a*) 356 and 2000, (*b*) 356 and 0.0000200; find the quotient of (*c*) 356 divided by 2000, (*d*) 356 divided by 0.0000200.

Solution

(*a*) $(3.56 \cdot 10^2)\,(2.000 \cdot 10^3) = 7.12 \cdot 10^5$ (*c*) $\dfrac{3.56 \cdot 10^2}{2.000 \cdot 10^3} = 1.78 \cdot 10^{-1}$

(*b*) $(3.56 \cdot 10^2)\,(2.00 \cdot 10^{-5}) = 7.12 \cdot 10^{-3}$ (*d*) $\dfrac{3.56 \cdot 10^2}{2.00 \cdot 10^{-5}} = 1.78 \cdot 10^7$

Problems for Review and Mind Stretching

Problem 1.35. Variables *y* and *x* are related by the equation

$$6y + 3x = 12 \tag{i}$$

(a)   Write y as a function of x.

(b)   Calculate the value of y at the following x values: $x = -2, -1, 0, 1, 2$.

(c)   Find the slope and y intercept of the straight-line graph of the function.

Solution

(a)   Isolate y by first subtracting $3x$ from each side of (i): $6y = -3x + 12$. Next, divide both sides by 6 to get

$$y = f(x) = -\tfrac{1}{2}x + 2 \tag{ii}$$

which is the desired result.

(b)   Substitute the values into (ii) to get

$$y = f(-2) = -\tfrac{1}{2}(-2) + 2 = 3 \qquad\qquad y = f(1) = -\tfrac{1}{2}(1) + 2 = 1.5$$
$$y = f(-1) = -\tfrac{1}{2}(-1) + 2 = 2.5 \qquad\qquad y = f(2) = -\tfrac{1}{2}(2) + 2 = 1$$
$$y = f(0) = -\tfrac{1}{2}(0) + 2 = 2$$

(c) $y = mx + b$, where m is the slope and b is the y-intercept. For our case, (ii) above, we have slope $= -\tfrac{1}{2}$, y intercept $= 2$.

Problem 1.36.   Find the equation of the straight line shown in Fig. 1-17.

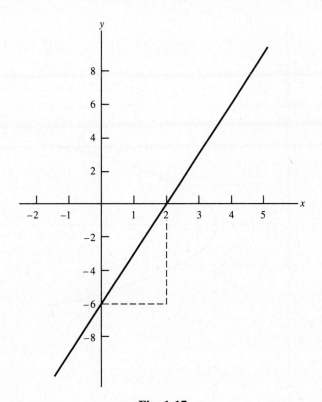

Fig. 1-17

Solution

For a general straight line, $y = Ax + B$. From the graph we see that when $x = 0$, $y = -6$, so the intercept is $B = -6$. The slope A can be obtained by considering the two points where the line crosses the axes and the right triangle formed by the dashed lines in the figure.

$$\text{Slope} = \frac{\text{vertical rise}}{\text{horizontal shift}} = \frac{6}{2} = 3$$

so $A = 3$. Then our equation is $y = 3x - 6$.

Problem 1.37.   Given the function $y = f(x) = 4x^2 + 2$.

(a)   Show that the graph of the function is symmetric about the y axis, and find the smallest value of y.

(b)   Find the inverse function $x = f^{-1}(y)$, and sketch what it looks like on a graph.

Solution

(a)   Since y takes on the same values at the points x and $-x$, the curve will be symmetric about a vertical line through $x = 0$, or in other words, about the y axis. y will be smallest when the term $4x^2$ is smallest, and that occurs at $x = 0$. Thus, $y_{min} = 2$.

(b) $y = 4x^2 + 2 \Rightarrow 4x^2 = y - 2 \Rightarrow x^2 = 0.25y - 0.5$ or $x = \pm\sqrt{0.25y - 0.5}$

So we have two branches of the inverse function:

$$x = f_1^{-1}(y) = \sqrt{-0.25y - 0.5} \quad \text{and} \quad x = f_2^{-1}(y) = -\sqrt{0.25y - 0.5}$$

defined for all values of $y \geq 2$. A rough graph of the inverse function is shown in Fig. 1-18.

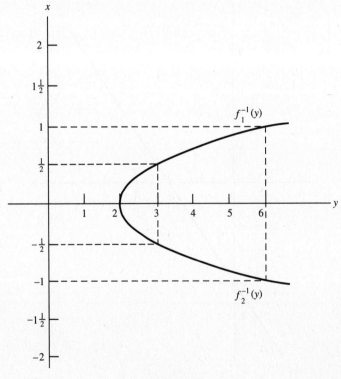

Fig. 1-18

Problem 1.38.

(a) Find the sine, cosine, and tangent of the angle θ shown in Fig. 1-19.

(b) Repeat for angle ϕ.

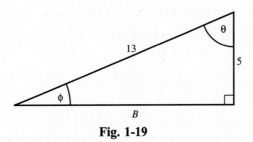

Fig. 1-19

Solution

(a) Since $\cos \theta = a/h$, we have $\cos \theta = \frac{5}{13} = 0.385$. To obtain $\sin \theta$ and $\tan \theta$ we need the side B opposite θ. Using the pythagorean theorem

$$5^2 + B^2 = 13^2 \quad \text{or} \quad B^2 = 13^2 - 5^2 = 169 - 25 = 144 \Rightarrow B = 12$$

Then $\sin \theta = \frac{12}{13} = 0.923$; $\tan \theta = \frac{12}{5} = 2.40$.

(b) We could repeat the calculations of part (a) for the case of ϕ. Instead we note that since $\phi = 90° - \theta$ (complementary angles), we have

$$\cos \phi = \sin \theta = 0.923 \qquad \sin \phi = \cos \theta = 0.385 \qquad \tan \phi = \frac{1}{\tan \theta} = 0.417$$

Problem 1.39. Determine the angles θ and ϕ in Fig. 1-19.

Solution

Using the results of Prob. 1.38, we have $\theta = \sin^{-1}(0.923)$. Utilizing the inverse sine function on a calculator (or looking up θ in a trigonometric table), we get $\theta = 67.4°$. Then, $\phi = 90° - \theta = 22.6°$. As a check we calculate $\tan 22.6° = 0.416$, which agrees with Problem 1.38(b) to within rounding errors.

Problem 1.40. Solve the simultaneous equations

$$\text{(i)} \quad y = 5t - 7 \qquad \text{(ii)} \quad y = t^2 - 1$$

Solution

Since both right sides equal y, they equal each other: $t^2 - 1 = 5t - 7$. Bringing all terms to the left side of the equation, we get

$$\text{(iii)} \quad t^2 - 5t + 6 = 0$$

This can be factored, yielding $(t - 3)(t - 2) = 0$, and the two solutions for t are $t_1 = 3$ and $t_2 = 2$. Then, from either (i) or (ii) we get the corresponding values of y:

$$y_1 = 8 \qquad \text{and} \qquad y_2 = 3$$

Problem 1.41.   Suppose in Eq. (1.8) (preceding Problem 1.27) we are given $a = 6.25$ m/s^2 and told that $x = 122$ m when $t = 3.15$ s. Find v_0.

Solution

$$x = v_0 t + \tfrac{1}{2}at^2$$
$$122 \text{ m} = v_0(3.15 \text{ s}) + \tfrac{1}{2}(6.25 \text{ m/s}^2)(3.15 \text{ s})^2$$
$$122 \text{ m} = v_0(3.15 \text{ s}) + 31.0 \text{ m}$$
$$91 \text{ m} = (3.15 \text{ s})v_0$$
$$v_0 = 28.9 \text{ m/s}$$

Problem 1.42.   Two measured lengths are recorded as $l_1 = 23.2$ m and $l_2 = 21.749$ m.

(a)   How big an uncertainty would you roughly estimate there is in the value of l_1? Repeat for l_2.

(b)   How big, roughly, are the percent uncertainties in l_1 and l_2?

(c)   If the two lengths are to be added, how would one record their sum L?

(d)   What is the uncertainty in the recorded sum?

Solution

(a)   Assume an uncertainty between 1 and 2 in the last significant digit of each number. Then for l_1 the uncertainty is 0.1 to 0.2 m. For l_2 it is 0.001 to 0.002 m.

(b)   For definiteness we use 0.2 m as the uncertainty in l_1. The percent uncertainty is then (0.2/23.2)(100) = 0.86%. Hence, there is about a 1% uncertainty in l_1. For l_2 we get about (0.002/22)(100) = 0.009%. Hence, l_2 has about a 0.01% uncertainty.

(c) $L = l_1 + l_2 = 23.2$ m $+ 21.749$ m $= 44.9$ m.

(d)   The uncertainty of the sum should be roughly that of the less precisely known length. Therefore the uncertainty in L is about 0.1 to 0.2 m. (Indeed, this is precisely why we keep the sum to three significant figures.)

Problem 1.43.   Assume l_1 and l_2 of Problem 1.42 are the length and width of a swimming pool.

(a)   How would you record the area A?

(b)   What is the percent uncertainty in the area?

(c)   What is the uncertainty in the area?

Solution

(a) $A = l_1 l_2 = (23.2$ m$)(21.749$ m$) = 505$ m.

(b)   The percent uncertainty in a product of two factors is about the same as the larger percent uncertainty of the two factors. In our case this is l_1, and from Problem 1.42 the percent uncertainty is about 1%.

(c)   Since the percent uncertainty in the area is about 1%, and the area is about 500 m^2, the uncertainty in the area is about 1% of 500 m^2 or about 5 m^2.

Problem 1.44.   Express in scientific notation (*a*) the lengths $l_1 = 436.37$ m and $l_2 = 0.00169$ m, (*b*) the product of l_1 and l_2, and (*c*) the ratio of l_1 to l_2.

Solution

(*a*) $l_1 = 4.3637 \cdot 10^2$ m $l_2 = 1.69 \cdot 10^{-3}$ m

(*b*) $l_1 l_2 = (4.3637 \cdot 10^2 \text{ m}) (1.69 \cdot 10^{-3} \text{ m}) = 7 \cdot 37 \cdot 10^{-1}$ m^2

(*c*) $\dfrac{l_1}{l_2} = \dfrac{4.3637 \cdot 10^2 \text{ m}}{1.69 \cdot 10^{-3} \text{ m}} = 2.58 \cdot 10^5$

Note that in parts (*b*) and (*c*) we keep three significant figures, and that in part (*c*) the answer has no units (is dimensionless) since it is the ratio of two lengths.

Supplementary Problems

Problem 1.45.   Given the function $y = f(x) = 10x - 24$, find (*a*) its slope and y intercept; (*b*) the inverse function $x = f^{-1}(y)$; (*c*) the slope and x intercept of the inverse function.

    Ans.   (*a*) 10 and -24; (*b*) $x = 0.1y + 2.4$; (*c*) 0.1 and 2.4

Problem 1.46.   Given the equation $12x + 16y = 24$, find y as a function of x, and x as a function of y. Are these two functions inverses of each other?

    Ans. $y = -0.75x + 1.5$; $x = -(\frac{4}{3})y + 2$; yes

Problem 1.47.   Find the inverse of the function found in (ii) of Problem 1.35.

    Ans. $x = -2y + 4$

Problem 1.48.   Find both branches of the inverse function of $z = t^2 - 4$. For what values of z is this defined?

    Ans. $\pm \sqrt{z + 4}$; $z \geq -4$

Problem 1.49.   In the triangle shown in Fig. 1-20, find sides A and B.

    Ans.   26.0; 15.0

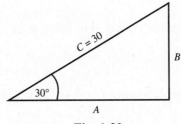

Fig. 1-20

Problem 1.50.   A student wants to determine the height of a flagpole in the schoolyard. She paces off 100 ft from the base of the flagpole and then measures the angle between the gound and a line of sight to the top of the flagpole to be $30°$.

(*a*)   What is the height of the flagpole?

(*b*)   If, instead, the flagpole had been 85 ft tall, what angle would she have gotten?

>   *Ans.*   (*a*) 57.7 ft.; (*b*) 40.4$°$

Problem 1.51.   If $\sin\theta = 0.90$ and θ is acute, find $\cos\theta$ and $\tan\theta$ without first finding θ.

>   *Ans.* $\cos\theta = 0.44$; $\tan\theta = 2.05$

Problem 1.52.   Convert each of the following to the sine of an acute angle: (i) $\cos 55°$, (ii) $\sin 135°$, (iii) $\sin 206°$, (iv) $\sin 340°$, (v) $\sin(-40°)$.

>   *Ans.*   (i) $\sin 35°$, (ii) $\sin 45°$, (iii) $-\sin 26°$, (iv) $-\sin 20°$, (v) $-\sin 40°$

Problem 1.53.   Convert each of the following to the cosine of an acute angle: (i) $\sin 15°$, (ii) $\cos 128°$, (iii) $\cos 199°$, (iv) $\cos 295°$, (v) $\cos(-130°)$.

>   *Ans.*   (i) $\cos 75°$, (ii) $-\cos 52°$, (iii) $-\cos 19°$, (iv) $\cos 65°$, (v) $-\cos 50°$

Problem 1.54.   Convert each of the following to the tangent of an acute angle: (i) $\tan 170°$, (ii) $\tan 250°$, (iii) $\tan 310°$, (iv) $\tan(-25°)$, (v) $\cot 22°$.

>   *Ans.*   (i) $-\tan 10°$, (ii) $\tan 70°$, (iii) $-\tan 50°$, (iv) $-\tan 25°$, (v) $\tan 68°$

Problem 1.55.   Find the solution of the pair of equations $5y + 8x = 1$ and $4y - 2x = 5$.

>   *Ans.* $x = -\frac{1}{2}, y = 1$

Problem 1.56.   Solve the simultaneous equations $6x + y = 2$ and $2x + 5y = 3$.

>   *Ans.* $x = \frac{1}{4}; y = \frac{1}{2}$

Problem 1.57.   Find the solutions of the pair of equations $y - 3x = 1$ and $y = x^2 - 9$.

>   *Ans.* $(x = -2, y = -5)$; $(x = 5, y = 16)$

Problem 1.58.   Find all the solutions to the pair of equations $y = 3x^2 - 4$ and $y = 2x^2 + 2x + 4$.

>   *Ans.* $(x = -2, y = 8)$; $(x = 4, y = 44)$

Problem 1.59.   A snail moves at a speed of 80 ft/h. How many meters will it travel in 100 s?

>   *Ans.*   0.677 m

Problem 1.60.   A rectangular block has dimensions $L = 3.24$ ft, $W = 39.2$ cm, $H = 1.62$ m. Find the volume V in m^3.

>   *Ans.*   0.627 m^3

Problem 1.61.

(a) If the length l_2 in Problem 1.42 were to be subtracted from the length l_1, how should the resulting length L' be recorded?

(b) What, roughly, is the uncertainty in L'?

(c) Estimate the percent uncertainty in the length L'.

   Ans. (a) 1.5 m; (b) 0.1 to 0.4 m; (c) 10 to 30%

Problem 1.62. Give a rough estimate of the uncertainty and a percent uncertainty in each of the following measured quantities: (a) 1.8307 m; (b) 321 s; (c) 12 ft; (d) 0.000223 m.

   Ans. (a) 0.0002 m, 0.01%; (b) 2 s, 1%; (c) 2 ft, 20%; (d) 0.000002 m, 1%

Problem 1.63. Assuming an uncertainty of 2 in the last digit of each measurement of Problem 1.62, find its range of possible values.

   Ans. (a) 1.8305 to 1.8309 m; (b) 319 to 323 s; (c) 10 to 14 ft; (d) 0.000221 to 0.000225 m

Problem 1.64. The length of a rug is measured to be 3.1944 m. The width is measured to be 6.22 ft.

(a) Find the area in m^2.

(b) Find the approximate percent uncertainty in the area.

(c) Give a rough estimate of the actual uncertainty in the area.

   Ans. (a) 6.06 m^2; (b) about 0.5%; (c) about 0.03 m^2

Problem 1.65.

(a) Find the perimeter of the rug in Problem 1.64 in meters.

(b) Is the percent uncertainty in the perimeter somewhat smaller or somewhat larger than the percent uncertainty in the width?

   Ans. (a) 10.18 m; (b) somewhat smaller

Problem 1.66. Referring to Problem 1.50(a), assume that the uncertainty in the measured angle is $2°$. If the 100-ft distance is known with great accuracy, what is the uncertainty in the calculated height of the flagpole?

   Ans. 5 ft

Problem 1.67. Given the formula $z = xy/t^2$, let $x = 132$, $y = 0.00736$, and $t = 0.0955$.

(a) Write x, y, and t, in scientific notation.

(b) Find z in scientific notation.

   Ans. (a) $1.32 \cdot 10^2$; $7.36 \cdot 10^{-3}$; $9.55 \cdot 10^{-2}$; (b) $1.065 \cdot 10^2$

Problem 1.68. Given the formula $x = v_0 t + \frac{1}{2}at^2$, suppose that $v_0 = 32.666$ m/s, $a = .00177$ m/s^2, and $t = 322$ s. Convert all quantities to scientific notation and determine the value of x.

   Ans. $3.2666 \cdot 10^1$ m/s; $1.77 \cdot 10^{-3}$ m/s^2; $3.22 \cdot 10^2$ s; $1.06 \cdot 10^4$ m

Chapter 2

Motion in a Straight Line

In this chapter we will assume that all quantities are correct to three significant figures. Thus 1 m = 1.00 m, 2 s = 2.00 s, 1.5 m/s = 1.50 m/s, etc.

2.1 TERMINOLOGY

Kinematics is the study of the physical quantities that describe the motion of an object. The most fundamental of these quantities are the *displacement* (*where* the object is) and the *time* (*when* it is there). From these two quantities we can define *velocity*, *speed*, and *acceleration*. To simplify the mathematics, in this chapter we restrict the discussion to straight-line, or one-dimensional, motion.

One-Dimensional Coordinate System

We call the straight line along which motion takes place the x-axis. It is conventional to label a horizontal axis by x and a vertical axis by y, but the choice is arbitrary. We pick a point on the axis and call it the *origin*. Each point of the axis is "labeled" with its coordinate which, numerically, is the distance of the point from the origin (expressed in, say, meters). Coordinates are taken positive in one direction (usually to the right of the origin along a horizontal axis) and negative in the opposite direction. The labeled axis constitutes our one-dimensional *coordinate system*.

Particle Description

For an object to be located at a definite point on the x axis at a given time, it would have to be infinitesimally small. Such an idealized object is called a *particle*. If we are dealing with a larger object that is not rotating, such as a block sliding on the floor, we can pick one particular point of the object and always use that point to specify the location of the object. We can thus always treat the motion as if it were that of a particle.

2.2 DISPLACEMENT

Absolute displacement specifies a particle's location as measured from the origin. It has both a magnitude and a sign. Its magnitude is the straight-line distance from the origin to the location of the particle. Its sign is positive if the particle is on the positive side of the axis, and negative if it is on the negative side. Absolute displacement thus corresponds exactly to the coordinate at which the particle is located on the axis. Figure 2-1 shows an x axis with positive chosen to the right. The absolute displacements when the particle is at the positions a, b, or c are x_a, x_b, or x_c, respectively. The arrows are drawn in to show if the displacement is to the right (positive) or to the left (negative).

Relative displacement is the location of a particle as measured from an *arbitrary* point of the axis. Thus, in Fig. 2-1, d_{ba} is the displacement of the particle at position x_b relative to position x_a. Note that $d_{ba} = x_b - x_a$. Similarly, d_{ca} is the displacement of the particle at x_c relative to position x_a, and $d_{ca} = x_c - x_a$. Like absolute displacement, relative displacement can be either positive or negative. If right has been chosen as the positive direction, then the relative displacement is negative when the position of the particle is to the left of the position from which it is measured.

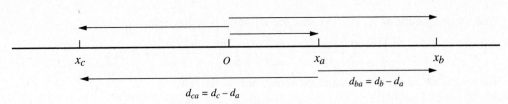

Fig. 2-1

Problem 2.1.   In Fig. 2-1 let $x_a = 3$ m, $x_b = 7$ m, $x_c = -5$ m. Find the magnitudes and signs of the relative displacements d_{ba}, d_{ca}, and d_{ac}.

Solution

$$d_{ba} = x_b - x_a = 7 \text{ m} - 3 \text{ m} = 4 \text{ m}$$

Thus the magnitude of d_{ba} is 4 m and the sign is *positive*.

$$d_{ca} = x_c - x_a = (-5 \text{ m}) - 3 \text{ m} = -8 \text{ m}$$

Thus d_{ca} has magnitude 8 m and is *negative* (x_c is to the left of x_a).

$$d_{ac} = x_a - x_c = +8 \text{ m}$$

(As expected, $d_{ac} = -d_{ca}$.)

2.3   VELOCITY AND SPEED

Average Velocity

If a particle is located at position x_1 at time t_1 and moves so that it occupies a different position x_2 at a later time t_2, then the *average velocity* v_{av} of the particle over that time period is defined as the relative displacement, $d_{21} = x_2 - x_1$, divided by the time elapsed, $t_2 - t_1$:

$$v_{av} = \frac{x_2 - x_1}{t_2 - t_1} \qquad (2.1)$$

Since t_2 is a later time than t_1 the denominator in (2.1) is always positive. The sign of v_{av} is thus the sign of the relative displacement, and thus it indicates whether the particle has moved to the right (plus) or to the left (minus). The magnitude, $|v_{av}|$, is just the *straight-line distance* from x_1 to x_2 divided by the elapsed time, $t_2 - t_1$. Average velocity is thus the "time rate of change of displacement" or the average change in displacement per unit time for the given time interval. The units are those of distance divided by time, and the SI units are meters/second (m/s). Other units commonly used are cm/s, ft/s, and mph (mi/h) (see Chap. 1).

Problem 2.2.   Refer to Problem 2.1. A moving particle passes point a at time $t_a = 4$ s, point b at time $t_b = 6$ s, and point c at $t_c = 9$ s. Find the magnitude and direction of the average velocity of the particle in the time interval from (a) t_a to t_b, (b) t_b to t_c, (c) t_a to t_c.

Solution

(a)   By applying (2.1)

$$v_{av} = \frac{x_b - x_a}{t_b - t_a} = \frac{7 \text{ m} - 3 \text{ m}}{6 \text{ s} - 4 \text{ s}} = \frac{4 \text{ m}}{2 \text{ s}} = 2 \text{ m/s}$$

Thus the magnitude of v_{av} is 2 m/s, and the direction is to the right.

(b)
$$v_{av} = \frac{x_c - x_b}{t_c - t_b} = \frac{-5 \text{ m} - 7 \text{ m}}{9 \text{ s} - 6 \text{ s}} = \frac{-12 \text{ m}}{3 \text{ s}} = -4 \text{ m/s}$$

The magnitude of v_{av} is 4 m/s, and the direction is to the left.

(c)
$$v_{av} = \frac{x_c - x_a}{t_c - t_a} = \frac{-5 \text{ m} - 3 \text{ m}}{9 \text{ s} - 4 \text{ s}} = \frac{-8 \text{ m}}{5 \text{ s}} = -1.6 \text{ m/s}$$

The magnitude of v_{av} is 1.6 m/s, and the direction is to the left.

Average Speed

Average speed is defined as the *total distance* traveled in a given time interval divided by that time interval. Since distance traveled is always positive, the average speed is always positive. Its units are the same as those of velocity. At first glance it might seem that the average speed is the same as the magnitude of the average velocity, but this is not always the case as will be illustrated by the following problem.

Problem 2.3. Find the average speeds over the three time intervals of Problem 2.2. Suppose the particle first moved to the right from point x_a to point x_b, and then moved to the left past x_a and on to x_c.

Solution

(a)
$$\text{Average speed} = \frac{\text{distance}}{\text{time}} = \frac{x_b - x_a}{t_b - t_a} = \frac{7 \text{ m} - 3 \text{ m}}{6 \text{ s} - 4 \text{ s}} = 2 \text{ m/s}$$

(b)
$$\text{Average speed} = \frac{\text{distance}}{\text{time}} = \frac{x_b + |x_c|}{t_c - t_b} = \frac{7 \text{ m} + 5 \text{ m}}{9 \text{ s} - 6 \text{ s}} = 4 \text{ m/s}$$

(c)
$$\text{Average speed} = \frac{(x_b - x_a) + (x_b + |x_c|)}{t_c - t_a} = \frac{4 \text{ m} + 12 \text{ m}}{9 \text{ s} - 4 \text{ s}} = 3.2 \text{ m/s}$$

Note. A comparison of Problem 2.2 and 2.3 shows that in one-way motion, average speed equals magnitude of average velocity. However, when a particle "backtracks," the distance covered exceeds the magnitude of the relative displacement, so average speed here exceeds magnitude of average velocity.

2.4 INSTANTANEOUS VELOCITY

Graph of Motion

The average velocity conveys a sense of how fast (on the average) and in what direction (on the average) a particle is moving. Can one do better than this?

The presumption of classical physics is that, at least in principle, one can know the precise location of a particle at any instant of time. (One might, for instance, make a videotape of the motion of a particle, and might then play it at normal speed while a clock with a moving second hand appears on screen.) Thus in principle, one knows the displacement x as *a function* (Chap. 1) of the time t; or what comes to the same thing, one can plot x vs. t on a graph such as that shown in Fig. 2-2. From the

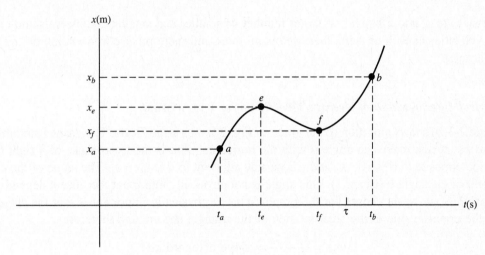

Fig. 2-2

graph (or the function) a much more precise description of velocity can be extracted. We start by exploring the graph.

Problem 2.4.   In Fig. 2-2, assume that $x_a = 3$ m at $t_a = 4$ s, $x_e = 5$ m at $t_e = 4.5$ s, $x_f = 4$ m at $t_f = 5.3$ s, and $x_b = 7$ m at $t_b = 6$ s.

(a)   In which direction is the particle moving, between t_a and t_e? t_e and t_f? t_f and t_b?

(b)   What is the average velocity from t_a to t_e? t_e to t_f? t_f to t_b? t_a to t_b?

Solution

(a) x is increasing in the entire interval between t_a and t_e, so the particle is moving to the right. Similarly, x is decreasing throughout the interval t_e to t_f; the particle is moving to the left. Clearly, t_e is the time and x_e is the point at which the particle first changed its direction of motion. Finally, x is increasing again throughout the interval t_f to t_b, and the particle is again moving to the right. Clearly, the direction of motion changed from left to right at (t_f, x_f). As can be seen, when a particle changes direction its displacement is either a maximum or a minimum point on the x vs. t graph.

(b)

$$v_{av,ae} = \frac{x_e - x_a}{t_e - t_a} = \frac{2 \text{ m}}{0.5 \text{ s}} = 4 \text{ m/s}$$

$$v_{av,ef} = \frac{x_f - x_e}{t_f - t_e} = \frac{4 \text{ m} - 5 \text{ m}}{5.3 \text{ s} - 4.5 \text{ s}} = \frac{-1 \text{ m}}{0.8 \text{ s}} = -1.25 \text{ m/s}$$

$$v_{av,fb} = \frac{7 \text{ m} - 4 \text{ m}}{6 \text{ s} - 5.3 \text{ s}} = \frac{3 \text{ m}}{0.7 \text{ s}} = 4.29 \text{ m/s}$$

Finally, for the entire interval,

$$v_{av,ab} = \frac{7 \text{ m} - 3 \text{ m}}{6 \text{ s} - 4 \text{ s}} = 2 \text{ m/s}$$

In Problem 2.4 the average velocities in the three subintervals collectively give us much more detailed information than does the average velocity in the overall interval t_a to t_b. Clearly, if we divide the interval t_a to t_b into a larger and larger number of smaller and smaller subintervals and calculate average velocities in each of them, then we obtain more and more precise information on the motion of the particle.

Geometrical Interpretation of Average Velocity on an x vs. t Graph

Figure 2-3(a) shows a portion of the graph in Fig. 2-2 on a larger scale. The dashed straight line is the chord ae, which makes an angle θ with the horizontal, and is the hypotenuse of a right triangle whose side opposite to θ is $x_e - x_a$ and whose side adjacent to θ is $t_e - t_a$. The *slope* of the chord is the tangent of the angle θ (Chap. 1). This angle is not physically important, because it depends on the particular units and scale chosen for the graph. What *is* physically important is that the slope is the ratio of the opposite side to the adjacent side of the triangle shown, and therefore

$$v_{\text{av}} = \frac{x_e - x_a}{t_e - t_a} = \text{slope of chord } ae$$

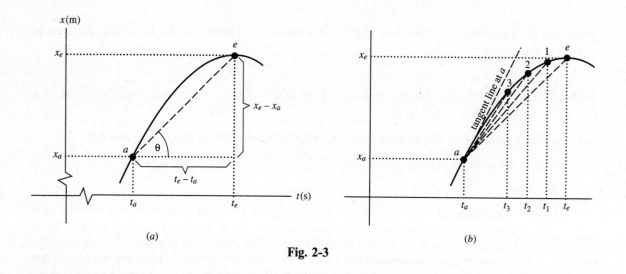

Fig. 2-3

Instantaneous Velocity

We are now prepared to define the most precise velocity possible—a velocity assignable not to an interval of time but to a given instant of time. In Fig. 2-3(b) we again show the x vs. t curve from t_a to t_e. Starting with t_e, we pick out a steadily decreasing sequence of times,

$$t_e > t_1 > t_2 > t_3 > \cdots$$

that approach t_a "from above." Over each time interval t_a to t_j ($j = 1, 2, 3, \ldots$) the average velocity v_{av} is defined in the usual way. As the intervals get smaller and smaller, the corresponding chords of the curve get closer and closer to the **tangent line** to the curve at the point a. The tangent line at a point on a curve is the line that just touches the curve at that one point; it is therefore the line whose direction is just the direction of the curve as it passes that point. Since the slope of each chord is just v_{av} over the associated time interval, we can say that the slope of the tangent line to the curve at point a represents the "ultimate" approximation to the velocity at point a. For this reason the slope of the tangent line at point a—often denoted the slope of the curve at a—is called the *instantaneous velocity* at point a, or at time t_a. Since any point of the x vs. t curve could have been used in this discussion instead of point a, we conclude that the slope of the tangent line to the curve at *any* time is just the instantaneous velocity at that time. The instantaneous velocity is usually given the symbol v without a subscript, and as with v_{av}, is completely specified by its magnitude and sign. The question of how to find the slope of the x vs. t curve at each point relates to the branch of mathematics called calculus. For simple enough x vs. t curves one can obtain the instantaneous velocity by algebraic means without formally using calculus, and we will do that below. But bear in mind that the determination of an instantaneous velocity generally requires the utilization of techniques of calculus.

Problem 2.5. Refer back to Fig. 2-2.

(a) What are the instantaneous velocities at points e and f?

(b) In the interval t_e to t_f, v_{av} was shown to be negative (Problem 2.4). How could this be determined using the slope-of-chord approach to v_{av}?

(c) Where in the interval t_f to t_b do you think the instantaneous velocity is well approximated by the v_{av} of that interval?

   Solution

   (a) Since point e is a maximum on the curve, the tangent to the curve at that point is horizontal and hence has zero slope. Thus the instantaneous velocity must be zero. Similar reasoning indicates that at point f, which is a minimum, the instantaneous velocity is also zero.

   (b) The chord ef will make an angle of greater than 90 ° with the horizontal graph axis. Indeed, the angle lies in the second quadrant where the tangent is negative; hence $v_{av, ef}$ is negative.

   (c) We can see with the eye that at a time τ approximately halfway between t_f and t_b the tangent to the curve will be nearly parallel to the chord fb. In other words, v (at time τ) $\approx v_{av, fb}$.

In general, if the x vs. t curve doesn't deviate much from a straight line in any given interval, then v at any point in the interval is nearly v_{av} for the interval as a whole. The ultimate example of this is a straight-line segment, where the instantaneous velocity is the same at each point (since the tangent to the curve is the same everywhere) and is the same as the average velocity over the whole straight-line segment.

Calculating v

   To actually calculate the instantaneous velocity we must use algebraic techniques. This means that we have to know the mathematical expression for x as a function of t, or, in other words, we must know the equation of the x vs. t graph. We call the value of x at time t, $x(t)$. Quite naturally, we use the notation $v(t)$ for the instantaneous velocity as a function of time. Suppose t_1 represents the time at which we wish to know the instantaneous velocity. That is, we want to know $v(t_1)$ (read as v at time t_1). Examining (2.1), the equation for average velocity between t_1 and some later time t_2, we have $v_{av} = [x(t_2) - x(t_1)]/(t_2 - t_1)$. Or, letting $x_2 = x(t_2)$ and $x_1 = x(t_1)$, $v_{av} = (x_2 - x_1)/(t_2 - t_1)$ [our Eq. (2.1) notation]. To get $v(t_1)$, the x component of the instantaneous velocity at time t_1, we let t_2 take on values closer and closer to t_1. We say that

$$v(t_1) = \text{limit as } t_2 \to t_1 \text{ of } \frac{x(t_2) - x(t_1)}{t_2 - t_1} \qquad (2.2a)$$

If we let $t_2 - t_1 = \Delta t$ and $x(t_2) - x(t_1) = \Delta x$, where Δt and Δx are read as "delta t" and "delta x" and represent the "increments" or changes in t and x, then (2.2a) can be reexpressed as

$$v(t_1) = \text{limit as } \Delta t \to 0 \qquad \text{of} \qquad \frac{\Delta x}{\Delta t} \tag{2.2b}$$

Observe that the conditions $t_2 \to t_1$ and $\Delta t \to 0$ are completely equivalent. Equations (2.2a) and (2.2b) are just different common notations for the same thing. But how do we take the limit and get an actual answer? We illustrate by example.

Problem 2.6. A particle moves along the x axis in such a way that its x vs. t equation is $x(t) = 5$ m $+ (2$ m/s$)t$. Find the velocity at (a) any instant t; (b) $t = 3$ s.

Solution

First we note that, unlike a pure mathematical equation, the numerical coefficients carry units (see Chap. 1) since the quantities x and t are physical quantities. Next we note that the whole expression must come out in correct units for x. The constant term is already in meters. The coefficient of the term with t in it has units of velocity (m/s); when this coefficient is multiplied by t in sec, the result is again in meters.

(a) Plotting x against t, we get a straight line whose slope is 2 m/s. From our graphical discussion of velocity it follows that the instantaneous velocity is constant at all times t and is just equal to the slope of the line: $v(t) = 2$ m/s. Let us apply Eq. (2.2a) to get the same answer. Let t_1 be the time at which we want the velocity, and let $t_2 = t_1 + \Delta t$ be our slightly later time. Applying Eq. (2.2a) to our case (leaving units out for the moment to avoid clutter) we have

$$v_{av} = \frac{(5 + 2t_2) - (5 + 2t_1)}{t_2 - t_1}$$

Substituting $t_2 = t_1 + \Delta t$ into this equation yields

$$v_{av} = \frac{(5 + 2t_1 + 2\Delta t) - (5 + 2t_1)}{\Delta t}$$

Canceling like terms with opposite signs in the numerator yields

$$v_{av} = \frac{2 \text{ m/s } \Delta t}{\Delta t} = 2 \text{ m/s}$$

where we have put the units back in the last equation. In this case the Δt has disappeared in our final expression for v_{av}. Thus, v_{av} is a constant and doesn't depend on the values of t_2 and t_1. Therefore, the instantaneous velocity at time t_1 is also $v = 2$ m/s.

(b) Since v is the same for any time t_1, we have solved for v at $t_1 = 3$ s, as called for.

Problem 2.7. Suppose $x(t) = 5$ m $+ (2$ m/s$)t + (4$ m/s$^2)t^2$. Find the velocity at any time t_1, and evaluate at $t = 1, 2,$ and 3 s.

Solution

Proceed as in Problem 2.6, temporarily ignoring the units.

$$v_{av} = \frac{x(t_2) - x(t_1)}{t_2 - t_1} = \frac{\Delta x}{\Delta t} \tag{i}$$

$$v_{av} = \frac{(5 + 2t_2 + 4t_2{}^2) - (5 + 2t_1 + 4t_1{}^2)}{t_2 - t_1} \tag{ii}$$

If we make the substitution $t_2 = t_1 + \Delta t$, and also note that

$$(t_1 + \Delta t)^2 = t_1{}^2 + 2t_1\,\Delta t + \Delta t^2 \tag{iii}$$

we then obtain

$$v_{\mathrm{av}} = \frac{(5 + 2t_1 + 2\Delta t + 4t_1{}^2 + 8t_1\,\Delta t + 4\Delta t^2) - (5 + 2t_1 + 4t_1{}^2)}{\Delta t} \tag{iv}$$

Simplifying the numerator and restoring the units leads to

$$v_{\mathrm{av}} = \frac{(2\ \mathrm{m/s})\Delta t + (8\ \mathrm{m/s^2})t_1\,\Delta t + (4\ \mathrm{m/s^2})\Delta t^2}{\Delta t} \tag{v}$$

Dividing out the Δt we get

$$v_{\mathrm{av}} = 2\ \mathrm{m/s} + (8\ \mathrm{m/s^2})t_1 + (4\ \mathrm{m/s^2})\Delta t \tag{vi}$$

Note that unlike the straight-line case, here v_{av} depends on both t_1 and Δt, or equivalently it depends on t_1 and t_2. For fixed t_1 and each different t_2, Δt is different and we get a different v_{av}. Letting $\Delta t \to 0$ in (vi) yields for the instantaneous velocity:

$$v(t_1) = 2\ \mathrm{m/s} + (8\ \mathrm{m/s^2})t_1 \tag{vii}$$

From (vii), we have $v(1\ \mathrm{s}) = 2\ \mathrm{m/s} + (8\ \mathrm{m/s^2})\ (1\ \mathrm{s}) = 10\ \mathrm{m/s}$, $v(2\ \mathrm{s}) = 2\ \mathrm{m/s} + (8\ \mathrm{m/s^2})\ (2\ \mathrm{s}) = 18\ \mathrm{m/s}$, and $v(3\ \mathrm{s}) = 2\ \mathrm{m/s} + (8\ \mathrm{m/s^2})\ (3\ \mathrm{s}) = 26\ \mathrm{m/s}$. In all our cases v is positive, so the velocity points in the positive x direction.

Note. It should be noted that taking

$$\text{limit } t_2 \to t_1 \text{ of } \frac{x(t_2) - x(t_1)}{t_2 - t_1} = \text{limit } \Delta t \to 0 \text{ of } \frac{\Delta x}{\Delta t}$$

is just part of the differential calculus and is called the *derivative of x with respect to t* at the point t_1 and is given the expression dx/dt. We won't discuss formal calculus in this book.

Figure 2-4 uses arrows to indicate the absolute displacement x (drawn below the axis) and the instantaneous velocity v (drawn above the axis, with tail at point of interest) for two positions of a particle moving along the x axis. The times are indicated in parentheses below the positions.

Instantaneous Speed

The instantaneous speed at time t_1 is defined as the limit as $t_2 \to t_1$ of the average speed, over the interval t_1 to t_2. As it turns out the instantaneous speed is *always* equal to the magnitude of the instantaneous velocity, so no new information is obtained.

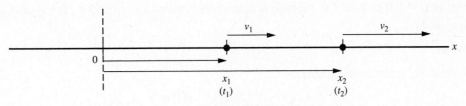

Fig. 2-4

Problem 2.8.   In Problem 2.3 we saw that the average speed sometimes differed from the magnitude of the average velocity. Why is it that there is never such a difference when instantaneous speed is compared with the magnitude of the instantaneous velocity?

Solution

Over any sufficiently tiny interval Δt the motion is necessarily in just one direction; the particle just doesn't have time to backtrack. Thus, average speed will equal magnitude of average velocity (Sec. 2.3) and, in the limit as $\Delta t \to 0$, instantaneous speed equals magnitude of instantaneous velocity.

2.5   ACCELERATION

Average Acceleration

Just as average velocity is the "time rate of change" of displacement [see (2.1)], so *average acceleration* is the "time rate of change" of velocity:

$$a_{av} = \frac{v(t_2) - v(t_1)}{t_2 - t_1} \qquad (2.3)$$

Like velocity, acceleration can be positive, negative, or zero. Letting $v(t_2) = v_2$; $v(t_1) = v_1$:

$$a_{av} = \frac{v_2 - v_1}{t_2 - t_1} \qquad (2.4)$$

The SI units are $(m/s)/s = m/s^2$. Other common units are cm/s^2, ft/s^2. Among auto enthusiasts we even have the "mixed" units mph/s (miles per hour per second). Thus a car going from 0 to 60 mph in 10 s has $a_{av} = 6$ mph/s.

If we know v at all times t (remember, v refers to instantaneous velocity), then we can plot v vs. t on a graph just as we plotted x vs. t. Figure 2-5 is an example of such a plot. Six points on the plot are noted with corresponding v and t values. The average acceleration between t_2 and t_5 is given by the slope of the chord joining points 2 and 5.

Instantaneous Acceleration

Instantaneous acceleration a at a given time (say t_2), is defined as the limit of the average acceleration over smaller and smaller time intervals each starting at t_2. In Fig. 2-5 it is seen that the chords from t_2 to t_5, t_2 to t_4, and t_2 to $t_3, \ldots$, get successively closer to the tangent line to the curve at point 2. Thus the instantaneous acceleration at time t_2, $a(t_2)$, is just the slope of the tangent line to the v vs. t curve at time t_2. This is completely analogous to the derivation of instantaneous velocity from the x vs. t curve.

Problem 2.9.   Assume the following values in Fig. 2-5: $v_1 = -2.0$ m/s at $t_1 = 1.0$ s; $v_2 = 1.0$ m/s at $t_2 = 2.0$ s; $v_3 = 3.5$ m/s   at $t_3 = 3.0$ s; $v_4 = 5.0$ m/s   at $t_4 = 4.0$ s; $v_5 = 6.0$ m/s   at $t_5 = 5.0$ s; $v_6 = 6.5$ m/s at $t_6 = 6.0$ s. Find the average acceleration between (a) t_1 and t_5, (b) t_2 and t_5, (c) t_2 and t_4, (d) t_2 and t_3.

Solution

Substitute in the defining equation (2.4).

(a)
$$a_{av} = \frac{6.0\ \text{m/s} - (-2.0\ \text{m/s})}{5.0\ \text{s} - 1.0\ \text{s}} = \frac{8.0\ \text{m/s}}{4.0\ \text{s}} = 2.0\ \text{m/s}^2$$

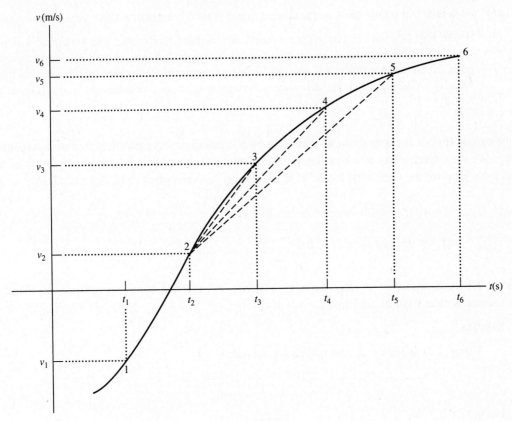

Fig. 2-5

For the remaining three intervals we get respectively:

(b)
$$a_{av} = \frac{6.0 \text{ m/s} - 1.0 \text{ m/s}}{5.0 \text{ s} - 2.0 \text{ s}} = 1.67 \text{ m/s}^2$$

(c)
$$a_{av} = \frac{5.0 \text{ m/s} - 1.0 \text{ m/s}}{4.0 \text{ s} - 2.0 \text{ s}} = 2.0 \text{ m/s}^2$$

(d)
$$a_{av} = \frac{3.5 \text{ m/s} - 1.0 \text{ m/s}}{3.0 \text{ s} - 2.0 \text{ s}} = 2.5 \text{ m/s}^2$$

Since a_{av} is positive in all four cases, the average acceleration in all four intervals points along the positive x axis.

Problem 2.10.   Refer to Problem 2.9.

(a)   Of the answers to (b), (c), and (d), which is the best approximation to $a(t_2)$, the instantaneous acceleration at time t_2?

(b)   What is the instantaneous acceleration at $t = 6.0$ s?

(c)   If the velocity is zero at some instant, does the acceleration have to be zero too?

   Solution

   (a)   The chord joining points 2 and 3, corresponding to the shortest time interval of the three, is most nearly parallel to the tangent line to the curve at point 2. Hence $a(t_2)$ is best approximated by a_{av} for the interval t_2 to t_3.

(b) At time t_6, v is a maximum, so the tangent line at point 6 is horizontal (zero slope). Thus $a(t_6) = 0$.

(c) No. In Fig. 2-5, the velocity v goes through zero as the curve crosses the horizontal axis of the graph sometime between t_1 and t_2. Yet the tangent to the curve is clearly not horizontal at that point, so the acceleration is *not* zero. In fact it is the nonzero acceleration which indicates that the velocity is changing from negative values, through zero, to positive values, as time progresses from t_1 to t_2.

The calculation of instantaneous acceleration by a limiting process parallels that of instantaneous velocity. We thus need to know v as a function of t, or in other words, we need the equation of the v vs. t graph. Suppose we want $a(t_1)$ (read "a at the time t_1"). Analogous to (2.2a) and (2.2b), we have

$$a(t_1) = \text{limit as } t_2 \to t_1 \quad \text{of} \quad \frac{v(t_2) - v(t_1)}{t_2 - t_1} = \lim_{\Delta t \to 0} \frac{\Delta v}{\Delta t} \qquad (2.5)$$

where $v(t_2) - v(t_1) = \Delta v$ and $t_2 - t_1 = \Delta t$.

Problem 2.11. Suppose v at any time t is given by $v(t) = 6.0$ m/s $- (2.0$ m/s$^2)t$. Find the instantaneous acceleration at any time t.

Solution

Using (2.5), we have, at time t_1 (leaving out units):

$$a = \frac{(6.0 - 2.0t_2) - (6.0 - 2.0t_1)}{t_2 - t_1}$$

Using $t_2 = t_1 + \Delta t$,

$$a = \frac{(6.0 - 2.0t_1 - 2.0\Delta t) - (6.0 - 2.0t_1)}{\Delta t} = \frac{(-2.0 \text{ m/s}^2)\Delta t}{\Delta t} = -2.0 \text{ m/s}^2$$

and a is constant for all t_1. The minus sign means the acceleration points in the negative x direction. It is no surprise that the acceleration is a negative constant—because the v vs. t curve is a straight line with negative slope.

Note. We have seen that if we know the x vs. t graph [or equivalently, the function $x(t)$], then we can find v at any time t; and if we know the v vs. t graph [or $v(t)$], then we can find a at any time t. We now ask if the reverse is true. Does a knowledge of the a vs. t curve [$a(t)$] lead to a knowledge of $v(t)$ and does a knowledge of $v(t)$ lead to a knowledge of $x(t)$? We will answer these questions by examining the very special case in which the acceleration is constant in time, $a(t) = a = $ constant. Not only does this example point the way to understanding more general cases, but it is very important in its own right. Many practical problems (and textbook problems) involve constant acceleration, including objects falling under gravity and objects sliding down inclines.

2.6 THE CASE OF CONSTANT ACCELERATION

Finding The Velocity

If we know that a is constant, we already know a great deal about the velocity v. In particular, we know that the slope of the v vs. t graph is a constant, and thus the graph must be a straight line with slope a. Figure 2-6(a) illustrates three possible graphs for a given value of a. Note that all candidates

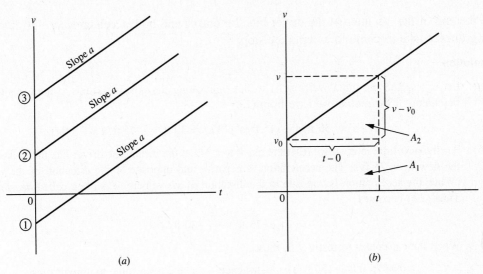

Fig. 2-6

are parallel straight lines. To know which one is the actual v vs. t graph we need one more piece of information, such as the intercept with the v axis. This point of intersection represents v_0, the velocity at $t = 0$, which is often called the **initial velocity**. To completely specify the v vs. t graph we thus need to know not only the value of the constant acceleration, but the initial velocity as well. In Fig. 2-6(b) we single out the straight line corresponding to the known initial velocity v_0. Since a is the slope of the line, we have

$$a = \frac{v(t) - v_0}{t - 0} \qquad \text{or} \qquad v(t) - v_0 = at$$

or, finally,

$$v(t) = v_0 + at \qquad\qquad\qquad (2.6)$$

which gives us the value of v at any time t, *provided a and v_0 are known.*

Problem 2.12.   A particle, starting with velocity $v_0 = 2$ m/s, moves along the x-axis with constant acceleration $a = 3$ m/s^2. Find v at times $t = 1$ s, 2 s, and 3 s.

> **Solution**
>
> Equation (*2.6*) becomes $v(t) = 2$ m/s $+ (3$ m/s$^2)t$. Thus
>
> $$v(1 \text{ s}) = 2 \text{ m/s} + (3 \text{ m/s}^2)(1 \text{ s}) = 2 \text{ m/s} + 3 \text{ m/s} = 5 \text{ m/s}$$
> $$v(2 \text{ s}) = 2 \text{ m/s} + (3 \text{ m/s}^2)(2 \text{ s}) = 8 \text{ m/s}$$
> $$v(3 \text{ s}) = 2 \text{ m/s} + (3 \text{ m/s}^2)(3 \text{ s}) = 11 \text{ m/s}$$
>
> The velocity increases by equal amounts in equal time intervals, just as is expected for constant acceleration.

Problem 2.13.

(a)   An automobile initially moving at 30 ft/s accelerates uniformly at 15 ft/s^2. How fast is it moving after 3 s?

(b) At the end of the 3-s interval the driver hits the brakes and now accelerates at -30 ft/s^2. How long does it take to come to a complete stop?

Solution

(a) Let us assume the initial velocity is to the right along the positive x axis. Setting $t = 0$ at the beginning of the motion we have from (2.6)

$$v(3 \text{ s}) = 30 \text{ ft/s} + (15 \text{ ft/s}^2)(3 \text{ s}) = 30 \text{ ft/s} + 45 \text{ ft/s} = 75 \text{ ft/s}$$

(b) For the new time interval we reset the clock to $t = 0$ at the instant the driver hits the brakes. Then the new v_0 is 75 ft/s. The acceleration is negative and opposite to the direction of the velocity. (When the acceleration is opposite to the direction of the velocity it is often called *deceleration*.) Thus (2.6) becomes

$$v = 75 \text{ ft/s} + (-30 \text{ ft/s}^2)t.$$

When the car comes to rest $v = 0$; thus,

$$0 = 75 \text{ ft/s} - (30 \text{ ft/s})t \quad \text{whence} \quad t = 2.5 \text{ s} = \text{time to come to rest.}$$

Finding the Displacement

We already know that constant acceleration ($a = \text{const}$) means $v = v_0 + at$, and the v vs. t graph is a straight line. Because of this, the average velocity over any time interval t_1 to t_2 will just be midway between the velocities at the beginning and end of the interval. In other words v_{av} is just the arithmetic mean of v_2 and v_1:

$$v_{av} = \frac{v_2 + v_1}{2} \tag{2.7}$$

Consider the time interval from 0 to t. Let the displacement and velocity at time 0 be labeled x_0 and v_0, and at time t, x and v. We now apply the definition of v_{av}, (2.1), to this interval, getting

$$v_{av} = \frac{x - x_0}{t - 0}$$

or $x = x_0 + v_{av}t$. Applying (2.7) to the same interval yields $v_{av} = (v + v_0)/2$. Substituting this into the previous equation we get

$$x = x_0 + \frac{(v + v_0)t}{2}$$

Since v is the velocity at time t, we can use the expression for v in (2.6) to get $x = x_0 + [v_0 + at) + v_0]t/2$, which, after multiplying out, becomes

$$x = x_0 + v_0t + \frac{at^2}{2} \tag{2.8}$$

If, as is often the case, we put our x-axis origin at the location of the particle when $t = 0$, then $x_0 = 0$, and (2.8) reduces to

$$x = v_0t + \tfrac{1}{2}at^2 \tag{2.9}$$

Problem 2.14. Find the absolute displacements of the particle of Problem 2.12 at $t = 1$ s, 2 s, and 3 s. Assume the particle is 3 m to the right of the x-axis origin at $t = 0$.

Solution

By (2.8), $x(t) = 3$ m $+ (2$ m/s$)t + \frac{1}{2}(3$ m/s$^2)t^2$. So,

$$x(1 \text{ s}) = 3 \text{ m} + 2 \text{ m} + 1.5 \text{ m} = 6.5 \text{ m}$$
$$x(2 \text{ s}) = 3 \text{ m} + 4 \text{ m} + 6 \text{ m} = 13 \text{ m}$$
$$x(3 \text{ s}) = 3 \text{ m} + 6 \text{ m} + 13.5 \text{ m} = 22.5 \text{ m}$$

Problem 2.15. How far did the automobile of Problem 2.13 travel (a) in the first 3 s? (b) in the *next* 2.5 s? (c) Find its absolute displacement after the entire 5.5 s.

Solution

Since the car continually moves to the right ($v > 0$), distance equals displacement in both (a) and (b).

(a) Here we set $x_0 = 0$ at $t = 0$. The displacement equation (2.9) gives

$$x(3 \text{ s}) = (30 \text{ ft/s})(3 \text{ s}) + \tfrac{1}{2}(15 \text{ ft/s}^2)(3 \text{ s})^2 = 90 \text{ ft} + 67.5 \text{ ft} = 158 \text{ ft}$$

(Only three significant figures are kept.)

(b) We now return to the problem at the end of the 3-s period, calling that instant $t = 0$ and that position $x = 0$. Then, from Problem 2.13, the new v_0 is 75 ft/s, and (2.9) yields

$$x = (75 \text{ ft/s})t + \tfrac{1}{2}(-30 \text{ ft/s}^2)t^2 = (75 \text{ ft/s})t - (15 \text{ ft/s}^2)t^2$$

Setting $t = 2.5$ s we get

$$x(2.5 \text{ s}) = (75 \text{ ft/s})(2.5 \text{ s}) - (15 \text{ ft/s}^2)(2.5 \text{ s})^2 = 187.5 \text{ ft} - 93.75 \text{ ft} = 93.8 \text{ ft} \quad (3 \text{ sig. fig.})$$

(c) The total displacement in the 5.5-s interval is just the sum of the displacements in the 3-s and 2.5-s intervals:

$$x = 158 \text{ ft} + 93.8 \text{ ft} = 252 \text{ ft}$$

Note. Equations (2.8) and (2.9) could not be used in one shot for the full 5.5 s because the acceleration was not constant for the full 5.5 s. Hence the problem had to be broken into two independent applications of (2.8) and (2.9).

Problem 2.16.

(a) Using the results of Problems 2.13 and 2.15, find the average velocity in the first 3-s interval from the definition (2.2), and see if it is consistent with what one gets from (2.8).

(b) Do the same thing for the last 2.5 s.

Solution

(a)
$$v_{av} = \frac{x - x_0}{t - 0} = \frac{157.5 \text{ ft} - 0 \text{ ft}}{3 \text{ s} - 0 \text{ s}} = 52.5 \text{ ft/s}$$

From Eq. (2.7), using the velocities in Problem 2.13,

$$v_{av} = \frac{v + v_0}{2} = \frac{75 \text{ ft/s} + 30 \text{ ft/s}}{2} = 52.5 \text{ ft/s}$$

which checks.

(b)   Using the notation of Problem 2.15(b) for the last 2.5 s, we again have

$$v_{av} = \frac{x - x_0}{t - 0} = \frac{93.75 \text{ ft}}{2.5 \text{ s}} = 37.5 \text{ ft/s}$$

From (2.7) we have

$$v_{av} = \frac{0 \text{ ft/s} + 75 \text{ ft/s}}{2} = 37.5 \text{ ft/s}$$

which again checks.

Finding the Displacement from the v vs. t Graph

In Fig. 2-7 we reproduce Fig. 2-6(b) with two arbitrary times t_1 and t_2, the corresponding velocities v_1 and v_2, and their average, $v_{av} = (v_2 + v_1)/2$, indicated on the graph. From its definition, Eq. (2.1),

$$v_{av} = \frac{x_2 - x_1}{t_2 - t_1} \quad \text{or} \quad x_2 - x_1 = v_{av}(t_2 - t_1)$$

The right-hand side of this equation is just the product of the height and width of the dotted rectangle on the v vs. t graph; in other words, $x_2 - x_1$ equals the area of the rectangle.

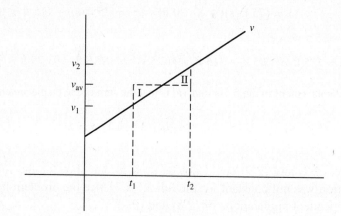

Fig. 2-7

It is easy to see that the area of the rectangle is the same as the area bounded by the v vs. t line above, by the two vertical dashed lines on the sides and by the horizontal axis below. This follows since triangles I and II have equal areas, and the new area differs from that of the rectangle in that triangle I is removed from the rectangle and triangle II is added. Thus for the case of constant acceleration (straight-line v vs. t graph), the displacement between two points x_2 and x_1, is just the area under the v vs. t curve between the corresponding times t_1 and t_2.

As an application, consider the case of Fig. 2-6(b). We consider the area under the curve from time 0 to t and the corresponding displacement $x - x_0$. As can be seen, the total area equals the sum of the areas of the rectangle (A_1) and triangle (A_2) shown. The rectangular area is $A_1 = v_0 t$. The triangular area is $\frac{1}{2}$ the base times the height: $A_2 = \frac{1}{2}t(v - v_0)$. But, from (2.6), $v - v_0 = at$ so that $A_2 = \frac{1}{2}t(at) = \frac{1}{2}at^2$. Thus, the total area $= x - x_0 = A_1 + A_2 = v_0 t + \frac{1}{2}at^2$, obtained earlier as (2.8).

General Case of Displacement from v vs. t Graph

It can be shown using the integral calculus that the statement "$x_2 - x_1$ equals the area under the v vs. t curve between t_1 and t_2" is true for *any* v vs. t curve—not just a straight line. Consider Fig. 2-8(a). The displacement from t_1 to t_2 is just the area under the v vs. t curve (shaded). While the rigorous proof of this requires calculus, we can see it intuitively as follows. We divide the interval along the time axis between t_1 and t_2 into tiny subintervals of width Δt, as in Fig. 2-8(b), and note that within each Δt the v vs. t curve is approximately a straight line. Then Δx for that time interval approximately equals the area under the curve within the Δt interval. Adding up all the successive Δx's is equivalent to adding up all the little areas under the successive Δt's so that $x_2 - x_1$ is approximately equal to the total area between t_1 and t_2. By letting the Δt's become infinitesimally small, the approximation becomes an exact equality. The result is true even if the velocity changes direction, as long as areas below the time axis are subtracted instead of added. Thus, in Fig. 2-8(a), we have that $x_4 - x_1$ equals the area from t_1 to t_3 *minus* the area from t_3 to t_4.

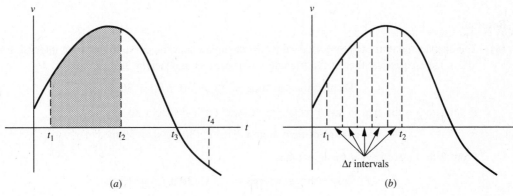

Fig. 2-8

Distance Traveled on v vs. t Graph

It is interesting to note the distinction between "distance traveled" and "displacement moved through" on a v vs. t graph. In Fig. 2-8(a), consider the time interval between, say, t_1 and t_4 for which we just obtained $x_4 - x_1$, the "displacement moved through." The "distance traveled" is the *sum* of the area between t_1 and t_3 and the area between t_3 and t_4, rather than their *difference*. This follows because, when v crosses the axis, the particle changes direction and starts to backtrack. Since the quantity $x_4 - x_1$ is the straight-line displacement from position 1 to position 4, we must *subtract* the backtracking between position 3 and 4. The "distance traveled," on the other hand, includes both the forward and backward travel as positive contributions.

Problem 2.17.

(a) For the curve depicted in Fig. 2-9, find the x displacement in the time intervals 0 to 2 s; 2 to 3 s; 3 to 4 s; 4 to 5 s.

(b) What is the total x displacement from 0 to 5 s, and what is the total distance traveled from 0 to 5 s?

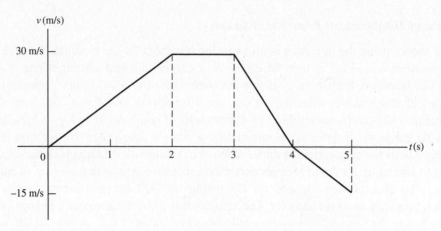

Fig. 2-9

Solution

(a) The displacement in each time interval is just the area under the curve in that time interval. From 0 to 2 s the area is just that of the triangle with base 2 s and height 30 m/s, so

$$\text{Displacement} = \text{area} = \tfrac{1}{2}(2 \text{ s})(30 \text{ m/s}) = 30 \text{ m}$$

From 2 to 3 s the area is just a rectangle of base 1 s and height 30 m/s, so

$$\text{Displacement} = \text{area} = (1 \text{ s})(30 \text{ m/s}) = 30 \text{ m}$$

From 3 to 4 s we have a triangle again:

$$\text{Displacement} = \text{area} = \tfrac{1}{2}(1 \text{ s})(30 \text{ m/s}) = 15 \text{ m}$$

For the period 4 to 5 s, we again have a triangle; this time, however, the area is below the time axis, so the velocity is in the negative direction and

$$\text{Displacement is minus the area} = -\tfrac{1}{2}(1 \text{ s})(15 \text{ m/s}) = -7.5 \text{ m}$$

(b) The total x displacement is the sum of the individual x displacements, or equivalently, the total areas above the axis minus those below the axis:

$$\textit{Total displacement} = 30 \text{ m} + 30 \text{ m} + 15 \text{ m} - 7.5 \text{ m} = 67.5 \text{ m}$$

The total distance traveled in the same time interval is the sum of all the areas, taken as positive, and

$$\textit{Total distance} = 30 \text{ m} + 30 \text{ m} + 15 \text{ m} + 7.5 \text{ m} = 82.5 \text{ m}$$

Finding Velocity in Terms of Displacement for Constant Acceleration

It is possible to eliminate the time between (2.6) and (2.8), obtaining a direct relation between v and x. First solve (2.6) for t, to get $t = (v - v_0)/a$. Then substitute this expression in (2.8) to obtain

$$x = x_0 + v_0 \frac{v - v_0}{a} + \tfrac{1}{2}a \left(\frac{v - v_0}{a}\right)^2$$

$$x - x_0 = \frac{v_0 v}{a} - \frac{v_0^2}{a} + \frac{\tfrac{1}{2}v^2}{a} - \frac{v v_0}{a} + \frac{\tfrac{1}{2}v_0^2}{a}$$

After some cancellation and combining of terms, we get

$$x - x_0 = \frac{\frac{1}{2}v^2}{a} - \frac{\frac{1}{2}v_0^2}{a} = \frac{v^2 - v_0^2}{2a}$$

which yields finally

$$v^2 = v_0^2 + 2a(x - x_0) \qquad (2.10)$$

If the particle is assumed to be the origin at $t = 0$, then $x_0 = 0$, and

$$v^2 = v_0^2 + 2ax \qquad (2.11)$$

Problem 2.18.   A truck having an initial velocity of 30 m/s accelerates uniformly at 3 m/s^2.

(a)   How fast is it moving after it has traveled 100 m from the initial position?

(b)   How long did it take to travel the 100 m?

Solution

(a)   We set $x_0 = 0$ at the initial time $t = 0$, when $v_0 = 30$ m/s. Then, from (2.11),

$$v^2 = (30 \text{ m/s})^2 + 2(3 \text{ m/s}^2)(100 \text{ m}) = 900 \text{ m}^2/\text{s}^2 + 600 \text{ m}^2/\text{s}^2 = 1500 \text{ m}^2/\text{s}^2$$

Taking the square root, we have $v = \pm 38.7$ m/s. Since both the initial velocity and the acceleration are positive the final velocity must be positive: $v = 38.7$ m/s.

(b)   We know v_0, and we just found v at $x = 100$ m. Substituting these values in (2.6) gives

$$38.7 \text{ m/s} = 30 \text{ m/s} + (3 \text{ m/s}^2)t \qquad \text{or} \qquad t = \frac{8.7 \text{ m/s}}{3 \text{ m/s}^2} = 2.9 \text{ s}$$

We could have also obtained t directly from (2.9), but then we would have had to solve a quadratic equation. Instead we will use (2.9) to check our results for v and t by solving it for x. From (2.9) we have

$$x = (30 \text{ m/s})(2.9 \text{ s}) + \tfrac{1}{2}(3 \text{ m/s}^2)(2.9 \text{ s})^2 = 87 \text{ m} + 12.6 \text{ m} = 99.6 \text{ m}$$

This differs from the correct result of 100 m only due to rounding errors, so our result checks out.

> ***Note.***   We discarded the negative square root of (2.11) in part (a) above. Does the negative square root ever have physical meaning? We investigate this question in the next problem.

Problem 2.19.   A truck is moving up a steep hill at 30 m/s when suddenly the engine conks out. The driver hits the brakes, but they don't work either. The truck starts to accelerate at -3 m/s^2.

(a)   How far does the truck move forward before it starts sliding back down the hill?

(b)   What is the velocity of the truck when it is 10 m forward of its initial position?

(c)   What two times do the answers to (b) correspond to?

Solution

Let us call the moment the truck starts its deceleration $t = 0$, and let the origin of the x axis (which runs parallel to the steep hill) be the truck's location at $t = 0$ so that $x_0 = 0$.

(a) Upon having moved the maximum distance forward, the velocity must be zero for an instant since the truck is changing its direction of motion. In other words, the velocity is changing from positive to negative and must pass through zero. Applying (2.11) allows us to solve for x directly without any reference to the time:

$$(0 \text{ m/s})^2 = (30 \text{ m/s})^2 + 2(-3 \text{ m/s}^2)x_{\text{max}} \quad \text{or} \quad (6 \text{ m/s}^2)x_{\text{max}} = 900 \text{ m}^2/\text{s}^2$$
$$\text{or} \quad x_{\text{max}} = 150 \text{ m}$$

(b) Here we apply (2.11) again, but now x is given and the corresponding v is to be determined:

$$v^2 = (30 \text{ m/s})^2 + 2(-3 \text{ m/s}^2)(100 \text{ m}) = 900 \text{ m}^2/\text{s}^2 - 600 \text{ m}^2/\text{s}^2 = 300 \text{ m}^2/\text{s}^2$$
$$\text{or} \quad v = \pm 17.3 \text{ m/s}$$

The positive velocity corresponds to passing the 100-m mark on the way up, while the negative velocity refers to passing the 100-m mark on the way down (after having reached the maximum position of 150 m).

Note. The magnitude of the velocity when the truck passes the given position is the same on the way up as on the way down. This is a general characteristic of motion under constant acceleration.

(c) Here we use (2.6) to get the two different times at which the truck passes the 100-m mark. On the way up

$$17.3 \text{ m/s} = 30 \text{ m/s} - (3 \text{ m/s}^2)t \quad \text{or} \quad (3 \text{ m/s}^2)t = 12.7 \text{ m/s} \quad \text{or} \quad t = 4.23 \text{ s}$$

On the way down

$$-17.3 \text{ m/s} = 30 \text{ m/s} - (3 \text{ m/s}^2)t \quad \text{or} \quad (3 \text{ m/s}^2)t = 47.3 \text{ m/s} \quad \text{or} \quad t = 15.8 \text{ s}$$

Freely Falling Bodies

Let us examine an important special case of constant acceleration in one dimension. Suppose an object is released either from rest or with an initial upward or downward velocity, and after release it is acted on *only* by the pull of gravity. (This assumes that air resistance is negligible.) Such an object is said to be in **free fall**. Examples are a ball dropped from a height, a rock thrown vertically upward, and an arrow shot straight downward from a height. As will be discussed in detail in Chap. 5, all objects in free fall have the same constant acceleration vertically downward. The magnitude of this acceleration, called the acceleration of gravity, is $g = 9.80 \text{ m/s}^2 = 980 \text{ cm/s}^2 = 32.2 \text{ ft/s}^2$.

Problem 2.20. A rock is dropped from rest from the roof of a building 100 m high.

(a) Find its velocity just before it hits the ground.

(b) Find the time it takes to hit the ground.

Solution

We choose the upward direction as positive and the roof as the zero of displacement. It is usual to label the displacement in the vertical direction by the letter y rather than x. Since the acceleration of gravity is in the negative y direction, we have $a = -g$. Also, $v_0 = 0$ and $y_0 = 0$. Equations (2.6), (2.9), and (2.11) take the forms

(i) $v = -gt = -(9.8 \text{ m/s}^2)t$

(ii) $y = -\frac{1}{2}gt^2 = -(4.9 \text{ m/s}^2)t^2$

(iii) $v^2 = -2gy = -(19.6 \text{ m/s}^2)y$

(a) At the ground, $y = -100$ m, and (iii) gives

$$v^2 = -(19.6 \text{ m/s}^2)(-100 \text{ m}) = 1960 \text{ m}^2/\text{s}^2 \quad \text{or} \quad v = \pm44.3 \text{ m/s}$$

Since it is moving downward, we choose $v = -44.3$ m/s.

(b) To find the time we use (i) with the value of v obtained above: $-44.3 \text{ m/s} = -(9.8 \text{ m/s}^2)t$ or $t = 4.52$ s.
[Or we could use (ii): $-100 \text{ m} = -(4.9 \text{ m/s}^2)t^2$ or $t^2 = 20.4 \text{ s}^2$ or $t = 4.52$ s, as before.]

Problem 2.21. An arrow is shot straight up from the edge of a cliff (Fig. 2-10) with an initial velocity of 50 ft/s.

(a) Find the time to reach the highest point.

(b) Find the displacement at the highest point.

(c) Find the height when the velocity is 25 ft/s.

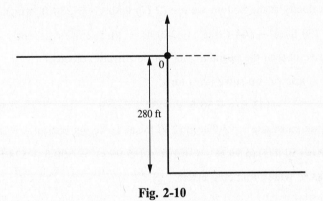

Fig. 2-10

Solution

In the English system of units $g = 32.2 \text{ ft/s}^2$. We choose the origin of the y axis to be the point at which the arrow is shot, so $y_0 = 0$.

(a) Equation (2.16) becomes in this case

(i) $v = 50 \text{ ft/s} - (32.2 \text{ ft/s}^2)t$

At the highest point, $v = 0$; so,

$$0 = 50 \text{ ft/s} - (32.2 \text{ ft/s}^2)t \quad \text{or} \quad t = \frac{50}{32.2}\text{s} = 1.55 \text{ s}$$

(b) Now that we know the time we can use (2.9), which for this case is

(ii) $y = (50 \text{ ft/s})t - (16.1 \text{ ft/s}^2)t^2$

Substituting the time to reach the top, we obtain

$$y = (50)(1.55)\ \text{ft} - (16.1)(1.55)^2\ \text{ft} = 38.8\ \text{ft}$$

[Or we could have used (2.11), with $v = 0$ for the highest point: $0 = (50\ \text{ft/s})^2 - (64.4\ \text{ft/s}^2)y$ or $y = 38.8$ ft, as before.]

(c)   We use (2.6) with $v = 25$ ft/s to get the time:

$$25\ \text{ft/s} = 50\ \text{ft/s} - (32.2\ \text{ft/s}^2)t \quad \text{or} \quad t = 0.776\ \text{s}$$

Next, we find the height using either (ii) with the time just obtained, or we use (2.11) with $v = 25$ ft/s. Choosing the latter, we get

$$(25\ \text{ft/s})^2 = (50\ \text{ft/s})^2 - (64.4\ \text{ft/s}^2)y \quad \text{or} \quad y = 29.1\ \text{ft}$$

Problem 2.22. If the arrow in Problem 2.21 just misses the edge of the cliff on the way down, find (a) the time for the arrow to reach the base of the cliff; (b) the velocity of the arrow just before it hits the ground.

Solution

(a)   We could use (ii) of Problem 2.21 to find the time by substituting in the displacement at the base of the cliff: $y = -280$ ft. Then $-280\ \text{ft} = (50\ \text{ft/s})t - (16.1\ \text{ft/s}^2)t^2$, and we can solve the quadratic equation for the time. Instead, we note that if the velocity at the bottom were known, we could use (i) of Problem 2.21 to get the time. Since this is a much easier way of getting the time, we try to solve (b) first and then return to (a).

(b)   To get the velocity at the bottom we use (2.11) with $y = -280$ ft, which gives

$$v^2 = (50\ \text{ft/s})^2 - (64.4\ \text{ft/s}^2)(-280\ \text{ft}) = 20,532\ \text{ft}^2/\text{s}^2 \quad \text{or} \quad v = -143\ \text{ft/s}$$

where we have chosen the negative root for downward velocity.

With v and v_0 known, we solve (2.6) for t;

$$-143\ \text{ft/s} = 50\ \text{ft/s} - (32.2\ \text{ft/s}^2)t \quad \text{or} \quad t = 5.99\ \text{s}$$

As a check we substitute $t = 5.99$s in (2.9) to see if we get back $y = -280$ ft:

$$y = (50\ \text{ft/s})(5.99\ \text{s}) - (16.1\ \text{ft/s}^2)(5.99\ \text{s})^2 = 300\ \text{ft} - 578\ \text{ft} = -278\ \text{ft}$$

which checks to within rounding errors.

Problems for Review and Mind Stretching

Problem 2.23. An automobile starts from rest as the light turns green and accelerates at 5 m/s² for 4.0 s. Find the final (a) displacement, (b) velocity.

Solution

Choose a coordinate system such that $x_0 = 0$ at $t = 0$, and note that $v_0 = 0$.

(a) $x = \frac{1}{2}at^2 = \frac{1}{2}(5\ \text{m/s}^2)t^2 = (2.5\ \text{m/s}^2)t^2$. At $t = 4.0$ s,

$$x = (2.5\ \text{m/s}^2)(4.0\ \text{s})^2 = 40\ \text{m}$$

(b) $v = at = (5.0\ \text{m/s}^2)t = (5.0\ \text{m/s}^2)(4.0\ \text{s}) = 20$ m/s.

Problem 2.24. At the end of 4 s the auto of Problem 2.23 stops accelerating and moves at constant speed for the next 10 s. Find the absolute displacement at $t = 14$ s.

Solution

In the final 10 s the automobile is moving at 20 m/s so that the relative displacement in that time interval is $x' = (20$ m/s$)$ $(10$ s$) = 200$ m. The absolute displacement is then 40 m $+ x' = 240$ m.

Problem 2.25. Suppose that at $t = 14$ s the car of Problems 2.23 and 2.24 starts to brake for a red light with acceleration $a_2 = -8.0$ m/s^2. How long will it take the car to come to rest?

Solution

The easiest approach is to consider the beginning of the braking period as a new starting time, $t = 0$, with $v_0 = 20$ m/s. Then $v = v_0 + at = 20$ m/s $- (8.0$ m/s$^2)t$. Upon coming to rest, $v = 0$.

$$0 = 20 \text{ m/s} - (8.0 \text{ m/s}^2)t \quad \text{whence} \quad t = \frac{20}{8.0} \text{ s} = 2.5 \text{ s}$$

Problem 2.26. With reference to Problems 2.23 to 2.25, what will be the entire displacement moved through by the car between the two lights?

Solution

As in Problem 2.25, we assume $t = 0$ at the beginning of the braking period. Then $v_0 = 20$ m/s, $x_0 = 240$ m (from Problem 2.24), and the motion ends at $t = 2.5$ s (Problem 2.25); by (2.8),

$$x = x_0 + v_0t + \tfrac{1}{2}at^2 = 240 \text{ m} + (20 \text{ m/s}) (2.5 \text{ s}) - \tfrac{1}{2}(8.0 \text{ m/s}^2) (2.5 \text{ s})^2$$
$$= 240 \text{ m} + 50.0 \text{ m} - 25.0 \text{ m} = 265 \text{ m}$$

Problem 2.27 A car is traveling at a constant speed of 60 ft/s in a 30 mph (44 ft/s) zone. A motorcycle cop bursts out from behind a bush at the instant the car passes, and accelerates from rest at 5.0 ft/s^2 until drawing alongside the car. How long does it take the cop to catch the car?

Solution

Let the instant the car passes the motorcycle be both our starting time and our zero displacement point. Then the equation for the displacement of the car is (i) $x_a = v_at$, where v_a is the constant velocity of the car. The equation for the displacement of the motorcycle is (ii) $x_m = \tfrac{1}{2}a_mt^2$, where a_m is the acceleration of the motorcycle and where we have used the fact that the initial velocity of the motorcycle is zero. Since we are interested in the time t at which $x_a = x_m$, we equate the right sides of (i) and (ii), to get

$$v_at = \tfrac{1}{2}a_mt^2 \quad \text{or} \quad (60 \text{ ft/s})t = (2.5 \text{ ft/s}^2)t^2$$

This is a quadratic equation, but a very simple one. The trivial solution $t = 0$ corresponds to the initial time when, indeed, the two displacements are the same (they are both zero). The other, nonzero, solution is the one we are interested in. To get it, divide both sides of the equation by t:

$$(2.5 \text{ ft/s})t = 60 \text{ ft/s} \quad \text{or} \quad t = 24.0 \text{ s}$$

Problem 2.28. A ball is dropped off a high cliff, and 2 s later another ball is thrown vertically downward with an initial speed of 30 m/s. How long will it take the second ball to overtake the first?

Solution

We label the first ball 1 and the second ball 2. Choose the origin for both balls to be the top of the cliff, and choose downward as positive for the displacements y_1 and y_2. Then the accelerations of the balls are $a_1 = a_2 = g = 9.8$ m/s^2. If t_1 and t_2 represent the times of fall, then

$$t_1 = t_2 + 2.0 \text{ s} \tag{i}$$

(For example, when t_2 equals 1 s, t_1 will already be 3 s.) The displacements for each ball are given by

$$y_1 = v_{01}t_1 + \tfrac{1}{2}gt_1{}^2 = (4.9 \text{ m/s}^2)t_1{}^2 \qquad y_2 = v_{02}t_2 + \tfrac{1}{2}gt_2{}^2 = (30 \text{ m/s})t_2 + (4.9 \text{ m/s}^2)t_2{}^2$$

When ball 2 catches up, $y_1 = y_2$,

$$(4.9 \text{ m/s}^2)t_1{}^2 = (30 \text{ m/s})t_2 + (4.9 \text{ m/s}^2)t_2{}^2 \tag{ii}$$

Substituting (*i*) into (*ii*) we get

$$(4.9 \text{ m/s}^2)\,[t_2 + (2.0 \text{ s})]^2 = (30 \text{ m/s})t_2 + (4.9 \text{ m/s}^2)t_2{}^2 \tag{iii}$$

Because $[t_2 + (2.0 \text{ s})]^2 = t_2{}^2 + (4.0 \text{ s})t_2 + (4.0 \text{ s}^2)$, (*iii*) becomes

$$(4.9 \text{ m/s}^2)t_2{}^2 + (19.6 \text{ m/s})t_2 + 19.6 \text{ m} = (30 \text{ m/s})t_2 + (4.9 \text{ m/s}^2)t_2{}^2$$

Canceling the $t_2{}^2$ terms, which are the same on both sides of the equation, we get

$$(19.6 \text{ m/s})t_2 + 19.6 \text{ m} = (30 \text{ m/s})t_2 \qquad \text{or} \qquad (10.4 \text{ m/s})t_2 = 19.6 \text{ m} \qquad \text{or} \qquad t_2 = 1.88 \text{ s}$$

Thus ball 2 catches up with ball 1 1.88 s after ball 2 is launched, or equivalently, 3.88 s after ball 1 is launched.

Supplementary Problems

Problem 2.29 A particle moving along the x axis reaches $x = 2.0$ m, 3.5 m, -8.0 m, 1.5 m at respective times $t = 0$ s, 1 s, 2 s, 3 s. Find (*a*) the absolute displacement for each of the four times; (*b*) the relative displacement in each of the time intervals 0 to 1 s, 1 to 2 s, 2 to 3 s, 0 to 2 s, and 0 to 3 s; (*c*) the average velocity in each of the time intervals of part (*b*).

    Ans.   (*a*) absolute displacement $= x$; (*b*) 1.5 m, -11.5 m, 9.5 m, -10.0 m, -0.5 m; (*c*) 1.5 m, -11.5 m, 9.5 m, -5.0 m, -0.167 m

Problem 2.30. In Problem 2.29 assume the particle moves in only one direction between successive given times.

(*a*)   Find the distance traveled in each of the time intervals of Problem 2.29(*b*).

(*b*)   Find the average speed in each of the time intervals.

(*c*)   In which interval(s) is the average speed different from the magnitude of the average velocity, and explain why?

    Ans.   (*a*) 1.5 m, 11.5 m, 9.5 m, 13.0 m, 22.5 m; (*b*) 1.5 m/s, 11.5 m/s, 9.5 m/s, 6.5 m/s, 7.5 m/s; (*c*) 0 to 2 s, 0 to 3 s; particle backtracks in these intervals.

Problem 2.31. For the motion graphed in Fig. 2-11, find the average velocities over the time intervals corresponding to (*a, b*), (*b, c*), (*c, d*), (*d, e*), (*e, f*), and (*f, g*).

    Ans.   4.0 m/s, 0 m/s, -10 m/s, 4.0 m/s, 3.0 m/s, -3.0 m/s

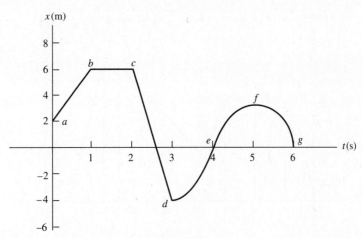

Fig. 2-11

Problem 2.32.   For the motion of Problem 2.31, find the instantaneous velocities at $t = 0.5$ s, 1.1 s, 2.4 s.

   Ans.   4.0 m/s, 0 m/s, -10 m/s

Problem 2.33   For the motion of Problem 2.31, find the average velocities over the intervals (t_a, t_c), (t_a, t_d), (t_b, t_f), (t_e, t_g).

   Ans.   2 m/s, -2 m/s, -0.75 m/s, 0 m/s

Problem 2.34.   Referring to Problem 2.32 and Fig. 2-11, estimate the instantaneous velocities at $t = 3.01$ s, 4.3 s, 5.0 s.

   Ans. ≈ 0 m/s, ≈ 3.5 m/s, ≈ 0 m/s

Problem 2.35.   A particle moves along the x axis in accordance with

$$x = -4 \text{ m} + (10 \text{ m/s})t - (3 \text{ m/s}^2)t^2$$

Find v_{av} for the interval 2 to 6 s.

   Ans. -14 m/s

Problem 2.36.   For the particle of Problem 2.35, find an expression for v_{av} over the interval $t = 2$ s to $t = (2 \text{ s}) + \Delta t$.

   Ans. $v_{av} = -2 \text{ m/s} - (3 \text{ m/s}^2)(\Delta t)$

Problem 2.37.   Referring to Problems 2.35 and 2.36, find the instantaneous velocity at $t = 2$ s.

   Ans. $v = -2$ m/s

Problem 2.38.   In the v vs. t graph of Fig. 2-12, assume the times shown are correct to three decimal places. Find the average accelerations over the time intervals (0 s, 1 s), (0 s, 2 s), (0 s, 3 s), (1.5 s, 3 s), (1.5 s, 3.5 s).

   Ans.   100 m/s^2, 75 m/s^2, 41.7 m/s^2, 0 m/s^2, -37.5 m/s^2

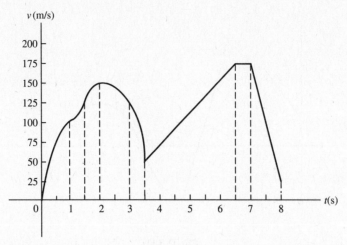

Fig. 2-12

Problem 2.39. Repeat Problem 2.38 for (3.5 s, 6.5 s), (6.5 s, 7 s), (7 s, 8 s), (0 s, 8 s).

   Ans.   41.7 m/s^2, 0 m/s^2, −150 m/s^2, 3.13 m/s^2

Problem 2.40. Referring to Problems 2.38 and 2.39, find the instantaneous accelerations at 2 s, 4.3 s, 5.2 s, 6.8 s, 7.4 s, 7.9 s.

   Ans.   0 m/s^2, 41.7 m/s^2, 41.7 m/s^2, 0 m/s^2, −150 m/s^2, −150 m/s^2

Problem 2.41. Refer to Problem 2.27. How far has the car traveled in the time it takes the motorcycle to catch up?

   Ans.   1440 ft

Problem 2.42. From Problem 2.27, what is the speed of the motorcycle when it catches up?

   Ans.   120 ft/s

Problem 2.43. In Problem 2.28, find the speeds of the two balls when the second overtakes the first.

   Ans. $v_1 = 38.0$ m/s, $v_2 = 48.4$ m/s

Problem 2.44. How far down from the top of the cliff will the balls of Problem 2.28 meet?

   Ans.   73.8 m

Problem 2.45. A coin is tossed vertically upward and reaches a maximum height of 90 cm. With what velocity was it thrown, and how long was it in the air?

   Ans.   4.2 m/s; 0.86 s

Problem 2.46. An arrow is shot vertically upward from the top edge of a 300-m cliff with a speed of 50 m/s, and it just misses the edge on the way down. What is its speed when it hits the base of the cliff?

   Ans.   91.5 m/s

Problem 2.47. How long does it take for the arrow of Problem 2.46 to hit the base of the cliff?

 Ans. 14.4 s

Problem 2.48. A bicycle traveling at constant speed is 50 m behind a bus that is just starting from rest with a constant acceleration of 2 m/s^2. What is the speed of the bicycle if it catches up with the bus in 6 s?

 Ans. 14.3 m/s

Problem 2.49. For the bus and bicycle of Problem 2.48, how long does it take for the bus to develop a speed equal to that of the bicycle, and how far will it have traveled in that time?

 Ans. 7.15 s, 51 m

Problem 2.50. A girl, standing still, tosses a ball vertically upwards. One second later she tosses up another ball at the same velocity. The balls collide 0.5 s after the second ball is tossed. With what velocity were they tossed?

 Ans. 9.8 m/s

Problem 2.51. In Problem 2.50, how high did the second ball rise before the collision, and what were the velocities just before collision?

 Ans. 3.68 m, ±4.9 m/s

Problem 2.52. A brick is dropped from rest from the roof of a building. On the way down it passes a 6-ft-high window and is observed to pass from top to bottom of the window in 0.25 s. How fast was it moving when it passed the top of the window?

 Ans. 20 ft/s

Problem 2.53. Refer to Problem 2.52. How far below the roof of the building is the top of the window?

 Ans. 6.25 ft

Chapter 3

Motion in a Plane

3.1 VECTOR QUANTITIES

To describe motion in a plane (two dimensions), one needs the same physical quantities as for motion in a straight line. The difference is that quantities that were described in one dimension by a magnitude and a *sign* must in two dimensions be described by a magnitude and a *direction*. Examples of such quantities are *displacement*, *velocity*, and *acceleration*. Any physical quantity that is described by a magnitude and a direction is called a **vector** quantity.

Definition

A vector is defined geometrically by means of an arrow. The length of the arrow is the magnitude of the vector, and the direction of the arrow is the direction of the vector. To specify the vector precisely, we can imagine a graph with an x and y axis at right angles to each other, and an arrow drawn to scale on the graph, with its direction specified by the angle it makes with one of the axes of the graph. In Fig. 3-1 we depict such a graph with three vectors **A**, **A′**, and **B**. The value of a vector does not depend on where it is located on the graph, *only* on its magnitude and direction. The vectors **A** and **A′**, which are parallel and have the same length, are therefore the same vector: **A** = **A′**. The length, or **magnitude**, of a vector **A** is often depicted as $|\mathbf{A}|$, or simply as A, and is always a positive number.

> *Note.* In general vectors will be denoted by **boldface** type to distinguish them from scalars (ordinary algebraic quantities).

Rules of Vector Algebra

1. Adding two vectors **A** and **B** gives another vector **C** = **A** + **B**, obtained as follows: Slide the arrow **B** parallel to itself until the tail of **B** touches the head of **A**; then draw an arrow from the tail

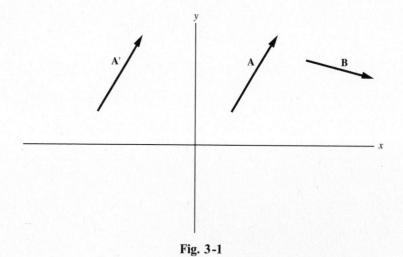

Fig. 3-1

of **A** to the head of **B**; this new arrow is the vector **C** [see Fig. 3-2(a)]. Vector **C** is called the **sum** of vectors **A** and **B**.

2. Multiplication of a vector **A** by a positive number h gives another vector, **B**, parallel to **A** and with a length that is h times the length of **A**. We write **B** $= h$**A** (and $B = hA$).

3. Multiplication of a vector **A** by a negative number, $-h$, gives another vector, **B**, whose direction is opposite to, or $180°$ from that of **A** and whose length is h times the length of **A**. We write **B** $= -h$**A** (and $B = hA$). See Fig. 3-2(b). Note that (-1)**A**, often written $-$**A**, is just the vector **A** turned $180°$, or upside down.

4. Subtracting a vector **B** from a vector **A** gives another vector **C** $=$ **A** $-$ **B**, which is obtained by turning **B** upside down and adding the result to **A**;   **C** $=$ **A** $+ (-$**B**$)$. See Fig. 3-2(c).

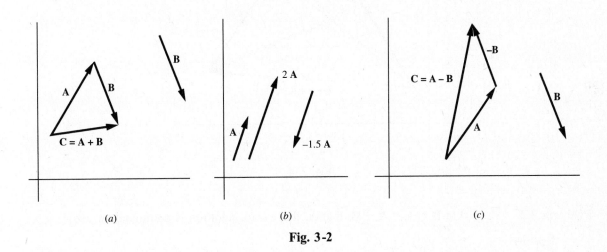

(a)   (b)   (c)

Fig. 3-2

Problem 3.1.   For the two vectors shown in Fig. 3-3(a), find **A** + **B** and **A** − **B**.

Solution

Since the tail of **B** is already by the head of **A**, we simply draw an arrow from the tail of **A** to the head of **B**. It is helpful to complete the parallelogram determined by **A** and **B**, as in Fig. 3-3(b). Then

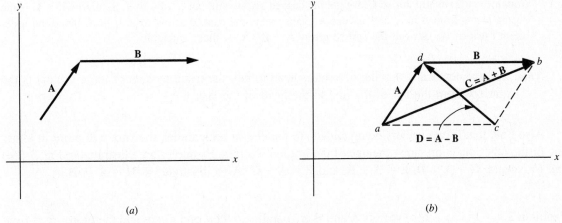

(a)   (b)

Fig. 3-3

C = **A** + **B** is just the diagonal arrow from point *a* to point *b*, as shown. This parallelogram law of addition can also be used to find **A** − **B**. The arrow from *c* to *b* is vector **A** and the arrow from *b* to *d* is −**B**. Therefore, **D** = **A** + (−**B**) = **A** − **B**, is the arrow from *c* to *d*, the other diagonal of the parallelogram.

Note.   We also can deduce that **A** = **B** + **D**, by adding the arrows from *a* to *c* and from *c* to *d*. Thus we can move a vector (in this case vector **B**) from one side of the equation to the other by changing the sign in front of it, just as in the case of numbers.

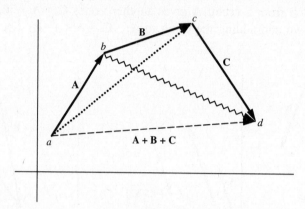

Fig. 3-4

Problem 3.2.   Show that **B** + **A** = **A** + **B**; that is, that vector addition is commutative.

Solution

The result follows from the parallelogram in Fig. 3-3(*b*). The arrow from *a* to *c* is **B**, and we already showed that the arrow from *c* to *b* is **A**, so **B** + **A** is the arrow from *a* to *b*, which is also **A** + **B**.

Problem 3.3.   Show that when you add three vectors it doesn't matter in what order you add them.

Solution

Consider the three vectors **A**, **B**, and **C** drawn head to tail in Fig. 3-4. **A** + **B** is the dotted arrow from *a* to *c*. If we add this to **C**, we get the dashed arrow pointing from *a* to *d*. Similarly, **B** + **C** is the zigzag arrow from *b* to *d*, and adding **A** again yields the dashed arrow from *a* to *d*. Since the order doesn't matter, we can call the dashed arrow **A** + **B** + **C** without ambiguity.

Note.   If one draws any number of vectors head to tail, the resulting sum of these vectors is the arrow from the tail of the first to the head of the last.

Also note that if two vectors being added are parallel or antiparallel, the sum will point in either one or the other direction along the line of the original vectors. Examples are illustrated in Fig. 3-5(*a*) and (*b*), where **G** = **A** + **D**, **E** = **A** + **B**, and **F** = **A** + **C**. Also illustrated is **H** = **A** − **B**.

Problem 3.4.   In Fig. 3-6(*a*) vectors **A** and **B** are parallel to the *x* and *y* axes and therefore are at right angles to each other. Find the magnitude and direction of the vector sum **C** = **A** + **B**.

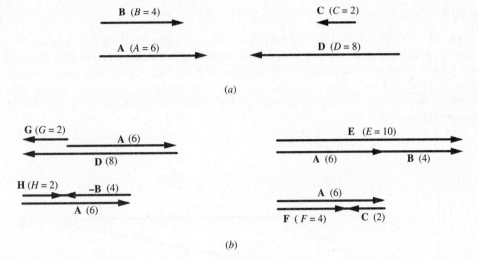

(a)

(b)

Fig. 3-5

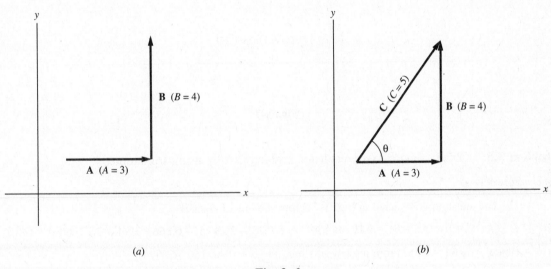

(a)   (b)

Fig. 3-6

Solution

In Fig. 3-6(b) the vector **C** is drawn in. The three vectors **A**, **B**, and **C** form a right triangle, with **C** being the hypotenuse. The angle θ gives the direction of **C**. From the pythagorean theorem, we have

$$C^2 = A^2 + B^2 = 3^2 + 4^2 = 25 \qquad \text{from which} \qquad C = 5.$$

Also,

$$\tan \theta = \tfrac{4}{3} \qquad \text{so that} \qquad \theta \approx 53\,^\circ$$

Problem 3.5. Assume that in Fig. 3-3(a) the vector **A** makes an angle $\theta = 30\,^\circ$ with the x axis and has a magnitude of 3. The vector **B** is parallel to the x axis and has a magnitude of 5. Find the magnitude of **C** = **A** + **B** and the angle that **C** makes with vector **A**.

Solution

We can solve this problem with a ruler and compass by drawing the graph to scale, as in Fig. 3-7. To get the magnitude of **C** we measure (with the ruler) the distances (ad) and (ab) in Fig. 3-7. Then, since these lengths are proportional to the lengths of **A** and **C**, respectively, we can set up the ratio $C/(ab) = A/(ad) = 3/(ad)$. This yields the result $C = 3(ab)/(ad) \approx 8$. To get the angle ϕ that **C** makes with the x axis, we use a compass to measure the angle between **B** and **C** in Fig. 3-7 and get the approximate result $\phi \approx 11°$.

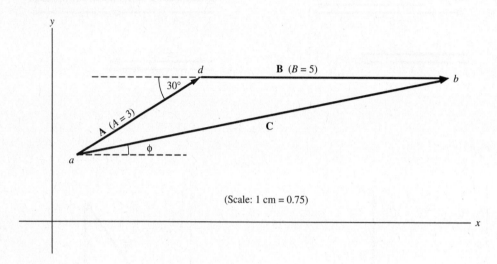

(Scale: 1 cm = 0.75)

Fig. 3-7

Problem 3.6.   Obtain a more exact result for Problem 3.5 by using trigonometry.

Solution

The situation is depicted in Fig. 3-7. From the law of cosines,
$$C^2 = A^2 + B^2 - 2AB \cos 150° = 9 + 25 - 2 \cdot 3 \cdot 5(-0.866) = 34 + 26 = 60.$$
Thus $C = \sqrt{60} = 7.75$. From the law of sines, $\sin \phi/A = \sin 150°/C$. Then
$$\sin \phi = \frac{3}{7.75} \cdot \frac{1}{2} = 0.193 \qquad \text{or} \qquad \phi = 11.1°$$

Components of a Vector

As can be seen from Problem 3.6, obtaining the sum of two vectors algebraically may require the use of complicated trigonometric formulas. Obtaining the sum of three or more vectors by such a trigonometric procedure could become unwieldy and confusing. There exists a more useful and manageable approach to adding vectors called the **component method**, which also gives valuable insight into the properties of vectors. We start by defining the component of a vector.

Consider an arbitrary vector **A** whose tail is made to touch an arbitrary directed line $\mathscr{P}$, as shown in Fig. 3-8. If sunlight were shining down perpendicular to line $\mathscr{P}$, vector **A** would cast a shadow on line $\mathscr{P}$ as shown. This shadow, A_p, is called the *projection*, or *component*, of **A** along $\mathscr{P}$. The projection is identified not only by a magnitude, or length, but also by a sign: positive if the sense of the shadow is in the positive sense of line $\mathscr{P}$ (as is the case for A_p), negative if the shadow is in the

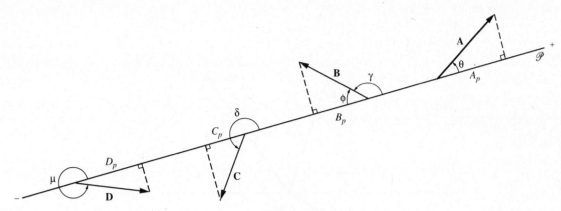

Fig. 3-8

negative line $\mathscr{P}$ direction (as for the case of B_p). If the vector **A** makes an acute angle θ with the line, as shown, we have $A_p = A \cos \theta$. Similarly, for vector **B** we have $B_p = -B \cos \phi$. If instead of ϕ, we used the angle γ, measured counter-clockwise from the positive $\mathscr{P}$ axis to **B**, then we would have $B_p = B \cos \gamma$, with the minus sign now contained in the cosine. The same would be true for vectors **C** and **D**: if one uses the counterclockwise angle from the positive $\mathscr{P}$ axis to the vector, one always gets the correct magnitude and sign.

In general it is easier to use the *acute angle* between any vector and the axis to get the magnitude of the component, and to put the sign in by eye. Thus for *any* vector, the component along $\mathscr{P}$ equals plus or minus ($\pm$) the magnitude of the vector times the cosine of the acute angle with line $\mathscr{P}$. The correct sign is then chosen by inspection.

Problem 3.7. In Fig. 3-8, assume the following data: $A = 6.0$, $\theta = 30°$; $B = 4.0$, $\phi = 60°$; $C = 5.0$, $\delta = 217°$; $D = 5.5$, $\mu = 320°$. Find the components of each vector on the line $\mathscr{P}$.

Solution

$$A_p = A \cos \theta = 6.0 \cos 30° = (6.0)(0.866) = 5.20$$
$$B_p = -B \cos \phi = -4.0 \cos 60° = (-4.0)(0.5) = -2.0$$
$$C_p = +C \cos \delta = -5.0 \cos 37° = (-5.0)(0.80) = -4.0$$
$$D_p = D \cos \mu = 5.5 \cos 40° = (5.5)(0.766) = 4.2$$

Problem 3.8. In Fig. 3-9 find the components of the vector **A** along the x axis (x component) and along the y axis (y component), if $A = 10$ and $\theta = 30°$.

Solution

$$A_x = A \cos \theta = 10 \cos 30° = (10)(0.866) = 8.66$$
$$A_y = A \cos(90° - \theta) = A \sin \theta = 10 \sin 30° = (10)(0.5) = 5.0$$

Problem 3.9. Assume now that the vector **A** in Fig. 3-9 has components $A_x = 3.0$ and $A_y = 4.0$. Find the magnitude of **A** and the angle θ it makes with the x axis.

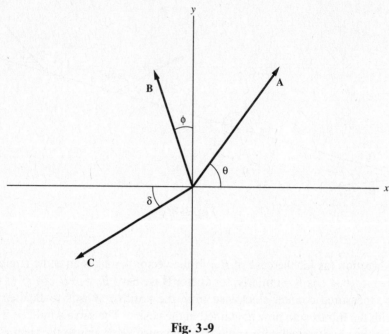

Fig. 3-9

Solution

The situation is depicted in Fig. 3-10. By the pythagorean theorem, $A^2 = A_x^2 + A_y^2 = (3.0)^2 + (4.0)^2 = 9.0 + 16.0 = 25$, so $A = 5.0$. Also, $\tan \theta = A_y/A_x = 4.0/3.0 = 1.333$. Taking the inverse tangent we get two possible answers: $\theta = 53°$ or $\theta = 53° + 180° = 233°$. Since we know **A** is in the first quadrant, because A_x and A_y are positive, we must take the solution $\theta = 53°$.

Note.   A knowledge of the two components of a two-dimensional vector uniquely determines the magnitude and direction of the vector.

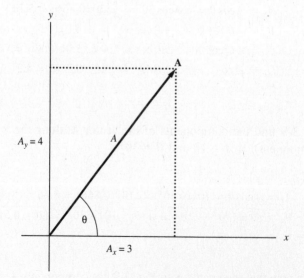

Fig. 3-10

Problem 3.10. In Fig. 3-9, assume $B = 7.0$, $\phi = 30°$, $C = 12$, and $\delta = 20°$. Find B_x, and B_y; C_x, C_y.

Solution

$$B_x = -B\cos(90° - \phi) = -B\sin\phi = (-7.0)\left(\tfrac{1}{2}\right) = -3.5$$
$$B_y = B\cos\phi = (7.0)(0.866) = 6.06$$
$$C_x = -C\cos\delta = -12\cos 20° = (-12)(0.940) = -11.3$$
$$C_y = -C\sin\delta = -12\sin 20° = (-12)(0.342) = -4.10$$

Adding Vectors by the Component Method

Consider the addition of two vectors, $\mathbf{C} = \mathbf{A} + \mathbf{B}$, as depicted in Fig. 3-11(a). It can be seen that $C_x = A_x + B_x$ and $C_y = A_y + B_y$. To convince yourself that this result is true no matter what the orientation of the two vectors, look at Fig. 3-11(b). Here B_x is positive as before, but B_y is negative. As can be seen from the figure, this is precisely what is required so that we still have $C_y = A_y + B_y = A_y - |B_y|$, as shown. The fact that the components can be positive or negative is just what is needed to ensure the generality of our result:

The component of the sum of two vectors along any axis is just the sum of the individual components along that axis.

This result can immediately be extended to the sum of any number of vectors (e.g., by adding a third vector to the sum of the first two, then a fourth to the sum of the first three, etc.). Thus, to add together a group of vectors, we first find their components along the x and y axes. Then we add the components along the x axis to obtain the component of the sum vector along the x axis; ditto for the y axis. From these components we obtain the magnitude and direction of the sum vector.

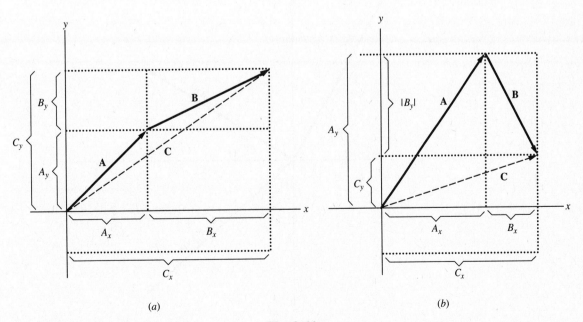

(a) (b)

Fig. 3-11

Problem 3.11. In Fig. 3-11(a), assume that vector **A** has a magnitude $A = 7.0$ and makes an angle $\theta = 40°$ with the x axis; similarly, assume that vector **B** has a magnitude $B = 8.0$ and makes an angle $\phi = 30°$ with the x axis. Find the magnitude and direction of the vector $\mathbf{C} = \mathbf{A} + \mathbf{B}$.

Solution

First we find the components of **A** and **B**.

$$A_x = A \cos \theta = 7.0 \cos 40° = 5.36 \qquad B_x = B \cos \phi = 8.0 \cos 30° = 6.93$$
$$A_y = A \sin \theta = 7.0 \sin 40° = 4.50 \qquad B_y = B \sin \phi = 8.0 \sin 30° = 4.00$$

Next we find the x and y components of **C**:

$$C_x = A_x + B_x = 5.36 + 6.93 = 12.3 \qquad C_y = A_y + B_y = 4.50 + 4.00 = 8.50$$

Finally, we follow the procedure used in Problem 3.9 to obtain the magnitude and direction of **C** from the components C_x and C_y.

$$C^2 = C_x{}^2 + C_y{}^2 = (12.3)^2 + (8.50)^2 = 223.5 \qquad \text{or} \qquad C = 15.0$$
$$\tan \delta = \frac{C_y}{C_x} = \frac{8.50}{12.3} = 0.691 \qquad \text{or} \qquad \delta = 34.6° \qquad \text{or} \qquad 214.6°$$

Since C_x and C_y are both positive, **C** is in the first quadrant, and we must choose $\delta = 34.6°$.

Problem 3.12. Find the sum of the three vectors shown in Fig. 3-12.

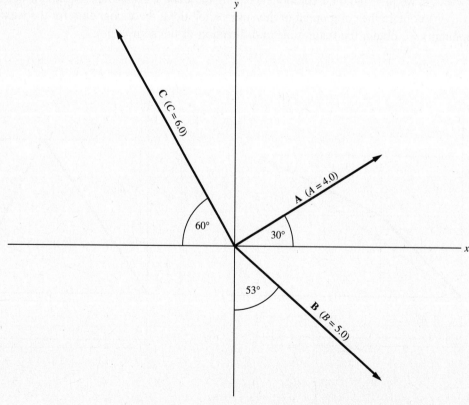

Fig. 3-12

Note. The sum of a group of vectors is often called the **resultant** vector **R**.

Solution

We first calculate the components of the three vectors:

$$A_x = 4.0 \cos 30° = 3.46 \qquad A_y = 4.0 \sin 30° = 2.00$$
$$B_x = 5.0 \sin 53° = 4.00 \qquad B_y = -5.0 \cos 53° = -3.00$$
$$C_x = -6.0 \cos 60° = -3.00 \qquad C_y = 6.0 \sin 60° = 5.20$$

The components of **R** are then

$$R_x = 3.46 + 4.00 - 3.00 = 4.46 \qquad R_y = 2.00 - 3.00 + 5.20 = 4.20$$

which give

$$R = (4.46^2 + 4.20^2)^{1/2} = 6.13 \qquad \tan \delta = \frac{4.20}{4.46} = 0.942 \qquad \text{or} \qquad \delta = 43.3°$$

where δ is the angle of **R** above the positive x axis.

Problem 3.13. Returning to Problem 3.11, find the magnitude and direction of the vector **C = A − B**.

Solution

Now we must find the components of **A** and −**B**, and then carry out the addition **C = A + (−B)** following the procedure of Problem 3.11. The components of **A** have already been obtained in Problem 3.11: $A_x = 5.36$; $A_y = 4.50$. The components of −**B** are just minus the components of **B**. This can be seen by noting that the shadows of **B** and "upside down" **B** have the same magnitude but opposite directions along the line. Thus the components of −**B** are $-B_x = -6.93$; $-B_y = -4.00$. Next we find the x and y components of **C = A − B**:

$$C_x = A_x + (-B_x) = 5.36 - 6.93 = -1.57 \qquad C_y = A_y - B_y = 4.50 - 4.00 = 0.50$$

Consequently,

$$C^2 = C_x{}^2 + C_y{}^2 = (-1.57)^2 + (0.50)^2 = 2.71 \qquad \text{or} \qquad C = 1.65$$

$$\tan \delta = \frac{C_y}{C_x} = -\frac{0.50}{1.57} = -0.319$$

whence $\delta = 162.3°$ or $342.3°$. Since C_x is negative and C_y is positive, the vector **C** is in the second quadrant, and we must choose $\delta = 162.3°$. (Alternatively, set $\tan \gamma = |C_y/C_x| = 0.50/1.57 = 0.319 \Rightarrow \gamma = 17.7° = $ acute angle made by **C** with the x axis. Then, **C** must lie $17.7°$ above the negative x axis.)

3.2 KINEMATICS IN A PLANE—PROJECTILE MOTION

Displacement

As a particle moves along a path in a plane, as depicted in Fig. 3-13, its **absolute displacement r** at any instant of time is the vector from the origin of coordinates to the location of the particle at that instant of time. If the particle has absolute displacements $\mathbf{r}_1$ at time t_1 and $\mathbf{r}_2$ at time t_2, as shown, then the vector from position 1 to position 2, $\Delta \mathbf{r} = \mathbf{r}_2 - \mathbf{r}_1$, is called the *relative displacement* that the particle has moved through in the time $\Delta t = t_2 - t_1$. The x and y components of $\mathbf{r}_1$ and $\mathbf{r}_2$ are also

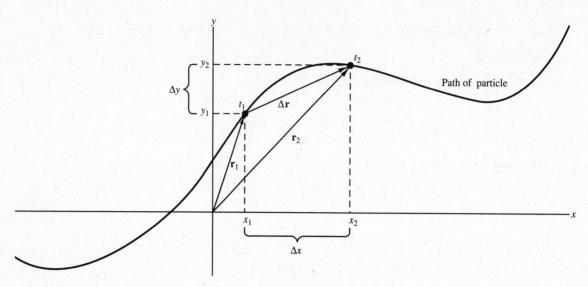

Fig. 3-13

shown in Fig. 3-13. Note that $\Delta x = x_2 - x_1$ and $\Delta y = y_2 - y_1$ are the changes in displacement of the shadows of the particles on the x and y axes, respectively.

Average and Instantaneous Velocities

The average velocity of the particle over the time interval $\Delta t = t_2 - t_1$ is defined as

$$\mathbf{v}_{av} = \frac{\mathbf{r}_2 - \mathbf{r}_1}{t_2 - t_1} = \frac{\Delta \mathbf{r}}{\Delta t}$$

Since Δt is a scalar quantity, multiplying a vector by $1/\Delta t$ does not change the direction of the vector, so $\mathbf{v}_{av}$ points in the direction of $\Delta \mathbf{r}$. The x and y components of $\mathbf{v}_{av}$ are

$$v_{av,x} = \frac{\Delta x}{\Delta t} \qquad v_{av,y} = \frac{\Delta y}{\Delta t}$$

and these are just the average velocities of the two shadow particles on the x and y axes, respectively.

As in Chap. 2, to find the instantaneous velocity $\mathbf{v}$ at the time t_1 we take the average over smaller and smaller time intervals, holding t_1 fixed. In other words, we let $\Delta t \to 0$ by choosing t_2 closer and closer to t_1. In Fig. 3-14 we see that the direction of $\Delta \mathbf{r}$ gets closer and closer to the tangent to the path of motion at time t_1. Since $\Delta \mathbf{r}$ is in the same direction as $\mathbf{v}_{av}$, we conclude that the instantaneous velocity $\mathbf{v}$ is tangent to the path of motion. From our discussion in the previous section we see that as $\Delta t \to 0$, $\Delta x/\Delta t$ and $\Delta y/\Delta t$ become v_x and v_y, the components of $\mathbf{v}$ along the x and y axes, respectively. They also become the instantaneous velocities of the shadow particles on the x and y axes. We conclude

$$v_x = \text{shadow velocity on } x \text{ axis} \qquad v_y = \text{shadow velocity on } y \text{ axis}$$

Average and Instantaneous Acceleration

Again as in Chap. 2, the average acceleration of the particle in the time interval $\Delta t = t_2 - t_1$ is defined as

$$\mathbf{a}_{av} = \frac{\mathbf{v}_2 - \mathbf{v}_1}{t_2 - t_1} = \frac{\Delta \mathbf{v}}{\Delta t}$$

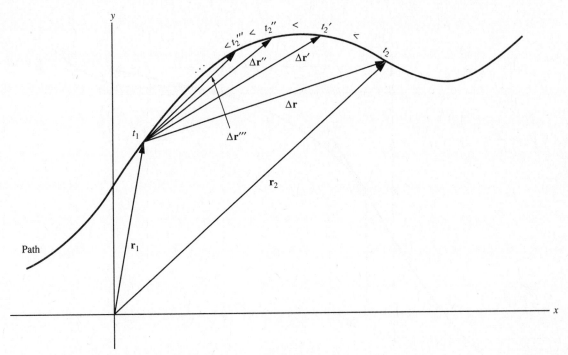

Fig. 3-14

where $\mathbf{v}_2$ and $\mathbf{v}_1$ are the instantaneous velocities of the particle at times t_2 and t_1, respectively. In Fig. 3-15 we show the path of the particle, with the instantaneous velocity displayed at the two times t_1 and t_2. The figure also displays the x and y components of the velocities and demonstrates their relationship to the x and y components of $\Delta \mathbf{v}$. Then, noting that

$$a_{\mathrm{av},x} = \frac{\Delta v_x}{\Delta t} \quad \text{and} \quad a_{\mathrm{av},y} = \frac{\Delta v_y}{\Delta t}$$

we have that $a_{\mathrm{av},x}$ and $a_{\mathrm{av},y}$ are just the average accelerations of the two shadow particles on the x and y axes, respectively. Taking the limit as $t_2 \to t_1$ (that is, $\Delta t \to 0$) in our expression for $\mathbf{a}_{\mathrm{av}}$ above, we obtain the instantaneous acceleration $\mathbf{a}$. Then, a_x and a_y, the x and y components of the instantaneous acceleration, are just the instantaneous accelerations of the shadow particles on the x and y axes, respectively.

Component Method for Planar Motion

We see that the motion of a particle in a plane can be analyzed by studying the motion of the particle's shadows on the x axis and the y axis, each of which is one-dimensional motion. If we know everything about the shadow motions along the two axes, we can reconstruct the full two-dimensional motion. This follows from the fact that the displacement, velocity, and acceleration of the shadows represent, respectively, the x and y components of the vector displacement, velocity, and acceleration for the full two-dimensional motion.

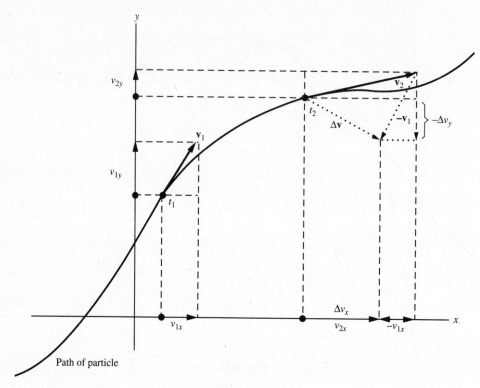

Fig. 3-15

Planar Motion with Constant Acceleration

A special case of motion in a plane is motion with constant acceleration. A very useful example of this is an object that moves under the influence of gravity near the earth's surface (neglecting air resistance). As discussed in Chap. 2, all such objects accelerate downward at a constant acceleration of magnitude

$$g = 9.8 \text{ m/s}^2 = 980 \text{ cm/s}^2 = 32.2 \text{ ft/s}^2$$

Let us assume that our particle indeed moves only under the influence of gravity, so it has a constant acceleration **a** whose magnitude is g and which points downward, perpendicular to the earth's surface. If we choose our y axis vertical (with upward positive) and our x axis horizontal, we have $a_x = 0$ and $a_y = -g$. Suppose the initial velocity of the particle at time $t = 0$ is $\mathbf{v}_0$, with components v_{0x} and v_{0y}, and the initial displacement of the particle is $\mathbf{r}_0$, with components x_0 and y_0. We now apply the straight-line motion equations developed in the last chapter for constant acceleration. The shadows on the two axes obey the equations

$$v_x = v_{0x} + a_x t \qquad x = x_0 + v_{0x}t + \tfrac{1}{2}a_x t^2 \qquad v_x{}^2 = v_{0x}{}^2 + 2a_x(x - x_0) \qquad (3.1a,\ b,\ c)$$

$$v_y = v_{0y} + a_y t \qquad y = y_0 + v_{0y}t + \tfrac{1}{2}a_y t^2 \qquad v_y{}^2 = v_{0y}{}^2 + 2a_y(y - y_0) \qquad (3.2a,\ b,\ c)$$

Let us choose our origin at the position of the particle when $t = 0$ so that $x_0 = y_0 = 0$. Then, noting $a_x = 0$, our shadow on the x axis moves at constant speed and our x equations become

$$v_x = v_{0x} \qquad x = v_{0x}t \qquad v_x{}^2 = v_{0x}{}^2 \qquad (3.3a,\ b,\ c)$$

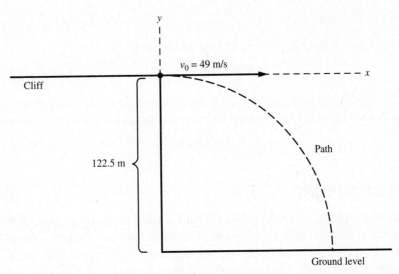

Fig. 3-16

The shadow on the y axis moves with acceleration $-g$ so that our y equations become

$$v_y = v_{0y} - gt \qquad y = v_{0y}t - \tfrac{1}{2}gt^2 \qquad v_y{}^2 = v_{0y}{}^2 - 2gy \qquad (3.4a, b, c)$$

Problem 3.14. A particle is projected horizontally from the edge of a cliff, as shown in Fig. 3-16.

(a) Find the x and y components of the displacement and the velocity 2 s later.

(b) Find the magnitude and direction of the velocity of the particle at $t = 2$ s.

> **Solution**
>
> (a) Choose the origin at the point of launch, with axes as shown. We apply Eqs. (*3.3a, b*) and (*3.4a, b*) with $v_{0x} = 49$ m/s, $v_{0y} = 0$. For the x direction at $t = 2$ s we get
>
> $$v_x = 49 \text{ m/s} \qquad x = (49 \text{ m/s})\,(2 \text{ s}) = 98 \text{ m}$$
>
> For the y direction at $t = 2$ s:
>
> $$v_y = -(9.8 \text{ m/s}^2)\,(2 \text{ s}) = -19.6 \text{ m/s}$$
> $$y = -(4.9 \text{ m/s}^2)\,(2 \text{ s})^2 = -19.6 \text{ m}$$
>
> The minus sign indicates it is below its starting position.
>
> (b) $$v^2 = v_x{}^2 + v_y{}^2 = 49^2 + 19.6^2 = 2785 \qquad v = 52.8 \text{ m/s}$$
>
> $\tan \theta = |v_y/v_x|$, where θ is the acute angle between **v** and the x axis. $\tan \theta = 19.6/49 = 0.40$ or $\theta = 21.8°$. Since v_x is positive and v_y is negative, **v** lies in the fourth quadrant, or $21.8°$ below the positive x axis.

Problem 3.15.

(a) For the particle of Problem 3.14, how much time elapses before it hits the ground?

(b) How far from the base of the cliff does the particle land?

Solution

(a)   We know that at the base, $y = -122.5$ m, so we use $(3.4b)$:

$$-122.5 \text{ m} = -(4.9 \text{ m/s}^2)t^2 \qquad \text{or} \qquad t^2 = (122.5/4.9) \text{ s}^2 = 25 \text{ s}^2$$

so that $t = 5$ s.

(b)   Now that we know the time elapsed before it hits the ground, from $(3b)$ we obtain

$$x = (49 \text{ m/s}) (5 \text{ s}) = 245 \text{ m}$$

3.3   PROJECTILE MOTION

The previous problem is a particular case of what is called projectile motion. A bullet fired from a gun, a ball thrown or batted, and an arrow shot from a bow are typical examples. In all cases something is projected with an initial velocity, but afterwards it moves solely under the influence of gravity (air resistance is ignored). The acceleration is thus directed vertically downward with constant magnitude g. It is often convenient to put the origin at the point of launch, and set the launch time at $t = 0$, as well as to express the initial velocity in terms of its magnitude and angle of elevation above the horizontal, as shown in Fig. 3-17. Then we have $v_{0x} = v_0 \cos \theta_0$ and $v_{0y} = v_0 \sin \theta_0$, and the equation of motion for the x and y shadow points are

$$v_x = v_0 \cos \theta_0 \qquad x = v_0 \cos \theta_0 t \qquad\qquad (3.5a, b)$$

$$v_y = v_0 \sin \theta_0 - gt \qquad y = v_0 \sin \theta_0 t - \tfrac{1}{2}gt^2 \qquad\qquad (3.6a, b)$$

$$v_y{}^2 = (v_0 \sin \theta_0)^2 - 2gy \qquad\qquad (3.7)$$

Problem 3.16.   In Fig. 3-17, the projectile is fired with an initial velocity $v_0 = 40.0$ m/s at an angle of elevation $\theta_0 = 30°$. At $t = 1.5$ s, find (a) the x and y components of the velocity; (b) the magnitude and direction of the velocity; (c) the vertical and horizontal positions of the projectile.

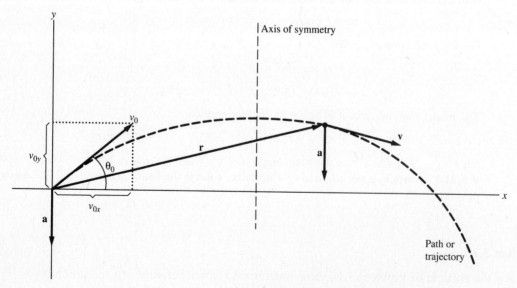

Fig. 3-17

Solution

(a)   We first find the components of the initial velocity

$$v_{0x} = v_0 \cos\theta_0 = (40 \text{ m/s}) \cos 30° = (40.0 \text{ m/s})(0.866) = 34.6 \text{ m/s}$$
$$v_{0y} = v_0 \sin\theta_0 = (40 \text{ m/s}) \sin 30° = (40.0 \text{ m/s})(0.50) = 20.0 \text{ m/s}$$

Then, applying the component equations for the velocity, [(3.3a) and (3.4a)], we have

$$v_x = v_{0x} = 34.6 \text{ m/s}$$
$$v_y = v_{0y} - gt = 20.0 \text{ m/s} - (9.8 \text{ m/s})(1.5 \text{ s}) = 5.3 \text{ m/s}$$

(b) $$v = (v_{0x}{}^2 + V_{0y}{}^2)^{1/2} = (34.6^2 + 5.3^2)^{1/2} = 35.0 \text{ m/s}$$

Also, since both components are positive, **v** points about the x axis at an angle

$$\tan\theta = \frac{v_y}{v_x} = \frac{5.3}{34.6} = 0.153 \qquad \text{or} \qquad \theta = 8.7°$$

Note that the particle is still on the way up after 1.5 s, but it is nearing the highest point.

(c)   Applying the x and y equations at the time $t = 1.5$ s, we get

$$x = (34.6 \text{ m/s})t = (34.6 \text{ m/s})(1.5 \text{ s}) = 51.9 \text{ m}$$
$$y = (20.0 \text{ m/s})t - (4.9 \text{ m/s}^2)t^2 = (20.0)(1.5) - (4.9)(1.5)^2 = 19.0 \text{ m}$$

Problem 3.17.   For the projectile in Problem 3.16:

(a)   Find the time for the projectile to reach the highest point and the velocity at that point.

(b)   Find the maximum height to which the projectile rises and the corresponding horizontal displacement.

(c)   Find the time for the projectile to return to the vertical level from which it was fired and the horizontal displacement R at that time (the horizontal range).

Solution

(a)   At the highest point $v_y = 0$, so (3.4a) yields

$$0 = 20.0 - 9.8t \qquad \text{or} \qquad t = \frac{20.0}{9.8} = 2.04 \text{ s}$$

(b)   Again at the highest point $v_y = 0$, and to find y we use the v_y vs. y equation (3.4c):

$$0 = 20.0^2 - 19.6y_{max} \qquad \text{or} \qquad y_{max} = \frac{400}{19.6} = 20.4 \text{ m}$$

To get the horizontal position at this point, we use the result of (a) and the x vs. t equation: $x = 34.6(2.04) = 70.6$ m.

(c)   To find the time to return to the same vertical level from which it is fired, we don't have to do any additional calculations. Instead we recall that the y shadow repeats its upward motion in reverse on the way down. Then the time taken by the projectile to go up and return to the starting level is just twice the time to reach the highest point, which we already calculated in (b). Thus, $t = 2(2.04 \text{ s}) = 4.08$ s. This same argument can be used to show that the path of motion (trajectory) of the particle (projectile) is symmetric about the highest point. Since the horizontal displacement sweeps out uniformly in time, the path on the way down will be a mirror image of the path on the way up. Hence, the horizontal range R is twice the horizontal distance to the highest point, and using the result of (b), we get $R = 2(70.7) = 141$ m.

As a check, we will directly obtain the time in part (b). We note that upon return to the starting vertical level we have $y = 0$. So (3.4b) yields $0 = 20.0t - 4.9t^2$. This has two solutions, one of which is $t = 0$, the starting time. The other is the time of interest. Dividing out t, we get $4.9t = 20.0$ or $t = 4.08$ s, as before. Then x can be obtained from the x vs. t equation: $x = 34.6\,(4.08) = 141$ m.

Problem 3.18. Assume that the projectile in Problem 3.16 is a baseball batted toward center field. The fielder is initially 150 m from the batter and starts running to meet the ball the moment it is hit. How fast must the fielder run to catch the ball at the same height from which it was batted?

Solution

From the results of the last problem, we see the fielder must run 150 m $-$ 141 m = 9 m in 4.08 s. Thus his average speed must be 9 m/4.08 s = 2.2 m/s.

Did you note how simple Problem 3.18 seems once you have solved Problem 3.17? Suppose Problem 3.17 were not given. Would you still have known how to handle Problem 3.18? The difference between a "difficult" and an "easy" (or straightforward) problem is often that the difficult problem requires you to figure out what information you need, not obviously stated in the problem, to ultimately get the answer.

Trajectory Equation

In addition to getting x vs. t and y vs. t equations, it is also possible to obtain an equation for the path of the projectile in the xy plane, that is, to obtain an equation for y in terms of x. Such an equation is called the **trajectory** equation. To obtain it, we eliminate the time between the x vs. t and the y vs. t equations above.

Problem 3.19.

(a) Find the equation of the trajectory of the projectile in Problem 3.16.

(b) Use this equation to find the horizontal range of the projectile.

Solution

(a) This is most easily done by first finding the trajectory equation for any v_0 and θ_0 and then substituting in the specific values for this problem. We first obtain the time t in terms of x from the x motion equation (3.5b) to get $t = x/(v_0 \cos \theta_0)$. We then substitute this into the y motion equation (3.6b) to get $y = v_0 \sin \theta_0[x/v_0 \cos \theta_0)] - \frac{1}{2}g[x/(v_0 \cos \theta_0)]^2$ or

$$y = \tan \theta_0 x - \frac{gx^2}{2v_0^2 \cos^2 \theta_0} \tag{i}$$

This is the equation of the parabola depicted in Fig. 3-17. For $v_0 = 40$ m/s and $\theta_0 = 30°$, we get $y = 0.577x - 0.00408x^2$.

(b) As can be seen there are two values of x for which y equals zero. One is the starting point, $x = 0$. The other is the horizontal range, $x = R$. To obtain a general expression for the range, we set $y = 0$ in the trajectory equation (i). Moving the negative term to the other side of the equation and dividing both sides by x, we get $\tan \theta_0 = gx/(2v_0^2 \cos^2 \theta_0)$. We then solve for x to get

$$x = R = \frac{2v_0^2 \sin \theta_0 \cos \theta_0}{g} \tag{ii}$$

where we have used $\tan \theta_0 = \sin \theta_0 / \cos \theta_0$. Substituting in the values of v_0 and θ_0 for our case, we get $R = 141$ m, the same result as obtained in Problem 3.17 using the time equations.

Note.   Since the trajectory equation is derived from time equations, nothing can be learned from it that can't also be learned directly from them.

3.4   UNIFORM CIRCULAR MOTION

Centripetal Acceleration

We now turn to a situation of great interest where we do not have constant acceleration. This is the case of an object moving with constant speed v around a circular path of radius r. Such motion is called *uniform circular motion* and has the peculiar property that while the magnitude of the velocity is just the constant speed v, the direction of the velocity is continually changing. This can be seen in Fig. 3-18, which shows the velocity at two times t_1 and t_2. The acceleration is thus due strictly to the change in the direction of $\mathbf{v}$. To obtain $\mathbf{a}$, we again note that $\mathbf{a}_{av} = (\mathbf{v}_2 - \mathbf{v}_1)/(t_2 - t_1)$. We can use this to deduce both the magnitude and the direction of the instantaneous acceleration $\mathbf{a}$ at time t_1 by examining the limit as $t_2 \to t_1$. First we get the direction of $\mathbf{a}$ by noting that $\mathbf{a}_{av}$ points in the direction of $\mathbf{v}_2 - \mathbf{v}_1 = \Delta \mathbf{v}$, as shown in the velocity triangle in Fig. 3-18. As $t_2 \to t_1$, the velocity $\mathbf{v}_2$ becomes more parallel to $\mathbf{v}_1$ and angle $\theta \to 0$. Since $v_1 = v_2 \equiv v$, the triangle is isosceles, and the other two angles each approach $90°$. Thus, $\Delta \mathbf{v}$ and $\mathbf{a}$ become more and more perpendicular to $\mathbf{v}_1$ and point downward, toward the center of the circle (Fig. 3-18). To get the magnitude of $\mathbf{a}$, we note that the two triangles shown in Fig. 3-18 are similar isosceles triangles, so $|\Delta \mathbf{v}|/v = |\Delta \mathbf{s}|/r$, where $\Delta \mathbf{s}$ is the displacement from the position of the object at time t_1 to that at time t_2. Multiplying both sides by v and then dividing by $\Delta t = t_2 - t_1$ yields

$$\frac{|\Delta \mathbf{v}|}{\Delta t} = \frac{v}{r} \frac{|\Delta \mathbf{s}|}{\Delta t}$$

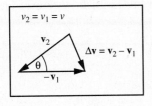

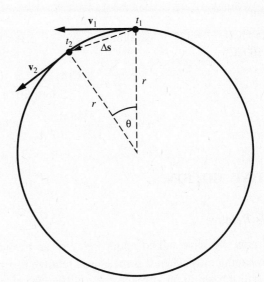

Fig. 3-18

The left side is just the magnitude of the average acceleration; in the limit as $\Delta t \to 0$ this becomes the magnitude of the instantaneous acceleration a. The right side is just vv_{av}/r, since $\Delta s/\Delta t$ by definition equals $\mathbf{v}_{av}$ for the time interval Δt. Thus, in the limit as $\Delta t \to 0$, the right side becomes v^2/r. Equating the two sides in the limit then gives the result

$$a = \frac{v^2}{r} \qquad (3.8)$$

The acceleration of a particle in uniform circular motion is called the *centripetal acceleration*. Since the time t_1 was chosen arbitrarily, the centripetal acceleration at any point in the motion always points in toward the center of the circle and has magnitude $a = v^2/r$. Thus, just as for the velocity, the acceleration has constant magnitude but changing direction.

Uniform circular motion is one example of *periodic motion*, motion that repeats itself over and over. The time for one repetition of such motion is called the *period T*. For uniform circular motion, the period T and the constant speed v are simply related since v equals the distance traveled in one revolution divided by the time to complete the circle, or $v = 2\pi r/T$. From (3.8) the centripetal acceleration can then be expressed as

$$a = \frac{4\pi^2 r}{T^2} \qquad (3.9)$$

Problem 3.20.   A rock is twirled at the end of a string of radius $r = 0.5$ m, at a speed of 10 m/s. Find (*a*) the magnitude of the centripetal acceleration of the rock, (*b*) the period of revolution.

Solution

(*a*) $a = v^2/r = (10 \text{ m/s})^2/0.5 \text{ m} = 200 \text{ m/s}^2$.

(*b*) $T = 2\pi r/v = 2(3.14)(0.5 \text{ m})/(10 \text{ m/s}) = 0.314$ s.

Problem 3.21.   The moon travels around the earth in a nearly circular orbit. The moon's period is 27.3 days, and its average distance from the earth is 240,000 mi. Find the velocity of the moon in its orbit, and its centripetal acceleration. Obtain your results in the English system of units.

Solution

We have $T = (27.3 \text{ days})(86,400 \text{ s/day}) = 2.36 \times 10^6$ s. Also $r = (240,000 \text{ mi})(5280 \text{ ft/mi}) = 1.27 \times 10^9$ ft.

$$v = \frac{2\pi r}{T} = \frac{2(3.14)(1.27 \times 10^9 \text{ ft})}{2.36 \times 10^6 \text{ s}} = 3380 \text{ ft/s}$$

$$a = \frac{v^2}{r} = \frac{(3380 \text{ ft/s})^2}{1.27 \times 10^9 \text{ ft}} = 0.00899 \text{ ft/s}^2$$

3.5 RELATIVE MOTION

All Motion Is Relative

Up until now we have talked about velocity as measured in some coordinate system. Indeed velocity has meaning only when it is measured relative to something that is assumed to be at rest. The velocity of a ball thrown in an airplane has a different value as measured by a passenger in the plane and by someone on the ground.

Relative Velocity in One Dimension

Consider a train moving along a straight track at constant velocity $v_{te} = 10$ m/s relative to the earth. (Fig. 3-19). (Take the direction of motion as the positive direction.) Suppose a child is running through a car of the train with a velocity $v_{ct} = 2$ m/s relative to the train. What is the velocity v_{ce} of the child relative to the earth, i.e., as seen by an adult on the ground watching the train go by? The answer is almost intuitive:

$$v_{ce} = \text{sum of the two velocities} = 2 \text{ m/s} + 10 \text{ m/s} = 12 \text{ m/s}$$

In general we have

$$v_{ce} = v_{ct} + v_{te} \qquad (3.10)$$

no matter what c, t, and e refer to.

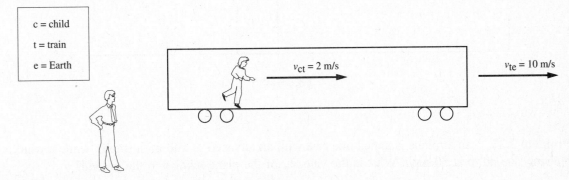

Fig. 3-19

Suppose that a person is sitting by a window seat in the train. What is the velocity v_{et} of the earth (and everything attached to it) as seen by this person? Clearly the person sees the earth go by at 10 m/s in the backward (negative) direction. Since the person is at rest relative to the train, v_{et} is just the velocity of the earth relative to the train, and again intuition correctly tells us

$$v_{et} = -v_{te} \qquad (3.11)$$

The velocity of the earth relative to the train is equal and opposite to the velocity of the train relative to the earth.

Relative Velocity in Two Dimensions

Figure 3-20 shows a situation involving relative velocity in two dimensions. A child is shown running on the deck of a ship with a velocity $\mathbf{v}_{cs}$, while the ship itself is moving relative to the earth with a velocity $\mathbf{v}_{se}$. What is the velocity of the child as seen by someone at rest on the shore? If we choose our coordinate axes on the ship and the shore parallel to each other, as shown, and we examine the shadows of the motion on the x axes and the y axes, respectively, we conclude that the shadows of the velocities obey the relative motion equations in one dimension: (c to e) = (c to s) + (s to e), and (e to s) = −(s to e). Since the shadows are just the components along the respective axes, we must have for the full vector velocities the same relations:

$$\mathbf{v}_{ce} = \mathbf{v}_{cs} + \mathbf{v}_{se} \qquad \text{and} \qquad \mathbf{v}_{es} = -\mathbf{v}_{se} \qquad (3.12a, b)$$

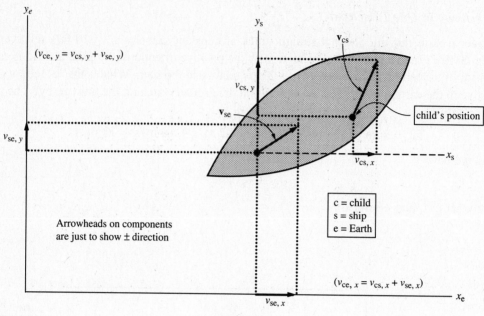

Fig. 3-20

Problem 3.22. An airplane is aimed due east with an airspeed of 200 mi/h (mph), while a wind is blowing due north at 80 mph. What is the velocity of the plane relative to the ground?

Solution

The velocity of the plane relative to the air, $\mathbf{v}_{pa}$, points in the tail-to-nose direction of the plane (east), and its magnitude is the airspeed 200 mph (Fig. 3-21). The velocity of the air relative to the earth,

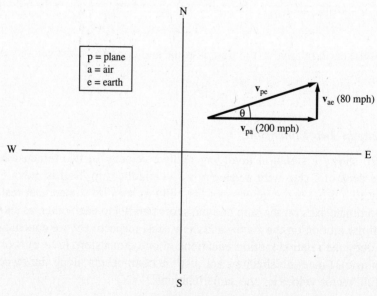

Fig. 3-21

$\mathbf{v}_{ae}$, is 80 mph due north. Then, as shown in Fig. 3-21, $\mathbf{v}_{pe} = \mathbf{v}_{pa} + \mathbf{v}_{ae}$. Since $\mathbf{v}_{pa}$ and $\mathbf{v}_{ae}$ are at right angles, the pythagorean theorem may be used, giving

$$v_{pe} = (200^2 + 80^2)^{1/2} = 215 \text{ mph} \qquad \tan \theta = \frac{80}{200} = 0.40$$

Hence $\theta = 21.8°$, so the direction is $21.8°$ N of E.

Problem 3.23. Suppose the pilot of the plane in Problem 3.22 wanted to fly to a city 800 miles due east of her starting point. Given the same airspeed and the same wind blowing, in what direction should she aim the plane and how long does the trip take (ignoring take off and landing times)?

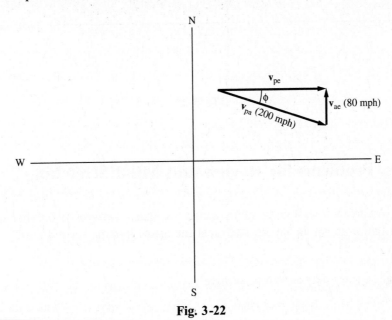

Fig. 3-22

Solution

She must aim her plane so that $\mathbf{v}_{pe}$ is due east (Fig. 3-22). As before, $\mathbf{v}_{pe} = \mathbf{v}_{pa} + \mathbf{v}_{ae}$. Now $\mathbf{v}_{pa}$ is the hypotenuse of the triangle, so $\mathbf{v}_{pe} = (200^2 - 80^2)^{1/2} = 183.3$ mph. In addition we have

$$\sin \phi = \tfrac{80}{200} = 0.40 \qquad \text{or} \qquad \theta = 23.6°$$

so that the plane is aimed $23.6°$ S of E. Note that this angle is *not* the same as the angle θ of Problem 3.22. The time of flight is

$$t = \frac{800 \text{ mi}}{183.3 \text{ mph}} = 4.36 \text{ h} = 4 \text{ h} \, 22 \text{ min}$$

Problem 3.24. Rain is falling vertically downward to the ground. The driver of a car traveling horizontally at 30 m/s observes that the rain forms streak lines on the side windows that make an angle of $50°$ with the vertical. What is the speed of the raindrops relative to the ground?

Solution

The streak lines represent the direction of the raindrops relative to the car. We are given that the raindrops fall vertically relative to the ground. Then $\mathbf{v}_{rg} = \mathbf{v}_{rc} + \mathbf{v}_{cg}$, as shown in Fig. 3-23. We know that $v_{cg} = 30$ m/s and that $\theta = 40°$. From this we can find the other sides of the triangle. In particular

$$v_{rg} = v_{cg} \tan \theta = (30 \text{ m/s}) (0.839) = 25.2 \text{ m/s}$$

80 MOTION IN A PLANE [CHAP. 3

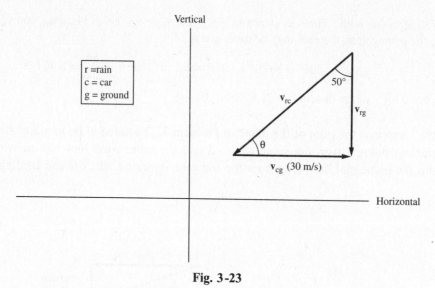

Fig. 3-23

Problems for Review and Mind Stretching

Problem 3.25. An arrow is shot horizontally across the chasm between two cliffs, as shown in Fig. 3-24. Find the height h above the chasm floor that the arrow hits the second cliff.

Solution

Choosing x and y axes as shown, we have

$$\text{(i)} \quad x = v_0 t = (80 \text{ m/s})t \qquad \text{(ii)} \quad y = -\tfrac{1}{2}gt^2 = -(4.9 \text{ m/s}^2)t^2$$

We set $x = 200$ m in (i) to find the time t for the arrow to reach the other cliff:

$$200 \text{ m} = (80 \text{ m/s})t \qquad \text{or} \qquad t = 2.5 \text{ s}$$

Then we solve (ii) for the corresponding y value: $y = -(4.9 \text{ m/s}^2)(2.5 \text{ s})^2 = -30.6$ m. Thus the arrow hits the second cliff 30.6 m below the starting point, and $h = 200$ m $- 30.6$ m $= 169.4$ m.

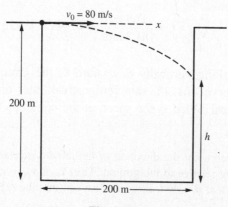

Fig. 3-24

Problem 3.26.   A cannon is fired from ground level with a muzzle velocity $v_0 = 2000$ ft/s at an angle $\theta_0 = 40°$ above the horizontal. Find the maximum height to which the shell rises, and the time to reach that height.

Solution

The coordinate system is shown in Fig. 3-17. We first find the components of the initial velocity along the standard x and y axes:

$$v_{0x} = (2000 \text{ ft/s}) \cos 40° = 1532 \text{ ft/s} \qquad v_{0y} = (2000 \text{ ft/s}) \sin 40° = 1286 \text{ ft/s}$$

Then we use (*3.3*) and (*3.4*), obtaining

$$\text{(i)} \quad v_x = v_{0x} = 1532 \text{ ft/s} \qquad \text{(ii)} \quad x = v_{0x}t = (1532 \text{ ft/s})t$$

$$\text{(iii)} \quad v_y = v_{0y} - gt = 1286 \text{ ft/s} - (32.2 \text{ ft/s}^2)t$$

$$\text{(iv)} \quad y = v_{0y}t - \tfrac{1}{2}gt^2 = (1286 \text{ ft/s})t - (16.1 \text{ ft/s}^2)t^2$$

$$\text{(v)} \quad v_y{}^2 = v_{0y}{}^2 - 2gy = (1286 \text{ ft/s})^2 - (64.4 \text{ ft/s}^2)y$$

To find the highest point, we set $v_y = 0$ in (v), obtaining

$$0 = (1286 \text{ ft/s})^2 - (64.4 \text{ ft/s}^2)y \qquad \text{or} \qquad y = 25{,}700 \text{ ft}$$

To find the time to reach the highest point, we set $v_y = 0$ in (iii), obtaining

$$0 = 1286 \text{ ft/s} - (32.2 \text{ ft/s}^2)t \qquad \text{or} \qquad t = 39.9 \text{ s}$$

Problem 3.27.   Referring to Problem 3.26, assume that an enemy helicopter is hovering 100,000 ft down range from the cannon. How high above the ground would it have to be for the shell to hit it?

Solution

First we find the time it would take the shell to cover that horizontal distance. Setting $x = 100{,}000$ ft in (ii) of Problem 3.26, we obtain

$$100{,}000 \text{ ft} = (1532 \text{ ft/s})t \qquad \text{or} \qquad t = 65.3 \text{ s}$$

Next we find what vertical height this corresponds to; using (iv), we obtain

$$y = (1286 \text{ ft/s})(65.3 \text{ s}) - (16.1 \text{ ft/s}^2)(65.3 \text{ s})^2 = 15{,}300 \text{ ft}$$

Problem 3.28.   Find the centripetal acceleration of a person standing at the equator, assuming that the earth is a sphere of radius $R = 6.38 \cdot 10^6$ m.

Solution

The centripetal acceleration is due to the rotation of the earth. The velocity of the person on the equator is given by $v = 2\pi R/T$, where $T = 24$ h $= 86{,}400$ s is the earth's period of rotation. Then

$$a = \frac{v^2}{R} = \frac{(2\pi R/T)^2}{R} = \frac{4\pi^2 R}{T^2} = \frac{39.4(6.38 \cdot 10^6 \text{ m})}{(86{,}400 \text{ s})^2} = 0.0337 \text{ m/s}^2$$

Problem 3.29.   A child tries to swim directly across a river that is flowing at 2.5 m/s. If the child's swimming speed is 1.0 m/s, find the speed and direction in which the child is moving as seen by someone on the shore.

Solution

The situation is depicted in Fig. 3-25. Let us use c, r, and e to stand for child, river, and earth, respectively. We are given that $\mathbf{v}_{cr} = 1.0$ m/s and $\mathbf{v}_{re} = 2.5$ m/s. Then, from the figure

$$\mathbf{v}_{ce} = (\mathbf{v}_{cr}{}^2 + \mathbf{v}_{re}{}^2)^{1/2} = [(1.0)^2 + (2.5)^2]^{1/2} \text{ m/s} = 2.69 \text{ m/s}$$

$$\tan \theta = \frac{2.5}{1.0} = 2.5 \qquad \text{or} \qquad \theta = 68\,°$$

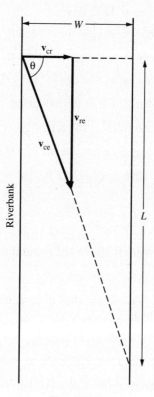

Fig. 3-25

Problem 3.30. A plane aims $30\,°$ east of north with an airspeed of $\mathbf{v}_{pa} = 800$ ft/s. A wind is blowing $20\,°$ north of east at $\mathbf{v}_{ae} = 100$ ft/s. Find the magnitude and direction of $\mathbf{v}_{pe}$, the velocity of the plane relative to the earth.

Solution

The situation is shown in Fig. 3-26. We have $\mathbf{v}_{pe} = \mathbf{v}_{pa} + \mathbf{v}_{ae}$. Since $\mathbf{v}_{pa}$ and $\mathbf{v}_{ae}$ are not at right angles, it is easiest to solve by the component method:

$$v_{pe,x} = v_{pa,x} + v_{ae,x} = (800 \text{ ft/s}) (\sin 30\,°) + (100 \text{ ft/s}) (\cos 20\,°) = 494 \text{ ft/s}$$
$$v_{pe,y} = v_{pa,y} + v_{ae,y} = (800 \text{ ft/s}) (\cos 30\,°) + (100 \text{ ft/s}) (\sin 20\,°) = 727 \text{ ft/s}$$

Then $v_{pe}{}^2 = (494)^2 + (727)^2$, or $v_{pe} = 879$ ft/s. Also, $\theta = \tan^{-1} (727/494) = 55.8\,°$ north of east.

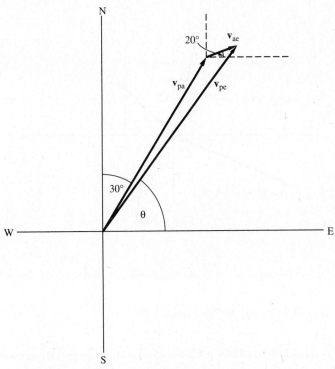

Fig. 3-26

Supplementary Problems

Problem 3.31.   For the three vectors shown in Fig. 3-27, find the magnitude and direction of their sum.

   Ans.   Magnitude 29.6; direction 51.8° above the negative x axis

Problem 3.32.   For the vectors shown in Fig. 3-27, determine $\mathbf{A} + \mathbf{B} - \mathbf{C}$.

   Ans.   Magnitude 62.9; direction 57.7° above the position x axis

Problem 3.33.   Given the vector equation $\mathbf{A} + \mathbf{B} + \mathbf{C} = \mathbf{D}$, with the following information: $A_x = -2.6$, $A_y = 4.2$; $B_x = 1.5$, $B_y = -4.0$; $C_x = 5.0$, $C_y = -3.3$.

(a)   Find the x and y components of $\mathbf{D}$.

(b)   Find the magnitude and direction of $\mathbf{D}$.

   Ans.   (a) $D_x = 3.9$, $D_y = -3.1$; (b) $D = 5.0$, 38.5° below positive x axis

Problem 3.34.   We are given the vector equation $\mathbf{A} + \mathbf{B} + \mathbf{C} = \mathbf{R}$, with $A_x = 3.0$, $A_y = 2.5$; $B_x = 4.2$, $B_y = -2.2$; $R_x = 3.5$, $R_y = 3.5$.

(a)   Find the x and y components of $\mathbf{C}$.

(b)   Find the magnitude and direction of $\mathbf{C}$.

   Ans.   (a) $C_x = -3.7$, $C_y = 3.2$; (b) $C = 4.9$, 40.9° above negative x axis.

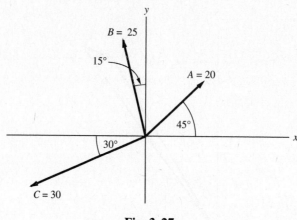

Fig. 3-27

Problem 3.35. Referring to Problem 3.25, find the magnitude and direction of the velocity of the arrow just before it hits the cliff.

    Ans.   83.7 m/s, 17.0° below the horizontal

Problem 3.36. A ball is thrown horizontally off the roof of a building directly at another building across an alleyway.

(*a*) If it drops 15.0 m before it hits the side of the second building, how much time has elapsed?

(*b*) If the alley is 10 m wide, what must have been the initial speed of the ball?

    Ans.   (*a*) 1.75 s; (*b*) 5.71 m/s

Problem 3.37. An arrow is fired into the air at an angle of 60° above the horizontal and reaches its highest point in 3.0 s

(*a*) What was the initial speed of the arrow?

(*b*) How high did it rise?

    Ans.   (*a*) 33.9 m/s; (*b*) 44.1 m

Problem 3.38. Find (*a*) the range of the arrow in Problem 3.37; (*b*) its height when it had traversed three-fourths of the range.

    Ans.   (*a*) 102 m; (*b*) 33.1 m

Problem 3.39. For the cannon shell of Problem 3.26, find the range and the time to return to ground level.

    Ans.   122,000 ft; 79.8 s

Problem 3.40. A quarterback throws a football at an angle of 30° above the horizontal with a velocity of 25 m/s toward a receiver who is 15 m away. Assume the receiver starts running to catch the ball, at a constant speed, the moment the ball is thrown. How fast must he run to just catch the ball at the height from which it was thrown?

    Ans.   15.8 m/s.

Problem 3.41. A bomber is flying horizontally at a speed of 800 ft/s and an altitude of 1000 ft when it drops a bomb.

(a) How far will the bomb move horizontally before it hits the ground?

(b) What will be the magnitude and direction of its velocity just before it hits the ground?

   Ans.   (a) 6300 ft; (b) 839 ft/s, aimed 17.5° below the horizontal

Problem 3.42. Refer back to Problem 3.41. The plane is trying to hit a tank directly ahead that is traveling at 60 ft/s in the same direction as the plane.

(a) How far back horizontally from the tank should the plane be when it drops the bomb?

(b) What would the answer be if the tank were moving toward the plane?

   Ans.   (a) 5830 ft; (b) 6770 ft.

Problem 3.43. A marksman is trying to hit a stationary target that is 100 m above the level of his rifle. He aims the rifle 5° above the horizontal, fires, and hits the target just as the bullet reaches the highest point in its trajectory. What is the muzzle velocity of the rifle? How far away, horizontally, was the target?

   Ans.   508 m/s; 2286 m

Problem 3.44. A space station in the form of a large wheel of radius $R = 200$ m rotates at such a rate as to simulate the earth's gravity for people working along the rim. The condition for this to happen is that the centripetal acceleration on the rim be equal to the earth's gravitational acceleration. Find the period of rotation.

   Ans.   28.3 s

Problem 3.45. Consider the space station of Problem 3.44.

(a) What must the period of rotation be changed to if the acceleration is to be double the acceleration of gravity?

(b) What is the new velocity of a point on the rim?

   Ans.   (a) 20.0 s; (b) 62.8 m/s

Problem 3.46. Find the centripetal acceleration of the earth as it moves in its nearly circular orbit of radius 1.49×10^{11} m about the sun.

   Ans.   5.91 mm/s^2

Problem 3.47. If the river in Problem 3.29 is 50 m wide, how far downstream will the child reach the other side?

   Ans.   125 m

Problem 3.48. An airplane pilot is to travel due south on a day that a wind of 80 km/h is blowing due west. His airspeed is 400 km/h.

(a) In what direction must he aim the airplane?

(b) What is his ground speed?

   Ans.   (a) 11.5° east of south; (b) 392 m/s

Problem 3.49.   A river is flowing due north at 3.0 m/s. A motorboat that travels through the water at 15 m/s leaves the western bank, heading due east. The river is 300 m wide.

(a)   How far north of its starting point will the boat be when it reaches the other shore?

(b)   How long will the trip take?

> *Ans.*   (a) 60 m; (b) 20 s

Problem 3.50.   Suppose the boat of Problem 3.49 were aimed 30° south of east. What are the components of its velocity relative to the earth in the northerly and easterly directions?

> *Ans.*   −4.5 m/s and 13.0 m/s, respectively

Chapter 4

Forces and Equilibrium

Note. In introductory mechanics it is usually assumed that all forces act in the same plane (usually called the *xy* plane). Such forces are said to be *coplanar*. This assumption simplifies the mathematics considerably but still allows for a substantial understanding of the underlying physics involved.

4.1 FORCES

A **force** is a mechanical effect of the environment on an object. It is either a push or a pull on an object, and has both a magnitude (in appropriate units such as newtons, dynes, or pounds—units of force are discussed in detail in Chap. 5) and a direction. It can thus be represented by a vector. A force has two basic effects on an object. (1) It can change the motion of the object, which is the subject of Newton's famous second law (Chap. 5). (2) It can distort the shape of an object such as by stretching, compressing, or twisting the object.

Types of Forces

A force can be either due to direct contact (**contact force**) such as a hand pushing a block or a rope dragging a box or due to influence from afar (**action at a distance**) such as the gravitational pull of the earth on a satellite or the push of one magnet on another not in contact with it. On the human scale there are many different forces of either type. But on the atomic scale there are only four fundamental forces: gravitational, electromagnetic, weak nuclear, and strong nuclear—all of them actions at a distance.

The Resultant of a System of Forces

The vector sum of the forces acting on an object is called the **resultant** force on the object. The laws of nature are such that when two or more forces are acting at the same point in an object, they can be replaced by their resultant acting at the same point, which will have the same exact effect on the object as the original set of forces.

Problem 4.1. In Fig. 4-1(a) two forces are shown acting at a point in an object. Find the magnitude and direction of the single force that can replace those two forces and have the exact same effect.

Solution

In Fig. 4-1(b) the resultant $\mathbf{R}$ and the replaced forces $\mathbf{F}_1$ and $\mathbf{F}_2$ (in dashed form), as well as $\mathbf{F}_2$ shifted parallel to itself so that it is tail to head with $\mathbf{F}_1$ (see Sec. 3.1). Since the two original forces are at right angles to each other, we can use the pythagorean theorem to obtain the magnitude of the resultant force: $R^2 = F_1^2 + F_2^2 = (30 \text{ lb})^2 + (40 \text{ lb})^2 = 2500 \text{ lb}^2$. Taking the square root, we obtain $R = 50$ lb. To get the direction of $\mathbf{R}$ we determine its angle θ with the horizontal. We have $\tan \theta = $ opposite/ adjacent $= 40/30 = 1.33$ or $\theta = 53°$. Thus $\mathbf{R}$ has magnitude 50 lb and acts at an angle $53°$ above the horizontal.

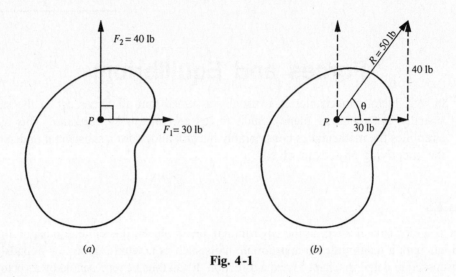

Fig. 4-1

Line of Action

When a force acts at a point in an object, one can draw an imaginary line through that point and parallel to the force. This is called the **line of action** of the force.

A rigid body refers to an object that doesn't change its shape when forces act on it. No real object is truly rigid, but the concept is a good approximation for stiff objects. In studying the relation of force and motion we will usually assume that we have rigid bodies. While in general the effect of a force on a rigid body depends on where it acts, a force acting on a rigid body can be applied anywhere along its line of action and still have exactly the same effect.

Problem 4.2.   In Fig. 4-2(a) we have the same two forces acting on a rigid body as in Fig. 4-1(a), but now they are acting at different points *B* and *C*. Can one still replace these two forces by a single resultant force that has exactly the same effect on the motion of the rigid body and, if so, give an example of such a resultant force?

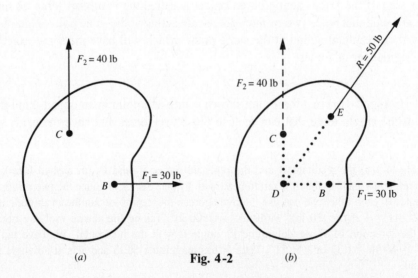

Fig. 4-2

Solution

The answer is *yes*. Since F_1 and F_2 can be moved anywhere along their lines of action without changing their effects, we can imagine moving them so that they both act at point D, the intersection of their lines of action (Fig. 4-21(*b*)). They can then be replaced by their resultant R, acting at the same point D. As already calculated in Problem 4.1, R is 50 lb acting 53° above the horizontal. Furthermore, this resultant force can be moved or slid anywhere along its own line of action without change in effect. Figure 4-2(*b*) shows the resultant R acting at point E, where it still has exactly the same effect as the original two forces (shown in dashed form) that it has replaced.

4.2   EQUILIBRIUM

Translational motion is the motion of the object *as a whole* through space, without regard to how it spins on itself. The translational motion of a very small object, idealized as a particle, is just the motion of the particle along its path. For a large, irregular body it is less clear what is meant by the motion of the object as a whole or the path of the object through space. Fortunately, the idea can still be defined precisely as the motion of a special point of the object, called the **center of mass**. For simple uniform symmetric objects, such as a disk, a sphere, a rod, or a rectangular solid, the center of mass is at the geometric center of the object (see Sec. 8.4).

Problem 4.3.   Describe the translational motion of the board eraser in Fig. 4-3.

Solution

The dashed parabolic line represents the path followed by the center of mass; it thus represents the translational motion of the eraser.

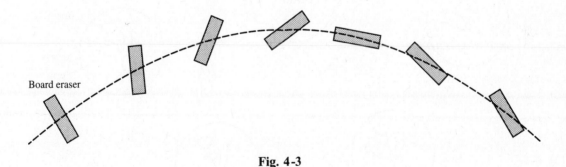

Board eraser

Fig. 4-3

Rotational motion is the spinning motion of an object, without regard to the motion of the object as a whole. Often rotational motion refers to the spinning of an object about a fixed axis, such as the spinning of a wheel on a shaft, but it can also refer to the spinning of an object on itself as the object as a whole moves through space.

Problem 4.4.   How does one describe the rotational motion of the board eraser from left to right in Fig. 4-3?

Solution

The change in the angular orientation of the eraser represents its rotational motion. Note that the eraser has rotated clockwise through 180°.

Problem 4.5.   Describe the translational and rotational motion of the cratered moon around the planet in Fig. 4-4.

Solution

The circular dashed line represents the translational motion of the moon. This moon has no rotational motion since its orientation does not change. The moon, in effect, stays parallel to itself throughout the motion.

Translational equilibrium means that the object as a whole, aside from rotation, has *uniform* translational motion, that is, its center of mass is either at rest or moving at constant speed in a straight line.

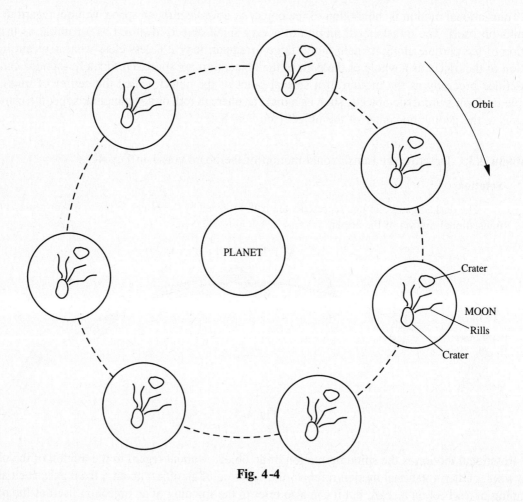

Fig. 4-4

Problem 4.6.   Does the motion of the eraser in Fig. 4-3 or of the moon in Fig. 4-4 correspond to translational equilibrium?

Solution

No. The translational motion of the eraser is a parabolic arc and that of the moon is a circle, whereas for translational equilibrium the motion must be in a straight line. An example of *approximate* translational equilibrium would be a block sliding on an ice-covered lake; the block would move in a straight line without slowing down.

Rotational equilibrium means that the object—whether it is undergoing translational motion or not—is either not spinning or it is spinning in a uniform fashion. For simple symmetric objects this means spinning at a constant rate about a fixed direction.

Problem 4.7.   Does the motion of the eraser in Fig. 4-3 and of the moon in Fig. 4-4 correspond to rotational equilibrium?

   Solution

   If the eraser were tumbling at a uniform rate, it would indeed be in rotational equilibrium; that, in fact, is a good approximation to what happens if air resistance is not an important factor. The moon is certainly in rotational equilibrium, since we are shown that the moon does not rotate at all.

A Frame of Reference refers to the "framework" that defines the coordinate system in which one's measurements and observations are made. If a coordinate system is fixed to the earth and another one is fixed to a rotating merry-go-round, one is going to observe things differently in each. Each of these coordinate systems is fixed in a different *frame of reference*.

An inertial frame of reference, by definition, is a frame of reference in which a completely isolated object (no forces) will appear to be in both translational and rotational equilibrium. For most purposes the earth can be considered an *inertial frame*; that is only an approximation, however, because the earth spins on its axis—although it is a very slow spin—once every 24 h. The importance of inertial frames is that Newton's laws hold only in such frames, and most of the other laws of physics take on simpler form when described in such frames. We will always assume that we are describing things in an inertial frame of reference unless otherwise indicated.

4.3   NEWTON'S FIRST LAW

A totally isolated object (no forces) is in both translational and rotational equilibrium in an inertial reference frame. However, even rigid bodies that *do* have forces acting on them can be in either translational or rotational equilibrium, or both, under suitable conditions. The condition for translational equilibrium is the statement of *Newton's first law*, also known as the *law of equilibrium*. We give here some simple cases.

Equilibrium with Only Two Forces Acting

If the two forces F_1 and F_2 (see Fig. 4-5) are equal in magnitude and opposite in direction (that is, $F_1 + F_2 = 0$), then the object is in translational equilibrium. If in addition the two forces act along a common line of action (*collinear forces*), as in Fig. 4-5(b), then the object is also in rotational equilibrium.

   Note.   It is also possible to have rotational equilibrium without translational equilibrium, a
        situation that will be discussed in a later chapter.

Problem 4.8.   A uniform rod is connected to two cords that exert the only forces on the rod, as depicted in Fig. 4-6; (i.e., we assume there is no pull of gravity on the rod). For each case determine whether the rod is in translational equilibrium. If so, can it also be in rotational equilibrium?

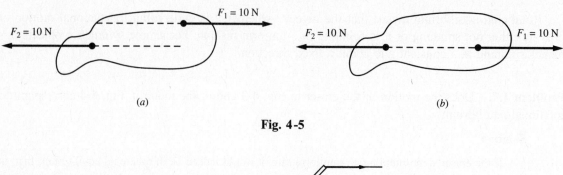

Fig. 4-5

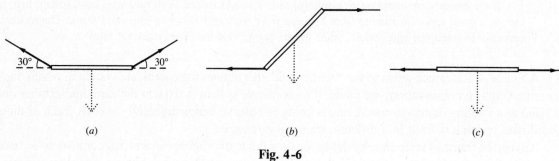

Fig. 4-6

Solution

   Since the cords are flexible and exert a force only when they are taut, they can only pull along their length, as is depicted by arrows. Case (a) cannot correspond to translational equilibrium because the two forces are not equal and opposite ($\mathbf{F}_1 + \mathbf{F}_2 \neq 0$), Case (b) can correspond to translational equilibrium, *if* the two forces have equal magnitude, but it cannot represent rotational equilibrium because the two forces don't have a common line of action. Case (c) corresponds to both translational and rotational equilibrium if the two cords pull with forces of equal magnitude.

Equilibrium with Three Forces Acting

   If the vector sum of the three forces is zero ($\mathbf{F}_1 + \mathbf{F}_2 + \mathbf{F}_3 = 0$), then the object is in translational equilibrium. If in addition the lines of action of the three forces pass through a common point, then the object is in rotational equilibrium as well. Such a system of forces is called *concurrent*.

Problem 4.9.   Consider the same cases as in Problem 4.8, except now take into account the weight of the rod. Which of the cases can now correspond to equilibrium?

   Solution

   Since the rod is uniform, we can assume the weight is a single force acting downward at its center (dotted arrows in Fig. 4-6). Now only case (a) can correspond to translational equilibrium since only in that case could the vector sum of the three forces add up to zero if the magnitudes were suitable (see Problem 4.10). The rod would also be in rotational equilibrium, because, by symmetry, the three forces are concurrent. In neither case (b) nor (c) could the three vector forces add up to zero since the weight is perpendicular to the vector sum of the two other forces and could never be balanced by them.

Problem 4.10.   For case (a) of Problem 4.9, if the weight is 100 N, find the force exerted on the rod by each of the two cords if the rod is in equilibrium (a) by geometric means; (b) by the component method.

Solution

(a) Newton's first law tells us that the resultant of the three forces acting on the rod must be zero. In Fig. 4-7(*a*) we redraw the rod as an isolated object and include only the forces acting on it (body diagram). The condition $\mathbf{F}_1 + \mathbf{F}_2 + \mathbf{F}_3 = 0$ implies that the three vectors, drawn head to tail, form a closed triangle. As can be seen in Fig. 4-7(*b*), the triangle is equilateral for our case, so $F_1 = F_2 = F_3 = 100$ N.

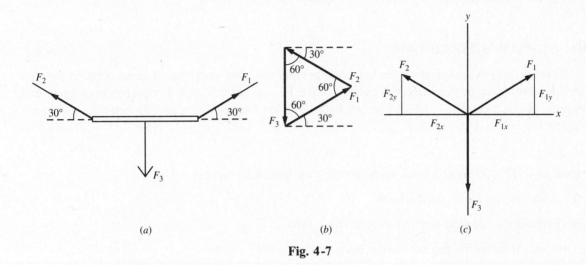

(a)   (b)   (c)

Fig. 4-7

(b) We now solve the problem algebraically. Choose the x axis along the rod and the y axis perpendicular to the rod at its center. Now slide the vectors parallel to themselves to the origin, for easier visualization Fig. 4-7(*c*). Since the vector sum of the three forces equals zero, we must have for the components

$$F_{1x} + F_{2x} + F_{3x} = 0 \quad \text{and} \quad F_{1y} + F_{2y} + F_{3y} = 0$$

From Fig. 4-7(*c*), we have

$$F_{1x} = F_1 \cos 30° \qquad F_{2x} = -F_2 \cos 30° \qquad F_{3x} = 0$$
$$F_{1y} = F_1 \sin 30° \qquad F_{2y} = F_2 \sin 30° \qquad F_{3y} = -100 \,\text{N}$$

Substituting into the x-component equation,

$$F_1 \cos 30° - F_2 \cos 30° + 0 = 0 \quad \text{or} \quad F_1 = F_2$$

Similarly, the y-component equation gives

$$F_1 \sin 30° + F_2 \sin 30° - 100 \,\text{N} = 0 \quad \text{or} \quad 0.5 F_1 + 0.5 F_2 = 100 \,\text{N}$$

Using $F_1 = F_2$ in the y-component equation gives

$$0.5 F_1 + 0.5 F_1 = 100 \,\text{N} \quad \text{or} \quad F_1 = 100 \,\text{N} = F_2$$

While this method of solving a vector equation seems more cumbersome than the geometric method, it can be applied to more general cases where the geometric approach is too difficult to use.

Equilibrium with Any Number of Forces

For the general case of any number n of forces, we again have two conditions for equilibrium. The first is the condition for translational equilibrium, or *Newton's first law*, which says that the vector sum of all the forces is zero: $\Sigma \mathbf{F}_i = 0$. For small objects or particles, where rotation can be ignored, it is the only condition of equilibrium. For extended objects, the second condition, for rotational equilibrium, is again needed. The general case of rotational equilibrium will be discussed in a later chapter. The rest of this chapter is concerned only with translational equilibrium.

4.4 NEWTON'S THIRD LAW

This law, otherwise known as the *law of action and reaction*, states that if some object A exerts a force $\mathbf{F}_{ab}$ on object B, then object B exerts a force $\mathbf{F}_{ba}$ on object A that is equal in magnitude and opposite in direction: $\mathbf{F}_{ba} = -\mathbf{F}_{ab}$. The law holds both for contact forces and for action-at-a-distance forces.

Problem 4.11. Consider a book lying at rest on a horizontal table.

(*a*) What are the forces on the book?

(*b*) What is the reaction force to each of these forces?

(*c*) What effect do the reaction forces have on the book?

Solution

(*a*) There are two forces acting on the book: its weight (the downward pull of gravity toward the center of the earth) and the force exerted upward on the book by the tabletop.

(*b*) The reaction to the weight is an upward pull of equal magnitude exerted on the earth by the book. The reaction to the table's force is a downward push of equal magnitude on the table by the book.

(*c*) The reaction forces have no effect on the book! By definition, any effect on the book is represented by a force *on the book*. The reaction forces act on the earth and on the table—not on the book.

Problem 4.12. An elephant and a teenager are having a tug-of-war, as shown in Fig. 4-8(*a*). Does Newton's third law imply a draw?

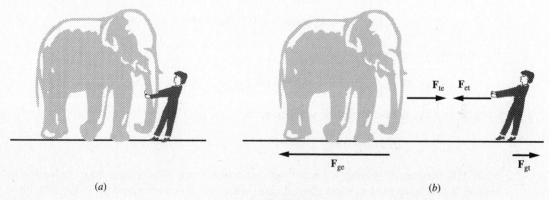

(*a*)   (*b*)

Fig. 4-8

Solution

No. Unless the elephant is very weak, the teenager will definitely lose. It is true that the force the elephant exerts on the teenager $\mathbf{F}_{et}$ is equal and opposite to the force the teenager exerts on the elephant $\mathbf{F}_{te}$, but the motion of either "object" depends on the resultant of *all* the forces acting on it. Both the teenager and the elephant are pushing the ground forward with their feet, and in each case the ground exerts an opposite reaction force. The situation is depicted in Fig. 4-8(b), where $\mathbf{F}_{gt}$ and $\mathbf{F}_{ge}$ represent the horizontal forces exerted by the ground on the teenager and on the elephant, respectively. Thus, for example, suppose that $F_{et} = F_{te} = 250$ lb. We might have $F_{gt} = 100$ lb and $F_{ge} = 650$ lb. Then a net force of 150 lb acts on the teenager to the left, and he moves leftward. Similarly, a net force of 400 lb acts on the elephant to the left, and the elephant also moves leftward. The next section deals with friction and shows why it is reasonable to assume that $F_{ge} > F_{gt}$.

Tension

At any given point in a taut rope (or cord, string, thread, or cable) we can ask: With what force does the segment of rope on one side of the point pull on the segment of rope on the other side? Consider the situation in Fig. 4-9(a), where a girl pulls on one end of a horizontal rope with a force $\mathbf{F}$, while the other end is attached to the wall. We consider an arbitrary point p of the rope that divides it into two segments A and B, as shown. Figure 4-9(b) shows the segments as separate bodies, with the horizontal forces on each drawn in. By Newton's third law, the forces with which the two segments pull on each other $\mathbf{F}_{ab}$ and $\mathbf{F}_{ba}$ are equal in magnitude and opposite in direction. The **tension** T at the point p is the magnitude of either of these forces: $T = F_{ab} = F_{ba}$. Since each rope segment is in equilibrium, we also have $F_{ab} = F$, and $F_w = F_{ba}$, where $\mathbf{F}_w$ is the force of the wall on the rope. Thus all these forces have the same magnitude T. Furthermore, since point p was chosen arbitrarily we conclude that the tension is the same everywhere in the rope.

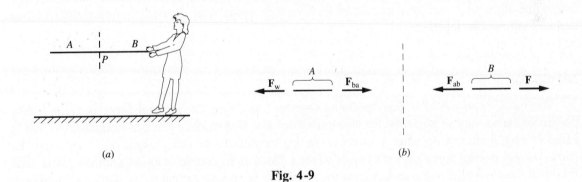

(a)   (b)

Fig. 4-9

"Weightless" Ropes

In general these results are true only for a horizontal rope in equilibrium. If the rope were vertical, with one end attached to the ceiling and the other end pulled down by the girl, then the weight of each segment of the rope would have to be taken into account, and the tension at a point p of the rope would equal neither the force with which the girl pulled down nor the force with which the ceiling pulled up. Indeed, the tension would vary from point to point in the rope. The same would be true if we had a horizontal rope that was not in equilibrium, because the forces applied to either end would not balance out.

There is, however, one circumstance where there is a common tension throughout the rope, and this tension always equals the magnitude of the forces acting at the ends of the rope—whether the rope is horizontal or vertical, whether the rope is in equilibrium or not. This is the circumstance where the rope is weightless. In most problems one characterizes such a rope as a cord, string, or thread to indicate its "lightness." Obviously no cord is completely weightless, but if it is very light in comparison to the other objects in the problem, it can be assumed weightless without much error.

Problem 4.13.   A block of weight $w = 15$ N hangs at the end of a (weightless) cord suspended from the ceiling. What is the tension in the cord, and with what force does the cord pull down on the ceiling?

Solution

The tension is the same at all points of the cord and is equal to the magnitude of the force pulling at either end. Since the block is in equilibrium under the action of two vertical forces (the weight downward and the pull of the cord upward), these two forces must have the same magnitude. Hence the upward pull of the cord = 15 N. By Newton's third law the magnitude of the pull of the block downward on the cord is also 15 N, so $T = w = 15$ N. The tension T also equals the magnitude of the pull of the ceiling on the cord, which by Newton's third law equals the pull of the cord downward on the ceiling. Thus the downward pull of the top of the cord on the ceiling is the same as the downward pull of the block on the bottom of the cord. Thus we see that a weightless rope transmits an applied force from one end to the other.

4.5   FRICTION

Friction is the rubbing force between two objects whose surfaces are in contact. The force of friction always acts parallel to the touching surfaces. By Newton's third law each surface exerts a frictional force that is equal in magnitude and opposite in direction to that exerted by the other. The magnitude of the frictional force exerted by each surface on the other depends on how tightly the two surfaces are pressed together.

Normal Force

The force responsible for this "pressing together" is called the **normal force** because it acts perpendicular to the two surfaces. By Newton's third law each surface exerts a normal force that is equal in magnitude and opposite in direction to that exerted by the other. Figure 4-10 indicates the frictional and normal force on each object when a block is in contact with an inclined plane. The frictional force (parallel to the surface) and the normal force (perpendicular to the surface) acting on a surface can always be thought of as the components of the overall force acting on that surface due to the other surface in contact with it.

Static Friction

When two surfaces are at rest with respect to one another, the frictional force each exerts on the other always opposes any tendency to relative motion. The frictional force on an object adjusts itself in magnitude and direction to oppose and counterbalance any other forces on the object that would tend to make the object start to slide. It varies, as needed, from zero magnitude up to some maximum value to stop such slippage. Such a frictional force is called a **static friction** force ($\mathbf{f}_s$). The maximum

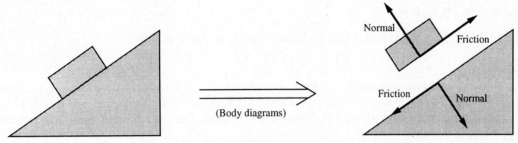

Fig. 4-10

static friction force $f_{s,max}$ that one surface can exert on another is proportional to the normal force **N** between the surfaces: $f_{s,max} = \mu_s N$, where N is the magnitude of the normal force, and μ_s is a proportionally constant, called the **coefficient of static friction**, that depends on the nature of the two surfaces. It is possible to force one object to slide over the other by applying a parallel force to one of the objects that is larger than $\mu_s N$, the maximum possible static friction force.

Problem 4.14. A book of weight $w = 10$ N rests on a horizontal table top, as shown in Fig. 4-11(a), and a horizontal force **F** is applied to it. If the coefficient of static friction μ_s between the book and the tabletop is 0.25, calculate (a) the normal force exerted by the tabletop on the book, and (b) the maximum value of the static friction force.

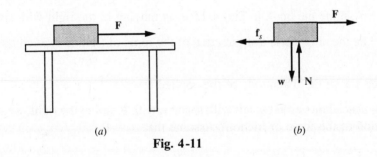

(a)   (b)

Fig. 4-11

Solution

(a)   Since the book is in equilibrium, the sum of the forces acting on it must equal zero. Figure 4-11(b) shows the body diagram for the book with all the forces acting on it. The frictional force is $\mathbf{f}_s$, and the normal force is **N**. Noting that $\mathbf{f}_s$ and **F** have no y components, from the condition that the sum of the y components equals zero we have $N - 10$ N $= 0$, or $N = 10$ N.

(b)   The maximum value attainable by the static friction force is

$$f_{s,\,max} = \mu_s N = (0.25)\,(10\,\text{N}) = 2.5\,\text{N}$$

Problem 4.15.

(a)   In Problem 4.14, if the magnitude of the applied force is $F = 2.0$ N, what is the magnitude and direction of the frictional force on the book?

(b)   What if $F = 1.0$ N; 0 N?

(c)   What is the biggest value that F can be before the book starts to slide?

Solution

(a)   The frictional force opposes the tendency to motion, so it is in the direction opposite to **F**, as shown in Fig. 4-11(b). The magnitude of the frictional force adjusts itself to keep the book at rest, which in this case means $f_s = F = 2.0$ N. This value is possible, since it is smaller than the maximum found in Problem 4.14(b).

(b)   If $F = 1.0$ N, then, by the same reasoning as in part (a), we have $f_s = 1.0$ N in the direction *opposite to* **F**. If $F = 0$, then $f_s = 0$, and there is no frictional force at all.

(c)   If F is bigger than $f_{s,max}$, then the frictional force cannot rise to match F and maintain equilibrium. Thus $F = 2.5$ N is the limiting value; beyond this value equilibrium cannot be maintained, and the book starts to move.

Kinetic Friction

Once two surfaces are in motion relative to one another, the frictional force, now called **kinetic friction** (f_k), acting on a surface is always in a direction opposed to the velocity of that surface. To a good approximation, its magnitude is independent of the magnitude of the velocity and is again proportional to the normal force between the two surfaces. Thus it can be expressed as $f_k = \mu_k N$, where μ_k, the **coefficient of kinetic friction**, depends only on the nature of the two surfaces. For any given pair of surfaces, $\mu_k \leq \mu_s$.

Problem 4.16.   Assume the book in Fig. 4-11(a) is moving to the right with speed v.

(a)   Now what are the magnitude and direction of the force of friction exerted by the tabletop on the book?

(b)   Does f_k depend on the magnitude of the applied force **F**?

(c)   If the book instead moves to the left with speed v, with **F** still to the right, what are the magnitude and direction of the force of friction? Assume that $\mu_k = 0.2$.

Solution

(a)   Once the book is moving the (kinetic) friction is of fixed magnitude, $f_k = \mu_k N$. Since we still have equilibrium in the y direction, we still have the same normal force; Thus $f_k = (0.2)(10$ N$) = 2.0$ N. The direction of the kinetic friction force is always opposite to the direction of motion, so it would be to the left.

(b)   No.

(c)   Since the normal force is still the same, the value of f_k is still 2.0 N. The direction of $\mathbf{f}_k$ is now to the right. Note that the direction of $\mathbf{f}_k$ depends only on the direction of motion and not on the direction of **F**.

4.6 CORDS AND PULLEYS

If a (weightless) cord is bent over a pulley, as in Fig. 4-12, there are two idealized situations in which the tension in the part of the cord on one side of the pulley will be the same as the tension in the part of the cord on the other side of the pulley.

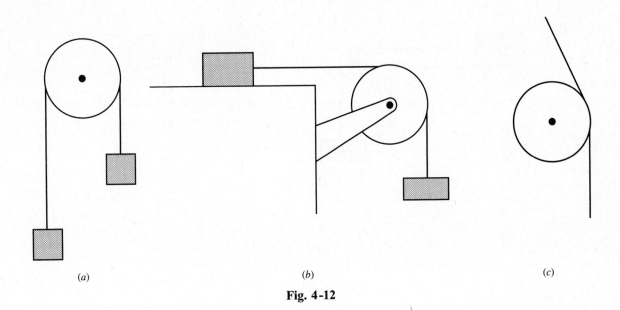

(a)   *(b)*   *(c)*

Fig. 4-12

1. The surface of the pulley is frictionless so that the cord slides effortlessly over it (frictionless pulley).

2. The surface of the pulley has friction, *but* the pulley has no weight *and* there is no friction between the pulley and the axle on which it rotates (**weightless pulley**).

In a problem, being told that the pulley is frictionless and/or weightless (massless) is generally shorthand for case 1 or case 2, and you can assume as much unless told otherwise.

Problem 4.17. In Fig. 4-13(*a*), the two blocks are connected by a light rope over a frictionless, weightless pulley. If the system is initially at rest, will it stay at rest? If so, what is the frictional force exerted by the table on block *A*?

Solution

Figure 4-13(*b*) gives the body diagrams for the two blocks. For block *B*, assuming equilibrium, the *y*-component equation gives $T - W_b = 0$ or $T = W_b = 10$ N. Since we have a rope and a frictionless, weightless pulley, the tension is the same on the block-*A* side of the pulley, and $T = 10$ N for block *A* as well.

Vertical equilibrium of block *A* requires that $N - W_a = 0$, or $N = W_a = 30$ N. Then the maximum possible static frictional force is

$$f_{s,\,max} = \mu_s N = (0.5)(30\,\text{N}) = 15\,\text{N}$$

Since $T < f_{s,max}$, the frictional force can balance *T* and the system remains at rest. The actual frictional force can be obtained from the equilibrium of block *A*:

$$T - f_s = 0 \qquad \text{or} \qquad f_s = T = 10\,\text{N}$$

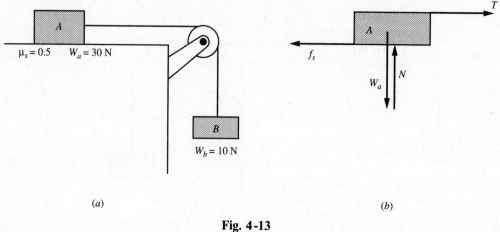

(a)   (b)

Fig. 4-13

Problems for Review and Mind Stretching

Problem 4.18.   Find the resultant **R** of the two forces shown in Fig. 4-14.

Solution

$\mathbf{R} = \mathbf{F}_1 + \mathbf{F}_2$. We choose x and y axes as shown in the figure and use the component method of addition.

$$F_{1x} = 0 \qquad F_{1y} = 20\,\text{N} \qquad F_{2x} = -(60\,\text{N})\cos 37° \qquad F_{2y} = -(60\,\text{N})\sin 37°$$

$$R_x = F_{1x} + F_{2x} = 0 - (60\,\text{N})(0.8) = -48\,\text{N}$$

$$R_y = F_{1y} + F_{2y} = (20\,\text{N}) - (60\,\text{N})(0.6) = -16\,\text{N}$$

$$R = [(-48)^2 + (-16)^2]^{1/2} = 50.6\,\text{N}$$

From the signs of its components, **R** is in the third quadrant. If θ is the acute angle that **R** makes with the negative x axis,

$$\tan\theta = \left|\frac{R_y}{R_x}\right| = \frac{16}{48} = \frac{1}{3} \qquad \text{or} \qquad \theta = 18.4°$$

Thus **R** has magnitude 50.6 N and points away from the origin at 18.4° below the negative x axis.

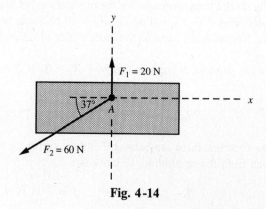

Fig. 4-14

Problem 4.19.   Three forces act on a rigid body, as shown in Fig. 4-15, with their lines of action passing through the common point B. Find their resultant and its point of application for equilibrium.

Solution

$\mathbf{R} = \mathbf{F}_1 + \mathbf{F}_2 + \mathbf{F}_3$. Choose the x and y axes as shown. Then

$$R_x = F_{1x} + F_{2x} + F_{3x} = (-50\,\text{N})\cos 30° + (40\,\text{N})\cos 45° + (0\,\text{N})$$
$$= (-50\,\text{N})\,(0.866) + (40\,\text{N})\,(0.707) = -15.0\,\text{N}$$
$$R_y = F_{1y} + F_{2y} + F_{3y} = (50\,\text{N})\sin 30° + (40\,\text{N})\sin 45° + (-30\,\text{N})$$
$$= (50\,\text{N})\,(0.5) + (40\,\text{N})\,(0.707) + (-30\,\text{N}) = 23.3\,\text{N}$$
$$R = [(-15)^2 + (23.3)^2]^{1/2} = 27.7\,\text{N}$$

$\mathbf{R}$ is in the second quadrant, with

$$\tan\theta = |R_y/R_x| = \frac{23.3}{15.0} \qquad \text{or} \qquad \theta = 57.2° \text{ above the negative } x \text{ axis}$$

$\mathbf{R}$ can act anywhere along a line of action through B.

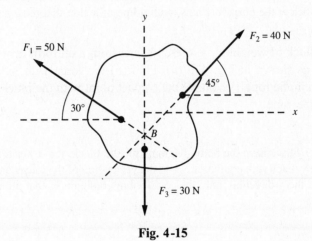

Fig. 4-15

Problem 4.20.   Refer to Problem 4.18.

(a)   What third force $\mathbf{E}$, must be exerted on the body for it to be in translational equilibrium?

(b)   Where must $\mathbf{E}$ be applied to give rotational equilibrium as well?

Solution

(a)   For translational equilibrium, $\mathbf{F}_1 + \mathbf{F}_2 + \mathbf{E} = 0$, or $\mathbf{E} = -(\mathbf{F}_1 + \mathbf{F}_2) = -\mathbf{R}$. Hence $E = 50.6$ N, and $\mathbf{E}$ points $18.4°$ above the positive x axis (see Fig. 4-16).

(b) $\mathbf{E}$ must have the same line of action as $\mathbf{R}$; that is, its line of action must also pass through point A.

Note.   The force which, when added to an existing set of forces on an object, will cause the object to be in equilibrium is called the *equilibrant* of the set. (The force $\mathbf{E}$ in the previous problem is thus an equilibrant.)

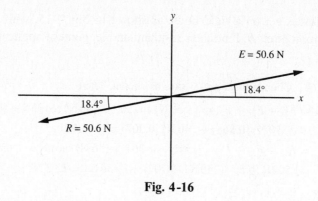

Fig. 4-16

Problem 4.21.   Find the equilibrant of the forces in Problem 4.19.

Solution

Here we have the concurrent forces F_1, F_2, and F_3 which can be replaced by the single resultant force $R = F_1 + F_2 + F_3$ with line of action through point B, as obtained in Problem 4.19. Clearly, to have equilibrium, the added fourth force, the equilibrant E, must obey $E = -R$. Thus $E = 27.7$ N pointing $57.2°$ below the positive x axis, with a line of action that must also pass through point B.

Problem 4.22.   A block of weight $w_1 = 400$ N hangs from a uniform heavy rope of length 3 m and weight $w_2 = 300$ N, as shown in Fig. 4-17(a). Find (a) the force with which the rope pulls on the block; (b) the tension in the rope 1 m above the contact point with the block; (c) the force with which the ceiling pulls on the rope.

Solution

In Fig. 4-17(b) we have the body diagrams for the block, the lower third of the rope, and the full rope, respectively. Each is in equilibrium, and the vector sum of the forces on each equals zero. Since the forces are all in the y direction, only the equilibrium condition in that direction need be applied.

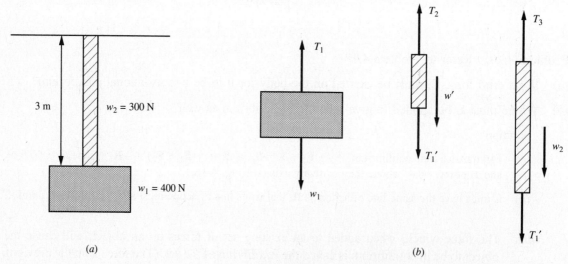

Fig. 4-17

(a) For the block, $T_1 - w_1 = 0$, or $T_1 = 400$ N equals the force of the rope on the block.

(b) For the lower third of the rope, $T_2 - T_1' - w' = 0$, where T_2 is the contact force of the upper two-thirds of the rope on the lower third and is the tension in the rope at that point; T_1' is the force of the block on the rope, given by Newton's third law as $T_1' = T_1 = 400$ N; w' is the weight of the lower third of the rope, or $w' = 100$ N. Thus $T_2 = T_1' + w' = 400$ N $+ 100$ N $= 500$ N.

(c) For the rope as a whole, $T_3 - T_1' - w_2 = 0$, or $T_3 = T_1' + w_2 = 400$ N $+ 300$ N $= 700$ N, equals the force of the ceiling on the rope.

Problem 4.23. For the weight-and-strings setup of Fig. 4-18(a), find the tensions T_1, T_2, and T_3.

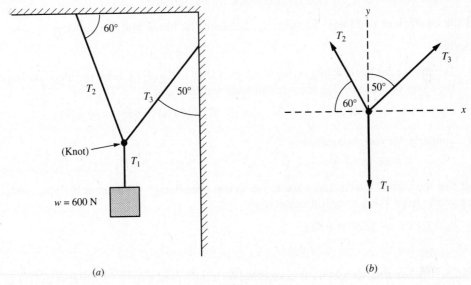

(a)   (b)

Fig. 4-18

Solution

From the equilibrium of the block, $T_1 = 600$ N. Since the knot is in equilibrium, the body diagram, Fig. 4-18(b), gives $\mathbf{T}_1 + \mathbf{T}_2 + \mathbf{T}_3 = \mathbf{0}$. Using the component method, we get

$$T_{1x} + T_{2x} + T_{3x} = 0 - T_2 \cos 60° + T_3 \sin 50° = 0 \qquad \text{or} \qquad 0.5T_2 = 0.766T_3$$

or $T_2 = 1.532\ T_3$. (A sine appears in the x-component equation because the angle of $\mathbf{T}_3$ is given relative to the y axis). Similarly,

$$T_{1y} + T_{2y} + T_{3y} = -T_1 + T_2 \sin 60° + T_3 \cos 50° = 0 \qquad \text{or} \qquad 0.866T_2 + 0.643T_3 = 600\,\text{N}$$

Substituting for T_2,

$$(0.866)(1.532T_3) + 0.643T_3 = 600\,\text{N} \qquad \text{or} \qquad 1.970T_3 = 600\,\text{N} \qquad \text{or} \qquad T_3 = 305\,\text{N}$$

Finally, $T_2 = 1.532T_3 = 467$ N.

Problem 4.24. A block of weight $w = 200$ N is pulled along a horizontal surface at constant speed by a force $F = 80$ N acting at an angle of $30°$ above the horizontal, as shown in Fig. 4-19.

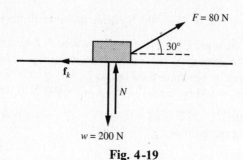

Fig. 4-19

(a) Find the frictional force **f** exerted on the block by the surface.

(b) Find the normal force **N** exerted on the block by the surface.

(c) Find the coefficient of kinetic friction, μ_k, between the block and the surface.

Solution

(a) The four vector forces acting on the block are shown in Fig. 4-19. Since the block is in equilibrium, their sum equals zero. For the x components we thus have

$$F \cos 30° - f_k = 0 \qquad \text{or} \qquad f_k = (80\,\text{N})(0.866) = 69.3\,\text{N}$$

(b) Similarly, for the y components,

$$F \sin 30° + N - w = 0 \qquad \text{or} \qquad N = 200\,\text{N} - (80\,\text{N})(0.5) = 160\,\text{N}$$

Note that the normal force is not equal to the weight even though the block is on a horizontal surface, because the force **F** has a vertical component.

(c) $\mu_k = f_k/N = 69.3/160 = 0.433$.

Problem 4.25.   A hanging weight w_1 is connected by a light cord over a frictionless pulley to a block on a frictionless incline of weight $w_2 = 500$ N, as shown in Fig. 4-20. If the block on the incline moves down at constant speed, what is the weight of the hanging block? How would your answer change if it were moving up the incline at constant speed?

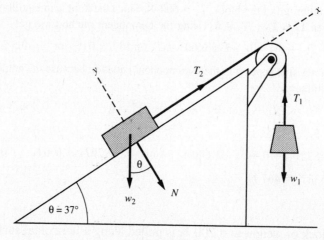

Fig. 4-20

Solution

In Fig. 4-20, all the forces on the respective blocks are shown right on the diagram for the system as a whole. Since both blocks move in straight lines at constant speed, they are each in equilibrium. For the hanging block, using y components, we have $T_1 - w_1 = 0$, or $w_1 = T_1$. To find T_1 we turn to the block on the incline. We choose x and y axes along the incline and perpendicular to it, respectively. We also note that the force of the cord on each block has the same magnitude, so $T_2 = T_1 = T$, since the cord is light and the pulley is frictionless. Then, for the x-component equilibrium equation we get

$$T - w_2 \sin\theta = 0 \quad \text{or} \quad T = (500\,\text{N})(\sin 37°) = 300\,\text{N}$$

Then from our earlier result $w_1 = T = 300$ N. Note that we did not need to solve the y-component equilibrium equation for the block on the incline to solve for T and w_1. This is because the y-component equation gives us the normal force N, which does not affect the x-component equation when there is no friction. If the block were moving up the incline, the blocks would still be in equilibrium under the action of the same forces, so the answer would remain the same.

Problem 4.26. Suppose that in Problem 4.25 there was friction between the block and the incline and that the coefficient of sliding friction was $\mu_k = 0.3$, but all the other data in the problem remained unchanged. Find the weight of the hanging block, w_1, if the other block moves at constant speed (a) down the incline; (b) up the incline.

Solution

(a) We can use Fig. 4-20 with the modification that there is an additional force on the block on the incline, a frictional force of magnitude f_k opposing the motion of the block and hence pointing parallel to the incline in the upward direction. From the rules for friction we have $f_k = \mu_k N$, where N is the normal force exerted on the block by the incline. Following the reasoning of Problem 4.25 we now have for the x components

$$T + \mu_k N - w_2 \sin 37° = 0 \quad \text{or} \quad T = (500\,\text{N})(0.6) - 0.3\,N$$

For the y components

$$N - w_2 \cos 37° = 0 \quad \text{or} \quad N = (500\,\text{N})(0.8) = 400\,\text{N}$$

Substituting into the previous equation we have

$$T = (500\,\text{N})(0.6) - 0.3(400\,\text{N}) = 300\,\text{N} - 120\,\text{N} = 180\,\text{N}$$

Since the hanging block obeys $w_1 = T$, we have our result, $w_1 = 180$ N.

(b) If the block is moving up the incline at constant speed, we proceed as before, noting that the frictional force is now directed down the incline although it still has the same magnitude $f_k = \mu_k N$. Furthermore the y-component equation for the block on the incline is unchanged, so we still have $N = 400$ N and $f_k = 0.3(400$ N$) = 120$ N. The x-component equation changes only in that the sign of the x-component of the frictional force changes, and we get

$$T - \mu_k N - w_2 \sin 37° = 0 \quad \text{and} \quad T = 300\,\text{N} + 120\,\text{N} = 420\,\text{N}$$

Finally, $w_1 = T = 420$ N.

Problem 4.27. For the setup in Fig. 4-18(a)—first discussed in Problem 4.23—the breaking point of the two cords attached to the wall and ceiling is 1500 N. How heavy can the block be without one of the cords snapping? Assume the cord attached to the block can handle any weight.

Solution

We first determine which of the two cords will reach a tension of 1500 N first. To do this we recall from Problem 4.23 that equilibrium in the x direction requires

$$T_3 \sin 50° = T_2 \cos 60° \qquad \text{or} \qquad 0.766 T_3 = 0.50 T_2 \qquad \text{or} \qquad T_3 = 0.653 T_2 < T_2$$

Clearly T_3 is always less than T_2, and hence T_2 will reach 1500 N first. We now set $T_2 = 1500$ N; from above, this immediately yields $T_3 = 0.653 \,(1500 \text{ N}) = 980$ N. We can now determine the corresponding weight w of the block using the equilibrium equation in the y direction:

$$w = T_1 = T_2 \sin 60° + T_3 \cos 50° = (1500 \text{ N})\,(0.866) + (980 \text{ N})\,(0.643) = 1929 \text{ N}$$

Supplementary Problems

Problem 4.28.

(a)   The earth's moon revolves about the earth once a month and always keeps the same side facing the earth. Describe the translational and rotational motion of the moon.

(b)   Is the moon in translational and/or rotational equilibrium?

> *Ans.*   (a)   The moon as a whole translates in a circular orbit about the earth; it rotates on its axis once a month.
>
> (b)   The moon is not in translational equilibrium; if the moon's monthly rotation on its axis is uniform (it is, approximately), then the moon is in rotational equilibrium.

Problem 4.29.   An automobile travels in a straight line with no skidding.

(a)   If the automobile travels at constant speed, are its wheels in translational and/or rotational equilibrium?

(b)   If the automobile accelerates from 0 to 60 mph, are its wheels in translational and/or rotational equilibrium?

(c)   Is a bit of chewing gum on the rim of a wheel of the automobile in translational and/or rotational equilibrium for the case of part (a) or part (b)?

> *Ans.*   (a) In both; (b) in neither; (c) not in translational equilibrium for either case; the bit of gum goes through one rotation every time the wheel makes one complete turn. For part (a) it is in rotational equilibrium, while for part (b) it is not.

Problem 4.30.   A uniform rod of weight 100 N is acted on by a force $\mathbf{F}_1$ as shown in Fig. 4-21. What force $\mathbf{F}_2$ must be added to the rod to ensure translational equilibrium?

> *Ans.*   56.6 N at an angle of 58.0° above the negative x axis

Problem 4.31.   In Fig. 4-22(a), assume the somewhat artificial condition that the strut is weightless and the wall is frictionless. The cord makes an angle $\theta = 37°$ with the strut.

(a)   What are the conditions imposed on T and N if the strut is to be in translational equilibrium?

(b)   Can the strut be in rotational equilibrium under the circumstances shown? Give your justification.

> *Ans.*   (a) $T = 83$ N, $N = 66$ N; (b) No. The three forces cannot possibly be concurrent.

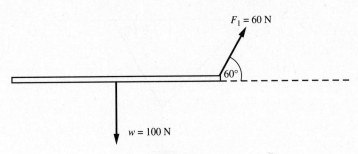

Fig. 4-21

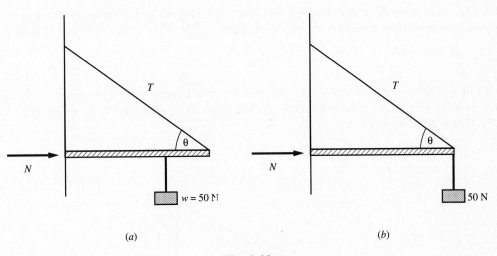

Fig. 4-22

Problem 4.32. Assume the same situation as in Problem 4.31, except that the weight now hangs from the end as shown in Fig. 4-22(*b*).

(*a*) Find the values of *T* and *N* for translational equilibrium.

(*b*) Is the strut now in rotational equilibrium and if so why?

> *Ans.* (*a*) The forces are as before: *T* = 83 N, *N* = 66 N.
>
> (*b*) Yes. If the forces are as in part (*a*), then the strut is also in rotational equilibrium since the three forces are concurrent.

Problem 4.33. A block weighing 200 N is suspended from the ceiling by means of three light cords joined in a knot (Fig. 4-23). Find the tensions in the cords and the forces the cords exert on the ceiling.

> *Ans.* $T_1 = 200$ N, $T_2 = 104$ N, $T_3 = 146$ N; 104 N and 146 N, downward along the cord directions

Problem 4.34. A block slides down a 30° incline at constant speed. Find the coefficient of kinetic friction.

> *Ans.* $\mu_k = 0.58$

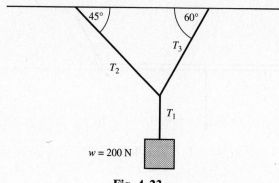

Fig. 4-23

Problem 4.35. The same block as in Problem 4.34, when placed at rest on the incline, does not move. When the angle of inclination is increased by $10°$, the block starts to slide. What is the coefficient of static friction?

Ans. $\mu_s = 0.84$

Problem 4.36. The block in Problem 4.34 is now connected to a hanging block by means of a light cord over a frictionless pulley (Fig. 4-24). If the block on the incline weighs 30 N, what must be the weight of the hanging block if it falls at constant speed?

Ans. 30 N

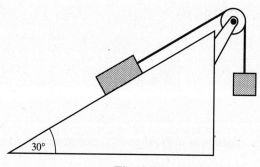

Fig. 4-24

Problem 4.37. Suppose that for the situation of Problem 4.26 (Fig. 4-20) the block is initially at rest and the coefficient of static friction is $\mu_s = 0.4$. For what range of weights w_1 will the block remain at rest?

Ans. 140 to 460 N

Problem 4.38. If the block in Problem 4.24 was initially at rest and $\mu_s = 0.6$, how big would the applied force have to be to just get the block moving?

Ans. $F = 103$ N

Problem 4.39. Suppose the rope in Problem 4.22 has a weak spot at its midpoint so that it will break if the tension at that point reaches 2000 N. What is the heaviest block that can be suspended by the rope?

Ans. 1850 N

Problem 4.40.   A block is pushed along a tabletop at constant speed by a force acting 20° below the horizontal as in Fig. 4-25(a). If the weight of the block is 100 N and the coefficient of kinetic friction is $\mu_k = 0.30$, find the magnitudes of (a) the pushing force, (b) the normal force due to the table.

>   *Ans.*   (a) 35.8 N; (b) 112 N

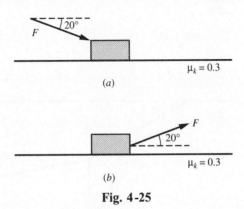

(a)

(b)

Fig. 4-25

Problem 4.41.   Repeat Problem 4.40 if the block is being pulled at constant speed by a force acting at an angle of 20° above the horizontal [Fig. 4-25(b)].

>   *Ans.*   (a) 28.7 N; (b) 90 N

Problem 4.42.   Find the tensions T_1 and T_2 in the two cords for the equilibrium situation depicted in Fig. 4-26(a).

>   *Ans.* $T_1 = 80$ N; $T_2 = 41$ N

Problem 4.43.   Repeat Problem 4.42 for Fig. 4-26(b).

>   *Ans.* $T_1 = 139$ lb; $T_2 = 160$ lb

Problem 4.44.   Repeat Problem 4.42 for Fig. 4-26(c).

>   *Ans.* $T_1 = 253$ N; $T_2 = 288$ N

Problem 4.45.   What is the minimum coefficient of static friction between table and block for which the blocks in Fig. 4-27 will remain in equilibrium? What is the tension T?

>   *Ans.*   0.29; 115 N

Problem 4.46.   A 50-N weight is hung symmetrically from the ceiling by two light cords, as shown in Fig. 4-28. The breaking strength of the cords is 1200 N. What is the minimum angle θ at which the weight can be hung without the cords breaking? (Assume the vertical cord is very strong.)

>   *Ans.*   1.19°

Problem 4.47.   In Fig. 4-26(b) the breaking point of the horizontal cord is 1000 lb, while that of the cord attached to the ceiling is 1200 lb.

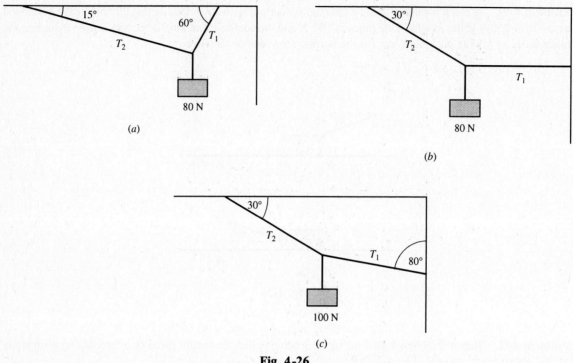

Fig. 4-26

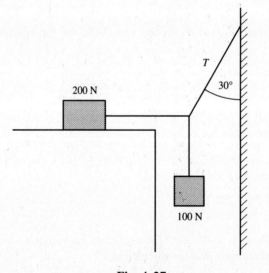

Fig. 4-27

(a)   If the weight of the hanging block is steadily increased, which cord will snap first?

(b)   What is the maximum weight that can be supported by the cords?

Ans.   (a) The horizontal cord; (b) 577 lb

Problem 4.48.   Referring to Fig. 4-20, suppose $\mu_k = 0.50$ and $w_1 = 900$ N. Find the weight w_2 such that the block just slides (a) up the incline at constant speed; (b) down the incline at constant speed.

Ans.   (a) 900 N; (b) 4500 N

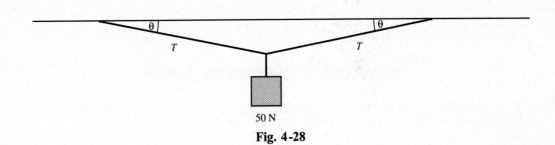

Fig. 4-28

Problem 4.49. A child pushes a block of weight $w = 300$ N against a wall with a force **F** acting upward at 45° to the horizontal to stop it from falling. The situation is shown in Fig. 4-29. $\mu_s = 0.6$ between the block and the wall.

(*a*) What is the minimum value of F for which the block will not fall?

(*b*) Would the child have an easier time of it by instead exerting a force in the horizontal direction?

    Ans. (*a*) 265 N; (*b*) no. The minimum force would now be 500 N.

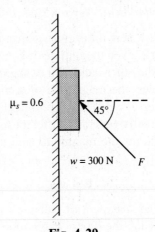

Fig. 4-29

Chapter 5

Newton's Second Law

In this chapter we concern ourselves only with the translational motion of objects.

5.1 RESULTANT FORCE AND ACCELERATION

In Chap. 4 it was found that if the vector sum of the forces on an object—the resultant force—is zero, then the object is in translational equilibrium; i.e., it has constant velocity, or, equivalently, zero acceleration. If the resultant force is not zero, then we should expect that the acceleration also would not be zero. Indeed, we should say that the unbalanced force on the object *caused* its acceleration. Newton's second law is the quantitative statement of this cause-and-effect relationship.

Experimental Facts and the Formulation of Newton's Second Law

When a nonzero resultant force **F** acts on a given object, the consequent acceleration **a** always points in the direction of **F**. Also, for a given magnitude of **F**, the magnitude of **a** is the same no matter what the direction of the force. On the other hand, if the magnitude of **F** doubles, the magnitude of **a** doubles; if the magnitude of **F** triples, the magnitude of **a** triples; etc. Thus the magnitude of **a** is proportional to the magnitude of **F**, or $F \propto a$. The proportionality constant is called the *mass m* of the object, and we write $F = ma$, where m is generally different for different objects. Since m is a scalar quantity, we can combine the results for the magnitude and the direction of the acceleration in the single equation

$$\mathbf{F} = m\mathbf{a}$$

This equation is the mathematical statement of Newton's second law. In Fig. 5-1(a) and (b), we show different resultant forces having the same magnitude acting on (a) the same object and (b) different objects, and the resulting accelerations of those objects.

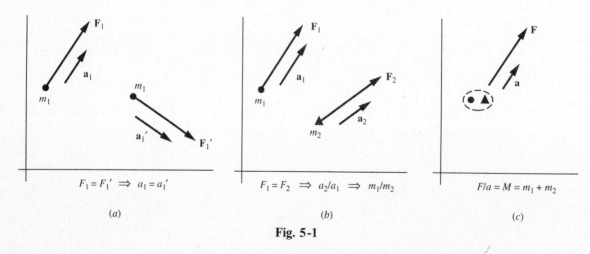

$$F_1 = F_1{}' \implies a_1 = a_1{}' \qquad\qquad F_1 = F_2 \implies a_2/a_1 \implies m_1/m_2 \qquad\qquad F/a = M = m_1 + m_2$$

(a)   (b)   (c)

Fig. 5-1

The Meaning of Mass

As can be seen in Fig. 5-1 the mass controls the response of the object to a given magnitude force: A small mass means a large acceleration, a large mass means a small acceleration. Because mass measures the resistance of an object to having its velocity changed ("being shoved around"), it is often referred to as the **inertia** of the object. The relative magnitude of different masses can easily be established by applying the same magnitude force to the different objects and measuring their accelerations. Then

$$m_1 a_1 = m_2 a_2 \qquad \text{or} \qquad \frac{m_1}{m_2} = \frac{a_2}{a_1}$$

The mass is clearly an intrinsic property of an object, but for it to be a truly fundamental property of all matter one needs to show that objects maintain this property even when they are combined with other objects. Figure 5-1(c) shows a resultant force being applied to two objects stuck together. The resulting acceleration is just what one expects if the mass of the combination is $M = m_1 + m_2$. The mass is thus an indestructible and unchanging property of any object that stays with the object even when it is combined into larger units. In the same way, when an object is broken into smaller parts, the sum of the masses of the parts equals the original mass.

Units of Force and Mass

In the International System (SI) units, the unit of force is already determined for us from Newton's second law, once we have a unit of mass and a unit of acceleration. The unit of mass is the kilogram, and the unit of acceleration is the meter per second squared. The corresponding unit of force is the Newton (N), and from $F = ma$ we have

$$1 \text{ N} = (1 \text{ kg})\,(1 \text{ m/s}^2) = 1 \text{ kg} \cdot \text{m/s}^2$$

In other words, a 1-N force gives a 1-kg mass an acceleration of 1 m/s^2. If one chooses the gram as the unit of mass and the centimeter per second squared as the unit of acceleration, then the unit of force is called the dyne. Again, from $F = ma$

$$1 \text{ dyn} = (1 \text{ g})\,(1 \text{ cm/s}^2) = 1 \text{ g} \cdot \text{cm/s}^2$$

Problem 5.1.   How many dynes are there in a newton?

Solution

$$1 \text{ N} = 1 \text{ kg} \cdot \text{m/s}^2 = (1000 \text{ g})(100 \text{ cm})/\text{s}^2 = 100{,}000 \text{ g} \cdot \text{cm/s}^2 = 10^5 \text{ dyn}$$

Problem 5.2.   What is the magnitude and direction of the acceleration of an object whose mass is 10 kg when it is acted on by a resultant force of 380 N at $30°$ above the positive x axis?

Solution

The direction is the same as that of the resultant force, $30°$ above the positive x axis. For the magnitude $F = ma$ gives

$$a = \frac{F}{m} = \frac{380 \text{ N}}{10 \text{ kg}} = 38 \text{ N/kg} = \frac{38 \text{ kg} \cdot \text{m/s}^2}{\text{kg}} = 38 \text{ m/s}^2$$

Problem 5.3.   A constant force acts on a 30-g object and produces an acceleration of 2 m/s^2. Find the force in dynes.

Solution

We are given mixed units, so we first convert the acceleration to the gram-centimeter-second system: $a = 2$ m/s^2 = 200 cm/s^2. Then $F = ma$ gives

$$F = (30 \text{ g}) (200 \text{ cm/s}^2) = 6000 \text{ dyn}$$

The English System and Weight

In the English system of units it is the unit of force, the pound (lb), that is fundamental, rather than the mass. One pound (1 lb) is defined as the pull of gravity on an object whose mass is 0.45359 kg at a specified latitude of the earth's surface. (The pull of gravity on an object is commonly called its weight.) The corresponding unit of mass is now defined using the second law, $F = ma$: A mass of 1 slug is that mass which when acted on by a force of 1 lb accelerates at 1 ft/s^2, or 1 slug = (1 lb)/(1 ft/s^2).

To convert from pounds to newtons we have to discuss the nature of weight. If an object near the earth's surface is acted on only by the force of gravity, it will accelerate with the acceleration $g = 9.8$ m/s^2. Calling the force of gravity, or weight, w, the second law gives $w = mg$. Since g is the same for all objects, $w/m = g$ is constant. Thus weight and mass are proportional at a given point on the earth's surface. As one changes position on the earth's surface, both w and g vary slightly, but m stays constant. This will be discussed in more detail when we discuss the law of universal gravitation.

We can now determine the conversion from the English to the metric system. From its definition: 1 lb = (0.45359 kg)(9.8 m/s^2) = 4.445 N. The mass 0.45359 kg is given a special name and called 1 pound-mass (i.e., the mass that weighs 1 lb). Since a force of 1 lb gives 1 lb-mass an acceleration $g = 9.8$ m/s^2 = 32.2 ft/s^2, while it gives 1 slug an acceleration of only 1 ft/s^2, it follows that 1 slug = 32.2 lb-mass = 32.2 (0.45359 kg) = 14.7 kg.

Problem 5.4.   What is the weight w, in pounds, of a 1-kg mass?

Solution

We can first get w in newtons. $w = (1 \text{ kg})(9.8 \text{ m/s}^2) = 9.8$ N. Dividing by 4.445 N/lb we get $w = (9.8 \text{ N})/(4.445 \text{ N/lb}) = 2.20$ lb. We could also get the result directly from the fact that 0.45359 kg weighs 1 lb, and therefore 1 kg weighs 1/0.45359 = 2.20 times as much.

Problem 5.5.   A resultant force of 50 lb acts on an object weighing 12 lb. Find the acceleration.

Solution

The mass of the object is $m = w/g = (12 \text{ lb})/(32.2 \text{ ft/s}^2) = 0.373$ slug. Then

$$50 \text{ lb} = (0.373 \text{ slug})a \quad \text{or} \quad a = 134 \text{ ft/s}^2$$

5.2 APPLICATIONS OF THE SECOND LAW

Whenever applying the second law it is essential to clearly identify the object being accelerated and to be sure that the force appearing in the equation is the resultant of all forces acting on the object. Also, because $\mathbf{F} = m\mathbf{a}$ as a vector equation, it may be useful to resolve it into components along convenient x and y axes.

Forces on a Single Object

Problem 5.6. A constant force $\mathbf{T}$ pulls horizontally on a block of mass $m = 2.0$ kg, which is free to move on a frictionless horizontal surface, as shown in Fig. 5-2(a). Starting from rest, the block is observed to move 20.0 m in 2.0 s. Find $\mathbf{T}$.

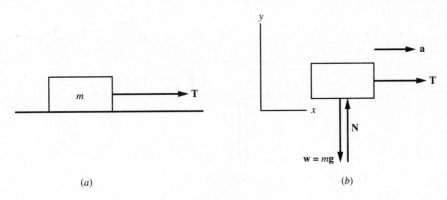

(a)   (b)

Fig. 5-2

Solution

We first draw a body diagram for the block, with all forces on the block drawn in, as shown in Fig. 5-2(b). Also shown is the acceleration $\mathbf{a}$. Since the acceleration is along the x direction (the block stays on the table), we have $a_x = a$ and $a_y = 0$. For the x direction we have $F_x = ma_x$. Since T is the only force with an x component, and it points in the x direction, we have $T = ma$ or $T = (2.0 \text{ kg})a$. Since T is constant, we know that a is constant, and we can use the kinematic equations for constant acceleration, together with the kinematic information given. Since the block starts from rest, we can set $x_0 = v_{0x} = 0$. We then have $x = \frac{1}{2}at^2$, which for our case yields $20.0 \text{ m} = \frac{1}{2}a(2.0 \text{ s})^2$ or $a = 10.0 \text{ m/s}^2$. Then

$$T = (2.0 \text{ kg}) (10.0 \text{ m/s}^2) = 20.0 \text{ N}$$

Problem 5.7. Redo Problem 5.6, if there is now friction between the block and tabletop and the coefficient of kinetic friction is $\mu_k = 0.3$.

Solution

The body diagram in Fig. 5-2 remains the same except that there is one additional force $\mathbf{f}_k$ in the negative x direction. Since $f_k = \mu_k N$, we need to find the normal force N. Considering the y direction we have (since $a_y = 0$) $N = mg = 19.6$ N. The x equation is now $T - f_k = ma$ or $T - \mu_k N = ma$. Substituting in the known values, we get

$$T - 0.3(19.6 \text{ N}) = (2.0 \text{ kg}) (10.0 \text{ m/s}^2) \qquad \text{or} \qquad T = 25.88 \text{ N}$$

Problem 5.8. A block of mass m = 5.0 kg slides from rest on a horizontal frictionless surface under the action of a force of 60 N in a direction $40°$ above the positive x axis. How fast is the block moving at the end of 6 s?

Solution

The situation is depicted in Fig. 5-3, where, instead of having a separate body diagram, all the forces acting on the block are directly drawn in. Only the x motion is of interest, and $F_x = ma_x$ yields

$$(60 \text{ N}) \cos 40° = (5.0 \text{ kg})a \qquad \text{or} \qquad a = 9.2 \text{ m/s}^2$$

Since we are starting from rest we have $v_x = at = (9.2 \text{ m/s}^2)(6 \text{ s}) = 55.2 \text{ m/s}$.

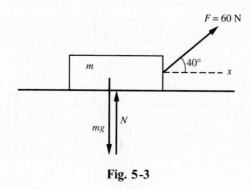

Fig. 5-3

Problem 5.9. A block of mass $m = 12$ kg slides down a frictionless inclined plane of angle 50°. What is the acceleration?

Solution

The situation is shown in Fig. 5-4. Since we know the motion of the block will be down the incline, we choose our x axis down along the incline. Since there is no friction, the only force with a component along the incline is the weight $w = mg$. Then

$$mg \sin 50° = ma \qquad \text{or} \qquad a = g \sin 50° = (9.8 \text{ m/s}^2)(0.766) = 7.51 \text{ m/s}^2$$

Note. The acceleration is independent of the mass, just as for the case of freely falling objects. Indeed, if the angle of the incline is any angle θ, the acceleration is $a = g \sin \theta$.

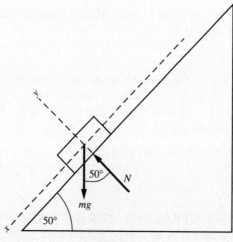

Fig. 5-4

Problem 5.10. Suppose that in Problem 5.9 there is friction, with $\mu_k = 0.2$. Find the acceleration.

Solution

A frictional force $f_k = \mu_k N$, acting up the incline (in the negative x direction), must be added to the forces already shown in Fig. 5-4. Since we have equilibrium along the y axis,

$$N = mg \cos 50° \qquad \text{and} \qquad f_k = \mu_k mg \cos 50°$$

Then, for the x motion, $mg \sin 50° - \mu_k mg \cos 50° = ma$. Dividing out the mass we obtain

$$a = g \sin 50° - \mu_k g \cos 50° = g(\sin 50° - \mu_k \cos 50°)$$
$$= (9.8 \text{ m/s}^2)(0.766 - 0.2 \cdot 0.643) = 6.25 \text{ m/s}^2$$

Problem 5.11. A child weighing 80 lb stands on a bathroom scale in an elevator. Find his "effective weight" as read on the scale, if the elevator is (a) moving downward at constant speed; (b) moving upward at constant speed; (c) accelerating upward at 8.0 ft/s²; (d) accelerating upward at 32 ft/s²; (e) accelerating downward at 8.0 ft/s²; (f) accelerating downward at 32 ft/s².

Solution

The child is under the action of two forces, the weight $w = mg$ downward and the normal force N of the scale upward. (The bathroom scale reads the value of N, which is what we call the "effective weight".) We choose our positive direction upward.

(a), (b) In these two cases the acceleration is zero, so the child is in equilibrium, and we must have $N = mg = 80$ lb, the true weight.

(c) Now $N - mg = ma$ or $N = m(g + a) = (w/g)(g + a) = w(g + a)/g = (80 \text{ lb})(32 + 8)/32 = (80 \text{ lb})\left(\frac{40}{32}\right) = 100$ lb.

Note. This "effective weight" is not just a mathematical result. The child will actually feel heavier. Just as the scale pushes up with a force greater than the weight to give the entire child an upward acceleration, so too the lower half of the child must push up on the upper half with a greater than usual force to give that half its acceleration. Indeed each part of the body must exert a proportionately greater force on every other part, hence the feeling of weighing more.

(d) We still have $N = w(g + a)/g$, but now $a = 32$ ft/s². Therefore $N = (80 \text{ lb})\left(\frac{64}{32}\right) = 160$ lb, or double the weight.

(e) Now $a = -8$ m/s², and $N = (80 \text{ lb})\left(\frac{24}{32}\right) = 60$ lb.

(f) Now $a = -32$ ft/s² and $g + a = 0$, so $N = 0$.

Note. The answer to part (f) is not surprising because the child is accelerating downward with the acceleration of gravity, which is called "free fall." The child in fact feels weightless since no forces other than gravity can be acting on any given part of his body. Thus, the usual forces exerted by different parts of the body on each other are not there, and it feels strange. A satellite moving around the earth is also in free fall, which is why the astronauts inside feel weightless.

Motion of Coupled Objects

In many situations objects are connected to each other by cords or directly make contact with one another. Newton's second law should be applied to each object and the simultaneous equations solved to obtain the motion of the two coupled objects.

Problem 5.12. Two blocks, of masses $m_A = 9$ kg and $m_B = 11$ kg, are connected by a light cord on a frictionless horizontal surface, as shown in Fig. 5-5(a). Block B is pulled to the right by a force of 12 N. Find the acceleration of the blocks and the tension in the connecting cord.

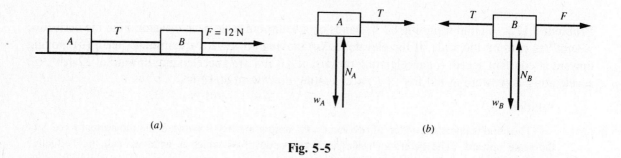

(a)   (b)

Fig. 5-5

Solution

We choose rightward as positive, and draw the body diagrams for the two blocks, as shown in Fig. 5-5(b). For each block there is no motion in the vertical direction, so the normal force in each case just balances the weight. In the horizontal direction, for block B we have

$$F - T = m_B a \tag{i}$$

where a is the acceleration. For block A we have

$$T = m_A a \tag{ii}$$

Adding the two equations (which means adding the left sides of the equations and setting the result equal to the sum of the right sides), we get

$$F = (m_B + m_A)a \quad \text{or} \quad 12 \text{ N} = (20 \text{ kg})a \quad \text{or} \quad a = 0.60 \text{ m/s}^2 \tag{iii}$$

Then

$$T = m_A a = (9 \text{ kg})(0.60 \text{ m/s}^2) = 5.4 \text{ N}$$

Problem 5.13. Two blocks, of masses $m_A = 5$ kg and $m_B = 12$ kg, are connected by a light cord over a frictionless pulley, as shown in Fig. 5-6(a). There is no friction between block A and the tabletop. Find the acceleration of each block and the tension in the cord between them.

Solution

By Sec. 4.6 the tension in a light cord is the same on both sides of a frictionless pulley. Figure 5-6(b) shows the body diagrams for the two blocks. For block B we choose downward as positive, since that is the direction of its acceleration. Then

$$m_B g - T = m_B a \tag{i}$$

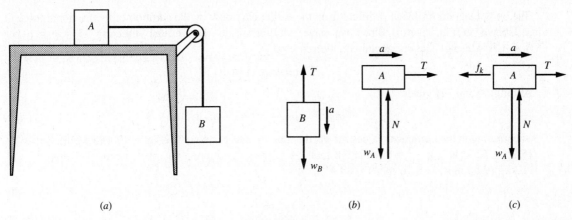

Fig. 5-6

For block A we note that the acceleration will have the same magnitude as for block B since the cord has a fixed length and the motion of block A to the right must be an exact replica of the downward motion of block B. To be able to use the same symbol a for acceleration for both blocks, we choose a consistent positive direction for each. Since we have chosen downward as positive for block B, we choose rightward as positive for A. Then, noting that the only force with a horizontal component is the tension **T**, we have

$$T = m_A a \tag{ii}$$

Since the masses are known we can solve Eq. (i) and (ii) simultaneously for a and T. By adding the two equations we obtain

$$m_B g = (m_A + m_B)a \tag{iii}$$

Note. This is the same form as Eq. (iii) of Problem 5.12. Indeed, if we let F in that equation equal $m_B g$ (instead of 12 N), the equations have identical form. Thus adding Eq. (i) and (ii) gives us an equivalent one-dimensional 1-D situation, with the "pulling" force just the hanging weight.

We can now solve for a in Eq. (iii) and put in the numbers:

$$a = \frac{(12 \text{ kg}) (9.8 \text{ m/s}^2)}{5 \text{ kg} + 12 \text{ kg}} = 6.9 \text{ m/s}^2$$

To obtain the tension in the cord we substitute our result for a into Eq. (ii):

$$T = (5.0 \text{ kg}) (6.9 \text{ m/s}^2) = 34.5 \text{ N}$$

One can check for numerical errors by substituting back into Eq. (i): $(12 \text{ kg})(9.8 \text{ m/s}^2) - 34.5 \text{ N} = (12 \text{ kg})(6.9 \text{ m/s}^2)$ or 83 N = 83 N. So it checks.

Problem 5.14. Suppose we have the same situation as in Problem 5.13, except that there is now friction between block A and the table with coefficient $\mu_k = 0.4$. Find the acceleration and tension.

Solution

The body diagram for block B is the same as before, so we have

$$m_B g - T = m_B a \tag{i}$$

The body diagram for block A differs from the earlier case only by the addition of the frictional force f_k, as shown in Fig. 5-6(c). Since we have equilibrium in the vertical direction, $N = m_A g$. Then $f_k = \mu_k N = \mu_k mg$. The horizontal equation is now

$$T - \mu_k m_A g = m_A a \tag{ii}$$

Adding (i) and (ii) yields

$$m_B g - \mu_k m_A g = (m_A + m_B)g \tag{iii}$$

Substituting in the numerical values for μ_k, the masses, and g, we get $[12 \text{ kg} - (0.4)(5 \text{ kg})](9.8 \text{ m/s}^2) = (5 \text{ kg} + 12 \text{ kg})a$ or $a = (10/17)(9.8 \text{ m/s}^2) = 5.76 \text{ m/s}^2$. From ($i$) we have $T = m_B(g - a) = (12 \text{ kg})(9.80 \text{ m/s}^2 - 5.76 \text{ m/s}^2) = 48.4 \text{ N}$.

Problem 5.15. Suppose blocks A and B of Problem 5.13 are still connected by a cord over a frictionless pulley, but with block A now free to slide on a frictionless incline, as shown in Fig. 5-7(a), instead of on a horizontal tabletop. Find the acceleration of the blocks and the tension in the cord between them.

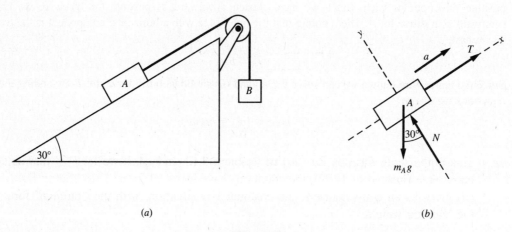

(a)   (b)

Fig. 5-7

Solution

The equation for the motion of block B is the same as in Problems 5.13 and 5.14:

$$m_B g - T = m_B a \tag{i}$$

For block A we draw the body diagram, Fig. 5-7(b), and choose axes along and perpendicular to the incline. Note that the positive x axis is again chosen consistently with the positive downward direction chosen for block B. For the x direction we have

$$T - m_A g \sin\theta = m_A a \tag{ii}$$

We again add (i) and (ii), which yields

$$m_B g - m_A g \sin\theta = (m_B + m_A)a \tag{iii}$$

Noting $\theta = 30°$, and $\sin 30° = 0.5$, we have

$$[12 \text{ kg} - (0.5)(5 \text{ kg})](9.8 \text{ m/s}^2) = (12 \text{ kg} + 5 \text{ kg})a$$

or
$$a = \frac{9.5}{17} (9.8 \text{ m/s}^2) = 5.48 \text{ m/s}^2$$
$$T = m_B(g - a) = (12 \text{ kg}) (9.80 \text{ m/s}^2 - 5.48 \text{ m/s}^2) = 51.8 \text{ N}$$

Problem 5.16. Two blocks on a frictionless horizontal surface are pushed to the right by a horizontal force $F = 46$ N, as shown in Fig. 5-8(a). Find the acceleration of the blocks and the normal force exerted by each block on the other.

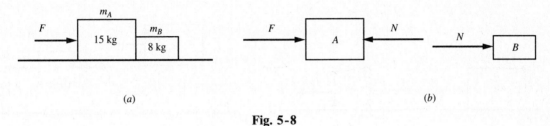

(a)   (b)

Fig. 5-8

Solution

The body diagrams showing the horizontal forces for the two blocks are shown in Fig. 5-8(b), where we recall that from Newton's third law, the normal forces exerted by each block on the other are equal and opposite. Then, applying Newton's second law to each block, we have $F - N = m_A a$ and $N = m_B a$. Adding the two equations yields $F = (m_A + m_B)a$. (This last result is obvious if we just treat the system as a single object acted on by the horizontal force **F**.) Hence,

$$a = \frac{46 \text{ N}}{23 \text{ kg}} = 2 m/s^2 \quad \text{and} \quad N = (8 \text{ kg}) (2 \text{ m/s}^2) = 16 \text{ N}$$

Thus block B exerts a force of 16 N to the left on block A, while block A exerts a force of 16 N to the right on block B.

Problem 5.17. Suppose the order of the blocks in Problem 5.16 were interchanged. How does that affect the answers for the acceleration and the forces between the blocks?

Solution

The situation is shown in Fig. 5-9(a), and the horizontal-force body diagrams in Fig. 5-9(b). The equations for the two blocks are now $F - N = m_B a$ and $N = m_A a$. Adding the equations yields $F = (m_A + m_B)a$, just as before. Thus the acceleration is the same: $a = 2$ m/s^2, which is to be expected. The situation is not the same, however, for the normal force between the blocks, as can be seen by solving for N:

$$N = m_A a = (15 \text{ kg}) (2 \text{ m/s}^2) = 30 \text{ N}$$

Now let's consider what happens if the mass of the cord connecting two blocks cannot be ignored.

Problem 5.18. A rope of mass $m = 1$ kg connects two blocks on a frictionless tabletop that are pulled to the right by a force $F = 48$ N, as shown in Fig. 5-10(a).

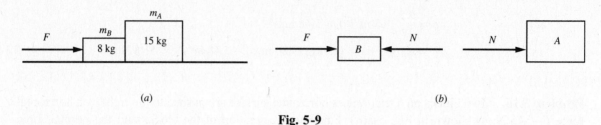

(a)   (b)

Fig. 5-9

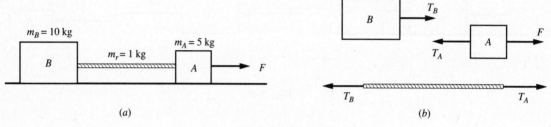

(a)   (b)

Fig. 5-10

(a) Find the acceleration of this three-object system.

(b) Find the forces T_A and T_B exerted by the rope on blocks A and B.

   Solution

   (a) Since the system moves as a unit, we can treat it as a single object of mass 16 kg acted on by a horizontal force of 48 N, yielding an acceleration of a = 48 N/16 kg = 3 m/s^2.

   (b) Applying Newton's second law to each object using the body diagrams (horizontal forces only) of 5-10(b) yields

$$F - T_A = M_A a \qquad T_A - T_B = ma \qquad T_B = M_B a$$

   Adding the three equations, we see that the T_A and T_B forces cancel out, yielding $F = (M_A + m + M_B)a = (16$ kg$)a$. This is just our earlier result that F = (combined mass)a, and a = 3 m/s^2. The first equation gives $T_A = F - M_A a$ = 48 N $-$ (5 kg)(3 m/s^2) = 33 N, and the third equation gives $T_B = M_B a$ = (10 kg)(3 m/s^2) = 30 N.

Uniform Circular Motion

   When an object moves in uniform circular motion, it has a centripetal acceleration $a = v^2/r$, where v is the magnitude of the instantaneous velocity (or speed) of the object and r is the radius of the circle on which the object is moving (see Sec. 3.4). From Newton's second law we know that there must be a resultant force, of magnitude mv^2/r, causing this acceleration. That resultant force is called the **centripetal force**.

Problem 5.19. A small block, of mass m = 100 g, is on a frictionless horizontal table. The block is attached to one end of a cord, of length L = 40 cm, whose other end is pinned to the center of the table, as shown in Fig. 5-11. If the block is spun so that it makes 2 revolutions per second (r/s), find the centripetal acceleration and the tension in the cord.

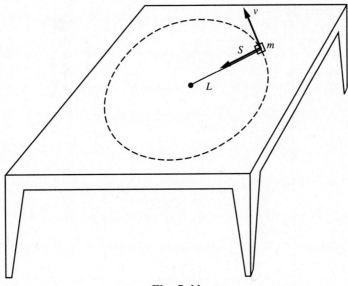

Fig. 5-11

Solution

First we find the constant magnitude of velocity, v. We are given the *frequency f* (number of revolutions per second) with which the mass twirls around on its circle of radius $L = 40$ cm. The *period T* (number of seconds per revolution) is just $T = 1/f$. Thus $f = 2$ r/s so that $T = 1/2$ s. Then

$$v = \frac{2\pi L}{T} = \frac{(6.28)\,(40\ \text{cm})}{\frac{1}{2}\ \text{s}} = 502\ \text{cm/s}$$

$$a = \frac{v^2}{L} = \frac{(502\ \text{cm/s})^2}{40\ \text{cm}} = 6300\ \text{cm/s}^2$$

with the acceleration directed toward the center of the circle.

The only force on the block in the plane of the tabletop is the tension in the cord S. Furthermore, since the cord is taut, it always exerts a force on the block radially inward toward the center of the circle. Thus S is in fact the centripetal force, and its magnitude is given by Newton's second law:

$$S = ma = (100\ \text{g})\,(6300\ \text{cm/s}^2) = 630{,}000\ \text{dyn} = 6.30\ \text{N}$$

Problem 5.20. Suppose the block and cord of Problem 5.19 are removed from the table, and the block is now twirled in a vertical circle with the same frequency as before, as shown in Fig. 5-12(a). Assume that the speed of the block is the same at all points of the circular motion. Find the tension in the cord at points A and B, the highest and lowest points of the circle.

Solution

The speed and acceleration are the same as in Problem 5.19, since the radius and the period of the motion are unchanged. Since the mass of the block is also unchanged, the centripetal force is unchanged as well, and, as before, is $ma = 6.30$ N. The difference here is that there are two forces contributing to the acceleration, the tension S in the cord and the force of gravity, or weight, $w = mg = (0.100\ \text{kg})(9.8\ \text{m/s}^2) = 0.98$ N. The resultant of these two forces is the centripetal force. The situation as the block passes the highest and lowest positions, point A and B, respectively, is shown

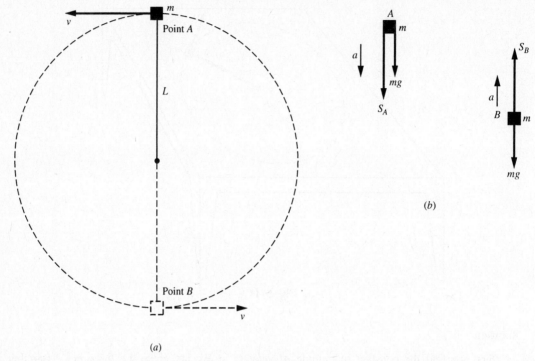

Fig. 5-12

in Fig. 5-12(b). For the highest point we choose the direction of the acceleration as positive, and (in SI units)

$$S_A + mg = ma \quad \text{or} \quad S_A = ma - mg = 6.30 \text{ N} - 0.98 \text{ N} = 5.32 \text{ N}$$

For the lowest point we again choose the direction of the acceleration as positive, so this time it is upward. We then get

$$S_B - mg = ma \quad \text{or} \quad S_B = ma + mg = 6.30 \text{ N} + 0.98 \text{ N} = 7.28 \text{ N}$$

The following aspect of circular motion often confuses students. In our everyday experience we feel ourselves being forced outward from the center as we move around a circular path. Does this contradict the fact that the centripetal force is always in toward the center of the circle? The answer is *no*. Consider the example of a woman sitting in the front passenger seat of an automobile that goes around a sharp curve to the left. She feels thrown out away from the driver and toward the right door of the car. The actual situation is depicted in Fig. 5-13. In the absence of a sideways force, the woman wants to travel in a straight line (Newton's first law). The automobile is curving toward the left, so the right door moves inward toward the passenger rather than the passenger moving outward toward the door. Only when the door makes contact is there an inward force on the passenger that gives the necessary centripetal acceleration for her to move around the curve with the automobile.

This leads to an interesting question: What force gives rise to the centripetal acceleration of a vehicle when it goes around a curve in the road? If the roadway is horizontal (no sideways slope), then the only force that can act horizontally on the vehicle is the force of friction due to the roadway. Furthermore, if there is no slippage (skidding) between the tires and the road, then this is a static frictional force. If, on the other hand, the road is sloped (i.e., the side of the road to the "outside" of the curve is higher than the side to the "inside" of the curve), then the normal force due to the

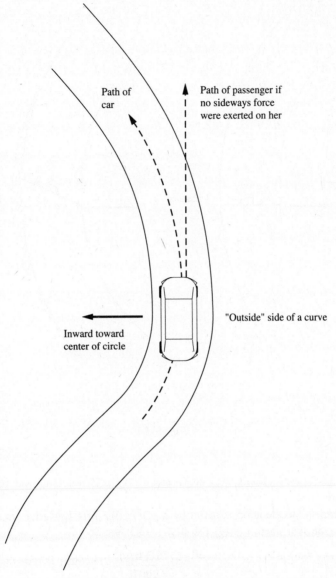

Path of
car

Path of passenger if
no sideways force
were exerted on her

"Outside" side of a curve

Inward toward
center of circle

Fig. 5-13

roadway has a horizontal component and contributes to the centripetal force. In this situation we say the road is **banked**. The banked and unbanked situations are shown in Fig. 5-14.

Problem 5.21.   A car travels around a curve on an unbanked road at 50 mi/h (mph).

(a)   If the radius of curvature (i.e., radius of the circle that best matches the curve) of the road is 200 ft, find the centripetal acceleration of the car.

(b)   If a man in the car weighs 160 lb, find the centripetal force exerted on him by the car.

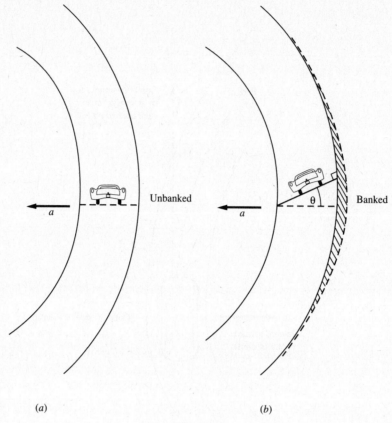

Unbanked

Banked

a

a

θ

(a)

(b)

Fig. 5-14

Solution

(a) The centripetal acceleration is given by $a = v^2/r$. We first convert from mph to ft/s. Recall that 60 mph = 88 ft/s. Then, $v = \left(\frac{5}{6}\right)$ (88 ft/s) = 73.3 ft/s. So

$$a = \frac{v^2}{r} = \frac{(73.3 \text{ ft/s})^2}{200 \text{ ft}} = 26.9 \text{ ft/s}^2$$

(b) The centripetal force on the man is $F = mv^2/r$, where v and r are the same as in part (a), since the man is moving with the car. Then $v^2/r = 26.9$ ft/s^2, as before. The man's mass is obtained from his weight by $m = w/g = (160 \text{ lb})/(32 \text{ ft/s}^2) = 5.0$ slugs. Then

$$F = (5.0 \text{ slugs}) (26.9 \text{ ft/s}^2) = 134 \text{ lb}$$

Problem 5.22. Find the minimum coefficient of friction μ_s for which the car in Problem 5.21 will not skid.

Solution

Since the car is on horizontal ground, the normal force N is vertical and just balanced by the weight of the car, $W = Mg$, or $N = Mg$. The frictional force f_s, which acts parallel to the ground, is the only horizontal force on the car and hence constitutes the entire centripetal force, so

$$f_s = Ma \qquad\qquad (i)$$

Since $f_s \leq \mu_s N$, in our case, $f_s \leq \mu_s Mg$, so the smallest μ_s will correspond to the case of equality:

$$f_s = \mu_s Mg \qquad (ii)$$

Comparing (i) and (ii), we have $Ma = \mu_s Mg$. Dividing both sides by Mg, we get

$$\mu_s = \frac{a}{g} = \frac{26.9 \text{ ft/s}^2}{32 \text{ ft/s}^2} = 0.84$$

where we have used the value of a from Problem 5.21(a).

Note. The fact that we don't know the mass M of the car did not stop us from solving the problem because ultimately the mass dropped out of the equations. This type of situation can often occur in a problem. At first glance there seems to be some information missing that is necessary to solve the problem, but by carrying the solution forward a couple of steps, one finds that the information is not necessary at all.

Problem 5.23. A truck travels around the curve of a banked road whose banking angle is $\theta = 20°$. If the radius of curvature of the road is $r = 100$ m, with what speed must the truck travel in order to go around the curve with no sideways frictional force acting on the tires?

Solution

The situation, as it appears to someone just behind the truck, is shown in Fig. 5-15. The forces acting on the truck are shown, and the direction of the curve in the road is shown by the centripetal acceleration vector. Note, that as required, we assume no frictional forces are acting. Since the acceleration is in the horizontal direction, it is most convenient to choose our x and y coordinate axes to be horizontal and vertical, as shown.

Note. In many inclined-plane problems it is most convenient to choose axes along and perpendicular to the incline. In this case, however, it is simpler to choose the axes as stated.

We now apply Newton's second law to the x and y directions.

$$N \sin \theta = Ma = \frac{Mv^2}{r} \qquad (i)$$

$$N \cos \theta - Mg = 0 \quad \text{or} \quad N \cos \theta = Mg \qquad (ii)$$

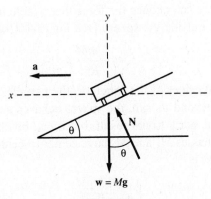

$$\mathbf{w} = M\mathbf{g}$$

Fig. 5-15

Since we don't know the mass M of the truck, we eliminate it from our equations. To do this we divide (*i*) by (*ii*) to obtain

$$\tan \theta = \frac{v^2}{rg} \qquad\qquad (iii)$$

We can now substitute in the value of θ, r, and g, to solve for v:

$$v^2 = (100 \text{ m}) (9.8 \text{ m/s}^2) (\tan 20°) = 357 \text{ m}^2/\text{s}^2 \qquad \text{or} \qquad v = 18.9 \text{ m/s}$$

Note.   Equation (*iii*) is called the *banking equation* because it gives the general relation among θ, v, and r that must hold in order to go around a curve, without the need for any frictional force. Note further that the mass of the vehicle doesn't enter the equation.

5.3   THE LAW OF GRAVITY

Newton's law of universal gravitation states that every particle of matter in the universe attracts every other particle of matter in the universe with a force directly proportional to the product of their masses and inversely proportional to the square of the distance between them. The situation is shown in Fig. 5-16(*a*) for two particles. If we assume the proportionality constant is G, the magnitude of this force is then

$$F = \frac{Gm_1 m_2}{r^2} \qquad\qquad (5.1)$$

The proportionality constant G is called the **universal gravitational constant** and has the value

$$G = 6.670 \times 10^{-11} \text{ N} \cdot \text{m}^2/\text{kg}^2 = 6.670 \times 10^{-8} \text{ dyn} \cdot \text{cm}^2/\text{g}^2$$

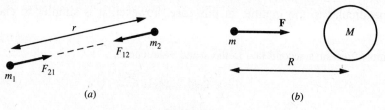

(a)   (b)

Fig. 5-16

From the general law (5.1) we can deduce the force that a large uniform sphere of mass M exerts on a particle of mass m located outside the sphere [see Fig. 5-16(*b*)]:

$$F = \frac{GmM}{R^2} \qquad\qquad (5.2)$$

where R is the distance from the center of the sphere to the particle. In other words, for purposes of gravitational pull on an object beyond its rim, the sphere behaves as if it were a particle of mass M concentrated at its center. This is not a trivial result, but it can be obtained by using calculus.

Similarly if two spheres of masses M_1 and M_2 have center-to-center separation R_{12}, then the force of attraction between the spheres is

$$F = \frac{GM_1 M_2}{R_{12}^2} \qquad\qquad (5.3)$$

Applying (5.2) to an object of mass m just at the earth's surface, we have $F = GmM_e/R_e^2$, where M_e and R_e are the earth's mass and radius, respectively. Since F is just the weight of the object, we also have $F = mg$. Thus $mg = GmM_e/R_e^2$, or

$$g = \frac{GM_e}{R_e^2} \qquad\qquad (5.4)$$

Since g and R_e were known quantities, even in Newton's time, G could be obtained if the mass of the earth were known, or conversely, the mass of the earth could be obtained if G were known. Since the mass of the earth was not known at that time, G had to be determined by experiments on earth with small known masses attracting each other with a measurable force. This was actually done, but not easily, given how tiny the value of G turned out to be.

Problem 5.24. Find the force of gravity between two lead balls of masses $m_1 = 20$ kg and $m_2 = 40$ kg, if the distance between their centers is $r_{12} = 10$ cm.

Solution

We use Eq. (5.1):

$$F = \frac{Gm_1m_2}{r_{12}^2}$$

Substituting in the equation, we obtain

$$F = \frac{(6.67 \times 10^{-11} \text{ N} \cdot \text{m}^2/\text{kg}^2)\,(20 \text{ kg})\,(40 \text{ kg})}{(0.10 \text{ m})^2}$$

$$= 5.34 \times 10^{-6} \text{ N}$$

Problem 5.25. Find the mass of the earth, given that the radius of the earth is $R_e = 6.38 \times 10^6$ m.

Solution

We use Eq. (5.4) above to get

$$9.8 \text{ m/s}^2 = \frac{(6.67 \times 10^{-11} \text{ N} \cdot \text{m}^2/\text{kg}^2)M_e}{(6.38 \times 10^6 \text{ m})^2}$$

Solving for M_e we get

$$M_e = \frac{(9.8)\,(6.38 \times 10^6)^2}{6.67 \times 10^{-11}} \text{ kg}$$

$$= 5.98 \times 10^{24} \text{ kg}$$

Problem 5.26. Find the acceleration of gravity g_x near the surface of planet X whose radius is four times the radius of the Earth and whose mass is 90 times the mass of the Earth.

Solution

Using Eq. (5.3), above, applied to planet X, we have $g_x = GM_x/R_x^2$. We are given that $M_x = 90M_e$ and $R_x = 4R_e$. Substituting these values into the equation for g_x we get

$$g_x = \frac{G(90M_e)}{(4R_e)^2} = 5.63\,\frac{GM_e}{R_e^2} = 5.63g_e = 5.63(9.8 \text{ m/s}^2) = 55.1 \text{ m/s}^2$$

Problem 5.27. Find the acceleration of an object immediately after it is dropped from a height of 2000 mi above the earth's surface.

Solution

Since this is a substantial height above the earth's surface, we cannot assume the acceleration is 9.8 m/s². Instead, we apply the law of gravitation and Newton's second law to the falling object. Since gravity is the only force acting on it once it is released, we have $F = GmM_e/r^2 = ma$, where r is the distance from the center of the earth to the object. Dividing out the mass of the object we get

$$a = \frac{GM_e}{r^2} \qquad (i)$$

At this point we could substitute in the numerical values for G, M_e, and r to get the result. This however is very tedious, and there is a trick that avoids having to even know the values of G and M_e. We recall from Eq. (5.3) that $g = GM_e/R_e^2$. Reworking this equation we get $GM_e = gR_e^2$. Thus for the problem at hand we have

$$a = \frac{gR_e^2}{r^2} \qquad (ii)$$

Noting that the radius of the earth is about 4000 mi and that $r = 6000$ mi, we get

$$a = (9.8 \text{ m/s}^2)\left(\tfrac{4000}{6000}\right)^2 = 4.36 \text{ m/s}^2$$

Problem 5.28. A rocketship with its engines off is at the exact midpoint between the earth and the moon. What is its acceleration? Assume that the distance from the center of the earth to the center of the moon is about 3.8×10^8 m, and the mass of the moon is 7.36×10^{22} kg.

Solution.

The situation is shown in Fig. 5-17. As can be seen, there are two competing forces acting on the rocket, the gravitational forces of the earth and moon, respectively. The net force points toward the earth, and applying Newton's second law, we have

$$\frac{GmM_e}{\left(\tfrac{1}{2}r_{em}\right)^2} - \frac{GmM_m}{\left(\tfrac{1}{2}r_{em}\right)^2} = ma$$

Dividing by m, and simplifying, we get

$$a = \frac{4G(M_e - M_m)}{r_{em}^2} = \frac{4(6.67 \times 10^{-11} \text{ N} \cdot \text{m}^2/\text{kg}^2)\,(5.98 \times 10^{24} \text{ kg} - 7.36 \times 10^{22} \text{ kg})}{(3.8 \times 10^8 \text{ m})^2} = 0.011 \text{ m/s}^2$$

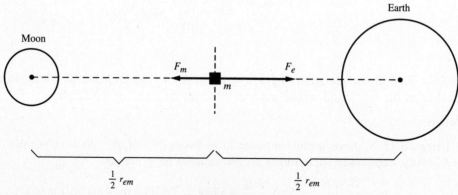

Fig. 5-17

Note.   Newton had some ideas that led him to the law of universal gravitation. We have already seen that near the earth's surface the force of gravity F on an object has the peculiar property that it is proportional to the mass m of the object being pulled. Newton realized that if the earth pulled on an object, then by the third law the object pulled with an equal and opposite force on the earth. This force, if it obeyed the same rules, would be proportional to the mass M_e of the earth. Thus the force of gravity on the object must be proportional to *both* masses; in other words, the force must be proportional to the product of the two masses: $F \propto mM_e$. From this idea Newton hypothesized the same result for any two particles in the universe. (No other force in nature has the property that the strength of the force depends on the intrinsic sluggishness of the object being pushed or pulled. Thus gravity has a special role in nature unlike any other force.)

Newton also had some basis for determining how the force of gravity varied with the distance between the particles. He knew that the moon has a centripetal acceleration toward the earth due to its orbital motion, and could even calculate its value. By comparing this to the acceleration of gravity at the earth's surface, he surmised the inverse square dependence on the distance. We carry through this reasoning in the next problem.

Problem 5.29.   Show how the acceleration of the moon toward the earth can be used to check that the force of gravity varies inversely as the square of the distance, and carry out the calculation.

Solution

The moon travels around the earth in a nearly circular orbit of radius $r_{em} = 3.84 \times 10^8$ m. It therefore has a centripetal acceleration toward the center of the earth a_m. If the universal law of gravity is correct, we must have

$$\frac{GM_mM_e}{r_{em}{}^2} = M_m a_m \qquad \text{or} \qquad a_m = \frac{GM_e}{r_{em}{}^2} \tag{i}$$

By the same token we already have seen that the acceleration of gravity at the earth's surface is given by

$$g = \frac{GM_e}{R_e{}^2} \tag{ii}$$

where R_e is the radius of the earth. Dividing Eq. (*i*) by Eq. (*ii*) we get

$$\frac{a_m}{g} = \frac{R_e{}^2}{r_{em}{}^2} \tag{iii}$$

The right side can easily be calculated from the known distances. The left side can also be calculated from known values.

First we calculate the left side. To do this we note that the centripetal acceleration is given by

$$a_m = \frac{v_m{}^2}{r_{em}} \tag{iv}$$

where v_m is the orbital velocity of the moon. The orbital velocity is related to the orbital period of the moon, $T_m = 27.3$ days, by

$$v_m = \frac{2\pi r_{em}}{T_m} \tag{v}$$

Substituting in numerical values, and noting there are 86,400 s in a day, we get

$$v_m = \frac{6.28(3.84 \times 10^8 \text{ m})}{27.3 \times 86,400 \text{ s}} = 1022 \text{ m/s}$$

Substituting into Eq. (iv) we get

$$a_m = \frac{(1022 \text{ m/s})^2}{3.84 \times 10^8 \text{ m}} = 0.00272 \text{ m/s}^2$$

Then, for the left side of Eq. (iii) we have

$$\frac{a_m}{g} = \frac{0.00272}{9.80} = 0.000278$$

For the right side of Eq. (iii) we have

$$\left(\frac{R_e}{r_{em}}\right)^2 = \left(\frac{6.38 \times 10^6}{3.84 \times 10^8}\right)^2 = 0.000276$$

Comparing the two numbers we see they agree to about 1%, which is consistent with the simplifying assumptions we have made.

Using the same basic approach as in Problem 5.29, we can calculate the orbital velocities and orbital periods of satellites moving in circular orbits of various radii about the earth.

Problem 5.30.   Find the period of an earth satellite moving in a circular orbit 1000 km above the earth's surface.

Solution

Applying Newton's second law, we have

$$\frac{GmM_e}{r^2} = \frac{mv^2}{r} \qquad \text{or} \qquad \frac{v^2}{r} = \frac{GM_e}{r^2}$$

Since we are asked for the period, we can substitute $v = 2\pi r/T$ directly into the last equation to get

$$\frac{4\pi^2 r}{T^2} = \frac{GM_e}{r^2} \tag{i}$$

Multiplying both sides of the equation by $r^2/4\pi^2$ we get

$$\frac{r^3}{T^2} = \frac{GM_e}{4\pi^2} \tag{ii}$$

Note.   Since the right side of Eq. (ii) is a constant, the left side must also be a constant: All earth satellites obey the rule that the ratio of the cube of their radii to the square of their periods is a constant. This is an example of Kepler's third law, which is true for elliptical as well as circular orbits.

Recalling that $GM_e = gR_e^2$, we solve Eq. (ii) for the period of our satellite: $T^2 = 4\pi^2 r^3/gR_e^2$. Noting that for our case $r = R_e + 10^6$ m $= 7.38 \times 10^6$ m, we have

$$T^2 = \frac{39.4(7.38 \times 10^6 \text{ m})^3}{(9.8 \text{ m/s}^2)(6.38 \times 10^6 \text{ m})^2} = 3.97 \times 10^7 \text{ s}^2 \qquad \text{or} \qquad T = 6300 \text{ s} = 105 \text{ min}$$

Problem 5.31.

(a)   Suppose the radius of the orbit of the satellite in Problem 5.30 were doubled. What would the new period be?

(b)   What would be the ratio of the orbital velocities for the two cases?

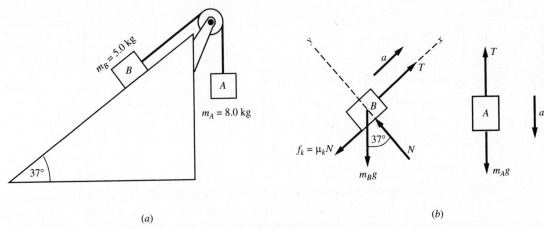

(a)   (b)

Fig. 5-20

Solution

The body diagrams for the two blocks are shown in Fig. 5-20(b). We choose downward as positive for block A, and upward, parallel to the incline, as positive for block B, as shown. For block A,

$$m_A g - T = m_A a \tag{i}$$

For block B,

$$T - m_B g \sin 37° - \mu_k N = m_B a \qquad \text{and} \qquad N - m_B g \cos 37° = 0 \tag{ii}$$

which together yield

$$T - m_B g \sin 37° - \mu_k m_B g \cos 37° = m_B a \tag{iii}$$

Adding Eqs. (i) and (iii) to eliminate T, we get

$$m_A g - m_B g \sin 37° - \mu_k m_B g \cos 37° = (m_A + m_B)a$$

Substituting in numbers we get

$$(8.0 \text{ kg}) (9.8 \text{ m/s}^2) - (5.0 \text{ kg}) (9.8 \text{ m/s}^2) (0.60) - 0.20(5.0 \text{ kg}) (9.8 \text{ m/s}^2) (0.80) = (13.0 \text{ kg})a$$

or

$$a = 3.17 \text{ m/s}^2$$

Substituting back into Eq. (i), we get

$$T = m_A g - m_A a = (8.0 \text{ kg}) (9.8 \text{ m/s}^2 - 3.2 \text{ m/s}^2) = 53 \text{ N}$$

Problem 5.36.   Block A of mass m_A = 5.0 kg rests on block B of mass m_B = 10.0 kg, which itself is on a horizontal tabletop. A horizontal force F = 100 N pulls on block B, while block A is constrained by a horizontal cord attached to a wall, as shown in Fig. 5-21(a). The coefficient of kinetic friction between all surfaces is μ_k = 0.2.

(a)   Find the acceleration of block B.

(b)   Find the tension in the cord.

Solution

(a)   The body diagrams for the two blocks are shown in Fig. 5-21(b) and (c). For block A, the normal force is due to block B. Since the frictional force is controlled by the relative motion of the two surfaces, f_{kA} opposes the motion of block A relative to B. Since block A moves to the left relative to

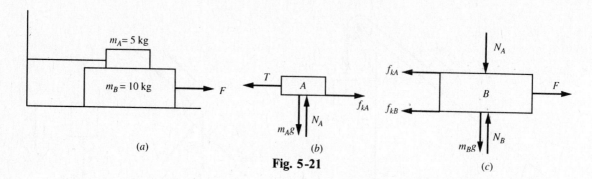

Fig. 5-21

B, f_{kA} is to the right. For block B, in addition to the usual normal and frictional forces due to the table (N_B and f_{kB}), Newton's third law requires a downward normal force N_A due to block A and a frictional force f_{kA}, acting to the left (equal and opposite to the frictional force on block A). Since both blocks are in equilibrium in the vertical direction, we have, for block A,

$$N_A = m_A g \qquad \text{and} \qquad f_{kA} = \mu_k N_A = \mu_k m_A g$$

Similarly, for block B,

$$N_B = m_B g + N_A = m_B g + m_A g \qquad \text{and} \qquad f_{kB} = \mu_k N_B = \mu_k (m_A + m_B)g$$

Substituting numerical values, we get

$$f_{kA} = 0.2(5.0 \text{ kg})(9.8 \text{ m/s}^2) = 9.8 \text{ N} \qquad \text{and} \qquad f_{kB} = 0.2(15.0 \text{ kg})(9.8 \text{ m/s}^2) = 29.4 \text{ N}$$

Newton's second law in the horizontal direction now gives

$$F - f_{kA} - f_{kB} = m_B a \qquad \text{or} \qquad 100 \text{ N} - 9.8 \text{ N} - 29.4 \text{ N} = (10.0 \text{ kg})a \qquad \text{or} \qquad a = 6.1 \text{ m/s}^2$$

(b)   For block A, $\Sigma F_x = 0$ implies

$$f_{kA} - T = 0 \qquad \text{or} \qquad T = f_{kA} = 9.8 \text{ N}$$

Problem 5.37.   A roller-coaster car passes point A in Fig. 5-22 at a speed of 40 ft/s, and point B at a speed of 20 ft/s. The radius of curvature of the track at both points is $R = 100$ ft. What is the normal force exerted by the car on a teenager, of weight $w = 96$ lb, standing in the car as it passes points A and B?

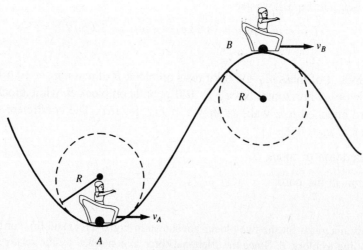

Fig. 5-22

Solution

The teenager moves in the same path as the car and with the same speed. As the teenager passes point A, she is moving, for an instant, on the bottom of a vertical circle of radius $R = 100$ ft with a speed of $v_A = 40$ ft/s. She therefore has a centripetal acceleration a_A vertically upward of magnitude

$$a_A = \frac{v_A{}^2}{R} = \frac{(40 \text{ ft/s})^2}{100 \text{ ft}} = 16 \text{ ft/s}^2$$

To find the normal force N_A we use Newton's second law, with upward chosen positive. In the vertical direction we have

$$N_A - w = ma_A$$

Noting that $m = w/g = (96 \text{ lb})/(32 \text{ ft/s}^2) = 3.0$ slugs, the above equation yields

$$N_A - 96 \text{ lb} = (3.0 \text{ slugs})(16 \text{ ft/s}^2) = 48 \text{ lb} \qquad \text{or} \qquad N_A = 144 \text{ lb}$$

At point B the teenager is moving on the top of a vertical circle of radius 100 ft, this time with velocity $v_B = 20$ ft/s. The acceleration is now vertically downward, and $a_B = v_B{}^2/R = (20 \text{ ft/s})^2/(100 \text{ ft}) = 4.0 \text{ ft/s}^2$. This time we choose downward as positive, so that Newton's second law gives

$$w - N_B = ma_B$$

Substituting values, we get

$$96 \text{ lb} - N_B = (3.0 \text{ slugs})(4.0 \text{ ft/s}^2) = 12 \text{ lb} \qquad \text{or} \qquad N_B = 84 \text{ lb}$$

Note that this implies the teenager feels "heavier" at point A and "lighter" at point B.

Problem 5.38. At what height h above the earth will a satellite moving in a circular orbit have half the period of the earth's rotation?

Solution

The earth's period is 24 h, or 86,400 s, so the period of the satellite must be $T = 43,200$ s. We need a direct relationship between the period and the radius of the satellite's orbit. We can obtain such a relationship from the two equations $GM_e/r^2 = v^2/r$ and $v = 2\pi r/T$. This was already done in Problem 5.30, and from Eq. (ii) of that example we have $r^3/T^2 = GM_e/4\pi^2$. Then, using $GM_e = gR_e{}^2$, we get

$$r^3 = \frac{gR_e{}^2 T^2}{4\pi^2} = \frac{(9.8 \text{ m/s}^2)(6.38 \times 10^6 \text{ m})^2 (43,200 \text{ s})^2}{39.4} = 1.889 \times 10^{22} \text{ m}^3$$

$$\text{or} \qquad r = 2.66 \times 10^7 \text{ m}$$

Since r is measured from the center of the earth, to find the height h above the earth we must subtract the earth radius R_e:

$$h = r - R_e = 2.66 \times 10^7 \text{ m} - 0.638 \times 10^7 \text{ m} = 2.02 \times 10^7 \text{ m} = 20,200 \text{ km}$$

Supplementary Problems

Problem 5.39.

(a) A constant resultant force of 20 N acts on an object of weight 10 N. Find the acceleration.

(b) An object of weight 16 lb is accelerating at 12 ft/s^2. Find the resultant force in lb.

(c) An object of weight 6.0 lb is accelerated by a force of 12 N. Find the acceleration in cm/s^2.

       Ans.   (a) 19.6 m/s^2; (b) 6 lb; (c) 438 cm/s^2

Problem 5.40.   A 96-lb block on a frictionless 45° inclined plane is pulled up the incline by a force of 160 lb that acts parallel to the incline.

(a) Find the acceleration of the block.

(b) If the block starts from rest, how far up the incline has it moved when its velocity reaches 100 ft/s?

       Ans.   (a) 30.7 ft/s^2; (b) 163 ft

Problem 5.41.   Suppose that in Fig. 5-2(a) the force T is 50 N and the coefficient of friction between the block and the surface is $\mu_k = 0.25$.

(a) Find m, if the block is observed to accelerate at 4 m/s^2.

(b) What would the acceleration be if $\mu_k = 0.50$?

       Ans.   (a) 7.75 kg; (b) 1.55 m/s^2

Problem 5.42.   Consider the situation in Fig. 5-23. If the block starts from rest, (a) how far will it travel in 5 s and (b) how fast will it then be moving?

       Ans.   (a) 103 m; (b) 41.1 m/s

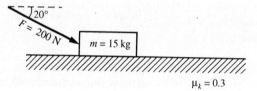

Fig. 5-23

Problem 5.43.   In Problem 5.42, at the end of the 5-s interval, the force F is removed. How long will it take the block to come to rest? [*Hint*:   The force of friction is no longer what it was in Problem 5.42.]

       Ans.   14.0 s

Problem 5.44.   Suppose that in Fig. 5-4 we have $\mu_s = \mu_k = 0.30$. If the block is given an initial velocity up the incline of 10.0 m/s, what is the maximum distance the block moves up the incline?

       Ans.   5.32 m

Problem 5.45.   After reaching its highest point, the block in Problem 5.44 starts back down the incline. Find its speed when it returns to its starting point.

       Ans.   7.73 m/s

Problem 5.46.   In the ideal setup of Fig. 5-6(a), $m_B = 6.0$ kg and $m_A = 5.0$ kg. The coefficient of friction between block A and the tabletop is $\mu_k = 0.30$. If the system starts from rest, how far will block B have fallen from its starting position when its speed is 10 m/s?

       Ans.   12.5 m

Problem 5.47.   In Fig. 5-6(a) let $m_A = 10$ kg and $m_B = 5$ kg. If block B descends with an acceleration of 2.0 m/s^2, what is the coefficient of friction μ_k between block A and the tabletop?

   Ans.   0.194

Problem 5.48.   In Fig. 5-7(a) assume that $m_A = m_B = 20$ kg and the coefficient of friction is $\mu_k = 0.2$. Find the acceleration of the system and the tension in the cord.

   Ans.   1.60 m/s^2, 164 N

Problem 5.49.   In Fig. 5-8(a), the coefficient of friction between all surfaces is $\mu_k = 0.25$ and $F = 100$ N. Find the acceleration of the blocks and the normal force between them.

   Ans.   1.90 m/s^2, 34.8 N

Problem 5.50.   In Fig. 5-11, $m = 0.150$ kg and $L = 0.300$ m. The tabletop is frictionless. If the breaking strength of the cord is 500 N, what is the maximum speed that the mass can have? What is the corresponding minimum period?

   Ans.   31.6 m/s, 0.0596 s

Problem 5.51.   Figure 5-24 shows a child ($m = 8.0$ kg) holding on tightly to a pole on the outer rim of a merry-go-round, as it spins out of control with period $T = 2.0$ s. The radius of the merry-go-round is $R = 10.0$ m.

(*a*)   Find the centripetal acceleration of the child and the force exerted by the pole on his hands.

(*b*)   Will the child be able to hold on?

   Ans.   (*a*) 99 m/s^2; 792 N; (*b*) no (792 N is about 10 times his weight)

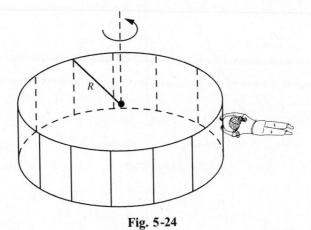

Fig. 5-24

Problem 5.52.   In an amusement park ride, people stand with their back to the inside surface of a circular vertical wall; the radius of this circle is 10 ft. The wall begins its spin about a vertical axis through the center of the circle, and the people move with it. Assume that the coefficient of friction between a person's back and the wall is no smaller than 0.8. At a certain speed the floor opens up beneath the people's feet. What minimum frequency of rotation f must be attained so that no one falls? (Recall that $f = 1/T$.)

   Ans.   0.319 r/s

Problem 5.53. A truck travels around a circular curve of radius $R = 200$ m; the road is banked at an angle $\theta = 15°$. The situation is depicted in Fig. 5-15. How fast must the truck travel if there is to be no sideways frictional force on the tires?

      Ans.   23 m/s

Problem 5.54. A circular speedway curve is banked at $60°$ so that cars traveling at 200 mph can negotiate the curve without the aid of friction.

(a) What is the radius of curvature of the curve?

(b) If the road were not banked and the coefficient of static friction were $\mu_s = 0.40$, what minimum radius of curvature would be needed to prevent skidding?

      Ans.   (a) 1550 ft; (b) 6720 ft

Problem 5.55. A conical pendulum consists of a bob of mass m, suspended from the ceiling by a light cord of length L, which is set in motion in a horizontal circle of radius R, as shown in Fig. 5-25.

(a) Find a relationship between the speed v of the bob, the half-cone angle θ, and the radius R.

(b) Recalling that the period T is given by $T = 2\pi R/v$ and noting that $R = L \sin \theta$. Find an expression for the period of the conical pendulum in terms of L and θ.

      Ans.   (a) $\tan \theta = v^2/Rg$; (b) $T = 2\pi(L \cos \theta/g)^{1/2}$

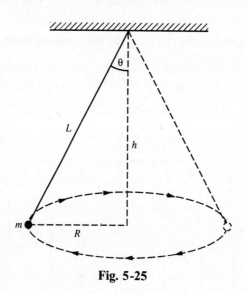

Fig. 5-25

Problem 5.56.

(a) Find the gravitational force exerted by the sun on a 1-kg mass on the earth's surface.

(b) Repeat, finding the gravitational force exerted by the moon. [Data: $G = 6.67 \times 10^{-11}$ N·m²/kg²; $M_{sun} = 1.99 \times 10^{30}$ kg; $r_{e, sun} = 1.50 \times 10^{11}$ m; $M_{moon} = 7.36 \times 10^{22}$ kg; $r_{e, moon} = 3.8 \times 10^8$ m.]

      Ans.   (a) $F_{sun} = 5.90 \times 10^{-3}$ N; (b) $F_{moon} = 3.40 \times 10^{-5}$ N

Problem 5.57. An asteroid of mass $m = 1.00 \times 10^{15}$ kg passes the earth at center-to-center distance of $r = 100,000$ km.

(a)   Find the force exerted on it by the Earth (R_e = 6380 km).

(b)   If this is the only force on it, what is its acceleration?

   Ans.   (a) 3.99×10^{13} N; (b) 0.0399 m/s^2

Problem 5.58.   The acceleration of gravity at the surface of planet X is g_x = 8.0 m/s^2. If the planet is of radius R_x = 3.0 R_e, what is the mass of planet X compared to the mass of the Earth?

   Ans.   7.34 Earth masses

Problem 5.59.   Find the acceleration of gravity on the surface of Neptune, given that the mass of Neptune is 16.7 times that of the Earth and the radius of Neptune is 3.89 times that of the Earth (R_e = 6380 km).

   Ans.   10.8 m/s^2

Problem 5.60.   Referring to Problem 5.59, find the orbital velocity and period of a satellite moving in a low-lying circular orbit about Neptune.

   Ans.   16.4 km/s, 2.64 h

Problem 5.61.   Find the velocity and period of a satellite revolving about the earth in a circular orbit of radius r = 8.0 R.

   Ans.   2800 m/s, 31.8 h

Chapter 6

Work and Mechanical Energy

6.1 INTRODUCTION

Note: There are many formal developments and new definitions in this chapter, and the point of the development probably will not be immediately obvious to the student. For that reason we attempt to put the new material in perspective. In the last chapter, we showed how Newton's second law can be applied to solve particular problems involving the motion of an object. In general, when the forces vary in both magnitude and direction, it may be very difficult to solve for the path of the motion, or for the velocity of the object.

The concept of work and its relationship to kinetic and potential energy gives us the ability to solve relatively easily many problems that would otherwise be difficult. The associated theorem of conservation of mechanical energy often can reduce otherwise complicated problems to a simple "bookkeeping" operation. Most importantly, our development of mechanical energy can be generalized so that the concept of energy, its transfer between systems and its overall conservation, applies beyond the subject of mechanics. Indeed, it has become one of the great underlying principles of the physical universe.

6.2 THE NATURE OF WORK

Work of a Constant Force

The work W_F due to a constant force $\mathbf{F}$ acting on an object while it moves through a displacement $\mathbf{s}$ is defined as the component of $\mathbf{F}$ along the $\mathbf{s}$ direction multiplied by the magnitude of $\mathbf{s}$:

$$W_F = F_s s = (F \cos \theta)s \tag{6.1}$$

See Fig. 6-1. Even though the work involves the two vector quantities $\mathbf{F}$ and $\mathbf{s}$, it itself has no direction and is thus a scalar. The units of work are those of force times distance. The SI unit of force is thus the newton-meter, which is given the special name the joule: $1 \text{ J} = 1 \text{ N} \cdot \text{m}$. Other units are the erg: $1 \text{ erg} = 1 \text{ dyne} \cdot \text{cm}$, and the foot-pound (which is not given a special name). Conversion between units gives:

$$1 \text{ J} = (1.0 \times 10^5 \text{ dyn})(1.0 \times 10^2 \text{ cm}) = 1.0 \times 10^7 \text{ dyn} \cdot \text{cm} = 1.0 \times 10^7 \text{ ergs}$$
$$1 \text{ ft} \cdot \text{lb} = (0.3048 \text{ m})(4.45 \text{ N}) = 1.356 \text{ N} \cdot \text{m} = 1.356 \text{ J}$$

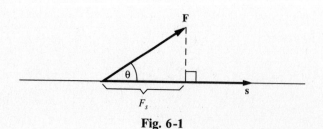

Fig. 6-1

Problem 6.1.   Find the work done by the force **F** in moving through the displacement **s** in each of the cases of Fig. 6-2(*a*), (*b*), and (*c*).

>   **Solution**
>
>   (*a*) $W_F = F \cos \theta \cdot s = (20 \text{ N})(\cos 30°)(6.0 \text{ m}) = (20 \text{ N})(0.866)(6.0 \text{ N}) = 104 \text{ N} \cdot \text{m} = 104 \text{ J}.$
>
>   (*b*) $W_F = (100 \text{ dyn})(\cos 37°)(12 \text{ cm}) = 960 \text{ dyn} \cdot \text{cm} = 960 \text{ ergs}.$
>
>   (*c*) $W_F = (40 \text{ lb})(\cos 50°)(6.0 \text{ ft}) = 154 \text{ ft} \cdot \text{lb}.$

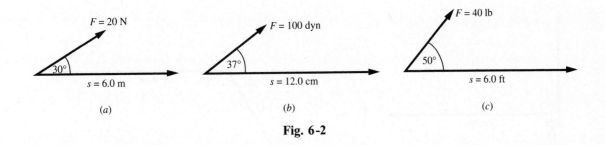

Fig. 6-2

Problem 6.2.   Find the work done by the force **F** in the cases of Fig. 6-3(*a*) to (*d*).

>   **Solution**
>
>   (*a*) $W_F = (50 \text{ N})(\cos 53°)(30 \text{ m}) = 900 \text{ J}.$
>
>   (*b*)   Here the component of **F** along **s** is negative, so $W_F = (50 \text{ N})(\cos 120°)(30 \text{ m}) = -(50 \text{ N})(\cos 60°)(30 \text{ m}) = -750 \text{ J}.$
>
>   (*c*)   Here the component of **F** along **s** is zero, since $\theta = 90°$. Thus $W_F = 0$. This is generally true when the force and the displacement are at right angles to each other.
>
>   (*d*) $W_F = -(50 \text{ N})(\cos 30°)(30 \text{ m}) = -1300 \text{ J}.$

>   ***Note.***   The work is defined so that it can be positive, negative, or zero, depending on whether the component of **F** along **s** is positive, negative, or zero.

Problem 6.3.   A block is moving on a horizontal frictional surface under the action of a number of forces, as shown in Fig. 6-4. Determine whether the work done by each force is greater than, less than, or equal to zero.

>   **Solution**
>
> $W_{F1} > 0, \ W_{F2} > 0, \ W_f < 0, \ W_w = 0, \ W_N = 0.$

Problem 6.4.   A man lifts a book vertically with his hand. Find the sign of the work done by (*a*) his hand on the book, (*b*) gravity on the book, (*c*) the book on his hand.

>   **Solution**
>
>   (*a*)   The hand exerts an upward force on the book as the book moves upward, so the work is positive.
>
>   (*b*)   The force of gravity is always pulling downward, so when the book is moving upward, gravity does negative work.

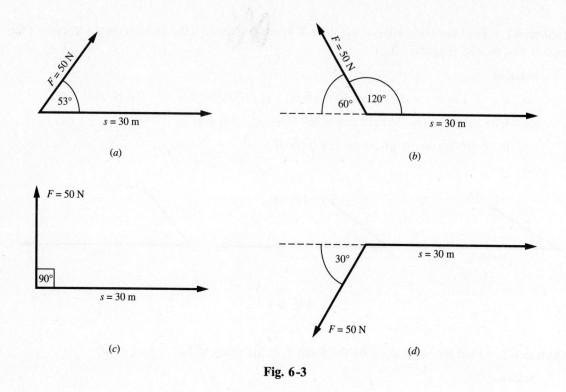

Fig. 6-3

(c)   The book exerts a reaction force downward on the hand. Since the hand is moving upward, the work done by the book on the hand is negative.

Total Work Done by a Number of Forces

The work done by each force is, by (6.1), the component of that force along the displacement of the object, times the magnitude of the displacement. Since the displacement is the same for all the forces acting, the total work is just the sum of the components of the individual forces times the magnitude of the displacement. But the sum of the components of individual vectors along a given direction is just the component of the resultant vector along that direction. We therefore conclude that the total work done is just the work by the resultant force.

Problem 6.5.   In Fig. 6-4, assume that $F_1 = 50$ N, $F_2 = 20$ N, $w = 100$ N, $\theta = 30°$, $\mu_k = 0.25$, and $s = 15$ m. Evaluate (a) N and f_k, (b) the work done by each force, (c) the total work due to all forces, (d) the x and y components of the resultant force, (e) the work done by the resultant force.

Solution

(a)   Since there is no acceleration in the vertical direction,

$$\Sigma F_y = 0 \qquad \text{or} \qquad F_1 \sin \theta + N - w = 0$$

So, $N = 100$ N $-$ (50 N) $\sin 30° = 75$ N. Then, $f_k = \mu_k N = (0.25)(75$ N$) = 18.8$ N.

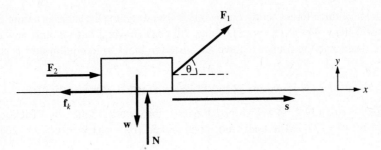

Fig. 6-4

(b) $W_{F1} = F_{1x}s = (F_1 \cos 30°)s = (50 \text{ N})(0.866)(15 \text{ m}) = 650$ J.
       $W_{F2} = F_{2x}s = F_2s = (20 \text{ N})(15 \text{ m}) = 300$ J.
       $W_f = f_{kx}s = -f_ks = -(18.8 \text{ N})(15 \text{ m}) = -282$ J.
       $W_w = w_xs = 0$ J.
       $W_N = N_xs = 0$ J.

(c) $W_{\text{total}} = W_{F1} + W_{F2} + W_f + W_w + W_N = 650 \text{ J} + 300 \text{ J} - 282 \text{ J} = 668$ J.

(d) $R_x = F_{1x} + F_{2x} + f_{kx} + w_x + N_x = 43.3 \text{ N} + 20 \text{ N} - 18.8 \text{ N} + 0 \text{ N} + 0 \text{ N} = 44.5$ N.
       $R_y = F_{1y} + F_{2y} + f_{ky} + w_y + N_y = 25 \text{ N} + 0 \text{ N} + 0 \text{ N} - 100 \text{ N} + 75 \text{ N} = 0$ N.

(e) $W_R = R_xs = (44.5 \text{ N})(15 \text{ m}) = 668$ J [checks with (c)].

Problem 6.6.   A block of mass $m = 5$ kg slides down an inclined plane of length $L = 15$ m and angle $\theta = 37°$, as shown in Fig. 6-5. Calculate the work done by each force acting on the block, as well as the total work done by all forces, as it traverses the incline from top to bottom, if (a) the incline is frictionless, (b) the coefficient of friction is $\mu_k = 0.30$.

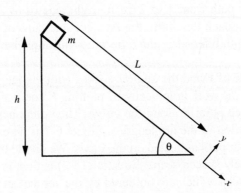

Fig. 6-5

Solution

(a)   The only forces acting on the block are the weight $w = mg$ and the normal force N. The normal force is perpendicular to the direction of motion so it does no work. The component of the weight along the incline is

$$w_x = mg \sin 37° = (5 \text{ kg}) (9.8 \text{ m/s}^2) (0.60) = 29.4 \text{ N}$$

Hence, $W_w = w_xL = (29.4 \text{ N})(15 \text{ m}) = 441$ J. This is also the total work done.

(b) There are now three forces acting on the block. The weight is the same as before and the work done by it is still $W_w = 441$ J. The normal force still does no work, but we must now obtain its value in order to determine the frictional force f_k. Since the block is in equilibrium in the y-direction, we have

$$N = mg\cos 37° = (5\text{ kg})\,(9.8\text{ m/s}^2)\,(0.80) = 39.2\text{ N}$$

Then $f_k = \mu_k N = (0.3)(39.2\text{ N}) = 11.8$ N. Finally, the work done by friction is $W_f = f_x L = -(11.8\text{ N})(15\text{ m}) = -177$ J. The total work done is then $W_T = 441$ J $-$ 177 J $= 264$ J.

Work of a Variable Force

Suppose the force **F** acting on a particle changes in magnitude and/or direction as the particle moves from position to position. The particle need not be moving in a straight line. We want to extend our definition of work to that done by this force as the particle moves between any two positions on its path of motion. Consider a particle moving along the path of motion shown in Fig. 6-6(a), which is acted on by the force **F** (in addition to possible other forces not shown). The force **F** is shown at a number of different points along the path.

We now imagine breaking up the path into a large number N of small intervals, each one of which is nearly a straight-line segment. If the segments are small enough, we can assume the force is nearly constant within each segment. We can approximate the path by a succession of small displacements, $\Delta \mathbf{s}_i$, $i = 1, 2, 3, \ldots, N$, as illustrated in Fig. 6-6(b), over each of which **F** is constant and the small amount of work done by **F** is $\Delta W_F = F\cos\theta \cdot \Delta s$, where θ is the angle between **F** and $\Delta \mathbf{s}$. Adding up the work over all the little displacements, we get

$$W_F = \Sigma\, F_i \cos\theta_i\, \Delta s_i \tag{6.2}$$

In the limit, as the number of intervals N approaches infinity and the size of each interval approaches zero, the approximation to the actual motion becomes exact. It is therefore natural to define the work done by the force **F** over the path from 1 to 2 as the right side of (6.2) in the limit as $N \to \infty$ and $\Delta s_i \to 0$. Note that as we approach this limit, the Δs's become tangent to the path (and their lengths are the corresponding arc length intervals), and θ becomes the angle between **F** and the tangent to the path at each point.

If we knew the magnitude of **F** and the angle it makes with the tangent to the path at every point along the path, we could find the work graphically by plotting $F\cos\theta$ as a function of the arc length S measured from some reference point R along the curve. The component of **F** tangent to the path at each point, $F\cos\theta$, is a function of the arc length s. Figure 6-7 is an example of the plot of $F\cos\theta$ vs. s, with points 1 and 2 of our path indicated on the s axis. We divide the s axis between points 1 and 2 into a large number of closely spaced strips. Equation (6-2) is then represented on the graph as the sum of the area of the rectangles, which are bordered by the vertical strips on the sides, the s axis on the bottom, and the average value of $F_i\cos\theta_i$ in each interval on the top. It is not hard to see that the sum of the areas of these rectangles approximates the actual area under the curve. Indeed, as the number of rectangles goes to infinity, and the width of each rectangle goes to zero, we get the exact area under the curve. (This is similar to our discussion of the v vs. t graph in Chap. 2.) Thus

$$W_F = \text{area under the } F\cos\theta \text{ vs. } s \text{ curve} \tag{6.3}$$

between the starting and ending points of interest (1 and 2 for our case).

Problem 6.7. What does the $F\cos\theta$ vs. s graph look like for the force $\mathbf{F}_1$ of Problem 6.5? Use the graph to calculate the work done by $\mathbf{F}_1$ in a displacement of 15 m.

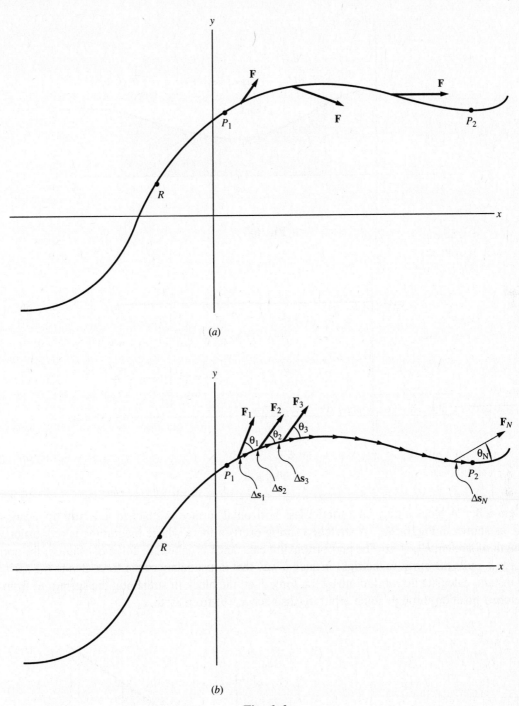

(a)

(b)

Fig. 6-6

Solution

In this case the path is a straight line along the horizontal (x) axis, so if we choose the origin as our reference point for s, then $s = x$. In this case $F_x = F_1 \cos \theta$ is constant and in fact equals (50 N)(0.866) = 43.3 N. The plot of F_x vs. x is thus the horizontal line shown in Fig. 6-8. The work done in a 15-m displacement, say from $x = 0$ to $x = 15$ m, is the area under the curve: (43.3 N)(15 m) = 650 J.

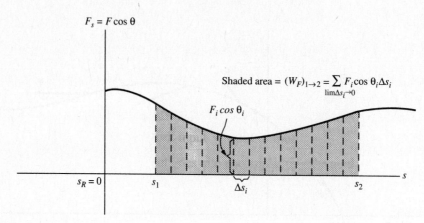

Fig. 6-7

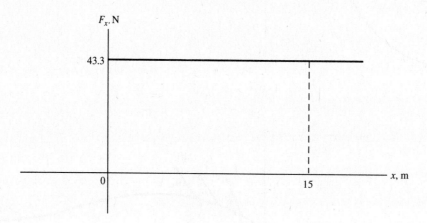

Fig. 6-8

Problem 6.8. A block sitting on a frictionless horizontal surface is attached to a wall by means of a spring, as shown in Fig. 6-9(a). A stretched spring exerts a force whose magnitude is proportional to the length of stretch: $F_{sp} = kx$. The proportionality constant k is called the force constant of the spring. If a force **F** pulls the block to the right in such a way that it just balances the force due to the spring at every instant, calculate the work done by the force F on the block in stretching the spring (a) from the unstretched position through some arbitrary distance x, (b) from x_1 to x_2.

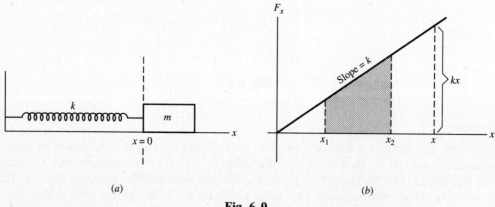

Fig. 6-9

Solution

(a)   As in Problem 6.7 the path is a straight line along the horizontal x axis, and again $s = x$. We take as the origin the position of the block when the spring is unstretched. Then the displacement of the block will always correspond to the stretch in the spring. Since F balances the spring force, $F = F_x = kx$. Our F_x vs. x graph is thus the straight line shown in Fig. 6-9(b). The work done in moving from the origin to point x is the area of a right triangle of base x and height kx, or

$$W_F = \tfrac{1}{2}(x)(kx) = \tfrac{1}{2}kx^2$$

(b)   The work done by F in going from x_1 to x_2 is the shaded area in Fig. 6-9(b). This equals the difference in the areas of the triangle from the origin to x_2 and the triangle from the origin to x_1:

$$(W_F)_{1 \to 2} = \tfrac{1}{2}kx_2{}^2 - \tfrac{1}{2}kx_1{}^2$$

Problem 6.9.   Repeat Problem 6.8 for the force F_{sp}.

Solution

Since F and F_{sp} are equal and opposite, the work done by F_{sp} is just the negative of the work done by F:

$$W_{\text{sp}} = -\tfrac{1}{2}kx^2 \qquad (W_{\text{sp}})_{1 \to 2} = \tfrac{1}{2}kx_1{}^2 - \tfrac{1}{2}kx_2{}^2$$

Problem 6.10.   Find the work done by each indicated force in Fig. 6-10.

Solution

Each force shown is perpendicular to the displacement at every moment, so it does zero work.

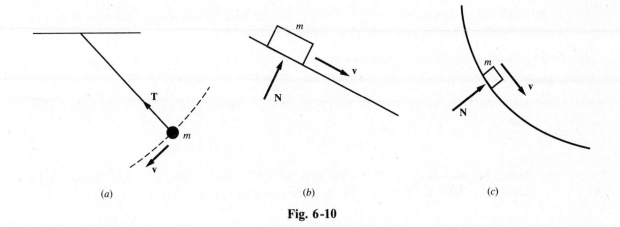

(a)   (b)   (c)

Fig. 6-10

6.3   KINETIC ENERGY AND ITS RELATION TO WORK

Consider a block on a frictionless horizontal surface, acted on by a *constant* horizontal force **F**, as shown in Fig. 6-11. The acceleration is then constant, and, by (2.10) $v^2 = v_0{}^2 + 2a(x - x_0)$. If we multiply both sides of the equation by half the mass, $m/2$, and bring the v_0 term to the other side, we get $ma(x - x_0) = \tfrac{1}{2}mv^2 - \tfrac{1}{2}mv_0{}^2$. Since **F** is the resultant force on the block, we have $F = ma$; thus $F(x - x_0) = \tfrac{1}{2}mv^2 - \tfrac{1}{2}mv_0{}^2$. The left side is just the total work W_T done on the block in moving from x_0 to x. If we relabel the initial position x_0 and velocity v_0 as x_1 and v_1, respectively, and relabel the final position x and velocity v as x_2 and v_2, respectively, we get

$$(W_T)_{1 \to 2} = \tfrac{1}{2}mv_2{}^2 - \tfrac{1}{2}mv_1{}^2 \tag{6.4}$$

The expression $\tfrac{1}{2}mv^2$ is called the **kinetic energy** of the mass m. The symbol for kinetic energy varies from textbook to textbook. Common symbols are K, KE, and E_k, and we will use the last in this book. Thus (6.4) becomes

$$(W_T)_{1 \to 2} = E_{k2} - E_{k1} \equiv \Delta E_k \tag{6.5}$$

where ΔE_k represents the change in E_k in going from the initial to the final position. The kinetic energy has units of work, and the SI units are joules. Equation (6.5) is called the **work–kinetic energy theorem**.

This result was derived by assuming constant acceleration, so we have shown its validity only when the resultant force acting on the object is constant.

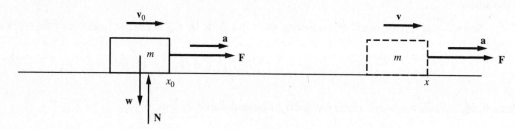

Fig. 6-11

Problem 6.11.   Assume the block in Fig. 6-11 has a mass $m = 10$ kg and the force $\mathbf{F} = 25$ N.

(a)   If the block has an initial velocity $v_1 = 20$ m/s, use the work–kinetic energy theorem to find its velocity v_2 after it has moved through a displacement of 20 m.

(b)   Redo part (a) using Newton's second law.

Solution

(a)   Using Eq. (6.4), we have $(W_T)_{1 \to 2} = (25 \text{ N})(20 \text{ m}) = 500 \text{ J} = \tfrac{1}{2}(10 \text{ kg})v_2{}^2 - \tfrac{1}{2}(10 \text{ kg})(20 \text{ m/s})^2$. Then

$$v_2{}^2 = 500 \text{ m}^2/\text{s}^2 \qquad \text{or} \qquad v_2 = 22.4 \text{ m/s}$$

(b)   Using $\mathbf{F} = m\mathbf{a}$, we have $25 \text{ N} = (10 \text{ kg})a$ or $a = 2.5 \text{ m/s}^2$. Then $v_2{}^2 = v_1{}^2 + 2a(x_2 - x_1) = (20 \text{ m/s})^2 + 2(2.5 \text{ m/s}^2)(20 \text{ m}) = 500 \text{ m}^2/\text{s}^2$ so $v_2 = 22.4 \text{ m/s}$, as before.

In the previous problem, the work–kinetic energy theorem does not seem to be any more useful than the standard $F = ma$ approach. This is because for constant-force problems it is very easy to apply Newton's second law. This is no longer the case for more complicated problems, where the acceleration varies in either magnitude or direction, or both.

It can be shown, using the calculus, that the work–kinetic energy theorem (6.5) is still true for the most general possible situation. No matter how complicated the path of motion, and no matter how complicated and how numerous are the forces acting on the object, *the total work done on the object in any interval equals the final minus the initial kinetic energy for that interval.* Thus, for example, if the particle moving along the path in Fig. 6.6(a) has a velocity of magnitude v_1 as it passes point 1 and a velocity of magnitude v_2 as it passes point 2, then those two speeds are related by Eq. (6.5), where $(W_T)_{1\rightarrow 2}$ is the total work due to all forces. The full power of this result will be recognized once we have introduced the concept of potential energy.

6.4 GRAVITATIONAL POTENTIAL ENERGY

Consider a block of cement being hoisted vertically by a crane (Fig. 6-12). The only two forces doing work are the tension **S** and the pull of gravity $\mathbf{F}_g$. Then in moving the block from position 1 to position 2, the total work is the sum of the work by the two forces, so (6.5) becomes

$$(W_T)_{1\rightarrow 2} = (W_S)_{1\rightarrow 2} + (W_g)_{1\rightarrow 2} = \Delta E_k$$

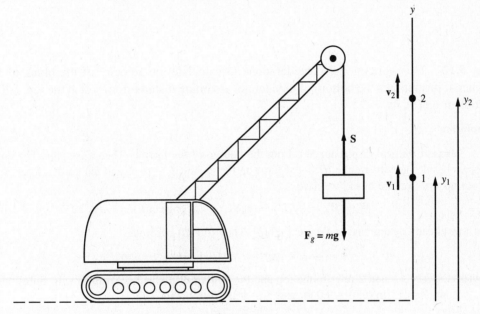

Fig. 6-12

Isolating the work done by **S** on the left side of the equation, we have

$$(W_S)_{1\rightarrow 2} = -(W_g)_{1\rightarrow 2} + \Delta E_k \qquad (6.6)$$

The work done by the force **S** depends on how the hoist is operated; **s** can vary from moment to moment and position to position. The work done by gravity, however, is predetermined, since (near the earth's surface) we have $F_g = mg$, pointing vertically downward, as shown. Then

$$(W_g)_{1\rightarrow 2} = -mg(y_2 - y_1) \qquad \text{or} \qquad -(W_g)_{1\rightarrow 2} = mgy_2 - mgy_1 \qquad (6.7)$$

We notice that $-W_g$ depends only on where one started and where one ended and not on the details of the block's motion. The quantity mgy is called the **gravitational potential energy** E_p of a mass m at height y. Then Eq. (6.7) becomes

$$-(W_g)_{1\rightarrow 2} = E_{p2} - E_{p1} \equiv \Delta E_p \qquad (6.8)$$

Substitution of (6.8) into (6.6) yields

$$(W_S)_{1\rightarrow 2} = \Delta E_p + \Delta E_k \qquad (6.9)$$

It can be shown that Eq. (6.7) is true for any path of motion of an object near the earth's surface.

Consider an object moving on an arbitrary path, such as in Fig. 6.6(a). We divide the total work W_T into two parts: the work done by gravity W_g and the work done by all other forces acting on the object W'. Then

$$(W_T)_{1\to2} = W'_{1\to2} + (W_g)_{1\to2} = E_{k2} - E_{k1}$$

and $$W'_{1\to2} = -(W_g)_{1\to2} + E_{k2} - E_{k1} \tag{6.10a}$$

or $$W'_{1\to2} = (E_{p2} - E_{p1}) + (E_{k2} - E_{k1}) = \Delta E_p + \Delta E_k = (mgy_2 - mgy_1) + (\tfrac{1}{2}mv_2{}^2 - \tfrac{1}{2}mv_1{}^2) \tag{6.10b}$$

Equation (6.10b) is a very general statement: The work done by all forces other than gravity on an object equals the sum of the changes in the gravitational potential energy and kinetic energy of the object.

Problem 6.12.   Use work-energy considerations to calculate the velocity of the block of Problem 6.6(b) when it just reaches the bottom of the incline, assuming it starts from rest at the top. All data are as in Problem 6.6(b).

Solution

Measure vertical displacement z from the bottom of the incline. Then $E_p = mgz$. The only acting forces besides gravity are the frictional force up the incline, $f_k = \mu_k N$, and the normal force N. Since N does no work on the block, we have

$$W' = W_f = -f_k L = -\mu_k N L = -\mu_k (mg\cos\theta) L = -177 \text{ J}$$

as was already determined in Problem 6.6(b). Then (6.10b) becomes

$$-177 \text{ J} = (mgz_2 - mgz_1) + (\tfrac{1}{2}mv_2{}^2 - \tfrac{1}{2}mv_1{}^2) \tag{i}$$

where the labels 1 and 2 refer to the top and the bottom of the incline, respectively. Substitute $v_1 = 0$, $z_1 = L\sin\theta = (15 \text{ m})(0.6) = 9.0 \text{ m}$, and $z_2 = 0$ in (i) to obtain

$$-177 \text{ J} = [0 - (5.0 \text{ kg})(9.8 \text{ m/s}^2)(9.0 \text{ m})] + [\tfrac{1}{2}(5.0 \text{ kg})v_2{}^2 - 0] \tag{ii}$$

Solving (ii) we obtain

$$v_2{}^2 = 106 \text{ m}^2/\text{s}^2 \qquad \text{or} \qquad v_2 = 10.3 \text{ m/s}$$

In Eqs. (6.9) or (6.10b), only the difference in the potential energy between two points appears. The definition of the potential energy can therefore be changed by adding or subtracting a constant without changing the energy equations.

Problem 6.13.   Consider the situation in Fig. 6-13, where a book of mass m is lifted above a tabletop, and y is the displacement measured from the tabletop to the bottom of the book. Choosing $E_p = mgy$ means that $E_p = 0$ when $y = 0$ (the book rests on the table). If we prefer our zero of potential to be at the floor level, find the new expression, E_p^*, for the potential energy.

Solution

$E_p^* = mgz$. Since $z = y + h$, we have $E_p^* = mg(y + h) = mgy + mgh = E_p + \text{const}$. Therefore potential-energy differences are the same for the old and new functions.

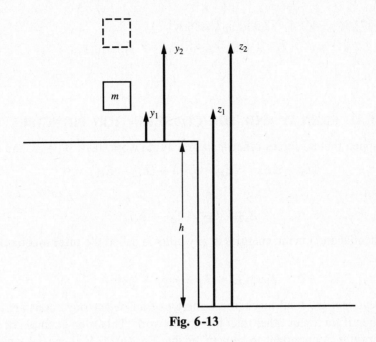

Fig. 6-13

Problem 6.14. Suppose the incline of Problem 6.12 were set on a tabletop of height $H = 2.0$ m, as shown in Fig. 6-14. Repeat Problem 6.12 if the zero of gravitational potential is set at the bottom of the table.

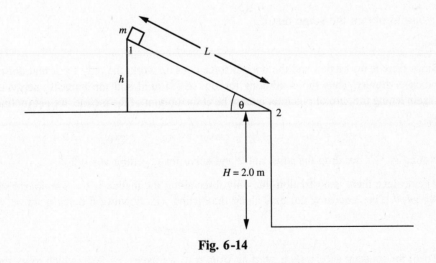

Fig. 6-14

Solution

We proceed as in Problem 6.12. Everything is the same as before except that the initial and final heights are z_1 and z_2 instead of y_1 and y_2. Then $z_1 = 2.0$ m $+ L \sin \theta = 2.0$ m $+ 9.0$ m $= 11.0$ m; $z_2 = 2.0$ m. Substituting into Eq. (*i*) of Problem 6.12, we get

$$-177 \text{ J} = [(5.0 \text{ kg}) (9.8 \text{ m/s}^2) (2.0 \text{ m}) - (5.0 \text{ kg}) (9.8 \text{ m/s}^2) (11.0 \text{ m})] + \left[\tfrac{1}{2}(5.0 \text{ kg})v_2{}^2 - 0\right]$$

Therefore -177 J $= -441$ J $+ (2.5$ kg$)v_2{}^2$, so that

$$v_2{}^2 = 106 \text{ m}^2/\text{s}^2 \quad \text{or} \quad v_2 = 10.3 \text{ m/s}$$

as before

6.5 MECHANICAL ENERGY AND THE CONSERVATION PRINCIPLE

If it should happen that no forces other than gravity do work, then $W' = 0$, and (*6.10b*) becomes

$$\Delta E_p + \Delta E_k = (E_{p2} - E_{p1}) + (E_{k2} - E_{k1}) = 0$$

which rearranges to

$$E_{p2} + E_{k2} = E_{p1} + E_{k1} \tag{6.11}$$

The sum of the potential and kinetic energies at any point is called the **total mechanical energy** E_T at that point:

$$E_T \equiv E_p + E_k = mgy + \tfrac{1}{2}mv^2 \tag{6.12}$$

Thus Eq. (*6.11*) says that the total mechanical energy of an object stays constant ("is conserved") throughout its motion if no forces other than gravity do work. This is an example of the conservation of mechanical energy. It is important to remember that Eq. (*6.11*) is a special case of Eq. (*6.10b*), which is the general work-energy theorem.

Problem 6.15. Assume that in Problem 6.12 the incline is frictionless, as in Problem 6.6(*a*).

(*a*) Use energy considerations to show that the velocity at the bottom of the incline is $v = \sqrt{2gh}$, where h is the height of the incline.

(*b*) Use $\mathbf{F} = m\mathbf{a}$ to obtain the same result.

Solution

(*a*) Since there is no friction and the normal force does no work, the only force that does work on the block is gravity. Thus the conditions for Eq. (*6.11*) hold and mechanical energy is conserved. Again letting the zero of potential energy be at the bottom of the incline, we get (noting $y_2 = 0$ and $v_1 = 0$)

$$mgy_1 + \tfrac{1}{2}mv_1{}^2 = mgy_2 + \tfrac{1}{2}mv_2{}^2 \quad \text{or} \quad mgy_1 + 0 = 0 + \tfrac{1}{2}mv_2{}^2$$

Noting $y_1 = h$, we drop the subscript 2 and solve for v, getting $v = \sqrt{2gh}$.

(*b*) Again, since there is no friction, the only force along the incline is the component of the weight, $mg \sin \theta$. Then choosing our axis along the incline with downward being positive, we have

$$a = \frac{F}{m} = g \sin \theta$$

Then, for constant acceleration, starting from rest, we have $v^2 = 2aL$, which gives the velocity at the bottom of the incline. Substituting for a, we get

$$v^2 = 2(g \sin \theta)L = 2gL \sin \theta = 2gh \quad \text{or} \quad v = \sqrt{2gh}$$

as before.

Problem 6.16. Suppose that instead of an inclined plane, as in Problem 6.15, we had a block sliding down a frictionless curved surface, as in Fig. 6-15. Assume the block starts from rest at a height h, as shown.

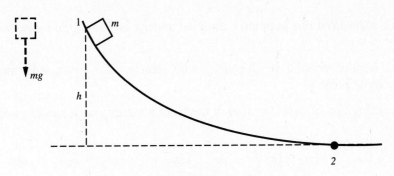

Fig. 6-15

(a) Find an expression for the velocity of the block at point 2 using energy considerations.

(b) Can you repeat part (a) using Newton's second law?

Solution

(a) As in Problem 6.15, we label the starting position 1 and the ending position 2 and choose the zero of potential energy to be the bottom of the curve. Since there is no friction, and since the normal force at any point on the curve is perpendicular to the path of motion and can do no work, we again have the conditions for conservation of mechanical energy. Then

$$mgy_1 + \tfrac{1}{2}mv_1{}^2 = mgy_2 + \tfrac{1}{2}mv_2{}^2$$

Therefore $\qquad\qquad mgh + 0 = 0 + \tfrac{1}{2}mv_2{}^2 \qquad$ or $\qquad v_2{}^2 = 2gh$

Dropping the subscript on the final velocity we have: $v = \sqrt{2gh}$.

Note that this is the same expression we got in Problem 6.15 with the frictionless incline. Indeed, this result was obtained without knowing the exact shape of the curve, and hence is true for all curves for which the block will reach the bottom point.

(b) We first note that the block is no longer traveling in a straight line, and the normal force varies in both magnitude and direction from point to point. Solution of the problem thus requires the full vector properties of Newton's second law, as well as dealing with variable forces. The problem can still be solved but requires the use of the calculus.

Problem 6.17. Consider a block sliding on the frictionless surface shown in Fig. 6-16.

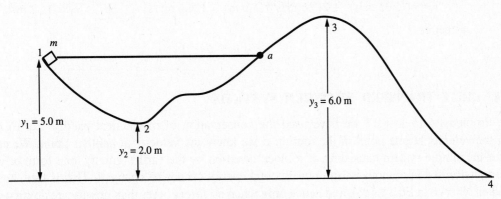

Fig. 6-16

(a) If the block starts from rest at point 1, find its velocity at point 2 and describe its subsequent motion.

(b) If the block were observed to reach point 3 with velocity $v_3 = 3$ m/s, what must have been its initial velocity at point 1?

(c) Under the assumption of part (b), what is the block's velocity as it reaches point 4?

Solution

(a) $mgy_1 + \frac{1}{2}mv_1^2 = mgy_2 + \frac{1}{2}mv_2^2$ or $mgy_1 + 0 = \frac{1}{2}mv_2^2 + mgy_2$ and

$$v_2 = \sqrt{2g(y_1 - y_2)} = \sqrt{2(9.8 \text{ m/s}^2)(5.0 \text{ m} - 2.0 \text{ m})} = \sqrt{58.8 \text{ m}^2/\text{s}^2} = 7.67 \text{ m/s}$$

The block will continue along the curve until it reaches the original height, 5.0 m, which will occur at some point a between points 2 and 3. At a it must have zero kinetic energy and hence zero velocity. It will then slide back down the curve, passing point 2 with the same magnitude of velocity as before but in the opposite direction. This follows by again applying Eq. (6.11). The block will continue slowing down, until it comes to rest at point 1. The motion will then repeat itself. This will go on forever as long as Eq. (6.11) truly holds, that is, as long as there is no friction or work done by any force except gravity.

(b) To reach point 3, which is higher than point 1, the block must have had an even greater velocity at point 1. In fact (6.11) gives

$$mgy_1 + \frac{1}{2}mv_1^2 = mgy_3 + \frac{1}{2}mv_3^2$$

from which

$$v_1^2 = v_3^2 + 2g(y_3 - y_1) = (3 \text{ m/s})^2 + 2(9.8 \text{ m/s}^2)(6.0 \text{ m} - 5.0 \text{ m}) = 28.6 \text{ m}^2/\text{s}^2$$

or $$v_1 = 5.35 \text{ m/s}$$

(c) Apply (6.11) between points 3 and 4:

$$mgy_3 + \frac{1}{2}mv_3^2 = 0 + \frac{1}{2}mv_4^2$$

$$v_4^2 = v_3^2 + 2gy_3 = (3 \text{ m/s})^2 + 2(9.8 \text{ m/s}^2)(6.0 \text{ m}) = 126.6 \text{ m}^2/\text{s}^2 \quad \text{or} \quad v_4 = 11.3 \text{ m/s}$$

We could equally well have applied Eq. (6.11) directly between points 1 and 4:

$$mgy_1 + \frac{1}{2}mv_1^2 = mgy_4 + \frac{1}{2}mv_4^2 \quad \text{or} \quad v_4^2 = v_1^2 + 2gy_1$$

Substituting, we get

$$v_4^2 = (5.35 \text{ m/s})^2 + 2(9.8 \text{ m/s}^2)(5.0 \text{ m}) = 126.6 \text{ m}^2/\text{s}^2 \quad \text{or} \quad v_4 = 11.3 \text{ m/s}$$

as before.

6.6 ENERGY TRANSFER BETWEEN SYSTEMS

In Problems 6.15 to 6.17 we have used the conservation of mechanical energy, Eq. (6.11), to obtain the velocity at one point in the motion if we know the velocity at another point. We can say that, for the simple system consisting of a block acted on by the earth's gravity, one form of energy can be transformed into another form but the total energy cannot be changed. This is true, however, only when $W' = 0$ in Eq. (6.10b), and hence only when no forces other than gravity are doing work on the system. In such a case our system's energy is **isolated** from, or **closed** to, the rest of the universe.

Isolation does not mean that other forces, such as the normal force, which keeps the block on track, have no effect on the system. They merely have no effect on the *total energy* of the system.

Suppose that some nongravitational force F does positive work on our block. Then $W' > 0$, and, according to Eq. (*6.10b*) the total mechanical energy of the system increases. On the other hand, if F does negative work, then $W' < 0$, and the mechanical energy decreases. If energy is a fundamental quantity, where did the extra energy of our system come from when $W' > 0$, and where did the lost energy go to when $W' < 0$? It can be shown that in the former case some other system which is the source of the force F gave up some of its energy; in the latter case some other system gained some additional energy. In either case the combined energy of the two systems remains constant. We can think of the work done by one system on the other as the mechanical transfer of energy between the systems.

Problem 6.18. Reconsider Problem 5.15, in which a hanging block of mass $m_B = 12$ kg is connected by a light cord over a frictionless pulley to another block of mass $m_A = 5$ kg on a frictionless inclined plane of angle $\theta = 30°$. Assume the apparatus starts from rest, with block A at the very bottom of the incline and block B 10 m above the base of the incline. Find the velocity v_2 of the blocks just before block B reaches the bottom using work-energy considerations, with the two blocks treated as two separate systems.

Solution

The situation is depicted in Fig. 6-17, with positions 1 and 2 being the initial and final positions for each block. We note that the tension in the cord does work on each system (A and B). But the work done by the cord on A is exactly the negative of the work done on B. (Overall, no net work is done by the cord.)

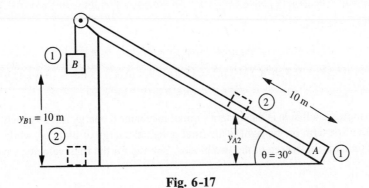

Fig. 6-17

Apply the work-energy theorem (*6.10b*) to system A (with $y_{A1} = v_1 = 0$ and $y_{A2} = (10 \text{ m})(\sin 30°) = 5 \text{ m}$):

$$(W'_A)_{1 \to 2} = \Delta E_p + \Delta E_k = (m_A g y_{A2} - m_A g y_{A1}) + (\tfrac{1}{2}m_A v_2{}^2 - \tfrac{1}{2}m_A v_1{}^2)$$
$$= (5 \text{ kg})(9.8 \text{ m/s}^2)(5 \text{ m}) + \tfrac{1}{2}(5 \text{ kg})v_2{}^2$$

We can solve for v_2 if we can calculate $(W'_A)_{1 \to 2}$. Since $T = 51.8$ N (from Problem 5.15) is along the direction of motion of system A,

$$(W'_A)_{1 \to 2} = (51.8 \text{ N})(10 \text{ m}) = 518 \text{ J}$$

and so

$$518 \text{ J} = (245 \text{ J}) + (2.5 \text{ kg})v_2{}^2 \quad \text{or} \quad v_2 = 10.4 \text{ m/s}$$

Although we have already obtained our result, it is informative to analyze system B in the same way:

$$(W'_B)_{1 \to 2} = \Delta E_p + \Delta E_k = (0 - m_B g y_{B1}) + (\tfrac{1}{2}m_B v_2{}^2 - 0)$$

Now T is opposite the direction of motion of system B so that $(W'_B)_{1 \to 2} = -518$ J. Hence the mechanical energy B is diminished by 518 J, and, by (6.5), B has considerably less kinetic energy than it would have had if it had dropped in free fall. Substituting the value of W'_B,

$$-518 \text{ J} = -(12 \text{ kg})(9.8 \text{ m/s}^2)(10 \text{ m}) + (6 \text{ kg})v_2{}^2 \quad \text{or} \quad v_2 = 10.5 \text{ m/s}$$

which is the same as our previous result to within rounding errors.

Note. The importance of Problem 6.18 lies in its demonstration that when system B does positive work (via a cord or whatever) on system A, then system A gains precisely the amount of mechanical energy lost by system B. In general, any system that does positive (negative) work loses (gains) energy.

Problem 6.19. Rework Problem 6.18 by considering the two blocks to make up a single isolated system.

Solution

If we treat the combination of A and B as a single system, then the cord is just an internal part of the system and we do not have to consider the tension at all. Thus, for the combined system, no forces other than gravity do work ($W' = 0$), and so total mechanical energy is conserved:

$$m_A g y_{A1} + m_B g y_{B1} + \tfrac{1}{2}m_A v_1{}^2 + \tfrac{1}{2}m_B v_1{}^2 = m_A g y_{A2} + m_B g y_{B2} + \tfrac{1}{2}m_A v_2{}^2 + \tfrac{1}{2}m_B v_2{}^2$$

But $y_{A1} = v_1 = y_{B2} = 0$, so

$$m_B g y_{B1} = m_A g y_{A2} + \tfrac{1}{2}(m_A + m_B)v_2{}^2$$
$$(12 \text{ kg})(9.8 \text{ m/s}^2)(10 \text{ m}) = (5 \text{ kg})(9.8 \text{ m/s}^2)(5 \text{ m}) + (8.5 \text{ kg})v_2{}^2$$
$$1176 \text{ J} = 245 \text{ J} + (8.5 \text{ kg})v_2{}^2$$

In the last equation the left side is the system's initial mechanical energy (all of which is potential energy of block B). The first term on the right is the final potential energy of block A, while the second term is the combined final kinetic energy of the two blocks. Solving for the final velocity, we get $v_2 = 10.5$ m/s, as before.

Note. Any force that has the property that the work done by the force depends only on the starting and ending points, and not on what happened in between, is called a *conservative force*. As we have seen, the force of gravity near the Earth's surface is clearly such a force. The name "conservative" comes from the fact that if an object moves in a path that returns to the starting point, the total work done by such a force must be zero, since the work is the same as if the object got there by not moving at all. Saying a force is conservative is equivalent to saying that we can define a potential energy for the force. Indeed, for a force whose work is described by a potential energy, we see immediately that if an object travels on a path that returns to the starting point, we have $\Delta E_p = 0$, and the work done equals zero.

6.7 OTHER CONSERVATIVE FORCES

If the gravitational force near the earth's surface were the only conservative force, and therefore the only force whose work can be treated from the point of view of potential energy, it would hardly have been worthwhile to introduce the idea. It turns out that many forces in nature are conservative. We will discuss two of them, the spring force and the general force of gravity.

Problem 6.20. Show that the spring force is conservative, and find a suitable expression for the spring potential energy.

Solution

In Problem 6.8 we calculated the work of an external force that is just strong enough to oppose the pull of a spring and that stretches the spring from x_1 to x_2, where x is measured from the unstretched position. At any point, this external force is equal and opposite to the force due to the spring. Hence for the work W_{sp} done by the spring we have

$$-(W_{sp})_{1\to 2} = \tfrac{1}{2}kx_2{}^2 - \tfrac{1}{2}kx_1{}^2 \tag{i}$$

Clearly this depends only on the starting and ending points; the spring force is conservative. Following our earlier definition of potential energy, we write

$$-(W_{sp})_{1\to 2} = E_{p2} - E_{p1} \tag{ii}$$

From (i) and (ii), $E_p = \tfrac{1}{2}kx^2 + C$, where C is an arbitrary constant. If we choose our zero point of potential energy to be at $x = 0$ (the unstretched position of the spring), then we get

$$E_p = \tfrac{1}{2}kx^2 \tag{iii}$$

Note. For loosely wound springs, the spring can be compressed as well as stretched, and the force formula $F_{sp} = -kx$ is valid for negative as well as positive values of x. Then it can be shown that the potential-energy formula, Eq. (iii), is valid for both positive and negative values of x.

Problem 6.21. A loosely wound spring of force constant $k = 100$ N/m is connected to a block of mass $m = 12$ kg on a frictionless horizontal surface, as shown in Fig. 6-18. The block is pulled to the right 15 cm and released. Assume the spring is light enough so that its own mass can be neglected.

(a) Find the velocity of the block at $x = 0$, the unstretched position.

(b) What is the maximum distance the spring will be compressed?

(c) What is the velocity of the block when $x = 10$ cm?

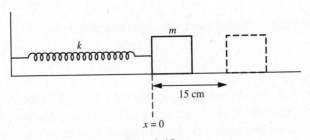

Fig. 6-18

Solution

(a) The only force that does work is the spring force, so we have conservation of mechanical energy:

$$E_{p1} + E_{k1} = E_{p2} + E_{k2} \qquad \text{or} \qquad \tfrac{1}{2}kx_1{}^2 + \tfrac{1}{2}mv_1{}^2 = \tfrac{1}{2}kx_2{}^2 + \tfrac{1}{2}mv_2{}^2$$

Letting 1 be the release point we have $x_1 = 0.15$ m, $v_1 = 0$, and letting point 2 be the unstretched position, we have $x_2 = 0$. Then

$$\tfrac{1}{2}(100 \text{ N/m})\,(0.15 \text{ m})^2 + 0 = 0 + \tfrac{1}{2}(12 \text{ kg})v_2{}^2 \qquad \text{or} \qquad v_2{}^2 = 0.1875 \text{ m}^2/\text{s}^2$$

$$\text{or} \qquad v_2 = \pm 0.433 \text{ m/s}$$

The plus (minus) refers to motion through $x = 0$ to the right (left).

(b) Now let 2 be the point of maximum compression ($x_2 < 0$). At this point the block must stop moving to the left; thus $v_2 = 0$ and

$$\tfrac{1}{2}(100 \text{ N/m})\,(0.15 \text{ m})^2 + 0 = \tfrac{1}{2}(100 \text{ N/m})x_2{}^2 + 0 \qquad \text{or} \qquad x_2{}^2 = 0.0225 \text{ m}^2$$

$$\text{or} \qquad x_2 = -0.15 \text{ m}$$

(c) With $x_2{}^2 = 100 \text{ cm}^2 = 0.01 \text{ m}^2$,

$$\tfrac{1}{2}(100 \text{ N/m})\,(0.15 \text{ m})^2 + 0 = \tfrac{1}{2}(100 \text{ N/m})\,(0.01 \text{ m}^2) + \tfrac{1}{2}(12 \text{ kg})v_2{}^2$$

$$\text{or} \qquad v_2{}^2 = 0.1042 \text{ m}^2/\text{s}^2 \qquad \text{or} \qquad v_2 = \pm 0.323 \text{ m/s}$$

The plus and minus signs refer to the block traveling to the right and left, respectively.

Note. Under conservation of mechanical energy, an object must always have the same magnitude of velocity every time it passes a given point, even though its direction of motion can be different. (This extends the "same place–same speed" rule of Chap. 2.)

Gravity at Large Distances from the Earth

We now turn to the gravitational force far from the earth's surface, where it can no longer be considered constant. This force can be shown to be conservative and thus has a potential energy. To obtain this energy we need the work done W_G by this force on an object as it moves along its path. Such a path is depicted in Fig. 6-19. To calculate the work done we can use the calculus, which gives the result

$$-(W_G)_{1 \to 2} = \left(\frac{-GM_e m}{r_2} \right) - \left(\frac{-GM_e m}{r_1} \right) \tag{6.13}$$

From (6.13) the gravitational potential energy is determined as

$$E_p = \left(\frac{-GM_e m}{r} \right) + C \tag{6.14}$$

Ordinarily we choose $C = 0$, thereby rendering E_p zero at $r = \infty$. Whether we do so or not, the minus sign in (6.14) makes physical sense. As r decreases, GMm/r increases; so $-GMm/r$ decreases. But a body approaching the earth (decreasing r) should indeed lose potential energy, since the attractive force of gravity is doing positive work on it.

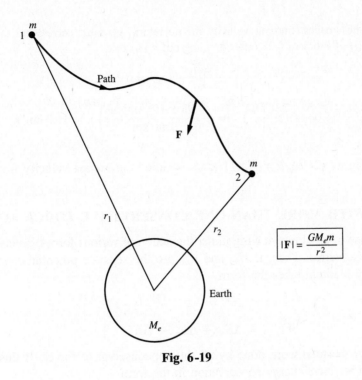

Fig. 6-19

Problem 6.22. A rocket is launched from the earth's surface. When the rocket engine burns out, the rocket is moving with a velocity of 6.0 km/s and is at an altitude of 10 km above the earth's surface. What is the maximum altitude to which the rocket rises? The radius of the earth is 6380 km.

Solution

From the moment of burnout, the rocket is acted on only by the force of gravity. Conservation of mechanical energy then holds, with the potential energy of gravity given by (*6.14*):

$$\frac{-GM_em}{r_1} + \tfrac{1}{2}mv_1{}^2 = \frac{-GM_em}{r_2} + \tfrac{1}{2}mv_2{}^2 \qquad\qquad (i)$$

[*C* has been canceled from both sides of (*i*).] Here $r_1 = 6380 + 10 = 6390$ km, and by (*5.4*),

$$GM_e = gR_e{}^2 = (9.8 \times 10^{-3}\ \text{km/s}^2)(6380\ \text{km})^2 = 3.99 \times 10^5\ \text{km}^3/\text{s}$$

At the highest point, r_2, we must have $v_2 = 0$. Noting that *m* divides out of (*i*), we get

$$-\frac{3.99 \times 10^5\ \text{km}^3/\text{s}^2}{6390\ \text{km}} + \tfrac{1}{2}(6.0\ \text{km/s})^2 = \frac{-3.99 \times 10^5\ \text{km}^3/\text{s}^2}{r_2} + 0$$

Solving, $r_2 = 8980$ km, for an altitude of $8980 - 6380 = 2600$ km.

Problem 6.23. Referring to Problem 6.22, what is the smallest velocity the rocket must have upon burnout (at altitude 10 km) such that it never returns to the earth?

Solution

For the rocket not to return, its velocity must never drop to zero while the rocket is a finite distance from the earth. If it did, the earth's gravitational attraction, however weak, would eventually pull it back down. Thus the smallest burnout velocity for no return, v_1, must correspond to $v_2 = 0$ at $r_2 = \infty$. Substitute in (*i*) of Problem 6.22 (after dividing out m) to find

$$-\frac{GM_e}{r_1} + \tfrac{1}{2}v_1{}^2 = 0 + 0$$

$$v_1 = \left(\frac{2GM_e}{r_1}\right)^{1/2} = \left(\frac{7.98 \times 10^5 \text{ km}^3/\text{s}^2}{6390 \text{ km}}\right)^{1/2} = 11.2 \text{ km/s}$$

Note.   The quantity $(2GM_e/R_e)^{1/2} \approx 11$ km/s is called the **escape velocity** from earth.

6.8   SYSTEMS WITH MORE THAN ONE CONSERVATIVE FORCE ACTING

Consider the case of an object moving under the action of various forces, precisely two of which, **F**$_a$ *and* **F**$_b$, are conservative. Then, if E_{pa} and E_{pb} are the separate potential-energy functions, the work–kinetic energy theorem takes the form

$$W'_{1 \to 2} = -(W_a)_{1 \to 2} - (W_b)_{1 \to 2} + \Delta E_k$$

or

$$W'_{1 \to 2} = \Delta E_{pa} + \Delta E_{pb} + \Delta E_k \tag{6.15}$$

where W' stands for the total work done by all the nonconservative forces. If this nonconservative work vanishes, then we have energy conservation in the form

$$\Delta E_T = \Delta(E_{pa} + E_{pb} + E_k) = 0 \tag{6.16}$$

It is obvious how (*6.15*) and (*6.16*) may be generalized to cover three, four, or more conservative forces.

Problem 6.24.   Two blocks are connected by a light cord over a frictionless pulley, as shown in Fig. 6-20. Block A rests on a horizontal frictionless surface and is connected to a light spring of force constant k. Initially, block A is at $x = 0$, the unstretched position of the spring.

(*a*)   If the apparatus is released from rest, what is the maximum distance through which block B falls?

(*b*)   What is the velocity of block B when it has fallen half that distance?

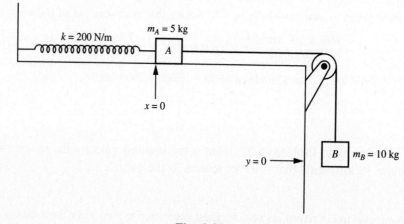

Fig. 6-20

Solution

(a) Consider the system composed of the linked blocks. Only gravity and the spring force—both conservative—do work on the system, so total mechanical energy is conserved. Let $E_{sp} = \frac{1}{2}kx^2$ be the spring potential energy (with x measured to the right from the unstretched position) and $E_g = m_B gy$ be the gravitational potential energy of block B (with y measured *upward* from the initial position of block B). Because the length of the cord is fixed, $x = -y$ and $v_A = v_B$. With subscript 1 denoting the starting position and subscript 2 the final position, we have $v_{A1} = v_{B1} = 0$ and $(E_{sp})_1 = (E_g)_1 = 0$. Also, for the maximum distance of fall $v_{A2} = v_{B2} = 0$. By (6.16),

$$0 + 0 + 0 = \tfrac{1}{2}kx_2{}^2 + m_B gy_2 + 0 = \tfrac{1}{2}kx_2{}^2 - m_B gx_2 + 0$$

or $\tfrac{1}{2}(200 \text{ N/m})x_2{}^2 - (10 \text{ kg})(9.8 \text{ m/s}^2)x_2 = 0$ or $(100x_2 - 98)x_2 = 0$

Dividing out by x_2 we get $100x_2 = 98$ or $x_2 = 0.98$ m.

(b) Now let point 2 correspond to $x = 0.49$ m. With $v_{A2} = v_{B2} = v_2$, gives

$$0 + 0 + 0 = \tfrac{1}{2}(200 \text{ N/m})(0.49 \text{ m})^2 - (10 \text{ kg})(9.8 \text{ m/s}^2)(0.49 \text{ m}) + \tfrac{1}{2}(5 \text{ kg} + 10 \text{ kg})v_2{}^2$$

or $7.5v_2{}^2 = 24.0$ or $v_2 = \pm 1.79 \text{ m/s}.$

Problems for Review and Mind Stretching

Problem 6.25.   A projectile ($m = 5.0$ slugs) is fired at an angle θ_o above the horizontal, as shown in Fig. 6-21. Use potential-energy considerations to find the work done by gravity in the projectile motions $o \to a$, $o \to b$, and $o \to c$.

Solution

$-(W_g)_{o \to a} = (E_p)_a - (E_p)_o$. Choose the zero of potential energy at the level of launch. Then $(E_p)_o = 0$ and

$$(E_p)_a = mgy_a = (5.0 \text{ slugs})(32 \text{ ft/s}^2)(6.0 \text{ ft}) = 960 \text{ ft} \cdot \text{lb}   \text{ or }   (W_g)_{o \to a} = -960 \text{ ft} \cdot \text{lb}$$

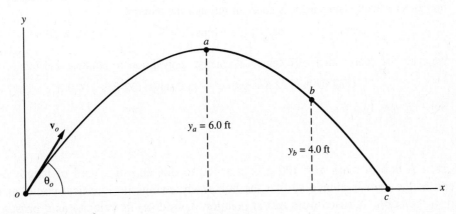

Fig. 6-21

Similarly,

$$(W_g)_{o \to b} = -(E_p)_b = -(5.0 \text{ slugs}) (32 \text{ ft/s}^2) (4.0 \text{ ft}) = -640 \text{ ft} \cdot \text{lb}$$

and $(W_g)_{o \to c} = -(E_p)_c = 0 \text{ ft} \cdot \text{lb}$.

Problem 6.26. An object moves along the x axis under the action of a force whose potential energy is given by $E_p = (2.0 \text{ J/m})x + (3.5 \text{ J/m}^3)x^3$, where x is in meters.

(a) Find the work done by this force as the object moves from $x = 1.0$ m to $x = 3.0$ m.

(b) If this represents the only work done on the object, and if its kinetic energy was 140 J at $x = 1.0$ m, use the work–kinetic energy theorem to find the kinetic energy of the object at $x = 3.0$ m.

Solution

(a) $-W_{1 \to 3} = (E_p)_3 - (E_p)_1 = [(2.0 \text{ J/m}) (3.0 \text{ m}) + (3.5 \text{ J/m}^3) (3.0 \text{ m})^3]$

$$- [(2.0 \text{ J/m}) (1.0 \text{ m}) + (3.5 \text{ J/m}^3) (1.0 \text{ m})^3] = 95 \text{ J}$$

or $W_{1 \to 3} = -95 \text{ J}.$

(b) $-95 \text{ J} = \Delta E_k = E_{k3} - E_{k1} = E_{k3} - 140 \text{ J}$ or $E_{k3} = 45 \text{ J}$

Problem 6.27. Referring to Problem 6.25, assume that the speed of the projectile at point a is 9.0 ft/s. Determine (a) the initial speed v_o; (b) the angle of launch θ_o; (c) the speed of the projectile as it passes point b.

Solution

(a) Once the projectile is launched, the only force acting on it (when we ignore air resistance) is gravity. Therefore we have conservation of mechanical energy: $(E_k)_o + (E_p)_o = (E_k)_a + (E_p)_a$ or

$$(2.5 \text{ slugs})v_o^2 + 0 = (2.5 \text{ slugs}) (9.0 \text{ ft/s})^2 + (5.0 \text{ slugs}) (32 \text{ ft/s}^2) (6.0 \text{ ft}) = 1163 \text{ ft} \cdot \text{lb}$$

from which $v_o^2 = 465 \text{ ft}^2/\text{s}^2$ or $v_o = 21.6 \text{ ft/s}$.

(b) The velocity at point a is horizontal since a is the highest point in the trajectory. Since the horizontal velocity component is constant through the motion,

$$v_o \cos \theta_o = v_a \quad \text{or} \quad (21.6) \cos \theta_o = 9.0 \quad \text{or} \quad \theta_o = 65.4°$$

(c) We again use conservation of mechanical energy, applied now to points a and b:

$$1163 \text{ ft} \cdot \text{lb} = (2.5 \text{ slugs})v_b^2 + (5.0 \text{ slugs}) (32 \text{ ft/s}^2) (4.0 \text{ ft})$$

Solving, $v_b = 14.5$ ft/s.

Problem 6.28. A bob of mass $m = 400$ g is attached to one end of a cord of length $L = 1.5$ m. The other end of the cord is pinned so that the bob freely swings in a vertical circle, as shown in Fig. 6-22(a). If the bob is released from rest at position A, find (a) its velocity as it passes positions B and C; (b) the tension in the cord as it passes position C.

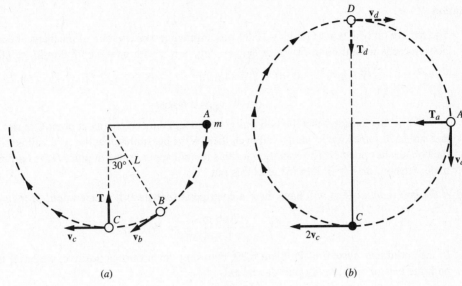

Fig. 6-22

Solution

(a)　Since the tension in the cord is always at right angles to the direction of motion, it does no work, and mechanical energy is conserved. Choosing the lowest point of the swing, point C, as the zero of potential energy (and the origin of our vertical coordinate y), we have

$$mgy_a + \tfrac{1}{2}mv_a{}^2 = mgy_b + \tfrac{1}{2}mv_b{}^2$$

Dividing out the mass m and multiplying by 2, we get

$$v_b{}^2 = 2gy_a - 2gy_b + v_a{}^2$$

Next we note that

$$y_a = L = 1.5 \text{ m} \qquad v_a = 0 \qquad y_b = L - L\cos 30° = (1.5 \text{ m})(1 - 0.866) = 0.201 \text{ m}$$

$$v_b{}^2 = 2(9.8 \text{ m/s}^2)(1.5 \text{ m}) - 2(9.8 \text{ m/s}^2)(0.201 \text{ m}) + 0 = 25.5 \text{ m}^2/\text{s}^2 \quad \text{or} \quad v_b = 5.05 \text{ m/s}$$

Similarly, for point C, $v_c{}^2 = 2gy_a - 2gy_c + v_a{}^2$ with $y_c = 0 = v_a = 0$. Then

$$v_c{}^2 = 2(9.8 \text{ m/s}^2)(1.5 \text{ m}) = 29.4 \text{ m}^2/\text{s}^2 \quad \text{or} \quad v_c = 5.42 \text{ m/s}$$

(b)　As the bob passes position C it has an upward centripetal acceleration

$$a = \frac{v_c{}^2}{L} = \frac{29.4 \text{ m}^2/\text{s}^2}{1.5 \text{ m}} = 19.6 \text{ m/s}^2$$

Then, from Newton's second law in the y direction,

$$T - mg = ma \quad \text{or} \quad T = m(g + a) = (0.400 \text{ kg})(9.8 \text{ m/s}^2 + 19.6 \text{ m/s}^2) = 11.8 \text{ N}$$

Problem 6.29.　The bob of Problem 6.28 is given an extra spurt as it passes point C so that its velocity at that point doubles.

(a)　Will it reach point D of Fig. 6-22(b)? If so, with what velocity?

(b)　If so, what is the tension in the cord as it passes point D?

Solution

(a) The new velocity at point C is $v_c = 10.84$ m/s. Applying conservation of mechanical energy as the bob proceeds toward point D; $v_d^2 = 2gy_c - 2gy_d + v_c^2$, with $y_c = 0$ and $y_d = 2L = 3.0$ m. Then

$$v_d^2 = 0 - 2(9.8 \text{ m/s}^2)(3.0 \text{ m}) + (10.84 \text{ m/s})^2 = (-58.8 + 117.5)\text{ m}^2/\text{s}^2 = 58.7\text{ m}^2/\text{s}^2$$

$$\text{or} \qquad v_d = 7.66 \text{ m/s}$$

While this indicates that the bob was given enough kinetic energy at point C to rise to point D and still have some kinetic energy left over, there is the possibility that the cord will go slack before the bob reaches point D. The condition for this to not happen is that at point D the cord will still be under tension, or $T \geq 0$. Part (b) tests this out.

(b) *If the bob reaches D*, it will have there a centripetal (downward) acceleration, of magnitude

$$a = \frac{v_d^2}{L} = \frac{(7.66 \text{ m/s})^2}{1.5 \text{ m/s}} = 39.1 \text{ m/s}^2$$

In the coordinate system of Problem 6.29, choosing downward as positive, we have, noting that both the tension and gravity pull downward,

$$T_d + mg = ma_y \qquad \text{or} \qquad T_d = m(a_y - g) = (0.400 \text{ kg})(39.1 \text{ m/s}^2 - 9.8 \text{ m/s}^2) = 11.7 \text{ N} > 0$$

so the cord did not go slack.

Problem 6.30. A block hangs from the end of a spring of force constant k. In the equilibrium configuration the spring is stretched a distance h (Fig. 6-23). Show that the *combined* potential energy of gravity and the spring force can be written as $\frac{1}{2}kx^2$, where x is the amount of stretch of the spring as measured from the *equilibrium* position.

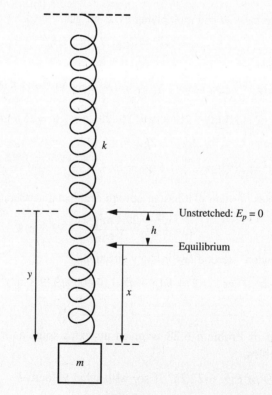

Fig. 6-23

Solution

With the origins of y and x as shown in the figure, the combined potential energy is given by

$$E_{sp} + E_g = \tfrac{1}{2}ky^2 - mgy \qquad (i)$$

(where the minus sign reflects the fact that downward has been chosen as positive for y). Noting that $y = x + h$, we substitute into Eq. (i) to get

$$E_{sp} + E_g = \tfrac{1}{2}k(x+h)^2 - mg(x+h) = \tfrac{1}{2}kx^2 + khx + \tfrac{1}{2}kh^2 - mgx - mgh$$

Now, at the equilibrium position, the downward force of gravity must just be balanced by the upward spring force: $mg = kh$. Then, $khx - mgx = 0$, and our expression reduces to

$$E_{sp} + E_g = \tfrac{1}{2}kx^2 + \tfrac{1}{2}kh^2 - mgh$$

Dropping the constant terms on the right, we get the desired result. Since adding or subtracting a constant from potential energy only changes the location of the zero point, we drop the constant terms on the right to get the desired result.

Problem 6.31. A block of mass $m = 10$ kg is first compressed 20 cm against a spring having force constant $k = 1000$ N/m, and then released, on a horizontal surface, as shown in Fig. 6-24. If the horizontal and inclined surfaces are both frictionless, through what maximum vertical height y will the block rise on the incline?

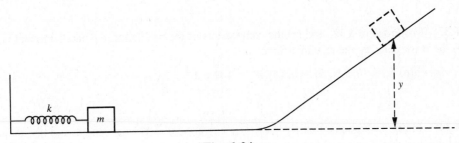

Fig. 6-24

Solution

Only gravity and the spring do work, so we have conservation of mechanical energy. The initial and final kinetic energies of the block are zero, so all the potential energy given up by the spring must appear as increased potential energy of gravity. Therefore we have

$$\tfrac{1}{2}(1000 \text{ N/m})(0.20 \text{ m})^2 = (10 \text{ kg})(9.8 \text{ m/s}^2)y \quad \text{or} \quad 20 \text{ J} = (98 \text{ N})y \quad \text{or} \quad y = 20.4 \text{ cm}$$

Supplementary Problems

Problem 6.32. A block on a frictionless inclined plane of length $L = 8.0$ m is acted on by the forces shown in Fig. 6-25.

(a) Find the work done by each force as the block moves down the entire length of the incline.

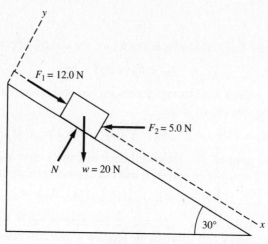

Fig. 6-25

(b) Find the total work done by all forces.

   Ans.   (a) $W_{F1} = 96.0$ J, $W_{F2} = -34.6$ J, $W_W = 80.0$ J, $W_N = 0.0$ J;

           (b) $W_T = 141.4$ J

Problem 6.33.   For Problem 6.32, find (a) the components of the resultant force parallel to and normal to the incline; (b) the work done by the resultant force.

   Ans.   (a) $R_x = 17.7$ N, $R_y = 0$; (b) $W_R = 141.6$ J

Problem 6.34.   In Fig. 6-4 assume that $F_2 = 40$ N, $w = 100$ N, $\theta = 37°$, $\mu_k = 0.25$, and that $\mathbf{F}_1$ points in the opposite direction to that shown and has magnitude 10 N. The displacement is $s = 12$ m. Calculate (a) N and f_k, (b) the work done by each force, (c) the total work done by all forces.

   Ans.   (a) $N = 106$ N, $f_k = 26.5$ N; (b) $W_{F2} = 480$ J, $W_{F1} = -96$ J, $W_f = -318$ J, $W_w = W_N = 0$;
           (c) $W_T = 66$ J

Problem 6.35.   For Problem 6.34, find (a) the x and y components of the resultant force, (b) the work done by the resultant force.

   Ans.   (a) $R_x = 5.50$ N, $R_y = 0$; (b) $W_R = 66$ J

Problem 6.36.

(a) For the situation of Problem 6.34, use the work–kinetic energy theorem to find the speed of the block at the end of the 12-m displacement, assuming the block started from rest.

(b) Through what additional displacement must the block move for the speed to be doubled?

(c) How would the answers to (a) and (b) change if there were no frictional force?

   Ans.   (a) 3.60 m/s; (b) 36 m; (c) 8.68 m/s, 36 m

Problem 6.37. A force **F**, varying in both magnitude and direction, acts on a block moving along the x axis. The $F \cos \theta$ vs. s curve for the block is shown in Fig. 6-26. Find the work done by the force in going from (a) $x = 0.0$ m to $x = 1.0$ m; (b) $x = 1.0$ m to $x = 2.0$ m; (c) $x = 2.0$ m to $x = 3.5$ m.

    Ans. (a) 40.0 J; (b) 30.0 J; (c) −22.5 J

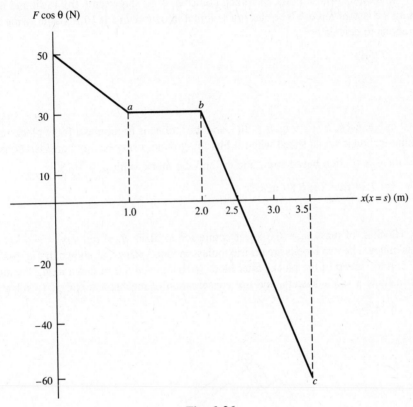

Fig. 6-26

Problem 6.38. Assume that the block in Problem 6.37 has mass $m = 5.0$ kg and that the given force represents the resultant force acting on the block. If the block is given an initial velocity $v_0 = 3.0$ m/s at $x = 0$, find its velocity at (a) $x = 1.0$ m, (b) $x = 2.0$ m, (c) $x = 3.5$ m.

    Ans. (a) 5.00 m/s; (b) 6.08 m/s; (c) 5.29 m/s

Problem 6.39. A block of mass $m = 20$ kg on a horizontal surface is given a speed of 30 m/s. The block comes to rest after traveling 150 m.

(a) Use work-energy considerations to determine the coefficient of kinetic friction μ_k.

(b) For the same μ_k, what would the block's initial speed have to be for it to stop after 75 m?

    Ans. (a) 0.306; (b) 21.2 m/s

Problem 6.40.

(a) Redo Problem 6.26(b) using the conservation of mechanical energy.

(b)   Assume now that, in addition to the given force, the object is acted on by a frictional force f_k = 15 N. Use the work–kinetic energy theorem to find the new value of the kinetic energy at x = 3.0 m.

Ans.   (a) 45 J; (b) 15 J

Problem 6.41.   An elevator whose mass, including contents, is 50 slugs starts from rest and is pulled upward by a cable exerting a constant force F. The elevator is found to be moving at 10 ft/s after rising 20 ft. Use work energy considerations to calculate F.

Ans.   1725 lb

Problem 6.42.

(a)   Assume that in Fig. 6-14, L = 1.5 m, θ = 30°, and the incline is frictionless. If the block starts from rest at the top of the incline, find its speed when it hits the ground, using energy considerations.

(b)   Redo (a) if there is friction between the incline and the block, with μ_k = 0.25.

Ans.   (a) 7.34 m/s; (b) 6.89 m/s

Problem 6.43.   Block A, of mass m_a = 6.0 kg, is connected to block B, of mass m_b = 4.0 kg, by a light cord over a frictionless pulley. The two blocks are on frictionless inclined planes, as shown in Fig. 6-27. If the system starts from rest, find the speed of the blocks after block A has moved 5.0 m down along the incline. Consider both blocks to constitute a single system, and use conservation of mechanical energy to solve the problem.

Ans.   4.84 m/s

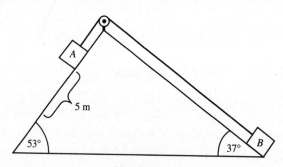

Fig. 6-27

Problem 6.44.   A 200-g block is compressed 10 cm against a spring of force constant k = 150 N/m while resting on a frictionless inclined plane. When the block is released, it is propelled by the spring up the incline. Through what vertical height will the block rise before coming to rest?

Ans.   38.3 cm

Problem 6.45.   Suppose that in Fig. 6-23 m = 15 kg and k = 400 N/m. If the block is stretched 40 cm below the equilibrium position and released, (a) what will its velocity be when it passes the equilibrium position?   (b) how high above the equilibrium position will it rise?

Ans.   (a) ±2.07 m/s; (b) 40 cm

Problem 6.46. Determine (*a*) the escape velocity from the surface of the moon, (*b*) the launch velocity for which a projectile will rise 500 km above the moon's surface. [Data: $G = 6.673 \times 10^{-11}$ N·m²/kg²; $M_{\text{moon}} = 7.36 \times 10^{22}$ kg; $R_{\text{moon}} = 1740$ km].

> *Ans.* (*a*) 2.38 km/s; (*b*) 1.12 km/s

Problem 6.47. A bead slides on a frictionless wire as shown in Fig. 6-28; the bead starts at a height of 5.5*R* above the base of the circular loop. Find the speed and the force exerted by the loop (*a*) at the topmost point, (*b*) at the bottommost point.

> *Ans.* (*a*) 351 cm/s, 1.47 N; (*b*) 440 cm/s, 2.94 N

Problem 6.48. A pendulum bob of mass $m = 1.2$ kg hangs at the end of a cord of length 2.2 m. The bob is drawn to one side until the cord makes an angle of 50° with the vertical, and then released. Find (*a*) the work done by gravity in moving the bob from the 50° position to the lowest point, (*b*) the tension in the cord at the lowest point.

> *Ans.* (*a*) 9.24 J; (*b*) 20.2 N

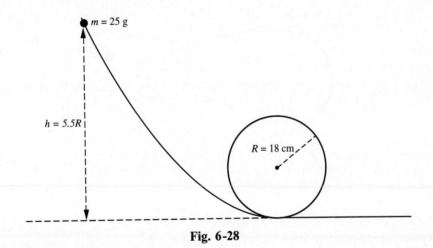

Fig. 6-28

Problem 6.49. A light spring ($k = 300$ N/m) rests on a horizontal frictionless surface with one end attached to a wall. A student slowly pulls the other end of the spring until it stretches 10 cm. She then hands it at that position to another student who slowly stretches it an additional 5.0 cm. Which student did more work, and how much more was it?

> *Ans.* The second student did 0.375 J more work.

Problem 6.50. Refer to Problem 6.45. (*a*) How high above equilibrium is the unstretched position? (*b*) What is the velocity of the block as it passes that point?

> *Ans.* (*a*) 36.8 cm; (*b*) ±0.81 m/s

Chapter 7

Energy, Power, and Simple Machines

7.1 GENERALIZATION OF CONSERVATION OF ENERGY

Thus far we have explored a number of conservative forces and the associated potential energies that can be used to represent the work they do. We have also encountered the force of friction and can ask if it too is conservative. Since friction always opposes the motion of an object, the work done by friction is always negative. If we move a block about on a tabletop where there is friction, as shown in Fig. 7-1, the work done by friction in going from a to b along path C_1 is negative, and so is the work done in going from b back to a along path C_2. Thus the total work done by friction in going around the closed loop (i.e., returning to its starting point) is not zero, and the force is not conservative.

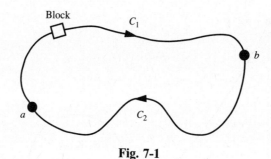

Fig. 7-1

Let us recall our earlier discussion of work being the mechanical transfer of energy between systems. A system doing positive work loses energy, and one doing negative work gains energy. Since friction always does negative work, the system that supplies the force of friction should always gain energy. But what sort of energy would this be? The source of friction is the interaction of the molecules in the surface layers of the two objects that are moving past each other and it is the energy of random jiggling of this vast number of molecules that increases. While such jiggling involves mechanical energy at the atomic level (including both kinetic energy of the molecules and potential energy of the forces between them), it is not mechanical energy on the macroscopic scale. Since the motion is random, it does not manifest itself in an organized group motion of all the molecules, as it does, for example, when a block is moving. When the block moves, all the molecules are also in motion, but in that case they are moving in unison. When the motion of the molecules is of a random nature, (describable, in fact, only by statistical means) we call the associated energy **thermal energy**. Such energy manifests itself macroscopically in various ways, most notably as a rise in temperature, and will be discussed in more detail in the section on heat and thermodynamics.

If we include in our considerations thermal energy, as well as other forms of energy such as electromagnetic radiation (light) and more subtle forms of mechanical energy such as sound, *the law of conservation of energy still holds*. Energy can be transformed from one type to another within a given system, and it can be transferred from one system to another system, but the total amount of energy stays the same.

Problem 7.1. Reexamine Problem 6.12(*b*) from the perspective of general energy conservation.

Solution

Consider the system composed of the block and the incline, as well as the gravitational interaction of the block with the earth. Initially, the system has zero kinetic energy, but the total energy includes the potential energy of the block at the top of the incline and whatever thermal energy the block and incline initially have. When the block reaches the bottom it has lost an amount of potential energy

$$mgh = (5.0 \text{ kg})(9.8 \text{ m/s}^2)(9.0 \text{ m}) = 441 \text{ J}$$

This energy must appear in the form of increased kinetic energy of the block and increased thermal energy of the system. The increase in thermal energy is a consequence of the negative work done by friction:

$$\text{Increase in thermal energy} = |W_f| = f_k L = (\mu_k mg \cos \theta)L = 177 \text{ J}$$

(as previously calculated in Problem 6.6(*b*)). The remainder of the potential energy lost by the block must appear as kinetic energy:

$$E_k = \tfrac{1}{2}mv_2{}^2 = 441 \text{ J} - 177 \text{ J} = 264 \text{ J} \qquad \text{whence} \qquad v_2 = 10.3 \text{ m/s}$$

(as before).

Problem 7.2. A block of mass $m = 6.5$ kg is released from rest at the top of a frictionless incline of height 3.0 m, as shown in Fig. 7-2. Upon reaching the bottom, the block slides a distance $L = 12$ m along a horizontal surface that has friction, until coming to rest.

(*a*) Using energy considerations, find the thermal energy gained by the system.

(*b*) Find the coefficient of friction μ_k between the block and the horizontal surface.

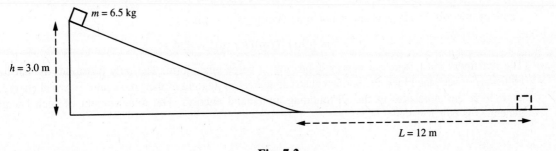

Fig. 7-2

Solution

(*a*) The kinetic energy of the block is zero at the beginning and at the end of the motion. Overall, the potential energy of the block decreases by an amount

$$mgh = (6.5 \text{ kg})(9.8 \text{ m/s}^2)(3.0 \text{ m}) = 191 \text{ J}$$

This energy thus reappears as 191 J of thermal energy gained along the horizontal section.

(*b*) Equating the gain in thermal energy to minus the work done by friction, we get

$$191 \text{ J} = -(-\mu_k mgL) = \mu_k(6.5 \text{ kg})(9.8 \text{ m/s}^2)(12 \text{ m}) = \mu_k(764 \text{ J}) \qquad \text{or} \qquad \mu_k = 0.250$$

Problem 7.3. A block of mass $m = 9.0$ kg is dropped onto a vertical light spring of force constant $k = 300$ N/m, as shown in Fig. 7-3(a). The block compresses the spring 1.7 m, as illustrated in Fig. 7-3(b). Find the amount of mechanical energy converted to thermal and sound energy due to the collision of the block with the spring.

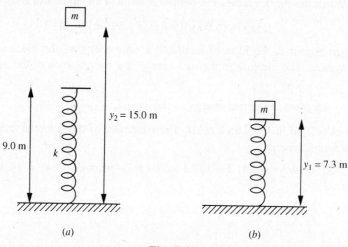

$$(a) \qquad\qquad\qquad (b)$$

Fig. 7-3

Solution

As in Problem 7.2, the initial and final kinetic energies of the block are zero. The amount of gravitational potential energy lost is

$$mg(y_2 - y_1) = (9.0 \text{ kg})(9.8 \text{ m/s}^2)(15.0 \text{ m} - 7.3 \text{ m}) = 679 \text{ J}$$

Some of this lost energy appears as potential energy of the spring:

$$\tfrac{1}{2}kx^2 = \tfrac{1}{2}(300 \text{ N/m})(1.7 \text{ m})^2 = 434 \text{ J}$$

The remainder must represent energy appearing in some other form. The only possibility is that the collision between the block and spring caused an increased jiggling of their molecules (thermal energy), as well as the molecules of the surrounding air (sound energy). The total amount of such energy generated is 679 J − 434 J = 245 J.

Problem 7.4. A ball of mass 1.5 kg is dropped from a height $h_1 = 3.0$ m above the floor, and the ball bounces straight back up. If 12.0 J of thermal energy is generated in the collision, to what height does the ball rebound?

Solution

The ball starts with no kinetic energy and with potential energy: $mgh_1 = (1.5 \text{ kg})$ $(9.8 \text{ m/s}^2)(3.0 \text{ m}) = 44.1$ J. When the ball rebounds to its maximum height h_2, it again has no kinetic energy, and its potential energy is mgh_2. Since 12.0 J disappears in the collision, we have $mgh_2 + 12.0 \text{ J} = 44.1$ J, or

$$(1.5 \text{ kg})(9.8 \text{ m/s}^2)h_2 = 32.1 \text{ J} \qquad \text{or} \qquad h_2 = 2.18 \text{ m}$$

7.2 POWER

Average Power

We now turn to the question of the *rate* at which work is done, that is, how much work is done per second by a force. The average power P_{av} delivered by a force in a time Δt is defined as the work ΔW done by the force in the time Δt, divided by Δt: $P_{av} = \Delta W/\Delta t$. The SI unit of power is the watt (W), where 1 W = 1 joule/second = 1 J/s. A related unit is the kilowatt, equal to 1000 W. Other units are ergs/s and ft·lb/s. In the English system of units a special unit of power called the horsepower (hp) is defined: 1 hp = 550 ft·lb/s. A calculation shows that 1 hp $\approx$ 0.75 kW.

Problem 7.5. A horizontal force $F = 10$ N pulls a block of mass $m = 2.0$ kg along a frictionless horizontal surface. If the block starts from rest, find the average power delivered by the force (*a*) in the first 5.0 s; (*b*) between $t = 3.0$ s and $t = 5.0$ s. (*c*) How would the answers to (*a*) and (*b*) change if the force made an angle of 30° with the horizontal?

Solution

(*a*) To find the work done in the first 5 s we need the displacement. Since the force is constant, the acceleration is also constant, and we have $x = x_0 + v_0 t + \frac{1}{2}at^2$; for our case $x_0 = v_0 = 0$ and $a = F/m = (10$ N$)/(2.0$ kg$) = 5.0$ m/s^2. Thus $x = (2.5$ m/s$^2)t^2$. Substituting $t = 5.0$ s we get $x = 62.5$ m, and $\Delta W = Fx = (10$ N$)(62.5$ m$) = 625$ J. Finally,

$$P_{av} = \frac{\Delta W}{\Delta t} = \frac{625 \text{ J}}{5.0 \text{ s}} = 125 \text{ W}$$

(*b*) Here $P_{av} = \Delta W/\Delta t = F\,\Delta x/\Delta t$, where $\Delta t = 5.0$ s $- 3.0$ s $= 2.0$ s, and $\Delta x = x_5 - x_3$. We have from (*a*) that $x_5 = 62.5$ m, and we find that $x_3 = (2.5$ m/s$^2)(3.0$ s$)^2 = 22.5$ m. Thus $\Delta x = 40.0$ m. Finally, we get

$$P_{av} = \frac{(10 \text{ N})(40.0 \text{ m})}{2.0 \text{ s}} = 200 \text{ W}$$

(*c*) In this case the work is due only to the horizontal component of the force **F**: $F_x = F \cos 30° = 0.866F$. The x displacements in a given time interval are all proportional to the acceleration (since $x = \frac{1}{2}at^2$ for our initial conditions), and the acceleration is now due to the force $F_x = 0.866F$, and is therefore reduced by the factor 0.866 as well. Calling the new acceleration **a**' we have **a**' = 0.866**a**. Thus the force doing the work is reduced by a multiplicative factor of 0.866, and the displacements are also down by a multiplicative factor of 0.866. Thus the work in any time interval is down by $(0.866)^2 = 0.75$, and the new average powers will just be 0.75 times the original ones.

Instantaneous Power

In the case of one-dimensional motion with the force along the direction of motion we saw in Problem 7.5 that

$$P_{av} = F \frac{\Delta x}{\Delta t} = F \frac{x_2 - x_1}{t_2 - t_1} \tag{7.1}$$

We define the instantaneous power P at the time t_1 as the limit as $t_2 \to t_1$ (or the limit as $\Delta t \to 0$) of P_{av}. But in this limit, $\Delta x/\Delta t \to v$, the instantaneous velocity. Then Eq. (*7.1*) becomes

$$P = Fv \tag{7.2}$$

This can easily be generalized to the case of an object moving on an arbitrary path and acted on by a force that makes an angle θ with the tangent to the path. The situation is depicted in Fig. 7-4. If Δs is a small incremental arc length moved through in the time interval Δt, then $\Delta W = F \cos \theta \, \Delta s$ and $P_{av} = \Delta W / \Delta t$, or

$$P_{av} = F \cos \theta \, \frac{\Delta s}{\Delta t} \qquad (7.3)$$

In the limit as $\Delta t \to 0$, we have that $\Delta s / \Delta t = v$, the magnitude of the instantaneous velocity. Thus, in general, the instantaneous power is given by

$$P = F \cos \theta \, v \qquad (7.4)$$

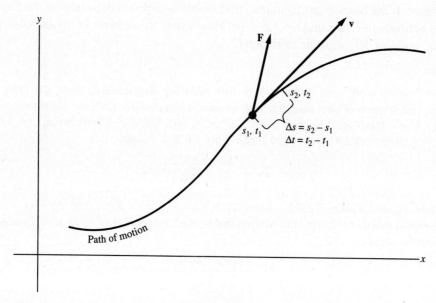

Fig. 7-4

Problem 7.6.

(a) Referring back to Problem 7.5, find the instantaneous power generated by the force F at $t = 2.0$, 3.0, 4.0, and 5.0 s.

(b) Repeat for the case of Problem 7.5, part (c)

Solution

(a) For this one-dimensional case we have Eq. (7.2): $P = Fv$. We also have that $v = v_0 + at$. Since $v_0 = 0$, $v = at = (5.0 \text{ m/s}^2)t$, from which we get $v_2 = 10.0$ m/s; $v_3 = 15.0$ m/s; $v_4 = 20.0$ m/s; $v_5 = 25.0$ m/s. Recalling that $F = 10$ N, we have $P_2 = 100$ W; $P_3 = 150$ W; $P_4 = 200$ W; $P_5 = 250$ W.

(b) In this case the power is $P' = F \cos \theta \, v' = 0.866Fv'$, where v' is the velocity for the new situation. Since the new acceleration is due to F_x, we have $a' = 0.866a \Rightarrow v' = a't = 0.866at = 0.866v$. Thus $P' = (0.866)^2 Fv = 0.75Fv = 0.75P$. Thus all values of power are reduced to 0.75 of their original values, just as was concluded for the average powers of Problem 7.5(c).

Problem 7.7.   A horse pulls a cart along a level road at 25 ft/s. If the net horizontal force exerted by the horse on the cart is 40 lb, how much horsepower is the horse delivering to the cart?

Solution

$P = Fv = (40 \text{ lb})(25 \text{ ft/s}) = 1000 \text{ ft} \cdot \text{lb/s}$. To convert to horsepower we divide by $(550 \text{ ft} \cdot \text{lb/s})/\text{hp}$ to get $P = 1.82$ hp.

Problem 7.8.   A truck travels along a level roadway at 60 mph (88 ft/s). At that speed, air resistance and internal frictional forces are such that an effective forward force of 3000 lb is necessary to keep the truck from slowing down. What power must be delivered by the truck's engine to keep the truck going at constant speed?

Solution

$$P = \frac{(3000 \text{ lb})(88 \text{ ft/s})}{550 \text{ ft} \cdot \text{lb}/(\text{s} \cdot \text{hp})} = 480 \text{ hp.}$$

Note.   This is really a much more complex situation than appears at first glance. The actual forward force is supplied by the static frictional force of the ground on the tires. Since the point of contact of the tires with the ground has no horizontal motion if there is no skidding, this force does no work! This is made more obvious by the fact that the ground is just a passive system and not one supplying energy to the truck. The actual work is done by the engine through the action of the drive shaft. This is an example of a system where "internal work" is done by one part of a complicated system on another. An even simpler example of this is the case of a child on ice skates pushing himself off from the ice rink wall. Clearly the force due to the wall accelerates the child, building up kinetic energy, but the wall force does no work since the hands it pushes are at rest against it. The energy is delivered by the internal work of the muscles of the child.

Problem 7.9.   In Problem 7.8, assume the truck engine has a maximum power capacity of 600 hp, and the truck weighs 8000 lb. What is the steepest incline that the truck can drive up and maintain its speed of 60 mph?

Solution

It takes 480 hp to just keep the truck moving at the constant speed on level ground. This leaves 120 hp to increase the potential energy E_p as the truck moves up the incline. Thus 120 hp = 66,000 ft $\cdot$ lb/s = $\Delta E_p/\Delta t$, the increase of potential energy per second. The situation is depicted in Fig. 7-5. $\Delta E_p/\Delta t = mg \, \Delta h/\Delta t$, where Δh is the increase in height in an infinitesimal time Δt. But $\Delta h/\Delta t$ is just the vertical component of the truck's velocity v_y, so $\Delta E_p/\Delta t = mgv_y$. If θ is the angle of the incline, then $v_y = v \sin \theta$, and $\Delta E_p/\Delta t = mgv \sin \theta = (8000 \text{ lb})(88 \text{ ft/s}) \sin \theta = 66,000 \text{ ft} \cdot \text{lb/s}$ (from before). Solving for $\sin \theta$ we get

$$\sin \theta = 0.0938 \quad \text{or} \quad \theta = 5.38°$$

Problem 7.10.   An electric light bulb rated at 100 W is left on for 10 days and nights.

(*a*)   How much energy was expended?

(*b*)   For how long must an electric heater rated at 3500 W be left on to expend the same amount of energy?

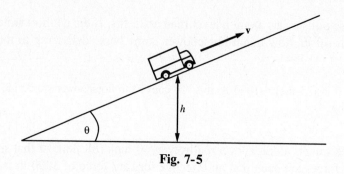

Fig. 7-5

Solution

(a) For the case of constant power, from the definition we have $E = Pt$, where E is the total energy expended in joules, P is the constant power generated in watts, and t is the elapsed time in seconds. A period of 10 days and nights corresponds to 240 h. Noting that there are 3600 s/h we get $t = (240 \text{ h})(3600 \text{ s/h}) = 8.64 \times 10^5$ s. Then

$$E = (100 \text{ W})(8.64 \times 10^5 \text{ s}) = 8.64 \times 10^7 \text{ J} = 86.4 \text{ MJ}$$

(b) Now

$$P't' = (3500 \text{ W})t' = 8.64 \times 10^7 \text{ J} \quad \text{or} \quad t' = 24{,}700 \text{ s} = 6.86 \text{ h}$$

Problem 7.11. For purposes of charging customers for energy usage, power companies use a special unit of energy, the kilowatthour (kWh) defined as the energy expended by a 1-kW power source operating for 1 hour.

(a) How many joules are there in 1 kWh?

(b) How many kilowatthours of energy are expended by the light bulb of Problem 7.10(a).
      Solution

(a) 1 kWh = (1000 J/s)(3600 s) = 3,600,000 J.

(b) $E = \dfrac{8.64 \times 10^7 \text{ J}}{3.60 \times 10^6 \text{ J/kWh}} = 24.0$ kWh.

7.3   SIMPLE MACHINES

A **simple machine** is any device that allows a small force to move an object against a larger resisting force, or a force in one direction to move an object against a resisting force in another direction. Many simple machines do both. Examples shown in Fig. 7-6 are (a) the **lever**, (b) the **inclined plane**, and (c) a **pulley system**. In all three cases we assume the applied force F_A is the minimum force needed to move the weight, (or "load"), w (that is, to move it with essentially zero acceleration).

Mechanical Advantage

The ratio of the load to the applied force is called the **mechanical advantage** (MA) of the machine. Clearly, the bigger the mechanical advantage the smaller the applied force necessary to accomplish the task. In any simple machine, the applied force F_A necessary when no frictional forces must be overcome will be smaller than F'_A, the applied force necessary when there are frictional forces.

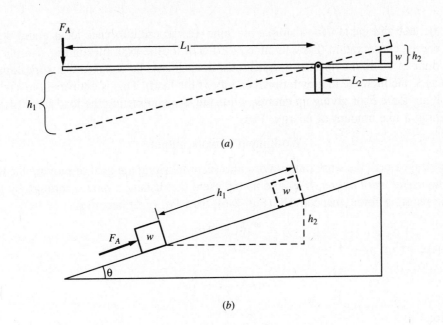

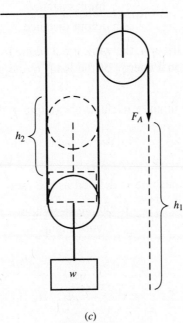

Fig. 7-6

When there is no friction we have the best or the "ideal" MA: (IMA)

$$\text{IMA} = \frac{w}{F_A} \qquad (7.5a)$$

The actual MA is given by

$$\text{MA} = \frac{w}{F_A'} \qquad (7.5b)$$

and is always smaller than the IMA because there are always frictional losses.

To find the IMA and the MA for a simple machine we can use our basic ideas about work-energy, and general energy conservation. If we assume no friction for the examples in Fig. 7-6, then the work input (work done by F_A in moving the weight) must in each case be equal to the work output (for our frictionless cases, the increase in gravitational energy of the load). This is equivalent to saying that the system supplying force F_A is giving up energy, while the system exerting the load force (gravity in our cases) is gaining a like amount of energy. Thus:

$$\text{Work input} = \text{work output} \qquad (7.6)$$

Since in this ideal case all the work output goes into accomplishing the goal of moving the weight, it is also called the *useful work output*. If h_1 and h_2 represent the distances moved through by the applied force and the resisting force, respectively (Fig. 7-6), then Eq. (7.6) becomes

$$F_A h_1 = w h_2 \qquad (7.7)$$

Then, from Eqs. (7.5a) and (7.7)

$$\text{IMA} = \frac{w}{F_A} = \frac{h_1}{h_2} \qquad (7.8a)$$

In other words

$$\text{IMA} = \frac{\text{input distance}}{\text{output distance}} \qquad (7.8b)$$

If, on the other hand, there is friction, the work input (done by F_A') must be larger than the useful work output (increase in gravitational energy of the load) by an amount equal to the thermal energy generated by the frictional forces:

$$\text{Work input} = \text{work output} = \text{useful work output} + \text{thermal energy increase} \qquad (7.9)$$

Efficiency

The efficiency e of a simple machine is defined as the ratio

$$e = \frac{\text{useful work output}}{\text{work input}} \qquad (7.10a)$$

For our examples this is just

$$e = \frac{w h_2}{F_A' h_1} \qquad (7.10b)$$

Using Eq. (7.7) this becomes

$$e = \frac{F_A h_1}{F_A' h_1} = \frac{F_A}{F_A'} \qquad (7.10c)$$

Thus

$$e = \frac{\text{ideal applied force}}{\text{actual applied force}} \qquad (7.10d)$$

From Eq. (7.10c) we can determine yet another expression for e, in terms of MA and IMA:

$$e = \frac{F_A}{F_A'} = \frac{w/F_A'}{w/F_A} = \frac{\text{MA}}{\text{IMA}} \qquad (7.10e)$$

Equations (7.8b), (7.9), (7.10a), (7.10d), and (7.10e) are general expressions that are true for any simple machines.

Problem 7.12. Assume that for the lever in Fig. 7-6(a), $L_1 = 6.0$ m and $L_2 = 1.5$ m, and that $w = 100$ N.

(a) If there is no friction in the pivot, find the force F_A necessary to just lift the weight w, and find the IMA of the machine.

(b) If the actual force needed is $F_A' = 28$ N, find the efficiency of the machine.

(c) For part (b), how much thermal energy is generated at the pivot if the weight is lifted 10 cm?

Solution

(a) If the weight is lifted through a small distance h_2, the force F_A will act through a corresponding distance h_1. Then from work-energy: $F_A h_1 = w h_2$ or $F_A = w(h_2/h_1)$. But by similar triangles we must have $h_2/h_1 = L_2/L_1 = 0.25$, so $F_A = (100 \text{ N})(0.25) = 25$ N. Also, IMA $= w/F_A = h_1/h_2 = L_1/L_2 = 4.0$. (This same result could be obtained by balancing torques about the pivot. Torques will be discussed in Chap. 9.)

(b) MA $= w/F_A' = 100/28 = 3.57$; $e =$ MA/IMA $= 3.57/4.0 = 0.893 = 89.3\%$.

(c) $h_2 = 0.10$ m $\Rightarrow h_1 = 0.40$ m $\Rightarrow$ work input $= F_A' h_1 = (28 \text{ N})(0.40 \text{ m}) = 11.2$ J.   Useful   work output $= w h_2 = F_A h_1 = (25 \text{ N})(0.40 \text{ m}) = 10.0$ J.   Therefore   the   thermal   energy $= 11.2$ J $- 10.0$ J $= 1.2$ J. [Or, since we have 89.3% efficiency, 10.7% of the work input is wasted as thermal energy: $0.107(11.2 \text{ J}) = 1.2$ J, as before.]

Problem 7.13. For the inclined plane in Fig. 7-6(b), assume $\theta = 30°$ and $w = 100$ N.

(a) Find an expression for the IMA of this simple machine.

(b) If the coefficient of friction between block and incline is $\mu_k = 0.25$, find the true MA and the efficiency of the machine.

(c) Using the results of part (b), find the thermal heat loss when $h_2 = 35$ cm.

Solution

(a) IMA $= w/F_A$. If there is no friction, then, balancing force components along the incline: $F_A = w \sin \theta \Rightarrow$ IMA $= 1.0/\sin \theta = 1.0/\sin 30° = 2.0$. [Or, from Eqs. (7.8) and Fig. 7-6(b), IMA $= h_1/h_2 = 1.0/\sin \theta$.]

(b) MA $= w/F_A'$. Again balancing components of force along the incline, but now including friction, we get $F_A' - w \sin \theta - f_k = 0$ or $F_A' - w \sin \theta - \mu_k W \cos \theta = 0 \Rightarrow F_A' = w(\sin \theta + \mu_k \cos \theta)$. Then

$$\text{MA} = \frac{1.0}{\sin \theta + \mu_k \cos \theta} = \frac{1/0}{0.50 + 0.25 \times 0.866} = \frac{1.0}{0.717} = 1.40$$

$$e = \frac{\text{MA}}{\text{IMA}} = \frac{1.40}{2.0} = 0.70$$

(Or, equivalently, $e = F_A/F_A' = 50/71.7 = 0.70$.)

(c) Work input $=$ (useful work output)$/e = w h_2/e = (100 \text{ N})(0.35 \text{ m})/(0.70) = 35$ J$/0.70 = 50$ J. Then the thermal loss $= 50$ J $- 35$ J $= 15$ J. (Or, thermal loss $= 30\%$ of work input, while useful work output $= 70\%$ of work input $\Rightarrow$ thermal loss $= \frac{3}{7}$ (useful work output) $= \frac{3}{7}(35 \text{ J}) = 15$ J.)

Problem 7.14. Consider the pulley system shown in Fig. 7-6(*c*), with weight $w = 100$ N.

(*a*) What is the value of the applied force and the IMA of the machine if both pulleys are massless and frictionless and the cord is light?

(*b*) If the movable pulley from which the weight w is suspended is now assumed to weigh $w_p = 5$ N, but all friction can still be ignored, what is the new value of the applied force, and the MA.

(*c*) What is the efficiency of the machine under the conditions of part (*b*)?

Solution

(*a*) As can be seen from Fig. 7-6(*c*), when the weight moves up a distance h_2, twice that length of cord has been pulled down by the applied force. Thus, $h_1 = 2h_2$. Then, using Eq (7.8) we have

$$\text{IMA} = \frac{w}{F_A} = \frac{h_1}{h_2} = 2.0 \quad \text{or} \quad F_A = 0.5w = (0.5)(100\text{ N}) = 50\text{ N}$$

(*b*) In this case, the applied force is $F_A' = 0.5(100\text{ N} + 5.0\text{ N}) = 52.5$ N. Even though there is no frictional loss, the useful work output relates only to the lifting of the weight w, so

$$\text{MA} = \frac{w}{F_A'} = \frac{100}{52.5} = 1.90$$

(*c*) The efficiency of the machine e is the ratio of useful work output to work input:

$$e = \frac{F_A h_1}{F_A' h_1} = \frac{F_A}{F_A'} = \frac{\text{MA}}{\text{IMA}} = \frac{1.90}{2.0} = 0.95$$

Note. There are many additional simple machines, such as the wedge, the screw, the jackscrew and more complicated pulley systems. In all cases, the basic work-energy approach discussed above can be used to analyze the IMA, the MA, and the efficiency e of the machine.

Problems for Review and Mind Stretching

Problem 7.15. Reconsider Problem 6.31 if there is friction and the frictional forces do a total of $W_f = -15$ J of work. To what maximum vertical height would the block rise on the incline?

Solution

We approach the problem from an energy balance point of view. As in the Problem 6.31 the kinetic energy is zero at the beginning and at the end. Now, however, the energy given up by the spring goes partly into building up the thermal energy of the surfaces so that less is available to build up gravitational potential energy. Thus $\frac{1}{2}(1000\text{ N/m})(0.20\text{ m})^2 = 15$ J $+ (98\text{ N})y$ or 20 J $= 15$ J $+ (98\text{ N})y \Rightarrow y = 5.1$ cm.

Problem 7.16. A 25,000-kg airplane starts from rest on the runway, takes off, and reaches an altitude of 5000 m and a speed of 250 m/s, all in a time of 8.0 min.

(*a*) Assuming no thermal losses, what is the average power generated by the airplane engines during this period?

(b)   Assuming that the average engine output was 1.3 times the power output of part (a), how much thermal energy loss was there during that period?

Solution

(a) $P_{av} = \Delta W/\Delta t$. From the work-energy theorem, $\Delta W = \Delta E_k + \Delta E_p$. Since the airplane starts from rest, ΔE_k = final kinetic energy = $\frac{1}{2}(25{,}000 \text{ kg})(250 \text{ m/s})^2 = 7.81 \times 10^8$ J. Choosing ground level as the zero of potential energy, ΔE_p = final potential energy = $(25{,}000 \text{ kg})(9.8 \text{ m/s}^2)$ $(5000 \text{ m}) = 1.23 \times 10^9$ J.   Then $\Delta W = 0.78 \times 10^9$ J $+ 1.23 \times 10^9$ J $= 2.01 \times 10^9$ J.   Noting that $\Delta t = (8 \text{ min})(60 \text{ s/min}) = 480$ s, we get

$$P_{av} = \frac{2.01 \times 10^9 \text{ J}}{480 \text{ s}} = 4.19 \times 10^6 \text{ W} = 4190 \text{ kW}$$

(b)   The average power lost to thermal sources is $0.3(4.190 \times 10^6 \text{ W}) = 1.26 \times 10^6$ W. The total thermal energy loss in 8 min is thus $(1.26 \times 10^6 \text{ W})(480 \text{ s}) = 6.05 \times 10^8$ J.

Problem 7.17.   A tugboat pulls a barge directly behind it at a speed of 4.0 m/s. The tugboat's engines generate 700 kW of power, of which 60% is needed just to keep the tugboat alone moving at that speed.

(a)   Find the tension in the rope connecting the tug and barge.

(b)   If the tugboat was in front but slightly to the side of the barge so that the connecting rope made a 20 ° angle with the direction of motion, what would the tension now be?

Solution

(a)   40% of the tugboat's engine power goes to moving the barge. So, calling this amount of power P_{barge}, we get $P_{\text{barge}} = 0.40(700 \text{ kW}) = 280$ kW. Let T be the tension in the rope.

$$P_{\text{barge}} = Tv \quad \text{or} \quad T = \frac{P_{\text{barge}}}{v} = \frac{280 \text{ kW}}{4.0 \text{ m/s}} = 70.0 \text{ kN}$$

(b)   Now $T \cos 20° = 70.0$ kN, or $T = 74.5$ kN.

Problem 7.18.

(a)   In Fig. 7-7 assume all the pulleys are massless and frictionless. Use energy considerations to determine the force F necessary to just lift a weight $w = 50$ lb.

(b)   If there were some friction in the pulleys and their mass were not negligible, the force F would have to be larger than in part (a). If the force F was in fact 20% larger than in part (a), what is the efficiency of this simple machine, and what fraction of the work done by F is converted into potential energy of the weight w?

Solution

(a)   If the weight and the two massless pulleys to which it is attached move up a distance h_2, the amount of slack let out in the cords is $2h_2$ about each moved pulley. Thus, $h_1 = 4.0h_2$ and

$$F = 0.25w = (0.25)(50 \text{ lb}) = 12.5 \text{ lb}$$

(b) $F' = 1.2F$, so $e = F/F' = 0.833$. This means that 83.3% of the work input is used to lift the weight and hence is converted to potential energy of the weight.

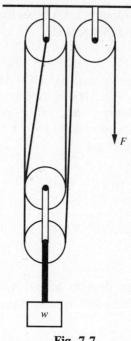

Fig. 7-7

Problem 7.19. A jackscrew that can be used to lift a weight w is shown in Fig. 7-8. The **pitch** p of the screw is defined as the vertical height through which the screw moves when it is turned through 360°. The lever arm L is measured from the axis of the screw. The turning force F_A is applied horizontally, and perpendicular to the lever arm.

(a) Find F_A in the ideal case of no friction, and find the IMA.

(b) If the jackscrew has an efficiency of 15.0%, find the MA and the actual force F'_A necessary to lift the weight.

Solution

(a) Work input = work output $\Rightarrow$ (for one complete turn) $F_A(2\pi L) = W(p)$ or $F_A(6.28)(0.30 \text{ m}) = (1200 \text{ kg})(9.8 \text{ m/s}^2)(0.0035 \text{ m}) \Rightarrow F_A = 21.8 \text{ N}$. IMA $= W/F_A = 2\pi L/p = 539$.

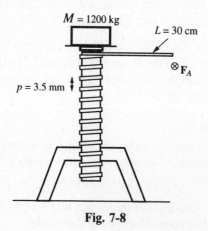

Fig. 7-8

(b) $e = F_A/F_A' \Rightarrow F_A' = F_A/e = 21.8$ N/0.15 = 145 N.   Also, $e = \text{MA}/\text{IMA} \Rightarrow \text{MA} = e(\text{IMA}) =$
0.15(539) = 81. [Or, MA $= W/F_A' = (1200$ kg)(9.8 m/s^2)/145 N = 81.]

Supplementary Problems

Problem 7.20.   Refer to Problem 6.47 and to Fig. 6-28. If the straightaway following the loop has friction ($\mu_k = 0.40$) and the rest of the track is smooth (a) how far along the straightaway will the bead slide? (b) Repeat (a) for a starting height of 11.0 R.

> *Ans.*   (a) 2.48 m; (b) 4.95 m

Problem 7.21.   A bullet of mass 150 g is fired with velocity 300 m/s into the trunk of a tree and penetrates to a depth of 8.0 cm. Find (a) the thermal energy generated; (b) the average resistive force of the tree over the 8.0-cm distance.

> *Ans.*   (a) 6750 J; (b) 84,400 N

Problem 7.22.   In Problem 6.48, how much work is done by a person moving the bob to the 50° position?

> *Ans.*   9.24 J

Problem 7.23.   A 5.0-kg projectile is fired vertically upward from the ground level with initial velocity $v_0 = 100$ m/s. By the time it reaches the highest point, 4 kJ of thermal energy has been generated due to air resistance. How high does the projectile rise?

> *Ans.*   429 m

Problem 7.24.   A rifle fires a 20-g bullet with a muzzle velocity of 3000 m/s. The barrel of the gun is 0.80 m long.

(a)   If a thermal energy of 40,000 J is generated when the gun is fired, what is the *total* energy released in the gunpowder explosion that projects the bullet out of the barrel?

(b)   What is the average force exerted on the bullet as it moves down the gun barrel?

> *Ans.*   (a) 130,000 J; (b) 112,500 N

Problem 7.25.   Assume that the net force acting on the bullet in Problem 7.24 while in the barrel is constant.

(a)   What is the time of flight down the barrel?

(b)   What is the time-average power exerted on the bullet?

> *Ans.*   (a) 533 μs; (b) $P_{av} = $ KE/$t = 169$ MW

Problem 7.26.   A water-skier is pulled by a motorboat in such a way that the towline makes a 40° angle with the skier's direction of motion. The skier is moving at a constant speed of 18 m/s, and the tension in the line is 40 N. How much power is needed?

> *Ans.*   552 W

Problem 7.27. When an object falls from a great height, the air resistance exerts an upward force that increases with the speed. Eventually the air resistance just balances the force of gravity, and from that moment on the object descends at a constant speed called the **terminal velocity**. Assume that an object weighing 80 lb has reached a terminal velocity of 110 ft/s when it is 1000 ft above the ground.

(a) Find the power, in hp, exerted on the object by the force of gravity as it descends with terminal velocity.

(b) Find the total thermal energy generated by the air resistance in the last 1000 ft before the object reaches the ground.

> *Ans.*   (a) 16.0 hp; (b) 80,000 ft · lb

Problem 7.28. An engine delivers a power of 30 kW in pulling a block horizontally along a level surface at a constant speed of 12 m/s. If the block has a mass of 500 kg, find (a) the frictional force between the block and the surface, and (b) the coefficient of friction.

> *Ans.*   (a) 2500 N; (b) 0.51

Problem 7.29. A 2000-lb car accelerates from 0 to 60 mph (88 ft/s) in 7.0 s on a straight, level track. Assuming no frictional losses, what minimum power must the engine have to accomplish this?

> *Ans.*   62.5 hp

Problem 7.30.

(a) A 5000-kg truck coasts down a steep (22°) hill in low gear without using the brakes and reaches a constant speed of 12.0 m/s. Find the thermal power generated due to friction in the drivetrain. (Ignore all other sources of friction, including air resistance). What is the source supplying that power to the truck?

(b) If the truck were "in neutral" (with the drivetrain disconnected from the wheels) and the brakes were used instead, how much thermal power would have to be generated in the brakes to keep the truck moving at 12.0 m/s?

> *Ans.*   (a) 220 kW, the force of gravity; (b) 220 kW

Problem 7.31. A student uses a pulley system to hoist physics lecture notes weighing 200 lb to a height of 20 ft. To accomplish this the student exerts a force of 30 lb and pulls a total of 200 ft of rope.

(a) Find the IMA, the MA, and the efficiency of the pulley system.

(b) If the student takes 25 s, what average power did he exert?

> *Ans.*   (a) 10.0, 6.67, 66.7%; (b) 240 ft · lb/s

Problem 7.32.

(a) For the lever system in Fig. 7-9(a), find the IMA and the force F needed to lift the weight in the ideal case.

(b) If the efficiency is 85%, find the MA and the actual force F' necessary to lift the weight.

> *Ans.*   (a) 3.0, 98 N; (b) 2.55, 115 N

Problem 7.33. Repeat Problem 7.32 for the machine of Fig. 7-9(b).

> *Ans.*   (a) 4.0, 12.5 lb; (b) 3.4, 14.7 lb

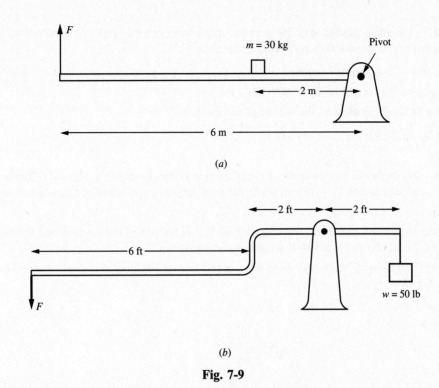

(a)

(b)

Fig. 7-9

Problem 7.34.   Water is pulled up from a well by means of a bucket connected to the handle-and-axle system shown in Fig. 7-10. The rope is wound on the axle as the handle is turned. If a force $F = 28$ lb is necessary to turn the handle while raising a 100-lb bucket, what is the efficiency of the simple machine?

Ans.   89%

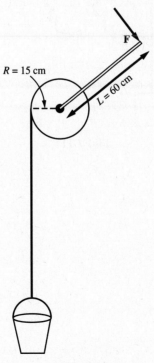

Fig. 7-10

Problem 7.35. A trunk is pushed up a 20° inclined plane from ground level to a platform 1.2 m above the ground by applying a force of 100 N parallel to the incline.

(*a*)   Find the IMA of this simple machine.

(*b*)   If this machine has an efficiency of 80%, find the MA.

(*c*)   Assuming 80% efficiency, find the weight of the trunk.

> *Ans.*   (*a*) 2.92; (*b*) 2.34; (*c*) 234 N

Problem 7.36. A simple machine consists of a meshed gear system as shown in Fig. 7-11. The handle on gear 1 sweeps out a circle of radius $R_1 = 40$ cm, while the axle on gear 2 (on which the rope winds up) has radius $R_2 = 10$ cm.

(*a*)   If there are 10 teeth on gear 1 and 50 teeth on gear 2, find the IMA of the machine and the turning force F needed on the handle to lift a 500-N weight in the ideal case.

(*b*)   If in general the ratio of the number of teeth on gear 2 to gear 1 is labeled N, find a general expression for the IMA for arbitrary R_1, R_2 and N.

> *Ans.*   (*a*) 20, 25 N; (*b*) IMA $= NR_1/R_2$

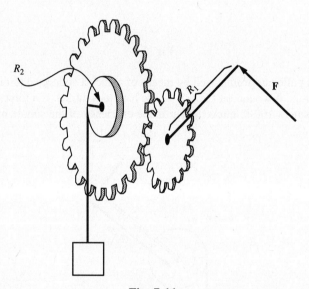

Fig. 7-11

Chapter 8

Impulse and Linear Momentum

8.1 IMPULSE

Impulse of a Constant Force

If a constant force $\mathbf{F}$ acts on an object for a time t, then the impulse $\mathbf{I}$ due to the force $\mathbf{F}$ is defined as

$$\mathbf{I} = \mathbf{F}t \tag{8.1}$$

Note that this is a vector equation, and $\mathbf{I}$ points along $\mathbf{F}$ since t is a positive scalar. If we restrict ourselves to two-dimensional problems (the xy plane), Eq. (8.1) is equivalent to the component equations

$$I_x = F_x t \qquad \text{and} \qquad I_y = F_y t \tag{8.2}$$

Figure 8-1(a) shows a simple situation in which a constant horizontal force $\mathbf{F}$ pulls a block along a tabletop. The impulse $\mathbf{I}$, due to $\mathbf{F}$, is depicted for the given time interval t. The units of impulse are those of force times time and therefore are $\text{N} \cdot \text{s}$, $\text{dyn} \cdot \text{s}$, or $\text{lb} \cdot \text{s}$, depending on the system of units being used.

If more than one constant force acts on the block for the time t, then the total impulse is just the vector sum of the impulses. Thus, in Fig. 8-1(b), the same block is shown again, but this time with the other forces acting: the weight, the normal force, and a kinetic frictional force. The total impulse is

$$\mathbf{I}_T = \mathbf{I}_F + \mathbf{I}_w + \mathbf{I}_N + \mathbf{I}_f = \mathbf{F}t + \mathbf{w}t + \mathbf{N}t + \mathbf{f}t = (\mathbf{F} + \mathbf{w} + \mathbf{N} + \mathbf{f})t$$

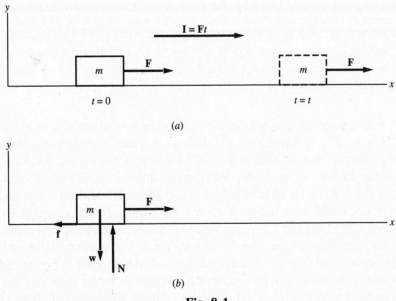

(a)

(b)

Fig. 8-1

Since the term in parentheses on the right is just the resultant force, we have that the total impulse equals the impulse of the resultant force.

From Fig. 8-1(*b*) we see that the *x* and *y* component equations for $\mathbf{I}_T$ are

$$(I_T)_x = (F - f)t \quad \text{and} \quad (I_T)_y = (N - w)t$$

Since there is equilibrium in the *y* direction, we have $N = w$ and $(I_T)_y = 0$. The total impulse is thus in the *x* direction and involves a positive contribution from $\mathbf{F}$ and a negative contribution from $\mathbf{f}$.

Problem 8.1.

(*a*) Assume that the force $\mathbf{F}$ in Fig. 8-1(*a*) has a magnitude of 100 N and the time $t = 8$ s. Find the impulse due to $\mathbf{F}$ in the 8-s interval.

(*b*) Suppose that after time $t = 8$ s the force $\mathbf{F}$ was changed to 300 N and acted on the block for an additional 8 s. What would the impulse be in the second 8 s?

(*c*) Suppose that after this second 8-s interval, the force $\mathbf{F}$ were changed again, this time to 400 N acting in the negative *x* direction, and that the force acted for an additional 4 s. What would the impulse be in this third time interval?

Solution

(*a*) The impulse clearly is in the *x* direction: $I_x = Ft = (100 \text{ N})(8 \text{ s}) = 800 \text{ N} \cdot \text{s}$.

(*b*) Again the impulse is in the *x* direction: $I_x = (300 \text{ N})(8 \text{ s}) = 2400 \text{ N}$.

(*c*) Here the impulse clearly points in the negative *x* direction: $I_x = (-400 \text{ N})(4 \text{ s}) = -1600 \text{ N}$.

Problem 8.2.   In Fig. 8-1(*b*) assume that $F = 50$ lb, $w = 30$ lb, and the coefficient of kinetic friction is $\mu_k = 0.5$. Find the total impulse in a 6-s time interval.

Solution

The impulses due to the weight and normal force are equal and opposite and therefore add up to zero. The impulses due to F and f are along the *x* axis, so the total impulse is in the horizontal direction. The *x* component of the impulse due to F is $(I_F)_x = (50 \text{ lb})(6 \text{ s}) = 300 \text{ lb} \cdot \text{s}$. The frictional force is given by $f = \mu_k N = 0.5(30 \text{ lb}) = 15 \text{ lb}$, so the impulse due to f is $(I_f)_x = (-15 \text{ lb})(6 \text{ s}) = -90 \text{ lb} \cdot \text{s}$. The total impulse is then $(I_T)_x = (I_F)_x + (I_f)_x = 300 \text{ lb} \cdot \text{s} - 90 \text{ lb} \cdot \text{s} = 210 \text{ lb} \cdot \text{s}$. [Alternatively, we could first find the resultant force F_T: $(F_T)_x = F_x + f_x = 50 \text{ lb} - 15 \text{ lb} = 35 \text{ lb}$. Then $(I_T)_x = (F_T)_x t = (35 \text{ lb})(6 \text{ s}) = 210 \text{ lb} \cdot \text{s}$, as before.]

Note.   There is an interesting similarity between the definition of impulse of a constant force and that of work of a constant force (as defined in Chap. 6). Work was defined as a force times a distance, and impulse is defined as a force times a time. We will see below that, just as for the case of work, the definition of impulse can be extended to the case of a variable force acting on an arbitrarily moving object. In addition, in our study of work, we saw that one could relate the work done to the change in kinetic energy (which is related to the change in velocity) over the interval in which the work was performed. We will soon see that impulse can also be related, through a quantity called momentum, to a change in velocity over the period during which the impulse is performed.

There is, however, a very fundamental difference in the nature of the definitions of work and of impulse. Work is defined as a scalar quantity; it has no direction. Impulse, on the other hand, is defined as a vector quantity. Whereas kinetic energy involves only the magnitude of the velocity, the quantity involving velocity to which impulse is related involves the velocity vector.

Impulse of a Variable Force

We now extend our concept of impulse to a variable force acting on an object moving on an arbitrary path. In Fig. 8-2 we depict the situation. We consider the time interval from the initial time $t_{init} = t_1$ to the final time $t_{final} = t_N$ and divide the path of the particle up into $N - 1$ small segments corresponding to small time intervals Δt. Thus, for example, $\Delta t_1 = t_2 - t_1$, $\Delta t_2 = t_3 - t_2$, ..., $\Delta t_i = t_{i+1} - t_i$, ..., $\Delta t_N = t_N - t_{N-1}$. The forces $\mathbf{F}_1$, $\mathbf{F}_2$, ..., $\mathbf{F}_i$, ..., $\mathbf{F}_{N-1}$ correspond to the average values of the forces in each of the corresponding small time intervals. Then by definition

$$\mathbf{I} = \lim_{\Delta t \to 0} \sum \mathbf{F}_i \, \Delta t_i \qquad (8.3)$$

where the sum is over all the $N - 1$ intervals between t_1 and t_N, and the limit means that all the Δt's get infinitesimally small (and, correspondingly, the number of intervals between t_1 and t_N get infinitely large). In terms of x and y components,

$$I_x = \lim_{\Delta t \to 0} \sum (F_x)_i \, \Delta t_i \qquad I_y = \lim_{\Delta t \to 0} \sum (F_y)_i \, \Delta t_1 \qquad (8.4)$$

If F_x and F_y are known functions of the time, Eqs. (8.4) can be understood graphically. In Fig. 8-3 we depict an example of F_x as a function of time by plotting F_x vs. t. (A similar depiction could be made

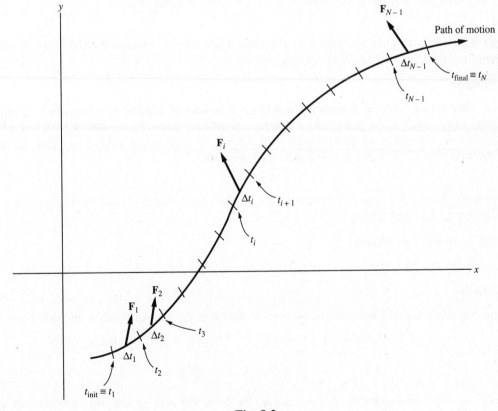

Fig. 8-2

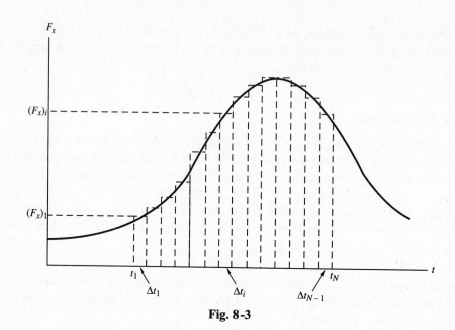

Fig. 8-3

for F_y.) By dividing the t axis into small intervals Δt, we see that the sum in the x component of (8.4) is approximated by the sum of the areas of the rectangles; in the limit as the Δt's go to zero this becomes the area under the F_x vs. t curve between the initial and final times. Thus, the *x component of the impulse* is the *area under the F_x vs. t curve*. A similar result holds for the y component. (Note the analogy between this and the $F\cos\theta$ vs. s curve for work in Chap. 6.)

Problem 8.3. Referring to Problem 8.1, find the total impulse exerted by the force **F** over the combined 20-s time interval of parts (a), (b), and (c).

Solution

The force **F** takes on three values during the 20-s interval. Labeling the intervals 1, 2, and 3 we have $F_1 = 100$ N, $\Delta t_1 = 8$ s; $F_2 = 300$ N, $\Delta t_2 = 8$ s; and $F_3 = -400$ N, $\Delta t_3 = 4$ s. Then $I_x = F_1\,\Delta t_1 + F_2\,\Delta t_2 + F_3\,\Delta t_3 = 800$ N $\cdot$ s $+ 2400$ N $\cdot$ s $- 1600$ N $\cdot$ s $= 1600$ N $\cdot$ s. This is just the algebraic sum of the impulses in the individual intervals.

Problem 8.4. Figure 8-4 depicts the time curves for the x component (a) and the y component (b) of a force acting on an object from $t = 0$ to $t = 20$ s.

(a) Find I_x for the 20-s interval.

(b) Find I_y for the 20-s interval.

Solution

(a) I_x equals the area under the F_x vs. t curve. We break the area up into two intervals 1 and 2.

$$(I_x)_1 = (60\text{ N})(10\text{ s}) = 600\text{ N}\cdot\text{s} \qquad (I_x)_2 = \tfrac{1}{2}(60\text{ N})(10\text{ s}) = 300\text{ N}\cdot\text{s}$$

$$I_x = (I_x)_1 + (I_x)_2 = 900\text{ N}\cdot\text{s}$$

(b) I_y is the area under the F_y vs. t curve. We break the area up into the four intervals shown. $(I_y)_1 = (40\text{ N})(5\text{ s}) = 200\text{ N}\cdot\text{s}$. To get $(I_y)_2$ and $(I_y)_3$ we note that areas 2 and 3 are similar

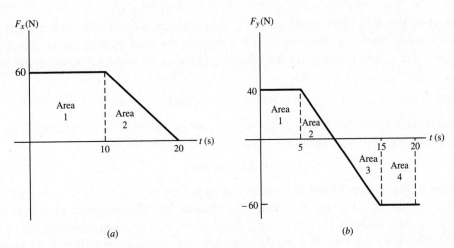

Fig. 8-4

triangles whose heights are in the ratio of 4 to 6. The bases must be in the same ratio, which makes the bases 4 s and 6 s, respectively, so the curve crosses the axis at $t = 9$ s. Then $(I_y)_2 = \frac{1}{2}(40 \text{ N})(4 \text{ s}) = 80 \text{ N} \cdot \text{s}$. Similarly, $(I_y)_3 = \frac{1}{2}(-60 \text{ N})(6 \text{ s}) = -180 \text{ N} \cdot \text{s}$. Next, $(I_y)_4 = (-60 \text{ N})(5 \text{ s}) = -300 \text{ N} \cdot \text{s}$. Finally,

$$I_y = (200 + 80 - 180 - 300)\text{N} \cdot \text{s} = -200 \text{ N} \cdot \text{s}$$

8.2 MOMENTUM AND THE IMPULSE-MOMENTUM THEOREM

Case of Constant Force

If there is no friction in the setup of Fig. 8-1(a), then the force **F** is the resultant force on the system, and $F = ma$. The acceleration of the block is then constant, so $v = v_0 + at$, where t is the time measured from the instant when the velocity is v_0. If we change our notation so that $v_0 = v_i$ at time t_i and $v = v_f$ at the later time $t_f = t_i + t$, our equation becomes

$$v_f = v_i + a(t_f - t_i) \qquad \text{or} \qquad a(t_f - t_i) = v_f - v_i$$

Multiplying this last equation by the mass of the block, we have

$$ma(t_f - t_i) = mv_f - mv_i \qquad \text{or} \qquad F(t_f - t_i) = mv_f - mv_i$$

Recalling that $F(t_f - t_i) = I$, the total impulse on the block in the time interval $(t_f - t_i)$, we have

$$I = mv_f - mv_i \qquad (8.5a)$$

The quantity mv is called the **linear momentum** or just the **momentum**. Therefore, ($8.5a$) states that impulse is equal to the change in linear momentum or

$$I = \Delta(mv) \qquad (8.5b)$$

Note that the units of momentum (in SI) are: $\text{kg} \cdot \text{m/s}$. This is the same as the units of impulse: $\text{N} \cdot \text{s} = (\text{kg} \cdot \text{m/s}^2)\text{s} = \text{kg} \cdot \text{m/s}$. Other units of momentum are the $\text{g} \cdot \text{cm/s}$ and the $\text{slug} \cdot \text{ft/s}$.

The concept of linear momentum can be generalized to two or three dimensions. By definition, if an object of mass m is moving at a given instant of time with velocity **v**, then

$$\text{Linear momentum} \equiv m\mathbf{v} \qquad (8.6)$$

We will now show that Eqs. (8.5) can be generalized to arbitrary motion of an object under the action of a variable resultant force. In other words, if **I** represents the total impulse on an object of mass m between times t_i and t_f, and $\mathbf{v}_i$ and $\mathbf{v}_f$ are the velocities at the initial and final points of the interval, we will have

$$\mathbf{I} = m\mathbf{v}_f - m\mathbf{v}_i = \Delta(m\mathbf{v}) \tag{8.7}$$

To demonstrate this result we recall that $\mathbf{F} = m\mathbf{a}$ can be expressed approximately in the form $\mathbf{F} \approx m\, \Delta\mathbf{v}/\Delta t$ for very small Δt, since $\mathbf{a} = \lim_{\Delta t \to 0} \Delta\mathbf{v}/\Delta t$. Then we must have

$$\mathbf{F}\,\Delta t \approx m\,\Delta\mathbf{v} \tag{8.8}$$

We now return to Fig. 8-2 and label the velocity at each time $(t_1, t_2, \ldots, t_i, \ldots, t_N)$ with the same index: $\mathbf{v}_1, \mathbf{v}_2, \ldots, \mathbf{v}_i, \ldots, \mathbf{v}_N$. For the change in velocity in the corresponding infinitesimal time intervals $\Delta t_1, \Delta t_2$, etc., we have $\Delta\mathbf{v}_1 = \mathbf{v}_2 - \mathbf{v}_1$, $\Delta\mathbf{v}_2 = \mathbf{v}_3 - \mathbf{v}_2$, etc. Then, applying Eq. (8.8) to each interval Δt, we have $\mathbf{F}_1\,\Delta t_1 = m\,\Delta\mathbf{v}_1$, $\mathbf{F}_2\,\Delta t_2 = m\,\Delta\mathbf{v}_2$, etc. Adding up all the $\mathbf{F}\,\Delta t$ terms, we get $\mathbf{I} = \sum \mathbf{F}_i\,\Delta t_i = \sum m\,\Delta\mathbf{v}_i = m(\sum \Delta\mathbf{v}_i)$. Adding up all the $\Delta\mathbf{v}$'s just gives the overall change in vector velocity, $\mathbf{v}_N - \mathbf{v}_1$. Thus, $\mathbf{I} = m\mathbf{v}_N - m\mathbf{v}_1$, which is just Eq. (8.7), with $\mathbf{v}_1 = \mathbf{v}_i$ and $\mathbf{v}_N = \mathbf{v}_f$.

Problem 8.5. Suppose that the block in Problem 8.1 moves on a frictionless surface so that F is the resultant force. Assume the mass of the block is 5.0 kg.

(a) If the block has a velocity of 40 m/s at the beginning of the first time interval, what is its velocity at the end of that interval (8 s later)?

(b) What is the velocity at the end of the full 20 s?

Solution

(a) From part (a) of Problem 8.1 we have $I_x = 800$ N · m. Then, using (8.5a) we get

$$800 \text{ N} \cdot \text{m} = (5.0 \text{ kg})v_f - (5.0 \text{ kg})(40 \text{ m/s}) \qquad \text{or} \qquad v_f = 200 \text{ m/s}$$

(b) We could solve this by letting v_f of part (a) be v_i for the second time interval and apply Eq. (8.5a) again to solve for v_f at the end of the second time interval. Then we would repeat the process for the last time interval. Instead we can use the general result (8.7) for the entire interval. The overall impulse in the full 20-s interval was calculated in Problem 8.3, so we have

$$1600 \text{ N} \cdot \text{s} = (5.0 \text{ kg})v_f - (5.0 \text{ kg})(40 \text{ m/s}) \qquad \text{or} \qquad v_f = 360 \text{ m/s}$$

Problem 8.6. Suppose in Problem 8.4 the force **F** represents the resultant force on a particle of mass 2.0 kg moving in the xy plane. Assume that at $t = 0$ the particle has a velocity of magnitude 100 m/s making an angle of $30°$ above the positive x axis. Find the magnitude and direction θ of the velocity at the end of the 20-s interval.

Solution

Here we split Eq. (8.7) into its x and y components:

$$I_x = mv_{fx} - mv_{ix} \qquad\qquad I_y = mv_{fy} - mv_{iy} \tag{i}$$

From Problem 8.4 we get $I_x = 900$ N · s and $I_y = -200$ N · s; from the data, $v_{ix} = (100 \text{ m/s})\cos 30° = 86.6$ m/s and $v_{iy} = (100 \text{ m/s})\sin 30° = 50.0$ m/s. Applying (i), we get

$$900 \text{ N} \cdot \text{s} = (2.0 \text{ kg})v_{fx} - (2.0 \text{ kg})(86.6 \text{ m/s}) \qquad \text{or} \qquad v_{fx} = 537 \text{ m/s}$$
$$-200 \text{ N} \cdot \text{s} = (2.0 \text{ kg})v_{fy} - (2.0 \text{ kg})(50.0 \text{ m/s}) \qquad \text{or} \qquad v_{fy} = -50.0 \text{ m/s}$$

Then $v_f = (v_{fx}^2 + v_{fy}^2)^{1/2} = 539$ m/s and $\tan \theta = |50/537| = 0.0931$. Solving for θ we get $\theta = 5.32°$. The vector $\mathbf{v}_f$ is in the fourth quadrant, has magnitude 539 m/s, and points $5.32°$ below the positive x axis.

Short Impulses

One of the most useful applications of the concept of impulse is to cases where very large forces act for very short time intervals. Consider, for example, a baseball game in which a batter hits the ball straight back at the pitcher. This is essentially a one-dimensional problem, with $I = \Delta(mv) = mv_f - mv_i$. Choose the positive direction from the batter toward the pitcher. For a given initial and final velocity the impulse is completely determined, even though we don't know the specifics of the force the bat exerts on the ball at any instant of time. Nonetheless we can draw a rough graph of the force vs. the time (Fig. 8-5). The solid line depicts the actual force exerted by the bat on the ball. Time t_a represents the instant when the pitched ball first makes contact with the bat. As the bat makes firmer contact with the ball the force rises rapidly to some maximum value. Thereafter the ball starts to separate from the bat, and the force drops rapidly until time t_c is reached, when the ball completely loses contact with the bat. The entire time interval $t_c - t_a$ is only thousandths of a second. Whatever the exact shape of the curve, we know that the impulse is the area under the curve. For a given impulse, the shorter the time interval over which the force acts, the higher the peak force must be, since the area under the F vs. t curve must stay the same. Another quantity that we can determine is the average force F_{av} giving rise to the impulse. This is defined as the constant force which, if acting for the same time interval, would give rise to the same impulse. The force F_{av} has a magnitude such that the area under the dashed rectangle in Fig. 8-5 is equal to that under the actual curve.

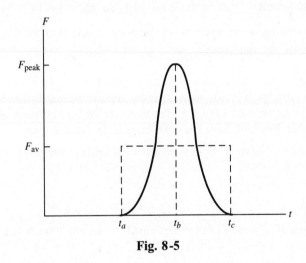

Fig. 8-5

Problem 8.7. A baseball, of mass 0.20 kg, is pitched at 40 m/s and is hit straight back at the pitcher at 90 m/s. Assume the positive x axis points toward the pitcher.

(a) Find the impulse exerted by the bat on the ball.

(b) If the ball is in contact with the bat for 0.0035 s, find the average force exerted on the ball.

(c) How would the result of part (b) change if the contact time were one-third as long?

Solution

(a) $I = mv_f - mv_i = (0.20 \text{ kg}) [(90 \text{ m/s}) - (-40 \text{ m/s})] = 26 \text{ N} \cdot \text{s}$

(We have used the fact that v_f is positive and v_i is negative.)

(b) $F_{av} \Delta t = I$

so that

$$F_{av}(0.0035 \text{ s}) = 26 \text{ N} \cdot \text{s} \quad \text{or} \quad F_{av} = 7430 \text{ N}$$

(c) Since the impulse is fixed, if Δt is one-third as long, F_{av} must be three times as great, so $F_{av} = 22,300 \text{ N}$.

Problem 8.8. A baseball catcher pulls her glove back as she catches the ball, rather than holding it stiffly. Explain as precisely as possible why this is advantageous.

Solution

The impulse that the catcher must impart in stopping the ball is fixed by the ball's initial momentum. Therefore, the longer she takes to bring the ball to rest, the smaller the average force she must exert, and hence the smaller the reaction force on her hand. It is to her advantage to lengthen the time of contact of ball with glove as much as possible.

Problem 8.9. A bullet hits a bone in the body. The bone is known to shatter if the peak force exerted on it exceeds 3000 N; otherwise the bone just brings the bullet to a stop. Assume the bullet has a mass of 10 g and is traveling at a speed of 500 m/s.

(a) If the bone does not shatter, what is the total impulse delivered to it by the bullet?

(b) Assuming that the average force exerted on the bone is one-third of the peak force, what is the shortest stopping time for the bullet?

Solution

(a) From Newton's third law it is easy to see that the impulse exerted by the bone on the bullet is equal and opposite to the impulse exerted by the bullet on the bone. Thus finding the former also gives the latter; in fact they both have the same magnitude. For our case

$$|I| = |\Delta(mv)| = |(0 - mv_i)| = (0.010 \text{ kg}) (500 \text{ m/s}) = 5.0 \text{ N} \cdot \text{s}$$

(b) We know that

$$I = 5 \text{ N} \cdot \text{s} = F_{av} \Delta t = \tfrac{1}{3}F_{peak} \Delta t \tag{i}$$

Since the largest F_{peak} without shattering is 3000 N, we put 3000 N in Eq. (i) to get the minimum Δt:

$$5 \text{ N} \cdot \text{s} = (1000 \text{ N}) \Delta t_{min} \quad \text{or} \quad \Delta t_{min} = 0.0050 \text{ s} = 5 \text{ ms}$$

Problem 8.10. Assume that in Problem 8.7 the batter hit the same pitch so that the ball left the bat with the same speed as before, but this time it was aimed 50 ° above the horizontal (so that it sailed directly over the pitcher's head).

(a) Choosing the x axis toward the pitcher and the y axis vertically upward, find the x and y components of the impulse exerted by the bat on the ball.

(b) Find the magnitude I and direction θ of the impulse exerted by the bat on the ball.

(c) Assuming the bat is in contact with the ball for the same length of time as in part (b) of Problem 8.7, find the magnitude and direction of the average force.

Solution

(a) We need the x and y components of the initial and final velocities. For the incoming pitch we have $v_{ix} = -40$ m/s, $v_{iy} = 0$. For the batted ball, immediately after it leaves the bat, we have $v_{fx} = (90 \text{ m/s}) \cos 50° = 57.9$ m/s, $v_{fy} = (90 \text{ m/s}) \sin 50° = 68.9$ m/s. Then for the impulse we have

$$I_x = mv_{fx} - mv_{ix} = (0.20 \text{ kg})\,[(57.9 \text{ m/s}) - (-40 \text{ m/s})] = 19.6 \text{ N} \cdot \text{s}$$
$$I_y = mv_{fy} - mv_{iy} = (0.20 \text{ kg})\,[(68.9 \text{ m/s}) - (0 \text{ m/s})] = 13.8 \text{ m/s}$$

(b) $I = (I_x^2 + I_y^2)^{1\backslash2} = [(19.6)^2 + (13.8)^2]^{1/2} \text{ N} \cdot \text{s} = 24.0 \text{ N} \cdot \text{s}$. If θ is the angle of elevation of the impulse above the x axis, we have

$$\tan \theta = \frac{13.8}{19.6} = 0.704 \qquad \text{or} \qquad \theta = 35.1°$$

(c) Since $\mathbf{I} = \mathbf{F}_{av}\,\Delta t$, the vector $\mathbf{F}_{av}$ has the same direction as $\mathbf{I}$, and

$$F_{av} = \frac{I}{\Delta t} = \frac{24.0 \text{ N} \cdot \text{s}}{0.0035 \text{ s}} = 6860 \text{ N}$$

Note. In the previous collision problems we have ignored the contribution of the force of gravity to the impulse during the collisions. This is because the impulse lasts such a short time that the contributions of an "ordinary" force such as gravity to the impulse will be very small when compared to the contribution of the huge (but short-lived) contact forces over the same time interval. In Problem 8.10, for example, the contact time is thousandths of a second. The force of gravity is about 2 N; the average force due to the bat, by contrast, is almost 7000 N and is thus the dominant contributor to the impulse during the collision. Once the ball leaves the bat, however, the force of gravity must be taken into account.

8.3 CONSERVATION OF LINEAR MOMENTUM

Case of Two Objects

Suppose we have two objects with no external forces acting on them, moving under their own mutual attraction or repulsion, as shown in Fig. 8-6. The force $\mathbf{F}_{ab}$ represents the force of object A on object B, and $\mathbf{F}_{ba}$ represents the force of object B on A. Then, by Newton's third law, $\mathbf{F}_{ab} = -\mathbf{F}_{ba}$ at any instant of time. Definition (8.3) then shows us that, over any time interval, $\mathbf{I}_{ab} = -\mathbf{I}_{ba}$. From the general impulse-momentum theorem, applied successively to each object, we get

$$\mathbf{I}_{ab} = \Delta(m_b \mathbf{v}_b) = m_b \mathbf{v}_{bf} - m_b \mathbf{v}_{bi} \qquad \text{and} \qquad \mathbf{I}_{ba} = \Delta(m_a \mathbf{v}_a) = m_a \mathbf{v}_{af} - m_a \mathbf{v}_{ai}$$

Then

$$m_b \mathbf{v}_{bf} - m_b \mathbf{v}_{bi} = -(m_a \mathbf{v}_{af} - m_a \mathbf{v}_{ai}) \qquad \text{or} \qquad m_a \mathbf{v}_{af} + m_b \mathbf{v}_{bf} = m_a \mathbf{v}_{ai} + m_b \mathbf{v}_{bi} \qquad (8.9)$$

The second of Eqs. (8.9) may be restated as total final momentum = total initial momentum. Thus, for our two objects, momentum is conserved, no matter what the forces between the two objects may be.

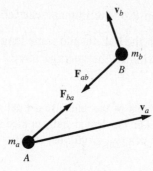

Fig. 8-6

Note. We will see later on, when we discuss center of mass, that conservation of momentum can be generalized to a system of any number of objects when no external forces (forces from outside the system) are acting on the system. It can even be extended to a system of objects that *do* have external forces acting on them, as long as the resultant of all the external forces adds up to zero.

For two-dimensional motion, Eq. (*8.9*) can be broken into its x- and y-component equations

$$m_a v_{afx} + m_b v_{bfx} = m_a v_{aix} + m_b v_{bix} \qquad (8.10a)$$
$$m_a v_{afy} + m_b v_{bfy} = m_a v_{aiy} + m_b v_{biy} \qquad (8.10b)$$

Collisions in One Dimension

Equations (*8.9*) and (*8.10*) are particularly useful in dealing with problems of collisions between objects, where the dominant forces are the forces of the collision itself and the external forces can be neglected (see the note following Problem 8.10). In this section we will discuss one-dimensional collisions, (i.e., those that occur in a straight line).

Problem 8.11. Two blocks are moving in the same direction along the x axis on a horizontal frictionless surface, as shown in Fig. 8-7. The blocks collide head-on (so that there is no change in the line of motion of either object). Find a relationship between the velocities of the two blocks after the collision.

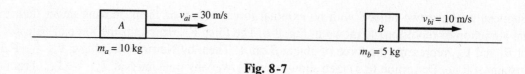

Fig. 8-7

Solution

Since there are no external forces in the x direction, momentum is conserved along the x axis, and we apply Eq. (*8.10a*) (but drop the x subscript for convenience).

$$(10 \text{ kg}) (30 \text{ m/s}) + (5.0 \text{ kg}) (10 \text{ m/s}) = (10 \text{ kg}) v_{af} + (5.0 \text{ kg}) v_{bf}$$

which reduces to $2v_{af} + v_{bf} = 70$ m/s.

Problem 8.12.   Assume the same situation in Fig. 8-7 except that now block B is initially moving to the left at 20 m/s. Find the new relationship between the final velocities of the two blocks.

Solution

The situation is similar to that of Problem 8.11, and we again apply Eq. $(8.10a)$:

$$(10 \text{ kg})(30 \text{ m/s}) + (5.0 \text{ kg})(-20 \text{ m/s}) = (10 \text{ kg})v_{af} + (5.0 \text{ kg})v_{bf}$$

or $2v_{af} + v_{bf} = 40$ m/s.

Note.   In a collision problem in which the initial velocities are known, momentum conservation gives us a relation between the final velocities, but not enough information to completely solve for those velocities, unless additional information is provided.

Elastic Collisions

An elastic collision is one in which the total kinetic energy of the colliding objects is the same just before and just after the collision:

$$\tfrac{1}{2}m_a v_{af}^2 + \tfrac{1}{2}m_b v_{bf}^2 = \tfrac{1}{2}m_a v_{ai}^2 + \tfrac{1}{2}m_b v_{bi}^2 \tag{8.11}$$

The implication of such a collision is that no thermal energy is generated during the collision and no energy is lost to the surroundings. Instead, as the two objects crush up against each other they are somewhat compressed, and, like springs, they store up potential energy which is released back in the form of kinetic energy as they separate. Since, by assumption, there are no energy losses, mechanical energy is conserved. Any external potential energy, such as that of gravity, is assumed to remain unchanged during the extremely short duration of the collision process.

While truly elastic collisions are believed to occur on the atomic scale, on the macroscopic scale they are always an approximation to the actual situation, since there are inevitably some thermal losses. Nonetheless, they are often excellent approximations to some collision processes.

Equation (8.11) is a quadratic equation in the velocities and therefore is often cumbersome to use. It turns out that by combining Eq. (8.11) with Eq. $(8.10a)$ one can derive a much simpler equation involving the velocities that holds for one-dimensional elastic collisions:

$$(v_{af} - v_{bf}) = -(v_{ai} - v_{bi}) \tag{8.12a}$$

You may recognize from our discussion of relative motion in an earlier chapter that the expressions in parentheses on the left and right are just the velocities of object A relative to object B, v_{ab}, after the collision and before the collision, respectively. Then Eq. $(8.12a)$ simply says that for a one-dimensional elastic collision the relative velocity of approach of the two objects is equal and opposite to their relative velocity of separation:

$$v_{abf} = -v_{abi} \tag{8.12b}$$

Problem 8.13.   Prove that Eq. $(8.12a)$ follows from Eqs. (8.11) and $(8.10a)$, as was stated above.

Solution

We again drop the x subscript in Eq. $(8.10a)$ since the whole problem is in one dimension. Rearranging Eqs. $(8.10a)$ and (8.11) so that terms with the same mass appear on the same side of the equation, we get

$$m_a(v_{af} - v_{ai}) = m_b(v_{bi} - v_{bf}) \tag{i}$$
$$\tfrac{1}{2}m_a(v_{af}^2 - v_{ai}^2) = \tfrac{1}{2}m_b(v_{bi}^2 - v_{bf}^2) \tag{ii}$$

Noting that $A^2 - B^2 = (A - B)(A + B)$ for any A and B, we can rewrite Eq. (*ii*) as

$$m_a(v_{af} - v_{ai})(v_{af} + v_{ai}) = m_b(v_{bi} - v_{bf})(v_{bi} + v_{bf}) \qquad (iii)$$

Using Eq. (*i*), we see that Eq. (*iii*) simplifies to

$$v_{af} + v_{ai} = v_{bi} + v_{bf} \qquad (iv)$$

Bringing all final velocities to the left and all initial velocities to the right, we finally get

$$v_{af} - v_{bf} = -(v_{ai} - v_{bi})$$

Problem 8.14.   Assume that the two blocks in Problem 8.11 had an elastic collision.

(*a*)   Find the final velocities of the two blocks, using Eq. (*8.12a*) for elastic collisions.

(*b*)   Verify that your answer truly corresponds to an elastic collision.

Solution

(*a*)   In Problem 8.11 the conservation of momentum yields

$$2v_{af} + v_{bf} = 70 \text{ m/s} \qquad (i)$$

Applying Eq. (*8.12a*), we have $v_{af} - v_{bf} = -(30 \text{ m/s} - 10 \text{ m/s})$ or

$$v_{af} - v_{bf} = -20 \text{ m/s} \qquad (ii)$$

We now solve the two simultaneous Eqs. (*i*) and (*ii*) for the final velocities, getting

$$v_{af} = 16.7 \text{ m/s} \qquad \text{and} \qquad v_{bf} = 36.7 \text{ m/s}$$

(*b*)   To show that our results are consistent with an elastic collision, we calculate the actual total kinetic energy before and after the collision, getting

$$E_{ki} = \tfrac{1}{2}(10 \text{ kg})(30 \text{ m/s})^2 + \tfrac{1}{2}(5 \text{ kg})(10 \text{ m/s})^2 = 4750 \text{ J}$$

$$E_{kf} = \tfrac{1}{2}(10 \text{ kg})(16.7 \text{ m/s})^2 + \tfrac{1}{2}(5 \text{ kg})(36.7 \text{ m/s})^2 = 4761 \text{ J}$$

These check to within rounding errors in our final velocities.

Problem 8.15.   Assuming that the collision described in Problem 8.12 is an elastic collision, find the final velocities of the two blocks.

Solution

From Problem 8.12 we already have the results of momentum conservation:

$$2v_{af} + v_{bf} = 40 \text{ m/s} \qquad (i)$$

From Eq. (*8.12a*) we get $v_{af} - v_{bf} = -(30 \text{ m/s} - [-20 \text{ m/s}])$ or

$$v_{af} - v_{bf} = -50 \text{ m/s} \qquad (ii)$$

Solving Eqs. (*i*) and (*ii*) for v_{af} and v_{bf}, we get

$$v_{af} = -3.33 \text{ m/s} \qquad \text{and} \qquad v_{bf} = 46.7 \text{ m/s}$$

Note that in this problem the final velocity of block A is in the negative x direction.

Problem 8.16.   Two blocks of equal mass make a head-on elastic collision, with one of the blocks initially at rest. Show that just after the collision the initially moving block will be at rest, and the block initially at rest will have exactly the same velocity as the initially moving block.

Solution

From Eq. (*8.10a*) we have $mv_{af} + mv_{bf} = mv_{ai} + 0$, which reduces to

$$v_{af} + v_{bf} = v_{ai} \qquad\qquad (i)$$

From Eq. (*8.12a*) we have

$$v_{af} - v_{bf} = -v_{ai} \qquad\qquad (ii)$$

Solving for the final velocities (e.g., by equating the sum of the left sides of the two equations to the sum of the right sides) yields

$$v_{af} = 0 \qquad \text{and} \qquad v_{bf} = v_{ai}$$

Problem 8.17.   Use Problem 8.16 to explain the behavior of the hanging steel-ball devices sold in novelty shops (Fig. 8-8).

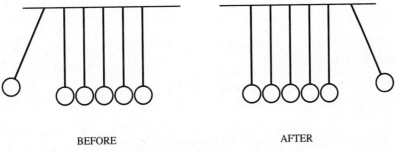

BEFORE   AFTER

Fig. 8-8

Solution

All the steel balls have the same mass. Steel balls collide *almost* elastically, so we assume the collisions between the individual balls are elastic. Also, we have conservation of momentum in the horizontal direction, because the tensions in the supporting strings are vertical during the collision process. Finally, though the balls actually may be in contact when they are in their rest positions, we may assume that they are slightly separated, to make Problem 8.16 more readily applicable.

When the first ball is moved to the side and released, it builds up a certain velocity with which it horizontally collides with its neighbor ball, which is at rest. Then, by Problem 8.16, the first ball comes to rest and the second ball picks up its velocity, but not for long. The second ball almost immediately collides with the third ball, and by the same reasoning it comes to rest and the third ball picks up the velocity. This process continues until the next-to-last ball hits the last ball. The next-to-last ball comes to rest, and the last ball moves off with the same velocity which the first ball had. It thus rises to the same height from which the first ball was let go. After reaching the highest point it descends and starts the collision process going again, with the same speed, but in the opposite direction. The balls in the middle always appear at rest because they have a negligible distance to travel from the time they are hit to the time they once again come to rest.

Inelastic Collisions

Any collision that is not elastic is called **inelastic**. An inelastic collision is characterized by a certain disappearance of kinetic energy in the collision process. In general, unless one knows precisely how much thermal energy is generated in the collision, one cannot write down an auxiliary equation to use together with the momentum conservation equation (8.10a) to solve for the unknown velocities. The best one can do is to account for the thermal energy loss in collisions of different objects by means of an empirical quantity called the **coefficient of restitution** e. The value of e is defined as the ratio of the magnitude of the relative velocity after the collision to that before the collision:

$$e = \left| \frac{v_{abf}}{v_{abi}} \right| = \frac{-(v_{af} - v_{bf})}{v_{ai} - v_{bi}} \qquad (8.13)$$

We see from Eqs. (8.12) that for an elastic collision, $e = 1$. Generally speaking, the smaller the e value, the more thermal energy is generated and hence the more kinetic energy is lost. The lowest possible value of e is $e = 0$, which corresponds to $v_{af} = v_{bf}$. This means that the two objects move as one after the collision; in other words, they stick together. The case of $e = 0$ is often called a *totally inelastic collision*. The value of the coefficient of restitution depends very heavily on the nature of the materials colliding, as well as other factors.

Problem 8.18.

(a) Redo Problem 8.14(a) if $e = 0.80$.

(b) What fraction of the initial kinetic energy is lost in this collision.

Solution

(a) Now momentum conservation and the definition of e give

$$2v_{af} + v_{bf} = 70 \text{ m/s}$$
$$v_{af} - v_{bf} = -(0.80)(30 \text{ m/s} - 10 \text{ m/s}) = -16 \text{ m/s}$$

Solve as before, to find

$$v_{af} = 18.0 \text{ m/s} \qquad \text{and} \qquad v_{bf} = 34.0 \text{ m/s}$$

(b) The initial kinetic energy was found in Problem 8.14(b) to be 4750 J. For the final kinetic energy we now have

$$E_{kf} = \tfrac{1}{2}(10 \text{ kg})(18.0 \text{ m/s})^2 + \tfrac{1}{2}(5 \text{ kg})(34.0 \text{ m/s})^2 = 4510 \text{ J}$$

Then $\text{Fraction lost} = 1 - (\text{fraction remaining}) = 1 - \dfrac{E_{kf}}{E_{ki}} = 0.051 = 5.1\%$

Problem 8.19.   If the collision described in Problem 8.12 is an inelastic collision with $e = 0.5$, find (a) the final velocities of the two blocks, (b) the total thermal energy generated in the collision.

Solution

(a) From Problem 8.12 and Eq. (8.13) we have

$$2v_{af} + v_{bf} = 40 \text{ m/s}$$
$$v_{af} - v_{bf} = -(0.5)[30 \text{ m/s} - (-20 \text{ m/s})] = -25 \text{ m/s}$$

Solving by addition, we get

$$v_{af} = 5.0 \text{ m/s} \qquad \text{and} \qquad v_{bf} = 30.0 \text{ m/s}$$

(b)   The thermal energy generated is just $E_{ki} - E_{kf}$:

$$E_{ki} = \tfrac{1}{2}(10 \text{ kg}) (30 \text{ m/s})^2 + \tfrac{1}{2}(5.0 \text{ kg}) (20 \text{ m/s})^2 = 5500 \text{ J}$$

$$E_{kf} = \tfrac{1}{2}(10 \text{ kg}) (5.0 \text{ m/s})^2 + \tfrac{1}{2}(5.0 \text{ kg}) (30 \text{ m/s})^2 = 2375 \text{ J}$$

$$\text{Thermal energy} = E_{ki} - E_{kf} = 3125 \text{ J}$$

Problem 8.20.   Repeat Problem 8.18 for a totally inelastic collision.

Solution

For this case the two objects stick together, and we immediately know that $v_{af} = v_{bf} \equiv v_f$. While we could proceed as in Problem 8.18 it is more informative to insert v_f directly into the momentum equation:

$$m_a v_{ai} + m_b v_{bi} = (m_a + m_b)v_f \qquad \text{or} \qquad (10 \text{ kg}) (30 \text{ m/s}) + (5.0 \text{ kg}) (10 \text{ m/s}) = (15 \text{ kg})v_f \qquad (i)$$

or $v_f = 23.3$ m/s. To obtain the fractional loss in kinetic energy, we again note that from Problem 8.18 (or Problem 8.14) we have $E_{ki} = 4750$ J. We get

$$E_{kf} = \tfrac{1}{2}(m_a + m_b)v_f{}^2 = \tfrac{1}{2}(15 \text{ kg}) (23.3 \text{ m/s})^2 = 4070 \text{ J}$$

Then, the fractional loss equals $1 - (4070/4750) = 0.143 = 14.3\%$.

The Ballistic Pendulum

A ballistic pendulum is a device that is used to measure the velocities of small swift projectiles, such as bullets. A typical schematic of such a device is shown in Fig. 8-9. A bullet of mass m is fired horizontally into a block of mass M and embeds itself in the block. The block, which is suspended from the ceiling by vertical cords, then rises, as indicated by the dotted lines, through some measurable vertical height h. From this information one can deduce the initial speed v_i of the bullet.

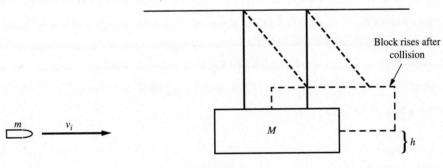

Fig. 8-9

Problem 8.21.   For a ballistic pendulum (Fig. 8-9), assume $m = 10$ g, $M = 3990$ g, and $h = 3.0$ cm.

(a)   Find the velocity V_f of the combined block-bullet body just after the collision.

(b)   Find the initial velocity of the bullet.

Solution

(a)   Here we use the fact that from the time immediately after the collision through the rise time, mechanical energy is conserved. This is a consequence of the fact that the tensions in the cords can do no work since the points of contact with the block move on the arcs of circles perpendicular to the cords. At the moment just after the collision we have $\frac{1}{2}(m + M)V_f^2 = (m + M)gh$. Solving for V_f we get

$$V_f = (2gh)^{1/2} = [2(9.8 \text{ m/s}^2)(0.030 \text{ m})]^{1/2} \quad \text{or} \quad V_f = 0.767 \text{ m/s}$$

Observe that momentum is not conserved when the block is rising owing to the combined actions of the external forces of gravity and cord tension.

(b) During the collision process we assume that conservation of momentum holds in the horizontal direction. This follows since the block does not move an appreciable distance during the collision time, and the tensions in the cords and force of gravity do not act in the horizontal direction. Then $mv_i = (m + M)V_f$. Substituting the known values, we get $v_i = 307$ m/s.

Problem 8.22. Suppose that the bullet in Problem 8.21 passes straight through the block and emerges out the other side with velocity $v_f = 250$ m/s. Assume that the block still rises through a height $h = 3.0$ cm. Find the initial velocity of the bullet. (Ignore the effect of any splinters that emerge with the bullet.)

Solution

The velocity of the block just after the bullet leaves it is again determined by conservation of mechanical energy, and we again have $V_f = 0.767$ m/s. Then, applying momentum conservation during the brief penetration time, we have $mv_i = mv_f + MV_f$, so

$$10v_i = 10(250 \text{ m/s}) + 3990(0.767 \text{ m/s}) \quad \text{or} \quad v_i = 556 \text{ m/s}$$

Problem 8.23. How much kinetic energy was lost in the brief collision time of (a) Problem 8.21(b)?   (b) Problem 8.22?

Solution

(a) $E_{ki} = \frac{1}{2}(0.010 \text{ kg})(307 \text{ m/s})^2 = 471$ J $E_{kf} = \frac{1}{2}(4.000 \text{ kg})(0.767 \text{ m/s})^2 = 1.18$ J

for a loss of $E_{ki} - E_{kf} \approx 470$ J. (Thus almost all the kinetic energy was lost to thermal energy even though momentum was conserved!)

(b) Here, $E_{ki} = \frac{1}{2}(0.010 \text{ kg})(556 \text{ m/s})^2 = 1546$ J

and $E_{kf} = \frac{1}{2}(0.010 \text{ kg})(250 \text{ m/s})^2 + \frac{1}{2}(3.990)(0.767 \text{ m/s})^2 = 314$ J

for a loss of 1232 J.

Collisions in Two Dimensions

Much of the discussion for one-dimensional collisions carries over to the two-dimensional case. Conservation of momentum, (8.9), is valid as a vector equation or can be expressed as a pair of component equations. Analogous to (8.12), we have as the definition of the coefficient of restitution

$$e = \frac{|\mathbf{v}_{abf}|}{|\mathbf{v}_{abi}|} = \frac{|\mathbf{v}_{af} - \mathbf{v}_{bf}|}{|\mathbf{v}_{ai} - \mathbf{v}_{bi}|} \qquad (8.12\,bis)$$

(See Eq. (3.11).] It can be shown that in a two-dimensional *elastic* collision,

$$|\mathbf{v}_{abf}| = |\mathbf{v}_{abi}| \qquad (8.11\,bis)$$

or $e = 1$ for an elastic collision. For a sticky collision we again have $e = 0$, just as in the one-dimensional case.

Problem 8.24. Two pucks of equal mass m have an elastic collision on a frictionless horizontal table, as shown in Fig. 8-10. Assume that puck B is initially at rest, and puck A has initial speed $v_{Ai} = 4.5$ ft/s and final speed $v_{Af} = 2.5$ ft/s. Choose your x axis along $\mathbf{v}_{Ai}$.

(a)   Show that the y components of the two final velocities are equal and opposite.

(b)   Find the final speed of puck B.

(c)   The angle θ can be shown to be $56.2°$. Find the angle ϕ.

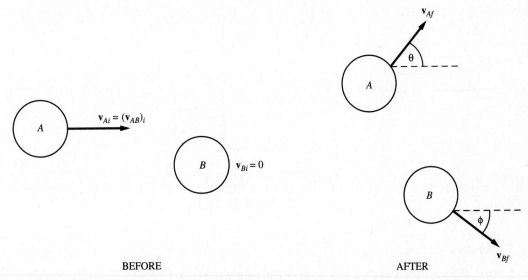

Fig. 8-10

Solution

(a)   The initial momentum in the y direction is zero, so

$$0 = mv_{(Af)y} + mv_{(Bf)y} \Rightarrow v_{(Af)y} = -v_{(Bf)y}$$

(b)   From kinetic energy conservation, we have

$$\tfrac{1}{2}mv_{Ai}^2 = \tfrac{1}{2}mv_{Af}^2 + \tfrac{1}{2}mv_{Bf}^2$$

or $v_{Bf}^2 = v_{Ai}^2 - v_{Af}^2 = (4.5 \text{ ft/s})^2 - (2.5 \text{ ft/s})^2 = 14.0 \text{ ft}^2/\text{s}^2$

Solving, we get $v_{Bf} = 3.74$ ft/s.

(c)   From part (a) $v_{Af} \sin\theta = -(-v_{Bf}\sin\phi) = v_{Bf}\sin\phi \Rightarrow 2.5 \sin 56.2° = 3.74 \sin\phi \Rightarrow \sin\phi = 0.556 \Rightarrow \phi = 33.7°$. (Alternatively,

$mv_{Ai} = mv_{Af}\cos\theta + mv_{Bf}\cos\phi \Rightarrow 4.5 =$

$$2.5 \cos 56.2° + 3.74 \cos\phi \Rightarrow \cos\phi = 0.831 \Rightarrow \phi = 33.8°$$

which is our previous result to within rounding errors.) One can in fact show that the sum of the angles, $\theta + \phi$, which represents the angle between $\mathbf{v}_{Af}$ and $\mathbf{v}_{Bf}$, is exactly $90°$ for any elastic collision between objects of equal mass, one of which is initially at rest.

Problem 8.25.   Two blocks, of masses $m_A = 5.0$ kg and $m_B = 12.0$ kg, are initially moving at right angles to each other on a frictionless horizontal surface, as shown in Fig. 8-11. Assume the blocks have a totally inelastic collision and that $v_{Ai} = 30$ m/s and $v_{Bi} = 15$ m/s.

(a)   Find the magnitude and direction of the final velocity $\mathbf{v}_f$ of the combination.

(b)   How much thermal energy is generated in this collision?

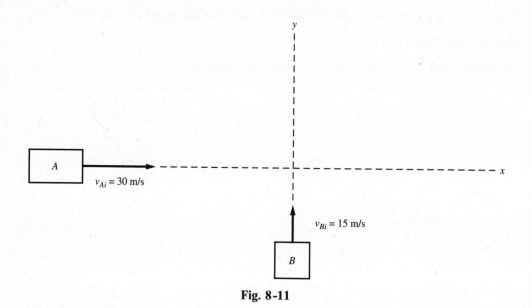

Fig. 8-11

Solution

(a)   We solve the x and y components of the momentum conservation equation. For the x direction, we have $m_A v_{Ai} + 0 = (m_A + m_B)v_{fx}$. Substituting, we get

$$5.0(30 \text{ m/s}) = 17.0 v_{fx} \qquad \text{or} \qquad v_{fx} = 8.82 \text{ m/s}$$

For the y direction, $0 + m_B v_{Bi} = (m_A + m_B)v_{fy}$, so

$$12.0(15 \text{ m/s}) = 17.0 v_{fy} \qquad \text{or} \qquad v_{fy} = 10.6 \text{ m/s}$$

$$v_f = [(8.82)^2 + (10.6)^2]^{1/2} \text{ m/s} = 13.8 \text{ m/s}$$

Letting θ equal the angle of $\mathbf{v}_f$ with the x axis, we have $\tan \theta = 10.6/8.82 = 1.20$, from which we get $\theta = 50.2°$.

(b) $E_{ki} = \frac{1}{2}(5.0 \text{ kg})(30 \text{ m/s})^2 + \frac{1}{2}(12.0 \text{ kg})(15 \text{ m/s})^2 = 3600 \text{ J}; \quad E_{kf} = \frac{1}{2}(17.0 \text{ kg})(13.8 \text{ m/s})^2 = 1619 \text{ J}.$ The thermal energy generated equals $E_{ki} - E_{kf} = 1981 \text{ J}.$

Recoil

In addition to collision problems, another class of problems that involves impulse and momentum is related to recoil. In recoil problems a system that is initially at rest, or moving as a unit, breaks up into two or more parts moving with different velocities as a consequence of rapid expenditure of some internal energy of the system. One example is a rifle and bullet. Initially both are at rest, with the bullet within the rifle barrel. When the rifle is fired, the gunpowder in the bullet casing explodes and drives the bullet forward. The forward impulse on the bullet is equal and opposite to the impulse imparted to the rifle. If the rifle is resting against the shoulder, the person firing it feels the "kick" of this impulse. In a rocket the burning fuel hurls hot gas out the back, and the reaction impulse pushes the rocket in the opposite direction (forward). If no external forces act on the rocket we have momentum conservation, and the increase in forward momentum of the rocket just balances the backward momentum gained by the ejected gases.

Problem 8.26.   Two blocks on a frictionless horizontal surface are pressed back to back so that they compress a spring of negligible mass held between them, as shown in Fig. 8-12. They are held in position by a connecting cord. Assume that $m_A = 14$ kg and $m_B = 8.0$ kg and that the stored potential energy in the spring is 1000 J. When the cord is cut, the two blocks move in opposite directions with speeds v_A and v_B.

(a)   Find the relationship between v_A and v_B.

(b)   Find the values of v_A and v_B.

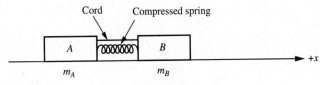

Cord   Compressed spring

A B $+x$

m_A m_B

Fig. 8-12

Solution

(a)   Considering the spring to be part of the two-block system, we see that there are no external forces acting on the system in the horizontal direction. We thus have momentum conservation in that direction. Choosing positive to the right, we have, since the system starts from rest

$$0 = -m_A v_A + m_B v_B \quad \text{or} \quad m_A v_A = m_B v_B \quad \text{or} \quad 14 v_A = 8.0 v_B \quad \text{or} \quad v_B = 1.75 v_A$$

(b)   All the spring energy goes into kinetic energy of the two blocks, so $\frac{1}{2}m_A v_A^2 + \frac{1}{2}m_B v_B^2 = 1000$ J, or, using the results of part (a) we get

$$\tfrac{1}{2}(14 \text{ kg})v_A^2 + \tfrac{1}{2}(8.0 \text{ kg})(1.75\, v_A)^2 = 1000 \text{ J}$$

or $(19.25 \text{ kg})v_A^2 = 1000$ J   or $v_A = 51.9$ m/s   and $v_B = 90.8$ m/s

Problem 8.27.   A machine gun fires bullets of mass $m = 25$ g at a muzzle velocity of 1200 m/s.

(a)   What is the recoil impulse on the gun due to each bullet that is fired?

(b)   If 300 bullets are fired per minute, what is the total recoil impulse imparted to the gun in 1 min?

(c)   What is the average recoil force acting on the gun?

Solution

(a)   The impulse I on the gun is equal and opposite to that acting on the bullet. The impulse on the bullet equals its change in momentum. Since the bullet starts from rest, we have

$$I = mv - 0 = (0.025 \text{ kg})(1200 \text{ m/s}) = 30 \text{ N} \cdot \text{s}$$

(b)   The total impulse in 1 min is just $300I = 9000$ N·s.

(c)   Over the 1 min period, $F_{av}t = 9000$ N $\cdot$ s so that

$$F_{av}(60 \text{ s}) = 9000 \text{ N} \cdot \text{s} \qquad \text{or} \qquad F_{av} = 150 \text{ N}$$

8.4   CENTER OF MASS

The concept of **center of mass** (CM) turns out to be useful in understanding the motion of large extended objects as well as of systems of particles.

Systems of Particles

The CM of a system of particles is defined as the position of the average displacement of the particles, weighted according to mass. The situation is depicted in Fig. 8-13, which shows a system of N particles. The ith particle has mass m_i and displacement from the origin $\mathbf{r}_i$. Then, the average displacement weighted according to the mass of each particle is just

$$\mathbf{R}_{CM} = \frac{\sum m_i \mathbf{r}_i}{\sum m_i} \tag{8.14}$$

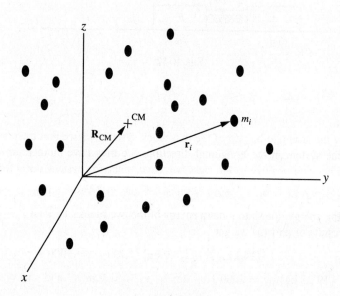

Fig. 8-13

where the sums are over all i from 1 to N. The sum in the denominator is just the total mass of the system M. Thus Eq. (8.14) can be rewritten as

$$M\mathbf{R}_{CM} = \sum m_i \mathbf{r}_i \tag{8.15}$$

If a (small) amount of time Δt elapses, the displacements $\mathbf{r}_i$ will change by (small) amounts $\Delta \mathbf{r}_i$. In other words, $\mathbf{r}_i \rightarrow \mathbf{r}_i + \Delta \mathbf{r}_i$ in the time Δt. The corresponding change $\Delta \mathbf{R}_{CM}$ in the displacement of the CM is given by $\mathbf{R}_{CM} \rightarrow \mathbf{R}_{CM} + \Delta \mathbf{R}_{CM}$. Examining Eq. (8.15) with the new values yields $M \Delta \mathbf{R}_{CM} = \sum m_i \Delta \mathbf{r}_i$. Dividing by Δt we get

$$M \frac{\Delta \mathbf{R}_{CM}}{\Delta t} = \sum m_i \frac{\Delta \mathbf{r}_i}{\Delta t} \tag{8.16a}$$

In the limit of infinitesimal Δt, the quantity $\Delta \mathbf{r}_i / \Delta t = \mathbf{v}_i$, the velocity of the ith particle. Similarly, $\Delta \mathbf{R}_{CM} / \Delta t = \mathbf{V}_{CM}$, the velocity of the CM. Thus

$$M \mathbf{V}_{CM} = \sum m_i \mathbf{v}_i \tag{8.16b}$$

The right side of $(8.16b)$ is just the total momentum of the system of particles. Therefore Eq. $(8.16b)$ states that the total mass of the system times the velocity of the CM equals the total momentum of the system. Thus, if momentum is conserved, $\mathbf{V}_{CM}$ is constant. If we now consider the small change in the velocity of each particle in a (small) time Δt, we could redo the steps that lead from (8.15) to $(8.16b)$, this time starting with Eq. $(8.16b)$, to get

$$M \frac{\Delta \mathbf{V}_{CM}}{\Delta t} = \sum m_i \frac{\Delta \mathbf{v}_i}{\Delta t} \tag{8.17a}$$

$$M \mathbf{A}_{CM} = \sum m_i \mathbf{a}_i \tag{8.17b}$$

where the $\mathbf{a}$'s are accelerations. From Newton's second law the right side of Eq. $(8.17b)$ is just $\sum \mathbf{F}_i$, where $\mathbf{F}_i$ is the resultant force on the ith particle and includes the forces due to all the other particles in the system on the ith particle, as well as the net external force on the ith particle, $(\mathbf{F}_{ext})_i$. In the $\sum \mathbf{F}_i$ all the internal forces cancel in pairs due to Newton's third law, so $\sum \mathbf{F}_i = \sum (\mathbf{F}_{ext})_i = (\mathbf{F}_{ext})_T$, the resultant external force on the system. Equation $(17b)$ thus becomes

$$(\mathbf{F}_{ext})_T = M \mathbf{A}_{CM} \tag{8.18}$$

In other words, the CM accelerates as if it were a particle of mass M acted on by a force equal to the resultant of all the external forces acting on the system of particles. We now can deduce our general rule for momentum conservation for an arbitrary system of particles: If $(\mathbf{F}_{ext})_T = 0$, then $\mathbf{A}_{CM} = 0$ and $\mathbf{V}_{CM} = $ constant. But, from Eq. $(8.16b)$ this is the same as saying the momentum of the system of particles is constant. Thus it follows that the momentum of a system of particles is conserved as long as the *resultant* external force on the system equals zero.

Note that Eqs. (8.15), $(8.16b)$, and (8.18) are vector equations; they can therefore be broken into component equations. For example, Eq. (8.15) can be expressed as

$$MX_{CM} = \sum m_i x_i \qquad MY_{CM} = \sum m_i y_i \qquad MZ_{CM} = \sum m_i z_i \tag{8.19a, b, c}$$

where x_i, y_i, and z_i are the components of $\mathbf{r}_i$, etc.

Rigid Bodies

In the case of an extended rigid body, Eq. (8.18) indicates that the CM of the body moves as if it were a particle having a mass equal to the total mass of the body acted on by the resultant force on the body. Thus, for any body, even for an irregular body, rotating and translating in space, we can describe the motion by studying the motion of its center of mass. To do this, we need to find the location of the CM of rigid bodies. This can be rather difficult when dealing with irregular objects; even for simple objects, such as a uniform cone, one needs calculus to find the CM. We will illustrate how to find the CM in some simple cases.

Problem 8.28. Find the center of mass of the three-particle system in the xy plane shown in Fig. 8-14.

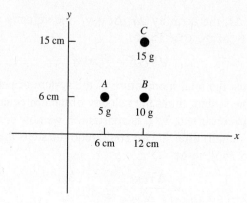

Fig. 8-14

Solution

We use Eqs. (8.19). For the x equation,

$$MX_{CM} = m_A x_A + m_B x_B + m_C x_C$$

$$(30 \text{ g})X_{CM} = (5.0 \text{ g})(6.0 \text{ cm}) + (10 \text{ g})(12 \text{ cm}) + (15 \text{ g})(12 \text{ cm}) = 330 \text{ g} \cdot \text{cm}$$

or
$$X_{CM} = 11 \text{ cm}$$

Similarly, for the y equation,

$$MY_{CM} = m_A y_A + m_B y_B + m_C y_C$$

$$(30 \text{ g})Y_{CM} = (5.0 \text{ g})(6.0 \text{ cm}) + (10 \text{ g})(6.0 \text{ cm}) + (15 \text{ g})(15 \text{ cm}) = 315 \text{ g} \cdot \text{cm}$$

or
$$Y_{CM} = 10.5 \text{ cm}$$

Problem 8.29. Find the CM of (a) a uniform sphere, (b) a uniform cylinder, and (c) a uniform donut (torus).

Solution

The CM of all three objects appear at their geometric centers by symmetry. To see this we consider the sphere. The CM of the uniform sphere must be at its center since if it were anywhere else it would change location upon rotation of the sphere. Since the mass distribution of the sphere is the same in the rotated position as in the original position, the CM of the same mass distribution would be in two different locations, which is impossible. Thus the CM must be at the center. Similar reasoning can be used for the uniform cylinder and the uniform donut. Note that in the case of the donut the CM is not in the object itself. The CM is a geometric point fixed in relation to a rigid body, but it is not necessarily in the body.

Problem 8.30. What can you say about the location of the CM of a uniform cone?

Solution

By symmetry, the CM must lie along the central symmetry axis of the cone. It is also clear that it will be closer to the base of the cone than to the apex, since there is more mass toward the base and the CM location is weighted by mass. To obtain the exact location one can use the calculus. The CM turns out to be one-fourth the way from the base to the apex.

Problems for Review and Mind Stretching

Problem 8.31. A rifle bullet of mass $m = 20$ g is fired with a muzzle velocity of 600 m/s. The length of the barrel is 80 cm.

(a) What is the total impulse imparted to the bullet?

(b) If the rifle were free to "kick" backward, what would its velocity be when the bullet has left the muzzle, assuming the mass of the rifle M was 3.0 kg?

Solution

(a) $I = mv_f - mv_i = (0.020 \text{ kg})(600 \text{ m/s}) - 0 = 12 \text{ N·s}$.

(b) Choosing the direction of the bullet as positive, from conservation of momentum (noting that the momentum before firing is zero), we have

$$0 = mv + MV = 12 \text{ N·s} + (3.0 \text{ kg})V \qquad \text{or} \qquad V = -4.0 \text{ m/s}$$

Problem 8.32. Show that when two objects A and B of equal mass m have an elastic collision in which one of the objects (say, B) is initially at rest, the final velocities of the two objects must be at right angles to each other. (See Problem 8.24 and the accompanying comments.)

Solution

The situation is similar to that in Fig. 8-10. From momentum conservation we have $m\mathbf{v}_{Ai} = m\mathbf{v}_{Af} + m\mathbf{v}_{Bf}$ or

$$\mathbf{v}_{Ai} = \mathbf{v}_{Af} + \mathbf{v}_{Bf} \tag{i}$$

This vector equation implies that the three velocities form a triangle, as shown in Fig. 8-15. Since the collision is elastic we also have $\frac{1}{2}mv_{ai}^2 = \frac{1}{2}mv_{Af}^2 + \frac{1}{2}mv_{Bf}^2$ or

$$v_{Ai}^2 = v_{Af}^2 + v_{Bf}^2 \tag{ii}$$

Equation (ii) implies that v_{Ai} is the hypotenuse of a right triangle whose other sides are v_{Af} and v_{Bf}. Thus the triangle in Fig. 8-15 is a right triangle, and $\mathbf{v}_{Af}$ and $\mathbf{v}_{Bf}$ are at right angles.

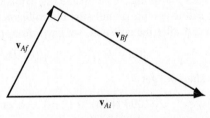

Fig. 8-15

Problem 8.33. A ball is dropped from rest at a height $h = 20$ ft onto a horizontal concrete floor.

(a) If the collision with the floor is perfectly elastic (coefficient of restitution $e = 1$), describe the subsequent events.

(b) Repeat parts (a) if $e = 0.7$.

Solution

(a) Assume the ball hits the floor with speed v_a. During the very brief collision period between the ball and the earth, we can ignore gravity and assume momentum is conserved in the vertical direction. Since $e = 1$, immediately after the collision the ball has the same magnitude and opposite direction relative to the earth. Since the velocity gained by the earth in the collision is so small, it contributes negligibly to the kinetic energy. Thus, the ball will have the same kinetic energy as before and will rise to the exact height from which it was dropped: $h = 20$ ft. The ball will repeat the bounce again and again.

(b) In this situation the ball loses some kinetic energy to thermal energy during the collision so that its rebound velocity is only $v_a' = 0.7v_a$. Therefore, it will rebound only to a height given by $v_a' = (2gh_a')^{1/2}$. Then $e^2 = (v_a'/v_a)^2 = 2gh_a'/2gh_a = h_a'/h_a$ or $(0.70)^2 = h_a'/h_a$. Solving, we get $h_a' = (0.49)h_a = (0.49)(20$ ft$) = 9.8$ ft. By the same reasoning, on each succeeding bounce the ball will rise to 0.49 times the previous height.

Problem 8.34. A bullet of mass $m = 15$ g is fired into a block of mass $M = 985$ g, which is attached to an uncompressed spring of force constant $k = 1000$ N/m. The spring is anchored to a wall, and the block rests on a horizontal frictionless surface as shown in Fig. 8-16. After the bullet embeds itself in the block, the block compresses the spring a maximum distance of $x = 12$ cm. Find the initial velocity of the bullet.

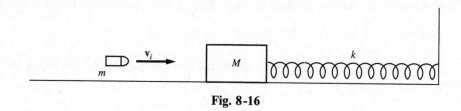

Fig. 8-16

Solution

This is similar to the earlier ballistic pendulum problems, except that now instead of rising against gravity the block compresses the spring. If we assume the collision of the bullet with the block is very rapid, the spring will not start to compress until after the collision is complete. If V_f is the velocity of the bullet-block combination just after the collision, we have, from conservation of mechanical energy,

$$\tfrac{1}{2}(m + M)V_f^2 + 0 = 0 + \tfrac{1}{2}kx^2$$

Substituting the known values we get

$$\tfrac{1}{2}(1.00 \text{ kg})V_f^2 = \tfrac{1}{2}(1000 \text{ N/m}) (0.12 \text{ m})^2 \quad \text{or} \quad V_f = 3.79 \text{ m/s}$$

Next we note that, during the brief collision process, the spring is negligibly compressed and exerts negligible horizontal impulse. We then have conservation of momentum from just before to just after the collision:

$$mv_i = (m + M)V_f \quad \text{or} \quad (0.015 \text{ kg})v_i = (1.00 \text{ kg}) (3.79 \text{ m/s}) \quad \text{so that} \quad v_i = 253 \text{ m/s}$$

Problem 8.35. A projectile is fired from ground level with a velocity v_0 of 600 ft/s, at an angle θ_0 of $30°$ above the horizontal. At the highest point in the trajectory the projectile suddenly explodes into two equal-mass fragments. One of the fragments continues to move horizontally immediately after the explosion, while the other falls vertically downward. Find the total horizontal distance traveled by the horizontally moving fragment.

Solution

The situation is depicted in Fig. 8-17. During the short explosion time, momentum is conserved. Just before the collision, the projectile, being at the highest point, is moving horizontally. Immediately after the collision, the first fragment continues to move horizontally, so the second fragment gains no vertical velocity either. The second fragment falls vertically, so it has lost all its horizontal momentum, and all the original momentum appears in the first fragment, which has half the original mass and thus double the velocity. To find how far this fragment travels horizontally, we first calculate the horizontal distance to the highest point. $v_0 = 600$ ft/s, so

$$v_{0x} = (600 \text{ ft/s}) \cos 30° = 520 \text{ ft/s} \qquad v_{0y} = (600 \text{ ft/s}) \sin 30° = 300 \text{ ft/s}$$

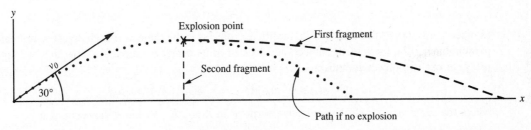

Fig. 8-17

The time to reach the highest point is given by $v_y = 0 = v_{0y} - gt \Rightarrow t = (300 \text{ ft/s})/(32 \text{ ft/s}^2) = 9.38$ s. The horizontal distance to this point is just $x_1 = v_{0x}t = (520 \text{ ft/s})(9.38 \text{ s}) = 4880$ ft. After the explosion, the first fragment has the doubled velocity of 1040 ft/s. Since the time of fall depends only on the height, it is the same as that of the original projectile had it not exploded. This is just the time it took to rise to that height, namely, 9.38 s. Then, the horizontal distance traveled by the fragment from the highest point until it reaches ground level is

$$x_2 = (1040 \text{ ft/s})(9.38 \text{ s}) = 9760 \text{ ft}$$

The total distance traveled by the first fragment is then

$$x_T = x_1 + x_2 = 4880 \text{ ft} + 9760 \text{ ft} = 14,640 \text{ ft}$$

Problem 8.36. Find the center of mass of the object shown in Fig. 8-18, which is made up of a uniform rod glued symmetrically to a rectangular block. Assume $L_R = 3.0$ ft, $L_B = 0.60$ ft, $M_R = 1.5$ slugs, and $M_B = 6.0$ slugs.

Solution

By symmetry (as explained in Problem 8.29) the CM lies somewhere along the symmetry axis (dotted line). Assume this is the x axis and measure x from the left end of the rod. To find the x coordinate of the CM, we note that the CM of the rod is located at its midpoint, at $X_A = 1.5$ ft, and the CM of the block is located at its midpoint, at $X_B = 3.0$ ft $+ 0.30$ ft $= 3.3$ ft. We now show that the CM of the composite object is given by

$$X_{\text{CM}} = \frac{M_A X_A + M_B X_B}{M_A + M_B} \qquad\qquad (i)$$

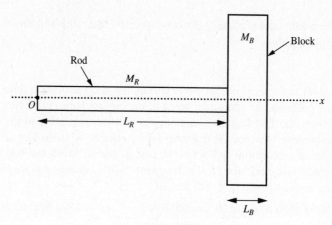

Fig. 8-18

In other words, the CM of a composite of different objects is the same as if each object were treated as a particle having the mass of the object, and located at its center of mass. To show this, we apply Eq. (8.19) to our two-object composite

$$\left(\sum m_{Ai} + \sum m_{Bi}\right)X_{CM} = \sum m_{Ai}x_{Ai} + \sum m_{Bi}x_{Bi} \qquad (ii)$$

where the sums go over all the respective particles in A and B. We know, however, that

$$\sum m_{Ai}x_{Ai} = M_A X_A \quad \text{and} \quad \sum m_{Ai} = M_A \qquad \sum m_{Bi}x_{Bi} = M_B X_B \quad \text{and} \quad \sum m_{Bi} = M_B$$

$$(iii)$$

Then substituting from (iii) into (ii) gives us (i). We can now solve for X_{CM} by substituting into (i):

$$X_{CM} = \frac{(1.5 \text{ slugs}) (1.5 \text{ ft}) + (6.0 \text{ slugs}) (3.3 \text{ ft})}{7.5 \text{ slugs}} = 2.94 \text{ ft}$$

Supplementary Problems

Problem 8.37.   A block of mass $m = 3.5$ kg, initially moving at a speed of $v_i = 12$ m/s to the right on a horizontal frictionless surface, is acted on by a variable horizontal force F as follows: For the first 10 s, $F = 10$ N to the right; for the next 5 s, $F = 25$ N to the left; and for the last 8 s, $F = 15$ N to right. Find the velocity of the block at the end of the 23-s interval.

   Ans.   39 m/s

Problem 8.38.   A baseball of mass 0.2 kg is pitched at 35 m/s and popped straight up by the batter. The ball rises to a maximum height of 120 m. Find (*a*) the speed with which the ball leaves the bat, and (*b*) the magnitude and direction of the impulse of the bat on the ball.

   Ans.   (*a*) 48.5 m/s; (*b*) 12.0 N · s, 54° above horizontal toward the pitcher

Problem 8.39.   In Problem 8.38, assume the average force exerted on the baseball by the bat is one-fourth of the peak force. If the peak force is $F = 12,000$ N, find the time of contact of the ball with the bat.

   Ans.   0.0040 s

Problem 8.40. Suppose that in Fig. 8-7 the initial velocities are $v_{ai} = -20$ m/s and $v_{bi} = -30$ m/s and the surface is frictionless. If the collision is elastic, find the final velocities of the two blocks.

   Ans. $v_{af} = -26.7$ m/s and $v_{bf} = -16.7$ m/s

Problem 8.41. Assume the same initial velocities as in Problem 8.40, and that the mass of block B is unchanged. For what mass of block A would the final velocity of block B be -25 m/s?

   Ans.   1.67 kg

Problem 8.42. Assume that in Problem 8.40 the collision is inelastic and the coefficient of restitution is 0.5. Find (*a*) the final velocities, (*b*) the loss in kinetic energy.

   Ans.   (*a*) $v_{af} = -25$ m/s, $v_{bf} = -20$ m/s; (*b*) 125 J

Problem 8.43. Assume that in Fig. 8-7 the surface is frictionless and the velocities are as shown, but the masses are $m_A = 15$ kg; $m_B = 10$ kg. If the collision is totally inelastic, find the final velocity and the loss in kinetic energy.

   Ans.   (*a*) 22 m/s; (*b*) 1200 J

Problem 8.44. In Fig. 8-9, assume that the masses are $m = 25$ g and $M = 8.2$ kg and that $v_i = 550$ m/s. If the bullet embeds itself in the block, find (*a*) the velocity of the block just after the collision and (*b*) the height through which the block rises.

   Ans.   (*a*) 1.67 m/s; (*b*) 14.2 cm

Problem 8.45. Suppose that in Problem 8.44 the bullet passes through the block and continues in a straight line. If the block rises through half the distance as that in Problem 8.44, what is the final velocity of the bullet?

   Ans.   161 m/s

Problem 8.46. In Fig. 8-10 assume the two pucks are on a frictionless horizontal surface and that $M_A = 50$ g and $M_B = 100$ g. Assume that $\theta = 30°$ and $\phi = 20°$ after the collision. If $v_{af} = 30$ cm/s: (*a*) find v_{Bf}, (*b*) find v_{Ai}, (*c*) was the collision elastic?

   Ans.   (*a*) 21.9 cm/s; (*b*) 67.1 cm/s; (*c*) no

Problem 8.47. Assume that Fig. 8-11 represents a bird's-eye view of a collision between two automobiles at an intersection. Assume $M_A = 2000$ kg, $M_B = 1500$ kg, $v_{Ai} = 20$ m/s, $v_{Bi} = 30$ m/s. The two cars stick together after the collision.

(*a*)   Find the magnitude and direction of the velocity immediately after the collision, ignoring the effects of pavement friction over the short collision time.

(*b*)   If the coefficient of kinetic friction between the locked wreckage and the pavement is 0.85, how far will it skid?

   Ans.   (*a*) 17.2 m/s, 48.4° with x axis; (*b*) 17.8 m

Problem 8.48. A ball of mass 40 g is dropped on a concrete floor from a height of 2.5 m. It is observed to rebound to a height of 1.5 m.

(a) Evaluate the coefficient of restitution

(b) How much kinetic energy is lost in the brief collision of the ball with the floor?

>   *Ans.*   (a) 0.775; (b) 0.392 J

Problem 8.49.   A 50-g cart is sliding without friction on a horizontal air track at a speed of 30 cm/s. A steel ball of mass 15 g is dropped vertically so that it lands in the cart. What is the new speed of the cart after the steel ball comes to rest in it?

>   *Ans.*   23.1 cm/s

Problem 8.50.   In Fig. 8-12 the spring is initially compressed 8.0 in and the blocks start at rest on a frictionless surface. The masses are $m_a = 2.5$ slugs and $m_b = 3.5$ slugs, and after the system is released, $v_{bf} = 20$ ft/s. Find v_{af} and the force constant of the spring.

>   *Ans.* -28 ft/s, 7560 lb/ft

Problem 8.51.   A boy, of mass 40 kg, is stranded on a frozen pond; the ice is so smooth as to be absolutely frictionless. He is trying to reach the closest bank, 50 m away, but keeps slipping in place. Suddenly he gets an idea: he takes off a boot, of mass 0.50 kg, and hurls it directly away from the bank at a speed of 12 m/s relative to the ice. how long will it take him to reach the bank?

>   *Ans.*   333 s

Problem 8.52.   A uranium 238 nucleus is unstable and decays into thorium 234 by emitting an α particle (helium nucleus). The relative masses of the thorium and α particle are 234 and 4, respectively. The thorium nucleus is observed to recoil at a speed of 2.39×10^4 m/s when the α particle is emitted from a uranium nucleus at rest. What is the speed of the α particle?

>   *Ans.* 1.4×10^6 m/s

Problem 8.53.   A uniform iron rod of length 1 m is bent at its midpoint to make a 90° angle. Find the location of the CM of the bent rod.

>   *Ans.*   17.7 cm from the midpoint along the symmetry axis (the line at 45° to each half of the rod)

Problem 8.54.   Two identical rods are rigidly connected to a disk at right angles to each other, as shown in Fig. 8-19. Find the center of mass of the system.

>   *Ans.*   10.2 cm from the center of the disk and midway between the rods (i.e., along a 45° line to the rods)

Problem 8.55.   A boy is in a cart which rests on a sheet of frictionless ice. The boy and cart are initially at rest. The boy runs from one end of the cart to the other, hurling himself against that end to get the cart moving. Will he succeed and if not why?

>   *Ans.*   No. The CM of the boy-cart combination is initially at rest, and there is no net external force on the system, so the CM remains at rest. Therefore, when the boy runs across the cart, the cart moves in the opposite direction at a speed that keeps the CM fixed. When he hits the other side, both he and the cart once more come to rest.

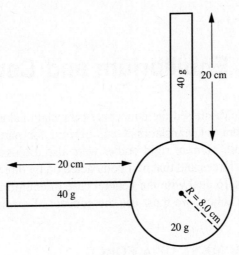

Fig. 8-19

Problem 8.56. The earth and the moon are separated by a distance (center to center) of 3.8×10^5 km. The CM of the system is known to be within the earth, at a distance of 4.62×10^3 km from its center. Find the ratio of the earth's mass to that of the moon.

Ans.   81.3

Chapter 9

Rigid Bodies I: Equilibrium and Center of Gravity

In Sections 4.2 and 4.3, we discussed the concepts of translational and rotational equilibrium, as well as the general requirement for translational equilibrium for particles and rigid bodies. The requirements for rotational equilibrium of rigid bodies were also discussed for two simple cases: that of a body acted on by only two forces and that of a body acted on by three forces. It would be useful to review those two sections now. To deal with the general case of equilibrium of rigid bodies, when an arbitrary number of forces are acting, we must use the concept of *torque*, or *moment*.

9.1 THE TORQUE OR MOMENT OF A FORCE

Definitions

The words *torque* and *moment* are synonymous, and we will use them interchangeably. In this chapter, as in Chapter 4, we deal almost exclusively with situations in which the forces acting on a rigid body are coplanar (in the same plane), allowing an algebraic definition of torque rather than the more general vector one. An important feature of the definition of the moment of a force is that it depends on the choice of a particular point in the plane relative to which the moment is defined. This will become clear from the definition.

In Fig. 9-1 we have a typical, rigid body and have displayed one of the coplanar forces **F** acting on it. We pick some arbitrary point A and define Γ_A, the moment of the force **F** about the point A, as follows: First, draw the line of action through the force **F** (represented by the dotted line in Fig. 9-1. Next, draw the perpendicular line from the point A to that line of action (represented by the dashed line of length d_A in Fig. 9-1). Then, by definition

$$\Gamma_A = \pm d_A F \tag{9.1}$$

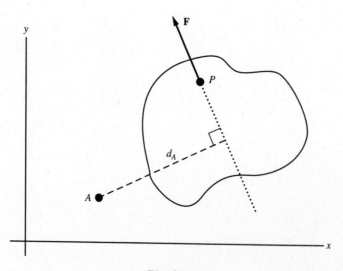

Fig. 9-1

218

where the choice of sign is determined by which way the force **F** would tend to rotate the body about A: clockwise or counterclockwise. (If point A is outside the body, as in Fig. 9-1, imagine that it is rigidly linked to the body and has a pin through it about which the whole system can rotate.) If point A were pinned, the force **F** would tend to rotate the body counterclockwise about the point. It is usual for such a counterclockwise moment to be considered positive, while clockwise moments are considered negative.

The distance d_A from point A to the line of action of **F** is given a special name. It is called the **moment arm** of the force **F** about A.

If more than one force is acting on a body, the total moment about A is the algebraic sum of the individual moments about A. In Fig. 9-2 we show three coplanar forces $\mathbf{F}_1$, $\mathbf{F}_2$, and $\mathbf{F}_3$ acting on a rigid body. The total torque is given as $\Gamma_A = d_{A1}F_1 - d_{A2}F_2 + d_{A3}F_3$, where the signs have been chosen as explained above.

Note that the units of torque are force times length, the same as the units of work, although torque has a quite different physical meaning. Typical units are N · m, dyn · cm, and lb · ft.

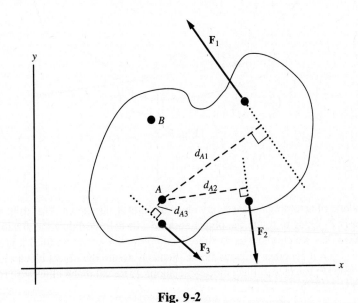

Fig. 9-2

Problem 9.1.

(a) Show that the torque Γ_A of the force **F** shown in Fig. 9-1 would not change if one slides **F** to a different location along its line of action.

(b) Show that if the force **F** were replaced by $-\mathbf{F}$ acting anywhere along the same line of action, the magnitude of the torque remains the same but the sign changes.

Solution

(a) From the definition, the torque depends only on the magnitude of the force and the moment arm to the line of action. Since **F** and d_A are unchanged, from Eq. (9.1) we see that Γ_A is unchanged.

(b) The magnitude of $-\mathbf{F}$ is the same as that of **F**, and d_A is unchanged, so the magnitude of Γ_A is unchanged. Now, however, the force $-\mathbf{F}$ tends to rotate the object about A in the direction opposite to that of the force **F**, so the sign of the torque must change.

Problem 9.2.

(a) Find the sign of the torques of $\mathbf{F}_1$ and $\mathbf{F}_2$ about A as shown in Fig. 9-3.

(b) What is the value of the torque of $\mathbf{F}_3$ about A?

(c) What are the signs of the torques of each of the three forces about point B?

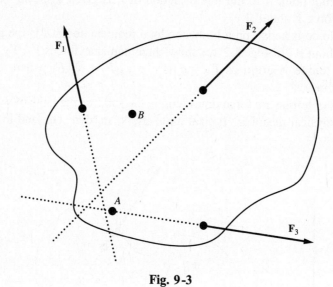

Fig. 9-3

Solution

(a) $\mathbf{F}_1$ has a line of action that passes very close to point A, as shown. This might make it less obvious which way $\mathbf{F}_1$ tends to rotate the object about A. To help visualize the situation we use the results of Problem 9.1, which allow us to slide $\mathbf{F}_1$ along its line of action until it is as close to point A as possible. Then it becomes obvious that $\mathbf{F}_1$ tends to rotate the object clockwise about A. Similarly, $\mathbf{F}_2$ also tends to rotate the object clockwise about A. Recall that a clockwise rotation has a negative sign.

(b) The line of action of $\mathbf{F}_3$ passes right through A. Then the moment arm $d_{A3} = 0$, and from Eq. (9.1) $\Gamma_{A3} = 0$. Thus, any force whose line of action passes through a given point has zero torque about that point.

(c) For point B it is not hard to see that $\mathbf{F}_2$ and $\mathbf{F}_3$ have counterclockwise moments ($+$), while $\mathbf{F}_1$ has a clockwise moment ($-$).

Problem 9.3. In Fig. 9-4 we have a force $\mathbf{F}$ acting at a given point in the body. Let $\mathbf{r}_A$ represent the relative displacement from point A to the point of application of $\mathbf{F}$. If $F = 15$ N, $r_A = 3.0$ m, and $\theta = 30°$, find the moment of $\mathbf{F}$ about point A.

Solution

Clearly $\mathbf{F}$ gives rise to a counterclockwise moment about A. To find the magnitude of the moment we must find the moment arm d_A. From the triangle we can see that $d_A = r_A \sin \theta$, so

$$\Gamma_A = d_A F = r_A F \sin \theta = (3.0 \text{ m})(15 \text{ N})(0.50) = 22.5 \text{ N} \cdot \text{m}$$

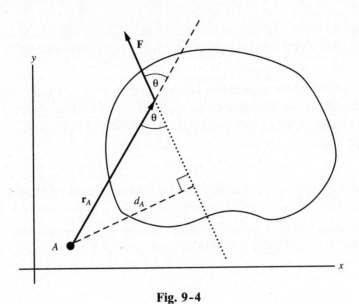

Fig. 9-4

Another View of Torque

Problem 9.3 gives us a way of expressing the torque in terms of r_A, the displacement from an arbitrary point A to the point of application of the force $\mathbf{F}$ (Fig. 9-4). The torque due to $\mathbf{F}$ about A is

$$\Gamma_A = \pm r_A F \sin \theta \qquad (9.2)$$

where θ is the angle between the vectors $\mathbf{r}_A$ and $\mathbf{F}$ when their two tails are together. This leads us to yet another expression for the torque. In Fig. 9-5 we reproduce Fig. 9-4 but now break $\mathbf{F}$ into components F_r, parallel, and F_t, perpendicular, to $\mathbf{r}_A$. As can be seen from Fig. 9-5, $F_t = F \sin \theta$. Thus, the torque from Eq. (9.2) can be reexpressed as $\pm r_A F_t$. We thus have three equivalent expressions for the torque:

$$\Gamma_A = \pm r_A F \sin \theta = \pm d_A F = \pm r_A F_t \qquad (9.3)$$

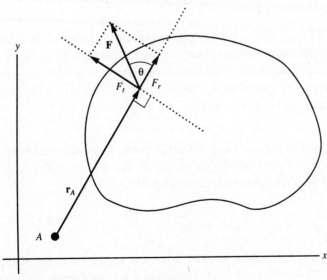

Fig. 9-5

Note the symmetry between the last two expressions of Eq. (9.3): F_t is the component of **F** perpendicular to $\mathbf{r}_A$, and d_A (as can be seen in Fig. 9-4) is the component of $\mathbf{r}_A$ perpendicular to **F**.

Problem 9.4. Figure 9-6(a) shows a ladder leaning against a smooth wall, with the various forces acting on the ladder drawn in. Find the moment of the force F about point A by (a) finding the moment arm d_A and using Eq. (9.1), and (b) finding the component of **F** perpendicular to $\mathbf{r}_A$ and using the right side of Eq. (9.3).

Solution

(a) d_A is just the perpendicular distance from A to the line of action of **F** and is shown in Fig. 9-6(b). Thus, $d_A = (20 \text{ m}) \sin 37° = 12 \text{ m}$. From Eq. (9.1): $\Gamma_A = (12 \text{ m})(30 \text{ N}) = 360 \text{ N} \cdot \text{m}$.

(b) Here we note that $\mathbf{r}_A$ is along the ladder from A to the contact point with the wall. Then, $F_t = F \sin 37° = (30 \text{ N}) \sin 37° = 18 \text{ N}$, and from Eq. (9.3); $\Gamma_A = r_A F_t = (20 \text{ m})(18 \text{ N}) = 360 \text{ N} \cdot \text{m}$.

9.2 THE LAWS OF EQUILIBRIUM FOR RIGID BODIES

Translational and Rotational Equilibrium

We are now able to express the necessary and sufficient conditions for translational and rotational equilibrium of a rigid body acted on by any number of coplanar forces. Two conditions must hold:

1. The vector sum of the forces must vanish.
2. The algebraic sum of the torques about a given point must vanish.

Mathematically:

$$(1) \quad \sum \mathbf{F}_i = 0 \qquad (2) \quad \sum \Gamma_{Ai} = 0 \qquad\qquad (9.4a, b)$$

The first condition (4a) can be expressed in component form:

$$\sum F_{ix} = 0 \qquad\qquad \sum F_{iy} = 0 \qquad\qquad (9.5a, b)$$

Note.   Equation (9.4a) [or Eqs. (9.5)] is the statement of Newton's first law applied to a particle. From our discussion of the center of mass of a system of particles in Chap. 8 these same equations are statements of the law of translational equilibrium for the CM of a rigid body. Equation (9.4b) can also be derived from Newton's laws for particles, as will be demonstrated in the next chapter.

Problem 9.5.   Suppose the ladder in Fig. 9-6(a) is at rest under the action of the forces shown. The ladder is uniform so that we can consider its weight **W** to act at its center. Calculate the values of the weight W, the normal force N, and the frictional force f.

Solution

Since the ladder is at rest, it is in both translational and rotational equilibrium. Therefore, Eqs. (9.4) must hold. If we take moments about A, the friction and normal forces don't contribute since their lines of action pass through A. Thus the only two forces contributing are F and W. The moment of F was

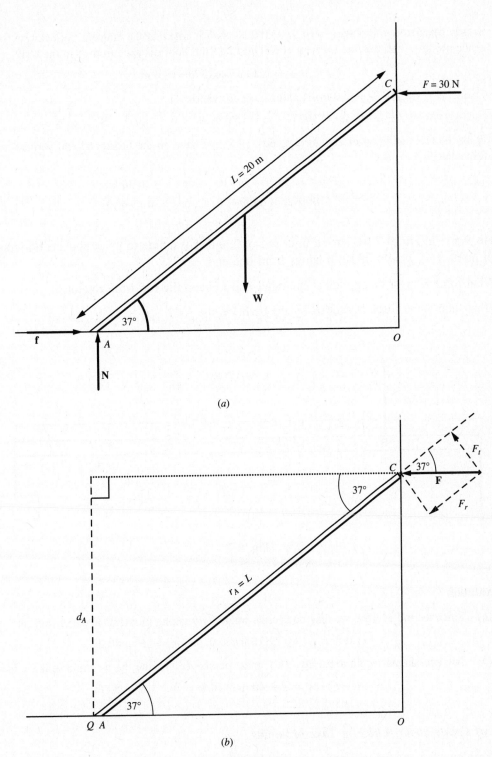

(a)

(b)

Fig. 9-6

already calculated in Problem 9.4: $\Gamma_{AF} = 360 \text{ N} \cdot \text{m}$. We note that the moment is clockwise for W, and hence negative, and that the moment arm is just half the floor distance from A to the wall:

$$d_{AW} = \tfrac{1}{2}(20 \text{ m}) \cos 37° = 8.0 \text{ m}$$

Then $\Gamma_{AW} = -d_{AW}W = -(8.0 \text{ m})W$, and Eq. (9.4b) yields

$$\Gamma_{AF} + \Gamma_{AW} = 360 \text{ N} \cdot \text{ m} - (8.0 \text{ m})W = 0 \quad \text{or} \quad W = 45 \text{ N}$$

From the first condition of equilibrium, Eqs. (9.5), we have, in the horizontal and vertical directions, respectively,

$$F - f = 30 \text{ N} - f = 0 \quad \text{or} \quad f = 30 \text{ N}$$
$$N - W = N - 45 \text{ N} = 0 \quad \text{or} \quad N = 45 \text{ N}$$

Problem 9.6. In Fig. 9-7 we have a light rod of length 5.0 ft free to pivot about a horizontal axis through point A. A weight of 10 lb hangs from one end.

(*a*)   What force F must be applied at the other end to keep the rod from rotating?

(*b*)   What then is the force N exerted by the pivot on the rod?

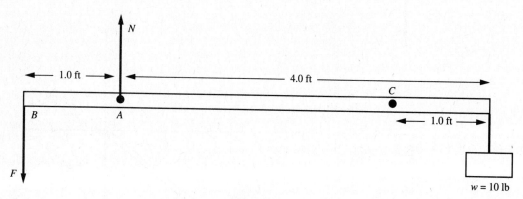

Fig. 9-7

Solution

(*a*)   Since the rod is light, we may neglect its weight. By taking moments about A, we get
$$(1.0 \text{ ft})F - (4.0 \text{ ft})(10 \text{ lb}) = 0 \quad \text{or} \quad F = 40 \text{ lb}$$

(*b*)   For translational equilibrium Eqs. (9.5) must be obeyed. Taking the y components we have
$$N - F - w = N - 40 \text{ lb} - 10 \text{ lb} = 0 \quad N = 50 \text{ lb}$$

Choice of Points about Which to Take Moments

In Problems 9.5 and 9.6 we made specific choices of the point about which moments were to be taken for use in Eq. (9.4b). Would we have gotten different results if we had taken moments about some other point? Is there a "correct" point about which to take moments in applying the laws of equilibrium?

The following result can be proved: If the first condition of equilibrium, Eq. (9.4a), holds, and if Eq. (9.4b) holds about a particular point A, then Eq. (9.4b) will also hold about every other point as well. Thus, once the vector sum of forces adds up to zero, the sum of the moments about one point will be zero if, and only if, the sum of the moments about every other point is zero.

This result is particularly useful for two reasons. One is that you can always check your solution to an equilibrium problem by taking moments about a different point and checking that they add up to zero. The other is that you have complete flexibility in picking the point about which to calculate moments for Eq. (9.4b). This means that you can pick the point that is most convenient for solving the problem. For example, in Problem 9.5, point A is a particularly convenient choice since it eliminates the forces $\mathbf{f}$ and $\mathbf{N}$ from the moment equation and hence leaves just one unknown, the weight W.

Problem 9.7.   Check your answer to Problem 9.5 by taking moments about point C in Fig. 9-6(a).

Solution

The sum of the moments about point C must add up to zero. The forces, as determined in Problem 9.5 are $F = 30$ N, $W = 45$ N, $f = 30$ N, $N = 45$ N. Referring to Fig. 9.6(a), we note that F has no moment about C; W and f have counterclockwise (positive) moments about C; N has a clockwise (negative) moment about C. The moment arms are easily obtained by looking at perpendicular distances from C to the lines of action of the forces: $d_{CW} = \frac{1}{2}(20$ m$)$ cos $37° = 8.0$ m; $d_{CN} = (20$ m$)$ cos $37° = 16$ m; $d_{Cf} = (20$ m$)$ sin $37° = 12$ m. Then

$$\Gamma_C = d_{CW}W + d_{Cf}f - d_{CN}N = (8.0 \text{ m})(45 \text{ N}) + (12 \text{ m})(30 \text{ N}) - (16 \text{ m})(45 \text{ N})$$
$$= 360 \text{ N} \cdot \text{m} + 360 \text{ N} \cdot \text{m} - 720 \text{ N} \cdot \text{m} = 0$$

Note.   In getting the moments of the forces acting on the ladder at point A we treated $\mathbf{f}$ and $\mathbf{N}$ as separate forces even though they are acting at the same point in the body. We could have replaced them by their vector sum and considered the moment of that single force. There was no point in doing so since the moment arms to the individual forces $\mathbf{f}$ and $\mathbf{N}$ are easily obtained, while getting the moment arm to the vector sum of $\mathbf{f}$ and $\mathbf{N}$ would have been harder. Actually, the reverse process is often more useful: If one is given a single force acting at a point, it is sometimes easier to break the force into a sum of two forces whose moment arms are easier to calculate.

Problem 9.8.   Check the results of Problem 9.6 (Fig. 9-7) by taking moments (a) about point B at the left end of the rod, and (b) about point C, which is 1 ft from the right end of the rod.

Solution

(a)   The force F contributes zero moment about the left end of the rod. Then

$$\Gamma_B = (1.0 \text{ ft})N - (5.0 \text{ ft})w = (1.0 \text{ ft})(50 \text{ lb}) - (5.0 \text{ ft})(10 \text{ lb}) = 50 \text{ lb} \cdot \text{ft} - 50 \text{ lb} \cdot \text{ft} = 0$$

(b)   About point C all three forces contribute:

$$\Gamma_C = (4.0 \text{ ft})F - (3.0 \text{ ft})N - (1.0 \text{ ft})w$$
$$= (4.0 \text{ ft})(40 \text{ lb}) - (3.0 \text{ ft})(50 \text{ lb}) - (1.0 \text{ ft})(10 \text{ lb})$$
$$= 160 \text{ lb} \cdot \text{ft} - 150 \text{ lb} \cdot \text{ft} - 10 \text{ lb} \cdot \text{ft} = 0$$

Problem 9.9.   A uniform rectangular block of weight $w = 40$ N moves at a constant speed along a frictionless horizontal surface, under the action of forces $\mathbf{F}_1$ and $\mathbf{F}_2$, as shown in Fig. 9-8.

(a)   Find the magnitude of the force $\mathbf{F}_2$ and of the normal force $\mathbf{N}$.

(b)   Find the point of application of the normal force, as measured from the left end of the block.

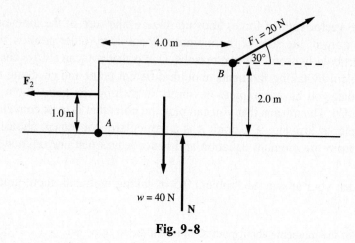

Fig. 9-8

Solution

(a) Since the block is undergoing translation at constant velocity and is not rotating, it is in equilibrium. We first consider the first condition of equilibrium, Eqs. (9.5). For the x direction

$$F_1 \cos 30° - F_2 = 0 \quad \text{or} \quad F_2 = 17.3 \text{ N}$$

For the y direction

$$F_1 \sin 30° + N - 40 \text{ N} = 0 \quad \text{or} \quad N = 30 \text{ N}$$

Thus, part (a) is solved without resort to the second condition of equilibrium.

(b) Here we need to find the location of the line of action of the normal force. Clearly only a moment equation will give us such information. We take moments about the point A at the left lower corner of the block. Since it will be difficult to find the distance of the line of action of the moment arm of $\mathbf{F}_1$ from A, we replace $\mathbf{F}_1$ by a pair of forces, one horizontal and one vertical, corresponding to the components F_{1x} and F_{1y}. These forces have magnitudes $F_{1x} = 17.3$ N and $F_{1y} = 10$ N. Then

$$\Gamma_A = (1.0 \text{ m})F_2 - (2.0 \text{ m})w + (4.0 \text{ m})F_{1y} - (2.0 \text{ m})F_{1x} + xN = 0$$

Substituting we get

$$\Gamma_A = (1.0 \text{ m})(17.3 \text{ N}) - (2.0 \text{ m})(40 \text{ N}) + (4.0 \text{ m})(10 \text{ N}) - (2.0 \text{ m})(17.3 \text{ N}) + x(30 \text{ N}) = 0$$

or

$$x = 1.91 \text{ m}$$

Problem 9.10. Check the results of Problem 9.9 by taking moments about point B.

Solution

The force $\mathbf{F}_1$ does not contribute a moment about point B, so

$$\Gamma_B = (2.0 \text{ m})w - (1.0 \text{ m})F_2 - (4.0 \text{ m} - x)N = 0$$
$$= (2.0 \text{ m})(40 \text{ N}) - (1.0 \text{ m})(17.3 \text{ N}) - (2.09 \text{ m})(30 \text{ N}) = 80 - 17.3 - 62.7 = 0$$

Problem 9.11. A weight $W = 500$ N hangs from one end of a uniform horizontal beam of weight $w = 100$ N and length L whose other end is pivoted at point A on the wall [Fig. 9-9(a)]. The beam is supported by a wire making an angle of 40° with the beam. Find (a) the tension in the wire, (b) the vertical and horizontal components of the force exerted by the pivot on the beam.

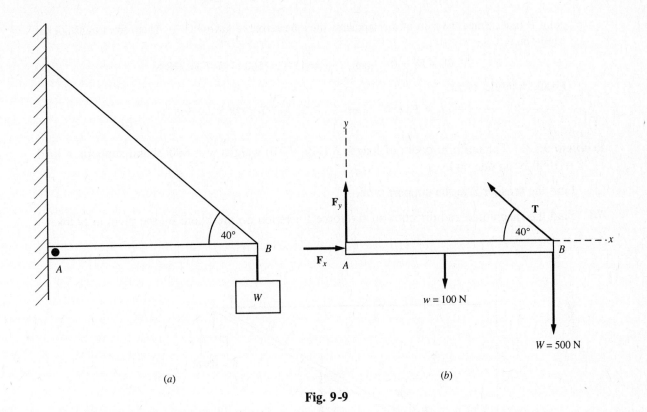

(a)   (b)

Fig. 9-9

Solution

(a) The forces acting on the beam are shown in Fig. 9-9(b). Since the beam is in equilibrium, Eqs. (9.4b) and (9.5a, b) must hold. If we take moments about point B, the forces **T**, **W**, and **F**$_x$ do not contribute since their lines of action pass through B. The only unknown force in the equation will then be F_y, so we can solve for it.

$$\Gamma_B = \left(\frac{L}{2}\right)w - LF_y = 0 \quad \text{or} \quad \tfrac{1}{2}(100 \text{ N}) - F_y = 0 \quad \text{or} \quad F_y = 50 \text{ N}$$

To find T we use Eq. (9.5b):

$$F_y - w - W + T\sin 40° = 0 \quad \text{or} \quad 50 \text{ N} - 100 \text{ N} - 500 \text{ N} + (0.643)T = 0$$

$$\text{or} \quad T = 855 \text{ N}$$

(b) We already obtained $F_y = 50$ N. To get F_x we use Eq. (9.5a)

$$F_x - T\cos 40° = 0 \quad \text{or} \quad F_x = (855 \text{ N})(0.766) = 655 \text{ N}$$

Problem 9.12.   If the beam in Problem 9.11 could be considered weightless, what would then be the values of T, F_y, and F_x?

Solution

We could redo the formal steps of Problem 9.11 with w set equal to zero, but it is easier to approach the problem more directly. First we note that if w = 0, the only force contributing any moment about point B is F_y. Since the sum of the moments must be zero, we have $F_y = 0$. Then, from translational equilibrium,

$$T_y - W = 0 \quad \text{or} \quad (0.643)T = 500 \text{ N} \Rightarrow T = 778 \text{ N}$$

Finally from Eq. (9.5a)

$$T_x - F_x = 0 \quad \text{or} \quad F_x = (0.766)(778 \text{ N}) = 596 \text{ N}$$

Problem 9.13. The uniform boom of length L (Fig. 9-10) weighs $w = 800$ N and supports a load of $W = 1000$ N on one end.

(a) Find the tension T in the support wire.

(b) Find the magnitude and direction of the force **F** exerted on the boom by the pivot at point A.

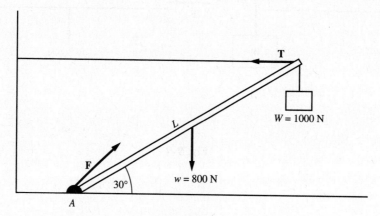

Fig. 9-10

Solution

(a) We take moments about point A, which eliminates the force **F** from the moment equation. Then
$\Gamma_A = (L \sin 30°)T - (L \cos 30°)W - \frac{1}{2}(L \cos 30°)w = 0$. Dividing out L we get

$$(0.50)T - (0.866)(1000 \text{ N}) - (0.433)(800 \text{ N}) = 0 \quad \text{or} \quad T = 2425 \text{ N}$$

(b) Breaking **F** into x and y components, we get from Eq. (9.5a):

$$F_x - T = 0 \quad \text{or} \quad F_x = 2425 \text{ N}$$

from Eq. (9.5b):

$$F_y - w - W = 0 \quad \text{or} \quad F_y = 1800 \text{ N}$$

Then

$$F = [(2425 \text{ N})^2 + (1800 \text{ N})^2]^{1/2} = 3020 \text{ N}$$

If θ is the angle of **F** above the positive x axis,

$$\tan \theta = \frac{F_y}{F_x} = \frac{1800}{2425} = 0.742 \quad \text{or} \quad \theta = 36.6°$$

Problem 9.14. A uniform ladder of length $L = 60$ ft and weight $w = 50$ lb leans against a frictionless wall. The ladder makes an angle of 50° with the floor, and the coefficient of friction between ladder and floor is $\mu_s = 0.50$. A painter, weighing (with bucket) $W = 160$ lb, starts to climb the ladder. What distance x along the ladder can the painter go before the ladder starts to slip?

Solution

The situation is depicted in Fig. 9-11, with all the forces on the ladder drawn in. So long as the ladder is in translational equilibrium

$$N = w + W = 210 \text{ lb} \qquad \text{and} \qquad f = F$$

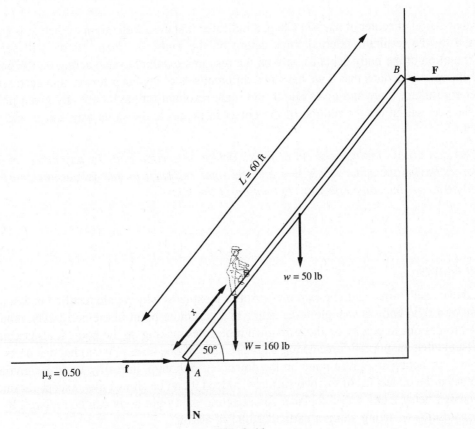

Fig. 9-11

independent of the position of the painter. In the moment equation (9.4b), about point A, only F appears as an unknown; furthermore, as the painter climbs the ladder, the clockwise torque about A due to **W** is increasing, because the moment arm is increasing. This can be balanced only by an increasing counterclockwise torque due to **F**. Since the moment arm from A to the line of action of **F** is fixed, the torque due to **F** can increase only if F increases. Since $f = F$, this means that f must keep increasing as the painter climbs the ladder, until it reaches its maximum value,

$$f_{max} = \mu_s N = (0.50)(210 \text{ lb}) = 105 \text{ lb} = F_{max}$$

Thus, just before slipping takes place, (9.4) gives

$$\Gamma_A = [(60 \text{ ft}) \sin 50°]F_{max} - [(30 \text{ ft}) \cos 50°]w - [x_{max} \cos 50°]W$$
$$= (60 \text{ ft})(0.766)(105 \text{ lb}) - (30 \text{ ft})(0.643)(50 \text{ lb}) - x_{max}(0.643)(160 \text{ lb}) = 0$$

whence $x_{max} = 37.5$ ft.

9.3   EQUIVALENT SETS OF COPLANAR FORCES

We have seen that to have translational and rotational equilibrium for a rigid body acted on by a set of coplanar forces, the set of forces must obey precisely two conditions, as expressed by Eqs. (9.4a, b). Nothing further need be known about the details of the set of forces to ensure equilibrium. The body will still be in equilibrium if our original set of forces is replaced by any other set of forces obeying the same equations. This leads us to an intriguing question. Suppose a rigid body acted on by a set of coplanar forces is *not* in equilibrium and we want to fully describe its translational and rotational motion. What do we need to know about the set of forces to completely describe the body's motion?

Our discussion of center of mass in Chap. 8 indicated that the acceleration of the CM is completely determined by the resultant external force acting on the body. In Chap. 10 we will see that the rotational motion of the body depends only on the resultant external torque acting on the body. From these results we can deduce that if we have two different sets of coplanar forces, and each set adds up to the same resultant force and gives rise to the same resultant torque (about any given point), then each of the sets will affect the motion of the object in precisely the same way. Let us state without proof that:

> One can always replace one set of forces acting on a rigid body by any other set of forces having the same vector sum and the same resultant torque (about any chosen point) to get the same effect on the motion of the body.

Center of Gravity

The above result turns out to be extremely useful. It explains why we are justified in assuming that the weight of a rigid body is a single force acting at a particular point in the body, even though there are myriad forces due to gravity on the individual molecules making up the body. It also explains why we can assume that the normal force acting on the surface of one object by another can be assumed to be a single force acting at a given point on the object, even though, in reality, there are myriad forces acting between the molecules of the two surfaces. Indeed it can be shown that, except for one special case (discussed below), any set of coplanar forces acting on a rigid body can be replaced by a *single force* (their resultant), acting along a particular line of action.

Problem 9.15.   Find the single force **F** that can replace the two parallel forces $\mathbf{F}_1$ and $\mathbf{F}_2$ acting on the body shown in Fig. 9-12, and find its point of application.

Solution

The single replacement force must equal the vector sum of the original forces. Since the forces are parallel, the force **F** points in the same direction and has magnitude $F = F_1 + F_2 = 30$ N $+ 20$ N $= 50$ N. Further, the moment of **F** about the origin must equal the combined moments of the original two forces: $\Gamma = \Gamma_1 + \Gamma_2 \Rightarrow xF = x_1 F_1 + x_2 F_2$

$$x(50 \text{ N}) = (6.0 \text{ m})(30 \text{ N}) + (12.0 \text{ m})(20 \text{ N}) \qquad \text{or} \qquad x = 8.40 \text{ m}$$

The force **F** can act anywhere along its line of action.

Problem 9.16.   Find the single force that can replace the three forces shown in Fig. 9-13, and find its line of action.

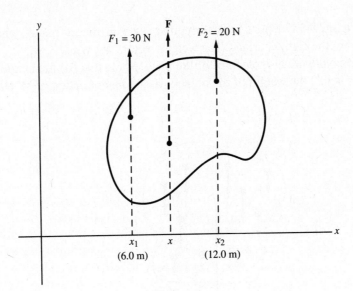

Fig. 9-12

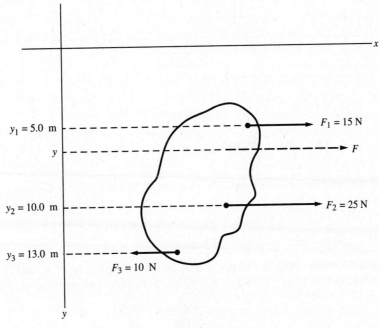

Fig. 9-13

Solution

Again, our single force is parallel to $\mathbf{F}_1$ and $\mathbf{F}_2$ and has magnitude

$$F = F_1 + F_2 - F_3 = 15\text{ N} + 25\text{ N} - 10\text{ N} = 30\text{ N}$$

The line of action is determined by equating moments about the origin:

$$yF = y_1F_1 + y_2F_2 - y_3F_3$$

Substituting, we get

$$y(30\text{ N}) = (5.0\text{ m})(15\text{ N}) + (10\text{ m})(25\text{ N}) - (13\text{ m})(10\text{ N}) \qquad \text{or} \qquad y = 6.5\text{ m}$$

Problem 9.17. Figure 9-14 depicts a flat irregular plate in the xy plane, where y is the vertical direction upward from the earth's surface. The weight vectors $\mathbf{w}_1, \mathbf{w}_2, \ldots, \mathbf{w}_i \ldots$, represent the pull of gravity on the various individual molecules of the plate. Show that (a) the single force $\mathbf{W}$ which can replace these forces is just the weight of the object; (b) the line of action of $\mathbf{W}$ passes through the CM of the plate.

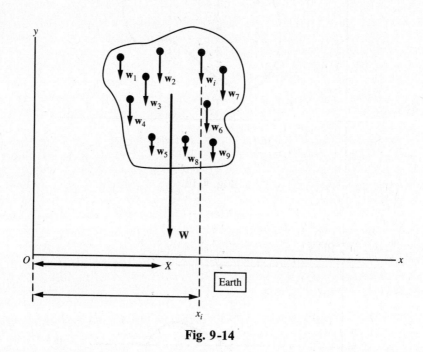

Fig. 9-14

Solution

(a) Since all the individual $\mathbf{w}$'s are parallel, their resultant $\mathbf{W}$ must point in the same direction and must be of magnitude

$$W = w_1 + w_2 + \cdots + w_i + \cdots = \Sigma w_i \tag{i}$$

where W equals the total weight of the plate.

(b) We equate moments about the origin. Let x_i be the moment arm of $\mathbf{w}_i$ and X the moment arm of $\mathbf{W}$. Then, $XW = \Sigma x_i w_i$. Dividing by W, using Eq. (i), and recalling that $w_i = m_i g$, we get

$$X = \frac{\Sigma m_i x_i}{\Sigma m_i} = \frac{\Sigma m_i x_i}{M} \tag{ii}$$

where M is the total mass of the plate. Comparing Eq. (ii) to Eq. ($8.19a$), we see that $X = X_{\mathrm{CM}}$.

The results of Problem 9.17 can be extended to any arbitrary orientation of the plate, in three dimensions as well as in two dimensions. For example, by considering the object to be rotated by 90° in the x, y plane and redoing the problem we find that the single force $\mathbf{W}$ which replaces all the individual weights is still the total weight of the object, and its line of action of $\mathbf{W}$ still passes through the center of mass. Thus, no matter what the orientation, one can always assume the weight of a rigid body acts at the CM. The point in a body where the total weight can be assumed to be acting is often called the **center of gravity** (CG). Thus the center of gravity and the center of mass are one and the same point.

Problem 9.18. Locate the CG of the composite object, made of three copper strips shown in Fig. 9-15.

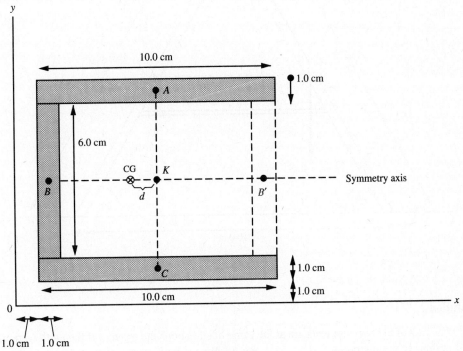

Fig. 9-15

Solution

The CM or CG of each strip lies at its geometric center. By symmetry we also know that the overall CG of the composite lies somewhere along a horizontal line through the CG of strip B. The total weight of the object passes through this overall CG, and it must have a moment about the origin equal to the sum of the moments of the weights of the individual strips:

$$X_{CG}W = x_A w_A + x_B w_B + x_C w_C$$

and
$$X_{CG} = \frac{x_A w_A + x_B w_B + x_C w_C}{w_A + w_B + w_C} \qquad (i)$$

From Fig. 9-15, we have $x_A = x_C = 6.0$ cm and $x_B = 1.5$ cm. While we are not given the weights of the strips, we do know they are all made of the same material, so their weights are proportional to their areas, and $w_B = 0.60w_A$; $w_C = w_A$. Substituting this into (i) and dividing out w_A, we get $X_{CG} = (x_A + 0.60x_B + x_C)/(1.0 + 0.60 + 1.0) = [6.0$ cm $+ 0.60(1.5$ cm$) + 6.0$ cm$]/2.6 = 4.96$ cm. Thus the overall CG is 3.46 cm to the right of the CG of strip B.

Problem 9.19. A ladder consists of two wood segments of equal length and a crosspiece of negligible weight, as shown in Fig. 9-16. When the ladder is open, both segments make an angle of 60° with the floor. Each segment is uniform but of different weight, as shown. Find the CG of the open ladder.

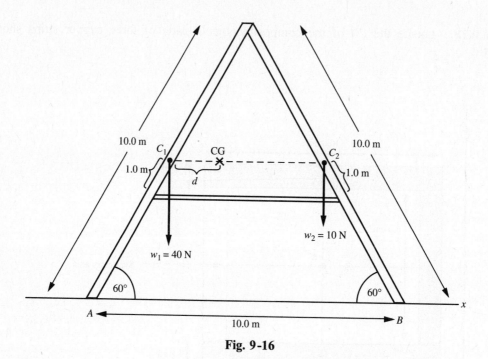

Fig. 9-16

Solution

The CGs of the two segments are at the same height above the ground. If the earth were tilted by $90°$ and pulling in the direction of the x axis, the weights of both segments would have a common line of action. The overall weight would, of course, have to have the same line of action. Thus we know that the overall CG must lie along the horizontal line between the two individual CGs. To find where along the line it acts, we go back to the actual situation with the earth pulling downward. Then, taking moments about point A, we get

$$X_{CG} = \frac{x_1 w_1 + x_2 w_2}{w_1 + w_2} \qquad (i)$$

where x_1 and x_2 are the moment arms to the weights w_1 and w_2, of left and right segments, respectively. We have $x_1 = (5.0 \text{ m}) \cos 60° = 2.5 \text{ m}$; $x_2 = (10 \text{ m}) \cos 60° + (5.0 \text{ m}) \cos 60° = 7.5 \text{ m}$. Substituting into Eq. (i), we get

$$X_{CG} = \frac{(2.5 \text{ m})(40 \text{ N}) + (7.5 \text{ m})(10 \text{ N})}{50 \text{ N}} = 3.5 \text{ m}$$

Couples

We return to the exceptional case in which a set of coplanar forces cannot be replaced by a single force. As long as the resultant of the set of coplanar forces is not zero, we can always find a point of application, far or near as needed, so that the torque of the resultant matches the torque of the set itself. But, what happens if the resultant force is zero, while the resultant torque is not zero? Then the zero resultant force can never give rise to the needed torque! Figure 9-17(a) depicts such a situation. Clearly the resultant of the three forces acting on the body is $F = F_1 + F_2 - W = 20 \text{ lb} + 10 \text{ lb} - 30 \text{ lb} = 0$. The sum of the torques about the origin is

$$\Gamma = (5.0 \text{ ft})(20 \text{ lb}) + (15 \text{ ft})(10 \text{ lb}) - (10 \text{ ft})(30 \text{ lb}) = -50 \text{ lb} \cdot \text{ft}$$

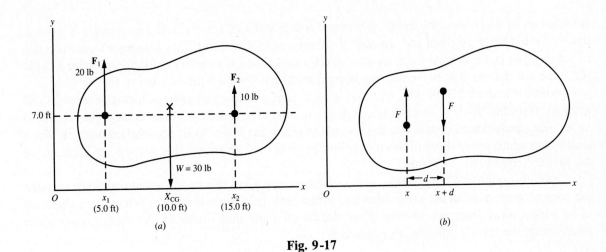

Fig. 9-17

For such situations, we can't replace the system by a single force, but we can replace the system by a pair of equal and opposite forces displaced a distance d from each other. Figure 9-17(b) shows such a pair of forces for the case at hand. Clearly the pair of forces sums to zero. In addition the torque due to the pair is $xF - (x + d)F = -dF$. For any choice of x one gets the same torque, so the location of the pair is unimportant. Furthermore, one has complete flexibility in the choice of F, as long as the product dF gives the desired result. A pair of equal and opposite forces giving rise to a torque is called a **couple**. In picking the couple for this example we chose the upward force to the left of the downward force to assure that the torque about the origin came out negative. As we saw earlier, the torque due to a couple does not depend on the absolute location of the couple, but rather only on the choice of d and F.

In Fig. 9-18 we depict three objects that are tilted slightly from their equilibrium positions on a horizontal table: a cylinder (a) and a cone (b) with broad support bases initially touching the table surface, and an inverted cone (c) with just the apex touching the table surface. In each case the objects

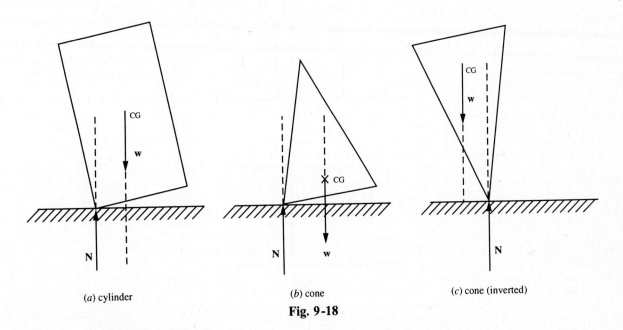

(a) cylinder   (b) cone   (c) cone (inverted)

Fig. 9-18

are acted on by two forces, the weight downward acting at the CG (or CM) and a normal force upward. In equilibrium these are equal and opposite. Furthermore, before tilting, they also have a common line of action. That is, the normal force appears directly under the CG to assure equilibrium. After a slight tilt to the left, for our first two cases, the normal force acts on the leftmost edge of the broad base, a point which is to the left of the CG. We have, in each case, a couple that gives a clockwise moment and tends to return the object to its equilibrium position. Similarly, had the tilt been to the right, we would have a counterclockwise couple that again tends to return the object to its equilibrium position. For a situation in which every slight tilt from equilibrium gives rise to a couple that restores equilibrium, we say that the equilibrium is **stable**.

Case (c) is quite different. Here, a slight tilt either way gives rise to a moment that tends to make the cone tilt even more in the same direction, so the cone falls over on its side. Whenever a slight tilt of an object away from equilibrium gives rise to a couple that continues the motion away from equilibrium, we say the equilibrium is *unstable*.

Problem 9.20.   Determine the kind of equilibrium we have for the three objects in Fig. 9-19.

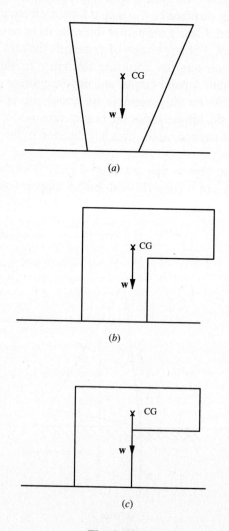

Fig. 9-19

Solution

(a) In the equilibrium position, the CG is between the two edges of the base touching the ground. A slight tilt to the left will therefore put the normal force under the left edge, while the CG will still be to the right of that point; the couple will therefore restore the object to the equilibrium position. The same reasoning holds for a slight tilt in the other direction. Thus we have stable equilibrium.

(b) The CG lies to the left of the right edge on the ground. A slight tilt to the right will leave it so, and we get a couple that restores equilibrium. The result is even more obvious for a tilt to the left. We thus again have stable equilibrium.

(c) The CG is directly over the right edge on the ground. Now even the slightest tilt to the right will put the CG to the right of the normal force, and the object will topple. We thus have unstable equilibrium.

Problem 9.21. What kind of equilibrium do we have for the two objects shown in Fig. 9-20, a uniform cylinder and a uniform cone lying on their sides?

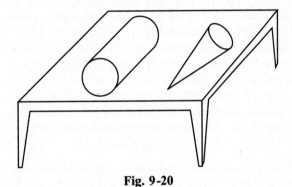

Fig. 9-20

Solution

A slight motion of either object leaves the normal force directly below the CG. Thus if one moves the cylinder by rolling it slightly to a new position and then releasing it from rest, it will stay in equilibrium in the new position. It will neither return to its original position nor move further away. It is thus in neither stable nor unstable equilibrium. It is said to be in **neutral equilibrium**.

Problem 9.22.

(a) Two identical heavy lead weights are suspended from the ends of a light, thin, bent aluminum rod, that is balanced at its center on a pivot. [Fig. 9-21(a)]. Describe the nature of the equilibrium of the system.

(b) A plastic horse and rider are connected rigidly by a stiff curved wire to a heavy iron ball, as shown in Fig. 9-21(b). The horse is supported by one foot on a narrow platform. Describe what happens when the horse and rider are tilted in any direction.

Solution

(a) In the equilibrium position the CG is located directly below the pivot point midway along and slightly above the line between the centers of the two weights. Although the CG is located outside

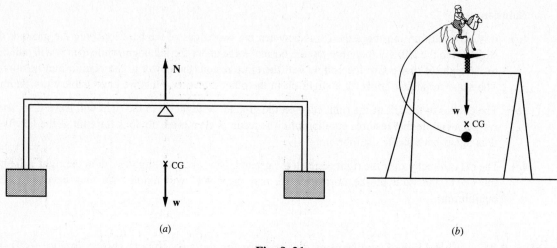

Fig. 9-21

the body, it maintains a geometrically fixed position relative to the body as the body moves. When the system is not touched, it is acted on by only two forces: gravity at the CG and the upward normal force at the pivot. At equilibrium these forces are equal and opposite and have a common line of action. When the body is rotated slightly in the counterclockwise direction about the pivot, the CG moves to the right, and the two forces form a clockwise couple, which returns the object to the equilibrium position when the object is let go. Similarly, after a clockwise rotation, the object will again return to the equilibrium position. The equilibrium is therefore stable. A slight tap on either side will set up oscillations about the equilibrium position because the object picks up speed as it returns to equilibrium and overshoots the equilibrium position, where the process is reversed. If friction is low, these oscillations can last a long time.

(b) The situation here is essentially the same as in part (a) because the heavy ball lowers the CG to below the pivot, as shown. Tilting the horse in any direction and letting go leads to oscillations about the equilibrium position.

Problems for Review and Mind Stretching

Problem 9.23.   Show that the statement of Chap. 4, that for a body to be in equilibrium under the action of three forces the forces must be concurrent, follows from Eqs. (9.4a, b).

Solution

From Eq. (9.4a) we have that the vector sum of the three forces adds up to zero, so the three vectors form a triangle and therefore are in the same plane. For them to be concurrent, their lines of action must pass through a common point. Consider the point of intersection of the lines of action of two of the forces, and call it point A. In taking moments about A, these two forces don't contribute. Equation (9.4b) then implies that the third force must have zero moment about A, so its line of action passes through A as well.

Problem 9.24.   A uniform horizontal rod 2.0 m long and weighing $w = 20$ N has weights of 80 and 40 N hanging from its ends (Fig. 9-22). Find (a) the magnitude and direction of the fourth force **F** necessary to keep the rod in equilibrium; (b) the point of application of the force F on the rod.

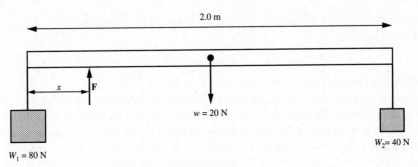

Fig. 9-22

Solution

(a) From the first condition of equilibrium, Eq. (*9.4a*), we must have that **F** is vertically upward and balances the other three forces:

$$F = 80 \text{ N} + 20 \text{ N} + 40 \text{ N} = 140 \text{ N}$$

(b) From the second condition of equilibrium, Eq. (*9.4b*),

$$x(140 \text{ N}) - (0 \text{ m})(80 \text{ N}) - (1.0 \text{ m})(20 \text{ N}) - (2.0 \text{ m})(40 \text{ N}) = 0 \qquad \text{or} \qquad x = 0.714 \text{ m}$$

Problem 9.25. A large wooden crate 8.0 ft high, 3.5 ft wide, and of weight $w = 100$ lb rests on a horizontal surface with coefficient of static friction $\mu_s = 0.60$. Assume the CG of the crate is at its geometric center. A horizontal force F is applied to the crate to get it moving. Below what height h must be force F be applied if the crate is to start to slide before it starts to tip over?

Solution

The situation is depicted in Fig. 9-23. The crate is acted on by the four forces: **w**, **N**, **f**, and **F**, where **f** is the retarding frictional force and **N** is the normal force of the floor on the crate. Let x represent the

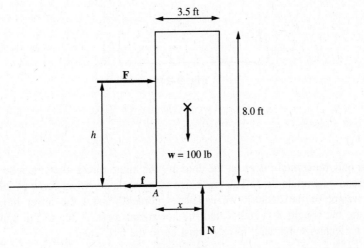

Fig. 9-23

distance from the left edge of the crate, point A, to the point of application of $\mathbf{N}$. To just get the crate to slide, we must have

$$F = f_{max} = \mu_s N \qquad (i)$$

From equilibrium in the vertical direction, $N = w = 100$ lb. Then (i) gives $F = 0.60(100 \text{ lb}) = 60$ lb. The question of whether the crate tips or not can be resolved by examining where the normal force acts. If $\mathbf{N}$ acts at the extreme right edge, the entire crate loses contact with the floor, except at that edge; this is the condition for just starting to tip. Taking moments about A, we see that $\mathbf{f}$ does not contribute, while $\mathbf{w}$ contributes a fixed clockwise moment. For fixed $F = 60$ lb, the clockwise moment of $\mathbf{F}$ increases with the height h at which it is applied. To balance the clockwise moments of $\mathbf{F}$ and $\mathbf{w}$, we have only the counterclockwise moment due to $\mathbf{N}$. For fixed $N = 100$ lb, this moment can get larger only by increasing the moment arm x. We therefore set x equal to its maximum possible value, 3.5 ft, to determine h_{max}:

$$\Gamma_A = (3.5 \text{ ft})(100 \text{ lb}) - h_{max}(60 \text{ lb}) - (1.75 \text{ ft})(100 \text{ lb}) = 0 \qquad \text{or} \qquad h_{max} = 2.92 \text{ ft}$$

Problem 9.26. A uniform door, of height 3.50 m and width 1.50 m and weighing 200 N, is supported by two small hinges, as shown in Fig. 9-24. The hinges are symmetrically placed, 20 cm from the top and bottom of the door. If the top hinge supports the full weight of the door, find the horizontal forces exerted by each hinge on the door.

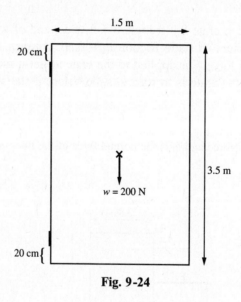

Fig. 9-24

Solution

Since the only horizontal forces on the door are the hinge forces, they must be equal and opposite; let their common magnitude be F. The top hinge also exerts a vertical force of 200 N on the door to balance the weight of the door. If we calculate moments about the lower hinge, the only forces contributing are the weight $w = 200$ N and the horizontal force F due to the upper hinge. Since the weight gives a clockwise moment, force F must be to the left. Then

$$\Gamma = (3.50 \text{ m} - 0.40 \text{ m})F - (0.75 \text{ m})(200 \text{ N}) = 0 \qquad \text{or} \qquad F = 48.4 \text{ N}$$

Problem 9.27.   Find the CG of the uniform disk of radius $R = 2.0$ m with a small disk of radius $r = R/3$, cut out, as shown in Fig 9-25.

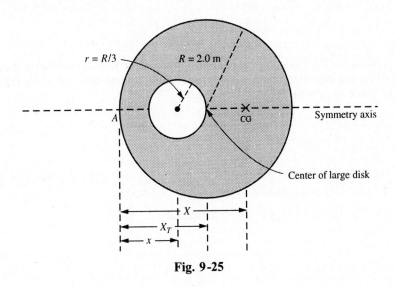

Fig. 9-25

Solution

At first this seems to be a formidable problem, but consider the disk with the piece missing. We know, by symmetry, that the CG (or CM) lies along the x axis, as shown, but we don't know where along the axis. If we put the cutout piece back in place, the CG of the *combination* would be just that of the whole disk and would be at its center. Assume that X is the moment arm from point A to the CG of the disk with the piece missing, and W is its weight. Similarly let x be the moment arm to the CG of the cutout piece and w be its weight. Then let X_T be the CG for the combined (complete) disk. We have

$$x = R - r = R - \frac{R}{3} = 1.33 \text{ m} \quad \text{and} \quad X_T = R = 2.0 \text{ m} \tag{i}$$

Also, the weights of the two pieces are proportional to their areas:

$$w = \sigma \pi r^2 \qquad W = \sigma \pi (R^2 - r^2) \tag{ii}$$

where σ is the proportionality constant. Note that in the second term, for W, we have subtracted out the area of the cutout. Then, solving for the CG of the combination of the two pieces, we get

$$X_T(w + W) = xw + XW \tag{iii}$$

Substituting and simplifying common terms, we get

$$X_T(R^2) = xr^2 + X(R^2 - r^2) \quad \text{or} \quad X_T = \frac{x}{9} + \frac{8X}{9}$$

so that $X = 2.08$ m.

Supplementary Problems

Problem 9.28.   Find the sign of the torques of the three forces in Fig. 9-2 about point B. Use the standard convention.

Ans. Γ_1 is positive; Γ_2 is negative; Γ_3 is positive

Problem 9.29. Assume that the moment of the force in Fig. 9-4 about A is $100 \text{ N} \cdot \text{m}$. If $d_A = 20$ m and $r_A = 60$ m, find (a) F; (b) θ.

    Ans.   (a) $F = 5.0$ N; (b) $\theta = 19.5°$

Problem 9.30. Assume that the rod of Fig. 9-7 is free to pivot about point A and that a 10-lb weight hangs at one end as shown. If the rod is uniform and has a weight of 3.0 lb, find the value of (a) the force F necessary for equilibrium; (b) the pivot force N necessary for equilibrium.

    Ans.   (a) 44.5 lb; (b) 57.5 lb.

Problem 9.31. For the boom-and-weight system of Fig. 9-26, find (a) the tension in the wire, (b) the magnitude and direction of the force exerted by the wall on the boom.

    Ans.   (a) 108 N; (b) 78 N, 46° above horizontal

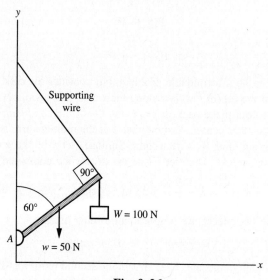

Fig. 9-26

Problem 9.32. Assume that the boom in Fig. 9-9(a) is weightless, that the maximum tension the wire can withstand without snapping is 3000 N, and that the maximum compressive force the boom can withstand without buckling is 2000 N.

(a) When the hanging weight W is increased, which will happen first: the wire snapping or the boom buckling?

(b) At what values of T and W will the event in part (a) occur?

    Ans.   (a) The boom will buckle; (b) $T = 2610$ N, $W = 1680$ N

Problem 9.33. How will the results of Problem 9.32 change if the uniform boom had a weight of 600 N?

    Ans.   (a) The boom will again buckle; (b) $T = 2610$ N, $W = 1380$ N

Problem 9.34.   Find the x and y components of the force **F** exerted on the boom by the wall for (a) Problem 9.32(b), (b) Problem 9.33(b).

   Ans.   (a) $F_x = 2000$ N, $F_y = 0$ N; (b) $F_x = 2000$ N, $F_y = 300$ N

Problem 9.35.   The ladder shown in Fig. 9-16 rests on a frictionless horizontal surface. The two segments of the ladder are hinged at the top and held together by a weightless horizontal crosspiece. Find the normal forces exerted by the floor on the ladder at points A and B.

   Ans. $N_A = 32.5$ N; $N_B = 17.5$ N

Problem 9.36.   Referring to Problem 9.35 and Fig. 9-16, assume that the crosspiece is attached at a point 4.0 m along the length of each ladder segment as measured from the bottom. Find the tension in the crosspiece. [*Hint*: Take one leg of the ladder as the system and apply the laws of equilibrium to it, using the results of Problem 9.35.]

   Ans.   12.0 N

Problem 9.37.   In Fig. 9-27 a block of weight $w = 80$ N is being pulled at constant speed along a horizontal surface by a force **F** acting at $20°$ above the horizontal. The coefficient of kinetic friction between surface and block is $\mu_k = 0.40$. Determine F and N, using only the first condition of equilibrium in the x and y directions.

   Ans. $F = 29.7$ N; $N = 69.8$ N

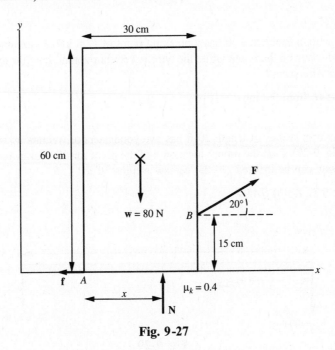

Fig. 9-27

Problem 9.38.   Referring to Problem 9.37, find the distance from the left edge of the block to the point of application of the normal force.

   Ans.   18.8 cm

Problem 9.39. Suppose that in Problem 9.37 the force **F** remained in the same direction but had a higher point of application B. How high could point B get before the block started to tip over?

    Ans. 43 cm

Problem 9.40. For the uniform boom of length L supported by a horizontal wire (Fig. 9-28), find (a) the tension in the wire, (b) the magnitude and direction of the force exerted on the boom at the pivot.

    Ans. (a) 8.74 kN; (b) 10.6 kN, 34.5° above horizontal

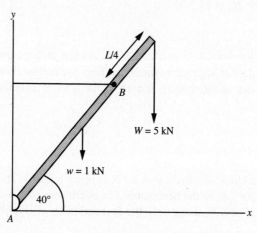

Fig. 9-28

Problem 9.41. The wire in Problem 9.40 has a breaking point of 12.0 kN. Assuming the point of attachment B of the wire is placed lower on the boom while the wire is kept horizontal, how far down along the boom can point B get before the wire snaps?

    Ans. $0.454L$ from the top

Problem 9.42. A uniform seesaw of length 20 ft has two youngsters of weights $w_a = 100$ lb and $w_b = 40$ lb, sitting on the ends (Fig. 9-29). Find the proper location x of the pivot for the seesaw to be just in balance, if (a) the weight of the seesaw can be ignored, (b) the seesaw weighs 30 lb.

    Ans. (a) 5.71 ft; (b) 6.47 ft

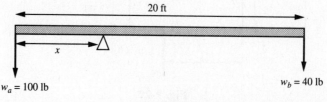

Fig. 9-29

Problem 9.43. A very thin rod bent into the shape of a right angle (90°) is made of a material which weighs 30 N per linear meter. In addition to gravity, there are two forces acting to keep the rod fixed: F_1 at the elbow and F_2 at point B (Fig. 9-30).

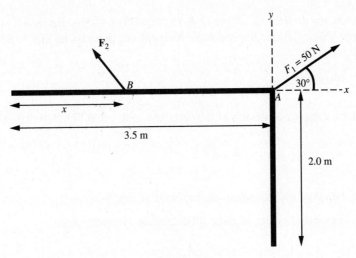

Fig. 9-30

(a) Find the magnitude and direction of $\mathbf{F}_2$.

(b) Find the distance x to the point of application of $\mathbf{F}_2$.

   Ans. (a) 147 N, 72.8° above negative x axis; (b) 2.19 m

Problem 9.44. In Fig. 9-31 a rigid object, whose weight can be ignored, is acted on by the three forces shown.

(a) Find the x and y components of the single force $\mathbf{F}$ that can replace these three forces.

(b) Find the total torque of the three forces about the origin.

   Ans. (a) $F_x = 88.5$ N, $F_y = 84.9$ N; (b) -15.9 N · m

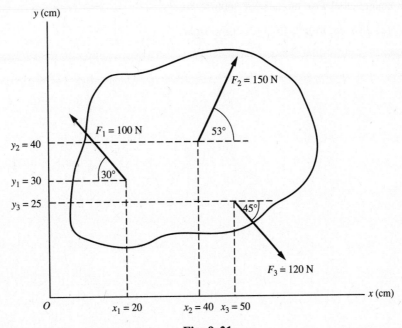

Fig. 9-31

Problem 9.45.   A point on the line of action of **F** in Problem 9.44 has abscissa $x = 30$ cm. What is the corresponding ordinate? [*Hint*: Assume that the force **F** acts at this point on its line of action, and determine y from the torque requirements.]

   Ans. $y = 46.7$ cm

Problem 9.46.   Find the x and y coordinates of the CG of the bent rod in Fig. 9-30. Use the coordinate system shown in the figure.

   Ans. $x = -1.11$ cm; $y = -0.36$ cm

Problem 9.47.   Find the CG of the asymmetrical dumbbell of Fig. 9-32.

   Ans.   14.7 cm left of center of large sphere, along symmetry axis

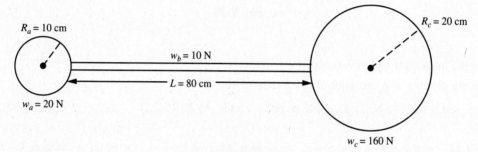

Fig. 9-32

Problem 9.48.   Suppose that in addition to the weight the only other force acting on the dumbbell of Problem 9.47 were an upward force **F** of magnitude 190 N. Find the horizontal distance to the line of action of **F**, as measured from the center of the large sphere, if the resulting couple gave (*a*) a clockwise moment of 1600 N · m, (*b*) a counterclockwise moment of 5600 N · m.

   Ans.   (*a*) 23.1 cm to left; (*b*) 14.8 cm to right

Chapter 10

Rigid Bodies II: Rotational Motion

10.1 ROTATION OF A RIGID BODY ABOUT A FIXED AXIS

In this section we will consider the motion of a rigid body that is free to rotate about a fixed axis. This means that all the particles of the body initially on this axis remain in fixed locations on this axis as the body moves. Our first task will be to describe the motion, or kinematics, of the body as a whole. Next we will relate the overall motion of the body to the motion of the individual particles making it up.

Description of Rotational Motion

In Fig. 10-1 we illustrate a rigid body free to rotate about a fixed axis, which we assume is perpendicular to the plane of the figure. We let the rotation axis be the z axis of our coordinate system. We can then choose x and y axes in the plane of the figure as shown. These axes are assumed to be *fixed in space in an inertial reference frame*; they do not rotate with the body. Since, by hypothesis, the particles of the body lying along the z axis stay fixed as the body rotates, every other particle in the body is constrained to move about the z axis on a circular arc with a radius equal to the perpendicular distance from the axis to the particle in question. These circular arcs are always parallel to the xy plane.

Angular Displacement

We now describe the motion of the body as a whole. We note that if we etch a series of straight-line segments parallel to the xy plane in the body, then as the body rotates, the etched lines will rotate as well (Fig. 10-2). In fact, since the body is rigid, the line segments must maintain their positions

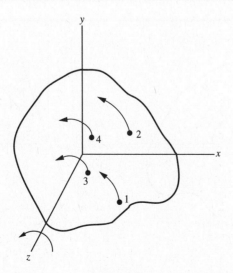

Fig. 10-1

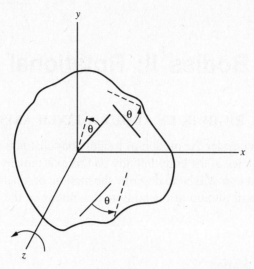

Fig. 10-2

relative to one another so that every such line segment will rotate through exactly the same angle in a given time interval. This is illustrated in Fig. 10-2, where the solid line segments correspond to one instant of time and the dashed lines correspond to the same line segments at some later instant. Thus the orientation of the rigid body can be completely specified by giving the orientation angle θ of a single chosen line segment etched in the body. For convenience we choose a segment that has one end (permanently) at the origin of our coordinate system, as shown in Fig. 10-3(a). We then let θ, measured in radians, be the angle the guideline makes with the x axis at time t. [Recall that the angle in radians between two line segments which meet at a point is defined as the ratio of the arc length of a circle centered on that point which is cut by the two segments to the radius R of the circle (for example, $\Delta\theta = \Delta s/R$ in Fig. 10-4). Thus, there are $2\pi R/R = 2\pi$ radians in a complete circle, and 2π radians = $360°$.] The angle θ is called the **angular displacement** of the rigid body. By convention, the angle θ is considered positive when it is measured counterclockwise from the x axis.

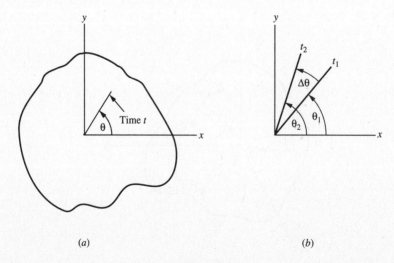

(a)   (b)

Fig. 10-3

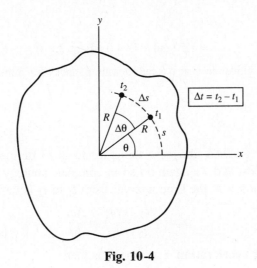

Fig. 10-4

Angular Velocity

To get an idea of how fast the body is rotating, we define the **average angular velocity** in a given time interval, say from t_1 to t_2, as

$$\omega_{av} = \frac{\theta_2 - \theta_1}{t_2 - t_1} \equiv \frac{\Delta\theta}{\Delta t} \tag{10.1}$$

(See Fig. 10-3(b).) Note how this definition mimics that of average velocity in one-dimensional translation, with ω and θ replacing v and x in Eq. (2.1). This analogy between straight-line and angular quantities is quite extensive, as will be seen. The units of angular velocity are rad/s.

The **instantaneous angular velocity** at time t_1, is defined as the limit of the average angular velocity as $t_2 \to t_1$ (or, equivalently, as $\Delta t \to 0$):

$$\omega(t) \equiv \lim_{\Delta t \to 0} \frac{\Delta\theta}{\Delta t} \tag{10.2}$$

Note that ω can be positive or negative, depending on whether θ is increasing or decreasing in time. For our angle convention, ω is positive for counterclockwise rotation and negative for clockwise rotation.

Problem 10.1.

(a) A body is rotating at a constant angular velocity of 4.0 rad/s. If the angle θ at $t = 0$ was $\theta_0 = 1.50$ rad, find θ at $t = 2.0$ s.

(b) What would the answer to (a) be if $\omega = -4.0$ rad/s?

Solution

(a) If ω is constant we have $\omega = \omega_{av} = (\theta_2 - \theta_1)/(t_2 - t_1)$. Letting $t_1 = 0$ and $\theta_1 = \theta_0$ and dropping the subscript on t_2 and θ_2, we get $\omega = (\theta - \theta_0)/t$ or

$$\theta = \theta_0 + \omega t \tag{i}$$

Substituting the data in (i),

$$\theta = 1.50 \text{ rad} + (4.0 \text{ rad/s})(2.0 \text{ s}) = 9.5 \text{ rad} \tag{ii}$$

(b)   We have

$$\theta = 1.50 \text{ rad} + (-4.0 \text{ rad/s})(2.0 \text{ s}) = -6.5 \text{ rad}$$

which means the guideline is at 6.5 rad measured clockwise from the x axis.

Angular Acceleration

As you probably have guessed, the next thing to do is to define the rate of change of the instantaneous angular velocity, and we again do so in complete analogy to straight-line motion. The **average angular acceleration** α in the time interval from t_1 to t_2 is defined as

$$\alpha_{av} = \frac{\omega_2 - \omega_1}{t_2 - t_1} = \frac{\Delta\omega}{\Delta t} \tag{10.3}$$

The **instantaneous angular acceleration** α at time t_1 is then

$$\alpha = \lim_{\Delta t \to 0} \frac{\Delta\omega}{\Delta t} \tag{10.4}$$

The units of α are rad/s^2. We note that θ, ω, and α are related to each other in precisely the same way as are x, v, and a. For this reason all formulas of Sec. 2.6 hold for constant angular acceleration if x, v, and a are replaced by θ, ω, and α.

Problem 10.2.   Find the general expressions for θ and ω as functions of time for the case of constant angular acceleration α.

Solution

From Chap. 2, for straight-line motion under constant acceleration a, we showed that

$$(i) \quad v = v_0 + at \qquad \text{and} \qquad (ii) \quad x = x_0 + v_0 t + \frac{at^2}{2}$$

where v_0 and x_0 are the initial velocity and displacement at $t = 0$. Thus, for rotation under constant acceleration α, we must have

$$(iii) \quad \omega = \omega_0 + \alpha t \qquad \text{and} \qquad (iv) \quad \theta = \theta_0 + \omega_0 t + \frac{\alpha t^2}{2}$$

where ω_0 and θ_0 are the initial angular velocity and angular displacement at $t = 0$.

Problem 10.3.   A wheel spinning on an axis through its center has a constant angular acceleration of 3.5 rad/s^2. Assuming the wheel started from rest, find (a) the angular velocity after 8.0 s, (b) the total angle turned through in 8.0 s.

Solution

(a) $$\omega = \omega_0 + \alpha t = 0 + (3.5 \text{ rad/s}^2)(8.0 \text{ s}) = 28 \text{ rad/s}$$

(b)   Assume our guideline is located on the x axis at $t = 0$, so we have $\theta_0 = 0$. Then

$$\theta = \theta_0 + \omega_0 t + \frac{\alpha t^2}{2} = \tfrac{1}{2}\alpha t^2 = \tfrac{1}{2}(3.5 \text{ rad/s}^2)(8.0 \text{ s})^2 = 112 \text{ rad}$$

Problem 10.4.   Through what angle must the wheel in Problem 10.3 turn for the angular velocity to reach $\omega = 140$ rad/s?

Solution

We first solve for the time:

$$\omega = \omega_0 + \alpha t \qquad \text{or} \qquad 140 \text{ rad/s} = 0 + (3.5 \text{ rad/s}^2)t \qquad \text{or} \qquad t = 40 \text{ s}$$

Next we get the angle, noting that, for our case,

$$\theta = \tfrac{1}{2}\alpha t^2 = \tfrac{1}{2}(3.5 \text{ rad/s}^2)(40 \text{ s})^2 = 2800 \text{ rad}$$

Problem 10.5.

(a) For the case of constant angular acceleration, find an expression for ω directly in terms of θ.

(b) Solve Problem 10.4 without first finding the time.

Solution

(a) From Chap. 2, we have, for straight-line motion at constant acceleration

$$v^2 = v_0{}^2 + 2a(x - x_0) \qquad\qquad (i)$$

By analogy, for fixed-axis rotation

$$\omega^2 = \omega_0{}^2 + 2\alpha(\theta - \theta_0) \qquad\qquad (ii)$$

(b) Applying Eq. (ii) and recalling that $\omega_0 = \theta_0 = 0$, we get $\omega^2 = 2\alpha\theta$. Substituting, we get

$$(140 \text{ rad/s})^2 = 2(3.5 \text{ rad/s})\theta \qquad \text{or} \qquad \theta = 2800 \text{ rad}$$

Problem 10.6. How many revolutions of the wheel does the answer of Problem 10.4 or 10.5 correspond to?

Solution

We recall that there are 2π rad in one complete circle. Therefore, the angle turned through equals 2π times the number of revolutions, or

$$2800 \text{ rad} = (6.28)(\text{no. of rev.}) \qquad \text{or} \qquad \text{no. of rev.} = 445.9 \text{ r}$$

Period and Frequency of Uniform Rotation

When an object spins on its axis it returns to any given position every time it rotates through $360° = 2\pi$ rad. The time to make one complete revolution is called the **period** T of the motion. For constant ω the period stays the same from one revolution to the next. Because $\Delta\theta = \omega\Delta t$, we have $2\pi = \omega T$, or

$$T = \frac{2\pi}{\omega} \qquad\qquad (10.5)$$

Next, one can define the **frequency** f as the number of revolutions per second, r/s. Therefore, T and f are reciprocals:

$$f = \frac{1}{T} \qquad\qquad (10.6)$$

For example, if $T = \tfrac{1}{2}$ s, then $f = 2$ r/s. From (10.5) and (10.6) we get

$$f = \frac{\omega}{2\pi} \qquad\qquad (10.7)$$

Note. The concepts of period and frequency are useful not only for rotations but for any kind of motion that repeats itself on a regular basis, such as oscillations. The period always refers to the time for one complete repetition of the motion and the frequency to the number of repetitions per second.

Problem 10.7. Find the period and frequency of the motion described in Problem 10.1(*a*).

    Solution

$$\omega = 4.0 \text{ rad/s} \Rightarrow T = \frac{2\pi}{\omega} = \frac{6.28 \text{ rad}}{4.0 \text{ s}} = 1.57 \text{ s}$$

$$f = \frac{1}{T} = 0.637 \text{ r/s}$$

Problem 10.8.

(*a*) Find the value of ω_{av} for the wheel of Problem 10.3 over the time interval from when it starts to when it reaches $\omega = 140$ rad/s.

(*b*) Find the period over the same time interval if the wheel had been rotating with constant angular velocity ω_{av}.

    Solution

(*a*) By definition, $\omega_{av} = \Delta\theta/\Delta t$. In Problem 10.4 we determined that $\Delta t = 40$ s and $\Delta\theta = 2800$ rad. Then $\omega_{av} = 70$ rad/s.

(*b*) T = (total time)/(number of revolutions). We already know from Problem 10.4 that the total time = 40 s. From Problem 10.6 we have that the corresponding number of revolutions = 445.9 r. Then

$$T = \frac{40 \text{ s}}{445.9 \text{ r}} = 0.0897 \text{ s}$$

[Or, directly from part (*a*), $T = 2\pi/\omega_{av} = (6.28 \text{ rad})/(70 \text{ rad/s}) = 0.0897 \text{ s}$.]

10.2 KINEMATICS OF INDIVIDUAL PARTICLES IN A ROTATING RIGID BODY

In Fig. 10-4 we depict a particular particle in a rigid body rotating about the z axis. The particle is constrained to move on a circle of radius R, where R is the perpendicular distance from the z axis to the particle. The velocity of the particle must always point along the tangent to the circle. Let s be the arc length of the circle of motion from the x axis to the position of the particle at time t_1, and let θ be the corresponding angle between the x axis and the radius line to the particle at t_1. At a time $t_2 = t_1 + \Delta t$, and additional arc length Δs and a corresponding angle $\Delta\theta$ will be swept through. As can be seen from the figure,

$$s = R\theta \qquad \text{and} \qquad \Delta s = R\,\Delta\theta \qquad\qquad (10.8a, b)$$

If we divide both sides of Eq. (*10.8b*) by Δt we get $\Delta s/\Delta t = R\,\Delta\theta/\Delta t$. In the limit as $\Delta t \to 0$ (holding t_1 fixed), we have $\Delta s/\Delta t \to v$, the magnitude of the velocity of the particle as it moves along its circular trajectory. Also, $\Delta\theta/\Delta t \to \omega(t)$, the angular velocity. Thus, in this limit we get

$$v = R\omega \qquad\qquad (10.9)$$

The acceleration of the particle consists of two parts. One part is the centripetal acceleration $\mathbf{a}_r$, which is due to the changing direction of the velocity vector $\mathbf{v}$, as the particle moves around the circle, and points radially inward along R to the center of the circle of motion with magnitude

$$a_r = \frac{v^2}{R} = \omega^2 R \tag{10.10}$$

where the last expression in Eq. (10.10) follows from Eq. (10.9). The other part of the acceleration is the tangential acceleration $\mathbf{a}_t$, which is due to the time variation of v, and which points along the tangent to the circle. By (10.9)

$$\Delta v = R \, \Delta\omega \qquad \text{whence} \qquad \frac{\Delta v}{\Delta t} = R \, \frac{\Delta\omega}{\Delta t}$$

Letting $\Delta t \to 0$ in the last equation gives

$$a_t = R\alpha \tag{10.11}$$

From Eqs. (10.9) to (10.11), we see that the velocity and acceleration of each particle in the body is completely determined from a knowledge of ω and α as well as of the radial distance R to the particle. The kinematic quantities for a typical particle are depicted in Fig. 10-5.

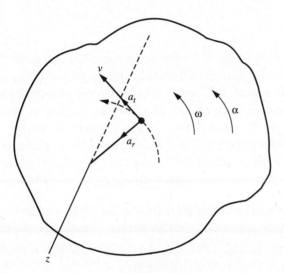

Fig. 10-5

Problem 10.9.   A disk of radius 40 cm is spinning at a constant angular velocity of $\omega = 30$ rad/s.

(a) Find the velocity of a point on the rim of the disk.

(b) Find the acceleration of a point on the rim of the disk.

(c) Repeat parts (a) and (b) for a point one-third of the radius out from the center of the disk.

   Solution

   (a) $v = \omega R = (30 \text{ rad/s})(0.40 \text{ m}) = 12$ m/s. (Note that the radian unit does not appear in the final answer because it is dimensionless, and when multiplied by a length it results in a length.)

   (b) Since there is no angular acceleration, $a_t = 0$, and only the centripetal acceleration a_r contributes:

$$a_r = \omega^2 R = (30 \text{ rad/s})^2 (0.40 \text{ m}) = 360 \text{ m/s}^2$$

(c) All that changes here is that the radius of the circle for the new particle is $r = R/3$. Therefore both v and a_r are reduced to one-third of the corresponding values for a point on the rim: $v = 4.0$ m/s; $a_r = 120$ m/s^2.

Problem 10.10. Assume that in Problem 10.9 the body has an angular acceleration of 4.5 rad/s^2. Assume also that at the instant in question ω has the same value as in Problem 10.9. How do the answers to Problem 10.9 change?

Solution

Since ω is the same as in Problem 10.9, the velocities and the centripetal accelerations are the same. The only change is that both particles now have a tangential component of acceleration: $a_t = R\alpha = (0.40$ m$)(4.5$ rad/s$^2) = 1.80$ m/s^2 for the particle on the rim, and $a_t = R\alpha/3 = 0.60$ m/s^2 for the particle at one-third the radius of the disk.

10.3 DYNAMICS OF A RIGID BODY ROTATING ABOUT A FIXED AXIS

Torque Revisited

As you might suspect from Chap. 9, the torque (or moment) of a force that acts on a rigid body is going to play a major role in the rotation of that body. Before showing this, however, we need to take a more sophisticated look at torque. In Chap. 9 we dealt only with coplanar forces and defined the torque as a positive or negative algebraic quantity. Actually, torque is generally defined as a three-dimensional vector quantity $\mathbf{\Gamma}$. Figure 10-6 shows a force $\mathbf{F}$ acting on a particle located at displacement $\mathbf{r}$ from the origin, where $\mathbf{F}$ is not necessarily in the xy plane. If θ is the angle between $\mathbf{F}$ and $\mathbf{r}$ (tail to tail), then the magnitude of the torque (on the particle) *about the origin* is defined as

$$|\mathbf{\Gamma}| = rF \sin \theta \qquad (10.12)$$

The vector $\mathbf{\Gamma}$ is, by definition, directed perpendicular to the plane formed by $\mathbf{r}$ and $\mathbf{F}$, as shown in Fig. 10-6. Note that there are two antiparallel choices for the direction perpendicular to a plane, and we must remove that ambiguity in the definition of $\mathbf{\Gamma}$. We agree that the force $\mathbf{F}$ will tend to rotate an object (pinned at the origin) counterclockwise about the positive $\mathbf{\Gamma}$ direction. An equivalent rule is to let the curved fingers of your right hand swing $\mathbf{r}$ through angle θ into $\mathbf{F}$; then your extended thumb points in the direction of $\mathbf{\Gamma}$. If $\mathbf{r}$ and $\mathbf{F}$ were in the xy plane, $\mathbf{\Gamma}$ would clearly point in the $\pm z$ direction. Indeed from Eq. (10.12) we see that the z component of such a torque would be $\Gamma_z = \pm rF \sin \theta$. By our convention, the sign is determined by whether the force tends to give rise to a counterclockwise or clockwise rotation about the positive z axis. Since all the forces in Chap. 9 were in the xy plane, the definition of torque given there was really the z component of the vector torque, as defined here.

When the forces acting on a rigid body are not coplanar, the vector torques can point in different directions, and the resultant torque can be quite complex. We will not deal with such general situations. We will restrict ourself to the effect of forces on a rigid body that is free to rotate about a fixed axis. For definiteness we will assume the fixed axis is the z axis of our coordinate system. The following statements can be shown to hold:

1. Only the z component of the torque due to a force has any effect on the rotation of a rigid body about the z axis. (The z component of the torque is often called the *torque about the z axis*.)

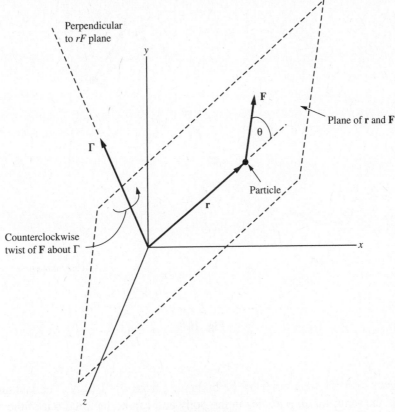

Fig. 10-6

2.   Only the x and y components of a force $\mathbf{F}$ can contribute to the z component of a torque. Thus any force (or part of a force) that points along the z axis cannot contribute to torque about that axis.

3.   The z component of the torque, due to a force $\mathbf{F}$ in the xy plane, is given by $\Gamma_z = rF \sin \theta$, where r stands for the *perpendicular distance* from the z axis to the point of application of the force and θ is the angle $\mathbf{F}$ and a line along r.

We will drop the subscript z in what follows, so Γ has the same meaning as in Chap. 9.

Torque, Angular Acceleration, and the Dynamic Laws of Rotation

In Fig. 10-7 we examine the ith particle, of mass m_i, in a rigid body that is rotating about the z axis. We assume the resultant force acting on that particle is $\mathbf{F}_i$, which includes both the forces due to all the other particles in the body and the external forces from outside the body. From Newton's second law, $\mathbf{F}_i = m_i \mathbf{a}_i$, where $\mathbf{a}_i$ is the acceleration of m_i. Thus, in the tangential direction, we must have

$$F_{it} = m_i a_{it} = m_i r_i \alpha \qquad (10.13)$$

where the last step follows from (10.11). Recognizing that $\Gamma_i = r_i F_{it}$ is the z component of the torque of the force $\mathbf{F}_i$, we find from (10.13) that $\Gamma_i = m_i r_i^2 \alpha$. Repeating the same procedure for every particle of the body and adding up all the Γ_i, we get

$$\Gamma_T = \sum \Gamma_i = \sum m_i r_i^2 \alpha = \left(\sum m_i r_i^2 \right) \alpha \qquad (10.14)$$

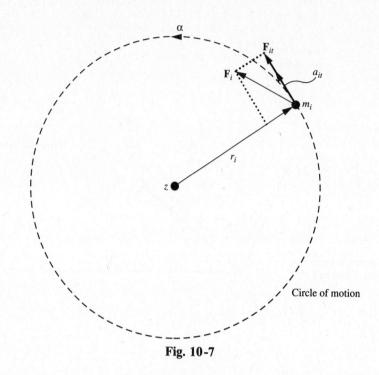

Fig. 10-7

where the sum goes over all N particles of the body, i.e., from $i = 1$ to N. The last term on the right follows since α is the same for all particles in the body and can be factored out of the sum. We define the **moment of inertia** I of the body about the z axis as

$$I = \sum m_i r_i{}^2 \qquad (10.15)$$

From definition (10.15), we see that I has dimensions of mass times distance squared = $\text{kg} \cdot \text{m}^2$ or $\text{g} \cdot \text{cm}^2$ or $\text{slug} \cdot \text{ft}^2$. The left side of Eq. (10.14) includes all the torques on all the particles, including the torques that the particles exert on each other. It is easy to see from Newton's third law that all these *internal* torques must add up to zero. This is shown in Fig. 10-8, where we examine the torques due to the action-reaction pair of forces on two arbitrary particles m_i and m_j. Since $\mathbf{F}_{ij}$ and $\mathbf{F}_{ji}$ are equal and opposite and have the same line of action, they must give rise to equal and opposite torques. Since all the internal torques are due to action-reaction pairs, all the internal torques must cancel in pairs. Thus, the only torque left in Γ_T is Γ_{ext}, the resultant torque due to external forces. Using Eqs. (10.14) and (10.15), we get

$$\Gamma_{\text{ext}} = I\alpha \qquad \text{or} \qquad \Gamma = I\alpha \qquad (10.16)$$

where on the right we have dropped the subscript, it being understood that we are referring to the resultant external torque. Note the analogy to the dynamic equation for one-dimensional motion $\mathbf{F} = m\mathbf{a}$. Equation (10.16) is Newton's second law for rotation about a fixed axis. Note that the quantity $I\alpha$ has dimensions $\text{kg} \cdot \text{m}^2/\text{s}^2 = (\text{kg} \cdot \text{m}/\text{s}^2)\text{m} = \text{N} \cdot \text{m}$. This is just the dimensions of torque, as required by Eq. (10.16). Table 10.1 is a table of analogs developed thus far between quantities related to rotational motion and translational (one-dimensional) motion.

Problem 10.11. Assuming that the analogies in the table can be extended further, find the rotational analog of the following equations: (a) $E_k = \frac{1}{2}mv^2$; (b) work $= F\Delta x = \Delta E_k$; (c) $P = Fv$; (d) $F\Delta t = \Delta(mv)$.

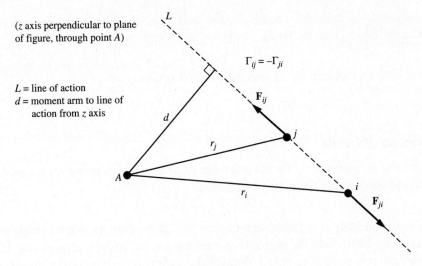

(z axis perpendicular to plane
of figure, through point A)

L = line of action
d = moment arm to line of
    action from z axis

$\Gamma_{ij} = -\Gamma_{ji}$

Fig. 10-8

Table 10.1

Rotation (Fixed-Axis)	Translation (One-Dimensional)
θ	x
ω	v
α	a
Γ	F
I	m
$\Gamma = I\alpha$	$F = ma$

Solution

    (a) $E_k = \frac{1}{2}I\omega^2$; (b) work = $\Gamma\Delta\theta = \Delta E_k$; (c) $P = \Gamma\omega$; (d) $\Gamma\Delta t = \Delta(I\omega)$.

Note.   The solutions to Problem 10.11 can all be shown to be true. $\Gamma\Delta\theta$ is the work done by the external forces in rotating a rigid body through an infinitesimal angle $\Delta\theta$, and the relation $\Gamma\Delta\theta = \Delta E_k$ is just the work-energy theorem applied to a rotating object. The power P is then just $\Gamma\Delta\theta/\Delta t = \Gamma\omega$, as expected. The quantity $\Gamma\Delta t$ is called the **angular impulse**, and the quantity $I\omega$ is called the **angular momentum**. The relationship $\Gamma\Delta t = \Delta(I\omega)$ is just the rotational analog of the impulse momentum theorem for linear motion.

Problem 10.12.   Show that $E_k = \frac{1}{2}I\omega^2$, the solution of Problem 10.11(a), is the kinetic energy of a rigid body rotating about a fixed axis.

Solution

    The rotational kinetic energy is given by $E_k = \sum (\frac{1}{2}m_i v_i^2)$, where the sum extends over all the particles of the rotating body, $i = 1 \rightarrow N$. We note that for the ith particle, $v_i = r_i\omega$. Substituting into our equation we get $E_k = \sum(\frac{1}{2}m_i r_i^2 \omega^2)$. Since ω is the same for all the terms in the sum, we can factor out ω^2 (and also the factor $\frac{1}{2}$), so we get $E_k = \frac{1}{2}(\sum m_i r_i^2)\omega^2 = \frac{1}{2}I\omega^2$, as required.

The other three results of Problem 10.11 may be verified similarly.

Calculating Moments of Inertia

To solve problems in rotational dynamics it is often necessary to determine the moments of inertia of the various rigid bodies about their axes of rotation.

Problem 10.13. A rigid body consists of four masses held at the corners of a rectangle by rigid bars of negligible mass (Fig. 10-9). Find the moment of inertia about (a) an axis through side 1; (b) an axis through side 2; (c) an axis parallel to side 1 through the geometric center of the object A.

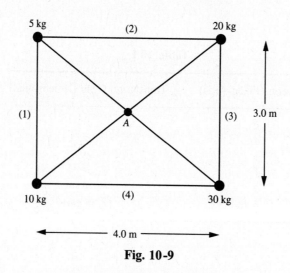

Fig. 10-9

Solution

(a) The 5- and 10-kg masses lie on the axis, so they don't contribute to the moment of inertia. The perpendicular distances to the 20- and 30-kg masses are each 4.0 m. Thus we get

$$I_1 = (20 \text{ kg})(4.0 \text{ m})^2 + (30 \text{ kg})(4.0 \text{ m})^2 = 800 \text{ kg} \cdot \text{m}^2$$

(b) Here the 5- and 20-kg masses don't contribute, and so

$$I_2 = (10 \text{ kg})(3.0 \text{ m})^2 + (30 \text{ kg})(3.0 \text{ m})^2 = 360 \text{ kg} \cdot \text{m}^2$$

(c) Each mass is 2.0 m from the axis.

$$I_{1A} = (5 \text{ kg})(2.0 \text{ m})^2 + (10 \text{ kg})(2.0 \text{ m})^2 + (20 \text{ kg})(2.0 \text{ m})^2 + (30 \text{ kg})(2.0 \text{ m})^2 = 260 \text{ kg} \cdot \text{m}^2$$

Problem 10.14. For the situation in Fig. 10-9, find the moment of inertia I_A about an axis through point A, and perpendicular to the plane of the figure.

Solution

The common distance of the four masses from the axis is one-half the diagonal. Since either diagonal and two connecting sides form a right triangle, we can use the Pythagorean theorem to obtain the diagonal length. In our case the sides are of length 3.0 and 4.0 m, respectively, so the diagonal has length 5.0 m. The distance to each mass is thus 2.5 m. Then

$$I_A = (5.0 \text{ kg} + 10 \text{ kg} + 30 \text{ kg} + 20 \text{ kg})(2.5 \text{ m})^2 = 406 \text{ kg} \cdot \text{m}^2$$

Problem 10.15. Figure 10-10 depicts a double wheel whose mass is concentrated in two concentric rims of equal mass, $M_1 = M_2 = 8.0$ kg. The rims are supported by a set of light spokes joining at the geometric center of the wheels. The radii of the two rims are $R_1 = 2.0$ m and $R_2 = 4.0$ m. Find (a) the moment of inertia of each rim about a perpendicular axis through the center of the wheel, (b) the total moment of inertia of the double wheel about the axis.

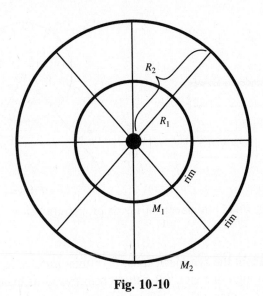

Fig. 10-10

Solution

(a) For the first rim, all the particles are at the same distance from the axis, so summing over all particles in this rim,

$$I_1 = \left(\sum m_i r_i^2 \right) = \left(\sum m_i \right) R_1^2 = M_1 R_1^2 = (8.0 \text{ kg})(2.0 \text{ m})^2 = 32 \text{ kg} \cdot \text{m}^2$$

Similarly for the outer rim, we sum over all particles in that rim:

$$I_2 = \left(\sum m_i r_i^2 \right) = \left(\sum m_i \right) R_2^2 = M_2 R_2^2 = (8.0 \text{ kg})(4.0 \text{ m})^2 = 128 \text{ kg} \cdot \text{m}^2$$

(b) The total moment of inertia is just the sum of the contributions from the two rims:

$$I_T = 32 \text{ kg} \cdot \text{m}^2 + 128 \text{ kg} \cdot \text{m}^2 = 160 \text{ kg} \cdot \text{m}^2$$

In general, obtaining the moment of inertia of even a simple, symmetric object is possible only by using the calculus. In Fig. 10-11 we show the moments of inertia for a few standard symmetric objects of uniform density: (a) a uniform disk of mass M and radius R about a perpendicular axis through its center; (b) a uniform cylindrical annulus (a hollowed-out concentric cylinder) of inner radius R_1 and

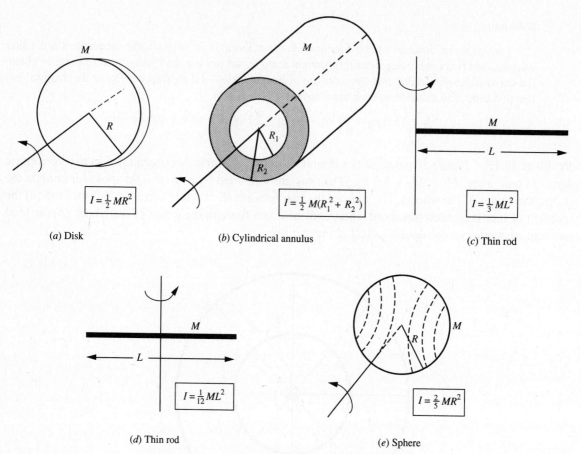

Fig. 10-11   Moments of inertia of uniform bodies.

outer radius R_2 and mass M about the symmetry axis; (*c*) a thin uniform rod of mass M and length L about a perpendicular axis through one end; (*d*) a thin uniform rod of mass M and length L about a perpendicular axis through its center; (*e*) a uniform sphere of mass M and radius R about an axis through its center.

Solving Dynamics Problems

We are now prepared to solve a variety of problems involving rigid-body rotation.

Problem 10.16.   A uniform disk of mass $M = 12.0$ kg and radius $R = 0.75$ m (Figure 10-12) is free to rotate about a frictionless axle through its center. A cord is wrapped around the rim of the disk and is pulled with a steady tension of $T = 100$ N. As the cord is unwound, the disk rotates, and we assume there is no slippage between the cord and the rim of the disk. If the disk starts from rest, find the angular velocity and the angle turned through after 6.0 s.

Solution

The only external forces acting on the disk are the tension T in the cord, the weight and the normal force due to the axle. The weight and normal force have no moment about the axis of rotation, so they do not contribute to the torque. The tension acts tangential to the rim, so the moment arm is just the radius

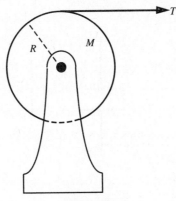

Fig. 10-12

of the disk. Then, from Eq. *(10.16)* and Fig. 10-11 we have $\Gamma = I\alpha$ or $TR = (\frac{1}{2}MR^2)\alpha$. Substituting, we get

$$(100 \text{ N})(0.75 \text{ m}) = (6.0 \text{ kg})(0.75 \text{ m})^2\alpha \qquad \text{or} \qquad \alpha = 22.2 \text{ rad/s}^2$$

Since α is constant, and the system starts from rest, we have

$$\omega = \alpha t = (22.2 \text{ rad/s}^2)(6.0 \text{ s}) = 133 \text{ rad/s}$$

Similarly, assuming we start measuring θ from $t = 0$, we have

$$\theta = \tfrac{1}{2}\alpha t^2 = (11.1 \text{ rad/s}^2)(6.0 \text{ s})^2 = 400 \text{ rad}$$

Problem 10.17.

(a)   Calculate the work W done by the tension T of Problem 10.16, in rotating the disk through 400 rad.

(b)   Using the work-energy theorem, find the angular velocity ω of the disk after it rotates through 400 rad., and compare to the result of Problem 10.16.

Solution

(a)   Since the torque is constant at 75 N · m, we have [Problem 10.11(*b*)]

$$\text{Work} = W = \Gamma\theta = (75 \text{ N} \cdot \text{m})(400 \text{ rad}) = 30{,}000 \text{ J}$$

[Or, we could calculate the work as $W = Tx$, where x is the distance through which the cord is pulled as the disk rotates through 400 rad. Now x is just the length of cord that unwinds from the rim, so $x = R\theta = (0.75 \text{ m})(400 \text{ rad}) = 300 \text{ m}$. Then $W = (100 \text{ N})(300 \text{ m}) = 30{,}000 \text{ J}$ as before.]

(b)   Since the disk starts from rest, we have $W = \tfrac{1}{2}I\omega^2$. We recall that $I = \tfrac{1}{2}MR^2 = (6.0 \text{ kg})(0.75 \text{ m})^2 = 3.375 \text{ kg} \cdot \text{m}^2$. Then

$$30{,}000 \text{ J} = \tfrac{1}{2}(3.375 \text{ kg} \cdot \text{m}^2)\omega^2 \qquad \text{or} \qquad \omega = 133 \text{ rad/s}$$

which is the same result as in Problem 10.16.

Problem 10.18.   A block of mass $m = 3.0$ kg hangs from one end of a cord, while the other end is wrapped around a uniform wheel of radius $R = 30$ cm and moment of inertia $I = 0.80$ kg · m². The wheel is free to rotate about a frictionless horizontal axle through its center, as shown in Fig. 10-13(*a*). The system starts from rest and the cord unravels with no slippage.

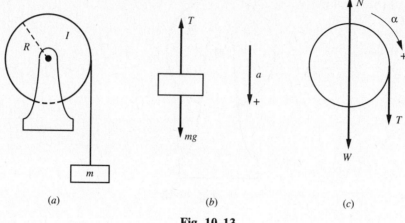

Fig. 10-13

(a) Find the acceleration a of the block.

(b) Find the angular velocity of the wheel after the block has dropped through a distance of 1.50 m.

Solution

(a) We first apply Newton's second law to the block. The free-body diagram, Fig. 10-13(b), gives

$$mg - T = ma \qquad (i)$$

This equation has two unknowns, the tension T and the acceleration a. We therefore need another equation, and we turn to the rotational law for the wheel. The body diagram for the wheel is shown in Fig. 10-13(c). For this problem we find it convenient to choose *clockwise* as our positive rotational direction—which is okay as long as we do so consistently for all rotational quantities, including the torque. We note that neither the normal force at the axle nor the weight of the wheel W, which acts at the center, can contribute to the torque about the axis of rotation. The only torque is due to the tension in the cord, and is clockwise, giving $\Gamma = TR$. Then

$$\Gamma = I\alpha \Rightarrow TR = I\alpha \qquad (ii)$$

Equation (ii) has two unknowns, T and α. Thus between (i) and (ii) we have two equations with three unknowns. We have, in addition, a relationship between a and α. Since there is no slippage between the rim and the cord, the velocity of the cord v (which is the same as the velocity of the block), must always equal the velocity of a point on the rim of the wheel. Similarly, the acceleration of the cord a (which is the same as the acceleration of the block) must equal the tangential acceleration of a point on the rim. Thus we have

$$v = R\omega \qquad a = R\alpha \qquad (iiia, b)$$

Equation (ii) can then be rewritten as $TR = Ia/R$ or

$$T = \left(\frac{I}{R^2}\right) a \qquad (iv)$$

Note that this looks just like Newton's second law for an object of mass $M' = I/R^2$ moving along a horizontal frictionless surface under the action of a horizontal force T. We can now solve Eqs. (i) and (iv) to obtain T and a. Adding, we get

$$mg = \left(\frac{I}{R^2} + m\right) a \qquad (v)$$

Substituting numerical values into (v) we get

$$(3.0 \text{ kg})(9.8 \text{ m/s}^2) = \left[\frac{0.80 \text{ kg} \cdot \text{m}}{(0.30 \text{ m})^2} + 3.0 \text{ kg}\right] a \qquad \text{or} \qquad a = 2.47 \text{ m/s}^2$$

(b)   The system starts from rest, and we can set $y = 0$ at the initial position of the block. Then,

$$v^2 = 2ay = 2(2.47 \text{ m/s}^2)(1.5 \text{ m}) = 7.41 \text{ m}^2/\text{s}^2 \qquad \text{or} \qquad v = 2.72 \text{ m/s}$$

Using ($iiia$), we have

$$\omega = \frac{v}{R} = \frac{2.72 \text{ m/s}}{0.30 \text{ m}} = 9.07 \text{ rad/s}$$

Problem 10.19.   Check Problem 10.18(b), using energy conservation.

Solution

The only external force that does work is gravity. (Note that the tension in the cord does positive work on the wheel but does an equal and opposite amount of work on the block, thus doing no net work on the system as a whole. This is to be expected, since the cord is not a source of energy but merely a device to transfer energy from one part of the system to the other.) The conservation of energy for the system as a whole then requires that the loss in gravitational potential energy as the block falls equals the gain in kinetic energy of the system. For our case, starting from rest, $mgy = \frac{1}{2}mv^2 + \frac{1}{2}I\omega^2$. Recalling that $v = \omega R$, we have $mgy = \frac{1}{2}(mR^2 + I)\omega^2$. Substituting, we set

$$(3.0 \text{ kg})(9.8 \text{ m/s}^2)(1.5 \text{ m}) = \frac{1}{2}[(3.0 \text{ kg})(0.30 \text{ m})^2 + 0.80 \text{ kg} \cdot \text{m}^2]\omega^2$$

Solving, we get $\omega = 9.08$ rad/s, which matches the result in Problem 10.18.

Problem 10.20.   The engine of an automobile delivers energy to the wheel via the driveshaft. Assuming that an engine delivers 180 hp while the driveshaft is spinning at a frequency of $f = 80$ r/s, find the torque exerted by the engine on the driveshaft.

Solution

We have $P = \Gamma\omega = \Gamma(2\pi f)$, so

$$(180 \text{ hp})(550 \text{ ft} \cdot \text{lb/hp}) = \Gamma(6.28 \text{ rad/r})(80 \text{ r/s}) \qquad \text{or} \qquad \Gamma = 197 \text{ lb} \cdot \text{ft}$$

Problem 10.21.   For Problem 10.18, find (a) the tension in the cord, (b) the instantaneous power delivered via the cord at the moment the block has fallen 1.50 m.

Solution

(a) From Problem 10.18, Eq. (i), we have $mg - T = ma$ or

$$T = m(g - a) = (3.0 \text{ kg})(9.8 \text{ m/s}^2 - 2.47 \text{ m/s}^2) = 22.0 \text{ N}$$

(b) $P = \Gamma\omega = TR\omega$. Substituting, we get [using the results of Problem 10.18(b)]

$$(22.0 \text{ N})(0.30 \text{ m})(9.07 \text{ rad/s}) = 59.9 \text{ W}$$

10.4   ANGULAR MOMENTUM

General Definition

We have already defined the angular momentum of a rigid body rotating about a fixed axis to be $I\omega$. The more general definition, however, like that of torque, is a vector quantity. Moreover, the formal definition is made in terms of a particle moving through space, not a rotating rigid body, and at first glance this definition appears to have nothing to do with $I\omega$. The definition of vector angular momentum is completely analogous to that of vector torque. The situation is shown in Fig. 10-14. There a particle of mass m moves with velocity **v** (not necessarily in the xy plane) and thus has momentum **p** = m**v**. At the instant in question the displacement of the particle from the origin is **r**. The magnitude of the angular momentum **l** *about the origin* is defined as

$$l = rmv \sin \theta = rp \sin \theta \qquad (10.17)$$

where θ is the angle between **r** and **p**.

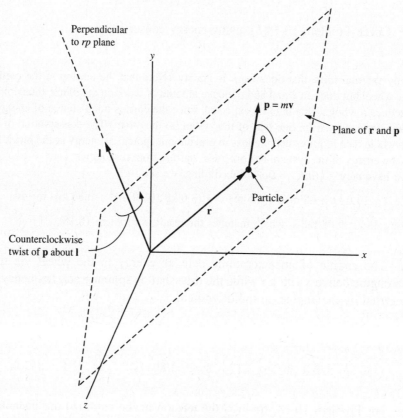

Fig. 10-14

The direction of **l** is defined to be perpendicular to the plane of **r** and **p**, and pointing in the same direction as a torque would point if **p** were a force instead of the momentum. Thus, for a particle moving in the xy plane, the angular momentum would point in the $\pm z$ direction, with the sign determined by whether the particle appears to be going "around" the z axis counterclockwise or clockwise. (Again, the standard convention is that counterclockwise is positive.) Because of the complete analogy of the definition of angular momentum to that of the moment of a force, the angular momentum is often called the **moment of momentum**.

Problem 10.22.

(a)   A particle of mass m = 2.5 kg moves in the xy plane with a velocity **v** of magnitude v = 30.0 m/s parallel to the x axis, as shown in Fig. 10-15. If the perpendicular distance from the origin to the

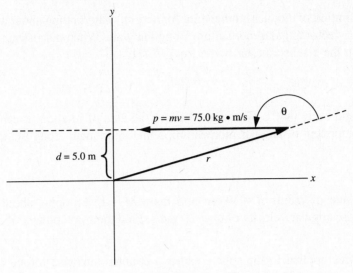

Fig. 10-15

line of motion is $d = 5.0$ m, as shown, find the magnitude and direction of the angular momentum $\mathbf{l}$ about the origin. Assume z is positive out of the paper.

(b)   If the particle continues to move with uniform velocity, how will the angular momentum change with time?

Solution

(a)   The direction of $\mathbf{l}$ is along the positive z axis, because the momentum vector, if thought of as a force, would give rise to a counterclockwise moment about the positive z axis. The magnitude of the angular momentum is given by $l = rmv \sin\theta$. We note that $r \sin\theta = r \sin(180° - \theta) = d$, so

$$l = dmv = (5.0 \text{ m})(2.5 \text{ kg})(30.0 \text{ m/s}) = 375 \text{ kg} \cdot \text{m}^2/\text{s}$$

(b)   For any position along the straight-line path of motion we have $r \sin\theta = d$. Also, mv remains constant by hypothesis. Thus $l = rmv \sin\theta = dmv = $ constant. The direction of $\mathbf{l}$ also remains constant, pointing along the positive z axis.

Rotation of a Rigid Body about a Fixed Axis

For a rigid body rotating about the z axis, all the particles are moving in concentric circles in planes parallel to the xy plane. The z component of the angular momentum of the ith particle, in analogy to the z component of a torque, can be shown to depend only on the perpendicular displacement r_i from the z axis to the particle and on the momentum of the particle in the xy plane. It is given by $l_{iz} = r_i m_i v_i \sin\theta_i$, where θ_i is the angle between the line r_i and the vector momentum $\mathbf{v}_i$. (For definiteness, we assume the object is rotating counterclockwise about the z axis, so l_{iz} has a plus sign.)

Since the ith particle is moving on a circle of radius r_i, the angle $\theta_i = 90°$ so that $\sin\theta_i = 1$ and $l_{iz} = m_i v_i r_i$. Since $v_i = r_i \omega$, this becomes $l_{iz} = m_i r_i^2 \omega$. The total z component of angular momentum is $L_z = \sum l_{iz} = \sum m_i r_i^2 \omega$. Since ω is the same for all particles in the body, and $I = \sum m_i r_i^2$, we get

$$L_z = I\omega \qquad\qquad (10.18a)$$

Thus, our earlier definition of angular momentum, for a rigid body rotating about a fixed axis, is really the component of the vector angular momentum along that axis. When discussing rotation about the z axis some texts drop the z subscript and write Eq. (*10.18a*) as

$$L = I\omega \qquad\qquad\qquad (10.18b)$$

Note.   For a rigid body that is symmetrical about the axis of rotation, it can be shown that the *only* component of angular momentum is the component along the axis.

Problem 10.23.

(*a*) A uniform sphere of radius $R = 30$ cm and mass $M = 15$ kg spins about the z axis with a counterclockwise angular velocity of $\omega = 20$ rad/s. Find the z component of angular momentum of the sphere.

(*b*) An external force applied to the sphere exerts a counterclockwise torque about the z axis of $\Gamma = 10$ N·m for a period of 3.0 s. The force then changes so that it exerts a clockwise torque of $\Gamma = 20$ N·m for the next 4.0 s. Find the total angular impulse in the 7.0-s interval.

(*c*) Find the angular velocity of the sphere at the end of the 7.0-s interval.

Solution

(*a*) $L = I\omega$. $I = \frac{2}{5}MR^2 = \frac{2}{5}(15$ kg$)(0.30$ m$)^2 = 0.54$ kg·m^2.   Then $L = (0.54$ kg·m$^2)(20$ rad/s$) = 10.8$ J·s.

(*b*) Angular impulse $= \Gamma_1\,\Delta t_1 + \Gamma_2\,\Delta t_2 = (10$ N·m$)(3.0$ s$) + (-20$ N·m$)(4.0$ s$) = -50$ J·s.

(*c*) Angular impulse $= \Delta(I\omega) = I\,\Delta\omega = I(\omega_f - \omega_i)$, since I is constant. Then

$$-50 \text{ J·s} = (0.54 \text{ kg·m}^2)(\omega_f - 20 \text{ rad/s}) \qquad \text{or} \qquad \omega_f = -72.6 \text{ rad/s}$$

Conservation of Angular Momentum

The general law of conservation of angular momentum for an arbitrarily moving system of particles is a rather complicated affair, but it is completely analogous to conservation of linear momentum for such a system. It may be stated as follows: If the resultant external vector torque (about the origin) $\mathbf{\Gamma}$ for a system of particles is zero, then the vector sum of the angular momenta of all the particles, $\mathbf{L} = \sum \mathbf{l}_i$, stays constant in time.

For the special case of objects rotating about a fixed axis, say the z axis, the law takes on a simpler form: If the total external torque about the axis is zero, then the total z component of angular momentum doesn't change.

Problem 10.24.   Two disks are freely rotating about a common frictionless axle, as shown in Fig. 10-16. The disks rest on frictionless pins in the axle. If the pin under the upper disk is suddenly removed, without otherwise disturbing the disk, the disk will fall onto the lower disk, and after a short time the friction between the two disks will bring them to a common angular velocity.

(*a*) Prove from basic principles that angular momentum is conserved in this case.

(*b*) Calculate the final angular velocity of the combination for the data of Fig. 10-16.

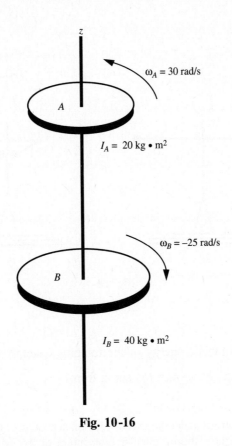

Fig. 10-16

Solution

(a) The external forces—the force of gravity and the normal force of the lower pin—do not contribute to the torque about the z axis. The only torques on the two disks as they collide are the frictional torques they exert on each other. These torques are equal and opposite, as a consequence of Newton's third law: Γ_{AB} (torque of disk A on disk B) $= -\Gamma_{BA}$. For any infinitesimal time interval Δt, we have $\Gamma_{AB}\,\Delta t = \Delta(I_B\omega_B)$ and $\Gamma_{BA}\,\Delta t = \Delta(I_A\omega_A)$. Thus

$$\Gamma_{AB} = -\Gamma_{BA} \Rightarrow \Delta(I_A\omega_A) = -\Delta(I_B\omega_B)$$

Since the changes in angular momentum of the two disks are equal and opposite, the combined angular momentum of the two disks must remain constant:

$$(I_A + I_B)\omega_f = I_A\omega_{Ai} + I_B\omega_{Bi} \tag{i}$$

(b) Setting the total angular momentum after collision equal to the total before, we obtain

$$[(20 \text{ kg} \cdot \text{m}^2) + (40 \text{ kg} \cdot \text{m}^2)]\omega_f = (20 \text{ kg} \cdot \text{m}^2)(30 \text{ rad/s}) + (40 \text{ kg} \cdot \text{m}^2)(-25 \text{ m/s})$$

from which $\omega_f = -6.67$ rad/s.

Problem 10.25.   A student stands on a light platform that is free to rotate without friction about a vertical axis. His arms are initially outstretched, as shown in Fig. 10-17(a), and he holds a 5.0-kg mass in each hand. His initial angular velocity is $\omega_i = 4.0$ rad/s.

(a) What is the new angular velocity ω_f when his elbows are bent as shown in Fig. 10-17(b)? [*Data*: The moment of inertia of the student (without the weights) about the rotation axis, with his arms outstretched, is 5.0 kg·m²; with his elbows bent, it is 4.5 kg·m². The weights are initially 0.90 m from the axis of rotation, and finally 0.30 m.]

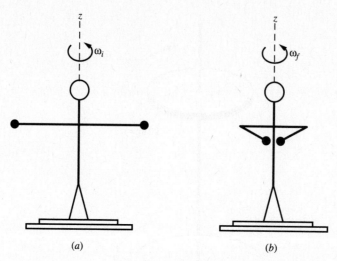

Fig. 10-17

(b) What is the increase in kinetic energy of the rotating system?

(c) Where does the extra energy in part (b) come from?

Solution

(a) Since no external torque about the axis of rotation acts on the system consisting of the student, the masses, and the light platform, angular momentum of the system about that axis is conserved: $I_i\omega_i = I_f\omega_f$. From the data,

$$I_i = 5.0 \text{ kg} \cdot \text{m}^2 + 2(5.0 \text{ kg})(0.90 \text{ m})^2 = 13.1 \text{ kg} \cdot \text{m}^2$$

$$I_f = 4.5 \text{ kg} \cdot \text{m}^2 + 2(5.0 \text{ kg})(0.30 \text{ m})^2 = 5.4 \text{ kg} \cdot \text{m}^2$$

Then, $(13.1 \text{ kg} \cdot \text{m}^2)(4.0 \text{ rad/s}) = (5.4 \text{ kg} \cdot \text{m}^2)\omega_f$ or $\omega_f = 9.70 \text{ rad/s}$.

(b) $$(E_k)_f = \tfrac{1}{2}I_f\omega_f{}^2 = \tfrac{1}{2}(5.4 \text{ kg} \cdot \text{m}^2)(9.70 \text{ rad/s})^2 = 254 \text{ J}$$

$$(E_k)_i = \tfrac{1}{2}I_i\omega_i{}^2 = \tfrac{1}{2}(13.1 \text{ kg} \cdot \text{m}^2)(4.0 \text{ rad/s})^2 = 105 \text{ J}$$

$\Delta E_k = 254 \text{ J} - 105 \text{ J} = 149 \text{ J}$.

(c) From the internal work done by the student in drawing in his arms with the held masses.

Problem 10.26. A wheel, of moment of inertia $I = 5.0 \text{ slug} \cdot \text{ft}^2$ and radius $R = 2.0 \text{ ft}$, is initially at rest and free to rotate about a frictionless vertical axis through its center. The wheel has horizontal cups attached to the rim which can catch and hold objects thrown at them tangential to the rim (Fig. 10-18). A ball of mass $m = 0.50 \text{ slug}$ is thrown at one of the cups with a velocity $v = 80 \text{ ft/s}$.

(a) Find the angular velocity of the wheel after the ball is caught in the cup.

(b) How much thermal energy was lost in the collision?

Solution

(a) Angular momentum about the z axis (through the center of the wheel) is conserved since there is no external torque about this axis on either the ball (in flight) or the wheel. Since the ball is moving tangentially, the z component of its angular momentum before the collision is mvR. Since the

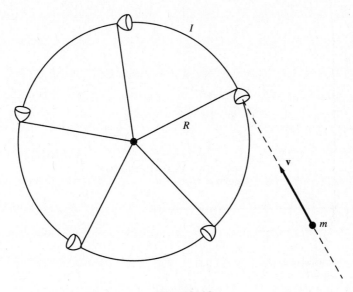

Fig. 10-18

wheel is initially at rest, its angular momentum is zero. The initial z component of angular momentum of the wheel-ball system is therefore

$$L_i = mvR = (0.50 \text{ slug})(80 \text{ ft/s})(2.0 \text{ ft}) = 80 \text{ slug} \cdot \text{ft}^2/\text{s}$$

After the collision, the moment of inertia of the wheel-ball system is

$$I_T = 5.0 \text{ slug} \cdot \text{ft}^2 + (0.50 \text{ slug})(2.0 \text{ ft})^2 = 7.0 \text{ slug} \cdot \text{ft}^2$$

and conservation gives

$$(7.0 \text{ slug} \cdot \text{ft}^2)\omega_f = 80 \text{ slug} \cdot \text{ft}^2/\text{s} \quad \text{or} \quad \omega_f = 11.4 \text{ rad/s}$$

(*b*) Thermal heat generated = loss of kinetic energy.

$$(E_k)_i = \tfrac{1}{2}mv^2 = \tfrac{1}{2}(0.50 \text{ slug})(80 \text{ ft/s})^2 = 1600 \text{ ft} \cdot \text{lb}$$

$$(E_k)_f = \tfrac{1}{2}I_T\omega_f{}^2 = \tfrac{1}{2}(7.0 \text{ slug} \cdot \text{ft}^2)(11.4 \text{ rad/s})^2 = 455 \text{ ft} \cdot \text{lb}$$

Thermal energy = $(1600 - 455)$ ft · lb = 1145 ft · lb.

10.5 ROTATION ABOUT AN AXIS THROUGH THE CENTER OF MASS

Until now we have been discussing rotation about a fixed axis. In general an object can translate through space and rotate at the same time; the dynamics of such motion can be very complicated. The special properties of the CM of a rigid body, however, simplify the analysis. In Fig. 10-19 we show an object moving through space. We imagine a coordinate system moving with the object so that its origin is fixed at the CM of the object, but its axes remain parallel to the axes of a coordinate system fixed in an inertial frame. (The moving coordinate system is called the **CM frame**.) From the point of view of someone moving with the CM frame, the CM is pinned at the origin, and therefore the object's only motion is its rotation about some axis through the origin. If this rotation axis has a fixed direction (does not pivot) as observed in the CM frame—if, for example, it always coincides with the z axis of the frame—then $\Gamma = I\alpha$ holds about this axis in the CM frame, as do the other laws of rotation. This is true even if the CM is accelerating relative to the inertial frame and therefore is not itself an inertial

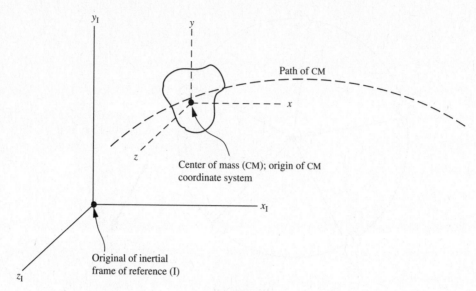

Fig. 10-19

frame. The laws of rotation generally *do not hold* in a coordinate system whose origin is fixed at a point in the body *other* than the CM.

Another special result for the CM frame is that the total kinetic energy of an object, as measured in the inertial frame, is given by

$$E_k = \tfrac{1}{2}MV_{CM}{}^2 + \tfrac{1}{2}I_{CM}\omega^2 \qquad\qquad (10.19)$$

Here, M is the mass of the object, V_{CM} is the velocity of the CM as seen in the inertial frame, I_{CM} is the moment of inertia about the CM axis of rotation, and ω is the angular velocity (which is the same in both coordinate systems, since their axes stay parallel). Note that the first term on the right of (*10.19*) is just the kinetic energy the body would have in the inertial frame if it were not rotating at all but merely translating with the velocity of the CM. The second term is just the rotational kinetic energy of the body as seen in the CM frame, i.e., the total kinetic energy in the CM frame.

Use of the CM frame and the energy decomposition (*10.19*) are particularly valuable in analyzing rolling motion.

Problem 10.27. In Fig. 10-20(*a*) a uniform disk, of mass $M = 2.0$ kg and radius $R = 0.45$ m, rolls without slipping down an inclined plane of length $L = 35$ m and slope 30 °. The disk starts from rest at the top of the incline. Find (*a*) the angular acceleration α of the disk and the linear acceleration a of the CM of the disk; (*b*) the time for the disk to reach the bottom of the incline; (*c*) the angular velocity at the bottom of the incline.

Solution

(*a*) Since there is no slippage between disk and incline, the point of contact translates a distance Δx along the incline when the disk has rotated through an arc length $\Delta s = \Delta x$. If $\Delta\theta$ is the corresponding angle of rotation, we have $\Delta s = R\,\Delta\theta$ and therefore $\Delta x = R\,\Delta\theta$. This leads to $v = R\omega$ and $a = R\alpha$, where ω and α are the angular velocity and angular acceleration of the disk, and where v and a are the linear velocity and acceleration of the point of contact along the incline. Since the CM of the disk is always in the same position relative to the point of contact, v and a are also the velocity and acceleration of the CM.

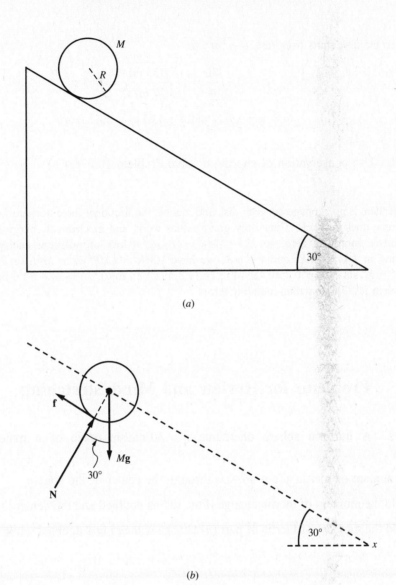

(a)

(b)

Fig. 10-20

Using the body diagram of the disk, Fig. 10-20(b), we have for the x motion of the CM

$$Mg \sin 30° - f = Ma \qquad (i)$$

Both f and a are unknowns, so a second equation is needed. For rotation *about the axis through the* CM we have $\Gamma = I_{CM}\alpha$. If we choose clockwise as positive and refer to Fig. 10-11(a), this becomes $fR = (\frac{1}{2}MR^2)(a/R)$, or

$$f = \tfrac{1}{2}Ma \qquad (ii)$$

Adding (i) and (ii) eliminates f and yields $Mg \sin 30° = [M + \frac{1}{2}M]a$, or

$$a = \tfrac{2}{3}g \sin 30° = \frac{9.8 \text{ m/s}^2}{3} = 3.27 \text{ m/s}^2$$

and $\alpha = a/R = (3.27 \text{ m/s}^2)/(0.45 \text{ m}) = 7.27 \text{ rad/s}^2$.

(b)   Since the disk starts from rest, $L = \frac{1}{2}at^2$, or

$$t = \sqrt{\frac{2L}{a}} = \sqrt{\frac{2(35 \text{ m})}{3.27 \text{ m/s}^2}} = 4.63 \text{ s}$$

(c) $\omega = \alpha t = (7.27 \text{ rad/s}^2)(4.63 \text{ s}) = 33.7 \text{ rad/s}$

Problem 10.28.   Use conservation of energy to solve Problem 10.27(c).

Solution

Since there is no slippage between disk and incline, the frictional force does no work. Similarly, the normal force does no work. Thus, only gravity does work, and mechanical energy is conserved. The initial kinetic energy is zero, so $E_{kf} = \frac{1}{2}Mv^2 + \frac{1}{2}I_{CM}\omega^2 =$ loss of potential energy $= MgL \sin 30°$. Substituting in $I_{CM} = \frac{1}{2}MR^2$ and $v = \omega R$, we have $\frac{1}{2}(MR^2 + \frac{1}{2}MR^2)\omega^2 = MgL \sin 30°$. Dividing out M, $\frac{3}{4}R^2\omega^2 = gL \sin 30° \Rightarrow 0.75(0.45 \text{ m})^2\omega^2 = (9.8 \text{ m/s}^2)(35 \text{ m})(0.50) \Rightarrow \omega = 33.6 \text{ rad/s}$, which agrees with Problem 10.27(c) to within rounding errors.

Problems for Review and Mind Stretching

Problem 10.29.   A uniform sphere of radius $R = 30$ cm is made of a material of density $\rho = 5000$ kg/m³.

(a)   Find the moment of inertia about an axis through the center of the sphere.

(b)   How would the moment of inertia change if the radius doubled and the density stayed the same?

(c)   How would the moment of inertia of part (a) change if the radius doubled while the mass stayed the same?

Solution

(a)   By Fig. 10-11(e),

$$I = \frac{2}{5}MR^2 \tag{i}$$

Recalling that the volume of a sphere is $V = \frac{4}{3}\pi R^3$, we get $M = \rho V = \frac{4}{3}\pi\rho R^3$. Therefore,

$$I = \frac{8\pi\rho R^5}{15} = \frac{8(3.14)(5000 \text{ kg/m}^3)(0.30 \text{ m})^5}{15} = 20.3 \text{ kg} \cdot \text{m}^2 \tag{ii}$$

(b)   From Eq. (ii) of part (a) we see that for constant ρ, I varies as R^5. Therefore, doubling R increases I by a factor of $2^5 = 32$. Then $I = 32(20.3 \text{ kg} \cdot \text{m}^2) = 650 \text{ kg} \cdot \text{m}^2$.

(c)   From Eq. (i) of part (a) we see that for constant M, I varies as R^2. Therefore doubling R increases I by a factor of $2^2 = 4$. Then $I = 4(20.3 \text{ kg} \cdot \text{m}^2) = 81.2 \text{ kg} \cdot \text{m}^2$.

Problem 10.30.   In an Atwood's machine (Fig. 10-21) two blocks are connected by a light cord over a pulley of radius R and moment of inertia I. Assume the pulley rotates without friction on a horizontal axis and there is no slippage between the cord and the pulley. Find (a) the acceleration of the blocks; (b) the tensions T_A and T_B on either side of the pulley.

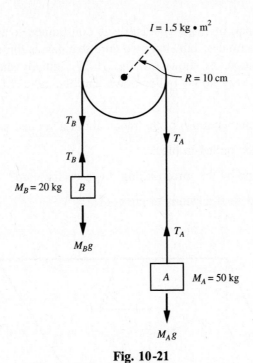

Fig. 10-21

Solution

(a) We apply the laws of motion to each of the three objects, for consistency choosing downward as positive for block A, upward as positive for block B, and clockwise as positive for the pulley. Then a can represent the acceleration of either block, and $\alpha = a/R$ represents the angular acceleration of the pulley.

for block A:

$$M_A g - T_A = M_A a \qquad (i)$$

for block B:

$$T_B - M_B g = M_B a \qquad (ii)$$

for the pulley:

$$\Gamma = I\alpha \Rightarrow T_A R - T_B R = \frac{Ia}{R} \qquad \text{or} \qquad T_A - T_B = \frac{I}{R^2} a \qquad (iii)$$

Adding (i), (ii), and (iii), the tensions cancel and we get

$$(M_A - M_B)g = \left(M_A + M_B + \frac{I}{R^2} \right) a$$

$$(50 \text{ kg} - 20 \text{ kg})(9.8 \text{ m/s}^2) = \left[50 \text{ kg} + 20 \text{ kg} + \frac{1.5 \text{ kg} \cdot \text{m}^2}{(0.10 \text{ m})^2} \right] a$$

$$a = 1.34 \text{ m/s}^2$$

(b) From (i), $T_A = M_A(g - a) = (50 \text{ kg}) (9.8 \text{ m/s}^2 - 1.34 \text{ m/s}^2) = 423$ N. Similarly, from (ii),

$$T_B = M_B(g + a) = (20 \text{ kg})(9.8 \text{ m/s}^2 + 1.34 \text{ m/s}^2) = 223 \text{ N}$$

Problem 10.31. A small block of mass $m = 200$ g is constrained to move in a circle of radius $R_i = 20$ cm on a horizontal frictionless tabletop by a cord that passes through a hole in the center of the table and is held in position, as shown in Fig. 10-22. Initially the block has a velocity of $v_i = 35$ cm/s. The cord is then very slowly pulled down until the radius of the circle of motion drops to one-half its original value.

(a) Find the initial angular momentum l_i of the block about a vertical axis through the hole.

(b) What is the velocity of the pulled-in block?

(c) How much work was done by the force pulling down on the cord?

(d) What were the initial and final tensions in the cord?

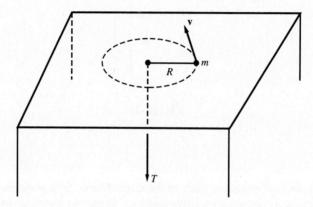

Fig. 10-22

Solution

(a) Since the radius is perpendicular to the velocity of the block,

$$l_i = mv_iR_i = (0.200 \text{ kg})(0.35 \text{ m/s})(0.20 \text{ m}) = 0.014 \text{ kg} \cdot \text{m}^2/\text{s}$$

(b) The only force in the plane of motion is the tension in the cord. Its line of action passes through the center of the circle and hence contributes zero torque about the vertical axis through that point. Thus, angular momentum about that axis is conserved:

$$mv_fR_f = mv_iR_i \qquad \text{or} \qquad v_f = \frac{R_i}{R_f} v_i = 2(35 \text{ cm/s}) = 70 \text{ cm/s}$$

(c) The only work done on the block is by the force pulling the cord down. Applying the work-energy theorem,

$$(E_k)_i = \tfrac{1}{2}mv_i^2 = \tfrac{1}{2}(0.20 \text{ kg})(0.35 \text{ m/s})^2 = 0.0123 \text{ J}$$
$$(E_k)_f = \tfrac{1}{2}mv_f^2 = \tfrac{1}{2}(0.20 \text{ kg})(0.70 \text{ m/s})^2 = 0.0490 \text{ J}$$
$$W = (E_k)_f - (E_k)_i = 0.0367 \text{ J}$$

(d) The initial tension is given by the centripetal force law:

$$T_i = \frac{mv_i^2}{R} = \frac{(0.20 \text{ kg})(0.35 \text{ m/s})^2}{0.20 \text{ m}} = 0.123 \text{ N}$$

Similarly, the final tension is given by

$$T_f = \frac{mv_f{}^2}{R} = \frac{(0.20 \text{ kg})(0.70 \text{ m/s})^2}{0.10 \text{ m}} = 0.980 \text{ N}$$

Problem 10.32. Ten girls, of mass $m = 35$ kg each, initially stand at different points on the rim of a merry-go-round; its moment of inertia is $I_0 = 800$ kg $\cdot$ m^2, and its radius is $R = 4.0$ m. The merry-go-round has an initial angular velocity of $\omega_i = 0.20$ rad/s and rotates freely on frictionless bearings.

(a) Find the velocity and the centripetal acceleration of each girl.

(b) On a signal the girls all start moving in toward the center of the merry-go-round until they reach a distance $R' = 1.5$ m from the center, where they again stand. Find the new angular velocity ω_f of the system.

   Solution

   (a) For each girl, $v = \omega R = (0.20 \text{ rad/s})(4.0 \text{ m}) = 0.80$ m/s, and **v** is tangential. Similarly, for each girl, the centripetal acceleration has magnitude

   $$a_R = \omega^2 R = (0.20 \text{ rad/s})^2 (4.0 \text{ m}) = 0.16 \text{ m/s}^2$$

   (b) Angular momentum about the axis of rotation is conserved: $I_i\omega_i = I_f\omega_f$. Here,

   $$I_i = 10(35 \text{ kg})(4.0 \text{ m})^2 + 800 \text{ kg} \cdot \text{m}^2 = 6400 \text{ kg} \cdot \text{m}^2$$
   $$I_f = 10(35 \text{ kg})(1.5 \text{ m})^2 + 800 \text{ kg} \cdot \text{m}^2 = 1588 \text{ kg} \cdot \text{m}^2$$

   Thus $\qquad\qquad (6400)(0.20 \text{ rad/s}) = 1588\omega_f \qquad$ or $\qquad \omega_f = 0.806 \text{ rad/s}$

Problem 10.33. In Problem 10.32, take the merry-go-round by itself as constituting the system. If 3.0 s was required for the girls to move from the rim to the final position, calculate (a) the time-average power and (b) the time-average torque exerted by the girls on the merry-go-round. (c) Assuming the torque was actually constant over the time interval, use it to find P_{av}.

   Solution

   (a) The average power P_{av} is given by the work-energy theorem as $P_{av} = \text{work/time} = \Delta E_k/\Delta t$, where ΔE_k is the change in kinetic energy of the merry-go-round. From Problem 10.32,

   $$\Delta E_k = \tfrac{1}{2}I_0\omega_f{}^2 - \tfrac{1}{2}I_0\omega_i{}^2 = (400 \text{ kg} \cdot \text{m}^2)[(0.806 \text{ rad/s})^2 - (0.200 \text{ rad/s})^2] = 244 \text{ J}$$

   Then,

   $$P_{av} = 244 \text{ J}/3.0 \text{ s} = 81.3 \text{ W}$$

   (b) The rotational impulse-momentum theorem gives $\Gamma_{av} \Delta t = I_0(\omega_f - \omega_i)$, or

   $$\Gamma_{av} = \frac{(800 \text{ kg} \cdot \text{m}^2)(0.806 \text{ rad/s} - 0.200 \text{ rad/s})}{3.0 \text{ s}} = 162 \text{ N} \cdot \text{m}$$

   (c) $P_{av} = \Gamma\omega_{av}$. If Γ is constant, then so is the angular acceleration α, and $\omega_{av} = (\omega_f + \omega_i)/2 = (0.806 \text{ rad/s} + 0.200 \text{ rad/s})/2 \quad$ or $\quad \omega_{av} = 0.503$ rad/s. Then $\quad P_{av} = (162 \text{ N} \cdot \text{m})(0.503 \text{ rad/s}) = 81.5$ W, which is consistent with our result in part (a).

Supplementary Problems

Problem 10.34.   A wheel having a uniform angular acceleration starts from rest and rotates through 150 rad in 2.5 s. Find (a) the angular acceleration; (b) the angular velocity at the end of the 2.5-s interval; (c) the number of revolutions turned through in the 2.5 s.

$\quad\quad$ *Ans.*   (a) 48 rad/s^2; (b) 120 rad/s; (c) 23.9 r

Problem 10.35.   The wheel of Problem 10.34 has a radius of 30 cm. At $t = 2.5$ s, find, for any point on the rim, (a) the linear velocity, (b) the tangential acceleration, and (c) the centripetal acceleration.

$\quad\quad$ *Ans.*   (a) 36 m/s; (b) 14.4 m/s^2; (c) 4320 m/s^2

Problem 10.36.   Referring to Problem 10.34, suppose that at the end of the 2.5-s interval the angular acceleration is suddenly changed to -144 rad/s^2. Find (a) the angular velocity 2.5 s later; (b) the overall angular displacement in the full 5.0-s interval.

$\quad\quad$ *Ans.*   (a) -240 rad/s; (b) 0 rad

Problem 10.37.   A rigid body in the xy plane consists of three identical spokes making angles of 120 ° with one another [Fig. 10-23]. Each spoke is of length $L = 2.0$ m and mass $m = 3.0$ kg and has a bob of mass $M = 5.0$ kg attached at the far end. Find the moment of inertia of the rigid body about the perpendicular (z) axis through its center. [*Hint*: See Fig. 10-11.]

$\quad\quad$ *Ans.*   72 kg · m^2

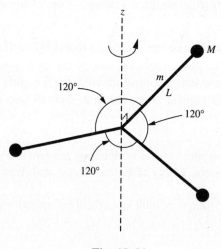

Fig. 10-23

Problem 10.38.   A force of constant magnitude $F = 12$ N is applied to one of the bobs in the rigid body of Problem 10.37. The force acts in the plane of the rigid body and always points at right angles to the spoke to which the bob is attached. If the rigid body is free to rotate about the z axis, and starts from rest, find (a) the torque about the rotation axis, (b) the angular velocity when the object has rotated through 80 rad.

$\quad\quad$ *Ans.*   (a) 24 N · m; (b) 7.30 rad/s

Problem 10.39.   A block of mass $M = 15$ kg starts from rest on a frictionless inclined plane of angle 40 °. The block is attached to a cord whose other end is wrapped around a wheel of moment of inertia $I = 15$ kg $\cdot$ m^2 and radius $R = 80$ cm, as shown in Fig. 10-24. The wheel is free to rotate about a frictionless horizontal axle. Find (a) the acceleration of the block down the incline; (b) the tension in the cord.

   Ans.   (a) 2.46 m/s^2; (b) 57.6 N

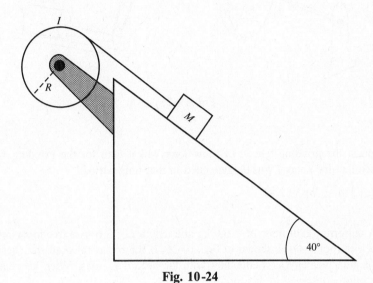

Fig. 10-24

Problem 10.40.   In Problem 10.39, use energy considerations to find the angular velocity of the wheel after the block has moved 3.0 m down the incline.

   Ans.   4.80 rad/s

Problem 10.41.   Referring to Problem 10.40, suppose that there were friction between the block and the incline. If the angular velocity of the wheel turned out to be 3.80 rad/s when the block moved the 3 m along the incline, (a) how much thermal energy was produced in the process? (b) What is the coefficient of kinetic friction between the block and the incline?

   Ans.   (a) 106 J; (b) 0.313

Problem 10.42.   A grinding wheel of radius $R = 20$ cm is rigidly connected to a long horizontal axle that is supported on both ends by frictionless pivots. The axle is driven by a belt over a pulley, which is also rigidly connected to the axle; the situation is shown in Fig. 10-25. A tool is pressed perpendicular to the grinding wheel with a force $N = 50$ N. Assume that μ_k between tool and wheel is 0.60 and that the wheel rotates at a steady rate of 10 r/s.

(a)   Find the torque on the grinding wheel, about the axis of rotation.

(b)   What must be the torque exerted by the belt on the wheel (or pulley)?

(c)   Assuming no losses in the shaft-belt-pulley system, how much power is supplied by the motor?

   Ans.   (a) 6.0 N $\cdot$ m; (b) −6.0 N $\cdot$ m; (c) 377 W

Problem 10.43.   Suppose that the moment of inertia of the wheel, shaft, and pulley of Problem 10.42 is 30 kg $\cdot$ m^2. Assume the same conditions as in Problem 10.42, and that the belt suddenly breaks. If the tool

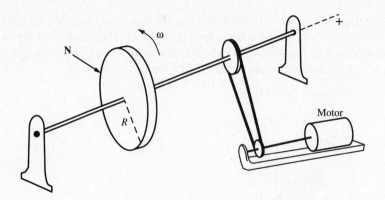

Fig. 10-25

remains pressed against the grinding wheel, (*a*) how long will it take for the grinding wheel to come to a stop? (*b*) how much thermal energy will be generated in that time period?

        Ans.   (*a*) 314 s; (*b*) 59.2 kJ

Problem 10.44. A uniform rod of mass $M = 6.0$ kg and length $L = 2.6$ m is free to swing in a vertical circle about a pivot at one end (point A), as shown in Fig. 10-26. If the rod is released from rest from the position shown, (*a*) find its angular velocity as it coincides with the negative *y*-axis. [*Hint*: Use energy conservation.] (*b*) Is angular momentum conserved in this motion?

        Ans.   (*a*) 4.12 rad/s; (*b*) no

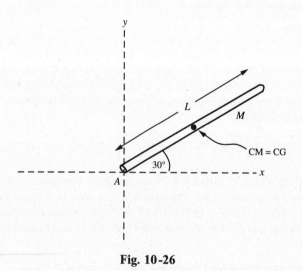

Fig. 10-26

Problem 10.45. A lump of clay, of mass $m = 0.20$ slug, is dropped from a height of 10.0 ft directly above one end of a uniform horizontal rod of length $L = 4.0$ ft and mass $M = 3.0$ slugs. The rod is free to rotate in a vertical circle about a horizontal axis through its center A (Fig. 10-27). Just before the collision, what is (*a*) the velocity of the clay, (*b*) the angular momentum of the clay (about the axis through point A)?

        Ans.   (*a*) 25.4 ft/s; (*b*) 10.2 slug·ft^2/s

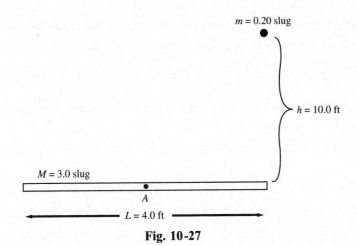

Fig. 10-27

Problem 10.46. Assume that the collision of Problem 10.45 is very rapid and that the clay sticks to the rod. Find (a) the angular velocity and (b) the kinetic energy, of the rod–clay combination immediately after the collision. (c) How much thermal energy is generated in the collision process?

>   *Ans.*   (a) 2.11 rad/s; (b) 10.7 ft · lb; (c) 53.7 ft · lb

Problem 10.47. Refer to Problem 10.24 and Fig. 10-16. Assume that the initial height difference between the two disks is 1.5 m and that the mass of the upper disk is $M_A = 100$ kg.

(a)   How much of the initial rotational kinetic energy is lost in the collision of the two disks?

(b)   How much thermal energy is generated?

>   *Ans.*   (a) 20.2 kJ; (b) 21.7 kJ

Problem 10.48. The mass of the earth is $M_e = 5.98 \times 10^{24}$ kg and its radius is $R_e = 6380$ km. Assuming the earth is a perfect sphere, find its angular momentum and rotational kinetic energy about its axis of rotation.

>   *Ans.* 7.08×10^{33} kg · m^2/s, 2.57×10^{29} J

Problem 10.49. Referring to Problem 10.48, imagine that an asteroid of mass $m = 5.0 \times 10^6$ kg, appears in the plane of the earth's equator. Traveling in a westerly direction at $v = 10$ km/s, the asteroid hits the earth just tangent to its surface, sticking to it.

(a)   What is the angular momentum of the meteor about the earth's axis before the collision?

(b)   Will this collision change the earth's angular momentum by a significant amount?

(c)   Assuming the same speed, what would the mass of the asteroid have to be to bring the rotation of the earth to a halt?

>   *Ans.*   (a) 3.19×10^{17} kg · m^2/s; (b) no (the change is insignificant; (c) 1.11×10^{23} kg (i.e., more massive than the moon)

Problem 10.50. A boy of mass $m = 30$ kg stands on the rim of a merry-go-round of moment of inertia $I = 200$ kg · m^2 and radius $R = 2.0$ m that is free to rotate without friction about a vertical axis through its center. Initially the angular velocity of the system is $\omega = 3.0$ rad/s. Suddenly the boy starts running around the rim in the direction *opposite* to the rotation, with a velocity relative to the earth of $v = 10$ m/s.

(a)   What is the angular velocity of the merry-go-round while the boy is running?

(b)   How fast does the boy seem to be running to someone at rest on the rim?

      Ans.   (a) 7.8 rad/s; (b) 25.6 m/s

Problem 10.51.   Redo Problem 10.27(a) if the disk is replaced by (a) a thin hoop and (b) a sphere of the same mass and radius.

      Ans.   (a) $a = 2.45$ m/s^2, $\alpha = 5.44$ rad/s^2; (b) $a = 3.50$ m/s^2, $\alpha = 7.78$ rad/s^2

Problem 10.52.   How would the results of Problems 10.27(a) and 10.51 change if the mass were different?

      Ans.   There would be no change, since the mass drops out of the equations.

Problem 10.53.   Write general expressions—in terms of mass M, radius R, and center-of-mass velocity V_{CM}—for the kinetic energies of the following uniform objects that are rolling without slipping: (a) a disk; (b) a hoop; (c) a sphere.

      Ans.   (a) $\frac{3}{4}MV_{CM}^2$; (b) MV_{CM}^2; (c) $\frac{7}{10}MV_{CM}^2$

Chapter 11

Deformation of Materials and Elasticity

11.1 DEFORMATION OF OBJECTS—STRETCHING AND COMPRESSING

So far we have investigated the motion of objects under the action of forces. Therefore we have ignored the deformation of extended objects—the distortion of their shapes. In previous chapters we assumed that extended objects were rigid bodies, but even the stiffest materials have some give in them. In this section we briefly explore the relationship between the forces acting on an object and the deformations they cause.

Horizontal Rods

Consider a horizontal rod of unstretched length L and cross-sectional area A, with one end firmly attached to a very strong wall. A horizontal force of magnitude F is applied to the other end, as shown in Fig. 11-1(a). (Since the rod remains attached to the wall, it is in equilibrium, and the wall exerts an equal and opposite force on the rod.) One would expect that under these circumstances the rod would stretch somewhat, with the amount of stretch depending on the strength of the force F. Let ΔL represent the amount of stretch. For a given force F, the stretch ΔL will depend on the intrinsic nature of the rod, i.e., the material of which it is made. It also will depend on the particular length and cross-sectional area of the rod in question. We would like to describe the stretching effect of a force on a rod in a way that doesn't depend on the particular cross section of the rod or on its length but only on the material of which it is made. We do this by defining the *stress* and the *strain*.

It is easy to see that the greater the area of our rod the greater the force necessary to get the same stretch. Indeed if we were to put another identical rod alongside the first and consider them as a unit, as shown in Fig. 11-1(b), a force F on the end of each would be needed to have the combination stretch the same ΔL as the single rod. If we had a single rod of the same length and cross-sectional area $2A$, as shown in Fig. 11-1(c), we would need the force $2F$ to stretch it by ΔL. Thus the force needed for a certain stretch is proportional to the cross-sectional area of the rod. If we define the **stress** as the ratio of the force to the cross-sectional area, we have a quantity that measures the effectiveness of a force in accomplishing a given stretch, independent of the cross-sectional area of the rod. To illustrate, we note that for the case of Fig. 11-1(a), we have stress = F/A. For the case of Fig. 11-1(c), we have stress = $2F/2A = F/A$. As we see, the stress is the same in both cases and gives rise to the same amount of stretch ΔL. The stress thus measures the effect of a force in stretching a rod without regard to how "thick" the particular rod is. The dimensions of stress are force per area (the same as for pressure). The SI unit of stress is the newton per square meter (N/m^2). This is given the special name the *pascal*: 1 Pa = 1 N/m^2. Other common units are dyn/cm^2, lb/ft^2, and lb/in^2.

Problem 11.1.

(a) If the cross-sectional area of the rod in Fig. 11-1(a) is $A = 2.50 \times 10^{-4}$ m^2 and the force is $F = 300$ N, what is the stress?

(b) If the cross-sectional area of the same-length rod were three times as great, what force F' would be necessary to get the same amount of stretch?

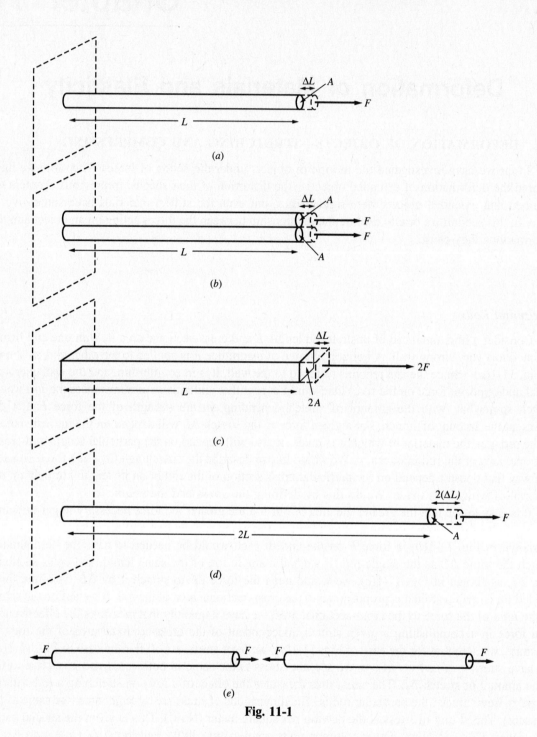

Fig. 11-1

Solution

(a) Stress = F/A = 300 N/(2.50 × 10^{-4} m^2) = 1.20 × 10^6 Pa.

(b) To get the same stretch the stress must be the same. Therefore, if we triple the area, we must also triple the force, so F' = 900 N.

We now turn to the effect of the length of the rod. If we had a rod of the same cross section as in Fig. 11-1(a) but of twice the unstretched length, the force F would stretch it twice as much; i.e., the extension would be $2\Delta L$, as shown in Fig. 11-1(d). To understand this, we consider the unstretched rod of length $2L$ to be made up of two equal sections, each of length L, as shown in Fig. 11-1(e). When the force F is applied, each half is under the action of equal and opposite forces at its two ends, because each is in equilibrium. By Newton's third law the magnitude of the forces on one half must be the same as those on the other half. Thus each half undergoes the same stretch ΔL, and the complete rod undergoes the stretch $2\Delta L$, as claimed. A given force will, therefore, cause a stretch that is proportional to the length of the unstretched rod. We define the **strain** as the ratio of the change in length of the rod to the unstretched length of the rod; for example, $\Delta L/L$ for the case of Fig. 11-1(a). As we have just seen, the strain due to a given force will be the same for any length rod of the same material and cross section. This is illustrated by comparing Fig. 11-1(a) and (d), where the force F is the same, and the strain is $\Delta L/L$ in the first case and $2\Delta L/2L = \Delta L/L$ in the second case. The strain is thus a measure of the stretch of a rod that is independent of the length of the rod. Note that strain is dimensionless, since it is the ratio of two lengths.

Problem 11.2.

(a)   If the rod in Problem 11.1 has length $L = 2.00$ m, and $\Delta L = 2.50 \times 10^{-5}$ m, find the strain.

(b)   What would the amount of stretch $\Delta L'$ be if the initial length of the rod were $L' = 1.50$ m, all else being the same?

   Solution

   (a)   Strain $= \Delta L/L = (2.50 \times 10^{-5}$ m$)/2.00$ m $= 1.25 \times 10^{-5}$.

   (b)   Since the stress is unchanged, the strain will be the same, and

$$\frac{\Delta L'}{L'} = \frac{\Delta L}{L} = 1.25 \times 10^{-5} \quad \text{or} \quad \Delta L' = (1.25 \times 10^{-5})(1.5 \text{ m}) = 1.88 \times 10^{-5} \text{ m}$$

Combining the ideas of stress and strain we conclude that:

   A given stress will give rise to a definite strain in a rod of a certain material irrespective of either the thickness or the length of the rod.

Hooke's Law, Elastic Limit, and Ultimate Strength

   We are now in a position to ask: What relation exists between the stress and the strain for a rod of a given material? It turns out that for many materials, as long as the stresses on the rod are not too large, upon removal of the stress the material returns to its original length. Any material that returns to its original shape after the distorting forces are removed is said to be **elastic**. For a rod of any given material there is a stress beyond which the material will no longer return to its original length. This boundary stress is called the **elastic limit**. For stresses below this elastic limit it is found that, to a good approximation, the strain is proportional to the stress; for example, if we double the stress, the strain will double. This result is called **Hooke's law**. Thus, in this "elastic" region, stress/strain = constant. The constant is called the **Young's modulus** Y, and its value depends on the material. Mathematically, we have

$$Y = \frac{\text{stress}}{\text{strain}} = \frac{F/A}{\Delta L/L} \qquad (11.1)$$

Young's modulus has dimensions of stress and can be measured in pascals.

Note. If a force tends to compress a rod rather than stretch it, Eq. (*11.1*) still holds with the same Young's modulus. In that case, ΔL represents a compression rather than a stretch.

If one applies a stress to a rod beyond the elastic limit, the rod will retain some permanent strain when the stress is removed. If the stress gets too great, the rod will break. The stress necessary to just reach the breaking point is called the **ultimate strength** of the material.

Problem 11.3.

(a) Assume that the rod in Fig. 11-1(*a*) obeys the conditions of Problems 11.1(*a*) and 11.2. Find the Young's modulus for the material of which the rod is made.

(b) Show that for a rod of definite cross section A and length L, the applied force F is proportional to the elongation ΔL and can therefore be expressed as $F = kx$, where k is the **force constant** of the system.

Solution

(a)
$$Y = \frac{F/A}{\Delta L/L} = \frac{1.20 \times 10^6 \text{ Pa}}{1.25 \times 10^{-5}} = 9.6 \times 10^{10} \text{ Pa} = 96 \text{ GPa}$$

(b) $F = (YA/L)\,\Delta L$, or $F = kx$, with $k = YA/L$ and distance x measured from the undeformed position.

Problem 11.4. For a certain steel beam of length 10 m and cross-sectional area 25 cm^2, the elastic limit is 400 MPa and the ultimate strength is 800 MPa; Young's modulus is 196 GPa.

(a) Find the maximum elongation in the elastic region.

(b) What stretching force is required to break the beam?

Solution

(a) $Y = (F/A)/(\Delta L/L)$ so that $\Delta L = (F/A)(L/Y)$. We get

$$\Delta L = \frac{(4.0 \times 10^8 \text{ Pa})(10.0 \text{ m})}{1.96 \times 10^{11} \text{ Pa}} = 0.0204 \text{ m}$$

(b) The ultimate strength = F/A so that

$$F = (8.0 \times 10^8 \text{ Pa})(25 \times 10^{-4} \text{ m}^2) = 2.0 \times 10^6 \text{ N}$$

Problem 11.5. A copper wire of length 3.0 m and diameter 4.0 mm has $Y = 1.18 \times 10^{11}$ Pa and elastic limit = 158×10^6 Pa.

(a) Find the force constant k [as defined in Problem 11.3(*b*)] of the copper wire.

(b) What tension T is necessary to stretch the wire 1.50 mm?

(c) Does this exceed the elastic limit?

Solution

(a) From Problem 11.3(*b*), we have $T = kx$, where $k = YA/L$. We have $A = \pi d^2/4 = 3.14(4.0 \times 10^{-3} \text{ m})^2/4 = 1.26 \times 10^{-5} \text{ m}^2$. Then

$$k = \frac{(1.18 \times 10^{11} \text{ Pa})(1.26 \times 10^{-5} \text{ m}^2)}{3.0 \text{ m}} = 4.96 \times 10^5 \text{ N/m}$$

(b)   Since $T = kx$, we get $T = (4.96 \times 10^5)(1.50 \times 10^{-3}) = 743$ N.

(c)   From part (b), $T/A = (743 \text{ N})/(1.26 \times 10^{-5} \text{ m}^2) = 59 \times 10^6$ Pa, so the answer is no.

11.2   SHEAR DEFORMATION AND SHEAR MODULUS

In addition to stretching or compressing, objects can be deformed in other ways, such as by shear deformation. A prototypical shear is shown in Fig. 11-2, where we have a rectangular solid whose base is held in place while parallel forces acting along one edge of the upper surface are applied. We assume the forces are distributed uniformly along the edge, their resultant being the *shear* force F. The base and top surfaces are each of area A, and the height of the solid is L. The deformation produced by F is a shifting of the top surface relative to the bottom surface by the amount Δx and the corresponding tilting of two of the vertical sides by the angle ϕ. We assume the distortion is very small compared to the original dimensions of the solid. Let us define the **shear stress** as F/A and the **shear strain** as $(\Delta x)/L = \tan \phi \approx \phi$ (rad). Then, by reasoning similar to that employed in the case for stretching, one can show that a given shear stress will give rise to a unique shear strain, irrespective of the dimensions of the rectangle. We find that for sufficiently small stresses the deformation is elastic and is governed by Hooke's law in the form

$$\frac{\text{Shear stress}}{\text{Shear strain}} = \frac{F/A}{\phi} = S \qquad (11.2)$$

where the **shear modulus** S is a constant for any given material and has the same dimensions as Y.

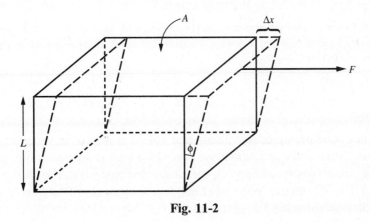

Fig. 11-2

Problem 11.6.   Two equal and opposite parallel forces each of magnitude 6 kN, are applied to a cubical metal block which is 40 cm on a side, as shown in Fig. 11-3. The shear angle is found to be $\phi = 0.00036°$. Find (a) the shear stress and the shear strain on the block, and (b) the shear modulus for the metal. (c) What would the shear angle be if the same forces were applied to a cubical block of the same metal that was 120 cm on a side?

Solution

(a)   The case at hand, with equal and opposite forces, is identical to the situation in Fig. 11-2, where the bottom is held fixed. Indeed, in Fig. 11-2 the surface in contact with the bottom supplies the equal

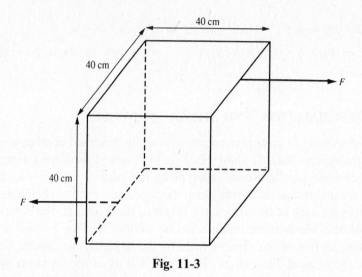

Fig. 11-3

and opposite force, since the block remains in equilibrium. Then,

$$\text{Shear stress} = \frac{6 \text{ kN}}{(0.40 \text{ m})^2} = 37.5 \text{ kPa}$$

$$\text{Shear strain} = 0.00036° \left(\frac{\pi \text{ rad}}{180°}\right) = 6.28 \times 10^{-6}$$

(b)
$$S = \frac{37,500 \text{ Pa}}{6.28 \times 10^{-6}} = 5.97 \text{ GPa}$$

(c) If the force is the same but the area increases ninefold, as it does for our case, the shear stress decreases by a factor of 9. Since S stays the same, the shear strain decreases by the same factor, and $\phi' = \phi/9 = 0.00004°$.

Twisting Deformation

Twisting a rod or a wire preserves its volume and indeed is a form of shear stress. Consider the situation in Fig. 11-4. When a torque Γ about the axis of the wire is applied at one end, and the other end is kept fixed (i.e., has an equal and opposite torque exerted on it), it can be shown that the angle of twist θ of one end of the wire relative to the other end is proportional to Γ. In fact, $\Gamma = \delta\theta$, where θ is in radians and the **torsion constant** δ is given by

$$\delta = \frac{\pi S R^4}{2L} \tag{11.3}$$

Here, S is the shear modulus for the material from which the wire is made. The units of δ are just those of torque, N · m.

By Newton's third law, the torque, Γ_w exerted by the wire on the external system is equal and opposite to the torque Γ exerted by the external system on the wire:

$$\Gamma_w = -\delta\theta \tag{11.4}$$

Problem 11.7. The steel driveshaft of an engine is 5.0 cm in diameter and 3.0 m long. The shear modulus for steel is 84 GPa.

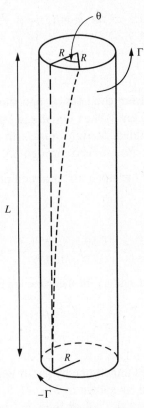

Fig. 11-4

(a) Find the torsion constant for the driveshaft.

(b) If one end is held fixed, what torque at the other end will give a twist angle of 22 °?

Solution

(a) From (*11.3*),

$$\delta = \frac{(3.14)(84 \times 10^9 \text{ Pa})(0.025 \text{ m})^4}{6.0 \text{ m}} = 17.2 \text{ kN} \cdot \text{m}$$

(b) $\Gamma = \delta\theta$. We must convert θ to radians, so $\theta = 22 °\,(\pi/180°) = 0.384$ rad. Then, $\Gamma = (17.2 \text{ kN} \cdot \text{m})$
(0.384) = 6.61 kN · m.)

Problem 11.8.

(a) How would the results of parts (a) and (b) of Problem 11.7 change if the length were doubled
and all else remained the same?

(b) What if the radius doubled instead and all else remained the same?

Solution

(a) From Eq. (*11.3*), we see that the torsion constant δ varies inversely with the length. Thus doubling
the length halves δ, and we have $\delta' = 8.6$ kN · m. Similarly, for the same angle of twist we have
that the new torque $\Gamma' = 3.3$ kN · m, half the old torque Γ.

(b) The torsion constant δ varies as the fourth power of R. Doubling R increases δ 16-fold, so $\delta' = 275.2$ kN $\cdot$ m. Then, for a 22° twist, $\Gamma' = 105.7$ kN $\cdot$ m.

Problem 11.9.

(a) A thin wire is hung vertically from the ceiling, and the lower end is tied to the middle of a horizontal crossbar of length 10 cm. When equal and opposite horizontal forces of magnitude 0.50 N are applied, and maintained, at right angles to the ends of the crossbar, the system reaches equilibrium when the bar has rotated through 65°. Find the torsion constant of the wire.

(b) If the wire is replaced by one of the same material and cross section, but twice as long, what is now the angle of rotation?

Solution

(a)
$$\delta = \frac{\Gamma}{\theta} = \frac{2(0.50 \text{ N})(0.05 \text{ m})}{65°(\pi/180°)} = 0.0441 \text{ N} \cdot \text{m}$$

(b) The torsion would be halved, and so for the same applied torque the angle of rotation would be doubled, to 130°.

Spring Deformation

A more complicated deformation is undergone by a stiff wire shaped into a spiral (in other words, a *coil spring*) that is pulled at one end, as shown in Fig. 11-5. Here the elongation x of the spring is primarily due to shear strain throughout the coiled wire and is therefore proportional to the applied force F. Thus we again have Hooke's law, $F = kx$, where k, the effective force constant, depends on the shear modulus and the geometry of the spring, and where x is the amount by which the length of the spring is changed from the unstretched position. Often one expresses Hooke's law not in terms of the external force F giving rise to the strain, but rather in terms of the force F_{sp} that the stretched spring exerts on the system pulling it. Since by Newton's third law $F_{sp} = -F$, we have

$$F_{sp} = -kx \qquad\qquad (11.5)$$

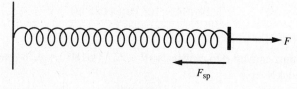

Fig. 11-5

in evident analogy to (11.4). Equation (11.5) shows F_{sp} to be a *restoring force*: If x is positive (a stretch), the force is in the negative direction, trying to pull the spring back to the unstretched position. If x is negative (a compression), the force is in the positive direction, now trying to push back to the uncompressed position.

Problem 11.10.   A light spring hangs vertically from the ceiling. A block of mass 40 kg is attached to the lower end of the spring, and the system is slowly let down until it comes to rest in the equilibrium position. (Fig. 11-6).

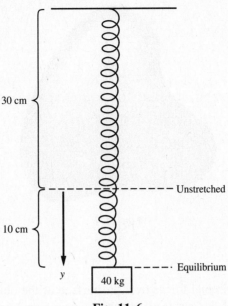

Fig. 11-6

(a)   Determine the force constant of the spring.

(b)   What is the force exerted by the spring on the block if the block is (i) pulled down 10 cm from the equilibrium position?   (ii) pushed up 15 cm from the equilibrium position?

Solution

(a)   We measure positive y downward from the unstretched position, and $F_{sp} = -ky$. For equilibrium of the block, we have $mg - ky = 0$, so that

$$k = \frac{mg}{y} = \frac{(40\,\text{kg})(9.8\,\text{m/s}^2)}{0.10\,\text{m}} = 3920\,\text{N/m}$$

(b) $F_{sp} = -ky$. In the first case $y = 20$ cm, so

(i) $F_{sp} = -(3920\,\text{N/m})(0.20\,\text{m}) = -784\,\text{N}$ (i.e., pulling upward)

In the second case, $y = -5.0$ cm, and

(ii) $F_{sp} = -(3920\,\text{N/m})(-0.050\,\text{m}) = 196\,\text{N}$ (i.e., pushing downward)

Note.   In the last case the spring is actually compressed 5.0 cm and hence pushes downward.

11.3   OVERALL COMPRESSION UNDER UNIFORM PRESSURE

Definitions

By definition, the **pressure** p at a point Q on the surface of an object is given by $\Delta F_n/\Delta A$, where ΔA is the area of a small patch of the surface centered on Q and ΔF_n is the *normal* force on the patch (see Fig. 11-7). The units of pressure are therefore those of stress.

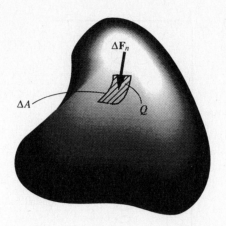

Fig. 11-7

Consider a distribution of normal forces over the surface of the object such that the pressure has the same value at each point of the surface. Let the pressure now increase everywhere by the same amount Δp, and let the corresponding change in volume of the object be ΔV. The change in pressure Δp is called the **volume stress**; the **volume strain** is then defined as $-(\Delta V)/V$, where V is the volume of the object before the change in pressure was applied. (The minus sign appears in the definition because ΔV is negative when Δp is positive, and we want a positive strain to be associated with a positive stress). With these definitions, the volume strain caused by a given volume stress will be independent of the size and shape of the particular object and will depend only on the material of which the object is made. It also turns out that, to a good approximation, Hooke's law again holds:

$$\frac{\text{Stress}}{\text{Strain}} = -\frac{\Delta p}{\Delta V/V} = B \tag{11.6}$$

in which the constant B, the **bulk modulus** of the material, has the dimensions of pressure or stress.

Compressibility of Liquids

Liquids cannot be stretched or sheared like solids, but like solids they are subject to volume compression. In fact, liquids are generally more easily compressed than solids, so a smaller Δp will produce the same fractional change in volume. In other words, bulk moduli will usually be smaller for liquids than for solids. It is often convenient to use the reciprocal of the bulk modulus, which is called the **compressibility** of the liquid:

$$\kappa \equiv \frac{1}{B} = -\frac{\Delta V/V}{\Delta p} \tag{11.7}$$

The various moduli are somewhat temperature-dependent. Table 11.1 gives room-temperature values.

Problem 11.11. Express (a) Young's modulus of brass in lb/in^2; (b) the compressibility of mercury in ft^2/lb.

Table 11.1

Substance	Y, GPa	S, GPa	B, GPa
Aluminum	70	24	70
Brass	91	36	61
Copper	118	42	140
Glass	55	23	27
Iron	91	70	100
Lead	16	5.6	7.7
Steel	196	84	160
Water	...	...	2.0
Glycerine	...	...	4.5
Carbon disulfide	...	...	1.5
Mercury	...	...	26
Ethyl alcohol	...	...	0.89

Note: 1 GPa = 10^9 Pa.

Solution

(a) Using the conversion factors from newtons to pounds and from meters to inches, we obtain from Table 11.1:

$$Y = (91 \times 10^9 \text{ N/m}^2) \frac{0.225 \text{ lb/N}}{(39.37 \text{ in/m})^2} = 1.32 \times 10^7 \text{ lb/in}^2$$

(b)

$$B = (26 \times 10^9 \text{ N/m}^2) \frac{0.225 \text{ lb/N}}{(3.28 \text{ ft/m})^2} = 5.43 \times 10^8 \text{ lb/ft}^2$$

$$\kappa = \frac{1}{B} = 1.84 \times 10^{-9} \text{ ft}^2/\text{lb}$$

Problem 11.12. A certain copper cube under ordinary atmospheric pressure (about 100 kPa) is 60 mm on a side. What would be the volume change in the cube if (a) it were subjected to a pressure increase of 50 MPa?   (b) The atmospheric pressure were removed?

Solution

(a) From (11.6) and Table 11.1,

$$\Delta V = -\frac{V \, \Delta p}{B} = -\frac{(0.060 \text{ m})^3 \, (50 \times 10^6 \text{ Pa})}{140 \times 10^9 \text{ Pa}} = -77.1 \text{ mm}^3$$

(b)

$$\Delta V = -\frac{(0.060 \text{ m})^3 \, (-100 \times 10^3 \text{ Pa})}{140 \times 10^9 \text{ Pa}} = +0.154 \text{ mm}^3$$

Problem 11.13. Compute the compressibility of glycerine if a pressure change of 2.0 MPa causes 128 mL of glycerine to change in volume by 0.0563 mL. [The *liter* (L) is the common unit for liquid and gaseous volumes: 1 L = 10^{-3} m^3.]

Solution

From (*11.7*),

$$\kappa = -\frac{(-0.0563)/128}{2.0 \times 10^6 \text{ Pa}} = 2.2 \times 10^{-10} \text{ Pa}^{-1}$$

which is consistent with Table 11.1.

Problems for Review and Mind Stretching

Problem 11.14.   An aluminum and a steel wire, each of length 3.0 m and diameter 2.8 mm, are fused together at one end to form a wire of overall length 6.0 m which is hung from a ceiling.

(*a*)   Compute the force constants for each wire.

(*b*)   If a 40-kg mass is hung from the end of the combined wire, what would the overall elongation be?

(*c*)   What is the "effective" force constant for the wire as a whole (i.e., the force constant which a single wire would need so that the same force would cause the same overall stretch)?

Solution

(*a*)   We note that the cross-sectional area A of each wire is $A = \pi d^2/4 = (3.14)(2.8 \times 10^{-3})^2/4 = 6.15 \times 10^{-6} \text{ m}^2$. Then, recalling the relationship between the force constant and the Young's modulus [from Problem *11.3(b)*)], we have

$$k_{\text{al}} = \frac{Y_{\text{al}}A}{L} = \frac{(0.70 \times 10^{11} \text{ Pa})(6.15 \times 10^{-6} \text{ m}^2)}{3.0 \text{ m}} = 1.43 \times 10^5 \text{ N/m}$$

$$k_{\text{st}} = \frac{Y_{\text{st}}A}{L} = \frac{(1.96 \times 10^{11} \text{ Pa})(6.15 \times 10^{-6} \text{ m}^2)}{3.0 \text{ m}} = 4.02 \times 10^5 \text{ N/m}$$

(*b*)   When the weight is hung, each of the two wires will be in equilibrium under the stretching action of equal and opposite forces at its end. These forces all have the same magnitude F, which is equal to the weight of the block: $F = W = Mg = (40 \text{ kg})(9.8 \text{ m/s}^2) = 392 \text{ N}$. Then, using the results of part (*a*), we can calculate the stretch of each wire:

$$\Delta y_{\text{al}} = \frac{F}{k_{\text{al}}} = \frac{392 \text{ N}}{1.43 \times 10^5 \text{ N/m}} = 2.74 \times 10^{-3} \text{ m}$$

$$\Delta y_{\text{st}} = \frac{F}{k_{\text{st}}} = \frac{392 \text{ N}}{4.02 \times 10^5 \text{ N/m}} = 0.98 \times 10^{-3} \text{ m}$$

The overall stretch is $\Delta y_T = \Delta y_{\text{al}} + \Delta y_{\text{st}} = 3.72 \times 10^{-3}$ m.

(*c*) $k_T = F/\Delta y_T = 392 \text{ N}/(3.72 \times 10^{-3} \text{ m}) = 1.05 \times 10^5 \text{ N/m}$.

Problem 11.15.   When any two wires (or rods or coil springs), each of arbitrary length and cross section, are attached end to end to form a single unit, as in Problem 11.14, the effective (or total) force constant k_T is defined by $F = k_T \Delta L_T$, where F is the applied force and ΔL_T is the overall elongation of the system.

(a) Find a general formula for the effective force constant in terms of the force constants of the individual wires (rods, or coil springs).

(b) Apply this result to obtain the answer to Problem 11.14(c).

Solution

(a) By definition, $\Delta y_T = \Delta y_1 + \Delta y_2$ so that $F/k_T = F/k_1 + F/k_2$, where 1 and 2 refer to the individual components. Dividing both sides by F we get

$$\frac{1}{k_T} = \frac{1}{k_1} + \frac{1}{k_2} \qquad (i)$$

(b) From Problem 11.14(a) we have $k_{al} = 1.43 \times 10^5$ N/m; $k_{st} = 4.02 \times 10^5$ N/m. Then $1/k_T = 1/(1.43 \times 10^5 \text{ N/m}) + 1/(4.02 \times 10^5 \text{ N/m}) \Rightarrow k_T = 1.05 \times 10^5$ N/m.

Problem 11.16. Assume the torsion constant for the driveshaft of a truck is $\delta = 20{,}000$ N · m. If the truck's engine delivers power $P = 105$ kW to the driveshaft which is rotating at a constant frequency of $f = 600$ r/min, find the angle of twist between the two ends of the driveshaft.

Solution

First we need to determine the torque exerted on the driveshaft by the engine. We recall from Chap. 10 that $P = \Gamma\omega$. We have that $\omega = 2\pi f = 2(3.14)$ (600 r/min) (1/60 s/min) $= 62.8$ rad/s. Then $\Gamma = P/\omega = (1.05 \times 10^5$ W$)/(62.8$ rad/s$) = 1670$ N · m. Next we recall that $\Gamma = \delta\theta$, from which we get

$$\theta = \frac{1670 \text{ N} \cdot \text{m}}{20{,}000 \text{ N} \cdot \text{m}} = 0.0835 \text{ rad} = 4.78°$$

Problem 11.17. Two containers, labeled 1 and 2, contain equal volumes of glycerine and ethyl alcohol, respectively. Both liquids are under an atmospheric pressure of 100 kPa. When the pressure on both liquids is increased by the same amount, Δp, the difference in volume of the liquids becomes 0.25 L. If the original volume of each liquid was 2000 L, find Δp.

Solution

For a given Δp, we have $\Delta V = -(V \Delta p)(1/B)$. We know the values of B and V for each liquid, but we are given only the difference in the ΔV's for the two liquids: $|\Delta V_2 - \Delta V_1| = 0.25$ L. Thus, by difference,

$$|\Delta V_2 - \Delta V_1| = (V \Delta p)\left|\frac{1}{B_2} - \frac{1}{B_1}\right|$$

$$0.25 \text{ L} = (2000 \text{ L})(\Delta p)\left|\frac{1}{0.89 \text{ GPa}} - \frac{1}{4.5 \text{ GPa}}\right|$$

$$\Delta p = 0.000139 \text{ GPa} = 139 \text{ kPa}$$

Problem 11.18. A printer stand having four solid aluminum legs is firmly epoxied to the top of a rigid table. Each leg has cross-sectional area $A = 5.0$ cm^2 and height $L = 10.0$ cm. A student, not realizing it is epoxied, tries to move the stand by pulling horizontally at the middle of one edge, as shown in Fig. 11-8. The student pulls harder and harder until he exerts a force of 160 N. Assuming the epoxy holds, how far will the top of the stand move?

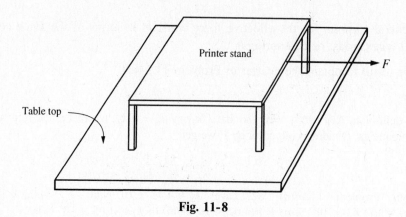

Fig. 11-8

Solution

Assume that the horizontal shear force on the top of each leg is $F = 40$ N. The top surface of each leg then moves by an amount Δx relative to the bottom surface (cf. Fig. 11-2). For each leg, *(11-2)* gives

$$\phi = \frac{\Delta x}{L} = \frac{F}{AS} \quad \text{or} \quad \Delta x = \frac{FL}{AS}$$

Substituting in the values of F, L, and A given above and the value of S for aluminum from Table 11.1, we get

$$\Delta x = \frac{(40 \text{ N})(0.10 \text{ m})}{(5.0 \times 10^{-4} \text{ m}^2)(24 \times 10^9 \text{ N/m}^2)} = 0.333 \text{ μm}$$

or about one-hundredth the thickness of a human hair!

Problem 11.19. A steel wire of length 1.0 m and cross-sectional area 1.0 mm² is tied horizontally between two rigid hooks. A heavy weight W is suspended from the middle of the wire, causing it to sag as shown in Fig. 11-9. If $\theta = 10°$, find the weight W.

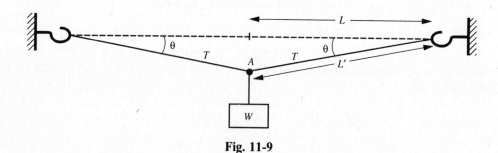

Fig. 11-9

Solution

Consider one of the halves of the wire, of unstretched length $L = 0.50$ m and under tension T. Then its stretched length is $L' = L/(\cos \theta)$, so

$$\Delta L = L' - L = L\left(\frac{1}{\cos \theta} - 1\right) = 0.0077 \text{ m}$$

From Hooke's law,

$$T = YA \frac{\Delta L}{L} = (196 \times 10^9 \text{ Pa})(1.0 \times 10^{-6} \text{ m}^2)\frac{0.0077 \text{ m}}{0.50 \text{ m}} = 3020 \text{ N}$$

Finally, since the junction point A is in equilibrium, $W = 2T \sin \theta = 1050$ N.

Supplementary Problems

Problem 11.20.

(a) An iron rod of length 5.0 m hangs vertically, with its top end firmly attached to a rigid ceiling beam. A 10-kN weight is hung from the lower end, and the rod is observed to stretch by 6.0 mm. Find the cross-sectional area of the rod.

(b) How would the answer change if the rod were steel?

(c) What is the ultimate strength of the iron rod if it breaks under a weight of 25 kN?

Ans. (a) 91.6 mm^2; (b) 42.5 mm^2; (c) 0.273 GPa

Problem 11.21.

(a) Find the force constants for the iron and steel rods of Problem 11.20.

(b) If the steel rod had the same cross section as the iron rod, what would its force constant be?

Ans. (a) $k_{ir} = k_{st} = 1670$ kN/m; (b) 3590 kN/m

Problem 11.22.

(a) If the iron rod of Problem 11.20 and the steel rod of Problem 11.21(b) were attached end to end to form a single rod of length 10.0 m, what would the effective force constant be?

(b) What force would increase the length of this combined rod by 8.0 mm?

Ans. (a) 1140 kN/m; (b) 9.12 kN

Problem 11.23. A light, rigid, horizontal bar is suspended from its ends by two equally long copper wires of cross-sectional areas A_1 and A_2, as shown in Fig. 11-10. A weight of 1200 N is then hung one-third of the way from the left end.

(a) If $A_1 = 2.0$ mm^2, what must A_2 be for the two wires to stretch by equal amounts?

(b) If each wire had an original length of 0.80 m, by what distance was the bar lowered when the weight was hung?

Ans. (a) 1.0 mm^2; (b) 2.7 mm

Problem 11.24. A steel rod of cross-sectional area 2.5 in^2 and length 3.0 ft is compressed by a force of 3000 lb. Find the distance of compression.

Ans. 0.0015 in

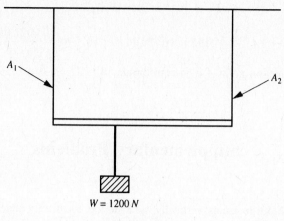

$W = 1200\,N$

Fig. 11-10

Problem 11.25. A 20-mm-thick brass disk of radius 50 mm has one face rigidly attached to a vertical wall, while the other face is attached to a 20,000-kg lead plate that is otherwise unsupported. By what vertical distance will one face of the disk be displaced relative to the other?

       Ans.   20.8 μm

Problem 11.26. The torsion constant of a cable is 300 lb $\cdot$ ft.

(*a*)   What torque at one end of the cable is necessary to twist it through 360°?

(*b*)   What torque would be necessary if the cable were twice as thick and twice as long?

       Ans.   (*a*) 1885 lb $\cdot$ ft; (*b*) 15,080 lb $\cdot$ ft

Problem 11.27. Suppose the cable in Problem 11.26(*a*) hangs from the ceiling, with its lower end attached to the center of a horizontal uniform disk of moment of inertia $I = 20$ slug $\cdot$ ft^2. If the disk is rotated through 360° and then released, find its angular acceleration (*a*) at the instant of release, (*b*) after it had rotated back through 180°

       Ans.   (*a*) 94 rad/s^2; (*b*) 47 rad/s^2

Problem 11.28. A coil spring, of force constant $k = 1000$ N/m, is at rest on a horizontal frictionless surface. One end is connected to a wall and the other end is connected to a block of mass $M = 30$ kg. Suppose the block is pulled back 20 cm and released.

(*a*)   Find the acceleration of the block at the moment of release.

(*b*)   How far from the unstretched position will the block be when the acceleration is 0.20 m/s^2?

       Ans.   (*a*) 6.67 m/s^2; (*b*) 0.60 cm

Problem 11.29. Two metal plates are connected by aluminum rivets, each of cross-sectional area 180 mm^2. The plates are expected to experience a shearing force of 120 kN. If each rivet can withstand a maximum shear stress of 70 MPa, and the rivets share the stress equally, what is the minimum number of rivets necessary?

       Ans.   10

Problem 11.30.

(a)   What increase in pressure is necessary to reduce a 100-mL volume of water by 0.002%?

(b)   What initial volume of glycerine would give the same absolute change in volume under the same pressure increase?

   Ans.   (a) 40 kPa; (b) 225 mL

Problem 11.31.   An iron rod of length 3.0 m and cross-sectional area 1200 mm^2 is brought from the earth's surface (where atmospheric pressure is 100 kPa) to a location on the ocean floor where the pressure is 10 MPa.

(a)   All else being the same, what is the decrease in the volume of the bar?

(b)   What is the decrease in the length of the bar?

   [*Hint*:   The fractional change in any linear dimension of the bar is one-third the fractional change in the volume.]

(c)   What stretching force would be necessary to return the bar to its original length?

   Ans.   (a) 356 mm^3; (b) 0.100 mm; (c) 3.60 kN

Chapter 12

Simple Harmonic Motion (SHM)

12.1 INTRODUCTORY CONCEPTS

In the last chapter we saw that Hooke's law is obeyed for a wide variety of systems. In the case of a coil spring this law takes on the simple form

$$\mathbf{F} = -k\mathbf{x} \tag{12.1}$$

where $\mathbf{F}$ is the force exerted *by* the spring, $\mathbf{x}$ is the displacement of the end of the spring from the unstretched position, and k is the force constant of the spring. In this chapter we will explore the motion of an object that is subjected to a Hooke's law type force. For definiteness we consider the motion of a block of mass m that is attached to one end of a loosely coiled spring of force constant k on a horizontal frictionless surface. The other end of the spring is fixed, such as by firmly attaching it to a wall, as shown in Fig. 12-1.

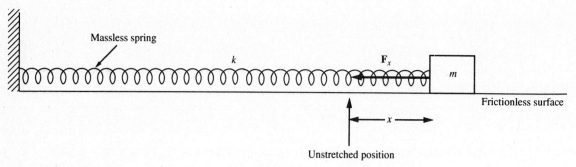

Fig. 12-1

The block is pulled to one side horizontally along the x axis, as shown in the figure, and then released from rest, or with an initial velocity along the x axis. We assume that after the block is released the only horizontal force acting on it is the spring force. The ensuing motion of the block is one-dimensional and is called **simple harmonic motion** (SHM). We want to find the precise description of that motion. (For simplicity we assume that the spring itself is light and that to a good approximation its mass can be ignored.)

12.2 NEWTON'S SECOND LAW APPLIED TO SHM

To determine the motion of the block acted on by the horizontal spring force, we first find an expression for the acceleration along the x axis. Recalling Newton's second law $\mathbf{F} = m\mathbf{a}$ and using Eq. (12.1), we get $-k\mathbf{x} = m\mathbf{a}$. Dividing by m we get, for the x component equation,

$$a = -\frac{k}{m}x \tag{12.2}$$

Here, a is the acceleration along the x axis, where the displacement x is measured from the unstretched position of the end of the spring. Since k and m are constants, we see that a is proportional to x in magnitude and always has the opposite sign. Thus, if x is positive (i.e., to the right in Fig. 12-1), then a is to the left. If x is negative (i.e., to the left), then the spring is compressed, and a is to the right. This behavior reflects the fact that the spring force always seeks to restore the object to the unstretched position of the spring, as can be seen from Eq. (12.1). Equation (12.2) implies that the acceleration varies with time, since x changes with time.

An equation such as Eq. (12.2) can be solved quite readily using the calculus. Although we cannot use the calculus approach in a course at this level, it is informative to note the significance of Eq. (12.2). Recalling that velocity v is the time rate of change of displacement x, and that acceleration a is the time rate of change of velocity v, Eq. (12.2) can be expressed in words as follows:

> The time rate of change of the time rate of change of the displacement is equal   (12.3)
> to a negative constant times the displacement

This is a precise mathematical relationship and completely defines the general solution of the ensuing motion, which gives us both x and v as functions of the time t. The specific solutions are obtained from the general solutions by putting in the initial conditions.

Problem 12.1.

(a) For the problem of the block acted on by a spring described by Eq. (12.2), find the position where the acceleration is smallest.

(b) Show that no matter which way the block is moving it will eventually turn around and move the other way.

(c) What is the block's velocity at the turning point of part (b)?

Solution

(a) From (12.2), a vanishes when $x = 0$, that is, at the unstretched position of the spring.

(b) If the block is moving to the right beyond the unstretched position, it will experience an acceleration that will slow it down. Furthermore, the strength of that acceleration will increase as x increases, guaranteeing that it will eventually be strong enough to reverse the direction of the velocity. The same reasoning applies when the block is moving to the left past the unstretched position. In that case the acceleration is to the right, and the block will again reverse its direction of motion.

(c) At the turning points the velocity is changing either from + to −, or from − to +. In either case, the velocity must pass through zero as it changes sign at the turning point.

Problem 12.2.

(a) If a bar at the end of a torsion wire (Fig. 12-2) is twisted through some angle and then released, what is the relationship between the angular acceleration α and the angular displacement θ?

(b) How would you describe the equation of motion for the angular displacement θ, and what relation would it have to that of the displacement of the mass at the end of the spring of Problem 12.1?

Solution

(a) From Eq. (11.4) we have $\Gamma = -\delta\theta$, where δ is the torsion constant. Recalling that $\Gamma = I\alpha$, where I is the moment of inertia of the rod about an axis along the wire, we have $I\alpha = -\delta\theta$, or

$$\alpha = -\frac{\delta}{I}\theta \qquad (i)$$

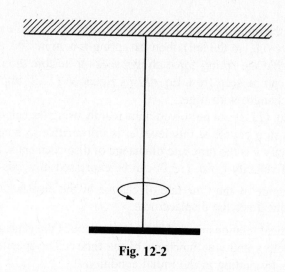

Fig. 12-2

(b)   Noting that α and θ in (i) are related in the same way as are a and x in Eq. (12.2), we see that the equation of θ vs. t is identical in form to that for x vs. t, and θ varies with time in accordance with the rules of SHM.

Conservation of Energy in SHM

Returning to our problem of the block at the end of a spring, as shown in Fig. 12-1, we note that the only force which can do work is that of the spring. Since the spring force is conservative, mechanical energy is conserved. Recalling that the potential energy of the spring is $E_p = \frac{1}{2}kx^2$, the constant total energy is

$$E = E_p + E_k = \tfrac{1}{2}kx^2 + \tfrac{1}{2}mv^2 = \text{constant} \qquad (12.4)$$

Using this relationship, one can learn a great deal about the SHM of the block. We explore this in the following problem.

Problem 12.3.

(a)   Show that as the block moves, its farthest position to the right of the origin is the same as its farthest position to the left. (The magnitude of this displacement is called the amplitude A of the motion.)

(b)   Show that the maximum displacements to both the right and the left are reached over and over again, and that the motion of the block repeats over and over.

(c)   Show that the maximum velocity $v_{\max}$, both positive and negative, occurs at the origin and has magnitude $v_{\max} = (\sqrt{k/m})A$.

Solution

(a)   From Problem 12.1(c), we see that at the farthest positions to either the left or right the velocity is zero. At those points, (12.4) becomes $E = \frac{1}{2}kx_{\max}^2$. Since E is constant, we must have the same magnitude of $x_{\max}$ on the left and right sides. Thus $x_{\max} = \pm A$.

(b)   At point $x = +A$, the velocity is zero and the acceleration is to the left, so the block will start moving to the left. From (12.4) we see that the velocity can be zero only when $|x| = A$, so the block will reach point $x = -A$ and come to rest momentarily. Since the acceleration is now to the right, it will start moving to the right and will next stop (momentarily) at $x = +A$. This is the exact situation we started with, so the next cycle of motion is identical to the preceding one (Fig. 12-3).

(c)   According to Eq. (12.4), v_{max} is attained when $x = 0$, at which point $\frac{1}{2}mv_{max}^2 = E$. Thus $v_{max} = \pm\sqrt{2E/m}$, which corresponds to the block passing the unstretched position in either direction. At the turning points, where $v = 0$, Eq. (12.4) gives $E = \frac{1}{2}kA^2$. Substituting into our equation for v_{max} we get our result.

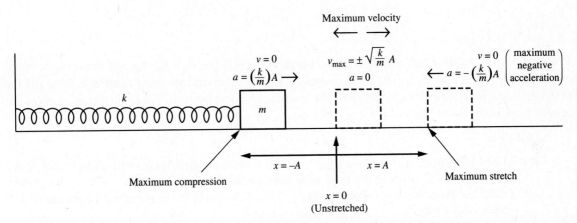

Fig. 12-3

Using Eq. (12.4), we can find an expression for the velocity v at any position x, in terms of x and the amplitude A. In Problem 12.3, we saw that $E = \frac{1}{2}kx_{max}^2 = \frac{1}{2}kA^2$. Substituting this for E in Eq. (12.3) we get

$$\tfrac{1}{2}kx^2 + \tfrac{1}{2}mv^2 = \tfrac{1}{2}kA^2 \qquad (12.5)$$

Simplifying, we get

$$v^2 = \frac{k}{m}(A^2 - x^2) \qquad (12.6)$$

Taking the square root, we get

$$v = \pm\sqrt{\frac{k}{m}}\sqrt{A^2 - x^2} \qquad (12.7)$$

The $\pm$ signs are indicative of the fact that the velocity of the block has the same magnitude at a given position x, whether it is passing to the left or to the right.

Problem 12.4.   For the motion illustrated in Fig. 12-3, find an expression, in terms of the amplitude A, for (a) the maximum acceleration in either direction; and (b) velocity in either direction when $x = 0.6\,A$.

Solution

(a) From Eq. (12.2) we have $a = -(k/m)x$, so that

$$a_{max} = \pm \frac{k}{m} A$$

where the plus sign holds for $x = -A$ and the minus sign for $x = +A$.

(b) From (12.7), we have

$$v = \pm \sqrt{\frac{k}{m}} \sqrt{A^2 - 0.36A^2} = \sqrt{\frac{k}{m}} \sqrt{0.64A^2} = 0.8 \sqrt{\frac{k}{m}} A$$

Problem 12.5.   Assume that the mass of the block in Fig. 12-1 is $m = 8.0$ kg and the force constant of the spring is $k = 200$ N/m. The block is pulled back 3.0 cm and released from rest. Find (a) the maximum acceleration in either direction, (b) the maximum velocity in either direction, and (c) the acceleration when $x = +2.0$ cm and $x = -1.5$ cm.

Solution

(a) From Problem 12.4(a), we have $a_{max} = \pm(k/m)A$. From the given data we have $k/m = (200 \text{ N/m})/(8.0 \text{ kg}) = 25 \text{ s}^{-2}$, where the final units were obtained by recalling that $1.0 \text{ N} = 1.0 \text{ kg} \cdot \text{m/s}^2$. Since the block is released from rest at $x = 3.0$ cm, this must be the maximum displacement A. It then follows that

$$a_{max} = \pm(25 \text{ s}^{-2})(3.0 \text{ cm}) = \pm 75 \text{ cm/s}^2 \qquad (\text{or} \pm 0.75 \text{ m/s}^2)$$

Note.   We appear to be using mixed units; k and m are in SI units while x is in cm. This is acceptable in this problem because in the ratio k/m, all length units have dropped out.

(b) From Problem 12.3(c), we have $v_{max} = \pm(\sqrt{k/m})A = \pm (5.0 \text{ s}^{-1})(3.0 \text{ cm}) = \pm 15.0 \text{ cm/s}$ (or ± 0.15 m/s).

(c) From Eq. (12.2) we have $a = -(k/m)x = -(25 \text{ s}^{-2})x$. For $x = 2.0$ cm this yields $a = -50 \text{ cm/s}^2$. For $x = -1.5$ cm, this yields $a = 37.5 \text{ cm/s}^2$.

Problem 12.6.   Referring to Problem 12.5, find (a) the velocity of the block at $x = 2.0$ cm and $x = -1.5$ cm; and (b) the values of x for which the block will have half its maximum velocity.

Solution

(a) From Eq. (12.7) we have $v = \pm(5.0 \text{ s}^{-1}) [(3.0 \text{ cm})^2 - x^2]^{1/2}$. Setting $x = 2.0$ cm and solving, this becomes $v = \pm 11.2$ cm/s. Similarly, setting $x = -1.5$ cm, we have

$$v = \pm(5.0 \text{ s}^{-1}) [(3.0 \text{ cm})^2 - (-1.5 \text{ cm})^2]^{1/2} = \pm 13.0 \text{ cm/s}$$

Note.   Unlike the case of acceleration, the velocity is determined to within a $\pm$ sign, as it should be, because the block can be passing a given point x in either direction.

(b) Starting from Eq. (12.7), and using the result of Problem 12.5(b) we have

$$7.5 \text{ cm/s} = (5.0 \text{ s}^{-1}) [(3.0 \text{ cm})^2 - x^2]^{1/2}$$

Squaring both sides and then solving for x we get $x = \pm 2.60$ cm. The $\pm$ indicates that the velocity can be half its maximum value on either side of the unstretched position.

Periodic Motion in SHM

Since SHM is a repetitive motion, it is called periodic motion. The period T is defined as the time to make one complete repetition of the motion. Thus, T is the time interval from when the object traverses any position x moving in a given direction to the next time the object traverses position x moving in the same direction. For example, T is the total time interval in going from $x = 0$, moving to the left, to the next time one passes $x = 0$, moving to the left. The period T is also the time it takes in going from the maximum displacement $x = A$ to the next time it reaches $x = A$. The frequency f of the periodic motion is the number of repetitions per second; it is the reciprocal of the period: $f = 1/T$. We have already encountered the concepts of period and frequency in our studies of other periodic motions: uniform circular motion and uniform rotation of a rigid body. Those cases, however, were not only periodic, but they were uniform as well; that is, the motion was always at the same rate at all points of the motion. Such uniformity of motion does *not* occur in SHM. The speed is changing from position to position and moment to moment during any given cycle of the motion.

Problem 12.7. Consider an object undergoing SHM with maximum amplitude A.

(a)   Compare the time it takes to go from $x = A$ to $x = 0$ to the time it takes to go the opposite way, from $x = 0$ to $x = A$.

(b)   Compare the time it takes to go from $x = 0$ to $x = A$ to the time it takes to go from $x = 0$ to $x = -A$.

(c)   What is the relationship between the times in (a) and (b) and the period T of the motion?

Solution

(a)   From (12.7) we see that for any position x, the velocity of the object has the same magnitude as the object passes that position in either direction. The time to travel between any two points in one direction is thus the same as the time to travel between those same two points in the other direction, and the time taken to go from $x = A$ to $x = 0$ equals the time to go from 0 to A.

(b)   From (12.7) we also see that the velocity of the object has the same magnitude as the object passes point x as when it passes point $-x$. Thus the motion from $x = 0$ to $x = -A$ is an exact replication of the motion from 0 to A, and the times are the same.

(c)   In analogy to part (a) the time go to from $-A$ to 0 is the same as the time to go from 0 to $-A$. Then, from (a) and (b) we conclude that the overall cycle of motion from A to $-A$ and back to A is divided into four equal time segments, t_s: $A \rightarrow 0$, $0 \rightarrow -A$, $-A \rightarrow 0$, and $0 \rightarrow A$. Thus, each of these time segments $t_s = T/4$.

12.3   TIME-DEPENDENT EQUATIONS OF SHM

While Eqs. (12.2) and (12.7) give us a great deal of information about simple harmonic motion, they will not give us the equations of motion, i.e., the relations between x and t and between v and t, without the use of calculus. Fortunately, it is possible to deduce the actual equations of motion in another way without having to resort to calculus.

The Reference Circle and Shadow Motion

Consider a particle undergoing uniform circular motion with speed v_0, on a circle of radius A, about the origin of a coordinate system, as shown in Fig. 12-4. The shadow, or projection, of the

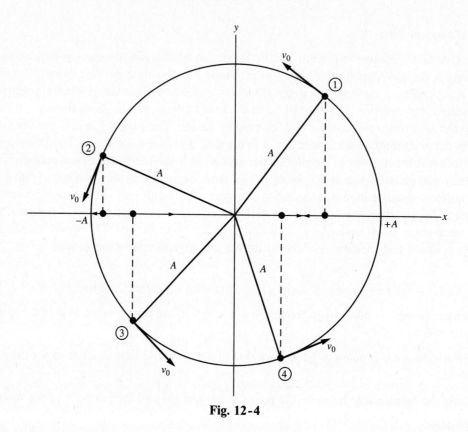

Fig. 12-4

particle on the x axis is shown for a few points along the circular trajectory (along with an arrow depicting the shadow's direction of motion). As the particle moves around the circle, its shadow moves back and forth along the x axis between $x = A$ and $x = -A$. The shadow undergoes periodic motion of amplitude A, with a period T that is identical to the period of uniform circular motion: one complete back-and-forth motion of the shadow corresponds to one complete 360° sweep of the particle. The shadow's motion is clearly symmetric about the origin and satisfies the same conditions of Problem 12.7 shown to be satisfied by SHM. We will soon see that the shadow motion is actually SHM. Thus, finding the time equations for the shadow's motion is equivalent to finding the time equations of SHM. For this reason the circle with the uniformly moving particle that gives rise to the shadow motion is called the *reference circle* for SHM.

Time Dependence of the Shadow Motion

To obtain the time dependence of the shadow motion we examine more closely uniform circular motion of radius A and speed $v_0 = \omega A$. The particle is shown at an arbitrary point in its uniform circular path in Fig. 12-5. At any point in its motion the particle's vector displacement **R** is of magnitude A and points out along the radial line to the particle. The particle's vector velocity **v** is tangent to the circle, and its vector centripetal acceleration **a** is inward along the radius. The magnitude of velocity **v** is v_0 and is constant. The magnitude of the acceleration **a** is $a_0 = v_0^2/A$, which is also constant. If θ represents the angle between the positive x axis and the radial line to the particle, then this radial line sweeps around the circle with a constant angular velocity ω, which is related to the speed of the particle by $v_0 = \omega A$. Substituting this into the expression for a_0 given above, we have $a_0 = \omega^2 A$.

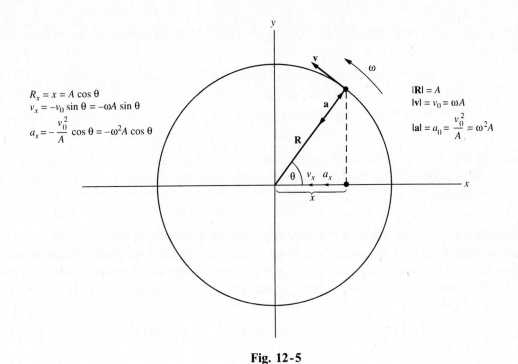

$R_x = x = A \cos \theta$
$v_x = -v_0 \sin \theta = -\omega A \sin \theta$

$a_x = -\dfrac{v_0^2}{A} \cos \theta = -\omega^2 A \cos \theta$

$|\mathbf{R}| = A$
$|\mathbf{v}| = v_0 = \omega A$

$|\mathbf{a}| = a_0 = \dfrac{v_0^2}{A} = \omega^2 A$

Fig. 12-5

Problem 12.8.

(a) Find an expression for the period of the shadow motion on the x axis described above.

(b) Show that the conditions of Problem 12.7 are indeed satisfied by the shadow motion.

Solution

(a) The time for one complete repetition of the shadow motion is the same as the time T for one complete revolution of the particle on the reference circle. Since ω is the constant angular velocity of the radial line to the particle, we have $\omega T = 2\pi$ or $T = 2\pi/\omega$.

(b) The shadow goes from $x = A$ to $x = 0$ in the time that the particle on the circle moves through one quarter circle. The elapsed time is the same when the shadow goes from $x = 0$ to $x = -A$, from $-A$ to 0, and from 0 to A. Thus each of these motions constitutes one quarter period.

We are now in a position to examine the motion of the shadow along the x axis in greater detail. We recall that the displacement, velocity, and acceleration of the shadow along the x axis are just the x components of the vector displacement, velocity, and acceleration of the particle moving on the circle. Figure 12-5 shows the relationship between the vector quantities and the components on the x axis at a particular instant of time. We have

$$x = A \cos \theta \qquad v_x = -\omega A \sin \theta \qquad a_x = -\omega^2 A \cos \theta \qquad (12.8a, b, c)$$

If we assume that at $t = 0$ the radial line to the particle is at angle θ_0, then (for constant ω) at any time t we get

$$\theta = \theta_0 + \omega t \qquad\qquad (12.9)$$

Substituting Eq. (*12.9*) into Eqs. (12.8) yields the time-dependent equations for the motion of the shadow:

$$x = A \cos (\omega t + \theta_0) \qquad (12.10a)$$

$$v = -\omega A \sin (\omega t + \theta_0) \qquad (12.10b)$$

$$a = -\omega^2 A \cos (\omega t + \theta_0) \qquad (12.10c)$$

Note.   In Eqs. (*12.10*) we have dropped the subscripts on the velocity v and acceleration a since the equations refer to the shadow's one-dimensional motion, and the subscripts are redundant.

The choice of θ_0 tells us where on the reference circle the particle is at time $t = 0$. This also tells us where the shadow on the x axis is at $t = 0$. If we agree to set our clock so that $t = 0$ corresponds to the shadow being at its maximum positive value, $x = A$, then the point on the reference circle clearly is at $\theta_0 = 0$. [This conclusion also follows directly from Eq. (*12.10a*), since if $x = A$ at $t = 0$, we have $A = A \cos \theta_0 \Rightarrow \cos \theta_0 = 1 \Rightarrow \theta_0 = 0$.] For this initial position of the shadow, Eqs. (*12.10*) become

$$x = A \cos \omega t \qquad v = -\omega A \sin \omega t \qquad a = -\omega^2 A \cos \omega t \qquad (12.11a, b, c)$$

Problem 12.9.

(*a*)   Use Eq. (*12.10a*) to verify that the period of the shadow's motion is $T = 2\pi/\omega$.

(*b*)   Using Eqs. (*12.10a, b*) show that the shadow velocity is zero at $x = \pm A$ and is a maximum at $x = 0$.

(*c*)   Show that if the shadow is at $x = A$ at $t = 0$, the velocity will be $v_x = -\omega A$ at $t = \pi/2\omega$ and $v_x = 0$ at $t = \pi/\omega$.

Solution

(*a*)   From Eq. (*12.10a*) we have $x = A \cos (\omega t + \theta_0)$. The quantity x will go through one complete repetition of the motion when the argument of the cosine $(\omega t + \theta_0)$ increases by 2π. Thus when $t \to t + T$, we must have $(\omega[t + T] + \theta_0) - (\omega t + \theta_0) = 2\pi \Rightarrow \omega T = 2\pi \Rightarrow T = 2\pi/\omega$.

(*b*)   From Eq. (*12.10a*) we see that at $x = \pm A$ we must have $\cos (\omega t + \theta_0) = \pm 1 \Rightarrow (\omega t + \theta_0) = 0$ or π. Then, since sine of either 0 or π vanishes, from Eq. (*12.10b*) we have $v_x = 0$. Similarly, at $x = 0$, Eq. (*12.10a*) implies $\omega t + \theta_0 = \pi/2$ or $3\pi/2$. Then, since $\sin (\pi/2) = 1$ and $\sin (3\pi/2) = -1$ we have from Eq. (*12.10b*), $v_x = \pm \omega A$.

(*c*)   If $x = A$ at $t = 0$, Eqs. (*12.11*) apply. Then, from Eq. (*12.11b*) we have, at $t = \pi/2\omega$, $v_x = -\omega A \sin (\pi/2) = -\omega A$. Similarly, at $t = \pi/\omega$, $v_x = -\omega A \sin (\pi) = 0$.

The Shadow Motion and SHM

A comparison of Eqs. (*12.8a*) and (*12.8c*) [or (*12.10a*) and (*12.10c*)] shows that

$$a = -\omega^2 x \qquad (12.12)$$

for all positions x. Since ω is a constant we see that Eq. (*12.12*) has the same mathematical form as Eq. (*12.2*), which refers to the SHM problem of a block at the end of a spring. Note that both Eq. (*12.2*) and Eq. (12.12) are described by the verbal equation (12.3) and thus satisfy the same mathematical requirements. Indeed, if we choose the ω of our reference circle so that

$$\omega = \sqrt{\frac{k}{m}} \tag{12.13}$$

then Eqs. (12.2) and (12.12) are identical. Furthermore if the radius of our reference circle is set equal to the amplitude of the motion of the block at the end of the spring, then the block's motion is in every way identical to that of the shadow of the reference circle. Thus, the block at the end of the spring obeys the general equations (12.10). Again, the choice of θ_0 is merely a determination of where along the motion we start our clock. As for the case of the shadow, if the block is at $x = A$, at $t = 0$, we get Eqs. (12.11) for the block's motion.

Note. The inclusion of such symbols as ω and θ_0 in the equation of motion for the block has nothing to do with angular motion of the block. They are just mathematical vestiges of the shadow motion for the reference circle. Any other symbols could be used. Indeed ω is just another name for $\sqrt{k/m}$. Thus, Eqs. (12.11) can be written as

$$x = A \cos\left(\sqrt{\frac{k}{m}}\, t\right) \tag{12.14a}$$

$$v = -\left(\sqrt{k/m}\right) A \sin\left(\sqrt{\frac{k}{m}}\, t\right) \tag{12.14b}$$

$$a = -(k/m) A \cos\left(\sqrt{\frac{k}{m}}\, t\right) \tag{12.14c}$$

but, it is traditional to use the symbol ω for $\sqrt{k/m}$.

Problem 12.10. Show that Eqs. (12.10a) and (12.10b), applied to the block at the end of the spring, can be used to derive Eq. (12.7).

Solution

Squaring Eq. (12.10b) we get

$$v^2 = \omega^2 A^2 \sin^2(\omega t + \theta_0) = \omega^2 A^2 [1 - \cos^2(\omega t + \theta_0)] = \omega^2 A^2 - \omega^2 A^2 \cos^2(\omega t + \theta_0)$$

Using Eq. (12.10a), we get

$$v^2 = \omega^2 A^2 - \omega^2 x^2 = \omega^2 (A^2 - x^2) \qquad \text{or} \qquad v = \pm \omega (A^2 - x^2)^{1/2}$$

Substituting in $\omega = \sqrt{k/m}$, we get Eq. (12.7).

Problem 12.11.

(a) Find an expression for the period of SHM for the case of the block and spring.

(b) Find the corresponding expression for the frequency f of the motion.

(c) Does the period of SHM depend on the amplitude of the motion?

Solution

(a) $T = 2\pi/\omega$, where $\omega = \sqrt{k/m}$. Then $T = 2\pi\sqrt{m/k}$.

(b) $f = 1/T = (1/2\pi)\sqrt{k/m}$.

(c) No. As can be seen, the amplitude does not enter into the expression for the period. This is a characteristic of SHM but is not true for periodic motion in general.

Problem 12.12. Referring to the block and spring of Problem 12.5, (a) find the period and the frequency of the SHM; (b) assuming $x = A$ at $t = 0$, find the equations of motion for the displacement x and velocity v.

Solution

(a) $T = 2\pi\sqrt{m/k} = 2\pi[(8.0 \text{ kg})/(200 \text{ N/m})]^{1/2} = (2\pi/5.0)$ s $= 1.26$ s; $f = 1/T = 0.796$ s^{-1}.

(b) For this situation, Eqs. (12.11) [or (12.14)] hold. Then, noting that $A = 3.0$ cm, we have $x = (3.0 \text{ cm}) \cos (5.0t)$; $v = -(15 \text{ cm/s}) \sin (5.0t)$, where the arguments of the cosine and sine are dimensionless, and in radians, when t is inserted in seconds.

Problem 12.13. Referring to Problem 12.12, find the position and the velocity of the block at (a) $t = 0.50$ s, $t = 1.15$ s, $t = 4.12$ s; (b) $t = T/12$, $t = T/6$, $t = T/4$.

Solution

(a) At $t = 0.50$ s:

$$x = (3.0 \text{ cm}) \cos 2.5 = -2.4 \text{ cm} \qquad v = -(15 \text{ cm/s}) \sin 2.5 = -8.98 \text{ cm/s}$$

At $t = 1.15$ s:

$$x = 2.58 \text{ cm} \qquad v = 7.62 \text{ cm/s}$$

At $t = 4.12$ s:

$$x = -0.536 \text{ cm} \qquad v = -14.8 \text{ cm/s}$$

(b) Recall that $\omega T = 2\pi$. Then the arguments, ωt of the cosine and sine in the expressions for x and v of Eqs. (12.11) are, at the three different times, respectively: $\omega T/12 = \pi/6$; $\omega T/6 = \pi/3$; $\omega T/4 = \pi/2$. Then the corresponding values of x are $x = (3.0 \text{ cm}) \cos (\pi/6) = 2.60$ cm; $x = 1.5$ cm; and $x = 0$ cm. Similarly, the corresponding values of v are $v = -7.5$ cm/s; $v = -13.0$ cm/s; and $v = -15$ cm/s.

Problem 12.14. Find the shortest time it takes the block of Problem 12.12 to go (a) from $x = A$ to $x = A/2$; (b) from $x = A/2$ to $x = 0$; (c) from $x = -A/3$ to $x = -A$.

Solution

(a) By hypothesis, $t = 0$ is one of the times at which the block is at $x = A$. To reach $x = A/2$, we note that $A/2 = A \cos (5.0t) \Rightarrow \cos (5.0t) = \frac{1}{2}$. This equation has an infinite number of solutions, but we are interested in the smallest time t, which corresponds to the acute angle solution: $5.0t = \pi/3$. Then $t = \pi/15$ s $= 0.209$ s.

(b) To find the time to go from $x = A/2$ to $x = 0$, we need only find the lowest time t corresponding to $x = 0$ and subtract the time found in (a). We have $0 = A \cos (5.0t) \Rightarrow$ (for the smallest solution for t): $5.0t = \pi/2 \Rightarrow t = \pi/10$ s $= 0.314$ s. Our time interval is then 0.314 s $- 0.209$ s $= 0.105$ s.

(c) Here the time to reach $x = -A/3$ is given by $-A/3 = A \cos (5.0t) \Rightarrow \cos (5.0t) = -\frac{1}{3} \Rightarrow$ (for the smallest time t): $5.0t = 1.91 \Rightarrow t = 0.382$ s. Then for the smallest time to reach $x = -A$, we have $\cos (5.0t) = -1 \Rightarrow 5.0t = \pi \Rightarrow t = 0.628$ s. Our time interval is therefore 0.628 s $- 0.382$ s $= 0.246$ s.

Obtaining Time Intervals by Using the Reference Circle

While Problem 12.14 illustrates how one can obtain time intervals by using the trigonometric time equations, this method can be tricky since there are multiple solutions for the "angles" corresponding to a given value of the trigonometric functions, and one has to know which one to choose. There is a simpler and more intuitive way of finding time intervals for SHM that uses only acute angles and allows one to quickly visualize the situation. This method returns us to the shadow motion of a particle on the reference circle. Consider a shadow motion that is the exact replica of the actual SHM we are interested in. The situation is illustrated in Fig. 12-6. We want to know the shortest time interval Δt to go from one point x_1 to another point x_2. The particle on the circle is always above its shadow, so the time interval Δt is just the time the particle takes in going along the arc of the circle from 1 to 2. Then the time interval Δt corresponds to the angle interval $\Delta \theta = \theta_2 - \theta_1$. Since the particle is moving uniformly, it sweeps out equal angles in equal times. Since it sweeps out the angle 2π in one period T, we can set up the ratio

$$\frac{\Delta t}{T} = \frac{\Delta \theta}{2\pi} \qquad (12.15a)$$

A knowledge of $\Delta \theta$ thus gives us the value of Δt.

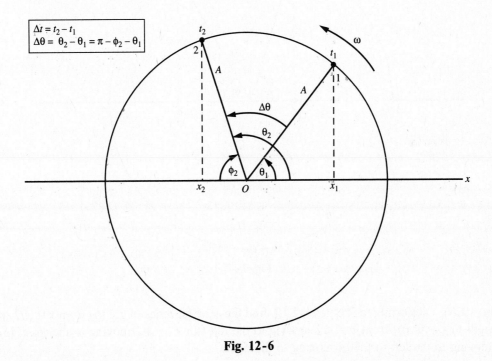

Fig. 12-6

If instead of using radians we measure all angles in degrees, Eq. (12.15a) becomes

$$\frac{\Delta t}{T} = \frac{\Delta \theta}{360°} \qquad (12.15b)$$

From Fig. 12-6 we see that $\Delta \theta = \pi - \phi_2 - \theta_1$. We also have $\cos \theta_1 = x_1/A$; $\cos \phi_2 = |x_2|/A$. Solving for θ_1 and ϕ_2, and substituting, we get $\Delta \theta$.

Problem 12.15. Redo Problem 12.14 by using the reference circle method.

Solution

The various points in question are labeled on the reference circle shown in Fig. 12-7. Then for part (a), we have $\Delta\theta_1 = \theta_1$, and $\cos\theta_1 = \frac{1}{2} \Rightarrow \theta_1 = 60°$. Therefore

$$\Delta t = \left(\frac{60}{360}\right) T = \frac{T}{6} = \frac{1.26\ \text{s}}{6} = 0.210\ \text{s}$$

For part (b),

$$\Delta\theta_2 = 90° - \theta_1 = 30° \Rightarrow \Delta t = \left(\frac{30}{360}\right) T = \frac{T}{12} = 0.105\ \text{s}$$

For part (c), let $\Delta\theta_3 = \phi$, and $\cos\phi = \frac{1}{3}$, so

$$\phi = 70.5° \Rightarrow \Delta t = \left(\frac{70.5}{360}\right) T = (0.196)(1.26\ \text{s}) = 0.247\ \text{s}$$

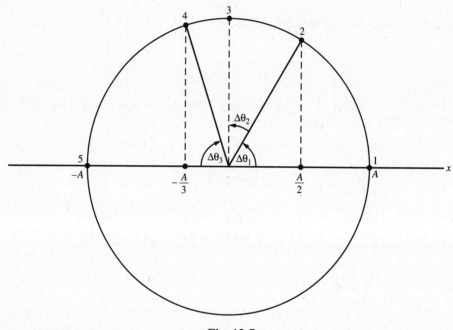

Fig. 12-7

Problem 12.16. Referring to Problem 12.12, find the shortest times to go: (a) from $x = A/2$ moving to the right to $x = 0$; (b) from $x = A/2$ moving to the left to $x = -A/2$ moving to the right; (c) from $0.60A$ moving to the left to $0.80A$ moving to the right.

Solution

The three situations are shown in Fig. 12-8 (a to c).

(a) $\Delta\theta = \phi + 90°$. $\cos\phi = \frac{1}{2} \Rightarrow \phi = 60°$. Thus $\Delta\theta = 150°$ and $\Delta t/T = \frac{150}{360}$. Since $T = 1.26$ s, we have $\Delta t = 0.525$ s.

(b) We see that $\Delta\theta = \pi \Rightarrow \Delta t = T/2 = 0.630$ s.

(c) We see that $\Delta\theta = 360° - \theta - \phi$. Also, $\cos\theta = 0.60 \Rightarrow \theta = 53°$, and $\cos\phi = 0.80 \Rightarrow \phi = 37°$. Then $\Delta\theta = 270°$, and $\Delta t/T = 270/360 = 0.75 \Rightarrow \Delta t = 0.75T = 0.945$ s.

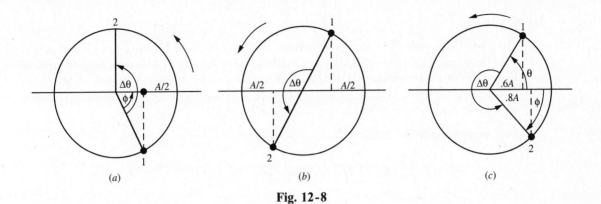

Fig. 12-8

12.4 OTHER EXAMPLES OF SHM

A Block Hanging from a Spring

In Problem 6.30 and Fig. 6-23, we considered a block of mass m hanging from one end of a vertical light spring of force constant k. It was shown in that problem that in determining the mechanical energy, the combined effect of gravity and spring was equivalent to considering the spring force alone—but measured from the equilibrium position. Indeed it is not hard to see that under the combined effect of gravity plus spring the block experiences a linear restoring force

$$F = -kx \qquad (12.16)$$

when it is displaced a distance x from its *equilibrium* position. It therefore executes SHM about $x = 0$, and our previous results apply to this situation. (Note that x is chosen as positive downward in Fig. 6-23.)

Problem 12.17. Assume the block in Fig. 6-23 has a mass of $m = 40$ kg and that the spring has a force constant $k = 36,000$ N/m. The block is pulled 2.5 cm below the equilibrium position and released from rest. Find (a) the distance h from the unstretched to the equilibrium position, (b) the period and amplitude of the motion, and (c) the velocity and acceleration of the block as it passes the equilibrium position.

Solution

(a)   For equilibrium, $kh = mg \Rightarrow h = mg/k = (40\text{ kg})(9.8\text{ m/s}^2)/(36,000\text{ N/m}) = 1.09$ cm.

(b) $T = 2\pi\sqrt{m/k} = 6.28(0.0333\text{ s}) = 0.209$ s;   Since it is released from rest 2.5 cm below equilibrium, and equilibrium is the zero point for our SHM, we have $A = 2.5$ cm.

(c)   Again, since the block executes SHM about the equilibrium point, the acceleration is zero at this point and the velocity is maximum:

$$v = \pm\sqrt{\frac{k}{m}}A = \pm\left(30\text{ s}^{-1}\right)(2.5\text{ cm}) = \pm75\text{ cm/s}$$

Problem 12.18. Referring to Problem 12.17, find (a) the acceleration of the block as it passes the unstretched position, and (b) the velocity of the block as it passes the unstretched position.

Solution

(a) The unstretched position is above equilibrium, and from Problem 12.17(a), this corresponds to $x = -1.09$ cm. Then $a = -(k/m)x \Rightarrow a = -(900 \text{ s}^{-2})(-1.09 \text{ cm}) = 981 \text{ cm/s}^2$. Since downward is positive, this corresponds to a downward acceleration equal to the acceleration of gravity, to within rounding errors. [This is not a surprise, since at its unstretched position the block is subject only to the force of gravity and is momentarily in free fall].

(b) Here we can use the formula

$$v = \pm\sqrt{\frac{k}{m}}(A^2 - x^2)^{1/2} = (30 \text{ s}^{-1})\,[(2.5 \text{ cm})^2 - (1.09)^2]^{1/2} = 67.5 \text{ m/s}$$

The Torsion Pendulum

Consider the bar at the end of the torsion wire referred to in Problem 12.2. If the bar is twisted and released, the ensuing rotational motion is SHM, as can be seen from Eq. (i) of Problem 12.2. The "displacement" is now the angular displacement θ of the bar from the untwisted position, the "velocity" is the angular velocity of the bar, and the "acceleration" is the angular acceleration of the bar.

> **Note.** These angle quantities have nothing to do with the reference circle. Here it is the actual angular motion itself that obeys the rules of SHM.

The period and frequency of the motion are given by

$$T = 2\pi\sqrt{\frac{I}{\delta}} \quad \text{and} \quad f = \frac{1}{2\pi}\sqrt{\frac{\delta}{I}} \qquad (12.17a, b)$$

The "amplitude" of the motion refers to the maximum angle of twist θ_A on either side of the untwisted position. If the bar is released from rest at θ_A, the time equation of motion for θ is

$$\theta = \theta_A \cos\left(\sqrt{\frac{\delta}{I}}\,t\right) \qquad (12.18)$$

Similar equations hold for the angular velocity and angular acceleration.

Problem 12.19. Assume in Fig. 12-2 that the torsion constant is $\delta = 1000 \text{ N} \cdot \text{m/rad}$ and the moment of inertia $I = 0.500 \text{ kg} \cdot \text{m}^2$. The bar is rotated through an angle of π rad and released from rest. Find (a) the period and amplitude of the motion, (b) the angular velocity ω as the bar reaches the angles $\pi/2$ and 0, respectively.

> **Note.** Again, this ω has nothing to do with the earlier use of the symbol from the reference circle.

(c) the shortest time it takes the rod to rotate from $\theta = \pi$ to $\theta = \pi/3$ rad.

Solution

(a)
$$T = 2\pi\left(\frac{I}{\delta}\right)^{1/2} = 2\pi\left(\frac{0.500 \text{ kg} \cdot \text{m}^2}{1000 \text{ N} \cdot \text{m/rad}}\right)^{1/2} = 0.140 \text{ s}$$

Since the bar is released from $\theta = \pi$ at rest this must be the maximum angle, and $\theta_A = 3.14$ rad.

(b)   We use the analog of Eq. (12.7), which is

$$\omega = \pm\sqrt{\frac{\delta}{I}}\left(\theta_A{}^2 - \theta^2\right)^{1/2} \qquad (i)$$

Then for $\theta = \pi/2$, we have

$$\omega = \pm(44.7 \text{ s}^{-1})\left[\pi^2 - \left(\frac{\pi}{2}\right)^2\right]^{1/2} = \pm 122 \text{ rad/s}$$

similarly, for $\theta = 0$ we get the maximum ω,

$$\omega = \pm\left(\sqrt{\frac{\delta}{I}}\right)\theta_A = \pm(44.7 \text{ s}^{-1})\pi = \pm 140 \text{ rad/s}$$

(c)   We choose $t = 0$ at $\theta = \theta_A = \pi$, so from Eq. (12.18), at $\theta = \pi/3$:

$$\frac{\pi}{3} = \pi \cos\left(\sqrt{\frac{\delta}{I}}\,t\right) \Rightarrow \cos(44.7t) = \tfrac{1}{3} \Rightarrow 44.7t = 1.23 \text{ rad} \qquad \text{or} \qquad t = 0.0275 \text{ s}$$

The Simple Pendulum

Consider a bob of mass M, hanging at the end of a cord of length L. If the bob is pulled back and released, how would we describe the ensuing motion? The situation is depicted in Fig. 12-9. To understand the motion we note that as long as the cord is taut, we can treat the cord-bob system as a rigid body rotating about a horizontal axis through the pivot point P. Then $\Gamma = I\alpha$ is the equation governing the motion. Since all the mass is concentrated in the bob, we have (about our axis through P) $I = ML^2$. The torque Γ about P is due only to the force of gravity, and in magnitude is just the component of the weight perpendicular to the cord times L. Choosing counterclockwise as positive, as

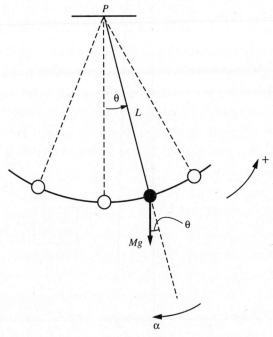

Fig. 12-9

shown, we have $\Gamma = -MgL \sin \theta$. Then, $I\alpha = -MgL \sin \theta$, and substituting for I and solving for α we get

$$\alpha = -\frac{g}{L} \sin \theta \qquad\qquad (12.19)$$

This is *not* the equation of SHM, since the right side contains $\sin \theta$ instead of θ. The motion described by Eq. (*12.19*) is a periodic motion, but it is more complex than SHM because the period depends on the amplitude θ_A. However, for small values of θ, we have $\sin \theta \approx \theta$ when θ is measured in radians. This result is good to 1% accuracy for angles up to 0.26 rad (or roughly 15°). The accuracy is even better for smaller angles. If we assume that our simple pendulum swings through a maximum angle of 15°, we can approximate Eq. (*12.19*) by the SHM equation

$$\alpha = -\frac{g}{L} \theta \qquad\qquad (12.20)$$

For this small-angle approximation, the bob moves on such a small portion of the arc of a circle that it can be approximated by a straight line, as shown in Fig. 12-10, and the approximations indicated there will hold: $x = L\theta$ and $a = L\alpha$, where x and a are the linear displacement and linear acceleration of the bob on the x axis. Substituting these results for x and a into (*12.20*), we get

$$a = -\frac{g}{L} x \qquad\qquad (12.21)$$

which is just (*12.1*) with a different proportionality constant.

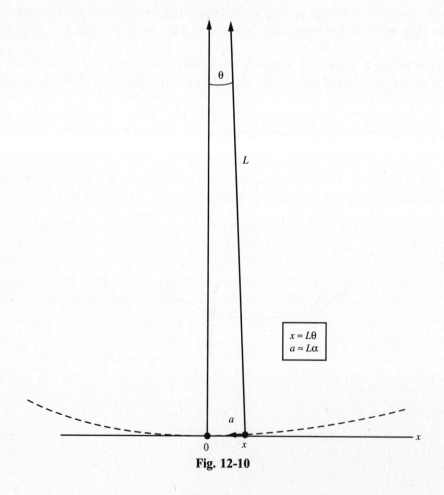

Fig. 12-10

Problem 12.20.

(a) Find expressions for the period, frequency, maximum angular velocity, and maximum angular acceleration for the simple pendulum obeying Eq. (*12.20*).

(b) What are the corresponding quantities if Eq. (*12.21*) is used?

   Solution

   (a)
$$T = 2\pi\sqrt{\frac{L}{g}} \quad \text{and} \quad f = \frac{1}{2\pi}\sqrt{\frac{g}{L}} \qquad\qquad (i, \, ii)$$

Note.   The period does not depend on the mass M of the bob. This is expected since only the force of gravity contributes to the torque and, as usual in such cases, the mass drops out of the dynamic equations.

$$\omega_{max} = \pm\sqrt{\frac{g}{L}}\,\theta_A \quad \text{and} \quad \alpha_{max} = \pm\frac{g}{L}\,\theta_A \qquad\qquad (iii, \, iv)$$

   where θ_A is the angular amplitude of the motion.

   (b) The period and frequency are the same, since the same constant appears in (*12.20*) and (*12.21*). For the velocity and acceleration we have

$$v_{max} = \pm\left(\sqrt{\frac{g}{L}}\right)A \quad \text{and} \quad a_{max} = \pm\frac{g}{L}\,A \qquad\qquad (v, \, vi)$$

   where A is the amplitude. (Since, $A = L\theta_A$, we see that, as expected, $v_{max} = \omega_{max}L$ and $a_{max} = \alpha_{max}L$.)

Problem 12.21.   A simple pendulum consists of a bob of mass $M = 30$ g and length $L = 80$ cm. The bob is pulled back $10°$ and released from rest.

(a) What is the period of the motion?

(b) What is the linear amplitude A of the motion of the bob?

(c) What is the velocity v of the bob as it passes the equilibrium (lowest) position?

   Solution

   (a) From Problem 12.20, we have

$$T = 2\pi\sqrt{\frac{L}{g}} = 6.28\left(\frac{80 \text{ cm}}{980 \text{ cm/s}^2}\right)^{1/2} = 1.79 \text{ s}$$

   (b) Again, from Problem 12.20, $A = L\theta_A = (80 \text{ cm})(10°)/(57.3 \text{ deg/rad}) = 14.0$ cm (where we converted θ_A to radians, as required).

   (c) Using Eq. (*v*) of Problem 12.20

$$v = v_{max} = \pm\left(\frac{80 \text{ cm}}{980 \text{ cm/s}^2}\right)^{1/2}(14.0 \text{ cm}) = 4.00 \text{ cm/s}$$

Problems for Review and Mind Stretching

Problem 12.22.

(a) Referring to Problem 12.17, find the shortest time it takes to go from equilibrium to the unstretched position.

(b) Find the time it takes to go from the unstretched position to the highest point in the motion.

Solution

(a) We want the time to go from $x = 0$ to $x = -1.09$ cm (recalling that downward is positive). If we drew a reference circle of radius $A = 2.50$ cm, this would correspond to a sweep of $\Delta\theta = 90° - \phi$ on the circle, where $\cos\phi = 1.09/2.50 \Rightarrow \phi = 64.2°$. Then, $\Delta\theta = 90° - 64.2° = 25.8°$, and $\Delta t = (25.8/360)T = 0.0717(0.209 \text{ s}) = 0.0150$ s.

(b) Since the time to go from equilibrium to the highest point is $(\frac{1}{4})T = (0.209 \text{ s})/4 = 0.0523$ s, and the time to go from equilibrium to the unstretched position is 0.0150 s, the time to go from the unstretched position to the highest point is just the difference: $0.0523 - 0.0150 = 0.0373$ s.

Problem 12.23. How would the quantities asked for in Problem 12.21 change if the length of the pendulum quadrupled, but the angular amplitude remained 10 °?

Solution

The period goes as the square root of L, so the period would double to $T = 3.58$ s. The linear amplitude A is proportional to L and would therefore quadruple if θ_A stayed the same, so $A = 56.0$ cm. Finally, the maximum linear velocity is proportional to both A and to $1/\sqrt{L}$, so it will increase by a factor of $\frac{4}{2} = 2$, and $v_{max} = \pm8.00$ cm/s.

Problem 12.24. For the situations shown in Fig. 12-11(a) and (b) the solid block represents the equilibrium position and the dashed-line block represents its position after a displacement x from equilibrium. For each case, find the equivalent force constant of a single spring that would have the same effect on the block, thus showing that the block undergoes SHM; find the period of SHM for each case.

Solution

(a) In stretching to position x from equilibrium, the restoring force to the left due to both springs is $F = -k_1 x - k_2 x = -(k_1 + k_2)x$. The equivalent single spring would give a force $F = -kx$. Thus

$$k = k_1 + k_2 \quad \text{and} \quad T = 2\pi\sqrt{\frac{m}{k_1 + k_2}}$$

(b) Here the two springs are pulling in opposite directions and just balance at the equilibrium position. If the block is pulled a distance x to the right of equilibrium, then spring one will *increase* its pull to the left by $k_1 x$, while spring two will *decrease* its pull to the right by $k_2 x$. Therefore, the net force at position x is $k_1 x + k_2 x$ to the left. Then, the equivalent single spring will again have force constant

$$k = k_1 + k_2 \quad \text{and again} \quad T = \sqrt{\frac{m}{k_1 + k_2}}$$

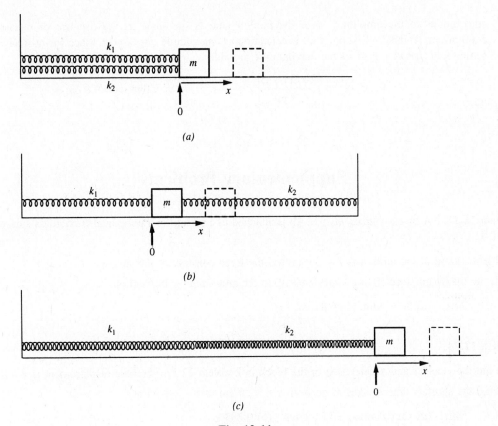

Fig. 12-11

Problem 12.25.   Repeat Problem 12.24 for the case of Fig. 12-11(c).

Solution

Here both springs were initially at their unstretched positions since the block was in equilibrium. When pulled to the right to position x, each spring will contribute to part of the stretch. If x_1 and x_2 are the stretches, respectively, of the two springs, then we must have $x_1 + x_2 = x$. Also, since the springs exert equal and opposite forces F on each other, we have, in magnitude, $F = k_1 x_1$ and $F = k_2 x_2$. The same force F is exerted on the block, so the equivalent spring has $F = kx$, in magnitude. Thus, $x_1 = F/k_1$, $x_2 = F/k_2$, and $x = F/k$. Then $x_1 + x_2 = x$ becomes $F/k_1 + F/k_2 = F/k$. Dividing both sides by F, we get $1/k = 1/k_1 + 1/k_2$. Making the common denominator $k_1 k_2$ on the right and inverting we have

$$k = \frac{k_1 k_2}{k_1 + k_2} \quad \text{and} \quad T = 2\pi \sqrt{\frac{m(k_1 + k_2)}{k_1 k_2}}$$

Problem 12.26.   A small object is placed on top of a block of mass $m = 20$ kg that is hung from one end of a vertical spring of force constant $k = 2000$ N/m and whose other end is attached to the ceiling. The block is pulled down a distance A below the equilibrium position and released from rest. What is the maximum value of A for which the small object remains in contact with the block throughout the subsequent SHM?

Solution

Contact will be lost only if the downward acceleration of the block momentarily exceeds the acceleration of gravity g. When that occurs the object will not be able to follow the motion of the block. The block's maximum downward acceleration occurs at the highest point in the motion, which corresponds to the amplitude A of the motion, and is the same as the distance of release below equilibrium. At this highest point the acceleration has magnitude $a = (k/m)A$. Since we must have $a \leq g$, setting $a = (k/m)A = g$ gives the maximum A possible:

$$9.8 \text{ m/s}^2 = \left[\frac{2000 \text{ N/m}}{20 \text{ kg}} \right] A \quad \text{or} \quad A = 0.098 \text{ m} = 9.8 \text{ cm}$$

Supplementary Problems

Problem 12.27. A block of mass $m = 12$ kg is attached to a spring on a horizontal frictionless surface, as in Fig. 12-1.

(a)   If the period of the motion is $T = 3.0$ s, find the force constant of the spring.

(b)   If the maximum acceleration is 30 cm/s^2, find the amplitude of the motion.

   Ans.   (a) 52.6 N/m; (b) 6.85 cm

Problem 12.28.

(a)   Find the velocity and acceleration of the block in Problem 12.27 when the displacement is $x = 3.9$ cm.

(b)   Find the shortest time it takes to go from $x = +2.0$ cm to $x = -2.0$ cm.

   Ans.   (a) ± 11.8 cm/s, -17.0 cm/s^2; (b) 0.283 s

Problem 12.29. A torsion pendulum executes SHM of amplitude 30 ° and frequency 5.0 repetitions per second.

(a)   Find the maximum torque exerted by the torsion wire if the moment of inertia of the system about the wire is $I = 0.75$ kg $\cdot$ m^2.

(b)   Find the maximum angular velocity of the system.

   Ans.   (a) 387 N $\cdot$ m; (b) 16.4 rad/s

Problem 12.30. Assume that a spring and block are set up vertically, with the block hanging from one end of the spring and the other end of the spring attached to the ceiling. The force constant of the spring is $k = 300$ N/m, and the equilibrium position is 20 cm below the unstretched position.

(a)   Find the mass m of the block.

(b)   If the block executed SHM of amplitude 30 cm, find the spring force on the block at the highest point.

   Ans.   (a) 6.12 kg; (b) 30 N, downward

Problem 12.31. For the spring of Problem 12.30, calculate (a) the acceleration at the highest point, (b) the acceleration at the unstretched position, (c) the velocity at the unstretched position.

   Ans.   (a) 14.7 m/s^2, downward; (b) 9.8 m/s^2, downward; (c) ± 1.40 m/s

Problem 12.32. For the system of Problems 12.30 and 12.31, (a) find the potential energy of the spring at the highest and lowest points, as measured from zero at the unstretched position; (b) find the potential energy of gravity at the highest and lowest points, as measured from zero at the unstretched position; (c) what is the relation between the total potential energy at the highest and lowest points, and why?

> *Ans.* (a) 1.50 J, 37.5 J; (b) 6.00 J, −30.0 J; (c) They are the same (7.5 J); since total mechanical energy is conserved and since the kinetic energy is zero at the highest and lowest points, the total potential energies must be the same.

Problem 12.33. A simple pendulum of length 1.20 m is used by a student to determine the acceleration of gravity. The pendulum swings back and forth through 10 complete swings in 22.2 s. What value of g is obtained?

> *Ans.* 9.61 m/s^2

Problem 12.34.

(a) Find the length of a simple pendulum that will have the same period as that of the block at the end of the spring in Problem 12.30.

(b) What is special about this length and why?

> *Ans.* (a) 20 cm; (b) This is the same as the distance h from the unstretched to the equilibrium position for the hanging block. Since $mg = kh$, we have $m/k = h/g$. Then, for the spring system, $T = 2\pi\sqrt{m/k} = 2\pi\sqrt{h/g}$; for the simple pendulum, $T = 2\pi\sqrt{L/g}$; and for equal periods we have $h = L$.

Problem 12.35. Assume in Fig. 12-11 that $m = 12$ kg, $k_1 = 300$ N/m, and $k_2 = 200$ N/m. Find the period of simple harmonic motion for the situation in (a) Fig. 12-11(a); (b) Fig. 12-11(b); (c) Fig. 12-11(c).

> *Ans.* (a) 0.973 s; (b) 0.973 s; (c) 1.99 s

Problem 12.36. A 96-lb weight hangs at the end of a spring of force constant 1500 lb/ft. The weight is pulled down 6.0 in and released from rest. Find (a) the period of the motion, (b) the maximum velocity and maximum acceleration, (c) the velocity when the distance from equilibrium is 4.0 in.

> *Ans.* (a) 0.281 s; (b) $v_{max} = \pm11.2$ ft/s; $a_{max} = \pm250$ ft/s^2; (c) ±8.33 ft/s

Problem 12.37.

(a) If the weight in Problem 12.36 is replaced by another weight that doubles the period of SHM, what is the new weight?

(b) If the original weight is retained, but the spring is replaced by a spring of identical construction, but twice as long, what is the new period? [*Hint*: Look at Fig. 12-11(c) and Problem 12.25.]

(c) If the original spring were cut in half and the original weight were hung from this "new" spring, what would the new period be? [*Hint*: Think hard about part (b).]

> *Ans.* (a) 384 lb; (b) 0.397 s; (c) 0.199 s

Problem 12.38. Equations (*12.14a, b, c*) are the equations of motion for x, v, and a for a block of mass m at the end of a spring of force constant k if the time $t = 0$ is taken as the instant the block attains its maximum positive value. What would these equations be if $t = 0$ corresponds to the block passing the equilibrium position moving in the positive direction? [*Hint*: Make use of the reference circle.]

Ans.

$$x = A \sin\left(\sqrt{\frac{k}{m}}\,t\right) \qquad v = \sqrt{\frac{k}{m}}\,A\,\cos\left(\sqrt{\frac{k}{m}}\,t\right) \qquad a = -\frac{k}{m}\,A\,\sin\left(\sqrt{\frac{k}{m}}\,t\right)$$

Problem 12.39.   Use the results of Problem 12.38 to find x and v at the following times: (*a*) $t = T/12$; (*b*) $t = T/6$; (*c*) $t = T/4$.

Ans.   (*a*) $A/2$, $\left(\sqrt{3k/2m}\right)A$; (*b*) $\left(\sqrt{\frac{3}{2}}\right)A$, $\left(\sqrt{k/4m}\right)A$; (*c*) A, 0

Chapter 13

Fluids at Rest (Hydrostatics)

13.1 INTRODUCTION

Liquids and gases are classified as fluids. In Chap. 11 we saw that solid objects are not perfectly rigid, but rather they respond to stress by distorting to some extent. In particular, if one applies a shear force to a solid, the solid responds to the stress that is created by distorting, as shown in Fig. 11-2.

Liquids resist compression in much the same way solids do, but they are unable to resist shear forces. As long as a shear force acts, the liquid will flow. Only when all shear forces are eliminated will the liquid cease to move. Indeed the fact that a liquid at rest takes the shape of its container and has a horizontal free surface is a consequence of the requirement that there be zero shear force between any two layers in the liquid, as well as between the liquid and the surfaces it is in contact with. A characteristic of liquids which distinguishes them from gases is that the molecules of a liquid are sufficiently bound to each other that the overall volume of a liquid doesn't significantly change even as the liquid changes shape to accommodate itself to different containers.

Gases, like liquids and solids, can resist compression, though much more weakly. Gases, like liquids, cannot resist shear forces, and in equilibrium no such forces are exerted by the walls of a closed container or by one part of the gas on another. Gases, however, differ from liquids in that the molecules of a gas have extremely weak interactions with each other. Gas molecules move about freely except for direct collisions with each other or with the walls of a confining container. A gas's resistance to compression comes not from intermolecular forces that resist the molecules being pushed closer together but rather from the collision of gas molecules with the walls of the container. Since the molecules of a gas have no grip on each other, a gas will expand to fill the volume of the container it is placed in.

In this chapter we will examine fluids at rest, the subject of *hydrostatics*. In the next chapter we will examine the properties of fluids in motion, the subject of *hydrodynamics*.

13.2 DENSITY AND PRESSURE OF FLUIDS

Density

The **density** d of any substance is defined as the mass per unit volume of the substance. If we have a uniform sample of materials (solid, liquid, or gas) of mass M and volume V, then

$$d = \frac{M}{V} \tag{13.1}$$

The density is an intrinsic property of a substance; that is, it does not depend on the size of the sample. Density, however, can vary with such factors as temperature and pressure. Table 13.1 gives the densities of a variety of substances at atmospheric pressure and room temperature (20 °C or 68 °F). The SI unit of density is the kg/m^3. Other units are g/cm^3 and slug/ft^3. In the foot-pound system of units it is usual to define the weight density d_w or weight per unit volume

$$d_w = \frac{W}{V} \tag{13.2}$$

Table 13.1. Densities

Material	Density, kg/m^3
Helium	0.18
Air	1.29
Benzene	880
Ethyl alcohol	810
Water	1,000
Aluminum	2,700
Brass	8,600
Gold	19,300
Ice	917
Iron	7,860
Lead	11,300
Mercury	13,600
Silver	10,500
Steel	7,860
Uranium	18,700

All figures at atmospheric pressure and room temperature; weight density of water, given for reference, is 62.5 lb/ft^3.

Since $W = Mg$, we have that

$$d_w = dg \tag{13.3}$$

The units of d_w are lb/ft^3, N/m^3, and dyn/cm^3.

Another quantity commonly used to describe densities is the specific gravity (sp gr) of a substance, which is defined as the ratio of the density of the substance to that of water:

$$\text{sp gr }(X) = \frac{d(X)}{d(H_2O)} \tag{13.4}$$

where X is the substance in question. This ratio is dimensionless and gives us a scale of densities relative to water. Since the density of water in CGS units is $d(H_2O) = 1.0$ g/cm^3, it follows that the specific gravity of any substance is numerically equal to its density in g/cm^3.

We can also express specific gravity in terms of weight density. Since $d_w = dg$, we have

$$\text{sp gr }(X) = \frac{d_w(X)}{d_w(H_2O)} \tag{13.5}$$

[Note that $d_w(H_2O) = 62.5$ lb/ft^3.]

Problem 13.1. A cubical block 10 cm on a side has a mass $M = 2700$ g.

(a) Find the density in kg/m^3; if the block is a pure substance listed in Table 13.1, what is it?

(b)   Find the specific gravity of the substance. If the weight density of water is $d_w = 62.5$ lb/ft^3, find the weight density of the substance in lb/ft^3.

(c)   What would the mass of the block be if it was made of iron?

Solution

(a) $d = M/V = (2.70$ kg$)/(0.10$ m$)^3 = 2.70 \times 10^3$ kg/m^3; the substance is aluminum.

(b)   sp gr $= d(Al)/d(H_2O) = (2.70 \times 10^3$ kg/m$^3)/(1.00 \times 10^3$ kg/m$^3) = 2.70$ [or $d_{Al} = (2700$ g$)/(10$ cm$)^3 = 2.70$ g/cm$^3 \Rightarrow$ (sp gr)$_{Al} = 2.70$.]; $d_w =$ (sp gr)$d_w(H_2O) = 2.70(62.5$ lb/ft$^3) = 169$ lb/ft^3.

(c)   If the block were of iron, we have $d(I) = M_I/V$, so that $M_I = d(I)V$. From Table 13.1, we get $M_I = (7.86 \times 10^3$ kg/m$^3)(0.10$ m$)^3 = 7.86$ kg.

Pressure

The pressure P on any surface is defined as the force per unit area acting perpendicular to that surface. We assume here that the forces are spread out smoothly over some area, instead of acting at discrete points. This is illustrated in Fig. 13-1. To be precise, the pressure at a point is defined by considering the total infinitesimal force ΔF acting perpendicular to an infinitesimal area ΔA around the point in question. Then

$$P = \lim_{\Delta A \to 0} \frac{\Delta F}{\Delta A} \qquad\qquad (13.6)$$

The pressure can, in general, vary from location to location along a surface. Unlike force, pressure is not defined as a vector. For our purposes we can think of pressure as a scalar quantity, keeping in mind that the action of the pressure on a given surface is always perpendicular to the surface. As discussed in Chap. 11, the international unit of pressure is the pascal (Pa): 1 Pa = 1 N/m^2. Other commonly used units of pressure are the dyn/cm^2, lb/ft^2, and lb/in^2.

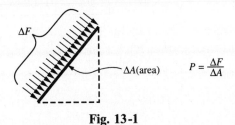

Fig. 13-1

We now examine some basic properties of the pressure in a fluid at rest (**hydrostatic pressure**). In Fig. 13-2 we examine a number of real and imaginary boundaries within such a fluid. In Fig. 13-2(a) we consider a small, infinitesimally thin and massless, disklike object placed somewhere in the fluid. We wish to compare the pressure due to the fluid on each side of the disk. The force on the disk due to the molecules of fluid pushing on its upper side is the same as the force those molecules would exert on the molecules of fluid on the other side of the disk if the disk were not there. From Newton's third law the molecules on the other side must exert an equal and opposite force. Since the area of the disk is the same as viewed from either side, we conclude that the pressure on each side of the disk is the same. Thus:

(a)   *For any point in a fluid at rest, the pressure on one side of a small surface is the same as the pressure on the other side.*

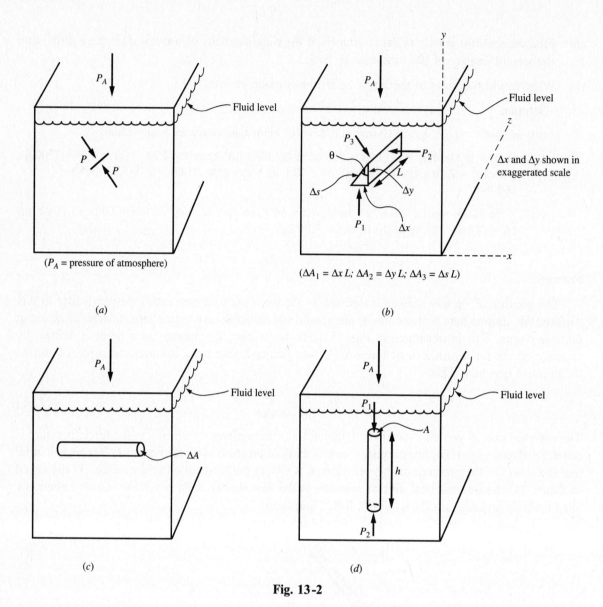

$(P_A = \text{pressure of atmosphere})$

(a)

$(\Delta A_1 = \Delta x\, L; \ \Delta A_2 = \Delta y\, L; \ \Delta A_3 = \Delta s\, L)$

(b)

(c)

(d)

Fig. 13-2

In Fig. 13-2(b) we have an imaginary triangular-shaped boundary enclosing some of the fluid. We assume the boundary is infinitesimal in the x and y directions, as shown, and extends a distance L in the z direction. The fluid inside the boundary is in equilibrium, so the x components of force on it add up to zero, as do the y components. Since there can be no shear forces, the forces in the xy plane are due only to the pressure perpendicular to the three surfaces ΔA_1, ΔA_2, and ΔA_3, which extend in the z direction, as well as due to gravity. (The forces on the end faces are only in the z direction and don't contribute to the x and y directions.) The magnitudes of the forces are $F_1 = P_1\,\Delta A_1 = P_1\,\Delta x\, L$, $F_2 = P_2\,\Delta A_2 = P_2\,\Delta y\, L$, $F_3 = P_3\,\Delta A_3 = P_3\,\Delta s\, L$, and $W = Mg = dVg$, where d = density of water and V is the triangular volume $V = \frac{1}{2}\Delta x\,\Delta y\, L$, so $W = \frac{1}{2}dg\Delta x\,\Delta y\, L$. If Δx and Δy are chosen small enough, W is negligibly small compared to the other forces because W depends on a product of two infinitesimals, while F_1, F_2, and F_3, each depend on one infinitesimal. We assume that Δx and Δy are chosen small enough so that W is negligible compared to the other forces. Then, for equilibrium in the y direction [from Fig. 13-2(b)],

$$F_3 \sin \theta = F_1 \qquad \text{or} \qquad P_3 \, \Delta s \sin \theta = P_1 \, \Delta x$$

Since $\Delta s \sin \theta = \Delta x$, we have $P_3 = P_1$. Similarly, for the x direction,

$$F_3 \cos \theta = F_2 \qquad \text{or} \qquad P_3 \, \Delta s \cos \theta = P_2 \, \Delta y$$

Since $\Delta s \cos \theta = \Delta y$, we have $P_3 = P_2$. Thus, $P_1 = P_2 = P_3$, and, since the angle θ was chosen arbitrarily, we conclude:

   (b)   *The pressure at a given point in a fluid at rest has a definite value that represents the force per unit area on a small surface placed at that point, oriented in any arbitrary direction.*

In Fig. 13-2(c) we consider a thin, imaginary, horizontal cylindrical boundary, with end faces of area ΔA. If we consider the fluid inside the cylinder to be our system, equilibrium requires that the sum of the horizontal forces on the cylinder add up to zero. The only horizontal forces are due to the pressure on the two end faces, since there can be no shear force along the length of the cylinder. Since ΔA is the same on both sides, we must have that the pressures at the two ends are equal in magnitude, so we conclude:

   (c)   *The pressure in a fluid at rest is the same at all points on a horizontal plane.*

In Fig. 13-2(d) we consider an imaginary vertical cylinder of height h and cross section A. Again, the fluid inside is in equilibrium, so the sum of the vertical forces must add up to zero. The vertical forces are those due to gravity, the pressure P_1 exerted downward on the top of the cylinder, and the pressure P_2 exerted upward on the bottom of the cylinder. Letting d be the density of the fluid, we have $P_1 A + dVg = P_2 A$. But, since $V = hA$, we have $P_1 A + dghA = P_2 A$, and

$$P_2 - P_1 = dgh \qquad\qquad (13.7)$$

(Here we have assumed that the density remains essentially constant at all depths in the cylinder. Unless h is very large this is a good approximation for most liquids, since liquids are not easily compressed.)

   Our overall conclusions about hydrostatic pressure can be summed up as follows: *The pressure in a fluid at rest varies only with the depth, in accord with Eq. (13.7), and at any given depth in a fluid the pressure exerted by the fluid in any direction is the same.*

Problem 13.2.   In Fig. 13-3, we show a rectangular tank filled with water to a depth of 20 m. The horizontal cross-sectional area of the tank is $A = 25 \text{ m}^2$, and the pressure on the top of the liquid is due to the atmosphere and is $P_A = 1.01 \times 10^5$ Pa. Find (a) the pressure at point 2, at a depth of 12 m, as shown; (b) the pressure exerted by the water on the wall of the container at point 3; (c) the pressure exerted by the water on the bottom of the container at point 4.

   Solution

   (a)   From Eq. (13.7), we have

$$P_2 = P_A + dgh = (1.01 \times 10^5 \text{ Pa}) + (1000 \text{ kg/m}^3)(9.8 \text{ m/s}^2)(12 \text{ m})$$
$$= 1.01 \times 10^5 \text{ Pa} + 1.18 \times 10^5 \text{ Pa} = 2.19 \times 10^5 \text{ Pa}$$

   (b)   Points 3 and 2 are at the same level, so $P_3 = P_2 = 2.19 \times 10^5$ Pa.

   (c) $P_4 = P_A + dgh' = (1.01 \times 10^5 \text{ Pa}) + (1000 \text{ kg/m}^3)(9.8 \text{ m/s}^2)(20 \text{ m}) = 1.01 \times 10^5 \text{ Pa} + 1.96 \times 10^5 \text{ Pa} = 2.97 \times 10^5 \text{ Pa}$.

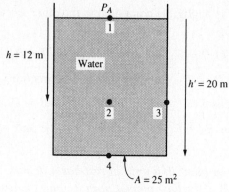

Fig. 13-3

Problem 13.3.

(a) For the situation of Problem 13.2, find the total force exerted by the water on the bottom of the tank.

(b) Do a similar calculation for the force on one of the sides of the tank, where the water covers an area $A_{side} = 50$ m^2.

Solution

(a) Since the pressure is the same everywhere along the bottom of the tank, the total downward force exerted by the water on the bottom is $F = PA = (2.97 \times 10^5$ Pa$)(25$ m$^2) = 74.3 \times 10^5$ N.

(b) To find the total force on the side of the container, one would have to take into account the fact that the pressure varies with depth. In general this type of problem would require the use of calculus. In this case, however, Eq. (13.7) tells us that the pressure varies linearly with the depth so that the average pressure P_{av} is

$$P_{av} = \frac{P_{top} + P_{bottom}}{2} = \frac{P_A + P_4}{2} = \frac{1.01 \times 10^5 \text{ Pa} + 2.97 \times 10^5 \text{ Pa}}{2} = 1.99 \times 10^5 \text{ Pa}$$

The force would then be

$$F_{side} = P_{av}A_{side} = (1.99 \times 10^5 \text{ Pa})(50 \text{ m}^2) = 99.5 \times 10^5 \text{ N}$$

Problem 13.4. It is often useful to refer to the difference between the actual, or absolute, pressure, P in a fluid, and the pressure exerted by the atmosphere P_A, which pervades the surface of the earth. This difference is called the **gauge pressure** P_g. Thus, $P_g = P - P_A$.

(a) Find the gauge pressure at points 2 and 4 of Problem 13.2.

(b) Find the gauge pressure at the top of the liquid surface in Problem 13.2.

(c) Assuming that the walls of the tank in Problem 13.3 are surrounded by air, show that the net force on the side of the tank due to all fluids, both inside and out, is equivalent to the force due to the gauge pressure of the water alone.

Solution

(a) From Problem 13.2, we have

$$P_{g2} = 1.18 \times 10^5 \text{ Pa} \qquad \text{and} \qquad P_{g4} = 1.96 \times 10^5 \text{ Pa}$$

(b) At the top surface of the water the only pressure is atmospheric, so $P_{g,\text{top}} = 0$.

(c) In Problem 13.3, we calculated the outward force on a side of the tank exerted by the water inside. In addition, however, the air outside the tank exerts an inward force on the side of magnitude $F' = P_A A_{\text{side}} = (1.01 \times 10^5 \text{ Pa})(50 \text{ m}^2) = 50.5 \times 10^5 \text{ N}$. The *net* force due to all fluids is thus

$$F_{\text{net}} = F - F' = 99.5 \times 10^5 \text{ N} - 50.5 \times 10^5 \text{ N} = 49 \times 10^5 \text{ N, outward.}$$

To see that this is equal to the force due to the gauge pressure of the water alone, we obtain the average gauge pressure: $P_{g,\text{av}} = \frac{1}{2}(0 \text{ Pa} + 1.96 \times 10^5 \text{ Pa}) = 0.98 \times 10^5 \text{ Pa}$. Then we have $F_g = P_{g,\text{av}} A_{\text{side}} = (0.98 \times 10^5 \text{ Pa})(50 \text{ m}^2) = 49 \times 10^5 \text{ pA}$, which is just F_{net} obtained above.

Problem 13.5.   In Fig. 13-4 we show an unusually shaped container filled with a liquid of density d.

(a) Show that Eq. (*13.7*) still holds for any two depths in the liquid.

(b) If $h_3 = 15$ m, and the liquid is benzene, find the pressure and the gauge pressure at the bottom of the container.

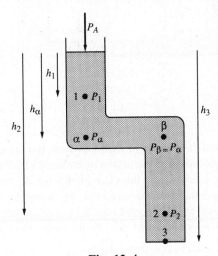

Fig. 13-4

Solution

(a) Choosing arbitrary points 1 and 2, we wish to show that $P_2 = P_1 + dg(h_2 - h_1)$. The arguments that led to Eq. (*13.7*) are valid for the points 1 and α, since they lie vertically above one another. Then $P_\alpha = P_1 + dg(h_\alpha - h_1)$. Furthermore, $P_\beta = P_\alpha$, since they are at the same horizontal level. We also know that

$$P_2 = P_\beta + dg(h_2 - h_\beta) \qquad \text{or} \qquad P_2 = P_\alpha + dg(h_2 - h_\alpha)$$

Substituting our previous expression for P_α, we get

$$P_2 = P_1 + dg(h_\alpha - h_1) + dg(h_2 - h_\alpha) = P_1 + dg(h_2 - h_1)$$

(b) From Eq. (*13.7*) we have

$$P_3 = P_A + dgh_3 = (1.01 \times 10^5 \text{ Pa}) + (8.8 \times 10^2 \text{ kg/m}^3)(9.8 \text{ m/s}^2)(15 \text{ m})$$

or $\qquad\qquad P_3 = 1.01 \times 10^5 \text{ Pa} + 1.29 \times 10^5 \text{ Pa} = 2.30 \times 10^5 \text{ Pa}$

Similarly, $P_{g3} = 1.29 \times 10^5$ Pa.

13.3 SOME PRACTICAL RESULTS

We now look at a number of practical consequences of the results we have obtained for fluids at rest. These include such rules as "water seeks its own level," Pascal's principle, and the hydraulic press, all developed in the framework of the problems presented below.

Problem 13.6. A set of Pascal vases, a number of unusually shaped containers open to the atmosphere at the top and connected by a horizontal tube at the bottom, is shown in Fig. 13-5. Show that when liquid is poured into the system, the liquid rises to the same level in all the containers. This phenomenon is described by the observation that "water seeks it own level."

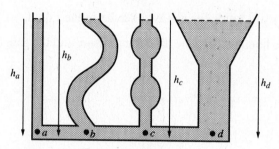

Fig. 13-5

Solution

Consider the pressures at the bottom of each container (points a, b, c, and d, respectively). From Eq. (13.7), and an obvious extension of the results of Problem 13.5(b), we see that each such pressure is just the sum of atmospheric pressure and the value of dgh for the container, where h is the depth from the top of the liquid to the bottom of the container. For example, for the second container we have $P_b = P_A + dgh_b$. For the liquid to be in equilibrium for the entire interconnected system, the pressure at each point along the bottom horizontal tube must be the same. Thus, $P_a = P_b = P_c = P_d$, which implies that $h_a = h_b = h_c = h_d$.

Problem 13.7. Show that in any container filled with a liquid, a change in pressure ΔP at any one point in the liquid leads to the same change in pressure at any other point in the liquid. This is commonly referred to as Pascal's principle.

Solution

We see from Eq. (13.7) that the pressure difference between any two points in a liquid depends only on the height difference of the two points. It follows that a change in pressure at one of the points must give rise to the same change in pressure at the other point, to ensure that the pressure difference between the two points will remain the same. This is the principle behind the hydraulic press.

Problem 13.8. Figure 13-6 shows a simple schematic setup for a **hydraulic press**. A nearly incompressible oil completely fills the container. One side of the container has a large cross-sectional area A and has a close-fitting light piston on top of the oil. The other side has a much smaller cross-sectional area a and also has a close-fitting light piston on top of the oil. By Problem 13.6, the height of the oil is the same in both sides of the container. Assume that a large weight W is placed on the large piston as shown, and that a pin holds the small piston in place.

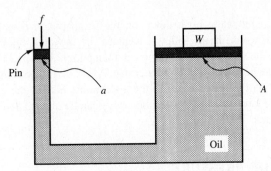

Fig. 13-6

(a) What is the change in pressure caused at every point in the fluid as a consequence of the weight W?

(b) What force f must be exerted downward on the small piston to ensure that it won't rise when the pin is removed?

(c) If $A = 150$ in² and $a = 1.0$ in², how much weight can be held up by a force $f = 25$ lb exerted downward on the small piston?

Solution

(a) The weight W is a downward force spread over an area A of the large piston. It therefore gives rise to an additional downward pressure on the oil of $\Delta p = W/A$. This additional pressure is transmitted to all points of the oil (Problem 13.7).

(b) Since there is an additional upward pressure $\Delta P = W/A$ exerted on the small piston by the oil, the total additional upward force of the oil on this piston is $(\Delta P)a = Wa/A$. Thus, the downward force f needed to counterbalance this is just $f = Wa/A$.

(c) Using the results of (b), we have

$$f = 25 \text{ lb} = W\left(\frac{1.0 \text{ in}^2}{150 \text{ in}^2}\right) = \frac{W}{150} \qquad \text{or} \qquad W = 3750 \text{ lb}$$

Problem 13.9. Referring to Problem 13.8(c) assume that a weight $W = 3750$ lb is being supported and that f is increased to slightly over 25 lb so that the small piston starts to move down.

(a) What distance h must the piston move to raise the weight 1 in?

(b) How much work is done by the force f, and where does this expended energy go?

(c) If one wants a hydraulic press that can lift a weight through a substantial distance, what change in design would make sense?

Solution

(a) Since the oil is incompressible, the volume decrease on one side must equal the volume increase on the other side. If the large piston moves up 1.0 in, the volume increase on this side is $(1.0 \text{ in})(150 \text{ in}^2) = 150$ in³. This corresponds to the volume reduction on the other side:

$$ha = 150 \text{ in}^3 \qquad \text{or} \qquad h(1.0 \text{ in}^2) = 150 \text{ in}^3 \qquad \text{or} \qquad h = 150 \text{ in}$$

(b) Work $= f h = (25 \text{ lb})(150 \text{ in})/(12 \text{ in/ft}) = 313 \text{ ft} \cdot \text{lb}$. This appears in the form of increased potential energy of the weight W: $\Delta E_p = (3750 \text{ lb})(1.0 \text{ in})/(12 \text{ in/ft}) = 313 \text{ ft} \cdot \text{lb}$.

(c) Clearly, it is not practical to push down on the small piston through huge distances. A more practical approach would be as follows. Replace the movable small piston by a valve that lets additional oil into the system. An oil pump can then pump oil from a reserve tank into the thin tube by exerting a gauge pressure slightly greater than $\Delta P = W/A$. The weight W will rise as the new oil is pumped in. When the weight rises to the appropriate height, the oil pump is shut off, and the valve is closed. To lower the weight, another valve can be opened, letting the oil slowly drain back into the reserve tank.

13.4 MEASUREMENT OF PRESSURE

A variety of instruments is available to measure pressure in a gas or a liquid. The use of liquids as the measuring device is discussed within the framework of the problems below.

Problem 13.10. The **open-tube manometer** is a simple instrument for measuring the pressure of gases or liquids in a container. The instrument (Fig. 13-7) consists of a flexible tube filled with a dense liquid, usually mercury. One end is open to the atmosphere, while the other end is exposed to a container filled with, for example, a hot gas at pressure P, so the mercury on the two sides of the tube is at different heights.

(a) Find an expression for the pressure P in terms of the density of mercury and the height difference $h_1 - h_2$.

(b) If $h_1 - h_2 = 85$ cm, find the gauge pressure of the gas.

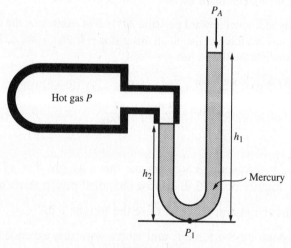

Fig. 13-7

Solution

(a) The condition for equilibrium is that the pressure at the bottom of the tube P_1 be the same whether determined from the left or right sections of the tube:

$$P + d_{Hg}gh_2 = P_A + d_{Hg}gh_1 \qquad \text{or} \qquad P = P_A + d_{Hg}g(h_1 - h_2)$$

(b) From (a),

$$P = P_A + (13.6 \times 10^3 \text{ kg/m}^3)(9.8 \text{ m/s}^2)(0.85 \text{ m}) = P_A + 113 \times 10^3 \text{ Pa}$$

The gauge pressure is just $P - P_A = 113 \times 10^3$ Pa.

Problem 13.11.   Referring to Problem 13.10, if the gas in the container cooled off and the pressure P started to drop, the mercury would start to rise in the left side of the tube. To stop this from happening one lowers the right side in such a way as to keep the height of the column of mercury on the left side fixed.

(a)   Assuming the gauge pressure of the gas drops to half of its value from Problem 13.10, find the new value of $h_1 - h_2$.

(b)   If the gas is allowed to cool further, it is found that the new equilibrium position is such that $h_1 < h_2$. What is the significance of that fact?

   Solution

   (a)   From Problem 13.10(b), the new gauge pressure is

$$P - P_A = 56.5 \times 10^3 \text{ Pa} = (13.6 \times 10^3 \text{ kg/m}^3)(9.8 \text{ m/s}^2)(h_1 - h_2) \quad \text{or} \quad h_1 - h_2 = 0.424 \text{ m}$$

   (b)   This indicates that $P - P_A$ is negative, so P is less than atmospheric pressure.

Problem 13.12.   A pressure gauge that measures the pressure of the atmosphere itself is called a **barometer**. A simple mercury barometer is shown in Fig. 13-8. A tall cylindrical tube open on one end is first filled with mercury. It is then carefully inverted into an open container of mercury and is supported by a stand with a clamp. The mercury starts to come out of the tube but comes to equilibrium at some height h above the mercury surface in the container. The space above the mercury is a near vacuum, filled only with low-pressure, mercury vapor.

(a)   Find the atmospheric pressure P_A in terms of the height h.

(b)   Determine the height h when the atmospheric pressure P_A has its normal value of 1.013×10^5 Pa.

   Solution

   (a)   The pressure at the surface level of the mercury in the container must have the same value as the pressure at that level in the tube. The value of the pressure at that level in the tube is just $d_{Hg}gh$, while in the container it is just atmospheric pressure P_A. Thus, $P_A = d_{Hg}gh$.

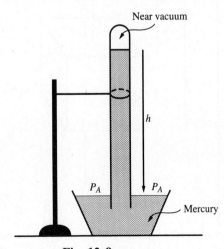

Fig. 13-8

(b)   From (a),

$$1.013 \times 10^5 \text{ Pa} = (13.6 \times 10^3 \text{ kg/m}^3)(9.8 \text{ m/s}^2)h \qquad \text{or} \qquad h = 0.760 \text{ m}$$

More commonly, the height is given in cm: $h = 76.0$ cm. It is quite common to actually quote the pressure in terms of the height of the supported column of mercury. Thus, the statement that atmospheric pressure is 75.5 cm of mercury means that the atmosphere supports a column of mercury 75.5 cm high.

13.5   ARCHIMEDES' PRINCIPLE

Another significant result of hydrostatics is Archimedes' principle, which will be discussed within the context of the following problems.

Problem 13.13.   A cubical block of iron of side $a = 15$ cm is suspended by a cord in a container of water, as shown in Fig. 13-9.

(a)   Show that the net upward force on the block due to the water has a magnitude equal to the weight of an amount of water that would occupy the volume of the block. (This volume is the volume of the liquid displaced by the block, also known as the *displaced* volume, and this net upward force is known as the *buoyant* force B due to the liquid. The fact that the buoyant force equals the weight of the displaced liquid is called **Archimedes' principle**: the law of buoyancy.)

(b)   Find the value of the buoyant force exerted on the block by the water.

(c)   Find the tension in the cord when the system is in equilibrium.

Solution

(a)   The vertical forces exerted on the block by the water are the forces F_1 and F_2, on the top and bottom faces due to the corresponding pressures P_1 and P_2. The net upward force is then

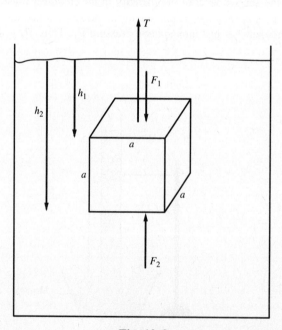

Fig. 13-9

$B = F_2 - F_1 = P_2a^2 - P_1a^2 = (P_2 - P_1)a^2$. But, from Eq. (13.7), $P_2 - P_1 = dga$, where d is the density of water, so $F_2 - F_1 = (dga)a^2 = dga^3$, which is the required result.

(b) $B = (1000 \text{ kg/m}^3)(9.8 \text{ m/s}^2)(0.15 \text{ m})^3 = 33.1 \text{ N}$.

(c)   If W is the weight of the block, then $T + B = W$. $W = d_1ga^3 = (7.86 \times 10^3 \text{ kg/m}^3)(9.8 \text{ m/s}^2)$
       $\times (0.15 \text{ m})^3 = 260 \text{ N}$. Then

$$T = W - B = 260 \text{ N} - 33 \text{ N} = 227 \text{ N}$$

Problem 13.14.

(a)   Show that Archimedes' principle holds for an arbitrarily shaped object submerged in an arbitrary fluid.

(b)   Find the statement of Archimedes' principle for a floating object.

Solution

(a)   The situation is shown in Fig. 13-10(a). At first glance it would seem almost impossible to get the desired result, since unlike the cube of Problem 13.13, the pressure acts at a variety of different angles, and has a variety of magnitudes, over the surface of the object. To get the buoyant force one would need to add up all the vertical components of the myriad different forces acting on all the infinitesimal surface elements of the object, a procedure that requires the calculus. Still, there is a much simpler way to obtain the result, one which Archimedes himself used many centuries before the invention of the calculus.

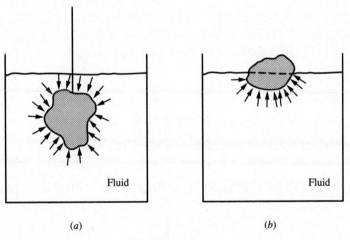

(a)   (b)

Fig. 13-10

   A hint as to the approach to take comes from our realization that there is no net horizontal force exerted by a liquid on an object that is submerged. This can be understood as follows. Suppose we replace the object by an identical volume of the same type liquid as is found in the container. We consider an imaginary boundary in the exact shape of the object separating this liquid from the rest of the liquid of the container. The old and new liquid together constitute a uniform liquid at rest in the container, and is therefore in equilibrium. The horizontal forces due to the liquid outside the boundary acting on the liquid inside the boundary must therefore add up to zero. Since the liquid outside the boundary is exactly the same as it was when the object was there, the force it exerts is unchanged, and the horizontal force on the object must have been zero also.

This same reasoning works for the vertical forces. For the liquid inside the boundary to be in equilibrium, the vertical forces due to the liquid outside must just balance the weight of the liquid inside. Again, these forces are unchanged if the object itself were inside the boundary, so we have our result: the net buoyant force of the liquid on the object is upward and equals the weight of the amount of liquid that would fill the space of the object, in other words, the amount of liquid displaced by the object. This is Archimedes' Principle.

(b)   Figure 13-10(b) depicts a floating object. We can use the same reasoning as before to get the expression for the buoyant force. Now, however, the force exerted by the liquid is due only to the pressure at points below the surface. Consider the object replaced by an amount of liquid which fills the space occupied by the part of the object which was submerged, i.e., the part of the object below the dashed line along the surface of the liquid, as shown. Again, we assume an imaginary boundary in the shape of the submerged portion of the object.

Since the old and new liquid together constitute a uniform liquid with a horizontal surface boundary at the top, it is a liquid in equilibrium. Let us ignore the effects of atmospheric pressure above the liquid surface for the moment. Then, the force exerted on the "new" liquid inside the boundary by the "old" liquid outside must just balance the weight of the liquid inside. This is just the weight of liquid that displaces the submerged part of the object. Since the outside liquid is exactly the same whether the "new" liquid or the object is within the boundary, it must exert the same force on each. Thus, the buoyant force on the object is still the weight of liquid displaced by the object. To include the effects of atmospheric pressure, we note that it pushes down on the object from above and pushes up on the object (through the increased pressure of the liquid) from below. These two effects can be shown to cancel, as they did in the case of the wall in Problem 13.4(c), so that Archimedes' principle holds also for a floating object.

Problem 13.15.   An iron ball of mass $M = 10$ kg is submerged in a container of liquid X by means of a cord as shown in Fig. 13-11. The tension T in the cord is found to be 65 N. Find (a) the buoyant force B acting on the ball; (b) the density of the liquid d_X.

Solution

(a)   For equilibrium, $T + B = W$. The weight of the ball $W = Mg = 98$ N. Therefore,

$$B = W - T = 98 \text{ N} - 65 \text{ N} = 33 \text{ N}$$

(b) $B = d_X g V$, where V is the volume of the iron ball. Since we know B and g, we could obtain d_X if we knew V. To obtain V, we use the density of iron d_I from Table 13.1, and we note that $d_I V = M$:

$$(7.86 \times 10^3 \text{ kg/m}^3)V = 10 \text{ kg} \qquad \text{or} \qquad V = 0.00127 \text{ m}^3$$

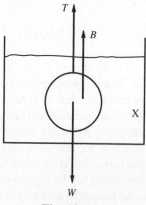

Fig. 13-11

Then, substituting in $B = d_X g V$, we get

$$33 \text{ N} = d_X (9.8 \text{ m/s}^2)(0.00127 \text{ m}^3) \quad \text{or} \quad d_X = 2.65 \times 10^3 \text{ kg/m}^3$$

Problem 13.16. The iron ball of Problem 13.15 is removed from liquid X and placed in a container of mercury, where it is found to float. What fraction of the volume of the ball is submerged?

Solution

For floating, the buoyant force (weight of the displaced liquid) just balances the weight of the ball:

$$d_I g V = d_{Hg} g V_s$$

where V and V_s are the total volume of the ball and the volume submerged in the mercury, respectively. Hence, the fraction submerged is

$$\frac{V_s}{V} = \frac{d_I}{d_{Hg}} = \frac{7.86}{13.6} = 0.578$$

Problem 13.17. A block of wood of mass 30 kg floats in seawater of density $d_{sw} = 1025 \text{ kg/m}^3$. When a child of mass 40 kg stands on the block, the block just barely floats with its top surface level with the water. Find (a) the volume V, and (b) the density d_{wd}, of the wood.

Solution

(a) From equilibrium considerations we have

$$B = W_{wd} + W_{ch} = (30 \text{ kg} + 40 \text{ kg})(9.8 \text{ m/s}^2) \quad \text{or} \quad B = 686 \text{ N}$$

We also know that

$$B = d_{sw} g V \Rightarrow 686 \text{ N} = (1025 \text{ kg/m}^3)(9.8 \text{ m/s}^2)V \quad \text{or} \quad V = 0.0683 \text{ m}^3$$

(b) $$d_{wd} = \frac{M_{wd}}{V} = \frac{30 \text{ kg}}{0.0683 \text{ m}^3} = 439 \text{ kg/m}^3$$

Problem 13.18. A beaker filled with water rests on a scale that reads $F = 50.0$ N. Next, an aluminum block of volume $V = 800 \text{ cm}^3$ is suspended from a cord in the water, as shown in Fig. 13-12. Find (a) the weight of the aluminum and the buoyant force exerted on it by the water; (b) the tension T in the cord; (c) the new reading F' of the scale.

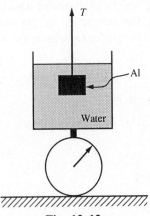

Fig. 13-12

Solution

(a) $W_{Al} = d_{Al}gV = (2.70 \times 10^3 \text{ kg/m}^3)(9.8 \text{ m/s}^2)(800 \times 10^{-6} \text{ m}^3) = 21.2 \text{ N}$

$B = d_wgV = (1000 \text{ kg/m}^3)(9.8 \text{ m/s}^2)(800 \times 10^{-6} \text{ m}^3) = 7.84 \text{ N}$

(b) From equilibrium of the aluminum, $T + B = W_{Al}$, so that

$$T = 21.2 \text{ N} - 7.8 \text{ N} = 13.4 \text{ N}$$

(c) By Newton's third law, the aluminum exerts a downward force of magnitude B on the liquid. The scale must balance the weight of the beaker and water, which was given to be 50.0 N, plus the downward reaction force to the buoyant force $B = 7.8$ N. The result is that the scale reads $F' = 57.8$ N.

Problem 13.19. A rectangular block of ice of cross-sectional area A and depth h floats at the interface of oil and water as shown in Fig. 13-13. Find the fraction of the ice that is in the water. (Assume $d_{oil} = 800 \text{ kg/m}^3$, and see Table 13.1 for d_{ice} and d_{water}.)

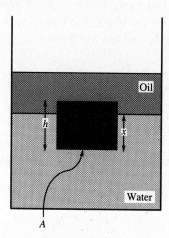

Fig. 13-13

Solution

The buoyant force is just the weight of displaced liquid, which is now a combination of oil and water. If x is the depth that the ice sinks in the water we have that the buoyant force $B = d_{water}gAx + d_{oil}gA(h - x)$. This force must balance the weight of the ice $W_{ice} = d_{ice}gAh$. Dividing by gA, we get

$$d_{ice}h = d_{water}x + d_{oil}(h - x)$$

Simplifying and then substituting, we get

$$d_{ice} = d_{oil} + (d_{water} - d_{oil})\frac{x}{h} \quad \text{or} \quad 917 = 800 + 200\frac{x}{h} \quad \text{or} \quad \frac{x}{h} = 0.585 = \text{fraction in water}$$

13.6 HYDROSTATICS OF GASES

As pointed out at the beginning of the chapter, the pressure due to a gas is a consequence of the bombardment of the surfaces of a confining container by the free-moving gas molecules. On the other hand, the actual value of the pressure of the atmosphere near the earth's surface is a consequence of the weight of the ocean of air above the surface. Thus the pressure near the ground is higher than that a thousand feet up in much the same way that the pressure of water at the bottom of a tank is greater than that near the top of the tank. The pressure difference of the air, however, cannot be expressed in the simple form $P_2 - P_1 = d_{air}gh$ because the density of a gas changes significantly with increasing pressure, so d_{air} is not even approximately constant over the height of the atmosphere. Nonetheless, although the formula is more complicated, the pressure increases in a definite way as one gets closer and closer to ground level, and this increase in pressure is accompanied by a greater density of air. The pressure of the atmosphere at ground level is exerted on all surfaces and is added to the hydrostatic pressure of liquids that are in contact with it.

The pressure exerted by the air at any given location is directly due to the bombardment of molecules and not directly due to the push of the air from above. This can be seen by considering an empty paper cup sitting on a table. If a steel plate is put across the top of the cup, there is no contact between the air above the cup and the air in the cup. Yet, the pressure of the air in the cup remains the same (otherwise the sides of the cup would get crushed in by the pressure of the air outside).

Problem 13.20.

(a) Find an expression for the force F exerted by the pressure of the atmosphere on the curved surface of a solid hemispherical object of radius R, as shown in Fig. 13-14(a).

(b) If $R = 2.0$ in, find the value of the force F. ($P_A = 14.7$ lb/in^2.)

(c) Two hollow hemispheres of radius $R = 10.0$ cm are brought together and make an airtight seal. The air inside is pumped out through a valve so that the pressure inside drops to zero. How large a force must be applied to each hemisphere to pull them apart?

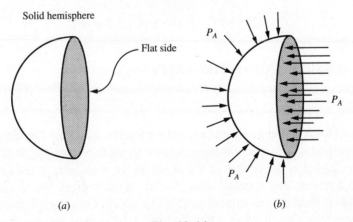

(a)   (b)

Fig. 13-14

Solution

(a) The pressure at any point on the hemisphere pushes perpendicular to the surface, as shown in Fig. 13-14(b). Thus, although the magnitude of the pressure is constant and equal to P_A, the net force due to that pressure is the resultant of myriad forces on the surface pointing in different directions. We can nonetheless obtain this resultant force simply by the following reasoning. The overall force of the atmosphere on the hemisphere must be zero, since otherwise the hemisphere would be accelerated, and we know this does not happen. Therefore, the net force on the curved surface must exactly balance the net force on the flat surface. This latter force is $P_A(\pi R^2)$ along the symmetry axis of the hemisphere. The force on the curved portion must therefore have the same magnitude, but point in the opposite direction.

(b) $F = (14.7 \text{ lb/in}^2)(3.14)(2.0 \text{ in})^2 = 185$ lb.

(c)   The force due to atmospheric pressure pressing in on each half is

$$F = P_A(\pi R^2) = (1.013 \times 10^5 \text{ Pa})(3.14)(0.10 \text{ m})^2 = 3.180 \text{ N}$$

This is the force that must be applied to pull the two halves apart.

Just as a liquid can exert a buoyant force, so can the air in the atmosphere. Although the buoyant force of the air is generally small (because the density of air is low), for hot-air balloons and blimps (dirigibles), which have large volume, the buoyant force of the air is the basis for their operation.

Problem 13.21.   A blimp has a frame and cargo that together weigh 10,000 N. Assume that the blimp is filled with helium at room temperature. What volume V must the blimp have to just float in the air near the earth's surface?

Solution

The blimp and its contents are in equilibrium when it floats, so the buoyant force B equals the total weight of the blimp. Assuming that almost the entire volume V of the blimp is taken up by the helium, we have

$$d_{\text{He}}gV + 10{,}000 \text{ N} = d_{\text{air}}gV \qquad \text{or} \qquad V = \frac{10{,}000 \text{ N}}{d_{\text{air}}g - d_{\text{He}}g}$$

Substituting in the densities we get

$$V = \frac{10{,}000 \text{ N}}{(1.29 \text{ kg/m}^3 - 0.18 \text{ kg/m}^3)(9.8 \text{ m/s}^2)} = 919 \text{ m}^3$$

13.7   SURFACE TENSION AND CAPILLARITY

Surface Tension

A droplet of water has a spherical shape because the surface of a liquid tends to pull itself in as if it were an elastic membrane. This phenomenon, known as **surface tension**, is ultimately caused by the pull of the molecules *below* the surface of the liquid on the molecules *at* the surface. This tends to pull the surface into a smooth and compact layer. Surface tension gives rise to such phenomena as a steel needle being able to float on a water surface [Fig. 13-15(a)], even though the density of the metal object is much greater than that of water. Other examples of surface tension are shown in Fig. 13-15(b) and (c). The surface tension γ is defined as the force per unit length exerted by a liquid surface on an object, along its boundary of contact with the object. This force is parallel to the liquid surface and perpendicular to the boundary line of contact. For a straight boundary of length L and a total force F we have $\gamma = F/L$. In Fig. 13-15(b) we show a soap membrane supporting a slide wire of weight W and length b. The surface tension pulls perpendicular to the wire and along the membrane. Because the soap membrane has two surfaces, the total upward force is $F = 2b\gamma$. Since the wire is in equilibrium, $W = F$, and so $\gamma = W/2b$.

Unlike an actual elastic membrane, the surface tension does not increase as the surface is stretched. Thus, if the soap membrane of Fig. 13-15(b) were stretched by pulling the wire down to a

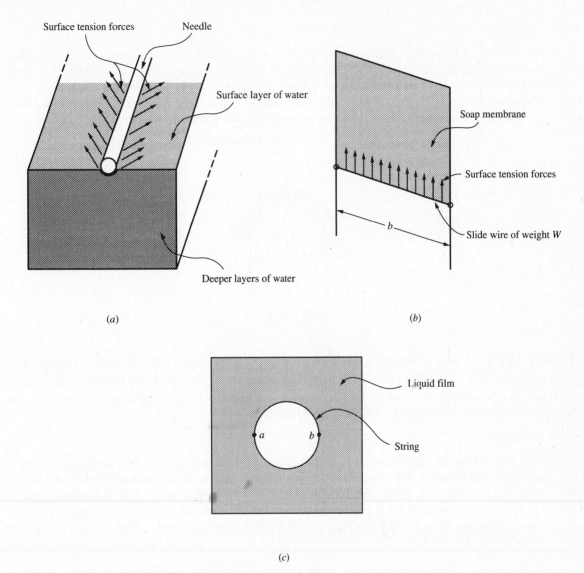

Fig. 13-15

lower position, the wire would remain in equilibrium in the new position upon release, since γ, and hence F, will not have changed. The value of the surface tension does not change because more molecules enter the surface from the interior as the membrane is stretched, and the intermolecular spacings stay the same. Surface tension does change when the liquid temperature or pressure changes, or when chemical substances are brought into contact with the surface.

Problem 13.22. In Fig. 13-15(c) a light string is pulled into a tight circular shape of radius $r = 3.0$ cm by the surface tension of a liquid film that extends between the string and the rectangular frame. If the surface tension of the film is $\gamma = 0.02$ N/m, find the tension in the cord. [*Hint*: It can be shown that the net force due to the film (which has two sides) pulling on the upper half of the string between points a and b is just $4r\gamma$ in the upward direction.]

Solution

In Fig. 13-16 we show half the string between points a and b. The upper arrows depict the surface tension pulling perpendicular to the string all around the string from a to b. From the hint we know that the net effect of the surface tension is an upward force of magnitude $4r\gamma$. The two downward arrows depict the tension in the string, which is exerted by the lower half of the string on the upper half at points a and b. Since the upper half of the string is in equilibrium, and its weight can be neglected, we have

$$4r\gamma = 2T \qquad \text{or} \qquad T = 2r\gamma = 2(0.030 \text{ m})(0.02 \text{ N/m}) = 0.0012 \text{ N}$$

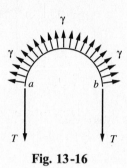

Fig. 13-16

Problem 13.23. A soap bubble of radius 0.60 cm filled with air has a surface tension in its inner and outer surfaces of $\gamma = 0.04$ N/m. Find the gauge pressure P_g of the air in the bubble. [*Hint*: From Problem 13.20(a), the net force on a hemisphere of radius r due to a uniform pressure P is $\pi r^2 P$ in the direction along the symmetry axis of the hemisphere.]

Solution

We consider the upper hemisphere of the bubble, as shown in Fig. 13-17. The surface tension pulls downward all around the rim with a force per unit length γ. Then the total downward force is $2\pi r\gamma$ due to each film surface (the inside and the outside). The total is thus $4\pi r\gamma$. This downward force is counterbalanced by the force due to the pressure of the air inside the bubble less the force due to the atmospheric pressure outside. From the hint, this is just an upward force of $\pi r^2(P - P_A) = \pi r^2 P_g$. For equilibrium we must have

$$4\pi r\gamma = \pi r^2 P_g \qquad \text{or} \qquad P_g = \frac{4\gamma}{r} = \frac{4(40 \times 10^{-3} \text{ N/m})}{0.60 \times 10^{-2} \text{ m}} = 26.7 \text{ Pa}$$

Capillarity

When a liquid is in contact with a surface of a container, there is a competition between the force of attraction of the molecules of the container on the molecules of the liquid (adhesion) and the force

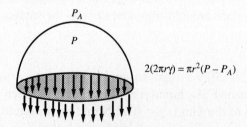

$$2(2\pi r\gamma) = \pi r^2(P - P_A)$$

Fig. 13-17

of attraction of the molecules of the liquid on each other (cohesion). If the adhesion forces are greater than the cohesion forces, the liquid surface will bend upward at the point of contact because of the liquid surface being pulled toward the wall of the container. This is illustrated in Fig. 13-18(a) for the case of water in a glass tube. The adhesive forces dominate in this case, and the water surface makes an angle θ with the walls of the container at the point of contact. The angle θ, called the contact angle, has an important effect when the liquid is in a very thin tube of radius r. Since the surface tension of the liquid is parallel to the surface of the liquid, by Newton's third law the glass exerts an upward force on the liquid all around the rim of the tube given by $F = 2\pi r \gamma \cos \theta$. This pulls the liquid up above its normal height in the tube, until the weight of the excess height h of liquid just balances the surface tension force F. If d is the density of the liquid, we have for the weight $w = dg\pi r^2 h$. Equating F and w, we get

$$h = \frac{2\gamma \cos \theta}{dgr} \qquad (13.8)$$

As can be seen, the smaller the radius r, the greater the capillary height h. Thus, for very thin tubes, the liquid can rise, in apparent defiance of gravity, to substantial heights, as shown in Fig. 13-18(b).

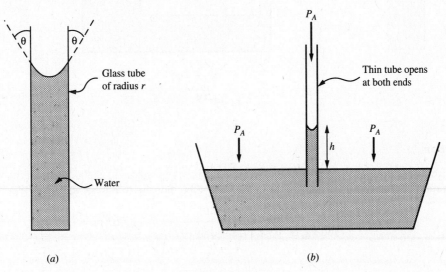

(a)　　　　　　　　　　(b)

Fig. 13-18

Blood flow in small blood vessels and flow of nutrients in plants are examples of this phenomenon in nature. The general name for the elevation or depression of a liquid surface under such conditions is **capillarity**, or **capillary action**.

Problem 13.24. Assume that in the Pascal vases of Fig. 13-5, the straight tube is very thin, with radius $r = 2.0$ mm. Assuming $\gamma = 0.07$ N/m and a contact angle of 20°, how high above the normal level will the water rise in this tube?

Solution

Calling the excess height Δh, from Eq. (13.8) we have

$$\Delta h = \frac{2(0.07 \text{ N/m}) \cos 20°}{(1000 \text{ kg/m}^3)(9.8 \text{ m/s}^2)(0.0020 \text{ m})} = 0.0067 \text{ m} = 0.67 \text{ cm}$$

Problem 13.25. In the case of mercury in a glass tube, the cohesive forces are greater than the adhesive forces, so the mercury surface is pulled down, as shown in Fig. 13-19(*a*). The contact angle in this case is obtuse, and the surface tension forces pull down on the liquid, making it drop below the normal level in the tube. The U-shaped container shown in Fig. 13-19(*b*) is filled with mercury. Find the height difference of the mercury in the two vertical tubes, if $\gamma_{Hg} = 0.545$ N/m and contact angle $\theta = 140°$.

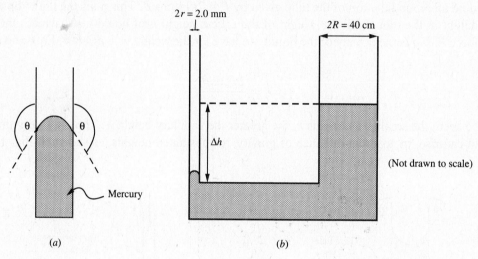

Fig. 13-19

Solution

Recalling from Eq. (*13.8*) that the capillary height varies inversely as the radius of the tube, we can ignore any change from normal height in the wide tube. For the thin tube, (*13.8*) yields

$$\Delta h = \frac{2(0.545 \text{ N/m}) \cos 140°}{(1360 \text{ kg/m}^3)(9.8 \text{ m/s}^2)(0.0010 \text{ m})} = -0.063 \text{ m} = -6.3 \text{ cm}$$

Problems for Review and Mind Stretching

Problem 13.26. A bent tube containing oil (of sp gr 0.750) and water is shown in Fig. 13-20. The tube cross sections are wide enough so that capillary action is negligible. The heights h_1 and h_2 are the height of the water and oil, respectively, above the oil-water interface. If $h_2 = 15$ cm, find the height difference Δh between the liquid in the two sides of the tube.

Solution

Since the pressure must be the same on both sides at the level of the interface, we have $P_A + d_w g h_1 = P_A + d_o g h_2$. Simplifying, we get $d_w h_1 = d_o h_2$ or

$$h_1 = \frac{d_o}{d_w} h_2 = (0.75)(15 \text{ cm}) = 11.3 \text{ cm} \qquad \text{and} \qquad \Delta h = h_2 - h_1 = 3.7 \text{ cm}$$

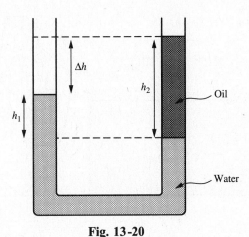

Fig. 13-20

Problem 13.27. Figure 13-21(a) depicts a dam of length $L = 100$ ft holding back the waters of a lake (with steep side walls) that is 60 ft deep.

(a) Find the force exerted by the water alone on the dam.

(b) If the dam were constructed so that its base just rests on the ground, with a coefficient of static friction between dam and ground of $\mu_s = 0.50$, what minimum weight W_{min} must the dam have if it is not to slip?

(c) Instead of a lake, assume the dam is holding back water filling a 3.0-in-wide ditch running the whole length of the dam, as shown in Fig. 13-21(b). Assume the water fills the ditch to a height of 60 ft. How would the answers to parts (a) and (b) change?

Solution

(a) The force of the water alone on the dam is due to the gauge pressure of the water, P_g. (This ignores the added effect of the atmospheric pressure on the water.) To find this force, we multiply the average pressure of the water on the dam by the area over which it acts: $F = P_{g,av}A$. Here, $P_{g,av} = \frac{1}{2}(0 + dgh)$, so

$$F = \frac{(62.5 \text{ lb/ft}^3)(60 \text{ ft})}{2}(60 \text{ ft})(100 \text{ ft}) = 11,250,000 \text{ lb}$$

(b) The net horizontal force due to the air and water on the dam is just the force of the water alone, as calculated in part (a). This is because the effect of the atmosphere pushing on the curved portion of the dam just balances the added force due to the pressure of the atmosphere on the water [see, e.g., Problem 13.4(c)]. The maximum static frictional force is just $f_s = \mu_s N$. Since $N = W$, we have $f_s = \mu_s W$. For equilibrium we must have $\mu_s W_{min} = F$, or

$$W_{min} = \frac{F}{\mu_s} = \frac{11,250,000 \text{ lb}}{0.5} = 22,500,000 \text{ lb} = 11,250 \text{ tons}.$$

(c) Since the pressure of the water depends only on depth, the answers to parts (a) and (b) are the same! The width of the column of water does not matter.

Problem 13.28. A hydraulic lift is to raise an automobile weighing $W = 12,000$ N. The radius of the lifting tube is $R = 30$ cm.

(a) What increase in pressure is necessary to lift the auto?

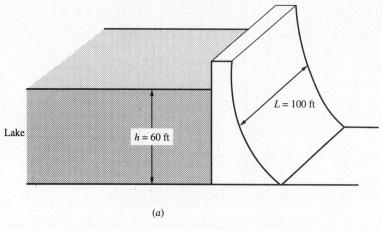

(a)

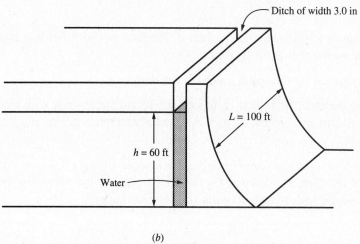

(b)

Fig. 13-21

(b)   If the maximum force that can be generated on the thin tube side of the lift is $F = 80$ N, what is the maximum radius r_{max} that the thin tube can have to lift the auto?

Solution

(a) $$\Delta P = \frac{W}{A} = \frac{W}{\pi R^2} = \frac{12{,}000 \text{ N}}{(3.14)(0.30 \text{ m})^2} = 42{,}500 \text{ N/m}^2$$

(b) $F/a_{max} = \Delta P \Rightarrow F = \Delta Pa_{max} \Rightarrow 80 \text{ N} = (42{,}500 \text{ N/m}^2)(3.14)r_{max}^2 \Rightarrow r_{max} = 0.0245 \text{ m}.$

Problem 13.29.   A block of wood floats in water with two-thirds of its volume V submerged in water. What fraction of its volume is submerged when it floats in benzene?

Solution

From Table 13.1, $d_B = 880$ kg/m^3, while for water $d_w = 1000$ kg/m^3. Whether floating in water or benzene, the buoyant force just balances the weight of the block W. Thus, $W = d_w g V_w = d_B g V_B$, where V_w and V_B are the displaced (submerged) volumes in the water and benzene, respectively. From this we get $d_B V_B = d_w V_w$, and dividing both sides by the volume of the block:

$$d_B \frac{V_B}{V} = d_w \frac{V_w}{V} \qquad \text{or} \qquad \frac{V_B}{V} = \left(\frac{d_w}{d_B}\right)\left(\frac{V_w}{V}\right) = \left(\frac{1.0}{0.880}\right)\left(\frac{2}{3}\right) = 0.758$$

Problem 13.30.　Two soap bubbles are formed from the same soap mixture, one having twice the radius of the other. What is the ratio of the gauge pressures of the air inside the two bubbles?

Solution

Assume the smaller and larger radii are r and R, respectively. As in Problem 13.23, we have $\pi r^2 P_{g1} = 4\pi r\gamma$, or

$$P_{g1} = \frac{4\gamma}{r}$$

Similarly, we have $\pi R^2 P_{g2} = 4\pi R\gamma$, or

$$P_{g2} = \frac{4\gamma}{R}$$

Taking the ratio P_{g1}/P_{g2} we get $R/r = 2.0$.

Supplementary Problems

Problem 13.31.　The specific gravity of mercury is 13.6. Find (a) the volume of 16 kg of mercury; (b) the weight density of mercury, in lb/ft³.

　　　Ans.　(a) 11.8×10^{-4} m³; (b) 850 lb/ft³

Problem 13.32.

(a) Find the absolute pressure at the bottom of a tall cylinder filled with a column of water 3.00 m high. Assume the top of the cylinder is open to the atmosphere, with $P_A = 1.013 \times 10^5$ Pa.

(b) How high a column of benzene must be poured in on top of the water to double the gauge pressure at the bottom of the cylinder?

　　　Ans.　(a) 1.307×10^5 Pa; (b) 3.41 m

Problem 13.33.　A light tank in the shape shown in Fig. 13-22 is filled with water to a height of 40 cm. The area of the bottom of the tank is 100 cm², and the cross-sectional area of the narrow neck is 4.0 cm². The tank rests on a scale.

(a) What is the reading of the scale?

(b) What is the total downward force on the bottom of the tank due to the water alone? (Neglect the effect of the atmosphere above the water.)

　　　Ans.　(a) 20.4 N; (b) 39.2 N

Prlblem 13.34.　Referring to Problem 13.33, shouldn't the answers to parts (a) and (b) be the same, and if not, why?

　　　Ans.　No. The water also exerts an upward force on the upper surface of the tank of area A'. The difference between the force on the bottom and this force is the net force of the water on the tank and must equal the weight of the water.

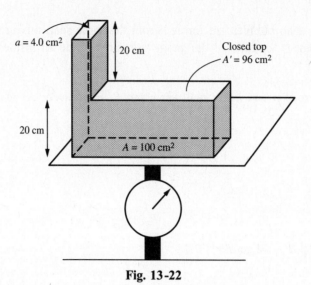

Fig. 13-22

Problem 13.35.   If the barometer of Fig. 13-8 used water instead of mercury, how high would the column of water have to be?

   Ans.   10.3 m

Problem 13.36.

(*a*)   What force, in pounds, is exerted by atmospheric pressure on the outside surface of an 8.0- by 4.0-ft door of a house?

(*b*)   Why doesn't the door cave in?

   Ans.   (*a*) 67,700 lb; (*b*) because an equal and opposite force is exerted due to air pressure on the other side of the door

Problem 13.37.   Assume that in the hydraulic press of Fig. 13-6, the diameters of the two vertical tubes are 2.0 in and 2.0 ft, respectively. How large a mass M, in kilograms, resting on the large piston can be lifted by a force $f = 35,000$ dyn.

   Ans.   5.14 kg

Problem 13.38.   If a stone feels exactly (*a*) one-half, (*b*) three-fourths as heavy when held under water as when in air, find its density.

   Ans.   (*a*) 2000 kg/m^3; (*b*) 4000 kg/m^3

Problem 13.39.   A nugget weighing 9.355 N is hung from the end of a sensitive balance and dipped until completely submerged in water contained in a cylinder of cross-sectional area 75 cm^2. The water is observed to rise in the cylinder, and the balance reads 8.870 N.

(*a*)   Find the density of the nugget and its likely composition.

(*b*)   How high does the water rise in the cylinder?

   Ans.   (*a*) 19,300 kg/m^3, pure gold; (*b*) 0.660 cm

Problem 13.40. A plank of wood, of area $A = 2000$ cm^2 and thickness 6.0 cm floats freely on seawater ($d_{sw} = 1024$ kg/m^3), with 4.0 cm submerged. When an aluminum weight is hung from a cord below the center of the plank, the plank is observed to just float with its top surface even with water.

(a)   What is the density of the wood?

(b)   What is the volume of the aluminum?

   Ans.   (a) 683 kg/m^3; (b) 0.00244 m^3

Problem 13.41. A ball (sp gr 0.35) is submerged in freshwater to a depth of 2.0 m and released.

(a)   Find the acceleration of the ball, ignoring viscous forces.

(b)   How fast will the ball be moving as it reaches the surface?

   Ans.   (a) 18.2 m/s^2; (b) 8.5 m/s

Problem 13.42. A large spherical reflecting ball of volume 4.0 m^3 and mass 50 kg is suspended from a light cable in a disco ballroom.

(a)   What is the buoyant force on the ball due to the air?

(b)   What is the tension in the cable?

   Ans.   (a) 50.6 N; (b) 439 N

Problem 13.43. A hot-air balloon consists of a large airtight canvas bag attached by ropes to a hanging gondola with passengers and equipment. The weight of all the above items is 2700 N. Assuming that the volume inside the bag is 400 m^3, find the density of the heated air inside the bag necessary for the balloon to float in equilibrium. Ignore the volume of the gondola and its contents.

   Ans.   0.60 kg/m^3

Problem 13.44. Suppose the needle of Fig. 13-15(a) is of steel, with a length of 30 mm and a radius of 0.20 mm. The surface tension of water is 0.07 N/m. Find (a) the weight of the pin; (b) the total vertical component of force that must be exerted by the surface tension on each side of the needle to keep it in equilibrium; (c) the angle this force makes with the vertical. (Assume buoyancy effects can be ignored.)

   Ans.   (a) 290 μN; (b) 145 μN; (c) 4.0°

Problem 13.45. A glass tube of inner radius 0.30 mm is dipped into a container of water. How high does the water rise in the tube assuming that $\gamma = 0.07$ N/m and the contact angle is 0°?

   Ans.   48 mm

Problem 13.46. A drop of water of radius 2.0 mm has the expected spherical shape because of surface tension ($\gamma = 0.07$ N/m). Evaluate the gauge pressure of the water inside the drop. [*Hint*: In a droplet, unlike a bubble, only one liquid surface exists.]

   Ans.   70 Pa

Chapter 14

Fluids in Motion (Hydrodynamics)

14.1 THE NATURE OF FLUID MOTION

In the last chapter we discussed the properties of fluids at rest. Their central feature was the lack of shear forces between layers of the fluid and between the fluid and the boundary surfaces. Partly as a consequence of that fact it was found that the pressure in a container of fluid varies only with the vertical depth of the fluid.

In this chapter we will discuss the properties of fluids in motion. In general, there are shear forces between layers of fluid that move past each other and between the moving fluid and the boundary surfaces. This property of fluids is called **viscosity**, and the shear forces, which are frictional in nature, are called **viscous forces**.

For some fluids, the viscous forces can be quite small, especially when they are moving slowly. In such cases one can ignore viscosity. Such a fluid is known as a **nonviscous fluid**.

We will first consider the properties of nonviscous fluid motion, and then the case of viscosity. Before doing either, however, we discuss the nature of fluid motion itself.

Fluids in motion occur in our everyday experience: the water moving through the pipes of a house; hot air moving through the heating ducts of a building; water flowing slowly in a quiet river; water cascading through rapids and over waterfalls; air rushing past an airplane wing, as seen in the frame of reference of the airplane; and winds moving clouds through the sky. Much fluid motion is quite complex, with the flow pattern at any given point changing over time. Such motion is called **turbulent** flow. In many cases, however, the flow pattern at any point stays the same from moment to moment. Such motion is called **steady-state** or just **steady** flow; it is also called **laminar** flow.

Consider a particle of water moving in a stream. The path it takes is called the **flow line** of the particle. In steady flow, any particle that is located on the flow line of a previous particle will repeat the motion of that particle. This means that all particles on the flow line not only follow the same path but speed up and slow down in precisely the same way from point to point along the path. The motion of a fluid in steady flow thus appears smooth and regular.

Another way of characterizing a fluid flow is not to look at the motion of a single particle, but instead look at the flow pattern of the entire fluid at a given instant. By freezing the motion at a given instant, while retaining knowledge of the velocities of all the particles at that instant, one could do the following tracing. Start with any particle, and see in which direction its velocity points. Draw an imaginary infinitesimal line segment to the next particle in that direction. Next, see in which direction the velocity of this new particle points, and repeat the process. If one draws a line through all the particles so chosen, one has what is called a **streamline** of the flow. Each particle of the fluid will lie on one or another streamline. For the instant of time in question, each streamline has been chosen so that all the particles on it all have velocities tangent to it. Although in general fluid motion, the streamlines constructed at different times typically change from moment to moment, in steady flow they remain constant in time.

For steady flow the streamlines and the flow lines are identical. Consider a particle at a point on a streamline and unfreeze the motion. Since the particle is moving tangent to the streamline, it will move the infinitesimal distance to the location of the next particle on the streamline. Since the flow is steady, the particle will now move in precisely the way that the previous particle was moving when it was there, which is again tangent to the original streamline. Continuing this reasoning, the particle will trace out a path, or flow line, which is identical to the streamline. In turbulent motion, however, the streamlines and flow lines can be very different. Turbulent flow is characterized by swirling and eddies and constantly changing patterns of motion.

Problem 14.1.   Show that for steady-state flow, two streamlines can never cross each other.

Solution

A particle of fluid at any point on a streamline must move tangent to the streamline for steady-state flow. If two streamlines crossed, it would mean that the particles reaching the point of crossing would have a choice of moving in either of two different directions, and the flow would not be repetitive and steady in time. This obviously cannot happen for steady flow.

Problem 14.2.   Consider the case of steady flow, and consider a small cross-sectional area through which some of the fluid is flowing. If we trace the streamlines of the fluid that pass through the perimeter of this area, we get what is called a *stream tube*, or *flow tube*. Show that the flowing fluid can never cross the boundary of the tube.

Solution

The situation is depicted in Fig. 14-1. The particles of fluid moving within the stream tube are moving along streamlines which cannot cross the boundary streamlines, as shown in Problem 14.1. Thus the fluid inside cannot cross the boundary. Similarly, particles of fluid outside the stream tube move along streamlines that never cross the boundary streamlines and thus cannot enter the stream tube.

Note.   In general, as a fluid flows, its density can vary from location to location. This is especially pronounced for gases, which are easily compressed. Densities can also change for liquids, but for most liquids these changes are small. If we can ignore the change in density of a liquid we say it is **incompressible**. (An incompressible fluid that has no viscosity is called an **ideal fluid**.) In the following section, we will assume steady or laminar flow, with zero viscosity, unless otherwise stated.

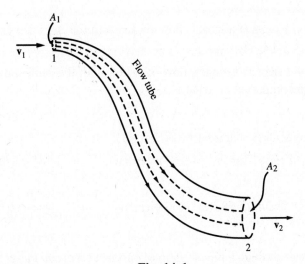

Fig. 14-1

14.2 THE LAWS OF FLUID MOTION

Equation of Continuity

  Consider the flow tube of Fig. 14-1. We assume that areas at each end are small and are chosen perpendicular to the direction of flow at each end. Let v_1 and v_2 be the velocities of the fluid at the two ends. The mass of fluid that flows into one end of the tube in a given time interval must be the same as the mass that flows out the other end in the same time interval. This follows from the conservation of mass, and the fact that for steady flow the mass inside the flow tube between the two ends must remain constant.

  Suppose that a short time interval Δt elapses. All particles that are to the left of the surface A_1 within a distance $v_1 \Delta t$ of it will pass through the surface in this time interval, as shown in Fig. 14-2. The volume of fluid entering the tube is thus $\Delta V_1 = v_1 \Delta t\, A_1$, and the mass is given by $\Delta m_1 = d_1 \Delta V_1 = d_1 v_1 \Delta t\, A_1$, where d_1 is the density of fluid at A_1. Similarly, the amount of mass leaving the tube through A_2 is $\Delta m_2 = d_2 \Delta V_2 = d_2 v_2 \Delta t\, A_2$, where d_2 is the fluid density at A_2. From $\Delta m_1 = \Delta m_2$, we get the equation of continuity

$$d_1 v_1 A_1 = d_2 v_2 A_2 \tag{14.1}$$

If the fluid is incompressible, we have $d_1 = d_2$, and (14.1) reduces to

$$v_1 A_1 = v_2 A_2 \tag{14.2}$$

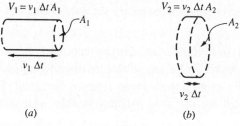

(a)   (b)

Fig. 14-2

Problem 14.3.

(a) Suppose that Fig. 14-1 depicts a steady flow of air. Assume $A_1 = 1.0$ cm^2, $A_2 = 3.0$ cm^2, and $v_1 = 12$ cm/s. If $d_2 = 1.3 d_1$, find v_2.

(b) Suppose that Fig. 14-1 depicts a steady flow of water, with the same values for A_1, A_2, and v_1. Assuming water is incompressible, what is v_2?

  Solution

  (a) By (14.1), after dividing both sides by d_1, we get

$$(12 \text{ cm/s})(1.0 \text{ cm}^2) = 1.3(3.0 \text{ cm}^2)v_2 \quad \text{or} \quad v_2 = 3.08 \text{ cm/s}$$

  (b) By (14.2),

$$(12 \text{ cm/s})(1.0 \text{ cm}^2) = (3.0 \text{ cm}^2)v_2 \quad \text{or} \quad v_2 = 4.0 \text{ cm/s}$$

Problem 14.4. Water flows through a pipe system of variable cross section as shown in Fig. 14-3(a). Assume that water completely fills all sections of the pipe and the flow is incompressible.

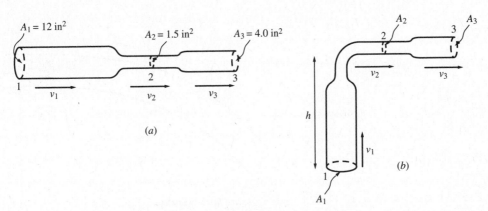

Fig. 14-3

(a)　If $v_1 = 0.80$ ft/s, find v_2 and v_3.

(b)　What volume, in cubic feet, passes through a cross section of the pipe each second?

(c)　How many pounds of water pass through a cross section of the pipe per second?

(d)　If the same pipe were bent into the shape shown in Fig. 14-3(b), with the same value for v_1, how will the result of part (a) change?

Solution

(a)　When water flows through a pipe and completely fills the pipe, the pipe itself is, in effect, a stream tube. Applying (14.2) to points 1, 2, and 3, we have

$$(0.80 \text{ ft/s})(12 \text{ in}^2) = v_2(1.5 \text{ in}^2) = v_3(4.0 \text{ in}^2) \quad \text{or} \quad v_2 = 6.4 \text{ ft/s} \quad v_3 = 2.4 \text{ ft/s}$$

(The equations were left in mixed units because area units cancel out).

(b)　$\Delta V_1 = v_1 \Delta t \, A_1.$　　$\Delta V_1 / \Delta t$ = rate of volume flow = $v_1 A_1 = (0.80 \text{ ft/s})(12 \text{ in}^2)/(144 \text{ in}^2/\text{ft}^2) = 0.0667 \text{ ft}^3/\text{s}$. (Here we must use consistent units.)

(c)　Recalling from Chap. 13 that the weight density of water is 62.5 lb/ft^3, we have

$$d_w \frac{\Delta V_1}{\Delta t} = (62.5 \text{ lb/ft}^3)(0.0667 \text{ ft}^3/\text{s}) = 4.17 \text{ lb/s}$$

(d)　The result is the same. Nothing changes because Eq. (14.2) is solely a consequence of conservation of mass and fluid incompressibility.

Bernoulli's Equation

We now turn to the question of how the pressure behaves in a flowing fluid. Again we will assume an incompressible fluid with constant density d. Consider the flow tube in Fig. 14-4. Let us apply the work-energy theorem to the fluid that at a given instant of time lies between points 1 and 2. This fluid constitutes our system, and everything else is external to it. At the end of a time interval Δt, our system (the same fluid) lies between points 1' and 2'. Since we are ignoring viscosity, the only forces other than gravity doing work on our system are those due to the pressure of the fluid to the left of our system at point 1 and to the right of our system at point 2. The force on our system at point 1 is $P_1 A_1$, acting to the right. During time Δt that force acts through a distance $v_1 \Delta t$, yielding the positive work $\Delta W_1 = P_1 A_1 v_1 \Delta t$. But, $A_1 v_1 \Delta t = \Delta V_1$, the volume moved through in time Δt, so $\Delta W_1 = P_1 \Delta V_1$.

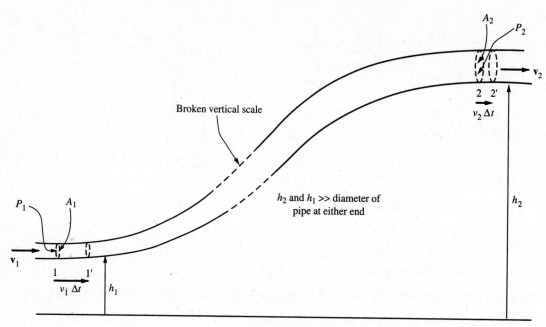

Fig. 14-4

The force from the fluid to the right of our system at point 2 is just $P_2 A_2$ acting to the left. In time Δt the fluid boundary moves a distance $v_2 \Delta t$ to the right. The work done is thus

$$\Delta W_2 = -P_2 A_2 v_2 \, \Delta t = -P_2 \, \Delta V_2$$

The net work done by all forces other than gravity is thus $\Delta W_T = P_1 \, \Delta V_1 - P_2 \, \Delta V_2$. Since the fluid is assumed incompressible, $\Delta V_1 = \Delta V_2$. Calling this common volume ΔV, we have

$$\Delta W_T = P_1 \, \Delta V - P_2 \, \Delta V \tag{14.3}$$

From the work-energy theorem, this must equal the net change in the kinetic and potential energy of our system in time Δt:

$$\Delta W_T = \Delta E_k + \Delta E_p \tag{14.4}$$

To find ΔE_k, we note that, in time Δt, our system has moved to the region between points 1′ and 2′. Because the flow is steady, the kinetic energy of the fluid lying between points 1′ and 2 is the same at the beginning and end of the time interval Δt. The net change is therefore due to the fact that the kinetic energy of the fluid that was originally between points 1 and 1′ has disappeared, and in its place we have the kinetic energy of the fluid that is now between points 2 and 2′. We already saw that the two volumes have common volume ΔV, so the mass in each region is $d \, \Delta V$, and we have

$$\Delta E_k = \tfrac{1}{2} d \, \Delta V \, v_2{}^2 - \tfrac{1}{2} d \, \Delta V \, v_1{}^2 \tag{14.5}$$

By the same reasoning, change in the potential energy of the system in the time interval Δt is due to the disappearance of mass between 1 and 1′ and the appearance of mass between 2 and 2′.

$$\Delta E_p = d \, \Delta V \, gh_2 - d \, \Delta V \, gh_1 \tag{14.6}$$

Substituting (14.3), (14.5), and (14.6) into (14.4) and canceling ΔV, we get

$$P_1 - P_2 = \tfrac{1}{2} dv_2{}^2 - \tfrac{1}{2} dv_1{}^2 + dgh_2 - dgh_1$$

or

$$P_1 + \tfrac{1}{2}dv_1{}^2 + dgh_1 = P_2 + \tfrac{1}{2}dv_2{}^2 + dgh_2 \qquad (14.7)$$

Equation (14.7) is called **Bernoulli's equation.**

Problem 14.5.   In Fig. 14-5 we show a section of a horizontal pipe with water flowing through it.

(a)   If the speed of the water at point 1 is $v_1 = 2.0$ m/s, find the velocity v_2 at point 2.

(b)   If the pressure of the fluid at point 1 is $P_1 = 2.0 \times 10^5$ Pa, find the pressure P_2 at point 2.

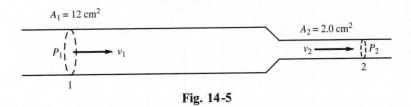

Fig. 14-5

Solution

(a)   We use (14.2), the equation of continuity for incompressible fluids:

$$v_1 A_1 = v_2 A_2 \Rightarrow (2.0 \text{ m/s})(12 \text{ cm}^2) = v_2 (2.0 \text{ cm}^2) \qquad \text{or} \qquad v_2 = 12 \text{ m/s}$$

(b)   To find the pressure we use (14.7), Bernoulli's equation. Since the pipe is horizontal, and the diameters of pipes are relatively small, we can assume $h_1 = h_2$. Then the potential-energy terms drop out, leaving

$$P_1 + \tfrac{1}{2}dv_1{}^2 = P_2 + \tfrac{1}{2}dv_2{}^2$$

or $P_2 = 2.0 \times 10^5 \text{ Pa} + \tfrac{1}{2}(1000 \text{ kg/m}^3)(2.0 \text{ m/s})^2 - \tfrac{1}{2}(1000 \text{ kg/m}^3)(12 \text{ m/s})^2$
$$= 2.0 \times 10^5 \text{ Pa} - 0.70 \times 10^5 \text{ Pa} = 1.30 \times 10^5 \text{ Pa}$$

Note.   Problem 14.5 shows that, in a horizontal pipe, the pressure is lower where the velocity is higher.

Problem 14.6.   Water flows through the pipe shown in Fig. 14-6. We examine two points, 1 and 2, a vertical distance $h = 5.0$ m apart. At point 1, the velocity of the water is $v_1 = 2.0$ m/s, the pressure is $P_1 = 2.0 \times 10^5$ Pa, and the cross-sectional area is $A_1 = 12$ cm^2.

(a)   If A_2, the cross-sectional area at point 2 is the same as A_1, find the pressure P_2 at point 2.

(b)   If the lower part of the pipe were narrower than shown and had a cross-sectional area at point 2 of $A_2 = 2.0$ cm^2, find the pressure at point 2.

Solution

(a)   Since $A_1 = A_2$ the continuity equation yields $v_1 = v_2$. Then, from Bernoulli's equation (14.7), the velocity terms cancel out, leaving $P_1 + dgh_1 = P_2 + dgh_2$. Since $h_1 - h_2 = h$, we get

$$P_2 = P_1 + dgh \qquad (i)$$

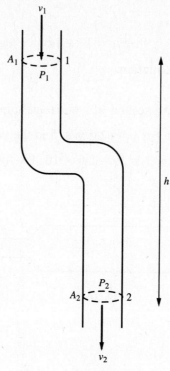

Fig. 14-6

Then
$$P_2 = (2.0 \times 10^5 \text{ Pa}) + (1000 \text{ kg/m}^3)(9.8 \text{ m/s}^2)(5.0 \text{ m})$$
$$= 2.0 \times 10^5 \text{ Pa} + 0.49 \times 10^5 \text{ Pa} = 2.49 \times 10^5 \text{ Pa}$$

Note. Equation (*i*) is just the equation for variation of hydrostatic pressure with depth. Thus, if the velocity is equal at two points in a flowing liquid, the pressure difference is the same as if the liquid were at rest.

(*b*) Now we need to find the new velocity at point 2. Since v_1, A_1, and A_2 are exactly as in Problem 14.5, we again have $v_2 = 12.0$ m/s. Then, by (*14.7*), we have

$$P_1 + \tfrac{1}{2}dv_1{}^2 + dgh_1 = P_2 + \tfrac{1}{2}dv_2{}^2 + dgh_2 \quad \text{or} \quad P_2 = P_1 + (\tfrac{1}{2}dv_1{}^2 - \tfrac{1}{2}dv_2{}^2) + (dgh_1 - dgh_2)$$

Substituting [see Problems 14.5(*b*) and 14.6(*a*)], we have

$$P_2 = 2.0 \times 10^5 \text{ Pa} - 0.70 \times 10^5 \text{ Pa} + 0.49 \times 10^5 \text{ Pa} \quad \text{or} \quad P_2 = 1.79 \times 10^5 \text{ Pa}$$

A special case of interest is that in which the cross-sectional area on one side of a stream tube is very large compared to the other side. An example is a tank with a small opening on the side or bottom.

Problem 14.7. In Fig. 14-7 we shown a tank of cross-sectional area $A = 500$ cm^2 open to the atmosphere and filled with a liquid of density d to a depth $h_1 = 1.5$ m. A small hole of cross-sectional area $a = 5.0$ cm^2 is drilled in the tank at a height $h_2 = 0.4$ m from the bottom.

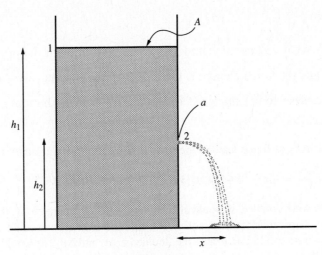

Fig. 14-7

(a) Find the velocity with which the liquid pours out of the hole.

(b) Ignoring air resistance, how far from the wall of the tank does the stream of liquid hit the ground?

Solution

(a) Applying (*14.7*) and noting that the liquid is open to the atmosphere at both points 1 and 2 so that $P_1 = P_2 = P_A$, we get

$$\tfrac{1}{2}dv_1{}^2 + dgh_1 = \tfrac{1}{2}dv_2{}^2 + dgh_2$$

From (*14.2*) we have $v_1 A_1 = v_2 A_2$ or $v_1 = v_2(A_2/A_1)$. For our case, $A_2 = a = 5.0 \text{ cm}^2$ and $A_1 = A = 500 \text{ m}^2$, so $A_2/A_1 = 0.01$. Therefore, $v_1 = 0.01 v_2$ and $v_1{}^2 = 0.0001 v_2{}^2$. Therefore, $\tfrac{1}{2}dv_1{}^2$ is completely negligible compared to $\tfrac{1}{2}dv_2{}^2$ and may be dropped. Letting $h_1 - h_2 = h$, we get

$$\tfrac{1}{2}v_2{}^2 = gh \Rightarrow v_2{}^2 = 2gh \Rightarrow v_2 = \sqrt{2gh}$$

Substituting, we get

$$v_2 = [2(9.8 \text{ m/s}^2)(1.5 \text{ m} - 0.4 \text{ m})]^{1/2} = 4.64 \text{ m/s}$$

(b) Since the fluid particles leave the tank with a horizontal initial velocity, the time it takes them to fall vertically from rest through a distance $h_2 = 0.40$ m is calculated as follows:

$$h_2 = \tfrac{1}{2}gt^2 \Rightarrow 0.40 \text{ m} = (4.9 \text{ m/s}^2)t^2 \Rightarrow t = 0.286 \text{ s}$$

Then the horizontal distance is

$$x = v_2 t = (4.64 \text{ m/s})(0.286 \text{ s}) = 1.33 \text{ m}$$

Note. $v_2 = \sqrt{2gh}$ in Problem 14.7 is the velocity that a drop of water would gain in free fall from rest through the distance h (which is the distance from the top of the liquid in the tank to the point of exit). This result is known as **Torricelli's theorem**. It is valid when the liquid is open to the atmosphere at both ends and the surface area of the tank is very large compared to the area where the liquid leaves the tank.

Problem 14.8.

(a) In Problem 14.7, what volume of liquid leaves the tank through the opening per second?

(b) How would the answer to (a) change if the area a of the opening were doubled?

(c) How would the answer to (a) change if the hole were near the bottom of the tank?

Solution

(a) The volume ΔV_2 of liquid leaving the tank at point 2 in a small time Δt is just $(v_2 \Delta t)a$. Hence,

$$\frac{\Delta V_2}{\Delta t} = v_2 a = (4.64 \text{ m/s})(5.0 \times 10^{-4} \text{ m}^2) = 0.0023 \text{ m}^3/\text{s} = 2300 \text{ cm}^3/\text{s}$$

(b) If the area a were doubled, it would still be very small compared to A, the cross-sectional area of the tank, so Torricelli's theorem still holds, and the velocity v_2 would be unchanged. Then the volume flow rate would just reflect the doubled area, and $\Delta V_2/\Delta t$ would double.

(c) If the hole were near the bottom, $v_2 = \sqrt{2gh'}$, where $h' = h_1 = 1.5$ m. Then

$$v_2 = [2(9.8 \text{ m/s}^2)(1.5 \text{ m})]^{1/2} = 6.64 \text{ m/s}$$

and

$$\frac{\Delta V_2}{\Delta t} = (6.64 \text{ m/s})(5.0 \times 10^{-4} \text{ m}^2) = 0.0033 \text{ m}^3/\text{s}$$

Problem 14.9.

(a) If the fluid in Problems 14.7 and 14.8(a) was water, what would be the rate at which mass left the tank?

(b) What would be the time rate of increase of momentum of the water as it left the tank?

(c) From your answer to (b) can you determine the reaction force on the tank exerted by the exiting water?

Solution

(a) From Problem 14.8(a) the volume rate was $\Delta V_2/\Delta t = 0.0023 \text{ m}^3/\text{s}$. Using the density of water d, the mass rate equals

$$\frac{\Delta M_2}{\Delta t} = \frac{d \, \Delta V_2}{\Delta t} = (1000 \text{ kg/m}^3)(0.0023 \text{ m}^3/\text{s}) = 2.3 \text{ kg/s}$$

(b) Each particle of water leaves the tank with horizontal velocity v_2. If ΔM_2 is the mass leaving in time Δt, the total momentum picked up in time Δt is $\Delta M_2 v_2$. Dividing by Δt gives the rate of increase of momentum of the water as it leaves:

$$v_2 \frac{\Delta M_2}{\Delta t} = (4.64 \text{ m/s})(2.3 \text{ kg/s}) = 10.7 \text{ kg} \cdot \text{m/s}^2 = 10.7 \text{ N to the right}$$

(c) Since the rate of increase of momentum of the water, as determined in (b), must be the force exerted on the exiting water by the water left behind, by Newton's third law the exiting water must exert an equal and opposite reaction force, $F_R = 10.7$ N, to the left.

Problem 14.10. A boy holds a garden hose as shown in Fig. 14-8. Water pours out of the hose at a speed of $v = 10$ m/s, and the cross-sectional area of the end of the hose is $a = 2.0 \text{ cm}^2$. What horizontal force must the boy exert on the hose to keep it in place?

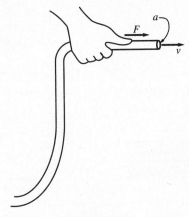

Fig. 14-8

Solution

From the previous problems we can see the essential approach to this problem. The water flowing up the vertical portion of the hose has no horizontal velocity component, so all the horizontal momentum gained by the water as it leaves the hose must have been caused by a horizontal force **F** exerted by the walls of the hose on the water as it goes around the bend. This same force is the force that the boy must exert on the hose to keep it in place. To calculate the magnitude of this force we need to determine the time rate of increase of momentum in the horizontal direction. The rate at which mass exits the hose is $\Delta M/\Delta t = d\,\Delta V/\Delta t$. Since $\Delta V/\Delta t = va$, we have $\Delta M/\Delta t = dva$. Each unit of mass picks up a horizontal velocity v. The horizontal force, which equals the time rate of increase of horizontal momentum, is then

$$F = v\,\frac{\Delta M}{\Delta t} = dv^2 a = (1000 \text{ kg/m}^3)(10 \text{ m/s})^2(2.0 \times 10^{-4} \text{ m}^2) = 20.0 \text{ N}$$

Venturi Tubes

When fluids flow through a pipe system, one often wants to monitor the pressure at various points in the pipe, as well as determine the flow velocity. One way of doing this is by means of transparent tubes attached to the pipe system, with a liquid such as water or mercury enclosed. Figure 14-9 gives the configuration of some venturi tube setups.

In Fig. 14-9(a) we have a vertical tube rising out of a pipe with water flowing through it under a positive gauge pressure. The upper end of the tube is open to the atmosphere. Water rises in the tube until the height of water produces a gauge pressure that just balances the pressure in the pipe. The pressure in the pipe is determined by observing the height of the water in the tube.

In Fig. 14-9(b) a thin bent tube with mercury in it is inserted in a pipe and sealed to prevent leakage. The left end of the tube has an opening on one side, with the fluid moving by at speed v, while the right end is open to the atmosphere. The tube acts like an open-tube manometer and measures the gauge pressure of the flowing fluid.

Figure 14-9(c) shows a more sophisticated venturi setup that can directly measure the velocity of flow in the pipe. We assume the diameter of the venturi tube is very small compared to that of the pipe so that it does not change the flow velocity in the pipe very much. The left end of the tube has an opening on its top, whereas the right end of the tube opens directly into the flowing fluid. Since the fluid must go around one or the other side of the tube, there is a small region or point right in front of the tube where the fluid is at rest. Such a point is called a **stagnation point**. Using Bernoulli's

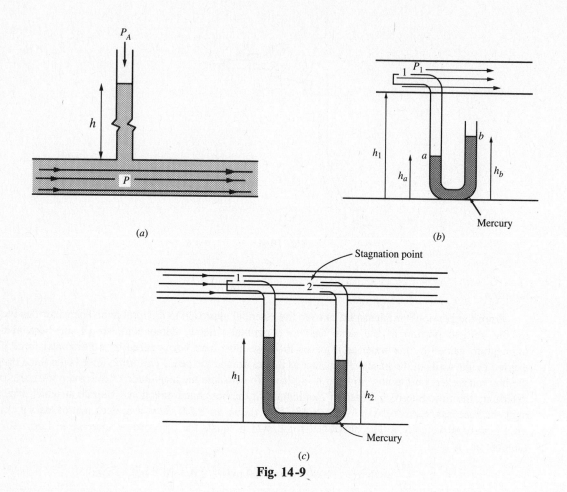

Fig. 14-9

equation, and assuming a horizontal pipe, the pressure difference between points 1 and 2 is $P_2 - P_1 = \frac{1}{2}dv_1^2$. The height difference of the mercury (corrected for the different heights of fluid above the mercury on the two sides) directly measures $P_2 - P_1$ and therefore yields the velocity v_1.

Problem 14.11.

(a) In Fig. 14-9(a) the water in the venturi tube rises 30 cm above the pipe level. Find the absolute pressure of the water in the pipe.

(b) In Fig. 14-9(b), water flows through the pipe at the same pressure as in (a). Assuming $h_1 = 30$ cm, find the height difference $h_b - h_a$ in the mercury.

Solution

(a) $P = P_A + dgh = 1.013 \times 10^5 \text{ Pa} + (1000 \text{ kg/m}^3)(9.8 \text{ m/s}^2)(0.30 \text{ m}) = 1.042 \times 10^5 \text{ Pa}$

(b)   We find the pressure at point a from the left and the right and equate them:

$$P_1 + d_w g(h_1 - h_a) = P_a = P_A + d_{Hg}g(h_b - h_a)$$

Substituting,

$$1.042 \times 10^5 \text{ Pa} + (1000 \text{ kg/m}^3)(9.8 \text{ m/s}^2)(0.30 \text{ m})$$

$$= 1.013 \times 10^5 \text{ Pa} + (13,600 \text{ kg/m}^3)(9.8 \text{ m/s}^2)(h_b - h_a) \qquad \text{or} \qquad h_b - h_a = 0.044 \text{ m}$$

Problem 14.12. In Fig. 14-9(c) the pipe contains air moving at velocity v. The mercury height difference is noted to be 18 mm. Find the velocity of the air, assuming that the density of the air is 1.3 kg/m^3.

Solution

The pressure difference in the two sides of the venturi tube is

$$P_2 - P_1 = d_{Hg}g(h_1 - h_2) = (13{,}600 \text{ kg/m}^3)(9.8 \text{ m/s}^2)(18 \times 10^{-3} \text{ m}) = 2400 \text{ Pa}$$

(Here we ignore the slight difference in the height of the air above the columns of mercury on the two sides). By Bernoulli's equation the difference in pressure at points 1 and 2 is also given by

$$P_2 - P_1 = \tfrac{1}{2}d_a v^2 \Rightarrow 2400 \text{ Pa} = \tfrac{1}{2}(1.3 \text{ kg/m}^3)v^2 \qquad \text{or} \qquad v = 60.8 \text{ m/s}$$

Aerodynamics

An airplane in motion is supported by the pressure difference between the top and undersides of the wing. This pressure difference is the consequence of Bernoulli's equation. In the frame of reference of the airplane, the air is rushing past the wing, which is designed to compress the streamlines above the wing much more than those under the wing. Figure 14-10 shows a cross section of the wing with the streamlines above and below.

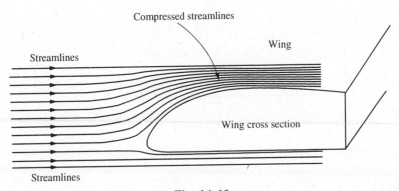

Fig. 14-10

Compression of the streamlines means that the stream tube above the wing has a smaller cross-sectional area than that in front of the plane and, from the continuity equation, the velocity of the air must therefore be greater above the wing. This greater velocity implies lower pressure than the normal pressure of the air in front of the plane. If we assume the flow lines under the wing are not compressed at all, the pressure under the wing is just the normal pressure of the air in front of the wing. Thus, there is a pressure difference on the two sides.

Problem 14.13. Consider an airplane moving through the air at velocity $v = 200$ m/s. Assume that the streamlines which move just over the top of the wing are compressed to eight-tenths their normal area, and that those under the wing are not compressed at all. ($d_a = 1.3$ kg/m^3.) Find (a) the velocity v_1 of the air just over the wing; (b) the difference in the pressure between the air just over the wing P_1 and that under the wing P_2; (c) the net upward force on both wings if the area of each wing is 40 m^2.

Solution

(a) Since the effective area of the stream tube is reduced to eight-tenths its original value, the velocity is increased to ten-eighths, or five-fourths its original value. So, $v_1 = 250$ m/s.

(b) From Bernoulli's equation, with both points at effectively the same elevation, we have $P_1 + \frac{1}{2}d_a v_1{}^2 = P_2 + \frac{1}{2}d_a v_2{}^2$. Here $v_2 = v = 200$ m/s, so

$$P_2 - P_1 = \tfrac{1}{2}(1.3 \text{ kg/m}^3)[(250 \text{ m/s})^2 - (200 \text{ m/s})^2] = 1.46 \times 10^4 \text{ Pa}$$

(c) The total net upward force is

$$(P_2 - P_1)A = (1.46 \times 10^4 \text{ Pa})(80 \text{ m}^2) = 1.17 \times 10^6 \text{ N}$$

Note. Similar aerodynamic effects occur when a horizontally moving ball simultaneously spins about a vertical axis. Because of drag effects the air flowing past the ball has different velocities on the two sides of the ball, leading to a pressure differential and a net sideways force on the ball. The detailed process involved are complex, but the net effect is shown schematically (top view), in the frame of reference of the center of mass of the ball (Fig. 14-11).

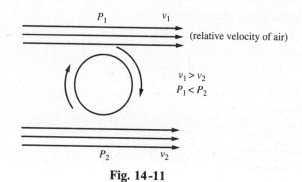

Fig. 14-11

14.3 VISCOSITY

Viscosity occurs both in steady flow and in turbulent flow and is, in effect, a frictional force between layers of fluid moving past each other. The nature of this force can best be understood by considering steady straight-line flow of a fluid. Figure 14-12(a) shows a fluid of thickness d between two very large plates, each of area A. We assume that the plates are large enough so that, over the time frame of the experiment, we can ignore the effects of fluid spilling out from between the plates at the edges. The bottom plate can be considered fixed, and the upper plate is being pulled to the right by a force F. The upper plate reaches equilibrium when it is moving at some velocity v. It is found that a thin layer of fluid in contact with each plate stays at rest relative to that plate. Thus, the uppermost layer of fluid moves to the right with velocity v while the bottommost layer is at rest. The velocities of the layers in between (which can be thought of as having very small thicknesses Δd) vary in proportion to their distances y from the bottom layer, as shown in Fig. 14-12(b). Since each layer is in equilibrium, the force F on the top surface of a given layer (pulling to the right) has the same magnitude as that on the bottom surface (pulling to the left). Thus the shear stress F/A is the same on all layers. While the absolute velocity is different for different layers, the rate of change of velocity with depth, or velocity gradient, stays the same: $\Delta v/\Delta y = v_y/y = v/d$, where v_y is the horizontal

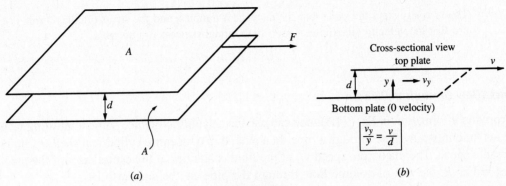

(a)   (b)

Fig. 14-12

velocity at height y. This is consistent with the observed result: For fluid in steady flow between parallel plates, the stress is proportional to the velocity gradient or

$$\frac{F}{A} = \eta \frac{v}{d} \qquad (14.8)$$

where η (the Greek letter *eta*) is the proportionality constant. This constant, which varies from fluid to fluid, is called the **coefficient of viscosity**, or, just the viscosity. From Eq. (*14.8*), we can see that the dimensions of η are $N \cdot s/m^2 = Pa \cdot s$. The unit of viscosity is called the poiseuille (Pl): $1\ Pl = 1\ Pa \cdot s$. The viscosities of all fluids decrease with increasing temperature. A few typical viscosities are given in Table 14.1.

Table 14.1. Viscosity

Substance	Temperature, °C	η, Pl
Air	20	1.8×10^{-5}
Water	20	1.0×10^{-3}
Whole blood	38	4.0×10^{-3}
Light oil	20	2.0
Heavy oil	20	9.9

Problem 14.14. The top plate in Fig. 14-12(*b*) has a constant velocity of 20 cm/s, when a shear stress of 300 N/m² is applied.

(a) If the distance between the plates is $d = 2.3$ mm, find the viscosity of the liquid between the plates.

(b) If the same liquid filled the space between the plates to a distance of $d = 4.6$ mm and the stress were increased to 600 N/m², what would the equilibrium velocity of the upper plate be?

Solution

(a)
$$\eta = \frac{F/A}{v/d} = \frac{300\ N/m^2 (2.3 \times 10^{-3}\ m)}{0.20\ m/s} = 3.45\ Pl$$

(b) The viscosity stays the same, but the distance d doubles, and the stress doubles. From (14.8), we see that the velocity quadruples under these circumstances: $v = 80$ cm/s.

Viscous Flow through a Pipe

From the information in Eq. (14.8), one can use the calculus to deduce some interesting results for a viscous fluid in steady flow through a pipe. In a pipe, thin concentric cylindrical shells of liquid flow at the same speed. The maximum speed v_m of the fluid is attained at the central axis of the pipe. For a pipe of radius R, the rate of volume flow through the pipe can be shown to be

$$\frac{\Delta V}{\Delta t} = \frac{v_m}{2}\,\pi R^2 \tag{14.9}$$

[Note that Eq. (14.9) implies that $v_m/2$ is the average velocity of the liquid in the pipe.]

It can also be shown that the net viscous force acting on a fluid in steady flow, due to the walls of a length L of pipe, is given by

$$F = 4\pi\eta L v_m \tag{14.10}$$

where the force F is in the direction opposite to the flow.

Since the flow through the pipe is steady, the net force on the length L of fluid must be zero. Assuming a horizontal pipe, the only other forces are due to the pressure on each end of the length L of fluid, and the difference in these pressures must give rise to a net force that balances the viscous force of Eq. (14.10). This implies that when a viscous fluid is in steady flow through a horizontal pipe of uniform cross section, there is a pressure difference at different points along the pipe. This is quite different than the result from Bernoulli's equation, where the pressure difference would be zero. The effect of viscosity on pressure is demonstrated in the next problem.

Problem 14.15.   Find an expression for the pressure difference between two points a distance L apart in a uniform horizontal pipe carrying a liquid moving with central velocity v_m and having viscosity η.

Solution

The situation is shown in Fig. 14-13. We consider our system to be the fluid in a length L of our pipe of radius R. Since the fluid is not accelerating, the net horizontal force must be zero. The only horizontal forces on our system are due to the pressure from the liquid to the left of the system P_1, the pressure due to the liquid to the right of the system P_2, and the viscous force due to the pipe. The force due to P_1 is $F_1 = P_1\pi R^2$ acting to the right. The force due to P_2 is $F_2 = P_2\pi R^2$ acting on the left. The viscous force is given by Eq. (14.10): $F = 4\pi\eta L v_m$ acting to the left. For equilibrium,

$$P_1\pi R^2 - P_2\pi R^2 - 4\pi\eta L v_m = 0 \qquad \text{or} \qquad P_1 - P_2 = \frac{4\eta L v_m}{R^2} \tag{i}$$

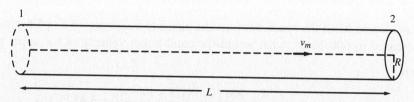

Fig. 14-13

Problem 14.16. Find the pressure drop across a 1.0-cm length of a small blood vessel 2.0×10^{-2} mm in radius, if the maximum speed of the blood in the vessel is 1.1 cm/s.

Solution

From Eq. (*i*) in Problem 14.15 (and Table 14.1), we have

$$P_1 - P_2 = \frac{4(4.0 \times 10^{-3} \text{ Pl})(0.010 \text{ m})(0.011 \text{ m/s})}{(2.0 \times 10^{-5} \text{ m})^2} = 4400 \text{ Pa}$$

Poiseuille's Law

By combining Eq. (*i*) of Problem 14.15 with Eq. (*14.9*) we can get a relationship between the volume flow $\Delta V/\Delta t$ and the pressure difference across a length L of pipe. From Eq. (*i*) we get

$$v_m = \frac{(P_1 - P_2)R^2}{4\eta L} \tag{14.11}$$

Substituting into Eq. (14.9) yields **Poiseuille's law**

$$\frac{\Delta V}{\Delta t} = \frac{\pi R^4 (P_1 - P_2)}{8\eta L} \tag{14.12}$$

Note that the volume flow rate depends on the fourth power of the radius R of the pipe, as well as on $(P_1 - P_2)/L$, the change in pressure per unit length along the pipe.

Problem 14.17. Water flows through a horizontal pipe of radius $R = 1.0$ cm and length $L = 300$ m. If the low-pressure end is at atmospheric pressure, what must the gauge pressure at the other end be if the water flows at a rate of 20 cm^3/s? (Assume the water is at a temperature of 20 °C.)

Solution

Solving (*14.12*) for $P_1 - P_2$, we get

$$P_1 - P_2 = \frac{(2.0 \times 10^{-5} \text{ m}^3/\text{s})(8)(1.0 \times 10^{-3} \text{ Pl})(300 \text{ m})}{(3.14)(0.010 \text{ m})^4} = 1530 \text{ Pa}$$

Since $P_2 = P_A$, we have $P_{1g} = P_1 - P_A = 1530$ Pa.

Problem 14.18.

(*a*) Assuming the same-length pipe and the same pressure difference $P_1 - P_2$ found in Problem 14.17, what would be the new volume flow rate of the water if the radius were doubled?

(*b*) Assuming the same length of pipe as in Problem 14.17, what would the gauge pressure P_{1g} have to be to maintain the same volume flow rate as in Problem 14.17 if the radius halved?

Solution

(*a*) According to (*14.12*), the volume flow varies as the fourth power of the radius. If all other factors are the same, then doubling R increases the volume flow 16 times. Then, $\Delta V/\Delta t = 320$ cm^3/s.

(*b*) According to (*14.12*), the pressure difference varies inversely as the fourth power of the radius. Then, if the radius drops by a factor of 2, $P_1 - P_2$ must increase 16-fold. So, the new value of $P_{1g} = 16(1530 \text{ Pa}) = 2.45 \times 10^4$ Pa.

Note. The radius of a pipe has an enormous impact on the pressure necessary to maintain a certain volume flow rate. This is a determining factor in a wide range of important phenomena, from the choice of diameters of water mains to the strain on the heart due to blood vessels narrowed by cholesterol buildup.

Stokes' Law

When an object moves through a viscous fluid in such a way that the fluid is in steady flow past it, the viscous forces on the object are, to a good approximation, proportional to the relative velocity and the coefficient of viscosity. As with all frictional forces, viscous forces oppose the direction of motion. The expression for the force will vary with the shape of the object, and, in general, is difficult to determine. However, for the case of a sphere of radius r moving relative to the fluid with velocity v, we have **Stokes' law**, the simple expression

$$F = 6\pi\eta r v \qquad (14.13)$$

Problem 14.19. A lead sphere of mass m and radius r drops from rest just below the surface in a tank of oil (sp gr 0.80).

(a) Assuming the relative motion of the oil past the sphere is steady flow, find an expression for the acceleration of the sphere. (Ignore the effect of buoyancy of the oil.)

(b) Show that at some point the velocity will reach a maximum value and stay constant thereafter; find an expression for this *terminal velocity*.

   Solution

   (a) The only downward force is the weight of the lead ball mg. Since we are ignoring buoyancy, the only upward force is that due to the viscous "drag" and is given by Stoke's law. Then, choosing downward as positive, we have

   $$mg - 6\pi\eta rv = ma \qquad \text{or} \qquad a = g - \frac{6\pi\eta rv}{m} \qquad (i)$$

   (b) The velocity increases until the acceleration becomes zero. This happens when v reaches the value given by $g = 6\pi\gamma rv/m$. Once that terminal velocity v_T is reached, the ball falls at constant speed

   $$v_T = \frac{mg}{6\pi\eta r} \qquad (ii)$$

Problem 14.20. Find the terminal velocity of the lead ball in Problem 14.19 if the radius of the lead ball is 2.0 cm and the viscosity of the oil is $\eta = 2.0$ Pl.

   Solution

   We need to determine the mass of the lead ball. Using the density of lead from Table 13.1, we get

   $$m = d_L\left(\frac{4\pi r^3}{3}\right) = (11.3 \times 10^3 \text{ kg/m}^3)\frac{(4)(3.14)(2.0 \times 10^{-2})^3}{3} = 0.379 \text{ kg}$$

   Substituting in the formula above for v_T of a sphere, we get

   $$v_T = \frac{(0.379 \text{ kg})(9.8 \text{ m/s}^2)}{6(3.14)(2.0 \text{ Pl})(2.0 \times 10^{-2} \text{ m})} = 4.93 \text{ m/s}$$

Problem 14.21.

(a)   How would the answer to Problem 14.19(a) change if buoyancy were included?

(b)   What is the new expression for the terminal velocity if buoyancy is included?

(c)   What is the solution to Problem 14.20 if buoyancy is included?

Solution

(a)   There is now an additional upward force due to buoyancy, $B = d_o g(4\pi r^3/3)$, where d_o is the density of oil. Thus, we get

$$mg - d_o g \left(\frac{4\pi r^3}{3} \right) - 6\pi\eta rv = ma$$

Solving for a and using $m = d_L(4\pi r^3/3)$, we get

$$a = g - \frac{d_o}{d_L} g - \frac{6\pi\eta rv}{m} \qquad (i)$$

(b)   The terminal velocity is attained when $a = 0$, which yields

$$v_T = mg \frac{1 - d_o/d_L}{6\pi\eta r}$$

(c)

$$v_T = 0.379 \text{ kg} \frac{(9.8 \text{ m/s}^2)(1.0 - 0.80/11.3)}{6(3.14)(2.0 \text{ Pl})(2.0 \times 10^{-2} \text{ m})} = 4.58 \text{ m/s}$$

Problem 14.22.   Suppose that a raindrop has a radius $r = 2.0$ mm and falls from rest from a cloud. Assuming steady flow, use Stokes' law to find the terminal velocity.

Solution

We ignore the buoyancy of air and use Eq. (ii) of Problem 14.19(b) and the value of viscosity of air from Table 14.1. The mass of the drop is

$$m = d_w V = d_w \left(\frac{4\pi r^3}{3} \right) = (1000 \text{ kg/m}^3) \frac{4(3.14)(2.0 \times 10^{-3} \text{ m})^3}{3} = 3.35 \times 10^{-5} \text{ kg}$$

Then

$$v_T = \frac{(3.35 \times 10^{-5} \text{ kg})(9.8 \text{ m/s}^2)}{6(3.14)(1.8 \times 10^{-5} \text{ Pl})(2.0 \times 10^{-3} \text{ m})} = 484 \text{ m/s}$$

Note.   This is much larger than the velocity of typical raindrops. This is a consequence of our assumption that the flow is steady and that Stoke's law holds. In fact, above a certain velocity, turbulence sets in, and our assumption is no longer valid.

Turbulence and Reynolds Number

When the velocity of a fluid in a pipe increases past a certain value, or the relative velocity of an object through a fluid increases past a certain velocity, the flow changes from steady to turbulent. Turbulent flow is characterized by local vortices of motion that randomly change from moment to moment. In such situations the viscous forces vary with velocity as v^2 or as higher powers of v. A crude but effective determination of the onset of turbulent flow is given by the **Reynolds number** R. This is a dimensionless quantity that depends on four factors: the density d of the flowing fluid, the coefficient of viscosity η, the average relative velocity of the fluid v, and the characteristic linear dimension L of the solid boundary. For flow through a pipe, L is the diameter of the pipe. For an object moving through a fluid, L can be taken as some average linear dimension of the object facing into the fluid flow. In all cases the expression for the Reynolds number is

$$R = \frac{dvL}{\eta} \qquad (14.14)$$

When R exceeds a certain value for the particular geometry at hand, the flow turns from steady to turbulent. A good rule of thumb for fluids flowing through a pipe is that when R exceeds 2000, the flow becomes turbulent. Similarly, for a sphere moving through a fluid, the critical value of R is about 10.

Problem 14.23.

(a) Find the Reynolds number for the ball falling through oil in Problem 14.19 and 14.20. Does the flow turn turbulent before the ball reaches critical velocity?

(b) Repeat for the raindrop of Problem 14.22.

Solution

(a) Letting L equal the diameter of the ball, we have, at the terminal velocity calculated in Problem 14.20,

$$R = \frac{(800 \text{ kg/m}^3)(4.93 \text{ m/s})(0.040 \text{ m})}{2.0 \text{ Pl}} = 79$$

The flow is turbulent.

(b) Here the diameter is 0.0040 m, and the density of air is found from Table 13.1. Thus, $R = (1.29 \text{ kg/m}^3)(484 \text{ m/s})(0.0040 \text{ m})/(1.8 \times 10^{-5}) = 139 \times 10^3$. Clearly, turbulence sets in long before a velocity of 484 m/s is reached. As a consequence the drag force increases much more rapidly with speed, and the terminal velocity of raindrops is much lower.

Problem 14.24.

(a) Assuming that at $R = 10$ we get turbulence, find the transition velocity for the raindrop in Problem 14.22.

(b) Find the transition velocity for water flowing through a pipe of diameter 5.0 cm, at a temperature of 20°C.

Solution

(a) We can find v from (14.14):

$$10 = \frac{[(1.29 \text{ kg/m}^3)(0.0040 \text{ m})]}{1.8 \times 10^{-5} \text{ Pl}} v \qquad \text{or} \qquad v = 3.49 \text{ cm/s}$$

(b) We proceed the same way, except that now we have

$$2000 = \frac{[(1000 \text{ kg/m}^3)(0.050 \text{ m})]}{1.0 \times 10^{-3} \text{ Pl}} v \qquad \text{or} \qquad v = 0.040 \text{ m/s}$$

Problems for Review and Mind Stretching

Problem 14.25. Referring to Problem 14.4 and the pipe in Fig. 14-3(a), assume zero viscosity and that the pressure at point 1 is $P_1 = 4.023 \times 10^3$ lb/ft^2.

(a) Find the pressure at points 2 and 3.

(b) How would v_2 change if the diameter of the middle section of pipe doubled?

(c) Assuming the changes of (b), how would the pressure and velocity change at point 3?

Solution

(a) From Problem 14.4, $v_1 = 0.80$ ft/s, $v_2 = 6.4$ ft/s, $v_3 = 2.4$ ft/s. Bernoulli's equation applied to a horizontal pipe, with $d = 1.94$ slugs/ft^3, gives

$$P_1 + \tfrac{1}{2}dv_1{}^2 = P_2 + \tfrac{1}{2}dv_2{}^2 \Rightarrow 4.023 \times 10^3 \text{ lb/ft}^2 + (0.97 \text{ slug/ft}^3)(0.80 \text{ ft/s})^2$$
$$= P_2 + (0.97 \text{ slug/ft}^3)(6.4 \text{ ft/s})^2$$

so that $P_2 = 3984$ lb/ft^2. Similarly, the pressure at point 3 is given by

$$P_1 + \tfrac{1}{2}dv_1{}^2 = P_3 + \tfrac{1}{2}dv_3{}^2 \Rightarrow 4.023 \times 10^3 \text{ lb/ft}^2 + (0.97 \text{ slug/ft}^3)(0.80 \text{ ft/s})^2$$
$$= P_3 + (0.97 \text{ slug/ft}^3)(2.4 \text{ ft/s})^2$$

so that $P_3 = 4018$ lb/ft^2.

(b) If the diameter doubles, the area quadruples. Then from the continuity equation $v_1 A_1 = v_2 A_2$, we deduce that if A_2 increases by a factor of 4, v_2 decreases to one-fourth its prior value, or 1.6 ft/s.

(c) The values of v_3 is unchanged since the value of A_3 hasn't changed, and from the continuity equation, applied to points 1 and 3, $v_1 A_1 = v_3 A_3$, which implies v_3 is the same. Since v_3 hasn't changed, Bernoulli's equation applied to points 1 and 3 implies P_3 hasn't changed either.

Problem 14.26. Assume that the cross-sectional areas at points 1, 2, and 3 of the pipe shown in Fig. 14-3(b) have the same dimensions as those of Problem 14.25(a) and that P_1 and v_1 are as given in that problem. If $h = 30$ ft, calculate the pressures at points 2 and 3.

Solution

Let the zero of gravitational potential energy be chosen at point 1. Then, Bernoulli's equation for points 1 and 2 becomes

$$P_1 + \tfrac{1}{2}dv_1{}^2 + dgh_1 = P_2 + \tfrac{1}{2}dv_2{}^2 + dgh_2$$

$$4.023 \times 10^3 \text{ lb/ft}^2 + (0.97 \text{ slug/ft}^3)(0.80 \text{ ft/s})^2 + 0 = P_2 + (0.97 \text{ slug/ft}^3)(6.4 \text{ ft/s})^2$$
$$+ (62.5 \text{ lb/ft}^3)(30 \text{ ft})$$

Solving, we get $P_2 = 2109$ lb/ft^2. Noting that $h_3 = h_2$, we follow a similar procedure to get $P_3 = 2143$ lb/ft^2.

Problem 14.27. Consider the situation in Fig. 14-7 (Problem 14.7), where the liquid is water. Show that the net force F exerted on the liquid leaving through the hole is exactly twice the net hydrostatic force exerted on the same area if no hole were there (e.g., assuming the hole is capped).

Solution

From Torricelli's theorem (Problem 14.7) we have that the velocity of the liquid leaving the tank is $v = \sqrt{2gh}$. The volume of liquid leaving per second is va, and the mass leaving per second is thus dva. Since the liquid acquires a velocity v perpendicular to the tank as it leaves, the total change in momentum per unit time for liquid leaving the tank is $(dva)v = dv^2a = d(2gh)a$. From Newton's second law the force F is the change in momentum per unit time, or $F = 2dgha$. If there were no hole in the tank, the hydrostatic pressure on the same area from the inside would be $P = P_A + dgh$. The atmosphere would be pushing from the outside with atmospheric pressure P_A. The net force F' on the area a is therefore just due to the gauge pressure and is

$$F' = (P - P_A)a = dgha = \tfrac{1}{2}F$$

Problem 14.28. Water flows through a thin horizontal tube (effects of viscosity *cannot* be ignored), and pours out of the right end (Fig. 14-14).

(a) If h_1, the height of water in the venturi tube above point 1, is 3.0 cm, find the gauge pressure P_{g1} at point 1.

(b) Find the maximum velocity v_m of the water in the tube.

(c) Find the volume rate of flow of the water out of the pipe.

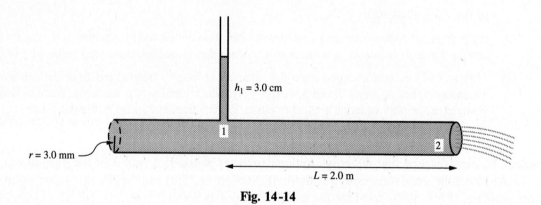

Fig. 14-14

Solution

(a) Since the venturi tube is open to the atmosphere, the gauge pressure is just due to the height of liquid:

$$P_{g1} = dgh_1 = (1000 \text{ kg/m}^3)(9.8 \text{ m/s}^2)(0.030 \text{ m}) = 294 \text{ Pa}$$

(b) To find the velocity v_m, we use Eq. *(14.11)* applied to points 1 and 2: $v_m = (P_1 - P_2)r^2/(4\eta L)$. Since $P_2 = P_A$, and $P_1 - P_A = P_{g1}$, we get

$$v_m = \frac{(294 \text{ Pa})(3.0 \times 10^{-3} \text{ m})^2}{(4)(1.00 \times 10^{-3} \text{ Pl})(2.0 \text{ m})} = 0.331 \text{ m/s}$$

(c) From Poiseuille's law *(14.12)* we have

$$\frac{\Delta V}{\Delta t} = \frac{\pi r^4 (P_1 - P_2)}{8\eta L} = \frac{(3.14)(3.0 \times 10^{-3} \text{ m})^4 (294 \text{ Pa})}{(8)(1.00 \times 10^{-3} \text{ Pl})(2.0 \text{ m})} = 4.67 \times 10^{-6} \text{ m}^3/\text{s} = 4.67 \text{ cm}^3/\text{s}$$

Problem 14.29.

(a) Referring to Problem 14.28, what would be the effect of doubling the radius r of the tube on the velocity and on the volume flow if everything else, including the pressure P_1 remained the same?

(b) What is the Reynolds number R for the water flowing in the tube of Problem 14.28? Is the flow steady or turbulent?

(c) Find the Reynolds number if the radius were doubled. Would the flow be steady or turbulent?

   Solution

   (a) From Eq. (*14.11*), we see that doubling r quadruples v_m. From Eq. (*14.12*) we see that the volume flow rate goes as r^4, so doubling r will increase $\Delta V/\Delta t$ 16-fold.

   (b) For our tube of radius r we have, using average velocity $v = v_m/2$:

$$R = \frac{d_w v (2r)}{\eta} = \frac{(1000 \text{ kg/m}^3)(0.1655 \text{ m/s})(6.0 \times 10^{-3} \text{ m})}{1.00 \times 10^{-3} \text{ Pl}} = 993$$

   Since the critical Reynolds number is 2000, the flow is steady in this case.

   (c) If the radius is doubled, then v increases fourfold, and R increases eightfold. Therefore, now $R = 7944$, and the flow is turbulent.

Supplementary Problems

Problem 14.30. Water flows without viscosity through a pipe at a rate of 12 cm³/s. Find the velocity of the water (a) at a point where the cross section of the pipe is 3.0 cm², (b) at a point where the radius of the pipe is 0.50 cm.

   Ans. (a) 4.0 cm/s; (b) 15.3 cm/s

Problem 14.31. If the pipe of Problem 14.30 is horizontal, find the pressure difference between the points of parts (a) and (b).

   Ans. 10.9 Pa

Problem 14.32. The venturi setup of Fig. 14.9(c) is used to calculate the speed of a gas of density 2.3 kg/m³ moving through the pipe. If the height difference of the mercury in the two sides of the tube is 15 mm, find the velocity of the gas.

   Ans. 41.7 m/s

Problem 14.33. A large tank filled with water to a height $h_1 = 2.0$ m is fitted with a pipe at its bottom (Fig. 14-15). Assume that $h_2 = 30$ cm and that the cross-sectional areas of the vertical and horizontal portions of the pipe are $a_2 = 25$ cm² and $a_3 = 15$ cm². Assuming that viscosity can be ignored, find (a) the velocity of the water leaving the pipe at point 3; (b) the velocity of the water at point 2, which is *just below* the bottom of the tank; (c) the gauge pressure at point 2.

   Ans. (a) 6.71 m/s; (b) 4.03 m/s; (c) 11.5 kPa

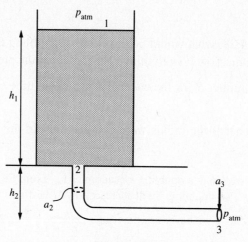

Fig. 14-15

Problem 14.34. Given the pressure p and the volume flow rate $\Delta V/\Delta t$ at a cross section of a pipe, find an expression for the instantaneous power exerted by the liquid behind the cross section on the liquid in front of it.

Ans. power $= Fv = pAv = p\,\Delta V/\Delta t$)

Problem 14.35. A **siphon**, as illustrated in Fig. 14-16, is a system in which one end of a tube rises above a tank in which it is immersed and the other end discharges fluid at a level below the surface of the liquid in the tank. Assume that the tube has a uniform cross sections and that viscosity can be ignored.

(a) If there is no liquid initially in the tube, the siphon will not work. Why not?

(b) Assume that liquid has been drawn up into the tube. How far along the tube must the liquid be before it will continue to flow on its own?

　　Ans. (a) The air in the tube will exert the same pressure as the air over the rest of the liquid surface in the tank, so the levels will remain the same; (b) Just below point 4 (the liquid must completely fill the tube, leaving no air gaps)

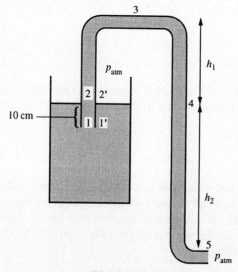

Fig. 14-16

Problem 14.36.   For the siphon of Fig. 14-16, assume the liquid is gasoline (sp gr 0.90); $h_1 = 40$ cm and $h_2 = 60$ cm. The gasoline flows out of the tube at point 5. Find: (*a*) the speed with which the gasoline leaves the tube, (*b*) the gauge pressure at point 4, (*c*) the gauge pressure at point 3, (*d*) the gauge pressure at point 2.

> *Ans.*   (*a*) 3.43 m/s; (*b*) -5.29 kPa; (*c*) -8.82 kPa; (*d*) -5.29 kPa

Problem 14.37.   For the situation in Problem 14.36, find the gauge pressure (*a*) at point 2′, at the same level as point 2 but outside the tube on the surface of the liquid of the tank; (*b*) at point 1, which is just inside the tube and 10 cm below the level of liquid in the tank; (*c*) at point 1′, which is at the same level as point 1 but in the bulk of the liquid. (*d*) If gasoline leaves the tube at 2.0 L/min, what is the cross-sectional area of the tube?

> *Ans.*   (*a*) 0; (*b*) -4.41 kPa; (*c*) 882 Pa; (*d*) 9.7 mm^2

Problem 14.38.   A firefighter holds a hose as in Fig. 14-8. The firefighter finds that it is necessary to exert a horizontal force of 50 N on the hose to keep it still. If the cross-sectional area of the nozzle is 12 cm^2, find the velocity with which the water leaves the hose.

> *Ans.*   6.45 m/s

Problem 14.39.   Heavy oil ($\eta = 9.9$ Pl) is forced through a horizontal pipe of radius 15 mm and length 0.80 m. The high-pressure end is at a gauge pressure of 50 kPa, while the other end is open to the atmosphere.

(*a*)   Find the velocity of the oil on the central axis of the pipe.

(*b*)   Find the volume of oil leaving the pipe per second.

> *Ans.*   (*a*) 0.355 m/s; (*b*) 125 mL/s

Problem 14.40.

(*a*)   Referring to Problem 14.39, what would the new gauge pressure have to be to push the oil through with the same velocity, if the radius were half as large and the length were twice as great?

(*b*)   Repeat (*a*) if the volume flow, not the velocity, stays the same.

> *Ans.*   (*a*) 400 kPa; (*b*) 1600 kPa

Problem 14.41.

(*a*)   Find the Reynolds number for the flow in Problem 14.39 and determine whether the assumption of steady flow is valid. Assume the specific gravity of the oil is 0.75

(*b*)   Repeat for the situation in Problem 14.40(*a*).

(*c*)   Repeat for the situation in Problem 14.40(*b*).

> *Ans.*   (*a*) 0.40 (assumption valid); (*b*) 0.20 (assumption valid); (*c*) 0.80 (assumption valid)

Problem 14.42.   Suppose that an oil additive reduces the viscosity of the oil in Problems 14.39–14.41 to one-sixtieth its original value.

(*a*)   Find the new value for the velocity of the oil in Problem 14.39.

(*b*)   Find the new value of the Reynolds number for this flow, and determine if the flow is steady or turbulent.

(*c*)   If the conditions of Problem 14.40 are imposed, find the new answers for Problems 14.41(*b*) and 14.41(*c*).

> *Ans.*   (*a*) 21.3 m/s; (*b*) 1440 (steady); (*c*) 720 (steady) and 2880 (turbulent)

Problem 14.43.   A sphere of radius 2.0 mm and mass 34.0×10^{-6} kg is released from rest underwater in a deep lake. Assuming Stokes' law holds, and including the effects of buoyancy of the water, find the terminal velocity of the sphere.

       Ans.   0.130 m/s

Problem 14.44.   Consider the droplet of Problem 14.22. Suppose the terminal velocity is found to be 0.30 m/s. If the drag force for turbulent flow is of the form $F_D = Bv^2$, where v is the relative velocity and B is a constant depending on the viscosity and other factors, find the value of B.

       Ans. $0.0036 \text{ N} \cdot \text{s}^2/\text{m}^2$

Problem 14.45.   Show that the Reynolds number is dimensionless.

Chapter 15

Thermodynamics I: Temperature and Heat

15.1 MACROSCOPIC SYSTEMS

In this chapter and the following three chapters we deal with the properties of *large systems,* also known as *macroscopic systems.* Such systems are characterized by their having myriad atoms and/or molecules. Some examples of macroscopic systems are (1) The earth and all its contents; (2) a pebble on the beach; (3) an elephant; (4) an ant; (5) the ant's brain; (6) the earth's atmosphere; (7) a cloud; (8) a mixture of gases confined in a container; (9) a single gas confined in a container; (10) a combination of solid, liquid, and vapor of a single substance; (11) a carbon electrical resistor; and (12) a bar magnet.

From these examples we see that a macroscopic system can vary from huge to relatively small and from extremely complex to relatively simple. The main requirement for a macroscopic system is that it contain large numbers of the various types of atoms and molecules of which it is composed. The typical linear dimension of an atom or molecule is less than 1 nanometer (1.0×10^{-9} m). Even a tiny cube 0.01 mm on a side would hold a trillion atoms or molecules.

In our previous work we dealt with large systems in the form of rigid bodies and fluids at rest and in motion. In those cases, however, we were concerned with the collective organized motion of the system as a whole (e.g., the translation or rotation of the entire rigid body; the organized flow of the liquid as a whole). What we turn to now are the large-scale measurable properties of a system that depend on the myriad random motions and interactions of the component atoms and molecules, rather than their lockstep behavior. The study of such properties constitutes the subject of **thermodynamics**.

Quasistatic Systems

The thermodynamics of most systems is extremely complex—particularly if the system is filled with fiery explosions due to chemical reactions, wildly turbulent flow of material, or pressures that vary from location to location and moment to moment. To allow some kind of simple description, we have recourse to the notion of a *simple system,* such as a gas in a container, a liquid in a tube, or a magnet made of a homogeneous material. Moreover, we generally confine ourselves to simple systems that are **quasistatic**. This means either that they are in mechanical, chemical, and thermal equilibrium (see Sec. 15.2), or that their properties vary so slowly that they can be described at any instant as if in equilibrium.

Thermodynamic Variables

For all systems (quasistatic or not) with well-defined boundaries, there are two quantities that can always be used to characterize the system as a whole. One is the volume V of the system. The other is the total energy associated with the system or, as it is called, the **internal energy** of the system U. Such physical properties as U and V, which describe the system as a whole, are called **macroscopic variables** or **thermodynamic variables**.

Most other thermodynamic variables can be defined only if the system is quasistatic. Thus, in a quasistatic system consisting of a gas, liquid, and/or solid confined to a container, the pressure—that of the gas on the walls of the container and on the liquid and solid surfaces—is a characteristic of the system as a whole. Another thermodynamic variable, important in all quasistatic systems, is the temperature T of the system (see Sec. 15.2).

While P, V, T, and U are among the most common and important thermodynamic variables, we should note that there are many others associated with systems with special properties. For example, the resistance R, the voltage drop $\mathscr{E}$, and the current I are additional thermodynamic variables for a quasistatic simple system in which electricity is flowing. Our discussion of thermodynamics will be restricted to systems for which P, V, T, and U provide the primary description; these are called **chemical systems**.

15.2 THERMAL EQUILIBRIUM AND TEMPERATURE

Types of Equilibrium

Consider a simple system that is in **mechanical equilibrium**. This will be understood to mean not only that the system as a whole does not accelerate, but that within the system the different parts are in mechanical equilibrium with one another—no churning of fluids and no pressure imbalances.

A system in mechanical equilibrium may still undergo change through a chemical reaction. Even if the reaction is so slow that the mechanical equilibrium is not disturbed, the chemical composition is changing, and chemical energy is being released. If we assume that there is no change in chemical composition taking place, we say the system is in **chemical equilibrium**.

If we have a system in both mechanical and chemical equilibrium, we notice that the system can still be changing! Consider a cold block of copper brought into close contact with a hot block of aluminum. After awhile the copper will feel hotter to the touch, even though it has remained in mechanical and chemical equilibrium. A careful examination will also show that its volume has gotten somewhat larger. Similarly, the aluminum block will soon feel cooler to the touch, and its volume will have gotten somewhat smaller. Eventually, the volume changes will stop, and the two blocks will feel equally cool (or hot) to the touch. The two blocks are then said to be in **thermal equilibrium** with each other, or in the same thermal equilibrium state. Two objects in thermal equilibrium with each other are also said to be at the same *temperature*.

A system that is in mechanical, chemical, and thermal equilibrium with its surroundings, as well as internally (one part of the system with another), is said to be in **thermodynamic equilibrium**. Thermodynamic equilibrium means that there is no change on the macroscopic level.

Temperature and The Zeroth Law of Thermodynamics

Experiments involving thermal equilibrium of systems show that all systems have a continuous range of possible thermal equilibrium states, which we qualitatively associate with the degree of "hotness" or "coldness" of the system. For a given system, a change in the thermal equilibrium state is characterized by changes in one or more of the physical properties of the system (such as the change in volume for the blocks discussed in the previous section).

With each thermal equilibrium state of a system we assign a numerical value called the **temperature**, as determined by some agreed-upon procedure. Once we have set up such a numerical temperature scale for one "standard" system (say our copper block), then we can assign temperature values to the thermal equilibrium states of any other system. To do this, we prepare our standard system in a particular thermal equilibrium state with a particular temperature value. Then we assign the same temperature value to any other system that is prepared so that it is in thermal equilibrium with the standard system. The concept of the temperature, or thermal equilibrium state of a system, has great importance as a consequence of the following fundamental law:

> *If two systems A and B are each found to be in thermal equilibrium with a third system C, then when the two systems A and B are brought into contact with each other, they are themselves found to be in thermal equilibrium.*

In other words, the concept of temperature has a universal meaning. All systems at the same temperature T are in fact in thermal equilibrium with each other. This result was so taken for granted by scientists that it was not assigned a name until after the famous first and second laws of thermodynamics were established. Since its truth lies at the very foundation of thermodynamics, it is now often called the **zeroth law of thermodynamics**.

Problem 15.1.

(a)   After the copper and aluminum blocks (referred to earlier in this section) came to thermal equilibrium, the copper block was quickly placed next to an iron block, and no changes in either block were observed. The iron block was then quickly moved into contact with the aluminum block. What changes do you expect in these two blocks?

(b)   If the temperature of the iron block is 30° on some scale, what were the temperatures of the copper and aluminum blocks after they came to equilibrium?

   Solution

   (a)   There would again be no changes, since, according to the zeroth law, the iron and aluminum are in the same equilibrium state.

   (b)   Each was at 30°, since they both were in thermal equilibrium with the iron block.

Temperature Measurement—Temperature Scales and Thermometers

   The procedures for setting up a temperature scale and measuring temperature were outlined in the previous section. We will now actually set up a temperature scale.

   First we single out a physical property of our standard system that varies with the thermal equilibrium states in a well-defined and reproducible way. Such a physical property of a system is called a **thermometric property**. Examples of thermometric properties are (1) the volume of a solid or liquid held under constant external pressure, (2) the length of a rod under constant pressure, (3) the resistance of a wire under constant pressure, (4) the pressure exerted by a constant volume of a confined gas, and (5) the volume of a container of gas held at constant pressure.

   For concreteness, let the standard system be a sample of mercury in a sealed glass container with gas at nearly zero pressure (as in the mercury barometer), and choose volume as the thermometric property. To make the change in volume easily visible, our glass container will consist of a hollow bulb attached to a long, thin, hollow glass stem. When the mercury expands, it is forced up the thin stem so that even small changes in volume are observable (Fig. 15-1).

   Now we are ready to develop the most widely used temperature scale, the **Celsius** (t_C) **scale**. We wish to assign the number $t_C = 0\,°C$ to the thermal equilibrium state (of our standard system) for which ice and water are in equilibrium at atmospheric pressure (the **ice point**). Thus, we dip the glass bulb into a large vat of ice and water in equilibrium, and when the mercury level stops changing, we make an etch mark on the glass tube and label it $0\,°C$. Similarly, we want $t_C = 100\,°C$ to represent the state in which the liquid and vapor phases of water are in equilibrium at atmospheric pressure (the

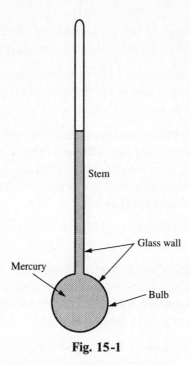

Fig. 15-1

steam point or boiling point), so we take the glass bulb and dip it into a large vat of boiling water. When the mercury level stops changing, we make another etch mark in the tube and label it $100\,°C$. We then divide the distance between the two etch marks into 100 equal marked intervals labeled in $1\,°C$ steps. We can also mark off intervals of the same size above $100°$ and below $0°$. Fig. 15-2(a) shows a schematic of system A with the Celsius scale.

The **Fahrenheit** (t_F) **scale** is defined in precisely the same way, except that the ice point and steam point are defined (for historical reasons) as $t_F = 32\,°F$ and $t_F = 212\,°F$, respectively, and the distance between the two etch marks is divided into 180 equal marked intervals, labeled in $1\,°F$ steps. [Fig. 15-2(b)].

Problem 15.2.   Find the conversion formula between the Fahrenheit and Celsius temperature scales.

Solution

From the definition of the two scales it is clear that a Celsius degree is larger than a Fahrenheit degree, and that, in fact, a $1\,°C$ interval corresponds to a $1.8\,°F$ interval. Consider any Fahrenheit temperature t_F and corresponding Celsius temperature t_C. A quick calculation shows that we must have

$$t_F - 32 = 1.8(t_C - 0) = 1.8 t_C \tag{i}$$

Noting that $1.8 = \frac{9}{5}$, we get

$$t_C = \tfrac{5}{9}(t_F - 32) \tag{ii}$$

$$t_F = \tfrac{9}{5} t_C + 32 \tag{iii}$$

Problem 15.3.   Find the temperature at which both Celsius and Fahrenheit have the same numerical value.

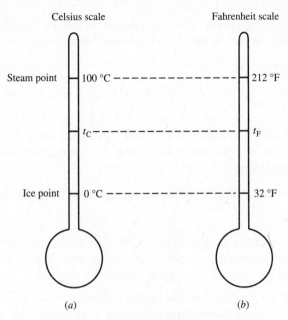

Fig. 15-2

Solution

Set $t_F = t_C$ in Eq. (*iii*) of Problem 15.2. Then

$$t_C = \tfrac{9}{5}t_C + 32 \Rightarrow -\tfrac{4}{5}t_C = 32 \Rightarrow t_C = -40°C = t_F = -40°F$$

Problem 15.4. Change the following temperatures to Celsius: (*a*) 128°F; (*b*) 60°F; (*c*) 0°F; (*d*) −459°F.

Solution

We substitute each value into Eq. (*ii*) of Problem 15.2 to get

(*a*) $t_C = \tfrac{5}{9}(128 - 32) = 53.3°C.$ (*b*) $t_C = \tfrac{5}{9}(60 - 32) = 15.6°C.$

(*c*) $t_C = \tfrac{5}{9}(0 - 32) = -17.8°C.$ (*d*) $t_C = \tfrac{5}{9}(-459 - 32) = -273°C.$

Our temperature-calibrated mercury system is called a **thermometer** because it can be used to measure the temperature of any other object. The procedure is simple: Let the object and thermometer, in contact, come to thermal equilibrium. Then, read their common temperature from the scale.

Problem 15.5. How can a thermometer measure the correct temperature of a system, since the thermal equilibrium of the system itself will change as a consequence of contact with the thermometer?

Solution

It is true that the thermometer records the temperature that corresponds to the final equilibrium state of the system, which is not the state it was in before contact with the thermometer. Nonetheless, if the thermometer is very small (in mass) compared to the system whose temperature is being measured, the change in the system will be negligible. Thus, for example, in using a mercury thermometer to measure the temperature of a child, the drop in the child's temperature due to contact with the cooler thermometer is negligible.

Problem 15.6.   Suppose that a Celsius thermometer was created with alcohol (instead of mercury) as the liquid.

(*a*)   Would the alcohol and mercury thermometers read exactly the same at every temperature being measured? Assume both thermometers are small in comparison with the objects whose temperatures are being measured.

(*b*)   What does your answer to (*a*) imply about measurements of temperature?

Solution

(*a*)   No. Only the two reference temperatures, $0\,^\circ$C (the ice point) and $100\,^\circ$C (the steam point), will definitely read the same. Only if the expansions of both liquids were perfectly linear with temperature would the readings at values in between be identical.

(*b*)   The definition of temperature depends on the particular physical properties of the "official" thermometer. If the official thermometer were taken to be the mercury one, we could still use an alcohol thermometer, but on it the etch marks for the $1\,^\circ$ intervals would not be equally spaced but would be calibrated against the readings of the official thermometer. As it turns out, the volumes of most liquids and solids vary nearly linearly with temperature (far from their melting or boiling points), so they do all give the same readings to a good approximation.

Problem 15.7.   Develop a Celsius gas thermometer, choosing as the thermometric property the pressure of the confined gas.

Solution

Figure 15-3(*a*) shows a gas confined to a fixed volume, with an open-tube manometer used to measure the pressure of the gas inside. We can set up the Celsius scale by noting the pressures corresponding to the ice point and the steam point, P_i and P_s [Fig. 15-3 (*b*) and (*c*)], respectively. Then we can take the temperature of any system by noting the equilibrium pressure of the gas when our gas thermometer is brought into close contact with that system. If the pressure is 40% of the way from P_i to P_s, we define the temperature as being 40% of the way from $0\,^\circ$C to $100\,^\circ$C, or $t_C = 40\,^\circ$C. We thus have a way of measuring Celsuis temperature with our gas thermometer. As in the cases of the alcohol thermometer there is no guarantee that this thermometer will read the same values as the mercury thermometer except at $0\,^\circ$C and $100\,^\circ$C.

As we have seen, our temperature scale is dependent on the particular material being used to define it. It would be nice to be able to set up our scale in a way that is completely independent of the nature of the substance of which the thermometer is made—a "universal" temperature scale. This turns out to be possible for materials in the gaseous state. It was experimentally shown that for all gases confined to fixed volumes and at very low density (dilute), the pressure varies linearly with the temperature, with great precision, over a much wider range of temperatures than for typical liquids. This means that very-low-density gas thermometers, of the type described in the last problem, all read the exact same temperature not only at $0\,^\circ$C and at $100\,^\circ$C but at all other temperatures as well. (For that reason the constant-volume gas thermometer is often considered the "standard" against which other thermometers are calibrated.) The graphs of pressure vs. temperature for all very-low-density gases at fixed volume are thus straight lines, as long as temperature is not so low that the gas is near the point of condensation to liquid or solid.

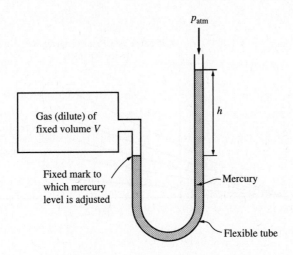

(a) Schematic of constant-volume gas thermometer

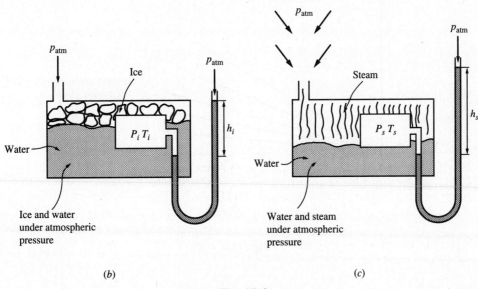

(b)

(c)

Fig. 15-3

If one extrapolates these straight lines until they intersect the temperature axis, a remarkable result is observed. All the lines cut the axis at the same point, $-273.15\,°C$, no matter what gas is involved [Fig. 15-4(a)]. On the basis of this result, one defines a new temperature scale T, known as the **absolute** or **Kelvin temperature scale**. A $1°$ interval—denoted 1 K—on this scale is the same size as a $1°$ interval on the Celsius scale ($1\,°C$), but the zero point is shifted to $-273.15\,°C$. Thus

$$T = t_C + 273.15 \qquad (15.1)$$

Figure 15-4(b) shows that the pressure P of a low-density gas at constant volume is directly proportional to its Kelvin temperature T. Since pressure cannot be negative, one might surmise that $T = 0\,K$ was the lowest possible temperature in the universe—"absolute zero." In fact, this is the case.

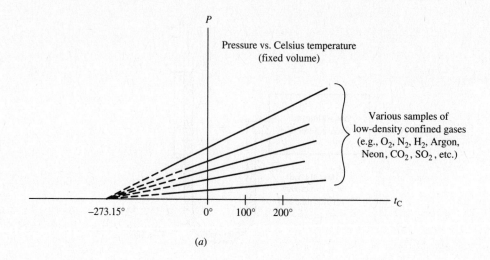

(a)

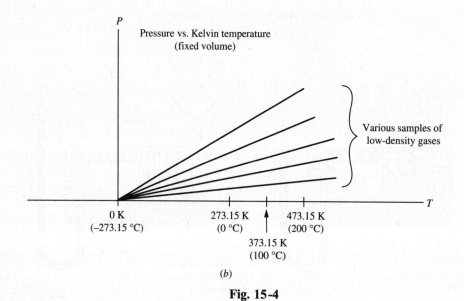

(b)

Fig. 15-4

Problem 15.8. Find the Kelvin temperature corresponding to (a) $t_C = 0\,°C$; (b) $t_C = 100\,°C$; (c) $t_F = 100\,°F$.

Solution

(a) Using Eq. (15.1), we get $T = 0 + 273 = 273$ K. (To three significant figures.)

(b) $T = 100 + 273 = 373$ K.

(c) We first convert from Fahrenheit to Celsius:

$$t_C = \tfrac{5}{9}(t_F - 32) = \tfrac{5}{9}(100 - 32) = 37.8\,°C$$

Next we convert to Kelvin: $T = 37.8 + 273.2 = 311$ K.

Problem 15.9. The entire development of the Kelvin scale can be redone using the Fahrenheit scale rather than the Celsius scale as the starting point. The resulting scale is called the Rankine scale, T_R.

(a)   Find the Fahrenheit temperature that corresponds to zero on the Rankine scale.

(b)   Find the formula that relates the Rankine and Fahrenheit scales.

Solution

(a)   This Fahrenheit temperature must correspond to $t_C = -273.15\,°C$. Then

$$t_F = \tfrac{9}{5}t_C + 32 = -459.67\,°F$$

(b)   Since the zero of the Rankine scale corresponds to $t_F = -459.67\,°F$ and the degree size is the same as the Fahrenheit degree, we must have $T_R = t_F + 459.67$.

Problem 15.10.   In setting up the Celsius and Fahrenheit temperature scales, we needed two reference points, which we took to be the ice point and the steam point. Show that the Kelvin scale can be completely defined with only one reference point.

Solution

We use a constant-volume gas thermometer to establish the scale, and we recall that P is proportional to T for such a thermometer. Let P^* be the pressure reading of the thermometer at some reference temperature T^*, and let P be the reading at any other temperature T. We must have

$$\frac{P}{T} = \frac{P^*}{T^*} \qquad \text{or} \qquad T = \frac{T^*}{P^*}\,P \tag{15.2}$$

Thus one reference temperature T^* allows us to use the thermometer to determine any temperature T.

The reference temperature in Problem 15.10, in principle, could be chosen as either the ice point or the steam point, but in fact it is not. Instead, it is chosen as the unique equilibrium state of water, called the **triple point**, the temperature at which all three phases of water—solid, liquid, and vapor—coexist. The temperature of the triple point is just slightly above the temperature of the ice point and corresponds on the Celsius scale to $t_C = 0.01\,°C$. For this reason the value of T^* (Problem 15.10) is defined to be 273.16 K, assuring that the newly defined scale will be essentially identical to the earlier version. Then

$$T = \frac{P}{P^*}\,(273.16\text{ K}) \tag{15.3}$$

where P^* is the pressure reading of our gas thermometer at the triple point of water, and P is the pressure reading at the temperature T.

Problem 15.11.

(a)   A constant-volume gas thermometer is immersed in water at the triple point, and the pressure is measured as $P^* = 2.5 \times 10^3$ Pa. The thermometer is next placed in an oven cavity, where its pressure is found to be 3.0×10^4 Pa. What is the Kelvin temperature of the oven?

(b)   What would be the pressure reading in the same oven for a gas thermometer whose pressure at the triple point was 1.0 kPa?

Solution

(a)   By (15.3),

$$T = \frac{30}{2.5}\,(273\text{ K}) = 3280\text{ K}$$

(b)   By Problem 15.10, the pressures of both thermometers must increase by the factor 30/2.5 = 12. The pressure of the new thermometer must then be 12(1.0 kPa) = 12 kPa.

Linear and Volume Expansivity

Among the most common thermometric properties of matter are the linear dimensions, surface area, and volume of solids, and the volume of liquids, all under constant pressure. If we have a rod of length L at a given absolute temperature and we increase the temperature by a small amount ΔT, we find that the length of the rod increases by an amount ΔL that is proportional to the original length L and to the temperature increase ΔT:

$$\Delta L = \alpha L \, \Delta T \qquad\qquad (15.4)$$

The proportionality constant α is called the **coefficient of linear expansion**; it depends on the material of which the rod is made. The units of α are those of reciprocal temperature, as can be seen from (15.4). Note that $\Delta T = \Delta t_C$, since the degree sizes are the same; it is common to give α in $°C^{-1}$. For most solids α will vary only slightly with temperature and pressure, so long as the solid is not close to the melting temperature. Equation (15.4) holds reasonably well, even when ΔT is substantial, as long as $\Delta L/L \ll 1$. Values of α for selected solids are given in Table 15.1.

Table 15.1. Linear Expansion

Solid	$10^5 \times \alpha$, $°C^{-1}$
Aluminum	2.55
Brass	1.93
Copper	1.67
Glass (Pyrex)	0.33
Iron (steel)	1.20
Platinum	0.90
Silver	1.90
Zinc	3.20

Problem 15.12.   An aluminum rod 3.0 m long is heated uniformly until its temperature rises by 20°C. Find the fractional change in the length of the rod.

Solution

By (15.4) and Table 15.1,

$$\frac{\Delta L}{L} = \alpha \, \Delta T = (2.55 \times 10^{-5}\,°C^{-1})(20\,°C) = 0.00051$$

Problem 15.13.   A railroad track is made of steel rails which are each 30 m long. If each rail can expand freely, how much space should be left between successive rails to avoid buckling? Assume that the maximum increase in temperature due to heating from the sun is 60°C.

Solution

The space should be sufficient to accommodate the maximum ΔL of each rail due to heating.

$$\Delta L = (1.2 \times 10^{-5}\,{}^\circ\mathrm{C}^{-1})(30\ \mathrm{m})(60\,{}^\circ\mathrm{C}) = 21.6\ \mathrm{mm}$$

Problem 15.14. A homogeneous material will have the same expansivity properties in every direction. Hence such an object changes its overall size upon heating, but not its shape.

(a) Given this fact, find the new diameter of a solid brass sphere of radius 0.9535 m when its temperature rises 200°C.

(b) If the sphere of (a) were hollow instead, with inner diameter 0.8535 m, what would be the new inside and outside diameters for the same temperature rise?

(c) In (b), by how much does the thickness of the spherical shell increase?

Solution

(a) Equation (15.4) applies to any diameter:

$$\Delta d = (1.93 \times 10^{-5}\,{}^\circ\mathrm{C}^{-1})(0.9535\ \mathrm{m})(200\,{}^\circ\mathrm{C}) = 0.0037\ \mathrm{m}$$

For a new diameter of 0.9572 m.

(b) The outer diameter still changes by 3.7 mm. Since all linear dimensions of the hollow sphere must expand in proportion, the inner diameter changes by

$$\Delta d_i = (1.93 \times 10^{-5}\,{}^\circ\mathrm{C}^{-1})(0.8535\ \mathrm{m})(200\,{}^\circ\mathrm{C}) = 0.0033\ \mathrm{m}$$

(c) We could reapply Eq. (15.4) to the 50-mm thickness of the brass shell. Instead we can just take the difference between the known expansions of the outer and inner *radii*, to obtain a

$$\tfrac{1}{2}(3.7\ \mathrm{mm} - 3.3\ \mathrm{mm}) = 0.2\ \mathrm{mm}$$

increase in shell thickness.

Note.   The hole (any hole) expands upon heating just like the homogeneous material itself.

Problem 15.15. A steel hoop at $t_\mathrm{C} = 20\,{}^\circ\mathrm{C}$ has inner diameter 100.005 cm. The hoop is to be placed over the rim of a wheel that is 100.044 cm in diameter. To what temperature t'_C should the hoop be heated to just fit over the wheel?

Solution

The inner diameter of the hoop must be increased by 0.039 cm. Then, from Eq. (15.4), 0.039 cm = $(1.2 \times 10^{-5}\,{}^\circ\mathrm{C}^{-1})$ (100.005 cm) ΔT. Solving for ΔT, we have $\Delta T = 32.5\,{}^\circ\mathrm{C}$, and $t'_\mathrm{C} = 52.5\,{}^\circ\mathrm{C}$.

Problem 15.16. A steel sphere of diameter 4.0025 cm is to be passed through a brass loop of inner diameter 4.0012 cm. If the steel and brass are heated together, by how many degrees must they be heated for the sphere to just fit through the loop?

Solution

Since the sphere starts off with a diameter 0.0013 cm larger than the loops, we must have

$$\alpha_b d_\mathrm{loop} \Delta T = \alpha_s d_\mathrm{sph} \Delta T + 0.0013\ \mathrm{cm}$$

The diameters are given, and the expansion coefficients are available from Table 15.1.

$$(1.93 \times 10^{-5}\,^\circ\mathrm{C}^{-1})(4.00 \text{ cm})\,\Delta T = (1.2 \times 10^{-5}\,^\circ\mathrm{C}^{-1})(4.00 \text{ cm})\,\Delta T + 0.0013 \text{ cm}$$

(Note that we approximated both diameters as 4.00 cm in the above expression, since these are to be multiplied by extremely small numbers, and the last decimal places of the diameters will contribute negligibly). Solving, we get $\Delta T = 44.5\,^\circ\mathrm{C}$.

Problem 15.17. Show that the change in volume of a homogeneous rectangular solid, due to a temperature rise ΔT, can be expressed as

$$\Delta V = \beta V\,\Delta T$$

where $\beta = 3\alpha$ is the coefficient of volume expansion of the solid.

Solution

If the dimensions of the solid are originally L_1, L_2, and L_3, then after heating, the new dimensions are

$$L_1' = L_1 + \alpha L_1\,\Delta\mathrm{T} = L_1(1 + \alpha\,\Delta\mathrm{T}) \qquad L_2' = L_2(1 + \alpha\,\Delta T) \qquad L_3' = L_3(1 + \alpha\,\Delta\mathrm{T})$$

The new volume is then

$$V' = L_1'L_2'L_3' = L_1L_2L_3(1 + \alpha\,\Delta T)^3 \tag{i}$$

We expand the term in parentheses, getting

$$(1 + \alpha\,\Delta T)^3 = 1 + 3\alpha\,\Delta T + 3(\alpha\,\Delta T)^2 + (\alpha\,\Delta T)^3 \tag{ii}$$

Recalling that $\alpha\,\Delta T$ is very small, even for reasonably large values of ΔT, we can ignore the last two terms to get $(1 + \alpha\,\Delta T)^3 \approx 1 + 3\alpha\,\Delta T$. Substituting into Eq. (i) we get

$$V' = V(1 + 3\alpha\,\Delta T) \qquad \text{or} \qquad \Delta V = V' - V = (3\alpha)V\,\Delta T = \beta V\,\Delta T \qquad \text{with} \qquad \beta = 3\alpha$$

Problem 15.18. Assume that the rectangular solid of the previous problem is made of aluminum and has dimensions $L_1 = 30$ cm, $L_2 = 20$ cm, and $L_3 = 50$ cm. Find (*a*) the volume expansivity of the rectangle; (*b*) the change in volume due to a ΔT of $40\,^\circ\mathrm{C}$.

Solution

(*a*) The volume expansivity of aluminum can be obtained from Table 15.1: $\beta = 3\alpha = 7.65 \times 10^{-5}\,^\circ\mathrm{C}^{-1}$.

(*b*) $V = L_1L_2L_3 = 30{,}000 \text{ cm}^3 \Rightarrow \Delta V = (7.65 \times 10^{-5}\,^\circ\mathrm{C}^{-1})\,(30{,}000 \text{ cm}^3)\,(40\,^\circ\mathrm{C}) = 91.8 \text{ cm}^3$.

The notion of linear expansion does not apply to liquids. Nevertheless, liquid volumes expand in accordance with the same law as for solids:

$$\Delta V = \beta V\,\Delta T \tag{15.5}$$

where β is now the volume expansivity of the liquid in question. Some values of β for liquids are shown in Table 15.2. Note that liquids generally have larger β values than solids.

Problem 15.19. The volume of the Pyrex glass bulb of a large mercury thermometer is $V = 0.30$ cm^3. The cross-sectional area of the inside of the stem is $A = 0.0020$ cm^2. If the temperature of the bulb increases by $30\,^\circ\mathrm{C}$, what is the increase Δh in the height of mercury in the stem?

Table 15.2. Volume Expansion

Liquid	$10^5 \times \beta$, °C^{-1}
Alcohol	110
Glycerine	53
Mercury	18.2
Turpentine	94
Water	30

Solution

We note that as the temperature increases, the volume of mercury increases, forcing mercury up the tube. However, the volume of the glass bulb also increases, and this must be taken into account. We ignore the expansion of the tiny amount of mercury already in the stem, as well as the slight change in cross section of the stem itself. The net volume that is forced up the stem, $A\,\Delta h$, is then the difference between the increase in volume of the mercury and the glass bulb:

$$A\,\Delta h = \Delta V_{\text{merc}} - \Delta V_{\text{bulb}} = \left(\beta_{\text{merc}} - \beta_{\text{glass}}\right) V\,\Delta T$$

From Tables 15.1 and 15.2, we get $(18.2 \times 10^{-5}\text{°C}^{-1} - 1.0 \times 10^{-5}\text{°C}^{-1})$ (0.30 cm^3) $(30\text{°C}) = 0.00155 \text{ cm}^3$. We must have $\Delta h\, A = \Delta V_{\text{net}} \Rightarrow \Delta h = \Delta V / A = 0.00155 \text{ cm}^3 \,/\, 0.0020 \text{ cm}^2 = 0.775 \text{ cm}$.

It should be noted that for liquids near the melting point, (15.5) can be quite a poor approximation. In fact, in some cases, β changes rapidly near the melting point; it can even change sign. This occurs for those few liquids that expand upon freezing, such as water. With decreasing temperature, the volume of water decreases until about 4°C, below which the volume increases until solidification at 0°C. The fact that water expands upon freezing explains why ice floats, since the ice is less dense than the water.

15.3 THERMAL ENERGY; HEAT CONSTANTS

Thermal Energy and Heat

As we have seen, when two systems in mechanical and chemical equilibrium, but at different temperatures, are brought into contact, changes in both systems take place until they reach a common temperature. Early scientists believed that some invisible and weightless substance, which they called **caloric**, flows from a hotter to a cooler object until both objects reach thermal equilibrium. Thanks to the work of Joule and others in the first half of the nineteenth century, it became clear that it is not a substance but **thermal energy** that is transferred between two macroscopic systems in contact.

At the interface between the two systems, the more energetic atoms and molecules of the hotter system interact with their less energetic counterparts in the cooler system. The net result of these interactions is a transfer of energy to the atoms and molecules of the cooler system. Such transfer of energy is called **heat**.

Viewed macroscopically, heat is a *nonmechanical transfer of energy*, since the interacting systems are in mechanical equilibrium. Heat, then, is the counterpart of *work*, which (Sec. 6.6) is the *mechanical transfer of energy* from one system to another. Heat is actually the statistical "summing up" of the mechanical work done by the random interactions of the individual atoms and molecules of our two systems. Like work, heat is not something that resides in a system but is the thermal energy transfer from one system to another. The related quantity that resides in a system is "disorganized" internal energy, or thermal energy, which is due to the random motion and jiggling of the myriad atoms and molecules making up our macroscopic system.

Problem 15.20.   The three common forms of internal energy are mechanical, chemical, and thermal. Figure 15-5 shows a system consisting of a container of hydrogen and oxygen gases and a long spiral spring. The container is slowly oscillating at the end of the spring. The entire system is at temperature T.

(a)   Describe the various internal energies of the system.

(b)   A spark causes the oxygen and hydrogen to explode, but the container doesn't burst. Is this process quasistatic? If not, explain why.

(c)   If no energy can escape from the system, what changes in the internal energy distribution would you expect after the system comes to internal equilibrium?

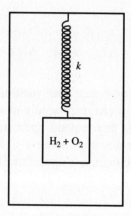

Fig. 15-5

Solution

(a)   This system possesses all three forms of internal energy. The *mechanical energy* is the sum of the kinetic energy, the gravitational potential energy, and the spring potential energy associated with the oscillation. The *chemical energy* is the potential energy of forces within the oxygen and hydrogen molecules that is available to be released in their combination into water molecules. The *thermal energy* is that associated with the jiggling molecules making up the gas mixture, the container, and the spring, at their common temperature T.

(b)   Prior to the explosion the system is quasistatic: the slow oscillations do not cause turbulence in the gas, which has a definite pressure associated with it. During and immediately after the explosion the system is, of course, not quasistatic. There is no common pressure in all parts of the container during the explosion, and the same is true for temperature. After the explosion, the contents of the container (water and any leftover gases) quickly reach a common pressure and temperature, but it takes a certain amount of time for thermal energy to travel from the gas and container to the spring, thereby bringing the entire system into equilibrium.

(c) The chemical potential energy will have been largely converted to thermal energy, as evidenced by the new higher temperature of the container and the spring. If the explosion occurred symmetrically within the container, no net force was exerted by the exploding gases on the container and the mechanical energy will remain unchanged. In an asymmetric explosion, however, some of the energy of the explosion could appear as increased mechanical energy of the system.

Heat Units

The historical unit of heat in the metric system is the **calorie** (cal), which originally was defined as the "amount of heat"—i.e., the amount of thermal energy in transit—necessary (at atmospheric pressure and a particular starting temperature) to raise the temperature of 1 gram of water $1\,°C$. In the English system the corresponding unit is the **British thermal unit** (Btu), which is the amount of heat necessary to raise 1 lb of water $1\,°F$. The conversion is 1 Btu = 252 cal. The fact that several definitions of the calorie have been in use, differing one from another in the fourth decimal place, may lead to some confusion. These calories are given separate labels and are now all defined in terms of the SI unit of energy, the joule. In this book we will employ only the "thermochemical" calorie, where $1\text{ cal} \equiv 4.184\text{ J}$.

> **Note.** The common food calorie is really 1000 heat calories, as defined above: 1 food calorie = 1 kcal or 4184 J.

Problem 15.21.

(a) A bunsen burner flame has been adjusted so that it generates 30 cal/s. Assuming that all this heat enters a container of water, what is the change, in J, of the internal energy of the container and water after 3.0 min?

(b) If instead the same change in internal energy were to take place through the work done on the water by a rotating paddle driven by a falling 100-kg mass (Fig. 15-6), through what distance would the mass have to fall? Assume that the mass falls at constant speed and that the pulley systems are frictionless.

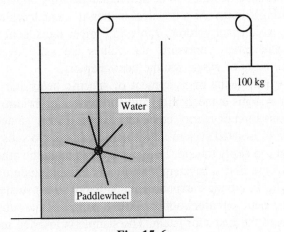

Fig. 15-6

Solution

(a) The increase in the internal energy of the system is just (30 cal/s) (180 s) = 5400 cal. Multiplying by 4.184 J/cal, we get 22,600 J.

(b) The falling mass must lose 22,600 J of gravitational potential energy. Thus, $mgh = 22{,}600$ J $\Rightarrow$ (100 kg) (9.8 m/s^2)$h = 22{,}600$ J $\Rightarrow h = 23$ m.

Specific Heats and Heat Capacities

The relationship between temperature and heat was already a major topic of investigation in the time of the caloric hypothesis. It was noted that for each different substance a characteristic amount of heat had to flow into a unit mass of the substance to produce a 1° rise in temperature. This characteristic property was quantified in the concept of **specific heat**. If ΔQ is the amount of heat entering a mass m of a pure substance and if the consequent temperature rise is ΔT, the specific heat c of the substance is given by

$$c = \frac{\Delta Q}{m\,\Delta T} \qquad \text{or} \qquad \Delta Q = mc\,\Delta T \qquad\qquad (15.6)$$

The working SI unit of specific heat is the kJ/(kg · K), in which °C may be substituted for K. Other commonly used metric units are cal/(g · °C) = kcal/(kg · °C), J/(g · °C) = kJ/(kg · °C), and J/(kg · °C) = 10^{-3} kJ/(kg · °C).

Clearly a substance with a high specific heat requires more heat energy to raise its temperature by a given amount than one with a low specific heat. The **heat capacity** C of our sample of material is the total amount of heat needed to produce a degree rise in temperature: $C = \Delta Q/\Delta T$. From Eq. (15.6),

$$C = mc \qquad\qquad (15.7)$$

Unlike heat capacity, which depends on the mass of the sample, specific heat is an intrinsic property. Nonetheless, it does depend to a slight degree on two other intrinsic properties, the material's temperature and pressure. For many substances the specific heat stays constant over moderate ranges of these variables. For water at atmospheric pressure, for example, the specific heat varies from about 4210 J/(kg · K) at $t_C = 0$°C down to about 4180 J/(kg · K) at $t_C = 30$°C and back up to about 4210 J/(kg · K) at $t_C = 100$°C. It thus varies by less than 1% over the full 100°C temperature range of water.

The specific heat also depends on the manner in which thermal energy is transferred to the substance. For example, the specific heat will be different depending on whether pressure or volume is held fixed during the heating process. As a practical matter, it is much easier to heat liquids and solids at constant pressure than at constant volume. Table 15.3 gives the specific heats of some solids and liquids under constant atmospheric pressure: the values are valid over a fairly wide range of temperatures. For specific heats of gases, see the next chapter.

Calorimetry is the experimental measurement of specific heats and other heat constants. It is based on the fact that, for systems in mechanical and chemical equilibrium, the thermal energy lost by one system must, by conservation of energy, equal the thermal energy gained by the other systems it is in contact with. Consider an isolated system that is composed of two subsystems in close "thermal" contact, meaning that heat can easily transfer from one subsystem to the other. If Q_{out} is the magnitude of heat transferring out of the first subsystem and Q_{in} is the magnitude of heat entering the second subsystem, then $Q_{\text{out}} = Q_{\text{in}}$. In a typical experimental situation, an insulated container holding water makes up the second subsystem, or **calorimeter**, while a sample of the substance whose specific heat is to be measured composes the first subsystem. The sample is inserted into the calorimeter and the two come to thermal equilibrium.

Table 15.3.   Specific Heats at Atmospheric Pressure

Substance	Specific Heat	
	kcal/(kg · °C)	kJ/(kg · °C)
Solids:		
Aluminum	0.22	0.92
Brass	0.090	0.377
Copper	0.093	0.389
Gold	0.031	0.130
Ice (near 0°C)	0.50	2.09
Iron (steel)	0.11	0.46
Lead	0.031	0.130
Platinum	0.032	0.134
Zinc	0.092	0.385
Liquids:		
Alcohol	0.55	2.30
Glycerine	0.58	2.43
Mercury	0.33	1.38
Turpentine	0.42	1.76
Water	1.00	4.184

Problem 15.22.   A lead brick, of mass $m_l = 3.0$ kg and at a temperature of $t_l = 300°C$, is dropped into an insulated copper vessel of mass $m_c = 1.5$ kg that contains $m_w = 2.0$ kg of water; the calorimeter temperature is $t_0 = 20°C$. If the final temperature at equilibrium is $t = 31.7°C$, find the specific heat of lead.

Solution

For the lead,

$$Q_{out} = m_l c_l(t_l - t) = (3.0 \text{ kg})c_l(300°C - 31.7°C)$$

For the calorimeter,

$$Q_{in} = m_w c_w(t - t_0) + m_c c_c(t - t_0)$$
$$= (2.0 \text{ kg})[4.184 \text{ kJ}/(\text{kg} \cdot °C)](31.7°C - 20°C) + (1.5 \text{ kg})[0.389 \text{ kJ}/(\text{kg} \cdot °C)](31.7°C - 20°C)$$

Equating Q_{out} and Q_{in}, and solving for c_l, we get $c_l = 0.130$ kJ/(kg · °C), which checks with Table 15.3.

Note.   In Q_{out} we subtract the final temperature from the hot temperature, while in Q_{in} we subtract the cold temperature from the final temperature, since both Q's are defined to be positive.

Problem 15.23.   An aluminum block, of mass 200 g and a temperature of 400°C, is dropped into an aluminum calorimeter of mass 1.0 kg filled with 100 g of water at a temperature of 5.0°C. Find the temperature when equilibrium is reached.

Solution

Using the specific heats from Table 15.3, we have

$$Q_{out} = Q_{in} \Rightarrow (0.200 \text{ kg})[0.22 \text{ kcal}/(\text{kg} \cdot {}^\circ\text{C})](400{}^\circ\text{C} - t_F)$$
$$= (0.100 \text{ kg})[1.00 \text{ kcal}/(\text{kg} \cdot {}^\circ\text{C})](t_F - 5.0{}^\circ\text{C}) + (1.00 \text{ kg})[0.22 \text{ kcal}/(\text{kg} \cdot {}^\circ\text{C})](t_F - 5.0{}^\circ\text{C})$$

We bring all terms involving t_F to the right and all numerical terms to the left, obtaining $19.2 = 0.364 t_F \Rightarrow t_F = 52.7{}^\circ\text{C}$.

Heat Constants

All substances have a solid, a liquid, and a vapor phase. For a solid substance under a fixed pressure, there is a definite temperature at which it will become liquid (melt) called the **melting point**. At the melting point one must add a definite amount of heat, called the **heat of fusion** L_f, to melt each unit mass of the substance. This process is reversible: if one extracts a like amount of heat from the liquid at the melting point (now renamed the **fusion point**), the liquid will become solid again.

Likewise, for a liquid under fixed pressure, there is a definite temperature, called the **boiling point**, at which the liquid will convert to vapor. Again, one must add a definite amount of heat, called the **heat of vaporization** L_v, to vaporize each unit mass of the substance at the boiling point. This process, too, is reversible, with the boiling point becoming the **liquefaction point**.

Melting and boiling points, and their associated heat constants, vary with pressure. The values given in Table 15.4 reflect normal atmospheric pressure.

Table 15.4. Heat Constants at Normal Atmospheric Pressure

Substance	Melting Point, °C	L_f, kJ/kg	Boiling Point, °C	L_v, kJ/kg
Hydrogen	−259	58.6	−253	452
Oxygen	−219	13.8	−183	213
Alcohol	−114	104.	78	854
Mercury	−39	11.8	357	272
Water	0	335.	100	2256
Lead	327	24.6	1750	871
Zinc	420	118.		
Gold	1064	64.5	2660	1578

A third phase transition—solid to vapor, or **sublimation**—must also be considered. For each substance there is a pressure below which there can be no liquid phase. Below that pressure, adding heat to a solid will lead directly to the vapor state. Again, for each fixed pressure, there is a definite temperature, or **sublimation point**, at which sublimation occurs, and a definite amount of heat, called the **heat of sublimation** L_s must be added to each unit mass of solid at that temperature to convert it to vapor. Again, the process is reversible.

A helpful means of keeping track of phase changes is a **pressure vs. temperature**, or *P-T*, **diagram**. For a pure substance (e.g., carbon dioxide, methane, mercury, water, or aluminum) the diagram will resemble Fig. 15-7(a) or (b). The three smooth curves separate the solid, liquid, and vapor domains. At any pressure and temperature to the left of the sublimation and fusion curves the

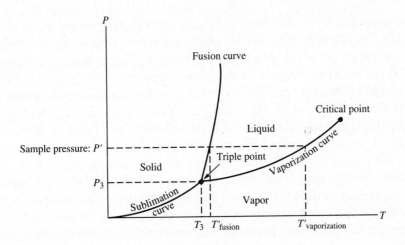

(a) Substance contracts on freezing

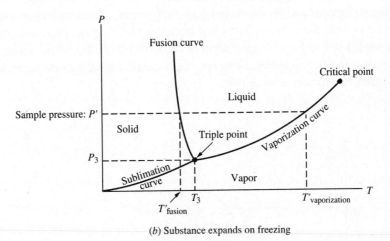

(b) Substance expands on freezing

Fig. 15-7

substance is in the solid phase. Similarly, any point below the sublimation and vaporization curves lies in the vapor domain. The liquid phase corresponds to the region between the fusion and vaporization curves above the triple point. For any given pressure P there is a corresponding temperature on the fusion curve, which is the melting point or fusion point for that pressure. For the same pressure there is also a corresponding (higher) temperature on the vaporization curve, and this is the boiling point or liquefaction point for that pressure. The graph clearly shows how the values of the melting and boiling points vary with pressure. Below the **triple point**, which is clearly the single point at which vapor, liquid, and solid coexist, we have only sublimation.

The P-T diagram (Fig. 15-7) also allows us to visualize the effects of heating. If we start at a given pressure, say P', and at $T = 0\,\mathrm{K}$, and we slowly add heat to the substance while holding the pressure constant, the solid's temperature will rise until it reaches the melting point on the fusion curve. The temperature will stay constant throughout the melting process. After all the solid has been converted to liquid, the temperature begins to rise again, and we slowly move along the dashed line until the vaporization curve is reached. At this point the liquid starts turning into vapor; the temperature remains at the boiling point until the vaporization is complete. After that the temperature continues to rise.

It should be noted that while the entire melting or vaporization process seems to take place at a single point on the P vs. T graph, in fact the volume of the system is changing during the process. The volume of the liquid at a given P and T on the fusion curve is different than the corresponding volume of the solid. This is even more dramatic for liquid and vapor on the vaporization curve.

Thus, for example, during the vaporization process, the volume changes from that of 100% liquid until it becomes that of 100% vapor. We must keep adding heat until all the liquid has become completely vapor. The same analysis is true of solid and liquid at a point on the fusion curve.

As shown above, crossing from one side of the vaporization curve to the other corresponds to a major change in the volume of the substance. As we repeat this process at higher and higher constant pressures, however, the difference in the volume between 100% liquid and 100% vapor decreases. At the pressure of the critical point (see Fig. 15-7) this difference in volume completely disappears, and the difference between liquid and vapor loses its meaning. Figure 15-8 illustrates the crossing of the vaporization curve at different fixed pressures (and corresponding temperatures) ranging from the triple-point pressure P_3 to the critical pressure P_c in a graph of P vs. V (pressure vs. volume). The dotted line on the left, called the **liquid saturation curve**, corresponds to points of 100% liquid, on the verge of starting to vaporize, while the dotted line on the right, called the **vapor saturation curve**, corresponds to points where the substance has just become 100% vapor. The horizontal dashed lines represent the changing volume for changing relative composition of the liquid-vapor mixtures at the given sample pressures and temperatures. Note how the volume differences between 100% liquid and 100% vapor decreases toward the critical point.

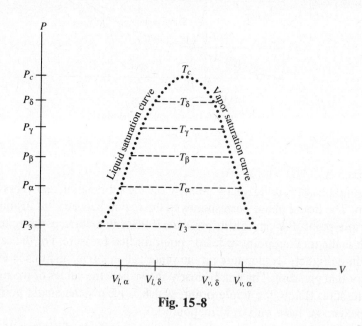

Fig. 15-8

Problem 15.24. The triple-point pressure of water is $P_3 = 0.006P_{atm}$, while the critical pressure is $P = 221P_{atm}$.

(a) What is the requirement for the sublimation of water?

(b) What is the difference between the densities of liquid and vapor water at the critical point?

(c) Are these phenomena observable in everyday life?

Solution

(a) One must reduce the pressure to below $0.006P_{atm}$; otherwise ice first melts into a liquid phase and then vaporizes.

(b) Zero (compare the volumes of a unit mass of liquid and a unit mass of vapor).

(c) Ice must be present in a highly evacuated chamber to reproduce the conditions for the triple point or for sublimation. Similarly, one would have to have water under extreme pressure to reproduce the conditions at the critical point or above. Thus these phenomena are not part of our normal experience.

Problem 15.25.

(a) Suppose the volume $V_{l,\delta}$ in Fig. 15-7 is 30.0 mL, while that of $V_{v,\delta}$ is 200 mL. What fraction, x, of the mass of the liquid has vaporized (at pressure P_δ) when the volume is $V'_\delta = 100$ mL?

(b) If the heat of vaporization of this fictitious substance is 600 kJ/kg and the mass is 80 g, how much heat must be added to the 30.0 mL of liquid to reach the volume 100 mL?

Solution

(a) $$V'_\delta = 100 \text{ mL} = (1-x)(30.0 \text{ mL}) + x(200 \text{ mL}) \qquad \text{or} \qquad x = 0.41$$

(b) From part (a), the amount of liquid vaporized is (0.41) (80 g) = 32.8 g. Then,

$$\text{Heat} = (600 \text{ kJ/kg})(0.0328 \text{ kg}) = 19.7 \text{ kJ}$$

We now apply the techniques of calorimetry to heats of fusion, vaporization, and sublimation.

Problem 15.26. A 0.500-kg block of ice, initially at $-50°C$, is placed in a large pot that is open to the atmosphere. The pot is heated at a constant rate of 20 W; all the heat enters the ice.

(a) Describe qualitatively the processes that occur as the ice is heated, from the start until it has turned into water vapor.

(b) How long does it take to raise the temperature of the ice to $0°C$?

(c) How long does it take to completely melt the block at $0°C$?

(d) How long does it take to raise the temperature of the liquid water from $0°C$ to $100°C$?

(e) How long does it take to vaporize the water at $100°C$?

Solution

(a) The ice will first warm up until it reaches $0°C$, the melting point at atmospheric pressure. At that point the ice will start to melt, and the temperature will remain at $0°C$ all through the melting process. After all the ice has melted, we have water at $0°C$, which will now absorb the incoming heat and rise steadily in temperature until it reaches the boiling point at $100°C$. At that point it will start to boil while it stays at $100°C$, until all the liquid has turned to vapor.

(b) From Table 15.3 we see that the specific heat of ice is 2090 J/(kg · °C). Then, the heat necessary to raise the temperature of the ice to $0°C$ is $Q = (0.50$ kg$)$ [2090 J/(kg · °C)] $(50°C) = 52.3$ kJ. At a rate of 20 J/s this will take 2615 s = 43.6 min.

(c) The heat of fusion of ice is 335 kJ/kg, so the heat necessary to melt the ice is $Q = (0.50$ kg$)$ (335 kJ/kg) = 167.5 kJ. The time is then 8375 s = 140 min.

(d)   The specific heat of water is 4.184 kJ/(kg · °C), so the heat to raise the water from 0°C to 100°C is

$$(0.50 \text{ kg})[4.184 \text{ kJ}/(\text{kg} \cdot {}^\circ\text{C})](100{}^\circ\text{C}) = 209 \text{ kJ}$$

and the time it takes is 10,500 s = 174 min.

(e)   The heat of vaporization of water is 2256 kJ/kg, so the heat to vaporize all the water is

$$(0.50 \text{ kg})(2256 \text{ kJ/kg}) = 1128 \text{ kJ}$$

and the time taken is 56,400 s = 940 min.

Problem 15.27.   A calorimeter has a shell of negligible heat capacity and contains 0.5 kg of ice and 0.5 kg of water in equilibrium. A 2.0-kg block of steel at 500°C is placed in the calorimeter, and the system is allowed to come to equilibrium.

(a)   What is the final equilibrium temperature t_0?

(b)   What would have happened if the mass of the steel block were 0.50 kg, all else being the same?

Solution

(a)   For the steel,

$$Q_{\text{out}} = m_s c_s (t_s - t_0) = (2.0 \text{ kg})[0.46 \text{ kJ}/(\text{kg} \cdot {}^\circ\text{C})](500{}^\circ\text{C} - t_0)$$

For the calorimeter,

$$Q_{\text{in}} = m_{\text{ice}} L_i + (m_{\text{ice}} + m_w) c_w (t_0 - 0{}^\circ\text{C}) = (0.50 \text{ kg})(335 \text{ kJ/kg}) + (1.0 \text{ kg})(4.184 \text{ kJ/kg} \cdot {}^\circ\text{C}) t_0$$

Setting $Q_{\text{out}} = Q_{\text{in}}$ and solving for t_0, we get $t_0 = 57.3{}^\circ\text{C}$.

[In equating Q_{out} and Q_{in} we assume that Q_{out} is sufficient to melt all the ice. If that had not been the case, we would have found that $t_0 < 0{}^\circ\text{C}$—which is absurd, because the equilibrium temperature has to lie between the highest and lowest initial temperature in the system. There is a more direct way to check whether all the ice melts or not; see (b).]

(b)   Let us first check to see if all the ice melts. The maximum value of Q_{out} is the heat necessary to drop the temperature to $t_0 = 0{}^\circ\text{C}$. Thus,

$$Q_{\text{out}} \le (0.50 \text{ kg})[0.46 \text{ kJ}/(\text{kg} \cdot {}^\circ\text{C})](500{}^\circ\text{C} - 0{}^\circ\text{C}) = 115 \text{ kJ}$$

The amount of heat needed to melt all the ice is $Q_{\text{melt}} = (0.50 \text{ kg})(335 \text{ kJ/kg}) = 164 \text{ kJ}$. Clearly, not all the ice melts. We can easily find the amount of ice that does melt, since we now know that the final temperature is indeed 0°C and that $Q_{\text{out}} = 115$ kJ. Thus,

$$(335 \text{ kJ/kg}) x = 115 \text{ kJ} \qquad \text{or} \qquad x = 0.34 \text{ kg}$$

Problem 15.28.   How many grams of live steam at atmospheric pressure must be injected into a calorimeter initially containing 100 g of ice and 200 g of water in equilibrium if the final temperature is to be 50°C? Ignore the heat capacity of the vessel.

Solution

$$\begin{aligned} Q_{\text{out}} &= m_s L_v + m_s c_w (t_s - t_0) \\ &= m_s (2256 \text{ kJ/kg}) + m_s [4.184 \text{ kJ}/(\text{kg} \cdot {}^\circ\text{C})](100{}^\circ\text{C} - 50{}^\circ\text{C}) = m_s (2465 \text{ kJ/kg}) \\ Q_{\text{in}} &= m_i L_f + (m_i + m_w) c_w (t_0 - 0{}^\circ\text{C}) \\ &= (0.10 \text{ kg})(335 \text{ kJ/kg}) + (0.30 \text{ kg})[4.184 \text{ kJ}/(\text{kg} \cdot {}^\circ\text{C})](50{}^\circ\text{C} - 0{}^\circ\text{C}) = 96.3 \text{ kJ} \end{aligned}$$

Equating Q_{out} and Q_{in}, we get $m_s = 0.039$ kg = 39 g.

Evaporation and Cooling

It has been seen that, for a given pressure, boiling will take place at a definite temperature. Boiling, which occurs within the bulk of the liquid, is a different phenomenon from **evaporation**, which takes place only at the *surface* of a liquid in contact with a gas at a given pressure. At temperatures well below the boiling point, molecules from the liquid that are particularly energetic can break free and rise above the liquid to form a vapor. If this vapor is trapped above the liquid surface, then eventually equilibrium is established, with as many vapor molecules reentering the liquid as leaving. But if the liquid is open to the atmosphere, the evaporation process continues unabated. The evaporating molecules carry off thermal energy with them—on average the amount of energy per unit mass is the same order of magnitude as the heat of vaporization for boiling. Thus the evaporation process removes heat from the liquid, cooling it and anything in contact with it.

Problems for Review and Mind Stretching

Problem 15.29.

(a) Find the relationship between the Kelvin and Rankine temperature scales, and find the triple-point temperature of water in the Rankine scale.

(b) Convert all the values of specific heats in Table 15.3 to units of Btu/(lb $\cdot$ °F).

Solution

(a) The two absolute temperatures are each directly proportional to pressure and hence directly proportional to each other. We know that the kelvin (or Celsius degree) is nine-fifths as large as the Rankine (or Fahrenheit) degree. It follows that $T_R = \frac{9}{5}T$. From this for the triple point of water, we get $T_{R,3} = \frac{9}{5}(273.16) = 491.69$ R.

(b) Recalling that the definition of the Btu is the amount of heat necessary to raise 1 lb of water 1 °F, we have $c_w = 1.0$ Btu/(lb $\cdot$ °F). This is numerically identical to the specific heat of water in kcal/(kg $\cdot$ °C) [or cal/(g $\cdot$ °C)]: $c_w = 1.0$ kcal/(kg $\cdot$ °C). This implies that all other specific heats must also have the same numerical values in both systems, and the first column of Table 15.3 already gives the correct values of the specific heats in Btu/(lb $\cdot$ °F).

Problem 15.30.   A flat plate of brass has area $A = 0.4500$ m². The temperature is raised by 100°C. Find the new area of the plate.

Solution

Just as for volume, the area expansion is related simply to the linear expansion. If we repeat the analysis found in Problem 15.17 for a flat rectangle of sides L_1 and L_2, we can quickly conclude that the area expansivity is just 2α. Then, for our brass plate,

$$\Delta A = 2\alpha A \, \Delta T = 2(1.93 \times 10^{-5} \, °C^{-1})(100 °C) = 0.0039 \text{ m}^2$$

The new area is $A' = A + \Delta A = 0.4500 + 0.0039 = 0.4539$ m².

Problem 15.31.   An aluminum pot of volume 600 cm³ is filled to the top with water at 20°C. The pot and contents are heated up to 60°C. What volume of water spills over the top of the pot during the heating?

Solution

The volume of the pot increases, but the volume of the water increases faster. The difference in the two volume increases, ΔV, is the volume of water that overflows. Recalling that the water and pot occupy the same initial volume V, we have

$$\Delta V = \beta_w V \Delta t - \beta_{Al} V \Delta t$$
$$= (30 \times 10^{-5}\,°C^{-1})(600\text{ cm}^3)(40°C) - (7.65 \times 10^{-5}\,°C^{-1})(600\text{ cm}^3)(40°C) = 5.36\text{ cm}^3$$

Problem 15.32. The **heat of combustion** of a fuel is defined as the amount of chemical potential energy converted to thermal energy for each kilogram of the fuel that burns up (completely combines with oxygen). To find the heat of combustion of gasoline, 2.0 g of gasoline is completely burned in an under-chamber of a 1.0-kg copper calorimeter containing 500 g of water initially at 20°C. The setup is such that all the energy from the combustion enters the calorimeter and contents as thermal energy. The final equilibrium temperature of the calorimeter is found to be 57°C.

(a) What is the heat of combustion h_g of the gasoline?

(b) If the energy content of 1.0 g of peanut butter is 12 kcal = 12 food calories, how does this compare to the combustion energy of gasoline?

Solution

(a) The amount of heat entering the calorimeter is

$$Q_{in} = m_w c_w \Delta t + m_c c_c \Delta t$$
$$= (0.500\text{ kg})[4184\text{ J}/(\text{kg}\cdot°C)](37°C) + (1.00\text{ kg})[389\text{ J}/(\text{kg}\cdot°C)](37°C) = 91{,}800\text{ J}$$

Then $m_g h_g = 91{,}800\text{ J} \Rightarrow (0.0020\text{ kg})h_g = 91{,}800\text{ J} \Rightarrow h_g = 45{,}900\text{ kJ/kg}$.

(b) We recall that 1 food calorie = 1 kcal = 4184 J. Dividing h_g by 4184 J/food calorie yields 10,970 food calories/kg, or approximately 11 food calories/g. The peanut butter, upon digestion, yields more energy per gram than the gasoline!

Problem 15.33. If a weighted wire rests on a block of ice, as shown in Fig. 15-9, the wire will slowly descend through the ice. When the wire has sliced completely through the ice, however, the block is still in one piece. Explain this example of **regelation** (refreezing).

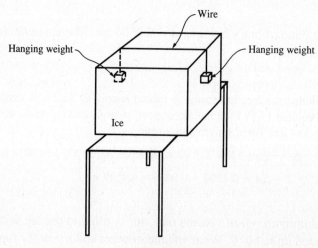

Fig. 15-9

Solution

The wire exerts great pressure on the ice immediately beneath it. Since the temperature of the ice is relatively constant, we can visualize what happens by following a vertical path in Fig. 15-7(b). As the pressure increases we move vertically upward on the graph from the solid region until we reach the fusion curve. If the pressure increases further, we are forced into the liquid region, which means that the ice melts. As the ice in the high-pressure region just below the wire melts, the wire displaces the liquid which rises above the wire. The liquid is now at lower pressure and resolidifies. The heat removed from the liquid then contributes to melting the next layer of ice under the wire, and the process repeats as the wire slices downward. At the end we are left with a solid block of ice.

Supplementary Problems

Problem 15.34.   Using Table 15.4, calculate the melting and boiling points of oxygen and mercury on (a) the Kelvin scale, (b) the Fahrenheit scale.

>   *Ans.*   (a) oxygen: 54 K and 90 K, mercury: 234 K and 630 K; (b) oxygen: $-362\,°F$, $-297\,°F$, mercury: $-38.2\,°F$, $675\,°F$

Problem 15.35.   A metal rod of length 3.000 m is uniformly heated so that its temperature rises 300 °C. The new length is found to be 3.015 m. Find the coefficient of linear expansion. What is a likely candidate for the metal of which the rod is made?

>   *Ans.* $1.67 \times 10^{-5}\,°C^{-1}$; copper

Problem 15.36.   A steel rod of length $L = 2.0$ m and cross-sectional area $A = 200$ mm^2 is held rigidly between two walls. Heating raises the rod's temperature by $\Delta t = 300\,°C$.

(a)   What would be the increase in length of the steel if it were free to expand?

(b)   If the walls hold the steel rigidly to its original length, find an expression for the force that must be exerted by each wall on the rod. [*Hint*:   Recall the definition of Young's modulus (Sec. 11.1).]

(c)   Find the numerical value for the force of part (b). (The Young's modulus for steel is $Y = 1.98 \times 10^{11}$ Pa.)

>   *Ans.*   (a) 7.2 mm; (b) $F = \alpha Y A\,\Delta t$; (c) 143 kN

Problem 15.37.   An aluminum hoop of inner diameter 1.0024 m is to be fitted over a steel disk of diameter 1.0045 m. Both the disk and the hoop are originally at 20 °C. If they are uniformly heated, at what temperature will the hoop just fit over the disk?

>   *Ans.*   176 °C

Problem 15.38.

(a)   Find the change in volume of a zinc sphere of radius $r = 20$ cm when the temperature increases by 250 °C.

(b)   What percentage change in volume does this correspond to?

(c)   What percentage change in density does this correspond to?

>   *Ans.*   (a) 804 cm^3; (b) 2.4%; (c) -2.4%

Problem 15.39.   A steel block weighing 10 lb and at a temperature of 450°F is dropped into a copper vessel weighing 1.0 lb filled with 3.0 lb of water; the calorimeter temperature is 40°F. Find the final temperature.

> *Ans.*   148°F

Problem 15.40.   100 g of steam at 100°C is fed into a calorimeter; the vessel has negligible heat capacity and is filled with 0.200 kg of ice and 0.500 kg of water in equilibrium. Find the final temperature of the system.

> *Ans.*   60°C

Problem 15.41.   A lead brick of mass 20 kg and temperature 300°C is placed on a 10-kg block of ice at 0°C. The system is well insulated from the environment. Describe the situation at equilibrium.

> *Ans.*   Final temperature is 0°C, 2.33 kg of ice having melted.

Problem 15.42.   A sealed 20-kg steel chamber contains 0.200 kg of gasoline [see Problem 15.32(*a*)] and enough air to completely burn it. This chamber is suspended in a larger, 40-kg steel chamber filled with 50 kg of water. The entire system, consisting of both chambers and their contents, is originally at 27°C and is well insulated from the outside environment. The gasoline is ignited and completely burns. Calculate the changes in the system's (*a*) chemical internal energy, (*b*) mechanical internal energy, (*c*) thermal internal energy, (*d*) total internal energy.

> *Ans.*   (*a*) −9.18 MJ; (*b*) 0 MJ; (*c*) +9.18 MJ; (*d*) 0 MJ

Problem 15.43.   Find the final temperature of the system of Problem 15.42. (Ignore the heat capacity of the products of combustion in the inner chamber.)

> *Ans.*   65.8°C

Problem 15.44.   1.0 kg of molten zinc at 420°C is poured onto a 2.5-kg lead brick initially at 27°C, resting in a calorimeter.

(*a*)   If the heat capacity of the calorimeter is negligible, find the final temperature of the mixture.

(*b*)   What fraction of each mass is liquid and what fraction is solid?

> *Ans.*   (*a*) 327°C; (*b*) zinc is 100% solid, while lead is 8.45% solid and 91.55% liquid.

Problem 15.45.   A solid steel cylinder, of radius $R = 20$ cm and mass $M = 5.0$ kg, rotates about its symmetry axis without friction at an angular velocity of 30.00 rad/s. The cylinder is then uniformly heated so that its temperature is raised by 100°C. What is the new angular velocity?

> *Ans.*   29.93 rad/s

Problem 15.46.   The density of mercury at 0°C is 13.6×10^3 kg/m³. Find its density at 200°C.

> *Ans.* 13.1×10^3 kg/m³

Problem 15.47.   An electric hot water heater takes in cool water at 10°C and heats it to 70°C. If the hot water is drawn off at 20 kg/min, what must be the minimum power rating of the heater?

> *Ans.*   83.7 kW

Problem 15.48. A lead bullet is fired into a very heavy block of wood in which it becomes embedded. Assume that all the heat generated goes into the bullet and that the bullet's temperature when it hits the wood is 127°C. What is the minimum velocity of the bullet that will cause it to completely melt in the wood?

> *Ans.*   318 m/s

Problem 15.49.

(a) Referring to Problem 15.48, what would the actual kinetic energy of the bullet be if the mass of the bullet was 20 g?

(b) How much gasoline ($h_g = 4.6$ MJ/kg) would have to burn to generate an equivalent amount of thermal energy?

> *Ans.*   (a) 1.011 kJ; (b) 22 mg

Problem 15.50. How much heat must be removed from 4.0 kg of water at 27°C to convert it to ice at (a) 0°C?   (b) −15°C?

> *Ans.*   (a) 1.792 MJ; (b) 1.917 MJ

Problem 15.51. A 15-kg child is running a fever of 3°C above her normal temperature of 37°C. Her father rinses her with water at 40°C, knowing that the water will evaporate, drawing heat from the girl. If the heat of vaporization of water at 40°C is 580 kcal/kg and the effective specific heat of the child is 0.85 kcal/(kg · °C) how much water must evaporate to restore her to normal temperature?

> *Ans.*   66 g

Chapter 16

Thermodynamics II: Gas Laws, the Atomic View, and Statistical Mechanics

16.1 THE MOLE CONCEPT AND AVOGADRO'S NUMBER

By the early nineteenth century the study of chemistry and chemical reactions led to the atomic view of matter. Any given substance is either an element, made up of identical indestructible atoms, or a compound, composed of identical molecules, or clusters, of two or more different atoms. From a study of the combining masses of different elements that formed compounds in various chemical reactions, it was possible to discover the relative masses of atoms and molecules. For many substances the results were approximately a whole-number multiple of the mass of the hydrogen atom. Deviations from this rule were attributed to the existence of isotopes—atoms of the same element with slightly different masses. The different isotopes of a given substance are identical chemically, despite their mass difference. When one examines atoms of individual isotopes of a given substance, their relative masses are indeed all very close to whole-number multiples of hydrogen.

We now know that all atoms consist of a massive tiny core, called the **nucleus**, made up of closely packed particles called **protons** and **neutrons**. Protons carry a fixed unit of positive electric charge e, while neutrons have no charge, but protons and neutrons have almost the same mass. Most of the volume of the atom is empty space, except for a swarm of **electrons** that can crudely be thought of as orbiting the nucleus at various distances. Electrons are particles that are very light compared to protons or neutrons, and they carry an electrical charge equal in magnitude and opposite in sign to that of the proton. An atom is electrically neutral and thus has exactly as many electrons as protons.

The number of protons in an atom is called the **atomic number** of the atom Z. The chemical behavior of an atom is completely determined by the number of electrons (or protons), making up the atom. Different isotopes of the same element involve atoms with the same Z but with different numbers of neutrons. The **mass number** A of each isotope is defined as the sum of the number of protons plus neutrons in the nucleus of that isotope. Figure 16-1 gives pictorial representations of various atoms. They are not drawn to scale and are not intended to show what atoms really "look" like.

Relative masses of atoms or molecules are now measured on the **atomic and molecular mass scale**, which is presently based on the assignment of the value 12 to the most abundant isotope of carbon (6 protons and 6 neutrons). On this scale, all the isotopically pure atomic and molecular

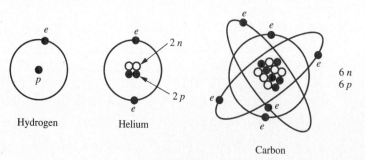

Fig. 16-1

masses are, again, very close to (but not exactly) whole numbers, which are just the mass numbers A for the isotope. See Table 16.1.

A mass of any substance whose numerical value in grams is the same as its atomic or molecular mass is called a *gram atomic or molecular mass* of that substance and often given the symbol $\mathcal{M}$.

Table 16.1

Atom or Molecule	Atomic or Molecular Mass (Approx.)
Hydrogen atom (H)	1
Hydrogen molecule (H_2)	2
Helium (He)	4
Carbon (C)	12
Oxygen atom (O)	16
Oxygen molecule (O_2)	32
Nitrogen atom (N)	14
Nitrogen molecule (N_2)	28
Carbon dioxide (CO_2)	44
Carbon monoxide (CO)	28

Note. Many texts still refer to the atomic or molecular mass by the misnomer "atomic or molecular weight," for historical reasons.

One gram atomic or molecular mass of any substance is called a *mole* (mol) of that substance. Thus, for oxygen gas (which is O_2, the molecular form of oxygen), $\mathcal{M} = 32$ g/mol, while for carbon $\mathcal{M} = 12$ g/mol.

Problem 16.1.   How many moles n are there in the following samples:

(a) 80 g of carbon dioxide?   (b) 26 g of water (H_2O)?   (c) 2.5 kg of gold ($A = 197$)?

Solution

(a) Since $\mathcal{M}$ is the mass of 1 mol, the total mass of our sample is $M = n\mathcal{M} \Rightarrow 80\text{ g} = n(44\text{ g/mol}) \Rightarrow n = 1.82$ mol.

(b) From Table 16.1, $\mathcal{M} = 2 + 16 = 18$. Then $M = n\mathcal{M} \Rightarrow n = 1.44$ mol.

(c) $M = n\mathcal{M} \Rightarrow 2500\text{ g} = n(197\text{ g/mol}) \Rightarrow n = 12.7$ mol.

From its definition, we can see that a mole of any substance has the same number of atoms or molecules as a mole of any other substance. The number of atoms or molecules in a mole of any substance is thus a universal constant and is called **Avogadro's number** N_A. The atomic mass scale was well known long before the value of N_A was determined. A variety of ingenious methods, including crystal x-ray diffraction, have been used to determine N_A:

$$N_A = 6.023 \times 10^{23} \text{ atoms/mol (or molecules/mol)} \qquad (16.1)$$

Problem 16.2.

(a) Use Avogradro's number to find the mass m_C of a carbon atom.

(b) Find the approximate mass of the hydrogen atom.

(c) The hydrogen atom consists of a nucleus of one proton, with one electron moving about it. If the mass of the electron is 1/1836 of the mass of the proton, find the mass of the electron.

Solution

(a) $m_C = \mathcal{M}_C/N_A = (12.00 \text{ g/mol})/(6.023 \times 10^{23} \text{ atoms/mol}) = 1.992 \times 10^{-23}$ g, where we have dropped the "per atom".

(b) $m_H = \mathcal{M}_H/N_A = (1.0 \text{ g/mol})/(6.023 \times 10^{23} \text{ atom/mol}) = 1.66 \times 10^{-24}$ g.

(c) Since a proton has a mass of 1836 electrons, the hydrogen atom has a mass of 1837 electrons, or

$$m_e = \tfrac{1}{1837} \, m_H = 9.04 \times 10^{-28} \text{ g}$$

(This is about 0.8% below the correct value because the atomic mass of hydrogen is really about 1.008.)

In the SI set of units the primacy of the kilogram has led to the use of the kilomole, which, for any substance, is a mass of that substance, in kilograms, whose numerical value is the atomic or molecular mass of the substance. Clearly then, 1 kilomole (kmol) is 1000 mol. In terms of the kilomole, Avogadro's number is $N_A = 6.023 \times 10^{26}$ atoms/kmol (or molecules/kmol).

Problem 16.3.   Refer to Problem 16.1.

(a) In 26 g of water, how many molecules are there?   How many hydrogen atoms?   How many oxygen atoms?

(b) How many atoms of gold are in 2.5 kg?

Solution

(a) From Problem 16.1(b) we have $n = 1.44$ mol. Multiplying by Avogadro's number we get 8.67×10^{23} molecules. Since there are two hydrogen atoms and one oxygen atom in each molecule, we have 17.3×10^{23} atoms of hydrogen and 8.67×10^{23} atoms of oxygen.

(b) From Problem 16.1(c), there are 12.7 mol in 2.5 kg of gold, or 0.0127 kmol. Then, the number of gold atoms is $(0.0127 \text{ kmol})(6.023 \times 10^{26} \text{ atoms/kmol}) = 7.65 \cdot 10^{24}$ atoms.

16.2 THE IDEAL GAS LAW

In Sec. 15.2, we saw that the pressure of a low-density (dilute) gas confined to a constant volume is directly proportional to the Kelvin temperature: $P \propto T$. In seventeenth century studies of confined gases, it was learned that at constant temperature the pressure of a dilute gas varies inversely as the volume: $P \propto 1/V$ (Boyle's law). Combining these two laws we have for any confined dilute gas

$$PV \propto T \qquad \text{or} \qquad PV = CT \tag{16.2}$$

where C is a proportionality constant. Clearly, at fixed T, Eq. (16.2) implies Boyle's law, and at fixed V it implies $P \propto T$. In general, C could be expected to depend on the amount of gas (number N of molecules) in the container, as well as, perhaps, on the particular gas involved.

Problem 16.4.   A gas confined in a cylinder with a tight-fitting piston is initially in the state $P_1 = 2000$ Pa, $V_1 = 2.0$ L, and $T_1 = 300$ K.

(a)   If the volume is decreased to 0.50 L while the temperature is held fixed, find the new pressure.

(b)   If in (a) the temperature instead rose to 400 K when the volume changed, what would be the new pressure?

(c)   Suppose that the gas is heated to 700 K while the volume is changed to a new value. If the final pressure is measured to be 6000 Pa, what is the new volume?

   Solution

(a)   If T is held fixed, then Eq. (16.2) implies $PV =$ constant, which is just Boyle's law. We then must have $P_1V_1 = P_2V_2 \Rightarrow$ (2000 Pa) (2.0 L) $= P_2(0.50$ L$) \Rightarrow P_2 = 8000$ Pa.

(b)   In this case we still have from Eq. (16.2) that $PV/T =$ constant. We must then have

$$\frac{P_1V_1}{T_1} = \frac{P_2V_2}{T_2} \tag{i}$$

from which we get

$$\frac{(2000 \text{ Pa})(2.0 \text{ L})}{300 \text{ K}} = \frac{P_2(0.50 \text{ L})}{400 \text{ K}} \qquad \text{or} \qquad P_2 = 10{,}700 \text{ Pa}$$

(c)   Again using Eq. (i), with 1 referring to the original situation and 2 to the new final situation, we have

$$\frac{(2000 \text{ Pa})(2.0 \text{ L})}{300 \text{ K}} = \frac{(6000 \text{ Pa})V_2}{700 \text{ K}} \qquad \text{or} \qquad V_2 = 1.56 \text{ L}$$

Equation (16.2) refers only to a confined sample of gas, and hence one with a fixed number of molecules. The constant of proportionality C will therefore differ from sample to sample of even the same gas, depending on how much gas is involved. We now seek a more general formula that includes, explicitly, the dependence on the number of molecules of gas. It is not hard to see that at a fixed temperature and pressure, the volume of a given gas must be proportional to the number of molecules N:

$$V \propto N \qquad (P \text{ and } T \text{ constant}) \tag{16.3}$$

In fact, suppose a container has a removable partition that divides it into two sections of equal volume, each section containing the same type of gas at the same pressure and temperature. Since the two sections are identical, they must contain the same number of molecules (to within macroscopic measure). If we remove the partition, we have a single container of gas, at the same temperature and pressure as each original section, with double the volume and double the number of molecules. Thus, we conclude that doubling the number of molecules at fixed pressure and temperature corresponds to doubling the volume.

   We can now combine (16.2), which says $PV \propto T$ (constant N) with (16.3), which says $V \propto N$ (constant P and T) to obtain $PV \propto NT$, or

$$PV = kNT \tag{16.4}$$

where k is a proportionality constant that depends only on the particular gas being used. For fixed N, (16.4) reduces to (16.2), and for fixed P and T it reduces to (16.3). As it turns out, k is the same no matter which dilute gas is being used. The universal constant k is called the **Boltzmann constant**. Its value is

$$k = 1.38 \times 10^{-23} \text{ J/(particle} \cdot \text{K)} \tag{16.5a}$$

Equation (*16.4*) is called the **ideal gas law** and is an excellent approximation to the behavior of all dilute (i.e., low-density) gases as long as the gases are not near liquification or solidification points.

Problem 16.5.

(a) Suppose that the piston of Problem 16.4 did not make a complete seal. Rework Problem 16.4(*c*) if 20% of the gas leaked out while the same pressure and temperature changes were being brought about.

(b) What would the change in pressure have been if the initial temperature and volume of the gas in Problem 16.4 were unchanged but 25% of the gas leaked out?

Solution

(a) Now we must use (*16.4*), which implies

$$\frac{P_1 V_1}{N_1 T_1} = \frac{P_2 V_2}{N_2 T_2} \tag{i}$$

We note that $N_2 = 0.80 N_1$, so

$$\frac{(2000 \text{ Pa})(2.0 \text{ L})}{300 \text{ K}} = \frac{(6000 \text{ Pa}) V_2}{(0.80)(700 \text{ K})} \quad \text{or} \quad V_2 = 1.24 \text{ L}$$

(b) If T and V are constant, (*16.4*) implies $P_1/N_1 = P_2/N_2$. For our case this reads

$$\frac{2000 \text{ Pa}}{N_1} = \frac{P_2}{N_2} = \frac{P_2}{(0.75) N_1} \quad \text{or} \quad P_2 = 1500 \text{ Pa}$$

It is usual to express the ideal gas law in terms of the number n of moles of gas rather than the number N of molecules. Recalling the definition of Avogradro's number, we clearly have $N = n N_A$, and (*16.4*) becomes $PV = n N_A k T$. Since both N_A and k are universal constants, we define the **universal gas constant** as their product R:

$$R = N_A k = 8.31 \text{ J/(mol} \cdot \text{K)} \tag{16.5b}$$

Thus, our ideal gas law takes the more usual form

$$PV = nRT \tag{16.6}$$

Problem 16.6.

(a) How many moles of gas were in the cylinder in Problem 16.4?

(b) How many moles leaked out in Problem 16.5(*a*)?

Solution

(a) Using the data from Problem 16.4 and the value for R in Eq. (*16.5b*) (and noting that $1.0 \text{ L} = 1.0 \times 10^{-3} \text{ m}^3$), Eq. (*16.6*) yields

$$(2000 \text{ Pa})(2.0 \times 10^{-3} \text{ m}^3) = n[8.31 \text{ J/(mol} \cdot \text{K)}] (300 \text{ K}) \quad \text{or} \quad n = 1.60 \times 10^{-3} \text{ mol}$$

(b) From Problem 16.5(*a*), we have that 20% of the molecules leaked out, which means that 20% of the moles leaked out, or $\Delta n = 0.20 n = 3.20 \times 10^{-4}$ mol.

Problem 16.7.   Show that 1 mol of an ideal gas at atmospheric pressure and a temperature of 0°C will occupy a volume of 22.4 L.

Solution

We apply (*16.6*), recalling the value of P_A from hydrostatics and noting that 0°C = 273 K. Then

$$(1.013 \times 10^5 \text{ Pa})V = (1 \text{ mol}) [8.31 \text{ J}/(\text{mol} \cdot \text{K})] (273 \text{ K}) \qquad \text{or} \qquad V = 0.0224 \text{ m}^3 = 22.4 \text{ L}$$

There is yet another common and useful form in which the ideal gas law is expressed:

$$P = \frac{dRT}{\mathcal{M}} \qquad\qquad (16.7)$$

where d is the density of the gas and $\mathcal{M}$ is its molecular mass.

Problem 16.8.   Derive Eq. (*16.7*) from Eq. (*16.6*).

Solution

If M is the mass of a sample of gas of molecular mass $\mathcal{M}$, then, as already seen in Problem 16.1, $M = n\mathcal{M}$. Substituting $n = M/\mathcal{M}$ into (*16.6*), we have

$$PV = \frac{MRT}{\mathcal{M}}$$

Dividing both sides by V, and recalling that the density d is M/V, this can be rewritten as $P = dRT/\mathcal{M}$, which is our result.

Problem 16.9.

(*a*)   For the gas in the initial situation of Problem 16.4, what is the density if the gas is oxygen? If the gas is hydrogen?

(*b*)   What is the density for the situation of Problem 16.5(*b*) if the gas is oxygen? If the gas is hydrogen?

Solution

(*a*)   Using (*16.7*) and the data from Problem 16.4, we have, for the case of oxygen,

$$2000 \text{ Pa} = \frac{d_O[8.31 \text{ J}/(\text{mol} \cdot \text{K})](300 \text{ K})}{0.032 \text{ kg/mol}} \qquad \text{or} \qquad d_O = 25.7 \text{ g/m}^3$$

Note that we had to convert the molecular mass to kg/mol for self-consistent units. Repeating for hydrogen, with $\mathcal{M} = 0.0020$ kg/mol, we get $d_H = 1.60$ g/m^3.

(*b*)   From Problem 16.5(*b*), we have that the final pressure is 1500 Pa and the temperature was unchanged from the original 300 K of Problem 16.4. Substituting into (*16.7*), we have

$$1500 \text{ Pa} = \frac{d_O[8.31 \text{ J}/(\text{mol} \cdot \text{K})](300 \text{ K})}{0.032 \text{ kg/mol}} \qquad \text{or} \qquad d_O = 19.3 \text{ g/m}^3$$

Repeating for hydrogen, we get $d_H = 1.20$ g/m^3. (Actually, these results can be obtained directly from the fact that the volume stayed the same and 25% of the gas leaked out. If 25% of the mass leaked out and the volume was unchanged, then the density must have dropped by 25% as well.)

16.3 EQUILIBRIUM STATES AND THE EQUATION OF STATE

Equilibrium States

As we have seen, for a confined ideal gas in equilibrium there is a definite relationship between P, V, and T. If we specify any two, we have the third. As we will see in the next section, the internal energy U of an ideal gas depends only on T. Thus, a knowledge of P, V, and T completely specifies the macroscopic state of our ideal gas.

If we made a graph of P vs. V for a confined sample of ideal gas, as shown in Fig. 16-2, every point on that graph (for positive P and V) uniquely specifies a possible macroscopic equilibrium state of our system. For each such point we could determine the value of T and the value of U. Other thermodynamic variables of interest could also be uniquely determined. Note that only *equilibrium* states can be identified with points on the graph. If the confined gas were in a state of turmoil, it could not be represented by any point on the P vs. V graph, since there would be no unique value of P for the entire sample of gas. Similarly, the temperature of the system would have no meaning for a thermally chaotic situation.

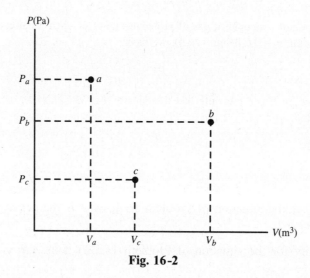

Fig. 16-2

In the case of quasistatic changes, however, we can trace out the changing equilibrium states of our system by drawing a curve of evolution of the system on the P vs. V graph. Examples of such evolutionary paths are shown in Fig. 16-3. Horizontal lines correspond to changes at constant pressure (called *isobaric* processes); vertical lines correspond to changes at constant volume (called *isovolumic* or *isochoric* processes). The curved hyperbolic lines correspond to a change at constant temperature (called *isothermal* processes). These last curves can be obtained from Boyle's law (Sec. 16.2).

Problem 16.10. Assume our confined ideal gas moves from point a to point b on the isobar shown in Fig. 16-3(a).

(a) If there is 3 mol of gas in our sample, what is the temperature corresponding to point a?

(b) What is the temperature corresponding to point b?

(c) If the temperature at point c is 900 K, what is the pressure?

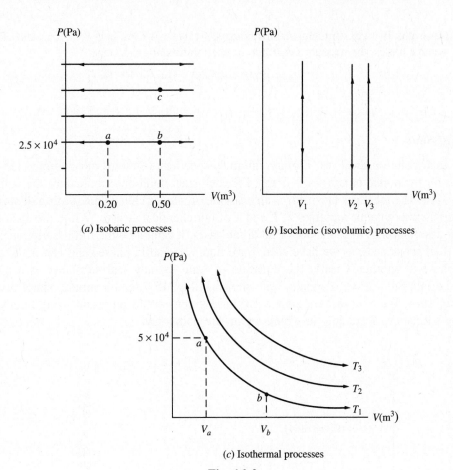

(a) Isobaric processes

(b) Isochoric (isovolumic) processes

(c) Isothermal processes

Fig. 16-3

Solution

(a) Using (*16.6*) we have

$$(2.5 \times 10^4 \text{ Pa})(0.20 \text{ m}^3) = (3.0 \text{ mol}) [8.31 \text{ J/(mol} \cdot \text{K)}] T_a \qquad \text{or} \qquad T_a = 201 \text{ K}$$

(b) Repeating the same calculation for point *b*:

$$(2.5 \times 10^4 \text{ Pa})(0.50 \text{ m}^3) = (3.0 \text{ mol}) [8.31 \text{ J/(mol} \cdot \text{K)}] T_b \qquad \text{or} \qquad T_b = 501 \text{ K}$$

(c) Again using (*16.6*), and noting that $V_c = V_b$, we have

$$P_c(0.50 \text{ m}^3) = (3.0 \text{ mol}) [8.31 \text{ J/(mol} \cdot \text{K)}] (900 \text{ K}) \qquad \text{or} \qquad P_c = 4.49 \times 10^4 \text{ Pa}$$

Problem 16.11.   Assume that our confined gas moves along the isothermal path from point *a* to point *b* shown in Fig. 16-3(*c*).

(a) If there is 2.0 mol of gas in our sample and $T_1 = 300$ K, find V_a.

(b) If V_b is three times V_a, find P_b.

Solution

(a) We use (*16.6*), with the given data:

$$(5.0 \times 10^4 \text{ Pa}) V_a = (2.0 \text{ mol}) [8.31 \text{ J/(mol} \cdot \text{K)}] (300 \text{ K}) \qquad \text{or} \qquad V_a = 0.100 \text{ m}^3$$

(*b*)   Since this is a constant-temperature process, we have Boyle's law PV = constant. Thus, if the volume triples, the pressure must drop to one-third its original value:

$$P_b = \tfrac{1}{3}(5.0 \times 10^4 \text{ Pa}) = 1.67 \times 10^4 \text{ Pa}$$

Equations of State

Just as each point on the P vs. V graph uniquely specifies a state of our confined ideal gas, the same is true for the points on a P vs. T graph. For each such point one can deduce the volume using the ideal gas law. The ideal gas law itself is an example of what is called an **equation of state**. It links the three key thermodynamic variables P, V, and T of our chemical system. While the ideal gas law is an excellent description of the behavior of all dilute gases, it cannot be the full description of any real substance. Real substances, as we have seen, have liquid and solid phases and can make transitions from one phase to another. Clearly the equation of state for any real substance is a much more complicated affair. Some P vs. T graphs were shown in Fig. 15-7, and a similar, simplified graph is given as Fig. 16-4. We note that the points on those graphs could represent solid, liquid, or vapor states of the substance, depending in which region the points lay.

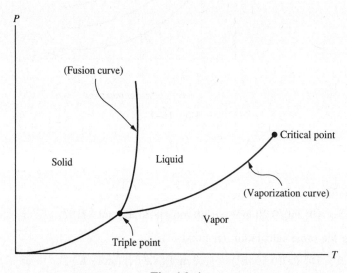

Fig. 16-4

Indeed, a point on the vaporization curve represents a whole range of states—from 100% vapor, through all fractions of vapor and liquid, to 100% liquid—all at a common P and T but covering a continuous range of volumes V. For an ideal gas, however, all points on a P vs. T curve are vapor states, and each point corresponds to a unique volume.

To further appreciate some of the complexity of the equation of state of a real substance, we can compare isotherms on a P vs. V graph for an ideal gas with those of a real substance that can liquify as the pressure increases and the volume decreases. Consider a gas confined in a piston-and-cylinder arrangement. If the piston slowly moves inward, thus decreasing the volume, while the temperature of the gas is held fixed (e.g., the whole cylinder is immersed in a constant-temperature bath), a quasistatic path will be traced out on the P vs. V curve. If the system is an ideal gas, we will get a hyperbolic path like those of Fig. 16-3(*c*). If the system is a real gas, then as the volume decreases, the density will increase since the mass is fixed. At first the pressure will also increase similarly to an ideal gas. As the density gets high, the curve will begin to deviate from the behavior of an ideal gas, and eventually liquification will begin.

Figure 16-5 traces the isothermal compressions (for a series of different temperatures) of such a real gas. Consider the curve corresponding to the definite temperature T_2. As the gas is compressed from *a* to *b*, the pressure rises, similar to an ideal gas. This general behavior continues until the pressure is reached at which the gas will liquify at the temperature T_2. This corresponds to point *c* on the isotherm. Further compression does not change the pressure since more and more of the gas is liquefying (at the fixed temperature T_2), and the density of the gas does not rise. This corresponds to the horizontal (isobaric) portion of the isotherm. Finally, point *d* is reached, at which all the gas is liquified. Further compression is now resisted by the liquid, which is difficult to compress, so the pressure of the liquid rises rapidly with compression. A similar process takes place if we repeat the process at different temperatures, and these are represented by the other isotherms in Fig. 16-5.

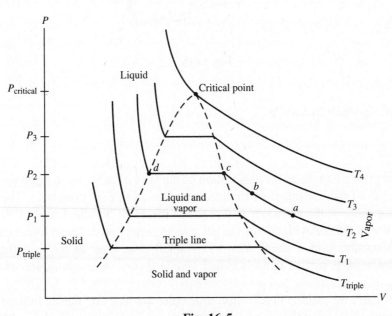

Fig. 16-5

As we go to higher-temperature isotherms, we see that the volumes at 100% vapor and 100% liquid get closer and closer to each other, until they become equal at the critical point. Above the critical point there is no clear distinction between vapor and liquid.

To mathematically describe the whole range of states of a real substance is very difficult, especially when there are phase transitions, where many different volumes correspond to the same *P* and *T* value. The relation between *P*, *V*, and *T* is often easier to describe on a three-dimensional graph in which each variable is along one of the axes. The entire range of possible equilibrium states of the system is then described by a "thermodynamic surface on such a graph." An example of such a graph is depicted in perspective in Fig. 16-6. The projection of this surface onto the *PT* plane gives us a picture like that of Fig. 16-4, while the projection onto the *PV* plane gives us a picture like that of Fig. 16-5.

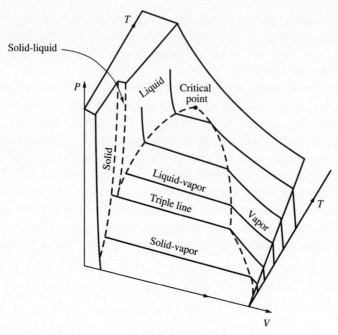

Fig. 16-6

16.4   STATISTICAL MECHANICS

The Ideal Gas Law

One of the first great triumphs of the application of the laws of statistics to large systems of atoms or molecules came from the derivation of the ideal gas law from first principles. The pressure of a confined gas on the walls of the container is due to the incessant bombardment of the walls by the molecules of gas. Each collision with the wall exerts a momentary force. These forces can be averaged over all collisions occurring in a small area and a small time interval to yield the macroscopic pressure. This calculation is part of what is called *kinetic theory*. A rough sketch of the procedure follows.

In the simplest case, we assume that the gas molecules act like tiny elastic billiard balls (a good model for monatomic gases) and that forces act between the molecules only during direct collision. We also assume that the average speed of a molecule in one direction is the same as in any other direction, that the collisions with the walls are completely elastic, and that for our dilute gas the volume of all the molecules taken together is still insignificant in comparison to the volume of the container. From these assumptions, and the ordinary laws of mechanics, we can obtain the pressure of the gas on the walls in terms of the **mean square velocity** $(v^2)_{av}$, the average value of the square of the magnitude of the velocity of the gas molecules. The result is

$$P = \frac{N}{V} \frac{m(v^2)_{av}}{3} \qquad (16.8)$$

where m is the mass of a molecule of the gas, N is the total number of molecules, and V is the volume of the container. Since the translational kinetic energy of a molecule is $\varepsilon = \frac{1}{2}mv^2$, the average kinetic energy per molecule (averaged over all gas molecules in the container) is just

$$\varepsilon_{av} = \frac{1}{2}m(v^2)_{av} \qquad (16.9)$$

Inserting (*16.9*) into (*16.8*), and rearranging, we get

$$PV = \frac{2N\varepsilon_{av}}{3} \tag{16.10}$$

This would be identical to the ideal gas law (*16.4*) if

$$\varepsilon_{av} = \frac{3kT}{2} \tag{16.11}$$

Using the fundamental laws of statistical mechanics, which are beyond the scope of this book, it can be shown that (*16.11*) indeed gives the average translational kinetic energy per molecule in a sample of ideal gas (monatomic or otherwise). Equation (*16.11*) is very important because it gives a fundamental meaning to the concept of temperature. The Kelvin temperature is a direct measure of the average translational kinetic energy of the gas molecules.

Problem 16.12.

(a) Find the average translational kinetic energy of the molecules of an ideal gas that are at a temperature of 300 K.

(b) Find the root-mean-square speed $\{v_{rms} \equiv [(v^2)_{av}]^{1/2}\}$ of the molecules of the gas for the cases of hydrogen, oxygen, and carbon dioxide.

Solution

(a) From (*16.11*) and (*16.5a*),

$$\varepsilon_{av} = 1.5[1.38 \times 10^{-23} \text{ J/(particle} \cdot \text{K)}] (300 \text{ K}) = 6.21 \times 10^{-21} \text{ J}$$

(b) From (*16.9*) we have

$$(v^2)_{av} = \frac{2\varepsilon_{av}}{m} \quad \text{or} \quad v_{rms} = \left(\frac{2\varepsilon_{av}}{m}\right)^{1/2} \tag{i}$$

We substitute ε_{av} from (*16.11*) into (*i*) to get $v_{rms} = (3kT/m)^{1/2}$. Multiplying numerator and denominator by Avogadro's number, we have $v_{rms} = (3N_A kT/N_A m)^{1/2}$. Recalling that $N_A k = R$ and $N_A m = \mathcal{M}$, we get finally

$$v_{rms} = \left(\frac{3RT}{\mathcal{M}}\right)^{1/2} \tag{ii}$$

Substituting in $R = 8.31$ J/(mol $\cdot$ K) and $T = 300$ K, for the three gases we have

Hydrogen :	$\mathcal{M} = 0.0020$ kg/mol	or	$v_{rms} = 1930$ m/s
Oxygen :	$\mathcal{M} = 0.0320$ kg/mol	or	$v_{rms} = 483$ m/s
Carbon dioxide :	$\mathcal{M} = 0.0440$ kg/mol	or	$v_{rms} = 412$ m/s

Note. At a given temperature the lighter molecules have greater velocities since the average kinetic energy is the same for all gases at a given temperature.

Heat Capacities

Equations (*16.10*) and (*16.11*) link our model of microscopic phenomena (how atoms and molecules behave) to the macroscopic temperature and to the experimentally determined ideal gas law.

Another such linkage comes from the study of the heat capacities of different gases. Recalling that the specific heat is the heat capacity per unit mass of a substance, we can ask: "Why are the specific heats of different substances different from one another?"

Suppose we add heat to a sample of a gas in a fixed-volume container, assuming no chemical reactions will take place. Since no work can be done (because the volume is fixed), all the heat goes into increasing the internal energy U of the gas, which in this case is purely thermal energy. Thus, if ΔQ is the heat entering the system, then $\Delta Q = \Delta U$. In our infinitesimal "billiard ball" model of a monatomic gas, the only energy is translational kinetic energy and, from (16.11) we must have

$$U = E_k = N\varepsilon_{av} = \tfrac{3}{2}NkT \qquad (16.12)$$

where, as usual, N stands for the number of molecules in our sample. If we add heat ΔQ to our system, we must have

$$\Delta Q = \Delta U = \tfrac{3}{2}Nk\,\Delta T \qquad (16.13)$$

where ΔT is the increase in temperature of the system. Recalling that the total heat capacity of a system is $C = \Delta Q/\Delta T$, Eq. (16.13) yields $C_V = \tfrac{3}{2}Nk$, where the subscript indicates that this is a constant-volume process. Recalling that $Nk = nR$, where n is the number of moles, we get

$$C_V = \tfrac{3}{2}nR \qquad (16.14)$$

If we divide C_V by the mass M of our sample of gas, we get $c_V = C_V/M$, the heat capacity per unit mass, or specific heat, at constant volume. Because of the form of Eq. (16.14) we find it more useful to define the heat capacity per mole, or *molar heat capacity*, $c_{V,mol}$, (at constant volume). For our simple billiard ball gas we have

$$c_{V,\,mol} \equiv \frac{C_V}{n} = \tfrac{3}{2}R = \frac{3(8.31\ \mathrm{J/(mol \cdot {}^\circ C)})}{2} = 12.5\ \mathrm{J/(mol \cdot {}^\circ C)} \qquad (16.15a)$$

For most monatomic gases, such as helium, neon, and argon, this in fact is an excellent approximation to the actual value of the molar heat capacity at constant volume (over a wide range of temperatures and pressures). Thus monatomic gases have the same molar heat capacity, even though they all have different masses, and their specific heats differ greatly.

The average energy per molecule [see Eq. (16.11)] depends only on the temperature T and not on the mass of the molecules involved. Therefore, the total internal energy of a sample of gas depends on the number of molecules, or equivalently, the number of moles, in the sample rather than on its mass. Since the heat entering a system is related to the change in the internal energy, this in turn means that the heat capacity per mole is more fundamental than the heat capacity per unit mass.

Since most heat measurements, such as those using calorimetry, involve knowledge of the mass of the samples, it is the specific heats that are experimentally determined. We therefore need to find the relationship between $c = C/M$ and $c_{mol} = C/n$. These two equations imply

$$C = Mc = nc_{mol} \qquad (16.16)$$

Recalling that $M = n\mathcal{M}$, where $\mathcal{M}$ is the molecular mass, and substituting this into Eq. (16.16), we get

$$c_{mol} = \mathcal{M}c \qquad (16.17)$$

Note that Eq. (16.17) also follows from the fact that since c is the heat capacity per unit mass and $\mathcal{M}$ is the mass per mole, multiplying the two gives the heat capacity per mole.

Problem 16.13.

(*a*) Find the specific heat at constant volume of the monatomic gas krypton (mass number $A = 84$), and compare it to that of helium.

(b) Find the molar heat capacities of aluminum ($A = 27$) and copper ($A = 63$) at constant pressure. (Table 15.3 gives specific heats of liquids and solids at constant pressure.)

Solution

(a) Since both krypton and helium are monatomic gases, we can assume that to a good approximation each has a molar heat capacity of $\frac{3}{2}R = 12.5$ J/(mol · K). Recalling that the molecular masses in g/mol are approximately the same as the mass numbers, we have $\mathcal{M}_{Kr} = 0.084$ kg/mol and $\mathcal{M}_{He} = 0.0040$ kg/mol. Applying (16.17), we get

$$c_{V,\,Kr} = \frac{12.5 \text{ J/(mol} \cdot \text{K)}}{0.084 \text{ kg/mol}} = 149 \text{ J/(kg} \cdot \text{K)}$$

$$c_{V,\,He} = \frac{12.5 \text{ J/(mol} \cdot \text{K)}}{0.0040 \text{ kg/mol}} = 3130 \text{ J/(kg} \cdot \text{K)}$$

(b) Equation (16.17) applies to all substances, whether gases or not. As in part (a) we get the molecular masses $\mathcal{M}_{Al} = 0.027$ kg/mol and $\mathcal{M}_C = 0.063$ kg/mol. Applying (16.17), and using the values of specific heat from the table, we get

$$c_{P,\,mol,Al} = (0.027 \text{ kg/mol})[920 \text{ J/(kg} \cdot \text{K)}] = 24.8 \text{ J/(mol} \cdot \text{K)}$$

$$c_{P,\,mol,C} = (0.063 \text{ kg/mol})[389 \text{ J/(kg} \cdot \text{K)}] = 24.5 \text{ J/(mol} \cdot \text{K)}$$

It should be noted that the specific heats or molar heat capacities of substances at constant pressure are generally larger than the corresponding ones at constant volume. For an ideal gas (as will be shown in the next chapter) we have

$$c_{P,\,mol} = c_{V,\,mol} + R \qquad (16.18)$$

Equipartition of Energy

Statistical mechanics can also be applied to multiatom ideal gases. If we assume that the ordinary laws of mechanics apply to molecules that are free to rotate and vibrate, as well as translate, we can still derive the same ideal gas law. Furthermore, the average energy per molecule of such gases depends on how many different "degrees of freedom" the molecules have that carry energy. Each such degree of freedom contributes $\frac{1}{2}kT$ to the average energy. A degree of freedom is any coordinate (linear, angular, etc.) that is needed to describe the motion of the molecule, and any "velocity" associated with that coordinate. For example, our monatomic gas of tiny "billiard balls" can move along the x, y, and z directions and can have velocities in each of those directions. That makes six degrees of freedom. Since we assume there is no potential energy between molecules, only the three velocity degrees of freedom contribute energy, and we have $\varepsilon_{av} = \frac{1}{2}kT + \frac{1}{2}kT + \frac{1}{2}kT = \frac{3}{2}kT$, our earlier result. For the case of a diatomic molecule that is free to rotate like a rigid dumbbell (see Fig. 16-7), in addition to the molecule as a whole translating through space, we have degrees of freedom for rotation about the two axes perpendicular to the symmetry axis, and the associated angular velocities (we assume the mass is so close to the symmetry axis that spinning about that axis can't contribute to the energy). Again, only the angular velocities contribute to the energy, through terms of the form $\frac{1}{2}I\omega^2$ for each axis. We thus have two "rotational" kinetic energy terms contributing to the average energy in additional to the translational kinetic energy, so $\varepsilon_{av} = \frac{5}{2}kT$. If the molecule is free to vibrate like a spring, in addition to rotating, we get two additional terms due to the vibrational potential energy and the vibrational kinetic energy. Adding these terms gives $\varepsilon_{av} = \frac{7}{2}kT$. More complex molecules can have additional degrees of freedom.

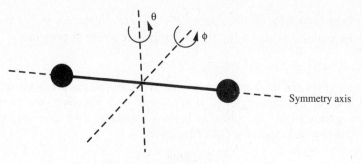

Fig. 16-7

These results, in which each degree of freedom that involves energy (with certain restrictions) contributes the same value ($\frac{1}{2}kT$) to the average energy, are called the law of **equipartition of energy**.

Applying the arguments leading to Eqs. (*16.12*) to (*16.15a*) for the case of diatomic molecules that can translate and rotate but not vibrate ($\varepsilon_{av} = \frac{5}{2}kT$), we conclude (see Problem 16.14 below)

$$c_{V,\,mol} = \tfrac{5}{2}R = 2.5R = 20.8 \text{ J/(mol} \cdot \text{K)} \qquad (16.15b)$$

Applying the same arguments to diatomic molecules that can both rotate and vibrate, we get

$$c_{V,\,mol} = \tfrac{7}{2}R = 3.5R = 29.1 \text{ J/(mol} \cdot \text{K)} \qquad (16.15c)$$

Problem 16.14.

(*a*) Show explicitly that $\varepsilon_{av} = \frac{5}{2}kT$ for a gas of diatomic molecules implies $c_{V,\,mol} = \frac{5}{2}R$.

(*b*) Having a higher molar heat capacity implies that more heat must be added to get a given rise in temperature. Explain, on the basis of the discussion above, why a gas of molecules with more degrees of freedom requires the addition of more heat to get a given rise in temperature than does a gas with fewer degrees of freedom.

Solution

(*a*) The total internal energy of our sample is now $U = N\varepsilon_{av} = \frac{5}{2}NkT = \frac{5}{2}nRT$. Since the volume is held fixed, no mechanical work is done, so the heat ΔQ added to the system all goes into an increase ΔU in the internal energy. Then $\Delta Q = \Delta U = \frac{5}{2}nR\,\Delta T \Rightarrow c_{V,\,mol} \equiv \Delta Q/(n\,\Delta T) = \frac{5}{2}R$.

(*b*) When adding heat to the gas, the average energy per molecule increases. According to the law of equipartition of energy, the average energy for each degree of freedom (that involves energy) is the same and equals $\frac{1}{2}kT$. Thus, part of the entering heat must increase the average energy in each degree of freedom. This means that for a given amount of heat input, the larger the number of degrees of freedom, the less the new energy is available to each, and the less is the increase in $\frac{1}{2}kT$. It therefore takes more heat to get a given rise in temperature than if there are fewer degrees of freedom.

In Table 16.2 we give the measured specific heats, molecular masses, and molar heat capacities at constant volume for a number of monatomic and diatomic gases at low pressure and moderate temperatures. An examination of the actual molar heat capacities at constant volume for various diatomic molecules show that the results are approximately consistent with Eq. (*16.15b*) at moderate temperatures. But the approximation is not as good as for monatomic molecules. Furthermore, experiments over an extended temperature range show that there is a clear temperature dependence of

Table 16.2.   Specific Heat, Molecular Mass, and Molar Heat Capacity for Gases at Constant Volume

Substance	c_V, J/(kg · K)	$\mathcal{M}$, kg/mol	$c_{V,mol}$, J/(mol · K)	$c_{V,mol}/R$
Monatomic:				
Helium	3120	0.0040	12.5	1.50
Neon	625	0.0200	12.5	1.50
Argon	313	0.0400	12.5	1.50
Diatomic:				
Hydrogen	10,200	0.0020	20.4	2.45
Nitrogen	743	0.0280	20.8	2.50
Oxygen	659	0.0320	21.1	2.54
Carbon monoxide	746	0.0280	20.9	2.51

molar heat capacities, while the values of Eqs. (*16.15a, b, c*) are fixed and independent of temperature. Closer comparison of more comprehensive theoretical calculations with the experimental values of molar heat capacities of gases indicated that the assumption of gas molecules completely obeying the laws of classical physics might be wrong. Thermodynamics and statistical mechanics thus allowed for the indirect study of the physics of the realm of atoms and molecules, which led to the realization that newtonian mechanics does not apply in this realm. This in turn led to the formulation of the new "quantum" mechanics in the early twentieth century.

Problem 16.15.   Under constant-pressure conditions, find (*a*) the molar heat capacity of neon, (*b*) the specific heat of nitrogen.

Solution

(*a*)   We use Eq. (*16.18*) and Table 16.2 to get

$$c_{P,\,mol} = 1.5R + R = 2.5R = 20.8 \text{ J/(mol · K)}$$

(*b*)   Here we first find $c_{P,\,mol}$ for nitrogen, as in (*a*):

$$c_{P,\,mol} = 2.50R + R = 3.50R = 29.1 \text{ J/(mol · K)}$$

Next, we use Eq. (*16.17*) to get

$$c_P = \frac{c_{P,\,mol}}{\mathcal{M}} = \frac{29.1 \text{ J/(mol · K)}}{0.0280 \text{ kg/mol}} = 1039 \text{ J/kg · K}$$

Molar Heat Capacities of Solids

In Problem 16.13(*b*) we calculated the molar heat capacities of two metals, copper and aluminum, and found that, although their specific heats were quite different, their molar heat capacities were very similar. This is not an accident but is a consequence of the equipartition law applied to solids. The simplest model of a crystalline solid is that of a three-dimensional matrix of identical molecules locked in fixed equilibrium positions, able only to vibrate somewhat about the equilibrium positions. In this model each molecule can be thought of as being held in place by springs in the *x*, *y*, and *z* directions (Fig. 16-8). Such a molecule has six degrees of freedom since it can vibrate in each of three

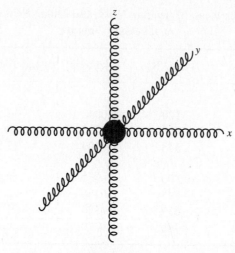

Fig. 16-8

directions and can have velocity in all three directions. Applying the equipartition of energy rule, the average energy per molecule of a sample of the solid at temperature T is

$$\varepsilon_{av} = 6\left(\tfrac{1}{2}kT\right) = 3kT \qquad (16.19)$$

If the sample has N molecules, we have for the total internal energy

$$U = 3NkT = 3nRT \qquad (16.20)$$

Again, if we add heat at constant volume, $\Delta Q = \Delta U = 3nR\,\Delta T$, which implies

$$c_{V,\,mol} = \frac{\Delta Q}{n\,\Delta T} = 3R = 24.9 \text{ J/(mol} \cdot \text{K)} \qquad (16.21)$$

This is fairly close to the values obtained in Problem 16.13(b). A study of the actual values of molar heat capacities of crystalline solids at constant volume shows that at high temperatures they all have essentially the same molar heat capacity $3R$ and satisfy Eq. (16.21). This is called the **law of Dulong and Petit**.

> **Note.** For most solids at low temperature, c_V and c_P have almost identical values. At higher temperatures they begin to deviate more significantly. For copper they are the same to within a few percentage points even at a temperature as high as 400 K. For our purposes we will assume that the two types of heat capacity of solids have the same values unless otherwise noted.

While the law of Dulong and Petit would seem to be a confirmation of our model in which a solid is made of molecules obeying the ordinary rules of newtonian mechanics, it turns out not to be so. Equation (16.21) implies that the molar heat capacity of solids should not vary with temperature, but all real crystal solids have molar heat capacities that decrease to zero as the Kelvin temperature decreases to zero (Fig. 16-9). It is therefore clear (even more strikingly than in the case of gases) that something basic is wrong: either our use of statistical concepts fails or our newtonian mechanics fails in the realm of atoms and molecules. In fact it is the newtonian mechanics that fails, and it must be replaced with **quantum mechanics**. In the quantum model, the energy of a system can assume only certain discrete values called quantum energy levels. Applying statistical ideas to such a system leads

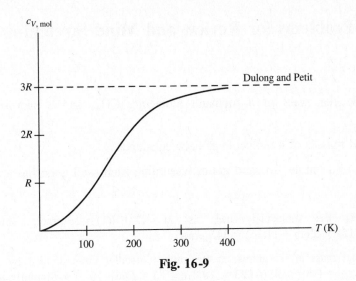

Fig. 16-9

to results consistent with the actual behavior of the molar heat capacities of solids. Many other forms of evidence indicate that discrete quantum energy levels exist within and between atoms and molecules. Examples are the discrete energies that electrons in an atom can have, and the discrete vibrational and rotational energy levels that a molecule can have.

Problem 16.16.   Consider a solid for which $c_{V, mol}$ has the temperature dependence shown in Fig. 16-9.

(a)   Find the approximate molar heat capacity at 300 K in J/(mol · K).

(b)   Suppose we have 2.0 mol of the solid. If adding 100 J of heat raises the temperature by 4 K, at what approximate temperature is the solid?

Solution

(a)   From the curve we see that 300 K corresponds to $c_{mol} \approx 2.75R = 2.75[8.31 \text{ J/(mol · K)}] = 22.85 \text{ J/(mol · K)}$.

(b) $c_{mol} = \Delta Q/(n \Delta T) = (100 \text{ J})/[(2 \text{ mol})(4.0 \text{ K})] = 12.5 \text{ J/(mol · K)}$. Since $R = 8.31 \text{ J/(mol · K)}$, this corresponds to $c_{mol} = 1.50R$. An examination of the curve in Fig. 16-9 indicates that this corresponds to a temperature of around 150 K.

Problem 16.17.   If a 2-mol block of metal at 400 K is placed in thermal contact with a container holding 1.5 mol of monatomic gas at 200 K, find the final temperature T_f. Assume that the container has negligible heat capacity, that the molar heat capacity of the metal is $3R$, and that no heat is lost to the surroundings.

Solution

This is a standard calorimetry problem, with $Q_{in} = Q_{out}$. Here, however, we use molar heat capacities instead of specific heats, since we are given the number of moles, rather than the masses. The amount of heat entering the gas is $Q_{in} = n_{gas}(c_{mol,gas})(T_f - 200 \text{ K})$. Similarly, Q_{out} is the amount of heat leaving the metal, which is $Q_{out} = n_{met}(c_{mol,met})(400 \text{ K} - T_f)$. Recalling that for a monatomic gas: $c_{mol,gas} = 1.5R$, and that the Dulong and Petit value yields $c_{mol,met} = 3R$, we get

$$(1.5 \text{ mol})(1.5R)(T_f - 200 \text{ K}) = (2.0 \text{ mol})(3R)(400 \text{ K} - T_f) \quad \text{or} \quad T_f = 345 \text{ K}$$

Problems for Review and Mind Stretching

Problem 16.18.

(a) Find the molecular mass of a methane molecule, CH_4, and a sucrose sugar molecule, $C_{12}H_{22}O_{11}$.

(b) Find the actual masses of a molecule of each substance.

(c) Find the mass of a "mole" of sand grains, assuming each sand grain has a mass of 0.05 g.

Solution

(a) For CH_4 the molecular mass is $M = 12 + 4(1) = 16$ g/mol. Similarly, for sugar, $M = 12(12) + 22(1) + 11(16) = 342$ g/mol.

(b) The actual mass m, in grams, is the gram molecular mass divided by Avogadro's number. Then, $m_{meth} = (16 \text{ g/mol})/(6.023 \times 10^{23} \text{ mol}^{-1}) = 2.66 \cdot 10^{-23}$ g. Similarly, $m_{sugar} = (342 \text{ g/mol})/(6.023 \times 10^{23} \text{ mol}^{-1}) = 5.68 \cdot 10^{-22}$ g.

(c) One mole of anything is 6.023×10^{23} units of that thing. For grains of sand, the mass of a mole of the sand is thus

$$(0.05 \text{ g})(6.023 \times 10^{23}) = 3.01 \times 10^{22} \text{ g} = 3.01 \times 10^{19} \text{ kg}$$

Problem 16.19.   A tank filled with helium has a volume of 4.0 ft^3 and is at a temperature of $0°C$. All the helium is used to fill a large, originally empty, balloon. The balloon has a final volume of 300 ft^3, final temperature $30°C$, and final pressure 0.15 MPa. If the ideal gas law holds, find (a) the original pressure, and (b) the original density, of the helium in the tank.

Solution

(a) Since no gas is lost or gained in the process, we must have $P_1V_1/T_1 = P_2V_2/T_2$. Since we are dealing with ratios, we can leave the mixed units, which will cancel out.

$$\frac{P_1(4.0 \text{ ft}^3)}{273 \text{ K}} = \frac{(0.15 \text{ MPa})(300 \text{ ft}^3)}{303 \text{ K}} \qquad \text{or} \qquad P_1 = 10.1 \text{ MPa}$$

(b) Use Eq. (16.7):

$$1.01 \times 10^7 \text{ Pa} = d_1 \left[\frac{8.31 \text{ J/(mol} \cdot \text{K)}}{0.004 \text{ kg/mol}} \right] (273 \text{ K}) \qquad \text{or} \qquad d_1 = 17.8 \text{ kg/m}^3$$

Problem 16.20.   A 400-L oxygen tank is at a temperature $T_1 = 300$ K and under a pressure $P_1 = 20$ atm. If 4.0 kg of oxygen leaks out when the temperature is raised to $T_2 = 400$ K, find the new pressure, P_2. (Assume the ideal gas law holds.)

Solution

We apply the ideal gas law in the form of (16.7) to obtain the initial density (recalling that $P_A = 1.013 \times 10^5$ Pa):

$$P_1 = \frac{d_1 R T_1}{M} \Rightarrow 20(1.013 \times 10^5 \text{ Pa}) = \frac{d_1 [8.31 \text{ J/(mol} \cdot \text{K)}](300 \text{ K})}{0.032 \text{ kg/mol}} \qquad \text{or} \qquad d_1 = 26.0 \text{ kg/m}^3$$

Next, we obtain the final density d_2. The initial mass is $M_1 = d_1 V_1 = (26.0 \text{ kg/m}^3)(0.400 \text{ m}^3) = 10.4$ kg. After the leakage, $M_2 = M_1 - 4.0 \text{ kg} = 6.4$ kg. Dividing M_2 by $V_2 = V_1 = 0.400 \text{ m}^3$, we get

$d_2 = 16.0 \, \text{kg/m}^3$. Finally, we use (16.7) to set up the ratio $P_1/d_1 T_1 = P_2/d_2 T_2$, from which we get

$$\frac{20 \, \text{atm}}{(26.0 \, \text{kg/m}^3)(300 \, \text{K})} = \frac{P_2}{(16.0 \, \text{kg/m}^3)(400 \, \text{K})} \qquad \text{or} \qquad P_2 = 16.4 \, \text{atm}$$

Problem 16.21.   Figure 16-10 depicts a fictitious polyatomic molecule that is free to rotate about each of three axes through its center. In addition, each outlying atom is free to independently vibrate in and out relative to the central atom. On the basis of equipartition of energy, what will be the molar heat capacity *at constant pressure* of an ideal gas of these molecules?

Solution

There are three translational degrees of freedom and three rotational degrees of freedom that have kinetic energy associated with them. In addition, each of the six outlying atoms has two vibrational degrees of freedom—one with potential energy and one with kinetic energy—for a total of 12 vibrational degrees of freedom. Altogether, there are 18 degrees of freedom, so

$$c_{V,\text{mol}} = \tfrac{18}{2}R = 9R \qquad \text{and} \qquad c_{P,\text{mol}} = c_{V,\text{mol}} + R = 10R$$

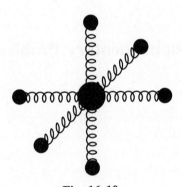

Fig. 16-10

Problem 16.22.   Dalton's law of partial pressures states that if a dilute mixture of different gases occupies a given volume at a given temperature, the total pressure exerted by the mixture is the sum of the pressures (called **partial pressures**) that each gas would exert alone if none of the other gases were there. Show why this is true.

Solution

We have seen that the ideal gas law holds irrespective of the nature of the molecules making up the gas (e.g., monatomic, diatomic, polyatomic) or of the masses of the molecules. We may therefore assume that a mixture of $N = N_1 + N_2 + N_3 + \cdots$ molecules of the different species of gases will obey $PV = NkT$, where P is the overall pressure. Hence,

$$P = \frac{NkT}{V} = \frac{N_1 kT}{V} + \frac{N_2 kT}{V} + \frac{N_3 kT}{V} + \cdots$$

The terms on the right are just the pressures $P_1, P_2, P_3, \cdots$ that each gas would exert alone in the same volume at the same temperature—in other words, the partial pressures. Thus we have Dalton's law: $P = P_1 + P_2 + P_3 + \cdots$.

Problem 16.23.   A cylinder of volume 30 L contains 4.0 mol of hydrogen and 6.0 mol of nitrogen at a temperature of 300 K.

(a) Find the partial pressures and the total pressure.

(b) Find the fraction of the total mass of the mixture that is hydrogen.

Solution

(a)
$$P(\text{H}_2) = \frac{n(\text{H}_2)RT}{V} = \frac{(4.0 \text{ mol}) \left[8.31 \text{ J/(mol} \cdot \text{ K)}\right] (300 \text{ K})}{30 \times 10^{-3} \text{ m}^3} = 332 \text{ kPa}$$

$$P(\text{N}_2) = \frac{6.0 \text{ mol}}{4.0 \text{ mol}} (332 \text{ kPa}) = 499 \text{ kPa}$$

$$P = 332 \text{ kPa} + 499 \text{ kPa} = 831 \text{ kPa}$$

(b) The two masses are

$$m(\text{H}_2) = (4.0 \text{ mol})(2.0 \text{ g/mol}) = 8.0 \text{ g}$$
$$m(\text{N}_2) = (6.0 \text{ mol})(28.0 \text{ g/mol}) = 168 \text{ g}$$

The fraction of hydrogen is then $8.0/176 = 0.0455$.

Supplementary Problems

Problem 16.24. Find the molecular mass of ethane (C_2H_6); find the actual mass, in grams, of an ethane molecule.

   Ans. 30 g/mol, 4.98×10^{-23} g

Problem 16.25.

(a) If 50 ft^3 of air at atmospheric pressure and 300 K is compressed to 8.0 ft^3 at the same temperature, find the new pressure, in pascals.

(b) With the new volume held fixed, the air is heated to 900 K. What is the new pressure, in Pa?

   Ans. (a) 633 kPa; (b) 1.90 MPa

Problem 16.26. Nitrogen gas occupies 15.0 L at a pressure of 1.50 MPa and a temperature of $-30°C$. If the volume doubles and the temperature rises to $180°C$, find the new pressure.

   Ans. 1.40 MPa

Problem 16.27. Find the mass of the nitrogen gas of Problem 16.26 and its final density.

   Ans. 0.312 kg; 10.4 kg/m^3

Problem 16.28. In the ideal gas law, $PV = nRT$, it is sometimes convenient to express P in atm and V in L.

(a) Find the value for R in the appropriate new units

(b) Find the pressure (in atm) exerted by 5.0 mol of an ideal gas that occupies 30 L and is at a temperature of 400 K.

   Ans. (a) 0.082 L $\cdot$ atm/(mol $\cdot$ K); (b) 5.47 atm

Problem 16.29. A 20-L cylinder contains oxygen at a pressure of 3.0 atm and at room temperature (300 K). The cylinder valve is opened and is kept open until oxygen stops leaking out, at which point it is closed.

(a)   What is the new pressure in the cylinder?

(b)   How many grams of oxygen have leaked out?

> *Ans.*   (a) 1 atm (room pressure); (b) 52 g

Problem 16.30. Assume that after the valve shuts in Problem 16.29, the temperature of the cylinder is raised to 500 K.

(a)   What is the density of the gas remaining in the cylinder?

(b)   What is the new pressure?

> *Ans.*   (a) 1.30 kg/m^3; (b) 1.67 atm

Problem 16.31.   (a)   For carbon monoxide (CO), $C_{V,mol} = 2.46R$. Calculate c_V and c_P.

> *Ans.*   0.730 kJ/(kg · K), 1.03 kJ/(kg · K)

Problem 16.32. For the data of Problem 16.31 and a temperature 500 K, find (a) the average molecular energy; (b) the root-mean-square molecular velocity.

> *Ans.*   (a) 1.70×10^{-20} J; (b) 667 m/s

Problem 16.33. Assume that Fig. 16-2 refers to 2 mol of a gas, with the following data: $P_a = 9.5 \times 10^5$ Pa; $P_b = 7.0 \times 10^5$ Pa; $P_c = 3.0 \times 10^5$ Pa.

(a)   If $V_a = 4.0$ L, find T_a

(b)   If $V_b = 10.0$ L, find the average translational kinetic energy of a molecule of the gas when it is in state b.

(c)   If $V_c = 7.0$ L, find v_{rms} of the gas in state c, if it is methane (CH$_4$).

> *Ans.*   (a) 228 K; (b) 8.71×10^{-21} J; (c) 444 m/s

Problem 16.34. A chunk of material at a temperature of 150 K has a molar heat capacity of half the Dulong and Petit value.

(a)   If 20 J of heat is necessary to raise the temperature of the chunk by 1.0 K, how many moles of material are present?

(b)   What is the thermal internal energy of the chunk at 150 K?

> *Ans.*   (a) 1.60 mol; (b) 3000 J

Problem 16.35. A mixture of 3.0 g of oxygen, 7.0 g of nitrogen, and 14 g of carbon dioxide (CO$_2$) are in a container of volume 3.0 L; the temperature is 500 K.

(a)   Find the number of moles of each gas in the container.

(b)   Find the total pressure exerted by the gases on the walls of the container. [*Hint*: See Problems 16.22 and 16.23.]

> *Ans.*   (a) O$_2$ − 0.094 mol, N$_2$ − 0.25 mol, CO$_2$ − 0.32 mol; (b) 0.92 MPa

Problem 16.36.   Recalling that the thermal internal energy of n mol of a gas at temperature T can be expressed as $U = nc_{V,mol}T$, find U for the mixture of Problem 16.35. [*Hint*: The molar heat capacities of O_2 and N_2 are in Table 16.2; assume that for CO_2, $c_{V,mol} = 3.39R$.]

   Ans.   8.10 kJ

Problem 16.37.   Consider a cylinder having a close-fitting massless piston as shown in Fig. 16-11. The cylinder contains a gas in thermal equilibrium, at 300 K, with the surrounding room air, which is at atmospheric pressure. Assume that 1000 N in weights is gently placed on top of the piston so that it moves down to its new equilibrium position without a change in temperature.

(*a*)   What is the new pressure exerted by the gas in the cylinder?
(*b*)   What is the new height h' of the piston above the base of the cylinder?

   Ans.   (*a*) 1.846×10^5 Pa; (*b*) 11.0 cm

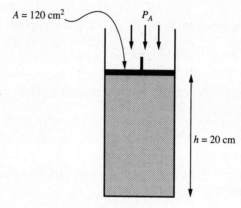

Fig. 16-11

Problem 16.38.   For the arrangement of Problem 16.37, if the temperature is increased to 400 K, how much additional weight must be put on the piston to keep its position unchanged?

   Ans.   738 N

Chapter 17

Transfer of Heat

17.1 CONDUCTION

In Chap. 15 we saw that heat is the nonmechanical transfer of energy. In examples we gave of objects at different temperatures being brought into contact, heat was transferred via the direct contact of more energetic, "hotter," layers of molecules with less energetic, "cooler," layers of molecules. This direct transfer of thermal energy from one layer of molecules to the next is called **heat conduction**. By definition, heat conduction is a nonequilibrium process, since it involves temperature differences between objects or between parts of a single object. The rate at which heat is conducted through an object is found to obey definite laws. Consider a bar of a uniform material of length L and cross-sectional area A, as shown in Fig. 17-1. Assume the two end faces are maintained at temperatures T_1 and T_2, respectively, where T_1 is the higher temperature. We assume that the long sides of the bar are well insulated so that heat cannot leak out the sides. We also assume a "steady-state" situation where the heat conducted through any given cross section of the bar will be the same as at any other cross section so that there is no accumulation of thermal energy at any location in the bar. The amount of heat transferred per unit time, $H = \Delta Q/\Delta t$, across a given cross section of the bar is directly proportional to the temperature difference $T_1 - T_2$ and to the area A and is inversely proportional to the length L:

$$H = \frac{kA(T_1 - T_2)}{L} \tag{17.1}$$

where k is a proportionality constant that is different for each material and is called the **coefficient of thermal conductivity** (or **conductivity**, for short). Since the SI unit of H is J/s = W, the SI unit for k is W/(m · K). In Table 17.1, we give the conductivities of a number of substances at room temperature.

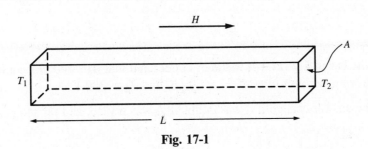

Fig. 17-1

Note that metals generally have larger conductivities than other solids and are therefore called good heat "conductors." The other materials listed clearly don't conduct heat well; they are called insulators. Stagnant liquids conduct heat to some extent, whereas stagnant gases are generally good insulators.

Problem 17.1. In constructing a calorimeter, one wants the container to be made of a substance that will allow the temperature of the container and its contents to quickly come to equilibrium. On the other hand, one doesn't want heat to be gained or lost to the surroundings during a calorimeter experiment. How would you design such a calorimeter?

Table 17.1.   Coefficients of Thermal Conductivity

Substance	k, W/(m · K)
Metals:	
Aluminum	205
Brass	109
Copper	385
Silver	406
Steel	50
Nonmetallic solids:	
Brick	0.7
Concrete	0.9
Cork	0.04
Glass	0.80
Rockwool	0.04
Styrofoam	0.01
Wood	0.10

Solution

The container should be made of metal so that heat rapidly flows through it, helping to bring it and its contents to a common temperature. To avoid heat losses, the container should be surrounded (including a cover) with insulating material, such as Styrofoam, which assures that heat leaks, in or out, occur very slowly.

Problem 17.2.

(a)   Assume that the bar in Fig. 17-1 is made of copper and that $A = 100$ cm^2 and $L = 60$ cm. Find H, the heat flowing per unit time, if $T_1 = 600$ K and $T_2 = 300$ K.

(b)   How would the answer change if A was doubled, L was tripled, and the temperatures stayed the same?

Solution

(a)   From Eq. (17.1) and Table 17.1 we get

$$H = \frac{[385 \text{ W/(m} \cdot \text{K)}] (100 \times 10^{-4} \text{ m}^2) (600 \text{ K} - 300 \text{ K})}{0.60 \text{ m}} = 1925 \text{ W}$$

(b)   If A doubles, so does H, and if L triples, H drops to one-third its original value, so combining these two effects, we see that H changes to two-thirds its original value: $H = 2/3$ (1925 W) = 1283 W.

Problem 17.3.   For the situation of Problem 17.2(a), find the temperature T' of the bar 20 cm from the left end.

Solution

Consider a cross section of the bar 20 cm from the left end. In a steady-state situation, T' remains constant as long as the end-face temperatures T_1 and T_2 are held fixed. We apply (17.1) to the part of the bar between the left end and the 20-cm position.

$$1925 \text{ W} = \frac{[385 \text{ W(m} \cdot \text{ K)}] \, (100 \times 10^{-4} \text{ m}^2) \, (600 \text{ K} - T')}{0.20 \text{ m}}$$

While we could solve this equation for T', it is more informative to note that, since the values of k, A, and H are the same as in Problem 17.2(a), we must have

$$\frac{T_1 - T_2}{0.60 \text{ m}} = \frac{T_1 - T'}{0.20 \text{ m}} \qquad \text{or} \qquad T_1 - T' = \tfrac{1}{3}(T_1 - T_2) = 100 \text{ K}$$

Thus $600 \text{ K} - T' = 100 \text{ K}$, so $T' = 500 \text{ K}$.

Note.   More generally, from (17.1) the steady-state temperature drops linearly (from T_1 to T_2) with distance along the rod.

Problem 17.4.   Two slabs α and β, of equal cross section $A = 80 \text{ cm}^2$ but made of different materials, are in close contact, as shown in Fig. 17-2. The left side of α and the right side of β are kept at temperatures $T_1 = 600 \text{ K}$ and $T_2 = 300 \text{ K}$, respectively. The lengths of the slabs are $L_\alpha = 20 \text{ cm}$ and $L_\beta = 30 \text{ cm}$. If slab α is made of steel and slab β is made of copper, find (a) the temperature at the interface between the two slabs, (b) the rate at which heat is transferred across the slabs.

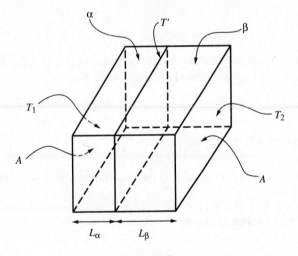

Fig. 17-2

Solution

(a)   In steady state the heat flow H must be the same in each slab. Thus

$$\frac{k_\alpha(T_1 - T')A}{L_\alpha} = \frac{k_\beta(T' - T_2)A}{L_\beta} \qquad\qquad (i)$$

Substituting in values from Table 17.1 and the data from the problem, we get

$$\frac{[50 \text{ W/(m} \cdot \text{ K)}] \, (600 \text{ K} - T')}{0.20 \text{ m}} = \frac{[385 \text{ W/(m} \cdot \text{ K)}] \, (T' - 300 \text{ K})}{0.30 \text{ m}}$$

Solving for T', we get $T' = 349 \text{ K}$.

(b)   Now that we have T' we can obtain H by using (17.1), $H = kA(T_1 - T_2)/L$, for either slab. For slab α, we have

$$\frac{[50 \text{ W}/(\text{m} \cdot \text{K})] \, (80 \times 10^{-4} \text{ m}^2) \, (600 \text{ K} - 349 \text{ K})}{0.20 \text{ m}} = 502 \text{ W}$$

[As a check we can apply (17.1) to slab β.]

Problem 17.5.   Equation (17.1) can be reexpressed as

$$\frac{H}{A} = \frac{T_1 - T_2}{L/k}$$

If we set $T_1 - T_2 \equiv \Delta T$, and define $L/k \equiv R$, we have $H/A = \Delta T/R$. The quantity R is called the **R-factor** of the slab.

(a)   Find the SI units of R.

(b)   Show that for a wall made up of multiple layers with R-factors $R_1, R_2, R_3, \ldots$, the rate of heat transfer is given by

$$\frac{H}{A} = \frac{\Delta T}{R} \tag{i}$$

where ΔT is the total temperature difference between the two sides of the wall, and $R = R_1 + R_2 + R_3 + \cdots$.

Solution

(a)   The units of R are those of $L/k = \text{m}/[\text{W}/(\text{m} \cdot \text{K})] = \text{m}^2 \cdot \text{K/W}$.

(b)   Consider a wall made up of three layers for definiteness. If ΔT_1, ΔT_2, and ΔT_3 represent the temperature differences across the respective layers, then

$$\frac{H}{A} = \frac{\Delta T_1}{R_1} \qquad \frac{H}{A} = \frac{\Delta T_2}{R_2} \qquad \frac{H}{A} = \frac{\Delta T_3}{R_3} \tag{ii}$$

Since $\Delta T = \Delta T_1 + \Delta T_2 + \Delta T_3$, we get

$$\Delta T = \frac{H}{A} R_1 + \frac{H}{A} R_2 + \frac{H}{A} R_3 = \frac{H}{A} (R_1 + R_2 + R_3)$$

Setting $R \equiv R_1 + R_2 + R_3$, we get $\Delta T = (H/A)R$, which implies that $H/A = \Delta T/R$. It is easy to generalize to any number of layers.

Problem 17.6.

(a)   Find the R-factor for each of the slabs in Problem 17.4.

(b)   Find the R-factor for the combination of both slabs.

(c)   Redo (b) of Problem 17.4 using the above result.

Solution

(a)   For slab α,

$$R_\alpha = \frac{L_\alpha}{k_\alpha} = \frac{0.20 \text{ m}}{50 \text{ W}/(\text{K} \cdot \text{m})} = 4.0 \times 10^{-3} \text{ m}^2 \cdot \text{K/W}$$

Similarly, $R_\beta = \dfrac{L_\beta}{k_\beta} = \dfrac{0.30 \text{ m}}{385 \text{ W}/(\text{K} \cdot \text{m})} = 7.79 \times 10^{-4} \text{ m}^2 \cdot \text{K/W}$

(b) $R = R_\alpha + R_\beta = 4.78 \times 10^{-3} \text{ m}^2 \cdot \text{K/W}.$

(c) $H = A \dfrac{\Delta T}{R} = \dfrac{(80 \times 10^{-4} \text{ m}^2)(300 \text{ K})}{4.78 \times 10^{-3} \text{ m}^2 \cdot \text{K/W}} = 502 \text{ W}$

as before.

Problem 17.7.   A wall of a house of area 25 m^2, is made up of three layers: 5.0 cm of wood, 4.0 cm of rockwool, and 2.0 cm of gypsum board [$k = 0.06$ W/(m · K)].

(a)   Find the R-value of the wall.

(b)   Find the rate of heat loss through the wall when the temperature difference between the inside and outside surfaces are 80 K.

Solution

(a)

$$R = R_1 + R_2 + R_3 = \frac{0.050 \text{ m}}{0.10 \text{ W}/(\text{m} \cdot \text{K})} + \frac{0.040 \text{ m}}{0.04 \text{ W}/(\text{m} \cdot \text{K})} + \frac{0.020 \text{ m}}{0.06 \text{ W}/(\text{m} \cdot \text{K})} = 1.83 \text{ m}^2 \cdot \text{K/W}$$

(b)

$$H = A\frac{\Delta T}{R} = \frac{(25 \text{ m}^2)(80 \text{ K})}{1.83 \text{ m}^2 \cdot \text{K/W}} = 1093 \text{ W}$$

Problem 17.8. R-values in the United States are often given in "common" units: $R = \text{ft}^2 \cdot {}^\circ\text{F}/(\text{Btu/h})$.

(a)   The R-value for a concrete wall is $R = 1.4$ ft$^2 \cdot {}^\circ$F/(Btu/h). If the wall has an area of $A = 120$ ft^2, and the temperature of the outside (colder surface) of the wall is $T_1 = 20\,^\circ$F, find the temperature of the inside surface of the wall T_2 if the rate of heat transfer across the wall is $H = 12{,}000$ Btu/h.

(b)   How many watts does H correspond to?

(c)   Find the conversion from common to SI units for R.

Solution

(a) $H = A \Delta T/R \Rightarrow 12{,}000 \text{ Btu/h} = (120 \text{ ft}^2)\,\Delta T/(1.4 \text{ ft}^2 \cdot {}^\circ\text{F} \cdot \text{h/Btu}) \Rightarrow \Delta T = 140\,^\circ\text{F} = T_2 - T_1 = T_2 - 20\,^\circ\text{F} \Rightarrow T_2 = 160\,^\circ\text{F}.$

(b)   Since there are 252 cal/Btu and 4.184 J/cal, we get

$$H = (12{,}000 \text{ Btu/h})(252 \text{ cal/Btu})(4.184 \text{ J/cal}) = 1.265 \times 10^7 \text{ J/h}$$

Converting hours to seconds we get

$$H = \frac{1.265 \times 10^7 \text{ J/h}}{3600 \text{ s/h}} = 3515 \text{ J/s} = 3515 \text{ W}$$

(c) $\text{ft}^2 \cdot {}^\circ\text{F} \cdot \text{h/Btu} = \dfrac{(0.305 \text{ m})^2 \left(\frac{5}{9}\,^\circ\text{C}\right)(3600 \text{ s})}{1054 \text{ J}} = 0.176 \text{ m}^2 \cdot \text{K/W}$

17.2   CONVECTION

Convection is a mechanism for the transfer of thermal energy that applies to fluids (liquids and gases). Unlike, conduction, where there is no macroscopic migration of molecules, in convection the thermal energy is transferred by the motion of material from one place to another. In convection the molecules of a gas or liquid pass a hot surface and gain thermal energy. The hot gas or liquid then travels to another location where the thermal energy is deposited in a cooler environment. Convection is the mechanism for heat transfer in the hot-air and hot-water home heating systems. If the circulation of the fluid is aided by a fan or pump, it is called *forced* convection. If the circulation is a consequence of the natural difference in density of the fluid (caused by a temperature difference) at different locations, it is called *natural* convection. An example of natural convection is the rising of the hot air near a steam radiator and its circulation through the room. Here, the hot fluid is less dense than the surrounding cooler fluid and so rises by buoyancy.

The rate at which a convective fluid removes heat from a hot surface and transfers it to the bulk of the fluid depends on the geometry of the surface and involves much more complicated expressions than does conduction. Nonetheless, to a good approximation the rate H of convective heat flow is proportional to the area A of the contact surface and to the temperature difference ΔT between the surface and the bulk of the fluid away from the surface. Thus,

$$H = hA\,\Delta T \tag{17.2}$$

where h, the **coefficient of convection**, depends on the fluid, the geometry, and a variety of other factors (including a slight dependence on ΔT). By (17.2) h has the same units as k. The following listing of hot surfaces and their corresponding h values applies to natural convection of air at atmospheric pressure.

1.   Horizontal plate with air passing the top surface:

$$h = 2.49\,(\Delta T)^{1/4}\ \text{W/(m}^2 \cdot \text{K)}$$

2.   Horizontal plate with air passing the bottom surface:

$$h = 1.31\,(\Delta T)^{1/4}\ \text{W/(m}^2 \cdot \text{K)}$$

3.   Vertical plate:

$$h = 1.77\,(\Delta T)^{1/4}\ \text{W/(m}^2 \cdot \text{K)}$$

4.   Horizontal or vertical pipe of diameter D:

$$h = 4.19\left(\frac{\Delta T}{D}\right)^{1/4}\ \text{W/(m}^2 \cdot \text{K)}$$

In the formulas, ΔT and D are treated as pure numbers, with ΔT the numerical value in K or °C and D the numerical value in cm.

Problem 17.9.   A bathroom is heated by a floor-to-ceiling steam pipe that is 10 cm in diameter. The ceiling height is $L = 3.0$ m and the temperature of the bulk of air in the room is 22°C. If the pipe surface is at 90°C, what is the rate of convective heat transfer?

   Solution

   Use (17.2) and the fourth formula above.

$$A = \pi D L = 0.942\ \text{m}^2 \qquad \Delta T = 90°\text{C} - 22°\text{C} = 68\ \text{K}$$

$$h = 4.19\left(\tfrac{68}{10}\right)^{1/4} = 6.77\ \text{W/(m}^2 \cdot \text{K)} \qquad H = [6.77\ \text{W/(m}^2 \cdot \text{K)}]\,(0.942\ \text{m}^2)\,(68\ \text{K}) = 434\ \text{W}$$

Problem 17.10.   The air outside a 1.50-m² glass window is at 8.0°C, and the air in the room is at 20°C. If the glass has thickness $L = 0.5$ cm, find the heat flow through the window and the temperatures of the inside and outside surfaces of the glass.

Solution

The problem is difficult because three heat-transfer processes are involved: the convection of air outside the window (H_1), the convection of air inside the room (H_2), and the conduction through the window (H_3). In steady state,

$$H_1 = H_2 = H_3 = H$$

and we can solve (17.1) and (17.2) simultaneously for the temperatures T_1 and T_2 of the inner and outer glass surfaces. Once these are known we can evaluate H.

Rather than do all that algebra, we make a simple approximation. A quick check shows that for conduction through the window

$$\frac{k}{L} = \frac{0.8 \text{ W/m} \cdot \text{K}}{0.0050 \text{ m}} = 160 \text{ W/m}^2 \cdot \text{K}$$

This is much larger than the h values for convection. Consequently (17.1) and (17.2) and the equality of the H values imply that the temperature difference across the glass must be much smaller than those between the glass surfaces and the inside and outside air. For purposes of calculating the convection rates we may therefore assume that the difference between temperatures T_1 and T_2 is negligible, and the glass is at a common temperature T'. This temperature must be midway between the temperatures of the inside and outside air if we are to have $H_1 = H_2$, so we take $T' = T_1 = T_2 = 14$°C. Applying (17.2) to the outside convection, with $\Delta T = 20$°C $- 14$°C $= 6.0$°C, we have

$$H = hA\,\Delta T = [1.77(6.0)^{1/4} \text{ W/(m}^2 \cdot \text{K})]\,(1.5 \text{ m}^2)\,(6.0 \text{ K}) = 24.9 \text{ W}$$

To check our approximate solution let us solve (17.1) for $T_1 - T_2$:

$$24.9 \text{ W} = \frac{[0.8 \text{ W/(m} \cdot \text{K})]\,(1.5 \text{ m}^2)\,(T_1 - T_2)}{0.005 \text{ m}}$$

or $T_1 - T_2 = 0.104$ K, which is indeed very small.

Problem 17.11.   Forced air flows over a heat exchanger in a room heater, with a convective heat-transfer coefficient $h = 150$ (Btu/h)/(ft² · °F). The surface temperature of the heat exchanger is held at 200°F while the air in the room is maintained at 72°F. Find the surface area of the heat exchanger if 20,000 Btu/h is delivered by the heater.

Solution

Here we are using English units, with power expressed in Btu/h. From the convection formula $H = hA\,\Delta T$, we have

$$20,000 \text{ Btu/h} = \left[150 \text{ Btu/(h} \cdot \text{ft}^2 \cdot °\text{F})\right]A(200 °\text{F} - 72 °\text{F}) \qquad \text{or} \qquad A = 1.04 \text{ ft}^2$$

17.3   RADIATION

The third, and last, form of thermal energy transfer is radiation. This is a process that involves electromagnetic waves, a concept that is beyond the scope of this book. In brief, every substance at any temperature T emits electromagnetic radiation, which carries energy with it. Light is an example of electromagnetic radiation, as are radio waves, microwaves, x-rays, and gamma rays. All these types of radiation are basically the same: rapidly oscillating transverse waves that can travel through empty space as well as through substances. They differ only in the frequency of the waves. Radio waves are relatively low-frequency waves, while light has a higher frequency, and x-rays are higher frequency yet. Since these waves all travel at the same speed—the speed of light—higher frequency means shorter wavelength. The sources of the radiation are the atoms and molecules that make up any system, and which all have electrical and magnetic properties. These atoms and molecules can release some of their energy by emitting electromagnetic radiation and undergoing transitions from higher to lower energy states. Similarly, atoms and molecules can absorb electromagnetic radiation impinging on them, undergoing transitions from lower to higher energy states. For a system to be in thermal equilibrium with its surroundings it must absorb as much radiation as it emits.

A study of radiation from solid objects shows that the total amount of radiation energy (summed over all frequencies) emitted per second H_{em} from an object at uniform Kelvin temperature T, and having total surface area A, obeys the **Stefan-Boltzmann law**

$$H_{em} = A\epsilon\sigma T^4 \qquad (17.3)$$

where σ is a universal constant called the **Stefan-Boltzmann constant** with the value

$$\sigma = 5.67 \times 10^{-8} \text{ W}/(\text{m}^2 \cdot \text{K}^4) \qquad (17.4)$$

and ϵ is a dimensionless constant, called the **emissivity**, that varies from substance to substance. The value of ϵ can vary from 0 to 1.

While (17.3) gives us the rate of emission of radiation by an object, we can quickly determine what the rate of absorption of radiant energy is for the same object when suspended in a large closed container whose inside walls are kept at some fixed temperature T. We first recognize that the rate of absorption is going to depend on the absorptive properties of the object, as well as on the intensity of the radiation that is impinging on it. This radiation, which fills the container like a bath, is emitted by the walls of the container. If we assume that the object is in thermal equilibrium with the walls of the container, then it absorbs radiation at the same rate as it emits radiation, $H_{em} = H_{abs}$, and is itself at temperature T. Then (17.3) leads to

$$H_{abs} = A\epsilon\sigma T^4 \qquad (17.5)$$

Now, (17.5) must hold even if the object is not at the temperature T (that is not in thermal equilibrium with the container), since the intensity of radiation in the container is determined by the temperature of the walls and not by that of the object. The presumption here is that the object is so small compared to the container that we can ignore its contribution to the "soup" of radiation within the container. It then follows that, for an object at temperature T_1 enclosed in a container with walls at temperature T_2, the *net* rate of flow of thermal energy out of the object is

$$H_{net} = H_{em} - H_{abs} = A\epsilon\sigma(T_1{}^4 - T_2{}^4) \qquad (17.6)$$

H_{net} can be positive or negative, depending on whether the object or the walls is the hotter.

Note from (17.3) that $\epsilon \approx 1$ for a good emitter. The same ϵ appears in (17.5), and so a good emitter is also a good absorber. Since, in almost all cases, the radiation hitting an object is either absorbed or reflected, a poor absorber-emitter must be a good reflector, and a good absorber-emitter must be a poor reflector. At normal temperatures a good absorber-emitter appears black when one shines a light on it, since so little of the light is reflected. A perfect or ideal absorber-emitter ($\epsilon = 1$) is called a **blackbody**. Substances such as charcoal behave very much like a blackbody, but no real object is a perfect blackbody.

A small hole in a container whose inside walls are in equilibrium at some temperature T emits radiation as if it were a blackbody at temperature T. This can be understood intuitively: the small opening is a near-perfect absorber—all radiation that falls on it gets lost inside the container and has negligible chance of reflecting back out again. Since a perfect absorber is a perfect emitter, the radiation energy from the hole is that of a blackbody.

Problem 17.12.

(a) A sphere of radius $R = 50$ mm acts like a blackbody. If the sphere is maintained at temperature $T = 300$ K, what is the rate of radiation from it?

(b) How would the answer to (a) change if the temperature were $T = 600$ K?

(c) How would the answer to (b) change if the radius were 150 mm?

Solution

(a) From (17.3), with $\epsilon = 1$,

$$H = A\sigma T^4 = (4\pi R^2)\sigma T^4 = [4(3.14)(0.0025 \text{ m}^2)][5.67 \times 10^{-8} \text{ W}/(\text{m}^2 \cdot \text{K}^4)](300 \text{ K})^4 = 14.4 \text{ W}$$

(b) If the temperature doubles, H goes up by $2^4 = 16$, so, $H = 230$ W.

(c) If the radius triples, the area A goes up by a factor of 9, so, $H = 2070$ W.

Problem 17.13. An incandescent lamp filament, with a surface area of 100 mm^2, operates at a temperature of 2300°C. Assume that the filament acts like a blackbody.

(a) What is the rate of radiation from the filament?

(b) If the walls of the room in which the lamp operates are at 27°C, what is the rate at which the filament absorbs radiation?

(c) At what rate does electrical energy have to be supplied to the filament to keep its temperature constant? (Ignore conduction and convection losses from the filament.)

Solution

(a) $H_{em} = A\sigma T^4 = (100 \times 10^{-6} \text{ m}^2)[5.67 \times 10^{-8} \text{ W}/(\text{m}^2 \cdot \text{K}^4)](2573 \text{ K})^4 = 249$ W

(b) $H_{abs} = A\sigma T^4 = (100 \times 10^{-6} \text{ m}^2)[5.67 \times 10^{-8} \text{ W}/(\text{m}^2 \cdot \text{K}^4)](300 \text{ K})^4 = 46$ mW. We see that the absorption due to the walls at room temperature is negligible.

(c) As energy radiated away from the filament, the filament would rapidly cool down unless the energy were continuously replenished. Thus 249 W of electrical power is required to keep the filament at constant temperature.

Problem 17.14. Assume that the steam pipe of Problem 17.9 has an emissivity of 0.60. Calculate the net rate of radiative thermal transfer from the pipe to the room, and compare it to the convective rate.

Solution

We apply (17.6), using the data from Problem 17.9:

$$H_{net} = (\pi DL)\epsilon\sigma(T_1{}^4 - T_2{}^4)$$

$$= (3.14)(0.10 \text{ m})(3.0 \text{ m})(0.60)[5.67 \times 10^{-8} \text{ W}/(\text{m}^2 \cdot \text{K}^4)][(363 \text{ K})^4 - (295 \text{ K})^4] = 314 \text{ W}$$

We note that more thermal energy is transferred by convection than by radiation. This is generally true for steam and hot water "radiators" despite their name.

Problem 17.15.   The surface area of the sun is about 2.4×10^{19} m^2, and its surface temperature is about 6000 K. Use this data to determine the total radiative power emitted by the sun, assuming it behaves like a blackbody.

Solution

$$H = A\sigma T^4 = (24 \times 10^{18} \text{ m}^2) \left[5.67 \times 10^{-8} \text{ W}/(\text{m}^2 \cdot \text{K}^4)\right] (6000 \text{ K})^4 = 1.76 \times 10^{27} \text{ W}$$

Problem 17.16.   Two objects at room temperature appear black and white, respectively, when light shines on them. The lights are turned off, and the two objects are then heated to the same high temperature until one of them glows brightly. Which one glows?

Solution

Since the object that appeared black is a good absorber, it is also a good emitter ($\epsilon \approx 1$), so at high temperature it will glow brightly. The object that initially appeared white is a good reflector and poor absorber, so it is also a poor emitter ($\epsilon \approx 0$) and will be much less bright at the higher temperature.

Problems for Review and Mind Stretching

Problem 17.17.   A metal cylinder, of length $L = 29$ cm and cross-sectional area $A = 300$ cm^2, has one end submerged in a shallow pool within an insulated vessel (Fig. 17-3). The pool consists of 0.600 kg of ice in equilibrium with water. The other end is kept at a constant temperature of 150°C. It is found that all the ice melts in 2.0 min. What is the conductivity of the metal, and what metal is it likely to be? Assume that there are no heat losses out the sides of the cylinder or from the vessel.

Solution

We can assume that the temperature of the submerged end remains at 0°C all through the melting process. To solve (*17.1*) for k, we need to know only the rate of heat transfer H; all the other quantities

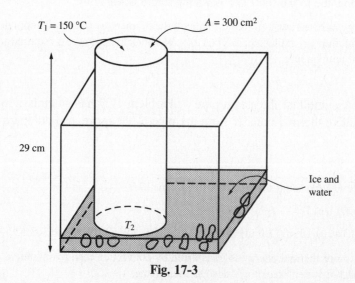

Fig. 17-3

are given. But H can be determined by figuring out how much heat must have been transferred to melt the ice and then dividing by the time taken. From Table 15.4 the heat of fusion of water is $L_f = 335$ kJ/kg. Thus,

$$H = \frac{mL_f}{\Delta t} = \frac{(0.600 \text{ kg}) (335 \text{ kJ/kg})}{(2.0 \text{ min}) (60 \text{ s/ min})} = 1.675 \text{ kW}$$

$$k = \frac{HL}{A(T_1 - T_2)} = \frac{(1675 \text{ W}) (0.29 \text{ m})}{(300 \times 10^{-4} \text{ m}^2) (150 \,^\circ\text{C} - 0 \,^\circ\text{C})} = 108 \text{ W/(m} \cdot \text{K})$$

Table 17.1 suggests *brass* as the metal.

Problem 17.18.   Compare the R-value of a single pane of glass 1.0 cm thick with that of a double pane, which consists of two 0.40-cm-thick panes separated by a 0.2-cm-thick layer of stagnant air $[k_{air} = 0.024$ W/(m $\cdot$ K)].

Solution

For the solid pane

$$R = \frac{L}{k} = \frac{0.010 \text{ m}}{0.80 \text{ W/(m} \cdot \text{K})} = 0.0125 \text{ m}^2 \cdot \text{K/W}$$

For each glass pane of the sandwich,

$$R_{glass} = \frac{0.0040 \text{ m}}{0.80 \text{ W/(m} \cdot \text{K})} = 0.0050 \text{ m}^2 \cdot \text{K/W}$$

For the dead-air space we have to concern ourselves only with conduction:

$$R_{air} = \frac{0.002 \text{ m}}{0.024 \text{ W/(m} \cdot \text{K})} = 0.0833 \text{ m}^2 \cdot \text{K/W}$$

The total R for the sandwich is then

$$R' = 2R_{glass} + R_{air} = 0.0933 \text{ m}^2 \cdot \text{K/W}$$

about 7.5 times larger than that of the solid glass.

Problem 17.19.   A space capsule has an outer shell of surface area 100 m^2 and average R-value 4.00 m$^2 \cdot$ K/W. If the inner walls are to be kept at 27°C, how much wattage must the capsule heaters generate? Assume an outer-wall temperature of 200 K.

Solution

The steady-state rate at which heat leaves the interior of the capsule is

$$H = \frac{A \, \Delta T}{R} = \frac{(100 \text{ m}^2) (300 \text{ K} - 200 \text{ K})}{4.00 \text{ m}^2 \cdot \text{K/W}} = 2500 \text{ W}$$

This must be the rate of heating to maintain the interior at constant temperature.

Problem 17.20.   Assume that the heat conducted to the outer wall of the capsule in Problem 17.19 leaves the capsule solely through radiation. Assume further that 800 W is absorbed by the capsule from "nearby" stars. What is the emissivity of the outer surface?

Solution

For steady state, the outer wall must radiate away the 2500 W from inside and reradiate the 800 W from outside, for a total output of 3300 W. The Stefan–Boltzmann law then yields

$$3300 \text{ W} = A\epsilon\sigma T^4 = (100 \text{ m}^2)\epsilon[5.67 \times 10^{-8} \text{ W}/(\text{m}^2 \cdot \text{K}^4)] (200 \text{ K})^4 \quad \text{or} \quad \epsilon = 0.364$$

Problem 17.21.

(a) An outside wall of a house has an area of 100 m^2. On a day when the outside air temperature is $-5.0°$C, the outside surface of the wall remains at 15°C. What is the rate of heat loss through the wall to the outside?

(b) Assuming that the other three walls and the roof each lose heat at the same rate as the wall in part (a), how much power must the house heating system deliver to maintain a steady state? Ignore losses other than through the walls and roof.

Solution

(a) The rate of heat loss is just the rate at which heat is removed from the wall due to convection of the outside air. For a vertical wall this is $H = hA \ \Delta T$, with $h = 1.77(\Delta T)^{1/4}$ W/(m$^2 \cdot$ K)]. For our case

$$H = [1.77(20)^{1/4} \text{ W}/(\text{m}^2 \cdot \text{K})] (100 \text{ m}^2) (20 \text{ K}) = 7490 \text{ W}$$

(b) The total rate of heat loss is 5(7490 W) = 37,450 W, and this must be the rate of power delivery of the heating system.

Supplementary Problems

Problem 17.22.   A small silver ingot measures 3 cm by 3 cm by 12 cm. The 9-cm^2 end faces are held at constant temperatures. T_1 and T_2, respectively, and no heat escapes out the other sides.

(a) Find the temperature differences $\Delta T = T_1 - T_2$ across the ingot if heat is conducted through it at the rate of 600 W.

(b) If the cooler end face had its temperature lowered by 20°C, how would the temperature of the hotter end face have to change to make the heat flow rate double that of (a)?

> *Ans.* (a) 197°C; (b) increase by 177°C

Problem 17.23.   Two 30-mm-diameter rods, one of brass and one of aluminum, are connected end to end. The aluminum rod has length 0.60 m and has its far end kept at 400°C; the brass rod has length 0.40 m and has its far end held at 20°C. Both rods are sheathed in highly insulating material. Calculate (a) the interface temperature, (b) the rate at which heat travels through the rods.

> *Ans.* (a) 231°C; (b) 40.6 W

Problem 17.24.

(a) Find the conversion of the coefficient of thermal conductivity from the mixed engineering units Btu $\cdot$ in/(ft$^2 \cdot$ °F) to SI units.

(b) What are the appropriate units for A, L, T, and H in (17.1) when k is in engineering units?

> *Ans.*   (a) 1 Btu $\cdot$ in/(ft$^2 \cdot$ h $\cdot$ °F) = 0.144 W/(m $\cdot$ K); (b) A (ft^2), L (in), T (°F), H (Btu/h).

Problem 17.25.   A glass window pane measuring 3 ft by 4 ft by 0.30 in has its outside surface kept at 12 °F and its inside surface at 80 °F. How many Btu per hour pass through the pane? (See Problem 17.24.)

   Ans.   15,100 Btu/h

Problem 17.26.   An insulating sandwich is made of four layers: an inner and outer layer of wood, each 1.0 cm thick; a layer of cork 3.0 cm thick; and a layer of Styrofoam 2.0 cm thick.

(*a*)   Find the *R*-value for the sandwich.

(*b*)   If the cross-sectional area of the sandwich is 2.0 m^2, what is the rate of thermal energy transfer through it when the temperatures of the two outside surfaces differ by 80 °C?

   Ans.   (*a*) 2.95 m$^2 \cdot$ K/W; (*b*) 54.2 W

Problem 17.27.   A room window pane is 80 cm wide, 120 cm high, and 0.70 cm thick. The air temperature inside the room is 20 °C, while the air outside is at -20 °C. Find (*a*) the rate at which heat flows through the pane; (*b*) the temperatures of the inside and outside surfaces of the glass.

   Ans.   (*a*) 71.9 W; (*b*) $+ 0.33$ °C and -0.33 °C

Problem 17.28.   A steam radiator in a room has the convection coefficient $h = 2.30(\Delta T)^{1/4}$ W/(m$^2 \cdot$ K). The surface area of the radiator is 3.0 m^2. If the room is kept at 22 °C and the radiator surface is at 90 °C, find the rate of convective heat transfer from the radiator to the room.

   Ans.   1.35 kW

Problem 17.29.   The filament of a light bulb emits 100 W of radiant energy when it is at its steady-state operating temperature of 2700 K.

(*a*)   If the emissivity of the filament is 0.35, find its surface area.

(*b*)   If the walls of the room are at 23 °C, find the radiant energy absorbed by the filament per second.

   Ans.   (*a*) 0.948 cm^2; (*b*) 15.2 mW

Problem 17.30.   A sphere of radius 25 mm and emissivity 0.40 is suspended by an electrical cord in an evacuated chamber whose walls are kept at 600 K.

(*a*)   How much electrical power must be supplied to the sphere to keep it at 650 K? Ignore losses due to heat conduction along the wire.

(*b*)   Redo the calculation if the sphere is blackened so that it behaves like a blackbody.

   Ans.   (*a*) 8.71 W; (*b*) 21.8 W

Problem 17.31.   If the sphere of Problem 17.30(*a*) were actually supplied with 400 W of electrical power, what would its steady-state temperature be?

   Ans.   1242 K

Problem 17.32.   If the emissivity of the radiator in Problem 17.28 is 0.25, find the *net* radiant power that is transferred from the radiator to the room.

   Ans.   416 W

Chapter 18

The First and Second Laws of Thermodynamics

18.1 THE FIRST LAW OF THERMODYNAMICS

We have seen that *work* is the mechanical transfer of energy from one system to another and that *heat* is the nonmechanical transfer of energy from one system to another. The **first law of thermodynamics** is the statement of the law of conservation of energy in its most general form. It presumes, as we have already described, that every system has a definite total energy content, called the internal energy of the system U, and that U changes only as a consequence of the transfer of energy into or out of the system from the "other" systems which represent the rest of the universe. Thus, the overall energy of the universe remains the same.

Let W represent the algebraic work done *by* the system on the outside world during some process; that is, W is positive when the system does positive work and thereby loses energy, and W is negative when the system does negative work and thereby gains energy. Let Q represent the algebraic heat *entering* the system during the same process; that is, Q is positive when energy is added to the system by nonmechanical means, and Q is negative when energy leaves the system by nonmechanical means. Then, if U_i and U_f are, respectively, the initial and final total internal energy of the system at the beginning and at the end of the process, we must have

$$U_f - U_i = Q - W \qquad (18.1)$$

This is the mathematical statement of the first law. It is schematically represented in Fig. 18-1. Equation (*18.1*) holds whether the process is turbulent and chaotic or gentle and quasistatic. The sign conventions for Q and W are historical, and they are standard in physics and most engineering.

> **Note.** Only the *difference* in internal energies of two states appears in Eq. (*18.1*). It is the difference in internal energies between states that is important, not the actual values. The actual values of the internal energy for the states of a system are obtained by arbitrarily assigning a numerical value to some chosen reference state, much as in the case of mechanical potential energy. Once such a value is assigned, the values of all the other states of the system are then fixed relative to that value.

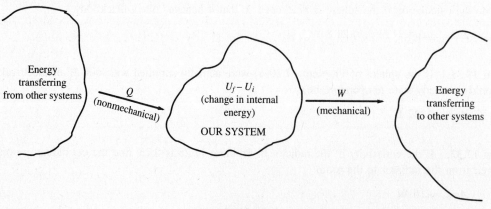

Fig. 18-1

436

Work and the P-V Diagram

In the case of a quasistatic process for a chemical system, the evolving states of the system can be tracked as a path on a P-V diagram (Fig. 18-2). In this situation, the initial and final states (points i and f, respectively) are completely defined by the thermodynamic variables, as are all the states passed through in between. Each state thus has a definite value for the internal energy. Such a track on a P-V diagram allows a simple calculation of the work W done by the system. To see this, assume that Fig. 18-2 refers to a system consisting of a gas in a cylinder with a close-fitting piston (Fig. 18-3). Suppose the piston is allowed to slowly move out under the pressure of the gas inside. If A is the area of the piston face, the force exerted by the gas (the system) on the piston (part of the environment) is $F = PA$. If the piston moves a small distance Δx, as shown, then the small amount of work done by the gas is $\Delta W = F \Delta x = PA \Delta x$. But $A \Delta x$ is just the change in volume of the gas: $\Delta V = A \Delta x$. So

$$\Delta W = P \Delta V \qquad (18.2)$$

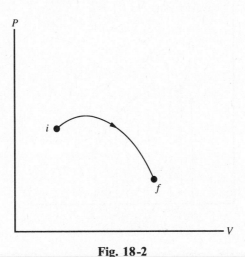

Fig. 18-2

As the gas continues to expand against the piston, the pressure of the gas will change, and the next small amount of work will be $P' \Delta V'$; this is followed by $P'' \Delta V''$, and so on. The total work done will be the sum of all these increments. If Fig. 18-2 represents the change of states of the gas during the expansion, we can see what the pressure is for each volume, and the work done between points i and f is clearly the total area under the curve on the P-V diagram (Fig. 18-4).

It is important to realize that the way the pressure changes with volume is not predetermined by the change in volume alone, since the pressure also depends on the temperature. The temperature can be separately manipulated as the gas in the cylinder slowly expands against the piston, by slowly heating or cooling the gas at various rates during the process. Thus, there are an infinite number of paths the gas can take on a P-V diagram in going between the same initial and final states. Figure 18-5 shows a number of alternative paths the system can take in going between the states i and f, in addition to the original path shown in Fig. 18-2.

For each of these paths the area under the curve is different, and, therefore, so is the work done. For that reason, we say that the work done in going between two states of a system "depends on path." However, the total change in energy depends only on the final and initial states and is just $U_f - U_i$ for all possible paths. Thus, the work done depends on the path, but the total energy change stays the same! How can this happen? The answer lies in Eq. (18.1), which implies that the value of Q will also depend on the path in such a way that $Q - W$ always is the same for given initial and final states.

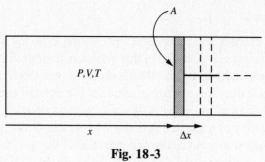

Fig. 18-3

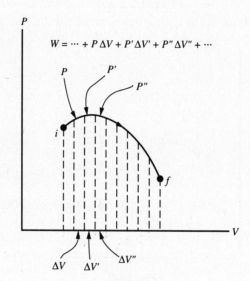

Fig. 18-4

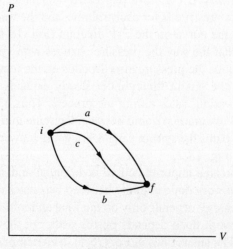

Fig. 18-5

(That Q depends on path is also implied by our description above of how to manipulate the pressure during the process by heating and/or cooling.)

What happens if one reverses the quasistatic process and returns from state f to state i? If, in Fig. 18-5, we retrace path a in the other direction, this corresponds to the piston slowly moving in, and the heat being added and subtracted in the exact reverse of the original process along path a. Clearly, from the P-V diagram (Fig. 18-4), we have

$$W_{a,fi} = -W_{a,if} \qquad (18.3a)$$

where the subscripts fi and if mean, respectively, from the final to initial state and from the initial to final state. From Eq. (18.1) and the fact that $U_i - U_f = -(U_f - U_i)$, it follows that

$$Q_{a,fi} = -Q_{a,if} \qquad (18.3b)$$

Reversing a given quasistatic path thus reverses the signs of the work done and the heat transferred.

Finally, it should be noted that while (18.2) was derived for the special case of a gas expanding against a piston, the result is true for any arbitrary shaped, flexible container that slowly changes shape.

Problem 18.1.

(a) Assuming that in Fig. 18-5 the work done along path a is 400 J and $U_f - U_i = -180$ J, how much heat entered or left the system during the process?

(b) If 60 J of heat enters the system along path b, how much work is done in that process?

Solution

(a) From Eq. (18.1) we have -180 J $= Q_{a,if} - 400$ J or $Q_{a,if} = 220$ J

(b) The change in internal energy is the same, so

$$-180 \text{ J} = 60 \text{ J} - W_{b,if} \qquad \text{or} \qquad W_{b,if} = 240 \text{ J}$$

Problem 18.2.

(a) If the heat entering the system along path c of Fig. 18-5 is the arithmetic mean of that entering along paths a and b (see Problem 18.1), then how much work is done in going from i to f along path c?

(b) How much heat leaves the system as it returns to state i by the reverse of path c?

Solution

(a) From Problem 18.1, the arithmetic mean is $Q_{c,if} = (220 \text{ J} + 60 \text{ J})/2 = 140$ J. Then, by applying (18.1),

$$-180 \text{ J} = 140 \text{ J} - W_{c,ij} \qquad \text{or} \qquad W_{c,ij} = 320 \text{ J}$$

(b) $Q_{c,fi} = -Q_{c,if} = -140$ J; that is, 140 J of heat leaves the system.

Problem 18.3. Suppose that the system described in Problems 18.1 and 18.2 goes along path a from state i to f in Fig. 18-5, and then returns to i along the reverse of path b. For such a **cyclical process**, find (a) the net change in internal energy; (b) the net amount of heat that enters or leaves the system; (c) the net work done.

Solution

(a) Since the initial and final states are the same, there is no change in internal energy: $U_i - U_i = 0$.

(b) From Problem 18.1, $Q_{a,if} = 220$ J and $Q_{b,fi} = -Q_{b,if} = -60$ J. The net heat in the cycle is thus $Q_{a,if} + Q_{b,fi} = 220$ J $- 60$ J $= 160$ J.

(c) The total, or net, work done is $W_{a,if} + W_{b,fi} = W_{a,if} - W_{b,if} = 400$ J $- 240$ J $= 160$ J. This result could also be obtained by noting that since $\Delta U = 0$, the first law gives $W = Q = 160$ J.

Problem 18.4. Show that in a cyclical process the work done is plus or minus the area enclosed by the closed cycle path on the *P-V* diagram.

Solution

We use Problem 18.3 as a model. The net work done in the cycle is $W_{a,if} - W_{b,if}$. In Fig. 18-5 this is just the area under path *a* minus the area under path *b*, which is the area enclosed between the two paths. This area is highlighted for more general paths *a* and *b* in Fig. 18-6. In this cycle the net work is positive because the system expanded at higher pressures (along path *a*) and contracted at lower pressures (along the reverse path *b*). If, instead, the system had expanded along path *b* and contracted along the reverse of path *a*, then the net work would have the same magnitude but a negative sign. Thus we have shown that the work in the cycle is plus or minus the area enclosed, depending on which way the cycle is traversed.

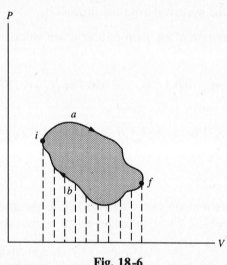

Fig. 18-6

Special Cases of Quasistatic Processes

In studying the various processes that can occur as a system evolves quasistatically, certain ones are of special interest. These (see Fig. 18-7) include a constant-volume process (isovolumic or isochoric), a constant-pressure process (isobaric), a constant-temperature process (isothermal), and a process in which no heat enters or leaves the system (adiabatic). The following problems apply the first law to these processes.

Problem 18.5.

(a) In an isochoric process [Fig. 18-7(*a*)], what is the work done? What is the statement of the first law for such a process?

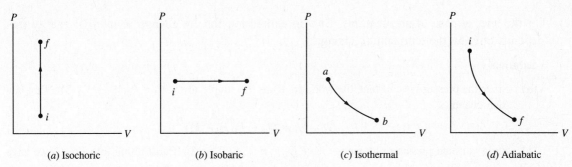

(a) Isochoric   (b) Isobaric   (c) Isothermal   (d) Adiabatic

Fig. 18-7

(b)   If the system consists of n mol of a substance whose molar heat capacity at constant volume is $c_{V,\text{mol}}$, find an expression for the first law that involves the temperature.

Solution

(a)   For a chemical system the incremental work done is given by $\Delta W = P\,\Delta V$. We see that for our case of no volume change, $\Delta V = 0$, and we can have no work done ($W = 0$). From (18.1), the first law becomes

$$Q_{if} = U_f - U_i$$

(b)   At constant volume we have $Q_{if} = nc_{V,\text{mol}}(T_f - T_i)$, so from (a) we have

$$U_f - U_i = nc_{V,\text{mol}}\left(T_f - T_i\right) \tag{i}$$

Note.   The direct relationship between internal energy and constant-volume heat capacities was discussed briefly in Ch. 16.

Problem 18.6.   Assume that Fig. 18-7(a) depicts a sample of 3 mol of an ideal gas with $c_{V,\text{mol}} = 2.5R$, where R is the universal gas constant. Find the change in internal energy between points i and f, given $V_i = 0.20$ m^3, $P_i = 2.0 \times 10^5$ Pa, and $P_f = 4.0 \times 10^5$ Pa.

Solution

We can use Eq. (i) of Problem 18.5 to obtain $U_f - U_i$. To do this we need the temperatures T_i and T_f. These can be obtained by rearranging the ideal gas law $PV = nRT$: $T_i = P_iV_i/nR$ and $T_f = P_fV_f/nR$. Since $V_f = V_i$ for a constant-volume process, the temperature interval is $T_f - T_i = V_i(P_f - P_i)/nR$. Substituting the expression into Eq. (i) of Problem 18.5, we get

$$U_f - U_i = nc_{V,\text{mol}}\frac{V_i\left(P_f - P_i\right)}{nR} = c_{V,\text{mol}}\frac{V_i\left(P_f - P_i\right)}{R} = 2.5V_i\left(P_f - P_i\right)$$

Now we can substitute in values to get

$$U_f - U_i = 2.5(0.20\text{ m}^3)\left(4.0 \times 10^5\text{ Pa} - 2.0 \times 10^5\text{ Pa}\right) = 1.0 \times 10^5\text{ J}$$

Problem 18.7.

(a)   For the isobaric process of Fig. 18-7(b), find an expression for the first law that involves the pressure and volume.

(b)   If the system consists of n mol of a substance with constant-pressure molar heat capacity $c_{P,\text{mol}}$, find an expression for the first law that also involves the temperature.

(c)   For the special case of an ideal gas, find an expression for the change in internal energy that depends only on the temperature change.

Solution

(a)   Since the pressure is constant, the work done has the simple form $W_{if} = P_i(V_f - V_i)$. The first law then becomes

$$U_f - U_i = Q_{if} - P_i(V_f - V_i) \qquad (i)$$

(b)   For a constant-pressure process we have $Q_{if} = nc_{P,\,\text{mol}}(T_f - T_i)$. Substituting into Eq. (i) we have

$$U_f - U_i = nc_{P,\,\text{mol}}(T_f - T_i) - P_i(V_f - V_i) \qquad (ii)$$

(c)   For an ideal gas, $PV = nRT \Rightarrow P_iV_i = nRT_i$ and $P_fV_f = nRT_f$. Recalling that $P_i = P_f$, we have $P_i(V_f - V_i) = nR(T_f - T_i)$. Substituting into Eq. (ii) we get

$$U_f - U_i = nc_{P,\,\text{mol}}(T_f - T_i) - nR(T_f - T_i) = n(c_{P,\,\text{mol}} - R)(T_f - T_i) \qquad (iii)$$

Problem 18.8.   Consider the isothermal process of Fig. 18-7(c).

(a)   What can one say about the internal energy of the system at points a and b, if the system is an ideal gas? If the system is more general?

(b)   Figure 18-8 shows an isotherm such as that of Fig. 18-7(c), with point a reached by an isochoric process from a point i and point b reached by an isobaric process from the same point i. Use the results of Problems 18.5(b) and 18.7(c) to prove that for an ideal gas $c_{P,\text{mol}} = c_{V,\text{mol}} + R$.

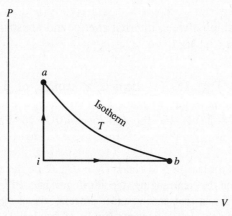

Fig. 18-8

Solution

(a)   In Sec. 16.4 it was seen that the internal energy of a sample of ideal gas depends only on the temperature. Thus, if the temperature remains constant, so does the internal energy. It follows that, for an ideal gas, the internal energy at every point along an isotherm is the same, so $U_a = U_b$. In the case of a more general system the internal energy typically depends on pressure as well as temperature, so different points along the isotherm will have different internal energies.

(b)   For the isochoric process, Eq. (i) of Problem 18.5(b) gives

$$U_a - U_i = nc_{V,\,\text{mol}}(T - T_i)$$

This equation is true not only for ideal gases but for more general systems as well.

For the isobaric process, Eq. (*iii*) of Problem 18.7(*c*) gives

$$U_b - U_i = n[c_{P,\,\text{mol}} - R](T - T_i)$$

for our ideal gas. But for an ideal gas, $T_b = T_a = T$ implies $U_b = U_a$. Since in our two equations the left-hand sides are the same, we can equate the right-hand sides to get the desired result. Note that this implies that c_P is greater than c_V. This makes intuitive sense, since at constant pressure positive work is done by the system as the heated ideal gas expands, giving up some of its energy to the environment. It therefore takes more heat input to get the same increase in internal energy than for a constant-volume process, where no work is done.

Problem 18.9.

(*a*)   Write the special form of the first law for the case of an adiabatic process.

(*b*)   Why is an adiabatic expansion of an ideal gas a steeper curve when plotted on a *P-V* diagram than that of an isotherm?

Solution

(*a*)   Since there is no transfer of heat into or out of the system, we have $Q_{if} = 0$, and the first law takes the form

$$U_f - U_i = -W_{if} \qquad (i)$$

(*b*)   In an adiabatic expansion, positive work is done by the system, and, as can be seen in Eq. (*i*), the internal energy drops. For an ideal gas this corresponds to a drop in temperature. All else being the same, lower temperature means lower pressure. Thus, as one plots *P* vs. *V* for an adiabatic process starting at some point on the *P-V* diagram, the pressure drops faster than it does along an isotherm starting at the same point (the temperature stays the same on the isotherm). Figure 18-9 shows a series of adiabatics and isotherms for an ideal gas. The lower isotherms correspond to lower temperatures.

Note.   For an ideal gas undergoing an adiabatic process it can be shown, using the calculus, that *P* and *V* are related by $PV^\gamma = $ constant, or

$$P_1 V_1{}^\gamma = P_2 V_2{}^\gamma \qquad (ii)$$

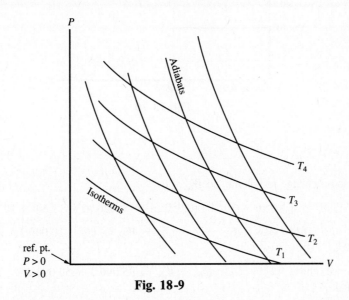

Fig. 18-9

where points 1 and 2 are anywhere along the adiabatic curve. Here $\gamma = c_{mol,P}/c_{mol,V}$, the ratio of molar heat capacities at constant pressure and constant volume. Using the ideal gas law, (ii) can be rewritten in terms of Kelvin temperature, as

$$T_1 V_1{}^{\gamma-1} = T_2 V_2{}^{\gamma-1} \tag{iii}$$

Since from the previous problem we saw $c_{mol,\,P} > c_{mol,\,V}$, we have $\gamma > 1$. Equation (ii) is the adiabatic analog of Boyle's law for an isothermal process of an ideal gas: $P_1 V_1 = P_2 V_2$.

Problem 18.10. Consider a system that is taken along the paths shown on the P-V diagram in Fig. 18-10. Assume $U_a = 30{,}000$ J.

(a) Find the work done by the system in going from a to b.

(b) Find the work done by the system in going from b to c.

(c) If 20,000 J of heat enters the system along the path from a to b, what is the internal energy at point b?

(d) If the internal energy at point c is 95,000 J, how much heat enters or leaves the system along the path from b to c?

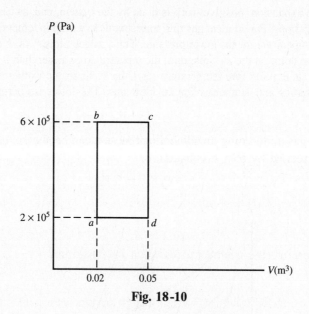

Fig. 18-10

Solution

(a) There is no change in volume, so $W_{ab} = 0$.

(b) $W_{bc} = P_b(V_c - V_b) = (6 \times 10^5 \text{ Pa})(0.050 \text{ m}^3 - 0.020 \text{ m}^3) = 1.80 \times 10^4$ J.

(c) From the first law, $U_b - U_a = Q_{ab} - W_{ab} \Rightarrow U_b - 30{,}000 \text{ J} = 20{,}000 \text{ J} - 0 \text{ J} \Rightarrow U_b = 50{,}000$ J.

(d) Here we have $U_c - U_b = Q_{bc} - W_{bc} \Rightarrow 95{,}000 \text{ J} - 50{,}000 \text{ J} = Q_{bc} - 18{,}000 \text{ J} \Rightarrow Q_{bc} = 63{,}000$ J.

Problem 18.11.   Refer to Problem 18.10 and Fig. 18-10.

(a)   If 21,000 J of heat enters the system in going from a to d, what is the internal energy at point d?

(b)   Find the heat that enters the system along the path from d to c.

(c)   If the system is taken along the closed loop $a \rightarrow b \rightarrow c \rightarrow d \rightarrow a$, how much work is done? What is the net heat that enters the system?

Solution

(a)   The first law gives $U_d - U_a = Q_{ad} - W_{ad}$. We first obtain the work W_{ad}. From Fig. 18-10, we have

$$W_{ad} = P_a(V_d - V_a) = (2.0 \times 10^5 \text{ Pa})(0.050 \text{ m}^3 - 0.020 \text{ m}^3) = 6000 \text{ J}$$

Then, using information given above and in Problem 18.10, we have

$$U_d - 30,000 \text{ J} = 21,000 \text{ J} - 6000 \text{ J} \quad \text{or} \quad U_d = 45,000 \text{ J}$$

(b)   We now have $U_c - U_d = Q_{dc} - W_{dc}$. We see that there is no change in volume along the path from d to c, so $W_{dc} = 0$. Recalling from Problem 18.10(d) that $U_c = 95,000$ J, we get

$$95,000 \text{ J} - 45,000 \text{ J} = Q_{dc} - 0 \text{ J} \quad \text{or} \quad Q_{dc} = 50,000 \text{ J}$$

(c)   Here, we add up the portions of the net work: $W_{\text{net}} = W_{ab} + W_{bc} + W_{cd} + W_{da}$. Recalling that $W_{ab} = 0$, $W_{bc} = 18,000$ J, $W_{cd} = -W_{dc} = 0$, and $W_{da} = -W_{ad} = -6000$ J, we have

$$W_{\text{net}} = 0 \text{ J} + 18,000 \text{ J} + 0 \text{ J} - 6000 \text{ J} = 12,000 \text{ J}$$

It is possible to obtain Q_{net} from the first law. Since we have returned to the starting point, the change in internal energy in the process is zero, and we must have $0 \text{ J} = Q_{\text{net}} - W_{\text{net}} \Rightarrow Q_{\text{net}} = W_{\text{net}} = 12,000$ J.

Problem 18.12.   A system consists of a sealed steel cylinder containing a volatile gas mixture. The system is surrounded by a thermal insulating material such as asbestos so that no heat can enter or leave the system (assume radiative losses are negligible). The mixture explodes, but the cylinder stays intact, and the system is allowed to settle down.

(a)   How has the temperature of the system changed?

(b)   What is the change in the internal energy of the system as a consequence of the explosion?

(c)   How would one describe the overall process on a P-V diagram?

Solution

(a)   In the explosion, stored chemical potential energy has been converted into thermal energy. Unless this thermal energy leaves the system or is converted to another form of energy, there will be a rise in temperature.

(b)   Since the sealed steel cylinder stays intact, there is essentially no change in volume and consequently no work done. Similarly, the insulation stops any transfer of heat to the outside world. From the first law, the amount of internal energy must be unchanged. Of course, the form of the internal energy has changed as described in (a).

(c)   The change in the system cannot be plotted on a P-V diagram, because the explosion is not quasistatic. One may be tempted to say that the system is describable by a vertical line on the diagram, corresponding to a constant-volume (isovolumic) process, but that would be wrong. The process is indeed isovolumic, but there is no well-defined "systemwide" pressure at any moment of the explosion. All one can do is to represent the initial and final states by two points (one directly above the other) on a P-V diagram, since these are equilibrium states of the system.

Problem 18.13. Consider a system undergoing a quasistatic cyclical process involving four legs, with two being isotherms and two being adiabats. Such a process is represented on the P-V diagram of Fig. 18-11 and is called a **Carnot cycle**.

(a)   If the system goes along path $a \rightarrow b \rightarrow c \rightarrow d \rightarrow a$, describe qualitatively the net work done.

(b)   Describe qualitatively the work done along each leg of the cycle.

(c)   Describe qualitatively the heat that enters or leaves the system along each leg of the cycle, and the net heat transferred by the system over the complete cycle.

(d)   How would the above answers change if the cycle were in the reverse direction: $a \rightarrow d \rightarrow c \rightarrow b \rightarrow a$?

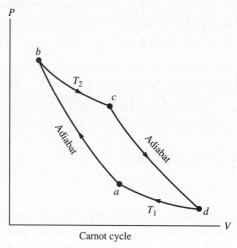

Carnot cycle

Fig. 18-11

Solution

(a)   From the discussion in the text and earlier problems, we note that the net work is the positive area enclosed by the cycle on the P-V diagram.

(b)   Since the system expands along $b \rightarrow c$ and $c \rightarrow d$, the work done in each of these two paths is positive. Similarly, the system contracts along $d \rightarrow a$ and $a \rightarrow b$, and the work done is negative on each of these two legs.

(c)   By definition, no heat enters or leaves the system along either adiabat. It is typical that heat would enter the system along path $b \rightarrow c$ because the system does positive work, and heat would have to enter the system to keep the temperature constant during the process. Likewise, along isotherm $d \rightarrow a$ heat ought to leave the system. On net, the total algebraic heat is $Q_{net} = Q_{bc} + Q_{da}$, where the first and second terms on the right are positive and negative, respectively. Furthermore, from the first law, at the end of the complete cycle the internal energy is back to its original value, so we must have $Q_{net} = W_{net}$, with both being positive quantities.

(d)   If the cycle is reversed, each leg is reversed, and we have that the work done and heat transferred during each leg simply changes sign. Similarly, the net work and net heat in the cycle must therefore change sign. In the reversed cycle, the net work done by the system is negative and the net heat entering the system is negative.

18.2   THE SECOND LAW OF THERMODYNAMICS

As we have seen, the First Law says that energy can only shift from one system to another (by means of work and heat transfer), but the total energy of the universe stays fixed. The second law of thermodynamics addresses the separate question of the feasibility of certain types of energy transfers. The fact that energy must be conserved when there is an energy transfer from one system to another doesn't say whether the transfer will in fact take place.

As an example of feasibility, consider the conductive heat transfer of energy between two systems at different temperatures that are brought into good thermal contact. Clearly, the heat will transfer from the hotter to the cooler body. From the point of view of the first law, there is no reason why energy could not transfer from the cool body to the hot body, with the cool body getting colder as it lost thermal energy and the hot body getting even hotter as it gained thermal energy. The only constraint placed on such a process by the first law is that the amount of energy leaving the cold body precisely equal the amount of energy entering the hot body. Nonetheless, such a process does not occur naturally by direct thermal contact. To accomplish the removal of thermal energy from a cool body and its transfer to a hot body requires an intermediary system called a **refrigerator**.

Another example is the conversion of mechanical energy of a system into thermal energy of the same system, or of another system. Clearly, it is always easy to convert mechanical energy into thermal energy because of friction: a block with kinetic energy sliding on a surface slowly comes to rest because of the frictional conversion of the mechanical energy into thermal energy. But what if we wanted the reverse to occur: the thermal energy of the block and surface to somehow give itself up, to expend itself, to get the block moving again. The first law does not prohibit such a process, as long as the total energy stays the same. Nonetheless, such a conversion will not simply occur. To convert thermal energy to mechanical energy requires the services of an intermediary system, called a **heat engine**, to accomplish the goal.

The central issue here lies in the fact that thermal energy, being statistically random in nature, does not have the ability to organize itself in a way to easily convert to mechanical energy (second example), or to transfer from a less energetic environment to a more energetic environment (first example). The second law is thus deeply connected to the concept of randomness, and therefore to the subject of statistical mechanics. It is a remarkable fact that the second law was developed on an empirical basis, quite independently of any understanding of the statistical behavior of the myriad atoms and molecules making up a macroscopic system.

The Engine Statement of the Second Law

We have referred, above, to intermediary systems to effect the transfers that don't occur naturally. We have already encountered such systems in our discussion of cyclical motion on a P-V diagram. Consider the systems described by the cycles $a \to b \to c \to d \to a$ in Figs. 18-10 and 18-11. Clearly, each time either system goes through a complete cycle, net work W_{net} is done by the system. This means that mechanical energy is transferred to somewhere in the environment. In that same cycle a net amount of heat has entered the system; that is, thermal energy has been drawn from somewhere in the environment. It follows that in this cyclical process, thermal energy from somewhere has been converted to mechanical energy somewhere, since the intermediary system has returned to its original state and therefore has not changed at all. As noted, such a device is called a heat engine. Since we can repeat the cycle over and over again, we can continuously transform thermal energy to mechanical energy.

There is a catch, however. In either of the engine cycles, heat $Q_{in} > 0$ is drawn in during part of the cycle (typically at the higher temperatures), but some heat Q_{out} is exhausted to the outside during another part of the cycle (typically at the lower temperatures). (For future reference Q_{in} and Q_{out} are understood to be the magnitudes of the heats involved and are therefore always positive.) This means that the conversion of thermal energy to mechanical energy is not 100% efficient. Only part of the thermal energy Q_{in} that had been pulled in from the "hot" outside systems has been converted to mechanical energy, since some of the thermal energy Q_{out} has been dumped to "cooler" outside systems as part of the process. Indeed, from the first law

$$Q_{in} = W_{net} + Q_{out} \tag{18.4}$$

The engine, or **Kelvin-Planck**, statement of the second law is a verbal formalization of this result:

> *It is impossible for a cyclical process to have no other effect than to draw thermal energy from some system or systems, and convert it completely into mechanical energy.*

In other words, Q_{out} in Eq. (18.4), is always greater than zero. The engine statement of the second law is expressed schematically in Fig. 18-12(a).

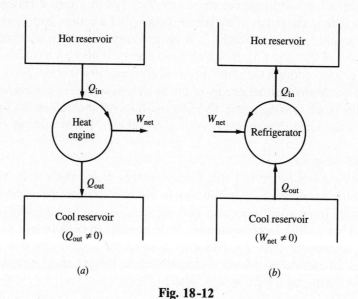

Fig. 18-12

The hotter system(s) which is the source of the thermal energy is often called the **hot reservoir(s)**, whereas the cooler system(s) to which thermal energy is exhausted is called the **cool reservoir(s)**. The efficiency e of any engine is defined as the ratio of mechanical energy obtained to the thermal energy extracted from the hot reservoir(s);

$$e = \frac{W_{net}}{Q_{in}} \tag{18.5a}$$

Using (18.4), this can be rewritten as

$$e = \frac{Q_{in} - Q_{out}}{Q_{in}} = 1 - \frac{Q_{out}}{Q_{in}} \tag{18.5b}$$

Problem 18.14. Referring to Problems 18.10 and 18.11, find the efficiency of the engine defined by the cycle $a \to b \to c \to d \to a$ in Fig. 18-10.

Solution

From Problems 18.11(c) and 18.10(c, d), we have, respectively, $W_{net} = 12{,}000$ J, $Q_{ab} = 20{,}000$ J, and $Q_{bc} = 63{,}000$ J. From Problem 18.11(a, b) we can deduce that $Q_{cd} = -50{,}000$ J and $Q_{da} = -21{,}000$ J. Then, from its definition, $Q_{in} = Q_{ab} + Q_{bc} = 83{,}000$ J. Similarly, from its definition, $Q_{out} = |Q_{cd} + Q_{da}| = 71{,}000$ J. Using ($18.5a$), we have

$$e = \frac{12{,}000 \text{ J}}{83{,}000 \text{ J}} = 0.145 = 14.5\%$$

Equivalently, we could use Eq. ($18.5b$) to get

$$e = 1 - \frac{71{,}000 \text{ J}}{83{,}000 \text{ J}} = 0.145 = 14.5\%$$

Problem 18.15.   Suppose that for the Carnot cycle of Fig. 18-11 we are given $Q_{bc} = 7{,}000$ J and $Q_{da} = -4800$ J. Find (a) the net work done in the cycle, (b) the efficiency of this Carnot engine.

Solution

(a) Since no heat enters or leaves the system along the other two (adiabatic) legs of the cycle, $Q_{net} = Q_{bc} + Q_{da} = 2200$ J. From the first law, for the complete cycle we must have $W_{net} = Q_{net} = 2200$ J.

(b) The efficiency is

$$e = 1 - \frac{|Q_{da}|}{Q_{bc}} = 1 - \frac{4800 \text{ J}}{7000 \text{ J}} = 0.314 = 31.4\%$$

The Refrigerator Statement of the Second Law

We now examine the intermediary systems that allow us to draw thermal energy from a cool system(s) and deposit it in a hot system(s). Again we have encountered such systems in the cycles of Figs. 18-10 and 18-11. This time we consider the cycles run in reverse order: $a \rightarrow d \rightarrow c \rightarrow b \rightarrow a$. In this case Q_{out} represents the magnitude of heat that enters the cyclical system at lower temperatures, and Q_{in} represents the heat expelled from the cyclical system at higher temperatures. Thus, thermal energy Q_{out} is being extracted from a cooler reservoir(s), and thermal energy Q_{in} is being deposited in a hotter reservoir(s). This is just what we want to accomplish. Our cyclical intermediary system, which like the engine is itself unchanged over a cycle, constitutes our refrigerator.

Again, as with the engine, there is a catch. The thermal energy Q_{in} deposited in the hotter reservoir is greater than the thermal energy Q_{out} extracted from the cooler reservoir. The difference is accounted for by the work done by the system, which is now negative and equals $-W_{net}$. In other words, positive work W_{net} must be done *by outside systems* to accomplish the refrigeration process. The relation of Q_{out}, Q_{in}, and W_{net} is given by the first law, $Q_{in} = Q_{out} + W_{net}$, which is algebraically the same as (18.4) but now has the interpretation given above for a refrigerator: The sum of the heat drawn from the cool reservoir(s) and the work done by outside systems equals the heat entering the hot reservoir(s).

The performance of the refrigerator is thus not ideal because some outside system has to do work to accomplish the thermal energy transfer. The refrigerator, or **Clausius**, statement of the second law is a verbal statement of this result:

> *It is impossible for a cyclical process to have no other effect than to extract thermal energy from a cooler system or systems, and eject that thermal energy to a hotter system or systems.*

In other words, W_{net} is never zero. The coefficient of performance κ of a refrigerator is defined as

$$\kappa = \frac{Q_{out}}{W_{net}} \qquad (18.6a)$$

Using Eq. (18.4) this becomes

$$\kappa = \frac{Q_{out}}{Q_{in} - Q_{out}} \qquad (18.6b)$$

Note. κ is defined so that it increases without limit as $W_{net} \to 0$ and is a measure of the amount of heat extracted from the cool reservoir per unit work done. Thus, for example, a coefficient, of performance κ of 20 means that for each joule of work done, 20 J of heat is extracted.

The refrigerator statement of the second law is expressed schematically in Fig. 18-12(b).

Problem 18.16. Referring to Problems 18.10 and 18.11, find the coefficient of performance κ of the refrigerator defined by the cycle $a \to d \to c \to b \to a$ in Fig. 18-10.

Solution

This is almost identical to Problem 18.14, except that the cycle is running in reverse. Recalling that Q_{out} and Q_{in} are defined as positive quantities, from Problem 18.14, we have $Q_{out} = 71,000$ J, $Q_{in} = 83,000$ J. Similarly the positive work done by outside systems is $W_{net} = 12,000$ J. From Eq. (18.6a), we get

$$\kappa = \frac{71,000 \text{ J}}{12,000 \text{ J}} = 5.92$$

Problem 18.17. Referring to Problem 18.15, suppose the same Carnot cycle is run in reverse. Find the coefficient of performance of the Carnot refrigerator.

Solution

$Q_{out} = |Q_{da}| = 4800$ J, and $Q_{in} = Q_{bc} = 7000$ J. From Problem 18.15, $W_{net} = 2200$ J. Then, from (18.6a) we have

$$\kappa = \frac{4800 \text{ J}}{2200 \text{ J}} = 2.18$$

Problem 18.18. Show that the engine and refrigerator statements of the second law imply each other and therefore are equivalent statements.

Solution

Both statements come from analysis of cyclical processes, but these processes operate in opposite directions. The standard method is to show that if either of the statements were false, then the other would also have to be false. Suppose the engine statement to be true and the refrigerator statement to be false. We will show that this cannot happen. Consider the engine operating between a hot reservoir and a cool reservoir, as shown schematically in Fig. 18-13(a). Since the engine statement is true, we must have that Q_{out} is not zero. We next construct a refrigerator that takes Q_{out} from the same cool reservoir and expels it to the same hot reservoir as that of the engine, with no outside work necessary, as depicted in Fig. 18-13(b). This is possible since the refrigerator statement of the second law is presumed false. The

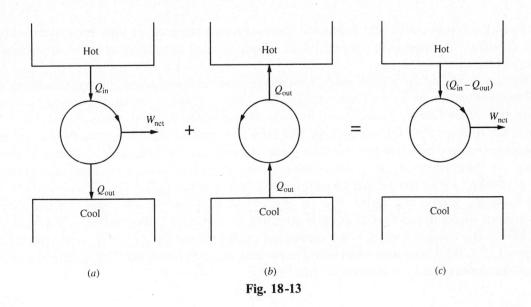

Fig. 18-13

combination of these two cycles is also a cyclical process between the same two reservoirs. The effect of the two cycles together is to take $Q_{in}' = Q_{in} - Q_{out}$ from the hot reservoir and convert it completely into work W_{net}, with no ejection of heat to any other place. This is shown in Fig. 18-13(c) and clearly represents an engine that violates the engine statement of the second law. Thus, if the refrigerator statement is false, so is the engine statement. The truth of the engine statement therefore implies the truth of the refrigerator statement.

A similar argument shows that if the refrigerator statement is assumed true and the engine statement false, a contradiction is again obtained.

Engine Efficiency and the Carnot Cycle

In any quasistatic cyclical process such as that of Fig. 18-10, one cannot have a single hot reservoir and a single cool reservoir interacting with the engine (or refrigerator) because the cycle generally passes through a range of temperatures; if the only reservoirs in contact with the cyclical system were at two fixed temperatures, there would be a finite temperature difference between the system and the reservoirs for most of the cycle. In that case the heat-transfer rate would not be infinitesimal and there would be no single temperature for the whole system at each instant. In other words the system would not be quasistatic and could not be represented on a P-V diagram. For such a cyclical process to be quasistatic, it is necessary to have a whole series of reservoirs, at incrementally different temperatures from one another, that are successively brought into contact with the system. Each such contact is allowed to occur as the system temperature just passes the temperature of that particular reservoir, and an infinitesimal thermal energy transfer takes place between the two. Such a cycle is an "ideal" cycle for theoretical analysis or possible laboratory study but is not practical as an actual engine or refrigerator.

There is, however, one quasistatic cyclical process that can indeed operate between a single hot reservoir and a single cool reservoir, and that is the Carnot cycle. The reason is easy to understand. Since the Carnot cycle is made up of two isotherms and two adiabats, heat transfers in or out of the cyclical system only at two temperatures, and these are the temperatures of the reservoirs that serve as the source and sink of the thermal energy being transferred. During the other parts of the cycle, the adiabats, when the temperature of the system is indeed changing, and different from that of the reservoirs, the system can remain quasistatic because no heat can enter or leave the system, and the finite difference in temperature compared with outside systems does not lead to the occurrence of nonequilibrium processes.

We now show that the second law implies that the most efficient engine operating between two fixed temperature reservoirs is a Carnot engine. Consider an arbitrary engine A operating between a hot reservoir at temperature T_H and a cool reservoir at temperature T_C, as shown in Fig. 18-14(a). We assume the reservoirs are sufficiently large that their temperatures are not noticeably changed as a consequence of any heat transfers that take place. Assume that the efficiency e_A of this engine is greater than the efficiency e_C of a Carnot engine operating between the same two reservoirs, as shown in Fig. 18-14(b). Let us assume that the engines are adjusted so that $Q_{out} = Q'_{out}$. Then, from ($18.5b$), $e_A > e_C \Rightarrow Q_{in} > Q'_{in}$, and hence $W_{net} > W'_{net}$. Now consider the combined cyclical system consisting of engine A, and the Carnot cycle operating in reverse, as a refrigerator $(-C)$, as shown in Fig. 18-15. The combined effect is the conversion of thermal energy $(Q_{in} - Q'_{in})$ into mechanical energy $(W_{net} - W'_{net})$, with no thermal energy exhausted to a cooler reservoir. This violates the second law, so our assumption $e_A > e_C$ must be false. Hence

$$e_C \geq e_A \qquad\qquad (18.7)$$

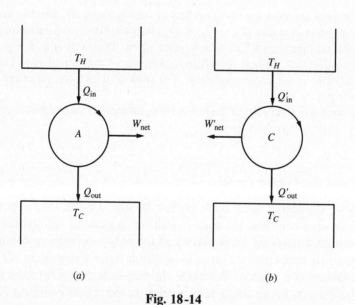

(a)   (b)

Fig. 18-14

where e_C is the efficiency of any Carnot engine operating between the two reservoirs at T_H and T_C and e_A is the efficiency of any other engine operating between the two same reservoirs.

Problem 18.19. Prove that all Carnot engines operating between the same two reservoirs, no matter what the operating substance making up the engine, are equally efficient.

Solution

Consider two Carnot engines A and B operating between the same two reservoirs. Since A is a Carnot engine, according to (18.7) we must have $e_A \geq e_B$. On the other hand, since B is also a Carnot engine we must have $e_B \geq e_A$. Therefore $e_A = e_B$.

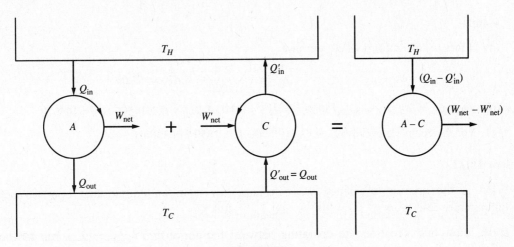

Fig. 18-15

Problem 18.20.   It can be shown, using the calculus, that for a Carnot cycle in a system consisting of a confined ideal gas (e.g., in a cylinder with a close-fitting piston), there exists a simple relationship between the ratio of heats entering (or leaving) along the two isotherms and the ratio of the Kelvin temperatures of the isotherms. Using the notation of Fig. 18-11, this relationship is $Q_{bc}/Q_{ad} = T_2/T_1$. Show that this implies that the efficiency of *any* Carnot engine operating between two reservoirs at Kelvin temperatures T_H and T_C, respectively, is

$$e_C = 1 - \frac{T_H}{T_C}$$

Solution

We recall, from Fig. 18-11, that for our ideal gas Carnot engine, $Q_{in} = Q_{bc}$ and $Q_{out} = Q_{cd}$. Furthermore, we note that in the notation of the problem, $T_2 = T_H$ and $T_1 = T_C$. Then, from the information in the problem, we have

$$\frac{Q_{in}}{Q_{out}} = \frac{T_H}{T_C} \qquad\qquad (i)$$

From (*18.5b*), we have

$$e_C = 1 - \frac{Q_{out}}{Q_{in}} = 1 - \frac{T_C}{T_H} \qquad\qquad (ii)$$

While this has only been determined for the special case of an ideal gas, we recall that all Carnot engines operating between the same two temperatures have the same efficiency, so (*ii*) is true for all Carnot engines.

Problem 18.21.

(*a*)   Find the efficiency of a Carnot engine that operates between two reservoirs at temperatures of 1000 K and 330 K, respectively.

(*b*)   If the engine absorbs 5000 J of heat from the hot reservoir in a cycle, how much heat is ejected to the cool reservoir?

(*c*)   How much work is done in the cycle?

Solution

(a) From (ii) of Problem 18.20, we have

$$e_C = 1 - \frac{T_C}{T_H} = 1 - \frac{330}{1000} = 0.670 = 67.0\%$$

(b) $Q_{out}/Q_{in} = T_C/T_H \Rightarrow Q_{out}/5000 \text{ J} = \frac{330}{1000} = 0.330 \Rightarrow Q_{out} = 0.330(5000 \text{ J}) = 1650 \text{ J}.$

(c) For the complete cycle, $W_{net} = Q_{net} = 5000 \text{ J} - 1650 \text{ J} = 3350 \text{ J}.$

Problem 18.22.

(a) What is the greatest efficiency we can hope for from an engine that operates between temperature reservoirs at $T_H = 900$ K and $T_C = 400$ K?

(b) If we know that a real engine operating between the above two temperatures has 40% of the efficiency of a Carnot engine, what is the efficiency of the real engine?

(c) Assuming the hot reservoir is fixed, what is an obvious way to improve the efficiency of an engine?

Solution

(a) The greatest efficiency is that of a Carnot engine, which is given by (ii) of Problem 18.20: $e_C = 1 - \frac{400}{900} = 0.556 = 55.6\%$.

(b) $e = (0.40)(0.556) = 0.222.$

(c) Again referring to (ii) of Problem 18.20, we see that for fixed T_H, we can increase the efficiency by decreasing T_C, the temperature of the cool reservoir (or, in other words, the temperature at which heat is exhausted). Thus, finding a cooler place to exhaust the heat improves efficiency.

Problem 18.23.

(a) Show how a Carnot engine can be used as a thermometer.

(b) We saw earlier that the Kelvin (or absolute) temperature scale was considered a "universal" scale because every constant-volume gas thermometer containing dilute gas gave rise to the same absolute scale, irrespective of the type of gas involved. Indeed the scale is defined as

$$T = (273.16 \text{ K}) \left(\frac{P}{P_{tr}} \right) \tag{i}$$

where P_{tr} is the pressure of any dilute constant-volume gas thermometer when immersed in a bath at the triple point of water, and P is the pressure of the same thermometer at T, the temperature of interest. Of course, not every system consists of a dilute gas. Show how the Carnot cycle can make the definition of the Kelvin temperature scale truly universal.

Solution

(a) If we want to measure the temperature of some system X, we let that system serve as one of the two reservoirs for our Carnot "thermometer." We next choose a "reference" reservoir at the triple point of water as our other reservoir. Then we operate our Carnot engine and measure the amount of heat entering or leaving at each reservoir. From Problem 18.20 we have

$$\left| \frac{Q_X}{Q_{tr}} \right| = \frac{T_X}{T_{tr}} = \frac{T_X}{273.16 \text{ K}}$$

Since the two Q's are measured, T_X is determined.

(b)   From part (a), we have

$$T_X = (273.16 \text{ K}) \left| \frac{Q_X}{Q_{\text{tr}}} \right| \qquad\qquad (ii)$$

This can be used as the new definition of the Kelvin temperature, replacing (i) above. Now, however, not only is this true for Carnot cycles involving an ideal gas, but for Carnot cycles involving any material—gas, liquid, or solid—and both chemical and nonchemical systems, including "magnetic" systems, where the work done involves thermodynamic variables other than P and V. Thus, the Kelvin scale can be defined in a truly universal way.

Problem 18.24.   One cylinder of a gasoline engine can be idealized by a quasistatic engine called the **Otto cycle**, shown in Fig. 18-16. Along path ab an ideal gas is compressed adiabatically from V_a to V_b. (In a real gasoline engine this is a rapid compression of gasoline and air, which is approximately adiabatic since there is very little time for heat to be conducted away.)

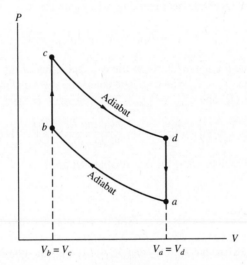

Fig. 18-16

Next, heat enters the system at constant volume along path bc, raising the temperature and pressure of the ideal gas. (In a real engine the gasoline is ignited and reacts with the oxygen in the air. The consequent explosion occurs over such a short time period that there is little expansion of the gas against the piston. The effect of the explosion is thus the isovolumic conversion of chemical potential energy to thermal energy. In the ideal engine this conversion is represented by the isovolumic absorption of heat from a series of outside reservoirs.)

Next, the heated ideal gas expands adiabatically along cd to the original volume. (This is the "power" stroke in a real engine, where the high-pressure hot gas expands rapidly against the piston, pushing it out to the end of the cylinder.)

Next, the ideal gas is allowed to cool at fixed volume along path da down to the original pressure. (In a real engine the hot exhaust gases are pushed out during another compression, and fresh gasoline and air are brought in during another expansion. This pair of steps does not involve any significant net work and accomplishes the same transfer of thermal energy out of the system as represented by the cooling of the ideal gas along da.)

(a) Find an expression for the efficiency e of the Otto cycle in terms of the temperatures T_a, T_b, T_c, and T_d.

(b) Find the efficiency of the Otto cycle in terms of the volumes V_d and V_c. [Hint: look at Eq. (iii) at the end of Problem 18.9.]

Solution

(a) First we note from Eq. (18.5b) that is suffices to determine the values of Q_{in} and Q_{out} to obtain the efficiency. In the Otto cycle, heat enters the system during the isovolumic increase in pressure along path bc, as is obvious from the fact that the temperature of an ideal gas at constant volume increases with pressure. The value of this can be determined from

$$Q_{bc} = nc_{mol,V}(T_c - T_b) \qquad (i)$$

where n is the number of moles of gas in our system, $c_{mol,V}$ is the molar heat capacity at constant volume, and T_c and T_b are the Kelvin temperatures at the respective endpoints of the path.

In similar fashion we see that heat leaves the system during the isovolumic decrease in pressure along path da. The algebraic heat entering along path da is

$$Q_{da} = nc_{mol,V}(T_a - T_d) \qquad (ii)$$

where T_a and T_d are the temperatures at the two endpoints of the path. We note that, as expected, Q_{da} is negative since $T_a < T_d$. Since no heat enters the system along the two adiabats ab and cd, we can identify $Q_{in} = Q_{bc}$ and $Q_{out} = |Q_{da}|$. The efficiency is then

$$e = 1 - \frac{Q_{out}}{Q_{in}} = 1 - \frac{nc_{mol,V}(T_d - T_a)}{nc_{mol,V}(T_c - T_b)} = 1 - \frac{T_d - T_a}{T_c - T_b} \qquad (iii)$$

(b) Recalling (iii) of Problem 18.9, for our adiabats we have

$$T_c V_c^{\gamma-1} = T_d V_d^{\gamma-1} \qquad (iv)$$

$$T_b V_b^{\gamma-1} = T_a V_a^{\gamma-1} \qquad (v)$$

Noting from Fig. 18-16 that $V_a = V_d$ and $V_c = V_b$, we can subtract (v) from (iv) to get

$$(T_c - T_b)V_c^{\gamma-1} = (T_d - T_a)V_d^{\gamma-1} \qquad (vi)$$

This implies $(T_d - T_a)/(T_c - T_b) = V_c^{\gamma-1}/V_d^{\gamma-1}$, and from (iii) above

$$e = 1 - \left(\frac{V_c}{V_d}\right)^{\gamma-1} \qquad (vii)$$

The inverse of V_c/V_d is called the **compression ratio** and is the ratio of the largest volume to the smallest volume of the engine cylinder as the piston moves in and out. The greater the compression ratio, the more efficient the engine.

Note. Problem 18.24 gives an example of a quasistatic cycle that mimics a real gasoline engine. Any real gasoline engine with the same compression ratio is much less efficient than this ideal engine because of factors such as friction, turbulent behavior, and heat-conduction losses.

Also, it can be shown that a Carnot engine operating between the highest and lowest temperatures achieved by another quasistatic engine (for example, T_c and T_a for the Otto cycle of Fig. 18-16) is always more efficient than that engine.

18.3 ENTROPY, DISORDER, AND THE SECOND LAW

The Macroscopic View

As we said at the outset, the second law is intimately related to the disordered nature of thermal energy and hence to statistical mechanics. It can be shown that for every equilibrium state of a system there is a definite quantitative measure of the disorder of the system in that state. This quantitative measure assigns a value to each equilibrium state of the system, which is called the entropy S. It follows that the entropy S, like P, V, T, and U, is a thermodynamic variable and can be expressed as a function of the other thermodynamic variables. The incremental change in entropy of a system ΔS when a small amount of heat ΔQ is slowly added can be shown to be given by

$$\Delta S = \frac{\Delta Q}{T} \tag{18.8}$$

where T is the Kelvin temperature of the system. The units of entropy are thus J/K. Equation (18.8) is true whether the heat is added at constant volume, at constant pressure, or in any other way. Equation (18.8) also implies that the entropy of a system increases with the increasing thermal energy. When heat leaves a system, ΔQ is negative, and the entropy of that system decreases. The second law of thermodynamics can be restated in terms of the overall entropy of the universe: *In any process or interaction of systems, the overall entropy change of the universe ΔS_{univ} obeys*

$$\Delta S_{\text{univ}} \geq 0 \tag{18.9}$$

where the equality occurs only in the case of quasistatic processes.

Problem 18.25.   Use (18.9), the entropy statement of the second law, to derive the engine statement of the second law.

Solution

Consider the schematic diagram of an engine shown in Fig. 18-12(a). Suppose that at the end of a cycle, Q_{in} is pulled in from the hot reservoir and converted completely into work so that $Q_{\text{out}} = 0$. We use (18.8) to examine the change in entropy. Since heat leaves the hot reservoir, ΔQ for that reservoir is negative, and ΔS must be negative as well, so the entropy of the hot reservoir decreases. The entropy of the engine itself is unchanged after a cycle because the system has returned to its original state. The work W_{net} represents an increase in the *mechanical* energy of some other system, so no heat transfer is involved and according to (18.8) the entropy of that system is unchanged. Thus, the overall change in entropy of the universe is negative, which contradicts (18.9). Therefore, if (18.9) is to hold, there must be a nonzero Q_{out} which enters the cool reservoir and increases its entropy so that (18.9) for the universe can hold. The fact that Q_{out} cannot be zero is just the engine statement of the second law.

Problem 18.26.   Use the law of entropy to show that the greatest possible efficiency of an engine operating between two reservoirs at temperature T_H and T_C, respectively, is that of a Carnot engine.

Solution

Consider any cyclical engine operating between two reservoirs at temperatures T_H and T_C. In a single cycle the amounts of heat Q_{in} pulled from the hot reservoir and the amount Q_{out} expelled to the cool reservoir are assumed to be sufficiently small that the temperatures of the reservoirs do not measurably change. Then, using (18.8), the change in entropy of the hot reservoir is $\Delta S_H = -Q_{\text{in}}/T_H$, and the change in entropy of the cool reservoir is $\Delta S_C = Q_{out}/T_C$. As discussed in Problem 18.23, there is no other change in entropy in any of the participating systems. Hence, by (18.9),

$$\Delta S_{univ} = \Delta S_H + \Delta S_C = \frac{Q_{out}}{T_C} - \frac{Q_{in}}{T_H} \qquad (i)$$

We see that from (18.9) the right side of (i) is ≥ 0, so we have

$$\frac{Q_{out}}{T_C} \geq \frac{Q_{in}}{T_H} \qquad (ii)$$

or

$$\frac{Q_{out}}{Q_{in}} \geq \frac{T_C}{T_H} \qquad (iii)$$

From (18.5b), we have for the efficiency of the engine

$$e = 1 - \frac{Q_{out}}{Q_{in}} \qquad (iv)$$

As can be seen, e is greatest when Q_{out}/Q_{in} is smallest. According to (iii), the smallest value of Q_{out}/Q_{in} is T_C/T_H, so the greatest efficiency is $e = 1 - (T_C/T_H)$, which is just the efficiency of a Carnot engine.

The Microscopic View

Considering the molecular level, the disorder of a system in equilibrium is measured by the number of different ways Γ that the molecules can arrange themselves so as to produce the value of the macroscopic variables that characterize the equilibrium state. The more such arrangements, the greater the disorder. The entropy of the system is formally defined as

$$S = k \cdot \ln \Gamma \qquad (18.10)$$

where k is Boltzmann's constant and $\ln \Gamma$ is the natural logarithm of Γ.

To understand the concept of Γ better, consider a box filled with 100 imaginary molecules that can exist in only one of two molecular states: state a or state b. Our box of imaginary "two-state" molecules is identical to the situation of a box filled with 100 coins with the state of each coin being determined by whether it has heads or tails facing up. A state of the macroscopic system, or system state, would correspond to specifying how many molecules are in molecular state a (the rest being in state b). One such "system" state would correspond to the case of all molecules in state a. There is only one way the molecules could arrange themselves like that, so $\Gamma = 1$, and this is a highly ordered state. Another system state would be the case of 99 molecules in molecular state a and 1 in molecular state b. Clearly there are 100 different ways that this could happen, so $\Gamma = 100$, and this system state has some disorder. For the case of 50 molecules in a and 50 in b, there are more ways for this to happen than Avogadro's number! This is a highly disordered system state. This is also a much more probable system state than the previous examples given. If we were to shake up the box of coins, there would be a much greater probability of getting 50 heads and 50 tails than of getting 100 heads, or even 99 heads and one tail. The macroscopic equilibrium state of our system corresponds to the most probable system state with its specific value of Γ, and hence S.

The same reasoning can be applied to a system made up of myriad real molecules N, with many more than two possible states for each molecule. By counting how many different ways the N molecules can arrange themselves in their varying molecular states, within certain physical constraints, one can find the most probable distribution of molecules among the molecular states. This corresponds to an actual macroscopic equilibrium state of the system. The number of different ways that the molecules can arrange themselves in this most probable configuration is the value of Γ for that macroscopic state. Equation (18.10) can be used to determine the value of S, or the disorder, of the macroscopic state.

The quantitative relationships that allow us to determine Γ for real systems of molecules, and the proof that the entropy S defined by (18.10) also obeys (18.8) and (18.9) are a consequence of the laws of statistical mechanics and are beyond the scope of this book.

Problems for Review and Mind Stretching

Problem 18.27. 3.0 kg of water at 100°C and atmospheric pressure (state a) is converted at constant temperature and pressure to 3.0 kg of steam (state b). Find the change in internal energy of the system, if the volume in the vapor phase is 1670 times that in the liquid phase.

Solution

By the first law,

$$U_b - U_a = Q_{a \to b} - W_{a \to b} \qquad (i)$$

Since, at atmospheric pressure and 100°C, the water is poised to undergo the phase transition to vapor, we know that the heat added is just

$$Q_{a \to b} = mL_V = (3.0 \text{ kg}) (2256 \text{ kJ/kg}) = 6768 \text{ kJ} \qquad (ii)$$

Since the process occurs at constant pressure, $W_{a \to b} = P_{\text{atm}}(V_b - V_a)$. Because the density of water is very nearly 1000 kg/m³ over the whole range from 0°C to 100°C, the volume of 3.0 kg of liquid water is

$$V_a = \frac{3.0 \text{ kg}}{1000 \text{ kg/m}^3} = 3.0 \times 10^{-3} \text{ m}^3$$

and the vapor volume is $V_b = (1670)V_a = 5.01$ m³. Then,

$$W_{a \to b} = (1.0 \times 10^5 \text{ Pa})(5.01 \text{ m}^3 - 3.0 \times 10^{-3} \text{ m}^3) = 501 \text{ kJ} \qquad (iii)$$

Substitute (ii) and (iii) in (i) to obtain $V_b - V_a = 6267$ kJ.

Problem 18.28. For the Otto cycle of Problem 18.24, assume that a diatomic ideal gas ($\gamma = 1.40$) is in the cylinder. Assume further that $V_c = 0.4 \, V_d$.

(a) Find the efficiency of this Otto engine.
(b) Given $P_c = 20 \, P_a$ find the efficiency of the Carnot cycle that operates between the highest and lowest temperatures of the Otto cycle.

Solution

(a) By Problem 18.24(b),

$$e = 1 - \left(\frac{V_c}{V_d}\right)^{\gamma - 1} = 1 - (0.4)^{0.40} = 0.307 = 30.7\%$$

(b) By Problem 18.21, $e_C = 1 - (T_a/T_c)$. But the ideal gas law tells us that (recalling that $V_a = V_d$)

$$\frac{P_a V_d}{T_a} = \frac{P_c V_c}{T_c} \quad \text{or} \quad \frac{T_a}{T_c} = \frac{P_a}{P_c} \frac{V_d}{V_c} = \left(\frac{1}{20}\right)\left(\frac{10}{4}\right) = 0.125$$

whence $e_C = 0.875 = 87.5\%$ (much superior to the Otto cycle).

Problem 18.29.   A home refrigerator must remove thermal energy at the rate of 1.5 kW to keep the interior temperature at 7.0 °C. Heat is expelled to the kitchen area, which is at 30 °C.

(a)   If the refrigerator operates in a Carnot cycle, what is its coefficient of performance κ?

(b)   How much electrical power P is needed to run the refrigerator?

Solution

(a)   By (18.6),

$$\kappa = \frac{Q_{out}}{Q_{in} - Q_{out}}$$

A Carnot refrigerator is just a Carnot engine run in reverse, so

$$\frac{Q_{out}}{Q_{in}} = \frac{T_C}{T_H} = \frac{280}{303} \quad \text{and} \quad \kappa = \frac{280/303}{1 - (280/303)} = 12.2$$

(b)   From Eq. (18.6a), $\kappa = Q_{out}/W_{net} \Rightarrow W_{net} = Q_{out}/\kappa$. Recalling the relationship between power and work, we have $P = (1500 \text{ J/s})/(12.2) = 123$ W.

Problem 18.30.

(a)   How is a quasistatic constant-entropy process represented on a P-V diagram?

(b)   If an ideal gas undergoes an isothermal compression, does the entropy of the gas increase or decrease?

(c)   Does the answer to (b) violate Eq. (18.9), the entropy statement of the second law?

Solution

(a)   If the entropy of the system stays the same, then (18.8) implies $\Delta Q = 0$. Thus, the process is represented by an adiabat.

(b)   In an isothermal compression, the work W done *by* the gas is negative. Since the internal energy of an ideal gas is constant during an isothermal process, the first law implies that the heat Q entering the system must equal the work done by the system: $Q = W$. Thus $Q = \Delta Q$ is also negative, and it follows from (18.8) that the entropy of the gas decreases.

(c)   No: (18.9) refers to the entropy *of the universe*. Since Q for the gas is negative, heat must be leaving it to enter some other system. The entropy of the other system will thus be increasing; overall, (18.9) will hold.

Problem 18.31.   An ideal gas is confined to one-half a rectangular container by a thin membrane, the other half of the container being completely empty. The container is well insulated so that no heat can enter or leave the system. When the membrane is broken, the gas rushes to occupy the whole container in a process called **free expansion** and then settles down to equilibrium in the new volume. Between the initial and final equilibrium, (a) what is the change in internal energy of the gas? (b) what is the change in temperature of the gas?

Solution

(a)   No change. No heat enters or leaves the container, and no work is done on or by the outside world, since the volume of the container is unchanged.

(b)   No change. For an ideal gas fixed internal energy means fixed temperature.

Problem 18.32.   In the free expansion of Problem 18.31 the entropy of the gas actually increases. How can this be, in view of (*18.8*) and the fact that no heat enters or leaves?

Solution

Equation (*18.8*) does not apply here, because the free expansion is turbulent and cannot be described by means of a quasistatic path. That the entropy *does* increase can be understood intuitively—the explosive expansion can only increase molecular disorder. To prove that the entropy has increased, we mark the initial and final equilibrium states on a *P-V* diagram. Since the two states have the same temperature, they can be connected by an isothermal quasistatic path. We then replace the real process with an expansion along the isotherm. As we expand along any ideal-gas isotherm, heat must enter the system, so $\Delta S = \Delta Q/T > 0$. Thus our final state has higher entropy than the initial state. Since the process occurs in an isolated system (our confined gas), the entropy change of the universe is the entropy change of the gas. Thus, in this real process the entropy of the universe increases.

Supplementary Problems

Problem 18.33.   In Fig. 18-5, assume the system absorbs 80 J of heat in going from $i \to f$ along path a and 50 J of heat in going from $i \to f$ along path b.

(*a*)   What is the net work done in going around the complete cycle: $i \to f$ along a and $f \to i$ along b?

(*b*)   If the work done by the system in going from $i \to f$ along path b is 170 J, what is the work done in going from $i \to f$ along path a?

   Ans.   (*a*) 30 J; (*b*) 200 J

Problem 18.34.   Referring to Problem 18.33, assume the internal energy at point i is 800 J and the work done in going from $i \to f$ along path c is 180 J.

(*a*)   What is the internal energy of point f?

(*b*)   How much heat enters or leaves the system as the system goes from point $f \to i$ along path c?

   Ans.   (*a*) 680 J; (*b*) 60 J leaves.

Problem 18.35.

(*a*)   Find the change in internal energy of 0.60 mol of oxygen as it is heated from $t = -50\,°C$ to $t = 80\,°C$ at constant volume. Assume the oxygen is an ideal gas. [*Hint*: See Problem 18.5.]

(*b*)   Repeat (*a*) if the oxygen undergoes the same change in temperature at constant pressure.

(*c*)   Find the work done by the oxygen in (*b*). [*Hint*: See Problem 18.7.]

   Ans.   (*a*) Increases 1650 J; (*b*) The same as part (*a*) (since U depends only on T); (*c*) 648 J

Problem 18.36.   When n mol of ideal gas undergoes an isothermal expansion, depicted in Fig. 18-7(*c*), the work done is given by $W_{a \to b} = nRT \ln(V_b/V_a)$, where T is the temperature of the isotherm. If 2.0 mol of an ideal gas expands along a 300-K isotherm until the volume doubles, find (*a*) the work done; (*b*) the heat entering the gas.

   Ans.   (*a*) 3.46 kJ; (*b*) 3.46 kJ

Problem 18.37.   Assume that 3.0 mol of a monatomic ideal gas undergoes an adiabatic expansion such as shown in Fig. 18-7(d). The temperature drops from $T_i = 400$ K to $T_f = 180$ K during the expansion.

(a)   Find the work done by the gas. [*Hint*: See Problem 18.8(b).]

(b)   Given $U_i = 12$ kJ, find U_f.

> *Ans.*   (a) 8.23 kJ; (b) 3.77 kJ.

Problem 18.38.   Refer to Problem 18.37.

(a)   Evaluate γ for the gas. [*Hint*:   Review Chap. 16 and see note at end of Problem 18.9.]

(b)   Given $V_i = 5.0$ L, determine V_f.

> *Ans.*   (a) $\frac{5}{3}$; (b) 16.6 L

Problem 18.39.   Suppose the adiabatic process described in Problems 18.37 and 18.38 is made part of a cycle with the other two paths being a constant-pressure and a constant-volume process, as shown in Fig. 18-17, with the three paths labeled a, b, and c.

(a)   Use the ideal gas law to find the pressure at points i and f, and the temperature at point k.

(b)   Find the work W_{fk} done by the system along path b from $f \rightarrow k$.

(c)   Find the heat Q_{fk} entering the system along path b from $f \rightarrow k$.

> *Ans.*   (a) $P_i = 1.99 \times 10^6$ Pa, $P_f = 2.70 \times 10^5$ Pa, $T_k = 54.2$ K; (b) $W_{fk} = -3130$ J; (c) -7840 J.

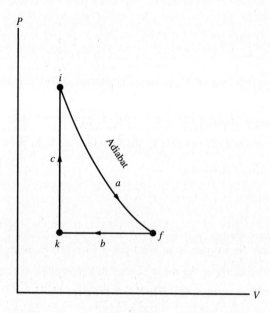

Fig. 18-17

Problem 18.40.   Refer to Problem 18.39 and Fig. 18-17.

(a)   Find the heat Q_{ki} entering the system along path c from $k \rightarrow i$ and the work done W_{ki} along the same path.

(b)   Using the results of (a) and Problem 18.39(c), find the net heat entering the system in the cycle.

(c) Using the results of (a), Problem 18.39(b), and Problem 18.37(a), find the net work done in the cycle. Is this consistent with the answer to part (b)?

  Ans. (a) 12,930 J, 0 J; (b) 5090 J; (c) 5100 J; in a complete cycle $W_{net} = Q_{net}$, which is our result to within rounding errors

Problem 18.41. A quasistatic engine cycle is represented on a P-V diagram by the triangle shown in Fig. 18-18. Assume that 500 J of heat enters the system along path a and that 300 J enters along path b.

(a) How much work is done in the cycle?

(b) How much heat must leave the system along path c?

(c) What is the efficiency of the engine?

  Ans. (a) 450 J; (b) 350 J leaves; (c) 56.2%

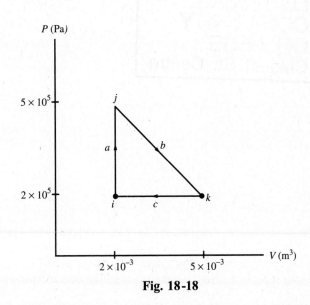

Fig. 18-18

Problem 18.42. Find the efficiency of the engines represented by the cycles of (a) Problem 18.33(a); (b) Problem 18.40. (Use the information given, and answers already obtained, in those problems.)

  Ans. (a) 37.5%; (b) 39.4%

Problem 18.43. Find the coefficients of performance of the backward-run engines of Problem 18.42.

  Ans. (a) 1.67; (b) 1.54

Problem 18.44. The efficiency of a Carnot engine is 85% and the hot reservoir is at 800 K.

(a) What is the temperature of the cool reservoir?

(b) If the engine performs 3 kJ of work per cycle, how much heat enters the system per cycle from the hot reservoir?

(*c*) How much heat is exhausted per cycle to the cool reservoir?

> *Ans.*   (*a*) 120 K; (*b*) 3.53 kJ; (*c*) 530 J

Problem 18.45.   For the quasistatic process of Problem 18.36, calculate (*a*) the change in the entropy of the gas; (*b*) the change in the entropy of the rest of the universe.

> *Ans.*   (*a*) 11.5 J/K; (*b*) -11.5 J/K (since $\Delta S_{unv} = 0$)

Index

SCHAUM'S SOLVED PROBLEMS SERIES

- ■ **Learn the best strategies for solving tough problems in step-by-step detail**
- ■ **Prepare effectively for exams and save time in doing homework problems**
- ■ **Use the indexes to quickly locate the types of problems you need the most help solving**
- ■ **Save these books for reference in other courses and even for your professional library**

To order, please check the appropriate box(es) and complete the following coupon.

❑ **3000 SOLVED PROBLEMS IN BIOLOGY**
ORDER CODE 005022-8/**$16.95 406 pp.**

❑ **3000 SOLVED PROBLEMS IN CALCULUS**
ORDER CODE 041523-4/**$19.95 442 pp.**

❑ **3000 SOLVED PROBLEMS IN CHEMISTRY**
ORDER CODE 023684-4/**$20.95 624 pp.**

❑ **2500 SOLVED PROBLEMS IN COLLEGE ALGEBRA & TRIGONOMETRY**
ORDER CODE 055373-4/**$14.95 608 pp.**

❑ **2500 SOLVED PROBLEMS IN DIFFERENTIAL EQUATIONS**
ORDER CODE 007979-x/**$19.95 448 pp.**

❑ **2000 SOLVED PROBLEMS IN DISCRETE MATHEMATICS**
ORDER CODE 038031-7/**$16.95 412 pp.**

❑ **3000 SOLVED PROBLEMS IN ELECTRIC CIRCUITS**
ORDER CODE 045936-3/**$21.95 746 pp.**

❑ **2000 SOLVED PROBLEMS IN ELECTROMAGNETICS**
ORDER CODE 045902-9/**$18.95 480 pp.**

❑ **2000 SOLVED PROBLEMS IN ELECTRONICS**
ORDER CODE 010284-8/**$19.95 640 pp.**

❑ **2500 SOLVED PROBLEMS IN FLUID MECHANICS & HYDRAULICS**
ORDER CODE 019784-9/**$21.95 800 pp.**

❑ **1000 SOLVED PROBLEMS IN HEAT TRANSFER**
ORDER CODE 050204-8/**$19.95 750 pp.**

❑ **3000 SOLVED PROBLEMS IN LINEAR ALGEBRA**
ORDER CODE 038023-6/**$19.95 750 pp.**

❑ **2000 SOLVED PROBLEMS IN Mechanical Engineering THERMODYNAMICS**
ORDER CODE 037863-0/**$19.95 406 pp.**

❑ **2000 SOLVED PROBLEMS IN NUMERICAL ANALYSIS**
ORDER CODE 055233-9/**$20.95 704 pp.**

❑ **3000 SOLVED PROBLEMS IN ORGANIC CHEMISTRY**
ORDER CODE 056424-8/**$22.95 688 pp.**

❑ **2000 SOLVED PROBLEMS IN PHYSICAL CHEMISTRY**
ORDER CODE 041716-4/**$21.95 448 pp.**

❑ **3000 SOLVED PROBLEMS IN PHYSICS**
ORDER CODE 025734-5/**$20.95 752 pp.**

❑ **3000 SOLVED PROBLEMS IN PRECALCULUS**
ORDER CODE 055365-3/**$16.95 385 pp.**

❑ **800 SOLVED PROBLEMS IN VECTOR MECHANICS FOR ENGINEERS
Vol I: STATICS**
ORDER CODE 056835-9/**$20.95 800 pp.**

❑ **700 SOLVED PROBLEMS IN VECTOR MECHANICS FOR ENGINEERS
Vol II: DYNAMICS**
ORDER CODE 056687-9/**$20.95 672 pp.**